D0984531

THEOLOGICAL
INVESTIGATIONS

Volume V

THEOLOGICAL INVESTIGATIONS

THEOLOGICAL INVESTIGATIONS

VOLUME V
LATER WRTINGS

by
KARL RAHNER

Translated by
KARL-H. KRUGER

CROSSROAD • NEW YORK

1983
The Crossroad Publishing Company
575 Lexington Avenue, New York, NY 10022

A translation of
SCHRIFTEN ZUR THEOLOGIE, V
published by Verlagsanstalt Benziger & Co. A.G., Einsiedeln

This translation © Darton, Longman & Todd Ltd. 1966
First published 1966
Reprinted 1969, 1975, and 1983

Library of Congress Catalog Card Number: 61-8189
ISBN: 0-8245-0381-3
Printed in the United States of America

CONTENTS

PART V   *The Christian Life*

ACKNOWLEDGEMENTS

I wish to express my most profound gratitude and appreciation to Rev Andrew Monaghan for his invaluable assistance in reading the manuscript and his many most helpful suggestions.

My sincere gratitude is also due to Miss Janet Westley, Mrs Patricia Purvey and Mrs Pearl Robertson for their patient work in typing the manuscript, to Mr Daniel Hainey for his help in reading the proofs and to many other friends who helped in different ways.

St Andrew's College   Karl-H. Kruger
Drygrange
Melrose
Scotland

ABBREVIATIONS

AAS   *Acta Apostolicae Sedis*

CIC   *Codex Iuris Canonici*

Denz Denzinger-Rahner, *Enchiridion Symbolorum* (1953)

DTC   *Dictionnaire de Théologie Catholique*

LThK *Lexikon für Theologie und Kirche*

NRT   *Nouvelle Revue Théologique*

RSR   *Recherches de Science Religieuse*

RT   *Revue Thomiste*

ZKT   *Zeitschrift für Katholische Theologie*

Note.—The author very rarely quotes Scripture directly in German, and when he does so appears to make his own translations. In the present translation, accordingly, the author's renderings are retained, though of course the standard English versions have been consulted.

PREFACE

This new volume of my *Theological Investigations* collects together those dogmatic reflections which I have published since the appearance of the first four volumes of these 'Investigations', i.e. since 1960. Although it does not represent any attempt at publishing some sort of 'Collected Works', the concept 'dogmatic reflections' has intentionally been taken in a wide sense: theology must serve the proclamation of the gospel, and it usually advances only when it springs from the exigencies and aim of this proclamation—in other words, when it does not experience pastoral-theological influences as to any extent lessening its scientific rigour.

The present volume is dedicated in gratitude to the Society of St Paul and in particular to its leading members. In their company I have once more experienced during the course of this year that 'a faithful friend is a stout shelter' (Ecclus 6.14).

Karl Rahner S J

PART I

QUESTIONS OF FUNDAMENTAL THEOLOGY AND THEOLOGICAL METHOD

I

THOUGHTS ON THE POSSIBILITY OF
BELIEF TODAY

I WOULD like to try to say a few words about the possibility of belief
today. I mean the possibility of belief in the infinite, unspeakable
mystery we call God—of belief in the fact that this infinite mystery,
as *our* mystery, has communicated himself to us absolutely, and has
come infinitely near to us, in Jesus Christ and his grace, even when one
does not realize it and thinks oneself to be falling into the dark abyss
of emptiness and nothingness—of belief in the fact that the legally constituted established community of those who confess the grace-giving
nearness of God in Christ for the salvation of the whole world is to be
found in the Catholic, Apostolic and Roman Church. Much could be
said about the possibility of such belief today. I can only make a few
remarks about it. And I do so with the ever-present fear that I may not
say exactly what would be decisive in giving the courage of his belief
to the individual listener. I sincerely want to speak with all honesty.
I also earnestly want to avoid confusing this plain honesty (which is of
obligation) with a cynical bitterness which is (as conscience testifies)
a danger in any heartfelt concern—in fact, the danger that one no
longer recognizes that whole truth which only a calm and humble heart
is allowed to approach.

The belief of which I wish to speak is belief in the real sense of the
word; it is, therefore, belief engaged in by personal decision, with
power to bring about a change of heart, and not a belief arising merely
out of middle-class convention and social antecedents. Hence the question as to what prospects this belief may have for the future can really
be answered only by asking what possibilities it has today in one's
own life. The future we are asking about in this connection grows out
of the individual decisions which today make us answerable for our
existence.

The fact that what I have to say is also meant to be an academic lecture (which is what I have been invited to give) causes me a certain amount of embarrassment. For I do not wish to give an erudite lecture but would rather try to say something more simple and, in my opinion, more important. For if there is a time when academic learning must take second place, then it is when we have to speak—falteringly—of God. And so I hope I may be forgiven if these words do not bear any very great resemblance to an academic lecture.

Where are we to start when it is a question of stating and showing that one may have the courage of one's belief? If it is impossible to say everything, then we must choose and also determine our starting-point somewhat arbitrarily.

I begin with the fact that I have—quite simply—always been a believer and that I have met with no reason which would force or cause me not to believe any more. I was born a Catholic because I was born and baptized in a believing environment. I trust in God that this faith passed on by tradition has turned into my own decision—into a real belief—and that I am a Catholic Christian even in my innermost being. This, in the last analysis, remains God's secret and an unreflected reality deep down within me which I cannot express even to myself. I say that—in the first place—I, this believer, have not encountered any reason which could cause me to cease being what I am.

I understand that one would have to have reasons for changing in a way contrary to the pattern according to which one has set out. For anyone who would change without such reasons—who would not even be willing in the first place to remain true to the situation in life in which he has been placed and to the definite commitment of his spiritual personality—would be a man falling into emptiness, and no more interiorly than the shadow of a man. If a man does not want to abandon his very self, then he must basically regard what is already there as something to be taken over and to be preserved until he has proof of the contrary. One can live and grow only out of those roots which already live, and precisely as they live—only out of that beginning in which one places one's original trust in life. What is transmitted to us may have provided us with lofty and sacred values; it may have opened up infinite vistas and taken hold of us by an absolute and eternal call. This alone, in the form of unreflected experience and simple practice without deceit or doubt, may not yet represent in the face of critical conscience and questioning reason any expressible and reflected proof of the simple truth of this tradition. One thing, however, has always remained clear to me—in spite of every temptation against the Faith which I, too, believe I have had to undergo—one thing has supported me as I kept fast to it: the conviction that we must not allow what has been inherited and transmitted to be consumed by the emptiness of the ordinary, of a spiritual indifference or apathetic and sombre scepticism, but at the most only by something stronger, something which calls us to greater freedom and into a more inexorable light. Inherited belief has certainly always also been faith tempted and liable to temptation. But I have always experienced it as the faith which asked me: 'Will you too go away?' and to which I could always merely reply, 'Lord, to whom shall I go?'; I have always experienced it as the faith, powerful and good, and the only possible reason permitting me to give it up would be the proof of the contrary. And nobody—nor even my experience of life—has furnished me with this proof. I realize that such a proof would have to go very deep and would have to be very comprehensive. There are, of course, many difficulties and many bitter experiences for the soul in life. But it is quite clear that no difficulty could claim consideration as a reason against my faith unless it were equal to the dignity and deep-rootedness of what it is trying to threaten and change. There may be many intellectual difficulties in the realm of the particular sciences—such as the history of religion, scriptural criticism, the early history of Christianity—for which I have no direct and—in every respect—satisfactory solution. But such difficulties are too particular and—compared to the reality of existence—too slight objectively speaking to be used as the basis for decisions about the ultimate questions of life; they are not weighty enough to be allowed to determine the whole, unspeakably profound depths of life. My faith does not depend on whether exegetes or the Church have or have not already found the correct interpretation of the first Chapter of Genesis —on whether some decision of the Biblical Commission or of the Holy Office is the last word in wisdom. Such arguments, therefore, are beside the point from the very start. There are, of course, other temptations, which go deeper. But these are the very ones which bring out true Christianity, provided one faces them honestly and, at the same time, humbly. They reach the heart, the innermost centre of life—they threaten it and confront it with the ultimate questionableness of man as such. But precisely in *this* way they can be for man the labour-pains of the true birth of Christian existence. The argumentation of human existence itself makes man feel lonely, as if placed into emptiness, as if

involved in an infinite fall. It delivers him up, as it were, to his freedom—and yet he does not feel assured of this freedom. It makes him
feel as if surrounded by an infinite ocean of darkness and an immense
unexplored night—always merely managing to survive from one contingency to an other. It leaves him fragile, poor, agitated by the pain of
his contingent nature. Always it leaves him convinced once more of his
dependence on the merely biological, on ridiculous social elements and
on the traditional (even when one contradicts it). He feels death living
within him in the midst of his life. He feels how death is the final limit,
beyond which he himself cannot pass. He feels the ideals of his life
grow weak and lose their youthful lustre. He experiences how one becomes weary of all the smart talk on the fairground of life and of science
—even of science. The real argument against Christianity is the experience of life, this experience of darkness. And I have always found that
behind the technical arguments levelled by the learned against Christianity—as the ultimate force and *a priori* pre-judgement supporting
these scientific doubts—there are always these ultimate experiences of
life causing the spirit and the heart to be sombre, tired and despairing.
These experiences try to objectify themselves and to render themselves
expressible in the doubts of scholars and of the sciences, no matter how
weighty these doubts may be in themselves and however much they
must be taken seriously. For this very experience is also the argument
of Christianity. For what does Christianity say? What does it proclaim? In spite of the complicated appearance of its dogmatic and
moral theology, it says something quite simple—something simple
which all particular dogmas of Christianity articulate in some way
(though perhaps it is seen to be simple only once these are given). For
what does Christianity really declare? Nothing else, after all, than that
the great Mystery remains eternally a mystery, but that this mystery
wishes to communicate Himself in absolute self-communication—as
the infinite, incomprehensible and inexpressible Being whose name is
God, as self-giving nearness—to the human soul in the midst of its
experience of its own finite emptiness. This nearness has become a
reality not only in what we call 'grace' but also in the historical
tangibility of the One whom we call the Godman. In these two ways of
divine self-communication—both by their radical, absolute nature,
and by reason of the identity of the 'existence-in-itself' of God and his
'existence-for-us'—there is also communicated, and thus revealed, to
us the duality of an inner-divine relationship: in other words, what we

profess as the trinity of Persons in the one Godhead. Man, however, experiences these three absolute mysteries of the Christian Faith (i.e. the Trinity, the Incarnation and grace) by his inescapable experience of the fact that he is grounded in the abyss of the insoluble mystery, and by experiencing and accepting this mystery (this is what we call 'faith'), as fulfilling nearness and not as a burning judgement, in the depth of his conscience and in the concreteness of his history (for both are constitutive elements of his existence). That this radical mystery is nearness and not distance, self-surrendering love and not a judgement which casts man out into the hell of his own nothingness—this man finds difficult to accept and to believe. It may appear to us as a light almost darker than our own darkness. Indeed, it may take, and in some sense consume, the whole power of our soul and heart, of our freedom and our whole existence, to accept it. And yet, is there not so much light, so much joy, love and glory, both internally and externally, in the world and in man, to make it possible for us to say that all this can be explained only by an absolute Light, Joy, Love and Glory—by an absolute Being and not by an empty nothingness which cannot explain anything—even though we cannot understand how there can be this our deadly darkness and nothingness if there is the Infinity of Fullness, albeit as a mystery? May I not say that I am right to hold on to the light (even though it is faint) rather than the darkness—to the happiness rather than the hellish torment of my existence? If I were to accept the arguments against Christianity to which human existence gives rise, what would they offer me for my existence? The valour of the honesty and the glory of the resolution to face up to the absurdity of human existence? But can one think of these as great, as obligatory and glorious, without implying once more (whether one really knows it or not, wants to or not), that there is something which is glorious and worthy of esteem? But how could this be, in an abyss of absolute emptiness and absurdity? In any case, anyone who courageously accepts life—even a shortsighted, primitive positivist who apparently bears patiently with the poverty of the superficial—has really already accepted God. He has accepted God as he is in himself, as he wants to be in our regard in love and freedom—in other words, as the God of the eternal life of divine self-communication in which God himself is the centre of man and in which man's form is that of the Godman himself. For anyone who really accepts *himself*, accepts a mystery in the sense of the infinite emptiness which is man. He accepts himself in the immensity of his unpredictable destiny and—silently, and without premeditation—he accepts the One who has decided to fill this infinite emptiness (which is the mystery of man) with his own infinite fullness (which is the mystery called God). And if Christianity is nothing other than the clear expression of what man experiences indistinctly in his actual being—which in the concrete is really always more than just spiritual nature but is spirit, illuminated from within by the light of God's gratuitous grace—what reason could I have then not to be a Christian? For when man accepts himself in this way wholly and entirely, he accepts this light (i.e. he believes) even though he does so unthinkingly and without expressing it. Thus, what reason should I have for not being a Christian, if Christianity means taking possession of the mystery of man with absolute optimism? I know of only one reason which weighs heavily on me—the despair, the lassitude, the sin I experience within me. This is the only reason which oppresses me—the crumbling away of human existence in the grey scepticism of our daily life, when we can no longer even raise a protest against mere existence, but just leave the tacit, infinite question which we ourselves are, well alone—a scepticism which cannot stand or accept this question but avoids it by losing itself in the wretchedness of everyday life. This is not meant to deny that even everyday existence lived in the quiet honesty of patiently doing one's duty can also be a form of 'anonymous' Christian living. Indeed, many a one (if he does not sceptically or stubbornly raise this way of living in its turn into an absolute system) may in actual fact grasp Christianity more genuinely in this way than in its more explicit forms which can often be so very empty and be used as a means of escape before the mystery instead of openly facing up to it. Nevertheless, the abyss opened up by the above reason could paralyse the infinite optimism which believes that man is a finite nature endowed with the infinity of God. If I were to give way to this argument, what could I put in the place of Christianity? Only emptiness, despair, night and death. And what reason do I have to consider this abyss as truer and more real than the abyss of God? It is easier to let oneself fall into one's own emptiness than into the abyss of the Blessed Mystery. But it is not more courageous or truer. This truth, of course, shines out only when it is also loved and accepted since it is the truth which makes us free and whose light consequently begins to shine only in the freedom which dares all to the very height. Yet this truth is there. I have called out to it and it has declared itself to me.

This truth gives me what I must give to it, that it may be and remain the happiness and strength of my human existence—it gives me the courage to believe in it and to call out to it when all the dark despairs and lifeless voids would swallow me up.

I see thousands upon thousands around me—I see whole cultures, whole epochs of history around me, before and after me—who are not explicitly Christian. I see the approach of times in which Christianity will no longer be a matter of course in Europe and in the whole world. I know all that, but ultimately it cannot really trouble me. Why not? Because I see everywhere a nameless Christianity, and because I do not see my own explicit Christianity as one opinion *among* others which contradict it. I see nothing other in my Christianity than the explicit recognition and home-coming of everything in the way of truth and love which exists or could exist anywhere else. I neither hold non-Christians to be more stupid than I am nor as having less good will than I have. If I were to fall into an empty and cowardly scepticism on account of the variety of philosophies of life, would I then have a better chance of attaining to the truth than if I remain a Christian? The answer must be in the negative, for even scepticism and agnosticism are only two opinions among others—in fact, the most cowardly and empty of all. They do not provide a way of escape from the multiplicity of philosophies of life in the world. Even 'refraining from making any decision regarding a philosophy of life' is a decision—and the worst at that.

Furthermore, I have no reason for regarding Christianity as *one* philosophy of life among others. Try to understand exactly what Christianity means! Make comparisons! Listen carefully to what Christianity has to say! Hear its message most exactly but also listen with all the breadth of the spirit and the heart. If you do this you will never hear anything elsewhere which is good, true and redemptive, which illuminates man's existence and opens up his reality into the infinity of the divine mystery—anything which is to be found in some other philosophy of life—which is not to be found also in Christianity. You may indeed hear something elsewhere which appeals to you, spurs you on, broadens the horizons of your mind, enriches and enlightens you. But all this is merely something transient which does not solve, and does not mean to answer, the ultimate question of human existence in view of death, and something which has its place also in the wide range of Christian existence, even though it has perhaps not been very much cultivated by Christians up till now. Or it is something which you will recognize as a part of authentic Christianity, if only you will study this Christianity more exactly and go more deeply and courageously into it. You will perhaps discover in the process that your conceptually reflex Christianity will never actually succeed in forming a complete and achieved synthesis of all these recognitions, experiences of life and realities of art, philosophy and poetry. Yet you will never discover any final and insurmountable contradiction between legitimate experiences, recognitions and things which make you happy, on the one hand—and authentic Christianity on the other. And this fact is quite sufficient. For in this sense you may be Christian and 'pagan' at once. It would after all be uncatholic to assert that there is only *one* source of experience and knowledge, when Christianity teaches a genuine pluralism (submitted to God) which ultimately is not absolutely controllable by man—and when consequently the synthesis of plurality and of human existence must always remain an uncompleted task in the short span of this life. You have, therefore, the right and the duty to hear Christianity as the universal message of truth which nothing can confine and which says 'no' only to the negations, but not to the genuine affirmations, of other outlooks on life. Give ear to Christianity as the universal message, as the one which 'gathers up' ('*aufhebt*') and thus preserves everything else. Listen to Christianity as the message which does not forbid anything except man's shutting-himself-off in his finite nature, except man's refusal to believe that he is endowed with the radical infinity of the absolute God and that the *finitum* is *capax infiniti*. I know this message of the infinity and the absolute truth and freedom of Christianity is often interpreted by its rabbis and scribes—with their miserable hearts—as a theology which must maintain its place beside others laboriously and by disputation with them—as a theology which loses itself in endless controversies and which merely consists in the dialectical opposition to some other opinion or form of experience. But do not let yourself be troubled by this wretched state of theology! Christianity is infinitely broad. For Christianity, among all religions, says the least in detail since it always says the one thing—but this with all the radiant splendour of truth and with the last ounce of that courage for living which only God can give—the absolute fullness itself, incomprehensible and nameless, infinite and unspeakable, has without diminution become the interior splendour of the creature, if only the creature will accept it. Hence, we

Christians do not regard non-Christians as those who, because they are less intelligent or more evil-willed or unhappy, have accepted error as truth. We regard their case as something not at all surprising in a world of history and becoming in which the 'final' is still on the way to perfection:—we regard them as those who have already been touched (or at least can be touched) in the depth of their being by the infinite grace of God in virtue of his universal saving purpose. They are merely those who are already being asked by God's eternal grace whether they will accept God, but who have not yet come to a reflex consciousness of what they already are:—men called by God, the God of eternal, triune life. If we are already aware of this, if we have already heard the news about what we and they are—which is given to us in the form of the human words of official revelation—then this is a grace we cannot yet attribute to these others. And this grace imposes a terrifying responsibility on us who must be now all the more freely what we necessarily are:—men sought by God. But this can certainly be no reason why we should not already be Christians explicitly and officially —simply because others are still only Christians anonymously, perhaps only in the sense of one who has been asked and not yet as one who has become a Christian in the reflex categories of an explicit profession of faith.

It is, of course, impossible to deduce *a priori* that God himself wished to enter into the world in a most radical and personal way, and that the idea of the Godman—which can be understood from this as being the at-least-hypothetical extension of man's being (understood as the empty openness to the infinite being of God)—became fact precisely in Jesus of Nazareth under the Emperor Augustus and Pontius Pilate, in this particular place and not somewhere else, at this particular moment in time and not at any other. Indeed, this concreteness—one might almost say concreteness *as such* and historical '*a posteriori*'—are proper to Christianity. But even beforehand—before any *a-posteriori* proofs of the evidence Jesus of Nazareth gave of what He is and the wonderful testimonies He gave us for this—it is easy to believe in Jesus as the Son of God (if one may think of anything so great as 'easy' —because where there really *is* love, the most difficult seems easy). Why? For one thing, this doctrine of the Hypostatic Union, understood in its truly Catholic sense (i.e. according to the teaching of Chalcedon), has nothing mythical about it. It is clearly not mythology to say that God's infinity is given to me in the absolute transcendence of the spirit, and that—since something is real according to the measure of its being by itself and by the absolute infinity of being—this presence of God is more actual and real than the reality of any finite thing. No more is it mythology to say that self-transcendence (which in us consists in principle always merely in becoming and beginning) has reached an absolute and insurpassable climax in a determinate man, who is an absolutely real man in every way—a man with a human consciousness, with free will and historicity, who worships and obeys and experiences the torments of death; in whom God's communication of himself to the spiritual nature of the creature took place in a unique and unsurpassable manner. It is not mythology to say:—there is a man by reason of whose existence I may dare to believe that God has promised to give himself irrevocably and finally to me; there is a man in whom God's absolute promise to give himself to every spiritual creature, and the acceptance of this promise by the creature, are both proved and rendered credible to me without ambiguity, irreparably and in a manner I can understand. If, however, one can really understand *this* proposition in its full ontological import, then one has given expression to the Hypostatic Union and yet has understood it as a realization—a realization which of course is unique and does not take place in any other instance, and which is God's doing—of what is meant by being a man as such. The mystery and divine freedom in the effecting of the Hypostatic Union do not thereby disappear. But it does thereby lose every taste of the mythical and it no longer gives the painful impression that it is a question of something analogous to Greek or other legends, to anthropomorphisms, according to which God, Infinity, the Incomprehensible, has made use of the livery of a human form in order to make, as it were, a second attempt to achieve what he had been unable to do as the ruler of the world at the creation of the world.

Furthermore, it must always be borne in mind that for a really Christian doctrine of the relationship of the world to God, the autonomy of the creature does not grow in inverse but in direct proportion to the degree of the creature's dependence on, and belonging to, God. It must, therefore, be borne in mind that Jesus is most truly and most independently man, that he has descended into the most profound depths of human reality, has most truly died and remains most decisively man, precisely because his human nature is most radically assumed and precisely because it belongs to the eternal Logos. Thus, if what we have just now been able merely to indicate is true—viz. that there certainly is an idea of divine humanity which is given together with the nature of man and his self-transcendence (even though this idea has perhaps come into its own in point of time only after the experience of the Incarnation), and if man understands himself best when he grasps himself as the *possible* self-expression of God which has become actual in the man Jesus, then it is no longer so difficult to recognize the actualization of this possibility in Jesus and no other. For where else is there a man in the clear tangible light of history who has ever made any claim that this event has taken place in him? Where is there anyone who by his human life, death—and, let us add, resurrection—and by the love numberless men have shown him, could give us the courage and the spiritual justification to make this claim—if it is not the Jesus of the Bible? Is it not true that I know myself to be the partner in an absolute, mutual self-engagement between God and the spiritual creature? Why should I not then acknowledge—if everything points to it and nothing militates against it—that this partnership of mutual self-engagement is so radical in Jesus from the very start that the human side belongs to God not only distantly, as to the Creator, but also to God as the One who gives expression to himself, and that the answer to God given in him is once more the Word of God himself—and that it is precisely in this way the most autonomous answer of man as a creature? Where apart from Jesus could I find the courage for such a belief—a courage which I want to have, and am permitted to have, because it springs from the depth of the experience of transcendence when filled with God's grace? If there must be an omega-point on which the whole history of the world converges—and if, on account of the experience of my own nearness by grace to God, I may expect that this omega-point already exists (to use Teilhard de Chardin's terminology) or at least that it cannot be presumption to look and ask whether it is not already present in history—must it then seem absurd to me to find it in Jesus of Nazareth? Does it seem absurd to find it in the One who even in death committed his soul into his Father's hands—in the One who convinced precisely because he did not need to discuss wise problems of a philosophy of life—in the One who knew all about the *mysterium* in itself, about the consuming Judgement, the death of man and his abysmal guilt, and yet called this *mysterium* his Father and us his brothers? Is it absurd to find the omega-point in Him who knew himself to be quite simply the Son and his death to be the reconciliation of the world? No one can be forced by arguments to believe in Jesus of Nazareth as the absolute presence of God. This belief is free, if only because it is belief in something historical and contingent. Anyone, however, who will accept ideas seriously, and as existentially true, only once they have become flesh and blood, can surely believe in Jesus of Nazareth—when he finds in the flesh that which is the most blessed project of the highest possibility of man, in the light of which one really begins to understand what ultimately is meant by 'man'.

One further aspect of this idea of the Godman and the fact of Jesus should be mentioned here. On the one hand, since he is God's pledge to the world and the acceptance of the world into God himself in person and as a person, he is certainly the unsurpassable and final event, the eschatological event. No other religious experience—no other prophet can come after him who could surpass him—nothing whereby something new or better could replace the old can now take the place of what has gone before—otherwise he would not be the Godman. How indeed could this be possible? There are after all two unsurpassable words and realities which consequently converge: there is man—the infinite question—and there is the infinite Mystery—the infinite and absolute answer by remaining a mystery: there is man and God. Hence, the Godman, is unsurpassable; a new prophet *cannot* achieve any more, can at best fall below the answer which the Godman is, or simply copy it. Yet through this unsurpassable, real formula of the world, of its meaning and its task, the world and history have reached their proper purpose (even in a conceptually and historically tangible way); but they have not come to their end in the sense that they cannot really have a history any more with regard to what is worth considering and doing. On the contrary, history (which after all should take place in knowledge and freedom) has now acquired its proper principle—it has experienced the central event of what is to come and has recognized its proper, infinite destiny as one which is already present within it as its own. Thus, history really only begins now—the unforeseeable, adventurous, incalculable history (incalculable, naturally, even with regard to its end). But it is a history which knows itself safe in God's love—a history which has already overtaken all His judgements and which may think of itself as glorious and victorious in spite of all the terrible things which have already happened and will still happen during it, and which will perhaps even increase apocalyptically. And the end of this history—which is supported by the Godman and is bound together in him, the absolute Mediator—is the absolute nearness to God of all those spiritual creatures who are saved, and their final, and utter immediacy to God, in the same way as this immediacy also constitutes of its nature the inner divinization of the Godman in his human reality. All this makes it quite clear that the goal and meaning of the incarnational unity is the direct union of the spiritual creature as such with God. It makes it clear that we are all conceived in very truth from the outset as the brethren of the Godman. The unique nearness of God and man in the Godman, therefore, cannot properly be conceived in this its first beginning as a negation of the nearness of the other spiritual creatures to the absolute Mystery. It must be conceived as the basis and the already radically realized pledge of the nearness of spiritual creatures to this Mystery. We may, therefore, speak of a true God-humanity as applicable to the human race as a whole.

There is, however, a further hindrance and danger to faith besides the deep bitterness of human existence and the great variety of philosophies of life in the world. I am referring to the assembly of believers itself—the Church. She is indeed the holy Church, even in the view of any unprejudiced student of history. She is the sign which, lifted up above all nations, bears her own testimony to her divine origin and life by her inexhaustible fruitfulness for all holiness. But she is also the sinful Church of sinners, the sinful Church, because we her members are sinners. And this sinfulness of the Church does not merely mean the sum total of the, as it were, private faults and failures of her members, including even those who bear her highest and most sacred offices. The sinfulness and inadequacy of the members of the Church have their effects also in the actions and conduct which, in so far as they take place within the sphere of human experience, must be designated as the actions and conduct of the Church herself. Sinful human nature, insufficiency, finiteness, shortsightedness, a falling short of the demands of the times, lack of understanding for the needs of the times, for her duties and for the trends of the future—all these most human characteristics also belong both to the office-bearers and to all the members of the Church and they also take effect by God's permissive will in what the Church is and does. It would be silly self-deceit and clerical pride, group-egoism and cult of personality as found in totalitarian systems—which does not become the Church as the congregation of Jesus, the meek and humble of Heart—if it were to deny all this, or tried to hush it up or to minimize it, or made out that this burden was merely the burden of the Church of previous ages which has now been taken from her. No, the Church is the Church of poor sinners; she is the Church which does not have the courage to regard the future as belonging to God in the same way as she has experienced the past as belonging to God. She is often in the position of one who glorifies her past and looks askance at the present, in so far as she has not created it herself, finding it all too easy to condemn it. She is often the one who, in questions of science, does not only proceed slowly and carefully—intent on preserving the purity of the Faith--but also often waits too long and who, in the nineteenth and twentieth century has sometimes been too quick to say 'no' when she could have pronounced a 'yes' earlier than she did—with, of course, the necessary nuances and distinctions. She has quite often in the past sided more with the powerful and made herself too little the advocate of the poor. Often she has not proclaimed her criticisms of the powerful of this world loudly enough, so that it looked as if she were trying to procure an alibi for herself without really coming into conflict with the great ones of this world. She often places more value on the bureaucratic apparatus of the Church than in the enthusiasm of her Spirit; she often loves the calm more than the storm, the old (which has proved itself) more than the new (which is bold and daring). Often in the past, she has in her office bearers wronged saints, thinkers, those who were painfully looking for an answer, and theologians—all of whom wanted merely to give her their selfless service. Often before, she has warded off public opinion in the Church, although according to Pius XII such public opinion is essential to the well-being of the Church. Not infrequently she has mistaken the barren mediocrity of an average theology and philosophy for the clarity of a good scholastic tradition. She has often shown herself more in the role of an anathematizing judge to those outside her fold, to the Orthodox and Protestants, than in the form of a loving mother who meets her child half-way—as far as she can possibly go— in all humility and without being controversial. She has frequently failed to recognize the spirit which is really her own when, as is its way, it has breathed where it would through the alleys of the history of the world and not merely through the sacred halls of the Church herself. Often before, she has let herself be pulled down by heresies and other movements—contrary to her proper nature and the fullness of her truth (although without ever denying that truth)—to the level of the onesidedness of her opponents. And often in such cases she has represented her teaching, not as the more comprehensive 'yes' to what was the 'proper' and latent meaning of the heresy, but rather as what appeared to be a purely dialectic 'no' given to such a heresy. According to every human estimation she has missed many a golden opportunity in the achievement of her task, or has wanted to seize it when the kairos for it was already past. Not infrequently, while being under the impression that she was championing the lofty inexorability of the divine law (which is certainly her sacred duty), she was really acting like a common, nagging governess, trying narrow-mindedly and with too average an understanding of human existence to regulate life by the typical 'Examination of Conscience' (*Beichtspiegel*) still found in devotional prayer-books which might have been suitable for the famous 'Lieschen Müller' in the even tenor of the provincial town of the nineteenth century. She has too often asked merely for well-ordered good breeding which never puts a foot wrong, instead of asking for a mind with high ideals, a loving heart and courageous life. To many minds she has not been able to give an authentic enough account of herself for people to see guilt and dark fate existing only outside her. All this is true. All this represents a temptation to faith, a burden which may impose itself on the individual and almost stifle him. But first of all, are we ourselves not part of this burden which weighs on us and threatens our faith? Are we not ourselves sinners too? Do we not also belong to the tired grey company of those in the Church who obscure the light of the Gospel by their mediocrity, their cowardice and their egoism? Do we really have the right to cast the first stone at the sinful woman who stands accused before the Lord and is called the Church—or are we not ourselves accused in her and with her, and delivered up to Mercy for good or ill? And furthermore, we surely know that reality and truth can be achieved only on earth, in history and in the flesh and not in an empty idealism. Surely we know today more than ever before that man finds himself only in a hard and clearly demanding community and that any kind of solipsism—every attempt at self-preservation by the precious, self-cultivating individual—is an ideal of the past which in any case was always wrong. Knowing all this, only one way is left open to modern man—he must bear the burden of the community seeing it in the true way, the real freedom of the person and of truth. Regarded in this light, the Church of sinners may indeed remain a heavy burden to us, but she will no longer be a scandal to us which destroys our courage of belief. Finally, we seek God in the very flesh and bones of our existence. We must receive the Body of the Lord. We want to be baptized into his death and be included in the history of the saints and great souls who loved the Church and remained loyal to her. One can achieve all this only if one lives in the Church and consequently helps to carry her burden—the burden which is our own. As long as the sacrament of the Spirit and the Body of the Lord is celebrated in her, all human insufficiencies are after all passing shadows which may frighten us but cannot kill. Our love, our obedience, our silence and our courage, where necessary, profess our belief in the true Church and her spirit of love and freedom to the official representatives of the Church, as did Paul to Peter. And these are much holier and hence always much more powerful realities in the Church than all mediocrity and all the traditionalism which will not believe that our God is the eternal God of all future ages. Our faith can be tempted by the concrete form of the Church—it can mature by it and does not need to be killed by it, unless we have already let it die beforehand in our own heart. It is difficult to judge one's own times. But I am of the opinion that the young people of today do not have an easy task. For there is one thing which is particularly difficult for them to understand, and yet it is essential that they should: they must learn to distinguish real Christianity, real faith in Jesus Christ, his Kingdom and his redeeming grace from things about which one is free to hold many different opinions and about which one may have to fight many hard, bitter and tragic battles to reach a decision—matters of science, culture, of the rebuilding of life in this world, of politics, matters concerning social conditions, earthly freedom, Europe's mission, Germany's place in the *one* world-history which is now beginning. Not that the two have nothing to do with one another. They are very much connected— if only because every man will be asked before the tribunal of eternity how he has fulfilled his very much earthly task and mission. Above all, the layman is a good Christian only if he loves the earth, man and his history, and only if he also hears in its call to him the call of his God who has created heaven and earth. But however much the teaching of Christianity embraces also an order of this earth, of the people—a social order and an order of history—it nevertheless is a fact that it is quite impossible to deduce a *clear* imperative for the shaping of the future in this earthly sphere from the message of Christianity *alone*. It therefore follows from this that even Christians may disagree amongst themselves—and disagree violently—about the things of this earth, about matters regarding the actual form political, public and social relations should take. They may disagree about the proper division between freedom and order, about the concrete pattern of tolerance, about the goals to which a people's march of history should be directed, about the analysis of the present situation and the conclusions to be drawn from it—and nothing may be left for them but to fight against one another with whatever lawful weapons God has given the human spirit. It is simply not true that we Christians and Catholics must or could always be at one in everything, or that the official Church could impose an obligatory norm on everyone about everything. It is true that the Church, in the person of her actual representatives, can be shortsighted and can go beyond what is justifiable by the true norms of Christianity and before the tribunal of history. Because such cases are always and everywhere possible, because we can and must expect this to happen in any age and any situation—since the members of the Church are finite and sinful—I am of the opinion that it will also not be possible to preserve the youth of today from such situations even in the present age. This is precisely the reason, however, why today's youth has the duty to put up calmly with such possible conflicts, in all patience, fairness, love for the Church, love for men of the Church, even when they are in disagreement with us on many points. The young people of today have a duty to avoid losing sight of the kingdom of God in their concern with their earthly duties: they have a duty to realize that one does not win a true future by disavowing the genuine past—and to grasp that even today the West has still the earthly and Christian mission to take the old truths with it on the way into the land of a better, freer and greater future. They have a duty not to let themselves become embittered or to lose courage, and a duty to reconcile the freedom of the children of God, the responsibility to one's own conscience and one's own mission and task, with obedience to the Church and the patience which can wait until the new age bears abundant fruit also in the Church. The youth of today must realize that the seed must die in order to bring forth fruit, and it must have the courage to overcome error by love. Anyone who lives his commission for the future in this way in the Church will bear with the historical face of the Church, without finding it an insurmountable temptation to faith. It may be that the official Church faces one with the dilemma to fall away from the Faith or to outgrow oneself and to practise a greater humility, a holier justice and a stronger charity in silence and patience than what we can learn from the living example of the official representatives of the Church. Why should not such a situation be possible? And why should we not be able to endure it? If we dare to rise above ourselves in this way and to die as the seed in the soil of the Church and not as a revolutionary outside her gates, then we will notice that only such an action can truly liberate us and bring us into the infinity of God. For faith—which is demanded of us even in this Church—is the action which, gifted to us by God, accepts the infinite mystery seen as the nearness of forgiving love; this cannot happen without a dying which engenders life. In this acceptance, however, is contained the whole Christian life in its proper and blessed essence. To dare such faith is possible even today. Indeed, today more than ever before.

Yet when all is said and done, only he will understand this message of the possibility of Christian belief today and tomorrow who not only listens to it but also practises it and gives himself to it in his very existence by prayer. This means having the courage to speak into that silent immensity which yet lovingly embraces us—with a will to trust oneself to it and with the belief that one has been accepted by this Holy Mystery we call God. This one achieves by taking pains to remain true to the demanding voice of conscience, by facing up to the questions of life, to *the* one silent, all-embracing question of one's existence, and by not running away from it but calling to it and addressing it oneself, opening oneself to it and accepting it as a mystery of infinite love. Let no one say that it is possible to live the teaching of Christianity only if one is already convinced of it, and that consequently one cannot prove the truth in *this* way. For we are all already disposed. And there is no man who is not already in some way or other a Christian in that reality which precedes his freedom and with which he can never quite catch up—which can never be utterly destroyed by this finite freedom. Man is always already a man of yearning, of love which still remains—a man who in his innermost being takes after all more pleasure in the truth than in lies, who still sees differences since even the worst positivist and the most sceptical materialist does not succeed in not seeing and hearing some demand and call somewhere in his life. He may not yet be a fully-grown Christian who has become reflexively conscious of himself—a Christian who has already in full consciousness accepted his pre-given Christianity in reflex freedom. But he cannot bring it about that the dynamism both of his human nature and of the grace of God does no longer orientate him to the Christian life. Hence, when we say that one should learn from the experience of one's life whether Christianity is the truth of life, this does not demand anything which is beyond us. It simply tells us: ally yourself with what is genuine, with the challenging, with what demands everything, with the courage to accept the mystery within you. It simply tells us: go on, wherever you may find yourself at this particular moment, follow the light even though it is as yet dim; guard the fire even though it burns low as yet; call out to the mystery precisely because it is incomprehensible. Go, and you will find—hope, and your hope is already blessed interiorly with the grace of fulfilment. Anyone who sets out in this manner may be far from the officially constituted Christianity; he may feel like an atheist, he may think fearfully that he does not believe in God—Christian teaching and conduct of life may appear strange and almost oppressive to him. But he should go on and follow the light shining in the innermost depth of his heart. This path has already arrived at the goal. The Christian is not afraid that he will not arrive, even though such a questioner and seeker did not succeed during his lifetime to give perfect expression to his anonymous Christianity in the explicit Christianity of the Church, and to integrate it into that explicit Christianity. It is no philosophical but a Christian truth that the one who seeks, has already been found by the One for whom, perhaps without knowing his name but with hopeful courage and sincerity, he searches. How blessed all this is; it is not so easy to run past the infinite Mystery, which embraces us in silent love, as the sceptic and the atheist, as well as the narrow-minded amongst Christians, may think—for they think of God too much in the image of their puny heart. But precisely because he silently embraces everything, because all paths lead to him, in whom we live, move and have our being, who is near to all of us, who bears and embraces everything and himself is not embraced or surpassed by anything—for that very reason Christianity and its belief are the simplest and most self-evident. This is true especially since the Christian Faith says nothing more than that we have been called into the immediacy of the mystery of God himself and that this mystery gives itself to us in unspeakable nearness. It tells us simply that this nearness has been revealed and consummated as something irrevocable in the Son of Man, who is the presence of the eternal Word of God among us. The Christian Faith merely announces to us that, in this finality of God's pledging himself which has become flesh and history, all those who have heard this pledge also in the historical and social dimension are called to the community (called 'Church') of those who wait in unity, truth and love—and in the celebration of the death of their Lord—for the *epiphaneia* of what already is: God, all and in all.

2
THEOLOGY IN THE NEW TESTAMENT

THE question we wish to pose here is whether there is already
a theology to be found in the New Testament itself, and—if
this question must be answered in the affirmative—what significance does this have for the task of present-day theology?

If the question posed is to be answered correctly, we must first of
all be clear about what is to be understood by 'theology' in this context.
There can be no question here of giving an exhaustive definition of this
notion. Nor can we be concerned with the problem of whether one
can speak of theology in several different senses to be carefully distinguished from one another, even abstracting from the notion of
'natural theology' and restricting oneself to that theology which refers
to Christian revelation and which tries to be 'ecclesiological'. Let us,
therefore, state quite simply at this point that we understand by
theology, at least in this context, a form of knowledge whose content
and certitude do not arise directly from the original event of revelation
which depends on nothing else for its content and evidence. By theology we mean knowledge which, although it does indeed in some way
ultimately come from this original event indirectly or derivatively, yet
arises directly rather from a thought process and a religious experience
which is not simply identical with the mere hearing of the revelation
as such. We do not maintain that such a definition is complete but just
that it is sufficient for us in the meantime. Indeed, it certainly presupposes that we have or may have sufficient understanding of what
we have just now called the immediate and original event of revelation.
We cannot enter into this question here. It will, however, suffice for
our purposes to state the following: the event of revelation of an
original kind which is referred to here means the direct effecting by
God of a kind of knowledge with a determined content in such a way
that the content of this knowledge is clearly grasped and is experienced
as being clearly and indubitably communicated by God, and yet that

this determined content is known only in this way because the event of revelation is effected by God directly with a view to this knowledge itself. How does this event take place? To what extent is it an interior and immediate intellectual illumination, and to what extent can it take place in the form of an experience of a divine revealing act? How far is the evidence of divine self-revelation obtained by interior spiritual events? Or does it require external attestation by miracles even in the case of the original bearer of revelation? How are we to conceive these miracles with regard to their function as criteria of the divine origin of a revelation? All these are questions which will not occupy us here. It suffices for our purpose if we distinguish this original revelation from ideas which are derived *from* such an original experience of the actual event of revelation itself and which build on it indeed but are not identical with it. Whether, why and in what sense such mediated knowledge can under certain circumstances still be called revelation in a proper sense will be discussed later on. There is at least no possible doubt about the fact that there is such a distinction and that it is justified. All the content of any theological reflection which has taken place, or is taking place, anywhere in the history of theology, has on the one hand the intention of building on the data of revelation, of starting from and returning to them, of explaining and developing them, of relating them to the totality of the one system of human consciousness and knowledge, etc. And, on the other hand, it does not lay any claim to having been received from God himself in a direct event of revelation in such a way that it would be the direct result of this divine activity in its content and correctness. If we give the name of theology quite simply to any such theological reflection understood in this way, in distinction to original revelation which builds no longer on something else, then the question arises: is there already theology in the writings of the New Testament—or is the latter in all its statements merely the objectification of an original event of revelation?

At first sight it might seem clear that this question must be answered in the negative. Holy Writ is inspired in all its parts, it is in everything it really states the object of faith and the norm of this faith in all its propositions. In other words, it is revelation and not theology.

But let us take a closer look before accepting this information as final. No Catholic theologian will dispute the fact that there are dogmas in the Church which as such are true statements of revelation and thus can and must be believed with divine and not merely ecclesiastical faith

—and which yet do not in themselves spring from an immediate event of revelation but are deduced from, or explained by, one or several propositions of original, or more original, revelation. We are not debating here about the conditions, presuppositions and limits under which such derived propositions still have the quality of 'being revealed by God', nor are we debating about the cases in which this is no longer possible (although even in these cases these propositions are perhaps absolutely certain and definable by the Church). It is quite enough for us in the present context that there are such derived propositions of faith in the pronouncements of the magisterium of the Church, i.e. propositions of which it *cannot* be said that they originate directly and as determined propositions from a divine revelation or that they are in the first place communicated knowledge dependent only on itself. There are truths of *faith* which are recognized as such by the Church because and as they are referred back to other truths of revelation in which they are 'implicitly' contained. Any development of dogma which is more than just history of theology would otherwise be impossible. For the history of dogmas means neither the history of a merely human effort of understanding concerning an always constant content of faith, nor the mere history of different formulations of the one truth which is always there as it were naked and independently of these formulations in which it is given, but which is now presented in different, changing verbal garbs simply by reason of some whim or on account of external circumstances in the history of the spirit. The history of dogmas is really a history of faith—of the same faith which always remains, which no longer experiences any real increase from outside. But it is a *history* of faith itself in which something happens which was up till then not given 'in that way'. The new justifies itself always and only through its origin from the old; the new truth is the old truth and not a truth added to the old one from outside. But it is a *new* truth in so far as there is given a statement which is presented as a proposition of faith itself only now and never before. And this newness of what is given only now can refer both to the content and to the reflected comprehension of the certain fact of its having been revealed as such. But precisely because the new truth of a revealed proposition proves itself to be the old truth by reverting to the old, already always-known and understood truth of faith, it tells us that it does not spring from a new divine revelation existing independently but that its hour of birth, its moment of revelation is the same as that of the other truth which itself is already the original revelation of God, resting on no other event of revelation, or stemming in its turn, as far as its own origin is concerned, from an original revelation of God. In brief, if there is any real history of dogmas, then there is a type of revelation which is not simply in itself original and yet is revelation, i.e. the word of God, which demands our faith infallibly and demands faith in the real sense of the word.

Once more, this is not the place for answering the question as to *how* this is possible—in other words, how a word derived from the word of God can still keep the quality of the word of God itself. This is a difficult question which certainly cannot be answered simply by the explanation given by the previously common textbook theology of the development and progress of dogma, viz. by maintaining that a new dogma says exactly the same in different words and that the communicated content is utterly and without any change whatsoever identical with the old content and therefore that it is for that precise reason the word of God. No—for instance, in the teaching that the sacraments are seven in number, that marriage has a sacramental nature, that the divine Persons have the nature of subsisting relations, etc., etc., expression is given to realizations in the form of dogmas which as such just were not there in earlier times—they have developed and yet were not given in any new revelation. They exist as the result of the real history of the old truth and are *therefore* and in *this* sense identical with it and share in its characteristics as the word of God, but they arise from the old source of a divine communication and not from a new one. And this communicated truth must have such a history. For since it is a truth heard and believed in a human manner (and only as such is it also the truth spoken by God), it must have a history. And a history in the realm of the spirit and of the person is always a history of a true becoming in the constant sameness of one and the same historically existing truth. As we have said, the more exact forms, conditions and causes of this becoming and of history with regard to any truth in general and with regard to a revealed truth, a word of God, in particular, cannot concern us here. All theories of the development of dogmas and of the history of dogmas are nothing other than attempts to give a more exact answer to this question of how a really new truth can be the old truth. The variety of such theories which have not yet by any means arrived at a *sententia communis* in theology, however, shows precisely by the fact of there being so many theories that it is true to say that Dogma as such can have a history. And this not only after the manner in which one normally tacitly conceives of the 'history of divine revelation' passing through the Old Testament into the New Testament, viz. in the sense that at different points in time new divine overtures are made which each time communicate new statements of the truth, each with their own proper moment of birth— but also in the sense that the truth, once communicated, has itself again its own history which does not necessarily lead it out of the sphere of divine revelation but which is itself the unfolding of that history.

If this historical character of revealed truth cannot be disputed in its general terms, and if this truth remains the same even in its new historical forms, then we can now pose the question as to whether there already is such a history of the original revealed truth even within the New Testament since in it there arise new developments of this truth which nevertheless lay claim to the quality of the Word of God without thereby demanding a proper origin of fresh revelation for themselves. The phrase 'within the New Testament' is meant here to indicate: already during the period of the New Testament, at the time of the Church of the Apostles, at which time, according to every theological conviction, revelation was still taking place (since it is declared to have terminated only with the 'death of the last Apostle')—so that such a derived but real revelation took place also (not 'only') at the time of the primitive Church and was proclaimed by the Apostles and by others appointed by them to proclaim the Christian message. But 'within the New Testament' is also meant to signify: while the writings of the New Testament itself were coming into existence—so that such developments in the field of the history of dogmas take place and become tangible in these writings themselves.

Our question can and must be clearly answered in the affirmative. It may first of all be asked: if we find this event in the later Church, why should it not have taken place also in the primitive Church? The inner power of development, the dynamism of self-explanation which is present within the truth and especially within a divine truth, cannot surely have been less at the time of the primitive Church than later on. After all, God did not need to do something at this stage by his own new initiative which the truth revealed by him could do itself. Of course, this would always take place (just as later on) under the continuous saving providence and the assistance of the Holy Ghost, and in accordance with a spiritual situation once more embraced by his will and wisdom—so that God really does not act 'less' when he expresses his truth in this way by an immanent unfolding of what has already been communicated than when he communicates it originally —he acts *differently*. Furthermore, it must be borne in mind that one cannot hear a truth—with understanding—without taking it in or assimilating it, without confronting it with the rest of what is already present in one's mind and consciousness, etc. In other words, the simple act of hearing and receiving, and the act of reflection are not at all acts and phases of a mental process of understanding which can be adequately distinguished from one another and arranged in temporal sequence one after the other. Thus theology, in as far as it is a condition of simple hearing, begins already in the first moment of hearing itself, and then it cannot but continue on and unfold itself.

In actual fact, if we read the New Testament itself attentively and without any prejudice, we will see that there is theology going on there. It would be absurd to try to reduce the whole difference between for example the theology of the Synoptics or of the Acts of the Apostles and that of St Paul to the intervention of a new, direct revelation of God. No, the men of the New Testament ponder and reflect on the data of their faith already known to them; they have 'problems' which they solve for themselves to the best of their ability in a theological reflection; they have heard objections which they answer and which give them new realizations of knowledge; they have different spiritual and theological origins, and these assert themselves in their perspectives of expression, in their choice of ideas, in the accentuation which they give to their exposition. They have personal experiences of life which they had first to gain, which were not always available to them and which now influence their theological thought and demand new answers on the basis of their old belief. Their teaching is different; this does not mean that it is contradictory. It would be impossible to speak of a theology of St Paul or the Johannine writings if they did not contain precisely—theology, human effort, human reflection, fermentation by a definite individuality and historical situation (of the Jewish environment, of the continuing activity of the baptist movement, of Hellenism, of the pre-Christian Jewish and pagan gnosticism). The authors of the New Testament obviously do not receive an answer to all these questions simply by ever new, separate revelations from God (in the sense of 'thus speaks Jahweh'). Rather, this answer is the result of their theology, of their own reflection on the basis of the last original data of revelation and of the most original recognitions of faith. This reflection (where it expresses itself in the New Testament understood as writing) is directly or indirectly the reflection of the authoritative messengers of Christ who have true authority to teach —it is a reflection which has the assistance of the Holy Spirit; this reflection is justified by its purely objective result, by its method and formal characteristics, by what we call 'Inspiration' (which after all is not necessarily the communication of a new, until now absent body of knowledge, to the inspired author); the result of this reflection remains properly speaking the word of God, on account of the authority of the authors and by reason of Inspiration. But there is this theological reflection in the New Testament, and it does not destroy the quality of the word of God in its expression; but it does mean that not everything which is said in the New Testament is based on a separate, new and autonomous event of revelation.

One might be afraid that these statements express and emphasize what is only too obvious. But when one looks at the work actually being done in Catholic theology even at the present time and notices, or thinks one notices, that in spite of this the proper conclusions are not being drawn, or at least are not being drawn clearly and precisely, from this simple fact, then one begins to have doubts again as to whether the simple principle of there being theology even already in the New Testament is after all as obvious as it ought to be or might be. We therefore pose the question as to what conclusions follow on this principle. We do not mean to develop these at length here but intend merely to name a few of them in brief outline.

First of all, since we can observe theology in the New Testament absolutely *a posteriori* and are not dependent for the establishing of this fact on the other insights which we have also made use of here, we may begin with by stating the following: since there already is theology in the New Testament which nevertheless is dogma, *such* theology can also be found in the Church of later ages. Protestant theology is largely (tacitly or explicitly) based on the axiom that there is indeed a significant history of theology even after the New Testament but not a real history of dogmas in which dogmas come into being of a type which impose an absolute obligation of faith and which possess finality: which obligation and which finality can be revised only 'in a forward direction' (in the sense of a better and more adequate form of expression) and not 'in a backward direction' (in the sense of casting doubts on their truth), and all having to be submitted again to the judgement of the New Testament which may perhaps disallow them. Against this position we may now state quite positively that if there is a theology in the New Testament which gives rise to dogmas binding in faith and not merely to theological opinions, then such a theology is also to be found outside the New Testament in the later ages of the Church—for the reasons and requirements are the same in both cases. Naturally, the New Testament considered as a period and especially the written word constitutes a norm for all later periods in so far as there is given in it the one foundation which is the permanent norm and the basis which must support the Church at every later date, as well as all later faith and every later theology; for this foundation is not just any collection of particular truths but a historical event of salvation (to which belongs also the formation of the Church herself). But this does not exclude the possibility of a process of developing new *dogmas* in the later history of the faith on this basis of the New Testament. If the 'making the faith one's own' is historical—and how could it be otherwise—and is not merely theological reflection on a consciousness of faith, then there must be a history of dogmas since this is nothing other than the history of the particular form of the absolute consent of faith at any particular time, made on the grounds of the one permanent divine revelation as it has been given once and for all in Jesus Christ and as it must remain in every situation of history —an actual event in the consent of faith and not merely of simple theology.

If there already is theology in the New Testament which, although a binding expression of revelation taken as the Word of God, is not an original event of revelation, then it must be possible in principle to get some idea as to *where* approximately the line of demarcation runs in the New Testament between the content of the original expression of revelation and the theology based on revelation. The fact that this question is hardly posed explicitly in Catholic theology shows that evidently the simple thesis expressed here has not been stated clearly enough in spite of its being so obvious. It can naturally be only a question of an *approximate* demarcation. Since the whole of the New Testament in all its parts and declarations is equally binding on later theology (even though in each case obviously with that particular binding force which is claimed by individual assertions in the New Testament itself), this matter of demarcation cannot be a question of providing us with a criterion as to which assertions of the New Testament are binding, 'Christ-compelling', or as to which correspond to the inner Canon of Scripture and which do not. And since it is extremely difficult in principle to determine the demarcation between an assertion stating something 'in other words' and an assertion which in relation to the original assertion is new and says something new— as is shown by the fact of all the differing theories about the development of dogma with their distinction between the formal and virtual inclusion, etc., of one declaration in another—the demand for such a demarcation cannot have the intention of establishing completely unmistakable limits. This cannot be the case particularly because a formulation of what is an original assertion and what is a derived assertion of revelation necessarily implies in both cases a comprehending interpretation of both classes of assertions by the one who makes the demarcation—in other words, because it itself implies theology again. Nevertheless, it is completely possible to pose the following question: what does that look like which is the real basic content of Christianity and can therefore be grasped as true when (and in as far as) it signifies a divine proclamation beyond which it is absolutely impossible to go? And what in the revealed Word of Scripture can itself be already conceived as 'unfolding', as a theological interpretation of these original, basic data with the help of the concepts, images and viewpoints which either grow out of the whole complex of problems of the basic data themselves or were already given as means of expression and as stimuli to theological reflection in the religious environment of the New Testament itself? Let us suppose (which certainly is not a strict hermeneutic principle but merely a sensible working hypothesis) that all the Christological and Soteriological declarations of the New Testament without exception go back to the declarations made by Jesus about himself and his Person (seeing these, it is true, in the light of the paschal experience) and that they do not contain beyond this any element which, in addition to the self-testimony of Jesus, would itself have to go back once more to a new content of a proper revelation. We may then ask, for example: what is the historical self-expression given by Jesus about himself which forms the basis of all the Christology and Soteriology of the other writings of the New Testament? No one with a Catholic understanding of Fundamental Theology will be able to say that such a question is impossible, unanswerable or not permissible and that one cannot go back beyond the Christological and

Soteriological faith of the Apostles and of the writings of the New Testament. If there is a Fundamental Theology in the Catholic sense, a Theology which ultimately, therefore, springs really from a historical assertion made by Jesus about himself or goes back to it (which comes to the same thing), then this question is completely legitimate and necessary. But in most cases this question is only posed quite incidentally.

This demand is not merely a demand of the historically curious, in order to know how everything has come about. Such a demarcation, the explicit and (as far as possible) clear consciousness of such relations of dependence and the sequences of origin in the case of the individual statements of the New Testament, has a much more essential function. For knowledge of these connections can serve to determine much better and more clearly the meaning of any statement, what it is really meant to convey, and the limits of what it is meant to convey. When one can tell the source *whence* a New Testament author actually learned what he is saying, then one can express much better what he wants to say. For then one can say in a case of doubt that he does not wish to say any more than the source of this declaration really warrants. This method, however, is not proposed as a critical principle which one could apply in order to reject the binding force of some statement of the New Testament whose meaning is already determined by some other source or simply by the wording itself. If this meaning is definite, then the dogmatic theologian can do nothing else but agree with the New Testament author even though he does not see how the supposedly original data of revelation really supply the meaning in this case, or is unable to give the sources from which the New Testament author actually knows what he is saying. But there are undoubtedly cases where the meaning of a statement, its scope and its limits, are not clear. In such a case it is an absolutely justifiable method to try to determine the exact meaning of the doubtful statement (or of a thought-complex which has to be interpreted) by asking oneself, 'from where' does the 'theologian of the New Testament' develop his thought?— what was the basis of his theological reflection as regards premises and self-evident presuppositions?—and by then asking what results from this and what does not. And if this meaning of the statement, determined from its source, is not repudiated by the meaning of the statement already fixed from elsewhere, then one is absolutely justified in saying that this meaning determined from the source is also the real meaning, and that in a doubtful case the real meaning also does not go beyond the meaning so determined. It is not possible here to give clear examples. But it is undoubtedly hermeneutically absolutely permissible—with careful use of the 'economy principle'—to presuppose that, for instance, St Paul had no more original revelation-data at his disposal for his doctrine of original sin than what is sufficiently available from the Old Testament and the rest of the Soteriology of the New Testament. It may then, however, be quite legitimately asked: what results from these original data? One can and must naturally answer this question (as is often necessary also elsewhere in the deeper questions of philosophy and theology) by as it were reconstituting the theology of St Paul. Obviously such a deduction can gain greater certitude by the fact that St Paul has thought it out for us in a binding way than if we had to think it out ourselves for the first time. But if we are thus to reconstitute pauline thought genetically, then (it would seem to me without my being able to give detailed reasons for this here) one would arrive at an originally pauline doctrine of original sin which makes a clearer connection between the first sin and personal sin than that of which St Augustine was aware: there would result an interpretation of the doctrine of original sin which would from the very start look on quite a few things differently from St Augustine, and quite a few important points would be brought out in it which in the traditional teaching on this matter (still far too dependent on St Augustine) are still incorporated too much as supplementary matter. But we cannot here do more than barely indicate the fact that this method can be fruitful.

There is a point at which modern Catholic exegesis and biblical theology uses the method just proposed, although under different catch-words. But as yet Catholic dogmatic theology in its inner-dogmatic work has hardly followed it at all in this. Present-day Catholic exegesis and biblical theology ask themselves very consciously indeed, when dealing with the words of Jesus, as to what in their formulation could be taken as the original word spoken by the historical Jesus himself—and what in such formulations (in the way they are 'beamed', in rendering the scope explicit, in drawing contours, in the conceptual material they use, etc.) is already formation of 'primitive-Church-theology' (*Gemeindetheologie*), correctly understanding the latter of course in a Catholic sense, viz. as the theology of the ecclesiastical *magisterium* of the primitive Church, based on the Apostles who were able to further the faith as the teachers of the primitive Church community authorized by Christ and under the assistance of the Holy Ghost—and not as an ultimately anonymous theological speculation which is not directed or guaranteed from any quarter. This is not meant to say simply that in every case, every word of Jesus itself seen historically must already be by itself an original event of revelation. But the closeness to such an event of revelation is at any rate so great in principle that the nevertheless conceivable distance which can sometimes still exist even in this case, is nearly always negligible—at least as far as the sayings of Jesus about himself are concerned, although (and this must not be overlooked) he presumably used theological concepts for this whose form and import had already been determined previously, and not merely theologically neutral concepts of a general human kind. In the eschatology of Christ there is already after all so much which is historically established from elsewhere that one can surely speak already of a theology of Christ which adds *one* thing and nothing more to the already traditional eschatology. Of course, it thereby revolutionizes the traditional eschatology fundamentally, for the one thing it adds is the fact that Christ himself is the pivotal point of world history, the Saviour in person and not merely a prophet. And so, for the reason just indicated, not every word of the historical Jesus can be identified with the notion of an original revelation (although it must certainly also be taken into consideration that Christ's absolute and original consciousness as the Son—direct vision of God, in the language of theology—must give to *all* his declarations a breadth of understanding which in its turn gives every one of his sayings, even if they are derived, an originality which cannot be surpassed). Thus in practice the labour of the exegete and biblical theologian, differentiating between the words of the historical Jesus and the work of 'primitive-Church-theology', does after all come to the same thing in many cases as what we have demanded here under the title of a method of differentiation (and not of separation). This work of differentiation which is undertaken by the exegete seems at first sight a superfluous method for the work of dogmatic theologians, since they do after all listen to the whole of Scripture with all it contains as the inspired and infallibly true Word of God, and since it does not seem to be essential for them to know where the exact wording of a statement comes from —whether it comes from Jesus himself or from 'primitive-Church-theology' (which already interprets the words of Jesus theologically

in the whole context of the Christ-faith). But when it is a question of
the exact, and perhaps otherwise very difficult to determine meaning
of one of Christ's words in the Gospels (and there can easily be cases
of this), then this distinction can become very significant indeed, even
for the dogmatic theologian. For example, whether texts like Mt 10.23
or Mk 9.1 are to be regarded as said by Jesus himself or not, 'just' as
they are written, is not simply indifferent for their meaning. For even
though these words must be regarded as inspired and inerrant under
both presuppositions, the choice between these two possibilities is not
unimportant for the exact determination of their meaning. In the case
of eschatological statements particularly, in order to determine their
meaning exactly, one should inquire very closely into the original
source of such statements. The same holds good, for instance, for the
trinitarian formula in Mt 28.19. If this is already the reflection of the
trinitarian theology of the primitive Church (*Urgemeinde*), then we
must simply seek for the meaning and scope of this formula from this
point of view. In this case it would not then be permissible to presuppose that the meaning of this formula should be interpreted as it
were in the light of Christ's direct vision of God. Rather, it would have
to be asked what moved the theology of the primitive Church to name
the Father, Son and Holy Ghost in a baptismal formula. This would
first of all demand an interpretation of this triad in the sense of the
economy of salvation, and only then could one arrive from this at the
immanent Trinity, with quite a few precisions which without the
realization of this starting-point could not perhaps be attained so clearly
and at the first attempt. And we could go on multiplying such examples
of the objective usefulness to hermeneutics of the principle laid down
above.

If this distinction were strictly carried through, it could provide us
with an even more basic benefit. Who has not had the impression that
the New Testament, and even more so the dogmatic theology taught
in our textbooks, present a bewilderingly complicated system of
assertions, a colossal complexity of statements, viewpoints, connections, distinctions, of opposing, often hard to harmonize movements
of thought whose synthesis calls forth even more complicated distinctions? It must, of course, be quite clear from the start that the truth
which tries to embrace and express (even if only from afar) the infinity
of God and the incalculable variety of the world and of saving history
cannot be so simple that its expression would not of necessity overtax

our powers. A system which would in a few formulas give the complete solution to everything with regard to the reality intended in the act of religion would by its simplifying simplicity and clarity already carry the stigma of falsehood within it. And yet, the message of the Gospel is addressed to the average man, it wants to help him to endure the hard struggle of his short life; the message of the Gospel is not meant to be the material on which man practises his dialectic acuteness of mind. Above all, the man of today gets the impression that one should be able to recognize in the true message of God that it testifies to the incomprehensible mystery we call God—that it does not claim to 'have got to the bottom of it' but, on the contrary, that it faces man inescapably with that greater God, with His mystery as such, in order to force him really to come out of himself and to transcend himself in that act which we call faith, adoration, surrender, love, etc. Reflection on the Christian message may be necessary and profitable *qua reflection*, i.e. as theology it may be complicated, subtle, abstract and in some way or other a secret science of an esoteric kind which is accessible only to the specialist. This is perhaps unavoidable, and the 'simple Christian' should not be too hasty in voicing cheap protests against it. Such a complicated theology may even have an indispensable function to perform by seeing to it that the message of the Gospel, the kerygma itself, is not reduced to a too simplified, 'enlightened' and utilitarian level in the unfathomableness *necessarily* belonging to it. But precisely this theology must not conceive the kerygma as theology *ad usum delphini*, as popularized theology, in the way microphysics is explained to the man in the street in our illustrated magazines. The simple message of the Gospel, the kerygma itself, must in its simplicity be the difficult, that which is nearer to the meant reality, the unfathomable and that which overtaxes the mind and heart, in spite of and because of its simplicity. The reflected system, as opposed to the kerygma, must always appear as something secondary and derivative because the kerygma, fully and properly understood, is not the more primitive language for this matter, but the meant reality and its experience itself, and therefore it can never be attained by the reflection of theology. For the kerygma, properly understood, is not an additional discourse about something, but is the reality itself. For in contrast to reflecting theology it is completely 'there' and properly received only when it includes the grace with which it is proclaimed and heard—only when it calls up the transcendency of man itself which is divinized by grace and plunged into the reality of God himself, i.e. the transcendency of man which is not there in words but in the experience of 'daily life', in the experience of love, death and the inescapable encounter with the mystery in whose unfathomableness everything is founded and whose night alone illumines every superficial brightness of human existence. But this kerygma (if it really is itself and not devitalized theology) is precisely in this way necessarily simple, for ultimately the simplest is also the most unfathomable and vice versa. Obviously this kerygmatic testimony to the mystery of the Godhead in which God gives himself and saves us, and which is aimed at in the Christian faith and made 'present' by the actual message of faith, has necessarily its own temporal modes, its own physiognomy bound up with different situations; for it must attain man in the concrete, just as he is. Let us note in parenthesis that it should not injure the dignity and permanent significance of Holy Scripture to take this historically, situationally conditioned physiognomy even of Scripture (which distinguishes and does not belittle it) more clearly into account, and hence to acknowledge more readily to ourselves the difficulty which it presents to us, the men of a different age. For our difficulty is to understand the meaning of Scripture as intended for us, and to make it really our own. And this we must do wherever we are placed in the cruelly sober reality of our actual life, and not somewhere up in the clouds where we escape from this reality into a romantic ideology which, when all is said and done, is merely an aesthetic enchantment deceiving us into thinking that we will derive the true comfort from Scripture which is really contained in it. If we were really proceeding along the right lines, then surely our word should reach more people today than it actually does. And so, even though this time-index of the kerygma may not be overlooked (or better, so that it may not be overlooked), it must always be asked again what is in actual fact the message, the meaning in our complicated theology. This must not be understood in the sense of a latitudinarianism or modernism, as if the answer to such a question were to determine what might be omitted without endangering the 'substance' of Christianity, or what might be excluded from the requirements of faith as of little importance. That would obviously be heresy. For, after all, God's simple and immense mystery displays itself—its very self—in everything said by complicated theology, and it would consequently be also injured in itself if one were to give up part of its self-explanation. But it must be proclaimed as kerygma and not as complicated theology, as primary and not as a simplified derivative of theology. And the Catholic doctrine of the '*fides implicita*' (which in the old days was an abomination to Protestant ears), and the question in theology as to what must be believed explicitly *necessitate medii* and *praecepti* and what not, are not in the last analysis casuistic questions looking for as easy a requirement for faith as possible. Rather, these questions are animated by a correct and most important conviction as to the fact that faith as such always only attains its true nature when it is a surrender to the incomprehensible God, an acceptance of the Unmanageable, a possession of the Incalculable—a real possession (and that is what is really meant by *fides implicita*). In these questions arises the conviction that the real possession of revealed reality does not always necessarily grow, but can even diminish with the growth of the conceptual unfolding of what is attained in the actual act of faith. For the act of faith does indeed attain what is meant through conceptual objectivity (to any extent whatsoever), yet not *in* it but rather in the experience of the divine grace of faith, in the light of faith, which is both the basis of faith and the actual object of faith; the grace of faith which is uncreated grace—the triune God himself—and as such also the content of faith possessed in the act of faith itself. It is therefore absolutely legitimate to ask about the nucleus of faith, about the right way for the kerygma to represent the meant reality conceptually, so that the act of listening acceptance of this kerygma, i.e. faith, may be as radical existentially and as much united in grace with the matter referred to as possible. This question is, however, most closely connected with the other question to which our present little reflection is devoted.

Naturally, the question just posed can be brought nearer to an answer in a way other than by the answer to our own question in the present investigation which has to try to uncover the genetic structure of the New Testament statements by *a posteriori* observation. One can also attempt to answer as well as possible the question just posed above by a more speculative process. One can more or less say in this connection that the real nucleus of Christian revelation, the unity of the mysteries in the strict sense, can be understood in the sense that the absolute mystery of God did not intend to be present to us merely as someone judging from a distance. Rather, God wished to give himself in an absolute, radical self-communication by grace as the innermost kernel of our existence and, precisely thus, as the permanent mystery always coming nearer for the acceptance in love. One could show—even though only subsequently on each defined and believed mystery of Christianity—that the three great Christian mysteries (the Trinity, Incarnation and Grace-Glory) can be understood as necessarily mutually connected articulations of the one basic mystery of our concrete existence, viz. that the mystery is quite simply that which has become near in grace and which as such should be accepted in faith and love. It may be that such a simplifying perspective is typically modern. We do not mean to dispute that this is so. No one will surely doubt the fact that the particular manner in which modern man experiences God is existential (and not merely theoretical, as it always was), that modern man experiences God as the Unspeakable, the Incomprehensible. And so it is only right to look at the simple incomprehensibility and the incomprehensible simplicity of the whole Christian message from this point of view. But if, as we have done in the present investigation, one poses the question about the difference between the kerygmatic and theological content of the New Testament, without answering it in content (since we were here concerned merely with the lawfulness of this question), then one may conjecture that the question thus posed, and the other question briefly indicated above both in itself and as regards its answer, converge in their conclusions, if they do not in fact become simply identified. For one thing must be noted: the distinction we have made here between original revelation and theology based on it (even though this theology is binding and revelation *quoad nos*) cannot ultimately be taken to mean that there simply are statements in the New Testament which are mere and (*sit venia verbo*) 'chemically' pure objectifications of the original event of revelation and nothing else, and which are in no way already theology. We have after all stressed the fact that the hearing of a revelation as such is already part of human activity and thus does necessarily imply theology. No doubt, the actual event of revelation in man begins also so 'profoundly' in his innermost centre (and indeed all the more so the more it is precisely revelation of the divine self-communication of divinizing grace and basically means nothing else than this whenever it has attained its climax and fulfilment), that every conceptual objectification of what is thus communicated is secondary in comparison, even though this objectification is also utterly willed in itself by God and guaranteed in its rightness (by a public revelation, in which this revelation must be passed on to others besides the direct bearer of revelation). One can get a clearer idea of what is meant by this from the example of the mystic. As is well known, a clear distinction must be made in mystical experience between the actual experience of God in the core of the person and the conceptual communication, interpretation and reflex objectification of that experience which the mystic undertakes for himself and then also for others with the aid of concepts, means of understanding, etc., available to him from elsewhere. Even though there is an essential difference as regards the divine guarantee for this conceptual objectification between the official public revelation and a mystical 'private revelation', it is nevertheless quite justifiable to conceive the actual and original central experience of the original bearers of revelation in the original event of revelation analogously to this central mystical experience. For grace, understood as the supernatural self-communication of God, is also light (light of faith, *illustratio et illuminatio mentis et cordis*), as the old theology had always acknowledged, since the New Testament teaching about the light, the unction, the experience of the *dynamis* of the spirit, the unspeakable groans of the spirit, etc., would simply be unintelligible without such a conception. Hence the simple inner bestowal of grace is already a kind of revelation, even though it only comes to its full being in the form of public and official revelation meant also for others, in the divinely guaranteed objectification of what is already contained in it but only as something which cannot be reflected on by man. This fundamental revelation in grace must, however, lie at the basis even of the original event of revelation in the case of revelation simply so called. This is because by definition there cannot be any higher form of revelation (before the Beatific Vision) than the self-communication by God in grace, with the result that this must also be at the basis of what is normally called revelation. The latter is then, of course, accompanied by a moment of official objectification, of conceptual representation and of binding concern to everyone, and extends to all the dimensions of human existence (both individual and social), all of which is not yet characteristic of the basic revelation by grace in the depth of the human being as such. If this is so, then it is easy to understand that this original process of revelation, which even in Scripture comes before theology, cannot be sought in, and simply identified with any particular objectification in chosen statements of the New Testament. It lies at the basis of these statements but is not identical with any determined, conceptually objectifying statements, even though these are the absolutely binding, and properly communicating objectification of the original event of revelation for us. If we bear this in mind, then we will be able to understand that the question about the pre-theological, kerygmatic content of the New Testament in distinction to the theology of the New Testament, and the question about the kerygmatic nucleus of the message of the New Testament to be proclaimed by us, are very closely connected. Of course, there is no way of *talking* about both these realities having to be distinguished from reflex theology except again in concepts, in more theology. But it is important for theology to understand that one of its own essential questions is to explain that it itself is not the original basis of Christian existence, just as metaphysics is not the original basis for intellectual existence, although both of them belong necessarily to human and Christian existence.

3
WHAT IS A DOGMATIC STATEMENT?[1]

WHAT is a dogmatic statement? This is the question I have been posed and which I am expected to answer in the framework of what is laid down in Catholic theology. It is a difficult question to expose and answer even for the simple reason that, as far as I know, it is hardly ever explicitly posed in this way in the usual Catholic textbook theology. Of course, the ecclesiological part of Fundamental Theology always includes a treatise on the Church's magisterium, its bearers and the binding force of its declarations—showing clearly the various grades of obligation imposed—as well as a treatise on the *loci theologici* and the primacy of Holy Scripture, the inspired Word of God. Also, we are once again beginning to reflect more deeply and exactly, and making the various delicate distinctions required, on the relationship between the *magisterium* and Scripture; there are signs that at last, after too much mere denial of Protestant theology, we are slowly developing something like a theology of the Word. In this connection reflection on the difference between Kerygma and Dogma, between the word of the magisterium and the real proclamation of the joyous, saving message of the Lord is gradually beginning. Yet it cannot be said that one has only to open a textbook to find there a clearer answer to the question as to what is a dogmatic statement. To this extent it is also clear that this subject is not already known and directly elaborated as a controversial theological theme, however much one may suspect *a priori* that any attempt to answer this question will once more bring to the fore all the doctrinal differences between Protestant and Catholic theology concerning the *magis-*

[1] The present essay was originally a lecture given at a specialists' meeting of the Protestant-Catholic ecumenical movement. Consequently, the fact that it was originally given in the framework of a report (which it was not thought desirable to extend subsequently) will explain the fragmentary nature of the various parts of its exposition.

terium, its relationship to Scripture, etc. Consequently, all I can do is to try to collect the *membra disiecta* of such a doctrine about the nature of a dogmatic statement from all the corners of Catholic theology. And it remains to be seen how far this is successful or to what extent I overlook many subjects connected with this question.

I presume that this question is meant in such a way that its answer must also draw the dividing line between a dogmatic statement and an utterance of the proper, direct kerygma. In other words, I presume that it is meant to make it quite clear whether, how and why there are intrinsically different forms of expression and speech in the realm of ecclesiastical Christianity, *one* of which is then called a dogmatic statement in the strict specific sense. But evidently, therefore, this distinction to be made within the language of faith of the Christian in the Church, and of the Church herself in her official representatives, cannot be the sole subject of the reflections required here. It is expected (I presume) that a dogmatic statement will not be only definitively distinguished from the kerygma and from proclamation and preaching in the strictest theological sense of these words, but will also be compared with ordinary statements (even those concerned with religious matters, if there are and can be such statements); in other words, it is presumably expected that what is shared in common by Kerygma and Dogma (up to and including theological statements) will be contrasted in this respect with ordinary discourse. In so far as a dogmatic statement must be most strictly distinguished from a kerygmatic one, a sufficiently clear demarcation is thus given between a dogmatic statement and *that* sort of statement which is to be found in Scripture. Of course, in this connection we must not overlook the fact that even Scripture does not simply express the most original revelation (in such a way that this is the original happening of this revelation as an event), but that there certainly is also that kind of theological reflection in Scripture which is not directly kerygma but rather (one might say) typical theological reflection. For all this finds a place in the Catholic conception of the Inspiration of the Scriptures, since this conception does not exclude the possibility of essentially different literary forms within the one Word of God. Let this suffice as preliminary 'method' reflections on what exactly we are supposed to be talking about here. I will try to fulfil my task in a series of theses, adding a certain amount of explanation in each case.

    1. A dogmatic statement is one which claims to be true even in that

formal sense which we are familiar with from ordinary everyday language and knowledge. Even a dogmatic statement should fulfil all those inner structures and laws which do or can belong to an ordinary statement: it is related to the person who makes it, has logic, its conceptual elements have their historicity, it is embedded in a historical and social fabric, contains different literary forms, presupposes those unreflected elements common to listener and speaker without which there would be no possibility of mutal understanding at all. Such and similar structures of a natural, ordinary statement must also be found in a dogmatic statement. Obviously we cannot develop these structures in greater detail here, for their reflex, explicit exposition—which is hardly ever undertaken in theology (which is not always too good)—would demand much more time and energy than are at our disposal. The thesis itself which we have formulated follows in its Catholic understanding not only from *a posteriori* experience of the fact that things are as the thesis states—in other words, that even in the expression of Christian proclamation and theology it is a question of human words and all that implies—but it follows also from the Catholic understanding of the relationship between nature and grace. This would be the point in theology where it would be easiest to find out something to help us with our Catholic understanding of the nature of a dogmatic statement in so far as it is also (but not only) a natural statement. But precisely from this point of view it would probably have to be asked and seen whether the Protestant view on the relationship between sinful creation and redeeming grace does not also have its repercussions in our present question. We would have to inquire into the question as to whether there is not (or whether we should not expect) a controversial-theological difference between the Catholic and Protestant conception even with regard to the natural, basic structures of a dogmatic and also kerygmatic statement. But perhaps in this sphere the difference has not been worked out consciously enough from the basic understanding of the relation between nature and grace which underlies it. Within the realm of Catholic thought itself we will, however, have to say that, in Catholic theology's reflections on the nature of the Word, the aspect of this Word which is determined by the sinfulness of man is hardly touched on. And yet it should touch on this. Much more should be done than simply to make a general statement about the clouding of the human mind as a result of original sin, and about the moral necessity of revelation for (clear and certain) knowledge of those truths which in themselves are open to natural human knowledge on the religious and moral plane. For these statements should not merely be used to determine the characteristics of human knowledge *apart from* revelation. They should be used also to inquire into the peculiarly 'infralapsarian' nature of human knowledge and expression *within* the realm of revelation and of the faith of the Church. Is it not Catholic doctrine that the justified man too, even though he is not *simul iustus et peccator* in the Protestant sense, still remains always co-determined by his origin from the state of sinfulness? In other words—using this particular formulation—can the *simul iustus et peccator* not be understood in an absolutely correct Catholic sense? If this is so, then it should not be interpreted merely as a determination of the *moral* dimension of justified man, but should be understood also as a determination of the 'noetic' element in man, and this precisely also as a determination of the true reality of the justified man in his faith. This divine truth is after all embodied in the natural spirituality of man—yet not in an abstract, neutral spiritual nature and noetic of man, but in a nature and noetic burdened with original sin and to be redeemed by the grace of Christ. But I cannot really find any information in the explicit subject matter of present-day Catholic theology, as to what precisely is meant in this connection by what we have just stated in a formal, abstract way. And yet, unless one favours the strange opinion (which is really senseless although probably tacitly very widespread) that human discourse and propositions cannot have any other properties than those of truth or error, one cannot brush aside the question as to whether dogmatic statements do not also bear the signature of guilty man in the state of original sin by the simple expedient of pointing out that since such statements are true, they are by this very fact already utterly withdrawn from the realm of sinful flesh. For God's truth has also in reality incarnated itself into this flesh of sin, if what our first thesis affirms quite innocently is true, viz. that dogmatic propositions are inevitably also propositions of a natural, noetic nature, and if it is true that this nature, too, like all natures, is not an abstract one (in the way it originates as itself from the hands of the creator) but a concrete and thus infralapsarian nature which bears the stamp of the guilt of man. One need only ask oneself whether a statement though in itself to be qualified as true cannot also be rash and presumptuous. Can it not betray the historical perspective of a man in such a way that this perspective reveals itself as an historically guilty one? Cannot even a truth be dangerous, equivocal, seductive, forward—can it not manœuvre a person into a position where he must make a decision for which he is not fitted? If such and many similar questions which could be asked are not to be rejected from the outset, then it becomes clear that even within the truth of the Church and of dogmatically correct statements it is absolutely possible to speak sinfully, with a sinfulness which may be either individual, or of humanity in general or of a particular period. Once again, it would be impossible to say that Catholic theology has given a great deal of thought up till now to this question which is not really so unimportant in itself and is of great interest also in the theology of 'concrete' nature in the infralapsarian order. If I were to ask myself, therefore, as to what within Catholic theology are the essential *basic* structures of this infralapsarian order of nature which are to be found also in every dogmatic statement, I would have to confess my ignorance and could merely make a guess unsystematically at some of these particular characteristics. But all this is not meant to obscure the more fundamental insight which our first thesis is intended to express:—a dogmatic statement has (like a kerygmatic one) also a natural substratum which makes such a statement analogous to ordinary statements and which is the *potentia obedientialis* even in a positive sense for the real nature and meaning of dogmatic statements as such. As has already been said, it is not possible to develop all these natural properties of a human statement precisely in so far as they are necessarily rediscovered in a dogmatic statement. All we want to do is to give a few more indications here.

First of all, a dogmatic statement is meant to be a true statement by the very fact that a human statement has this intention and makes this claim. It intends a definite objective content which has its own existence opposite the speaker—it is not merely the publication of a subjective state of the speaker; it does not ultimately wish to objectify the subjectivity of the speaker but rather to bring the objectivity of the matter referred to nearer to the listener and thus to subjectify in this sense. In as far as these dogmatic statements to a great extent do not refer simply to objects of direct sense experience and are also not concerned simply with one's own spiritual experience, such statements can only be analogous, i.e. they point to the meant object with the help of positive representations and point the way to surpassing those representations by transcendence and negation. They do this, however, in the consciousness that this transcendental way of surpassing the original data does not lead simply to absolute darkness and the nameless. For even what is unexperienced still has an objective likeness to what is experienced, and the transcendental affirmation of a similarity of analogy, in spite of the greater dissimilarity which obtains between divine and finite reality, belongs to those original intellectual data which are implicitly reaffirmed in every affirmation and negation. Under these presuppositions a dogmatic statement involves also the fact that not all dogmatic statements can be equally true or false. In other words, it involves the recognition that it is completely possible to pose the question of truth in this objective sense with regard to such statements and that not all statements are equally true or false simply because they refer to what is beyond sense experience. This will probably seem quite self-evident to the normal Christian. But if one thinks along the lines of absolute modernism (as understood in Catholic theology) or of absolute existentialism, then one ought to see in the truth of a dogmatic statement the final success in representing the subjective and always unique religious experience aptly—which means then, however, representing it productively both in an inward and outward direction. One may indeed have varying degrees of success in this, but this success can never be opposed to non-success in the same way as is the case between a logical affirmation and negation and between truth and falsehood as such. Certainly, a dogmatic statement must be allowed to have all those possibilities of ordinary statements, possibilities which exist in its case on account of a difference between the truth which is grasped in a properly personal act and that truth (or error) which is present in the objective-conceptual statement of that unobjectified, pre-conceptual truth—implied transcendentally or in some other way—and which is grasped in a personal, spiritual act. This pre-conceptual, pre-propositional knowledge, which may be true even though the conceptual-objective expression is false (the converse is of course also true), is, without detriment to its property of being non-propositional, an absolutely objective knowledge which refers to an object which stands quite independently of the exercise of this knowledge. The fact that this peculiar tension between what is meant and what is said (if we may put what we are trying to say in this, though perhaps misleading way) which is present in ordinary knowledge can be also present and indeed present above all in a theological statement, follows not only from the universal validity of our basic thesis but also from many other, specifically theological reasons. It follows from the possibility of being a person who really believes in Christ even where, judging merely from the objective meaning of an objectified statement, there seems only non-belief. It follows finally from the impossibility of knowing reflexly with absolute certainty the reality of one's own or someone else's belief, even though one seems to hold fast absolutely—according to the testimony of one's reflection—to the statement of faith declared to be absolutely true. It is not possible to enter further into this problem which we have just indicated.

2. A dogmatic statement is a statement of faith. In our fifth thesis we will indeed have to separate and distinguish the dogmatic statement from a direct and original kerygmatic statement. This must not prevent us, however, from qualifying the dogmatic statement in the stricter sense as also a statement of faith. A dogmatic statement, whenever it is genuine and lives up to its true being, is thus not merely an ordinary statement about some theological object (about something to which the Christian faith itself referred originally) but is also even in its execution —in as much as it is the self-accomplishment of the subject—an exercise of faith. In other words, it is a statement of faith not only in as far as it is *fides quae creditur* but also in as far as it is *fides qua creditur*. Catholic theology usually expresses what is meant here by stating that theology is not in fact merely an exercise of the *habitus fidei* purely as such but an exercise of the *habitus scientiae* which is however permeated and supported by the *habitus fidei*, so that theology always is and must be '*fide illustrata*' (Denz 1796: 1st Vatican Council). Because, and in so far as, faith is always the listening by a concrete human being to the Word of God, the real fact of having heard, the success of the listening to the Word of God which is actually present only when it is heard and understood, can always happen solely in a simultaneous understanding of faith, i.e. in a confrontation (which naturally admits of many degrees) of God's message with what man already is, with man in so far as he is a spiritual being and with the man as he is listening to this message. Since the analysis by the hearer of what he is told is an inevitable moment in the process of hearing itself, and since utter non-understanding destroys even the hearing itself, a certain degree of theology belongs as an inner moment to hearing itself, and the mere hearing in faith is already a human activity in which man's own subjectivity, together with its logic, its experience, native concepts and perspectives, already enters into play. What we call theology and hence dogmatic statement in the strict sense is therefore merely a further

development, an unfolding, of that basic subjective reflection which already takes place in the mere obedient listening to the Word of God, i.e. in faith as such. From this it follows, however, that dogmatic reflection and its statement can and must never separate themselves completely from the source from which they spring, i.e. from faith itself. This refers always, as has been said, not merely to the object of faith but also to its exercise. The latter remains the basis and support of the dogmatic statement as such itself. Self-evident as what has just been said may seem to be, it must nevertheless be admitted that it is in fact not really self-evident in Catholic theology. For one may hold— in company with not a small part of post-tridentine theology—that grace, in so far as it is strictly supernatural, is something of which we cannot at all be conscious. And in this case one will be of the opinion that the 'light of faith', even where one retains this expression, really means either that purely non-experiential, supernatural elevation of the spiritual acts of man by which these acts become saving acts, or that empirically exterior instruction by historical revelation whose fact and content (since these two are inseparable) can be grasped also by purely natural, speculative and historical reasoning. In other words, if one denies that the supernatural saving acts have a formal object which cannot be grasped by any natural act, *then* the object of theology (as even that of faith) can in principle be grasped also by purely natural reason in exactly the same way as by believing reason. The unbeliever will not in general actually occupy himself with such propositions, since they do not interest him. But, presupposing the theory about the nature of the grace of faith just indicated, he can basically do so just as well as the believer, and he grasps exactly the same when he occupies himself with these statements as the believer. There could, therefore, be a dogmatic statement which would be a statement of faith in its object but not in its exercise. *Against* this conception, which in a nominalistic and rationalistic fashion removes the actual supernatural nature of faith (which, of course, it does not deny) into a dimension conceived purely objectively and conceived as a state beyond consciousness and situated outside the exercise of the spirit as such, we hold fast to the thomistic doctrine of the proper formal object of the act elevated by grace and adhere to the doctrine of the proper light of faith and the incommensurability of faith with an ordinary act referring to some religious matter. It must then, however, be truly said that even where it is a question of pure 'listening to' and stating God's

message in Christ as such, and where it is a matter of a dogmatic statement in the sense of a self-justifying reflection (and in this sense a
matter of theology), it is always still a question of a statement of faith,
an exercise of faith. As soon as this is no longer the case, there may still
indeed be science of religion, but not theology. It may be—indeed it is a
fact—that this difference is not properly speaking subject to conscious
reflection and that, therefore, the profane student of religion and the
Christian theologian seemingly meet on exactly the same plane and
hence are distinguished from each other merely by the existential
acceptance and non-acceptance of that about which both of them speak
to one another. But in actual fact this is merely apparent. In fact this
existential acceptance or refusal opens up or shuts out the whole view
of the reality, even though it seems that the profane theoretician of
religion can know and say just as much or as little about Christianity as
the believing theologian. It is not easy to make it reflectively clear *why*
this is nevertheless not the case—*how*, in the case of apparently similar
propositions formulated by both, the profane scientist really misses
the whole point and does not really express it at all, although he reads
the dogmatic statements of the theologian and thinks he understands
them; and even though it is impossible to prove on the plane of objective concepts as such that he has not really understood at all. The truth
of the matter is that this incomprehension goes deeper and is rooted at
the point where knowledge is activated in the exercise of the person
accepting grace, and before it is on reflection expressed in propositions.
It must, of course, be noted also with regard to this conception that it
is not as if the unbeliever were simply one without the grace for
Christian understanding, 'pure nature' (in the Catholic theological
sense). He, too, comes under the influence of the grace which seeks
and enlightens every man; hence, in any case, he sees more than would
be seen by someone without grace, even though he does not want to
see what he sees and even though he 'represses the truth' and pushes it
aside. He, too, stands therefore under the light of grace—although by
self-closure from it. And to this extent there is after all a difference
between the statement of the theologian and that of the profane,
unbelieving theoretician of religion. (Of course, it must once more be
noted in this connection that nobody can say absolutely in practice
who among the speakers belongs to the one or the other category.)
If it is correct to say that the dogmatic statement, even where it is
already real theology, is and remains a statement of faith not merely

with regard to its object but also in the subjective act as such, then the dogmatic statement is determined by all the theological characteristics of the *fides qua creditur*. This would again provide the starting point for the development of a whole theology of the dogmatic statement. And again we must state that this is not possible here. At any rate it follows from this beginning that even a dogmatic statement still participates in its own way in the expressed profession and praise of the message Christ has given us about himself and which leads us to him—in the expression of that message listened to and accepted. The dogmatic statement leads towards the historical event of salvation, in spite of all its conceptual reflection. It renders this event present by confessing that it is brought about by it. It does not merely speak 'about' this event but tries to bring man into a real relationship with it. And despite all its abstractness and theoretical, reflective nature, it is essentially dependent on the fact that this not merely theoretical but also existential and supernatural relationship of the whole man to the historical event of salvation—and not merely to some proposition about it—is really preserved and that the theological statement, even in its theoretical-reflex character, is *ex fide ad fidem*. Since we cannot do more here than to indicate the *locus theologicus* of the question about the nature of a dogmatic statement—which is the same as the nature of the act of faith —we will now pass on to the further determination of dogmatic statements from a different angle. Before doing so, let us merely note that until quite recently the theological description of the act of faith itself regarded the latter far too much and almost exclusively from the point of view of the theological nature of the dogmatic proposition. If there is more concern in Catholic theology today with trying to bring out other moments of the act of faith than merely the holding fast to a proposition guaranteed by the authority of God, then it will no doubt be easier in future to clarify the proper characteristics of the theologically dogmatic statement by contrasting it with the act of faith as such. We will then have to avoid the danger, it is true, which might incline us to make a separation out of the distinction, to the detriment of both the act of faith itself (whose theoretical aspect might become obscured) and of the theological statement (whose property of referring back to the act of faith might disappear from view).

3. A dogmatic statement is in special measure an ecclesiological statement. Already the act of faith and the kerygma of Jesus Christ himself have an ecclesiological aspect which is essential to them.

Proclamation and belief take place in the Church, since she is (in an indissoluble union with the personal uniqueness of the individual and his decision of faith) the object of the redeeming, saving act of God and of the faith itself. For the act of faith is by hearing and remains dependent on the testimony of the message of Christ and this testimony takes place in the assembly of believers, originates from it and is destined for it. The dogmatic statement, however, is ecclesiological in an ever more special manner and measure. For theology, in so far as it is distinguished from the original message and simple faith, arises precisely because there is and must be the Church. Since belief must take place in the Church, from the Church and towards the Church, there is theology. Presumably there would, of course, be theology even if the individual had an absolutely individualistic history of salvation and faith, i.e. if the latter were possible: the message which he has heard and always hears anew, would be in continuous dialogue with the rest of his experience of life and would always have to be heard anew in relation to the rest of this spiritual history. And since his experience of salvation has a *history* both in itself (naturally it has this too) *and* through the continual encounter with the rest of his *historical* reality, there would already be theology in this way. For theology is the historical permanence of a revelation existing in ever new encounters and transforming everything into itself, with a spatio-temporal position in time. Suppose there were no eph'hapax of the event of saving history, that there were always just revelation and never any theology related to a localized event of salvation but not identical with it. Then, if there were no theology, the saving history which takes place but once would not be capable of really reaching later humanity in a saving way. Or at least later humanity would not be reached by it in the whole breadth and extent of its existence—anyone living later on would have to strip himself of his own historical uniqueness and seek to enter into a relationship with this past event of salvation in the form of the abstract man-in-himself. This consideration shows by the way (to make this already explicit here) that theology and a non-binding opinion resulting from a merely subjective reflection on a saving event or a proposition of the original revelation are not the same. For, particularly if theology is to be the absolutely obedient confrontation of one's own existence with the kerygma of salvation found in the unique person of Jesus Christ, it must be able to carry the obligation of faith in itself. It must be possible to have a theology which is authoritatively binding. Wherever it does not (yet) possess this character, this is not because theology *cannot* have this character but because it is itself still in the process of finding itself and of accomplishing what it means to accomplish, viz. of being the concrete form of faith in a new spiritual situation. But however much there is and must already be theology on account of the individual history of the faith of individual men, theology has still a particularly *ecclesiological* character. For in the Church men must believe in common, profess in common and praise God for his grace in a tongue which can be spoken by all. And this must always be done anew at each moment. Confronted with a common spiritual situation which, being common, must always be grasped and understood again in common, the traditional message must always be grasped anew in common. There must be theology in the Church for which the Church herself is responsible. It will, of course, always be due also to the initiative of individuals, since this is the only way in which there can be history and the life of a community. But even theology and theological statements by the individual always address themselves to the Church (explicitly or implicitly). Such a statement by the individual is always a question posed by the individual to the Church as to whether she can make this statement her own or at least can support it as being a possible statement in the one Church. Apart from this always ecclesiological theology of the individual, and superior to it, there is the theology of the Church in which the Church as a whole engages in theological activity through the bearers of her established *magisterium*. This means that here the Church reflects on the message—given by and received from Jesus Christ and transmitted in the belief of the primitive Church—in relation to each particular, historically conditioned situation and based on her consciousness of faith and its original source. She reflects on this message and proclaims the one permanent faith anew in the form of this new theological reflection, in such a way that this faith retains and acquires once more as inevitable a presence as possible for the one who hears the message of the Church to make a decision. This theological form of the proclamation of the Church is theology, for this proclamation always retains its reference to another *norma normans* to which it knows itself bound and which it wants merely to interpret, viz. the message of the first witnesses of the Lord, the faith of the primitive Church in the normative, concrete form in which it is found in Holy Scripture. And precisely this theology is a real proclamation of the faith which demands obedience, in so far as the Church claims and can claim in her *magisterium* that this her message constituted in this way (i.e. become theology) *is* (and does not merely speak about) the here and now valid form of the Word in which God has spoken to us in our heart. In this connection, too, it must again be stated that all we can do here is to determine the *locus theologicus* which could be the starting point for an essential determination of the nature of the dogmatic statement. For nothing very precise is said about the dogmatic statement simply by calling it ecclesiological. It would still be necessary to develop what exactly is meant by this. This again is impossible here.

Only in one regard should we make at least an attempt to clarify our meaning. Since a dogmatic statement—this is the way I would formulate it—has an ecclesiological character, it always signifies inevitably a communal *linguistic* ruling on terminology which, on the one hand, can be obligatory and, on the other hand, must be taken into account in any interpretation of the declarations made by the Church, and which must not be mistaken for the thing itself or respectively must not be confused with a statement which can be made only by starting from the thing itself. Let me explain myself and the sub-thesis I have just formulated. I regard this thesis as important, particularly because it is not reflected on in the usual theology of the *magisterium* and its binding force, and because this oversight leads to unnecessary misunderstandings in the internal Catholic teaching practice and in controversial theology. The reality referred to by theological statements is of incalcuable richness and infinite fullness. The terminological material available for characterizing this reality is extremely limited. It remains limited even when it grows in the course of the history of concepts and terms. It remains particularly limited when, and because, it is a question of that store of terminology which can be used for a theological statement for it ought to be brief, understandable by all and accommodated to the consciousness of faith of a wider audience. With this very limited material of communally usable concepts, we must keep open the view into the infinite fullness of what is meant by faith, and with it must be expressed the infinite fullness and differentiation of the matter under consideration. Such a limited terminology can never be adequate for what is meant. We do not, however, intend to think here about why and how one can be conscious of this inadequate relation between the statement and what is meant by it when the reality itself can be laid hold of only in the word itself and not side by side with it or beyond it.

What we are concerned with here is the following: the word which is inadequate for expressing the thing—always, solely, inevitably and most frequently indeed, in its communal use—brings out certain characteristics of the matter referred to and equally inevitably leaves other characteristics in the background. It creates new relations to certain other matters, and equally does not bring out certain existing relations with other realities of the faith. The historically conditioned, limited terminology lends historical finiteness, concreteness and contingence to the statement of faith itself, particularly in its theological form. Added to this there is the fact that it is basically impossible to furnish every time an absolutely unequivocal, reflectively expressed definition of associated terms, together with the terminology used. For theology cannot take its departure, like geometry, from a finite number of axioms which can be strictly defined in concepts used by them (quite apart from the fact that even these sciences are not absolutely successful in this). This is the reason why ecclesiastical declarations of doctrine, ecclesiastical statements of dogma, also contain implicitly a determined terminology about which one cannot pose the question of truth but at the most the question of aptness. Of course, those who teach and define are not always conscious of this; indeed, most of the time they are not conscious of it and *cannot* even be conscious of it in an adequately reflective way. Here and there, but only right at the fringes, this problem is recognized in some way in Catholic theology. This is the case, for instance, when it is said that the Church calls the event taking place at the Lord's supper '*aptissime*' transubstantiation, or when Pius XII defends the aptness of many of the scholastic concepts which we may not presume the Church will ever abandon again in the future, although we know that they are of historical origin (Denz 2312). But the problem we have referred to here is felt very much in the Church's teaching practice. When it is taught (to give at least a few examples) that man is already a sinner by descent from Adam, the word 'sinner' is used very much in an analogous sense which differs most essentially from the sinfulness brought about by one's own personal decision. This is dealt with at length by scholastic theology in the treatise on Original sin. But in the concise formulation given by the Church, which states that man is a sinner by reason of his origin from Adam, the merely analogous nature of this term is not made explicit. It is not treated by itself as a special theme and is not clearly present in the reflex consciousness of faith in the majority of Christians. Theologians

for the most part forget it since their theology too is very much reduced in normal practical life to the catechetical, undifferentiated elements of the usual statements made by the Church. Anyone who is
really conscious of what analogy means in such a case understands
also that one could equally well say in the nature of things and *in
abstracto* that man is not a sinner through Adam—without necessarily
teaching something thereby which is objectively contradictory to the
Church's teaching on original sin, since such a statement in a different
terminology would merely dispute that man is a sinner by his origin
from Adam in the *same* sense as he is by his own decision. There are
indeed some examples which show that the Church has not only
gradually given different nuances to her terminology here and there,
but has even changed that terminology in the strict sense (without
making any change in what is meant by it). The augustinian terminology, for instance, which at one time was the terminology of the
Church with regard to the sinfulness of every act done by someone in
the state of original sin, was implicitly abandoned through the declarations of Pius V. St Augustine could and had to say—and the Church
of his day also said so as part of her teaching—that every non-justified
person in the state of original sin sins by every one of his acts; in the
language of the post-tridentine Church we may no longer formulate
the matter in this way, although it can be shown that these opposing
formulations do not contradict each other in what they mean—even
though this must not be allowed to obscure the fact that even such a
change in terminology is extremely significant in the field of theology
and the history of thought. There are many such determinations of
terminology contained implicitly in definitions. For instance, the
Church's teaching on the Trinity *as a whole* requires a conception of
'person' in *this* connection which (if one is honest) has relatively little
to do with what one understands by this word in other connections.
And yet this word says what is meant, and it is not permissible within
the Church's teaching to express the matter intended by completely
circumventing this concept and word, although a terminology such
as would be proposed by Barth in this matter might not perhaps be
liable in itself to more misunderstandings though perhaps different
ones. When the Holy Office declared recently that only a consecrating
priest can concelebrate, this was more a determination of terminology
than a dogmatic statement clarifying the matter itself. This is at least
true in so far as this declaration does not explain what is meant by con-

celebration. Thus, this particular statement practically came to this that one may only call that way of celebrating Mass a concelebration in which several priests pronounce the words of consecration together. This leaves it open, however, whether or not a priest who celebrates Mass together with other priests without co-consecrating in this way can nevertheless exercise his priestly function as such in some other way. Let us take another, better-known example: the question as to who according to Catholic teaching possesses membership of the Church is for the greater part a matter of linguistic determination of terminology. '*Mystici Corporis*' reserved the term of 'Church membership' to Catholics. Today those concerned with the teaching authority of the Church seem rather to be inclined once more to describe that reality as membership of the Church which is already given by baptism alone. The interesting thing about this is merely the fact that nowhere in these declarations of the Church's *magisterium* is this question seen explicitly as one of terminology but that this matter is taught with the impression and presupposition that one is speaking about the reality itself. It must moreover be noted in this connection that this terminology is inevitably exposed to continual historical change. This historical change has indeed itself been influenced by the *magisterium* of the Church which has to a certain extent helped in directing its course, has arrested it and to a certain extent has diverted it—and rightly so— into other paths. But it must also be remembered that this historical process of change in terminology cannot be completely steered by the authorities of the Church's *magisterium*, not even in the ecclesiastical field. This process therefore takes place independently, at least partly so, of the official Church and her conscious regulating power, and this fact implies in its turn the duty (and the right) of the Church to take account of this terminological process going on independently of her. This she can do in a great variety of ways into which I do not wish to enter here. But it can happen for these reasons that the Church does not take these changes in terminology clearly and decisively enough into account. As a result there may arise theological controversies both within the Church and with non-Catholic theology which do in fact rest basically on a mutual misunderstanding of terminology. Hence it may also happen—speaking from the Catholic viewpoint— that a Catholic theologian remains obliged to use an officially adopted terminology even though he cannot blind himself to the problematic nature of this terminology, its misleading nature, its lack perhaps of perspectives which are of essential import and similar limitations of such, as of any, terminology. This again is not meant to say that the theologian takes up a passive attitude towards these regulations of the language of theological terminology undertaken by the Church. No, wherever he is engaged in a living theology by looking at the reality itself, the theologian contributes also actively (even though perhaps almost imperceptibly) towards the continual historical changes of the terminology of the Church. And conversely, by keeping in this process to the Church's rules of language in his statements, he enters into the communal, historical conditionality of the particular consciousness of faith existing at the time—a conditionality which at the same time (if it is accepted and endured) keeps the individual view open to the Church's consciousness of faith as it also expects that renunciation of the individual without which there can be no unity of truth and love in this world.

4. A theological statement is a statement which leads into the *mysterium*. This, too, is meant to refer for a start to a characteristic which the theological and dogmatic statement has in common with the direct, kerygmatic statement. If the kerygmatic statement, with and in spite of all its determined and indispensable content—which belongs to it and rightly so, if only because it always refers also to a historical event within the human dimension—is already a statement which directs its hearer beyond himself into the mystery of God as it is in itself, then this is true also of the dogmatic statement since the latter must never abandon its original relation to the real kerygmatic statement of faith. The dogmatic statement—it is true—is a reflected statement in which man (if we may put it this way) is also explicitly alone with himself in his own process of knowledge and not only alone with the thing. And so the dogmatic statement can only be what it must be if it does not forget that the object to which it refers is only properly known when it is grasped as something infinite and incomprehensible —as a permanent mystery—in the very act of taking hold of its finite concept. The dogmatic statement must not forget, therefore, that for this very reason its object is given not only in a concept but also in the effect of God's touching man both by lifting him up and by his grace which goes beyond any conceptual procedure. The dogmatic statement—like the kerygmatic one—is basically possessed of an element which (in the case of intramundane categorical statements) is not identical with the represented conceptual content. Without injuring

its own meaning, the represented conceptual content is in this case merely the means of experiencing a being referred beyond itself and everything imaginable. That this reference is no mere empty, frustrated desire to transcend, that it is not simply the formal horizon for the possibility of objective conceptualization, but, the way in which man really moves towards the self-communication of God as he is in himself—is brought about by what we call grace, and is grasped and accepted in what we call faith. We do not refer here to the *concept* of transcendence or the *concept* of grace, but to these realities themselves. Naturally, these realities do not permit of any simple objective presentation in the dogmatic statement; it cannot be determined objectively whether they have come into play in the dogmatic statement itself. The theologian himself can only be told repeatedly that what enters into his conceptually composed statements as such is not everything that should be present in them. It can be indirectly tested by critical conjectures as to this or that indication, whether there is the spirit as well as the letter and—besides talking about the matter—also the matter itself. Seen in the totality of what is said, and taking a deeper view, certain signs offer themselves for a distinction of spirits, indicating whether someone merely mentions the fact that he is concerned with a mystery when in reality he manipulates his concepts and statements as if they were the reality itself and not merely signs which speak most clearly and perceptibly when they silently refer the believing man beyond themselves into the impenetrable light of God himself. These criteria have not yet been properly developed in Catholic theology. (We prescind here from the subject of analogy which is itself most frequently misunderstood inasmuch as the analogous concept is conceived as an odd hybrid between an univocal and an equivocal concept, i.e. as something derived, in contrast to which the univocal predication is the more original and proper—when in reality the radical openness of the movement of the spirit in analogy really makes the spirit a spirit.) The theories of paradox, of dialectic discourse and of the merely indirect discourse—and presumably not without some justification— have not found any real echo, and have certainly not established their right of being at home, in Catholic scholastic theology. As far as the doctrine of analogy is concerned, we will have to admit if we are honest that it was E. Przywara who first elevated it from being a modest study somewhere in logic or general ontology to being a really important nodal point of theological discourse. And it is still far from having been developed to the point where one could say in this respect that its meaning has been generally understood. This is clear from the fact that it is not yet agreed as to whether this doctrine is what Barth used to describe as something specifically Catholic and absolutely to be denied, or whether this analogy is the name given by Catholic theology to something which is recognized by everyone as an essential characteristic of theological discourse (although perhaps under different names), and which for us signifies a first starting point for what is of importance here, viz. the fact that the theological discourse does not only speak about the mystery but that it only speaks properly if it is also a kind of instruction showing us how to come into the presence of the mystery itself. At any rate—to be more concise—one must not imagine that one has already arrived at the reality in theological dogmatic discourse when one possesses its conceptual term. This term is mystagogical quite apart from its function of substituting for the reality and of being its image. Over and above this, it invokes the experience granted by grace of the absolute mystery itself, to the extent in which this mystery communicates itself to us in that grace which is the grace of Christ. Yet once more it cannot here be more than a question of announcing a theme and of pointing out regretfully that it is not a subject found in scholastic theology—by which we naturally do not mean that it is found nowhere in our theological tradition.

5. A dogmatic statement is not identical with the original Word of revelation and the original statement of faith.

Perhaps I am only now coming to the subject I have been expected to treat of and so cannot deal adequately with it at the end of a long lecture. But in the Catholic understanding of theology and faith, of scriptural and dogmatic statements, this relationship is extremely many-sided, entangled and very difficult to express merely by a nice distinction. Hence, what we have said so far has also been a necessary preparation after all for the section on which we are about to embark, i.e. the section about the distinction between the original proclamation of revelation and the original statement of faith, on the one hand, and reflex dogmatic statements on the other. We find the prototype of the first kind of statement in Scripture, although we should perhaps note that even here there is once more the distinction between the original event of revelation with its direct testimony, on the one hand, and on the other hand the reflection on it found in Scripture. If we are to contrast the dogmatic statement with the statements of Scripture—

and we are absolutely justified in doing this—then we must now proceed to work out the differences between the two. This is not as easy
as it might seem at first sight. After all, we have already said that even
the dogmatic statement is supported objectively and subjectively by
faith. We have already seen that it remains a statement and an act of
faith and is therefore qualified in exactly the same way by the *magisterium* of the Church even though it is not always and in every case
the statement of a binding explanation given by the *magisterium*, but
may also be the statement of a *quaestio disputata*—for even then it still
tries to look to the Church's consciousness of faith as a whole and even
in this case knows itself to be dependent on the Church's *magisterium*.
And conversely: there is no *proclaimed* revelation except in the form of
a *believed* revelation. A *believed*, i.e. heard, revelation, always already
includes also—in so far as it is a revelation understood, accepted and
assimilated—a synthesis of the Word of God and the word of a particular man which *he* in particular can and indeed must speak in his
historical situation and from his particular standpoint. Every Word of
God which is spoken by men is already, therefore, to a certain extent a
reflected word, and to that extent also already a beginning of theology.
The difference between the original kerygma and a dogmatic statement,
therefore, does not lie in the fact that in the former there is as it were the
pure Word of God alone and in the latter only human reflection. If
this were the case, then there could be indeed merely non-binding
theological discourse talking round about this Word of God, but not
a statement of faith which though different from the original Word of
God is yet absolutely binding and through which the Word of God,
as announced originally, receives its real binding presence in the
course of history. There could only be a history of theology in this
case and not a history of dogmas. The fact that the latter exists can be
explained only because the original statement of faith already includes
that moment of genuine human reflection which makes it legitimate
and necessary and which continues to be effective and to unfold itself
in later theology. What has just been said—it must be stressed once
more—is valid also of Holy Scripture. Thus, even in the simplest
kerygmatic statement there is already a beginning of theology; and this
theology, understood as reflection and as derived from the most direct
experience of revelation, is undoubtedly already given an extensive
place in Scripture. It is regrettable that Catholic theology hardly reflects
on this in fact. One practically never asks oneself about the source from

which the author of certain parts of Holy Scripture has received what he says. One does not reckon with the undoubtedly real possibility that even a scriptural statement can already be secondary in relation to another such statement—that it can be derived from this other statement. One puts every Scripture text on the same plane of meaning and treats it as an entirely original datum which has sprung absolutely directly from the revelation of God and cannot be derived from anything else. And yet no one can seriously deny this other possibility in principle; it is a real possibility, for we can already observe a development of dogma within the New Testament. And to take such possibilities into account in practice could contribute a great deal to the exact determination of the meaning of certain texts of Scripture.

And yet there is an essential difference between a theological statement (even in its binding form of a real testimony of faith and of actual proclamation) and the original testimony of faith to which *quoad nos* Scripture as a *whole* does after all belong. The reason for this lies in the peculiar and unique position of Holy Scripture. Revelation has a history. Christian understanding, however, means by this first and last that there are certain quite definite events fixed in place and time in which this revelation (which is determined for all later ages) takes place in such a way that later ages remain permanently bound by this historical event, and that they really attain this divine revelation only if and in so far as they refer back to this historical event of revelation. Hence there are certain events and statements for future ages (statements which in their turn belong to the constitutive elements of these events themselves) which form the enduring and unsurpassable *norma normans, non normata* for all later dogmatic statements, viz. none other than the original statements just mentioned. Even if and when these statements have *also* all those elements which we have elsewhere attributed to dogmatic statements, they nevertheless have one thing no other statement has—they belong to that unique historical event of salvation itself to which all later proclamation and theology are referred. They are in this very definite sense more than theology, and even more than absolutely binding theology. They are not merely any statement of faith but here that statement which remains the permanent ground of all other, future statements—they are what is handed down and not the unfolding tradition of what has been handed down. It is true, of course, that the latter statement of the already derived and standardized type is a form and aspect of the original statement, without which later Christians could no longer hear and repeat that original statement obediently without becoming unhistorical and unecclesiastical. It is true, in other words, that the later Christian will always hear the original statement in terms of its later statement by the Church's *magisterium* and consciousness of faith. Yet he really hears that original statement of faith itself, not although but precisely because he hears it by means of the present Church. For the *ultimate* guarantee of being able to hear the original statement is not the historical skill of man, (i.e. his 'being able to understand' historically in matters of revelation and faith), but the exercise of faith in community with the present-day Church. But as has been said, it is *thus* that the *original* statement of faith is heard, and this statement remains a moment in the historical event of salvation to which all ages, past and future, remain constantly referred. It can therefore be merely a question of the form in which this original statement of faith, understood as the *norma normans, non normata*, is given to us today, both in binding and non-binding statements of faith. We do not intend to answer this question by a theological deduction, although this would presumably be possible. Our question can be answered by saying quite simply that the original statement of faith understood in this way is given to us in Holy Scripture. We are quite justified in making this assertion even though we do not commit ourselves regarding what has been and still is (today more than in preceding centuries) a controverted question in Catholic theology, viz. the question as to whether Tradition—which according to the Council of Trent is a norm of our Faith and of the Church's proclamation of doctrine—is basically and abstractly speaking a source of the material content of the faith in addition to Scripture, or whether it is only a formal criterion for the purity of the faith, after the material content of the apostolic proclamation had settled adequately and objectively in Scripture. The reason for our being justified in making the above assertion is quite simple. For, even if we suppose that there is another source *besides* Scripture which serves as testimony for us of certain material contents of the faith not found also in Holy Scripture, this other source known as Tradition would nevertheless be such in fact as to contain only the testimony (guaranteed by God as pure) of the actual apostolic traditions in accord with relevation and unmixed with human tradition. For it goes without saying: revelation, right from the very start of the historical movement of revelation, was accompanied by human, theological reflection, by non-binding *theologumena*, by purely human knowledge and opinions and by errors. It is not indeed necessary to dispute the fact that the Church can distinguish, within the mixed up mass of what is human and what is divine in Tradition, between that which really represents a handing on properly-so-called of the original tradition and the rest which cannot make any such claim. One will absolutely have to concede this instinct to her because of the assistance of the Holy Spirit promised to her. But this does not yet answer the question as to *how* the Church makes this necessary distinction, a distinction always necessary if the revealed truth is always to be recognized *anew* by the Church and she nevertheless knows herself always bound to the original revelation. Let us suppose that the Church is able to do this by the light of faith granted to her or by an instinct of faith alone, without any extrinsic criteria. Let us suppose, furthermore, that the Church simply adopts this critical distinction with regard to the literature passed on to her from the apostolic age—in other words, that she says where, in this literature, she recognizes the genuine objectification and the pure expression of her faith, and that she says in what other literature of this age she does not recognize this. Then, even under these presuppositions, she would delimit precisely *that* pure objectification of the original apostolic testimony which we call Holy Scripture. Yet, be this as it may, Christians are agreed (at least in essentials) about the fact that the pure (even though absolutely historical) written objectification of the apostolic kerygma *is* given to the Church in Holy Scripture—no matter what may be said about the just mentioned *a priori* considerations. Otherwise the Church would not possess any such objective norm when she wishes to determine by the gift of distinction what in the concrete totality of her actual Tradition is actually tradition of revelation and what is merely human tradition which has also existed from the beginning of the Church. There is, therefore, a *norma normans, non normata*, and this norm is identical with Scripture and it alone. This is primarily a norm for the consciousness of faith of the Church as a whole and for the Church's *magisterium*, but not for the individual (much less for his fight against the consciousness of faith of the whole Church attested authoritatively by the *magisterium*). And to this extent the original word of revelation and of faith in—and of—the Church is essentially distinct from every later, theological statement of—and in—the Church, even though the latter be a kerygmatic testimony of faith, something demanding the assent of faith, and not merely a theological reflection. Hence, one could say that the theological word is *only* a theological word, in as much as it is not the word of Scripture. Naturally, even the statements of scriptural exegesis and biblical theology are merely theological statements, even when they deal *with* the words of Scripture. It would naturally be also still possible and necessary to make explicit, and to give reasons for and to estimate the significance of, a distinction within the theological word which we have up till now always only mentioned in passing and presupposed. We mean the distinction which is based on the fact that there is, *on the one hand*, a dogmatic statement made by the Church in her ordinary and extraordinary proclamation of doctrine, which demands obedience and faith—and this right up to the real, absolute assent of faith but also below this—even where such an absolute consent of faith is not demanded of him, or at least not demonstrably so— in the different degrees in which the individual Christian and theologian knows himself to be bound by the proclamation and teaching of the Church—and that there is, *on the other hand*, the merely private word of the individual theologian. The borderlines between these different kinds of theological statement are fluid. This is so even merely because the theologian, even in his private statements, if they are truly dogmatic, wants still to refer himself to the Church's consciousness of faith. For under certain circumstances he has the absolutely correct impression (based on sufficient grounds) that he does after all factually reproduce the teaching of the ordinary *magisterium*, i.e. of the normal proclamation of faith, and that he addresses himself by his statement to his hearer in such a way that he directs him to the faith of the Church and gives him sufficient certainty to respond on his part to the thus attained belief of the Church not only theologically but believingly. Even where in actual fact a statement is proposed as a *quaestio disputata*, or a *sententia libera*—and this fact is even explicitly stated—such a statement, if it is to remain theological at all, can only be meant in the sense that it wants to ensure or facilitate the grasping and assimilating of properly dogmatic statements of faith at least for the one who pronounces it and, in the form of an offer, for the one who hears it. For even free theological opinions cannot seriously find their sole meaning in being simply additional knowledge with regard to the real content of the faith. Whether there is in this sense a real deductive theology attaining absolutely new knowledge and declaring it not to be part of the content of the Faith and non-binding is certainly something doubtful which should at any rate make one ask more earnestly the question whether, if there were such a thing, it could still be theology. The theologically decisive function of the theologically free statement is surely that of helping us to see better and to confess what we really believe—of being a help, in other words, for faith itself. It must not be overlooked, moreover, that it is quite impossible for the individual, here and now, to make everywhere an absolute and adequate distinction between the proper content of faith and a merely theological, free opinion. It must not be forgotten that even the definitions of the Church are understood by everyone especially when they do not reflect on it, *also* by means of their total consciousness and hence also by theologically free opinions. What has been said so far in connection with this fifth thesis of our lecture does not imply that everything has thereby been said concerning this distinction between a kerygmatic and a dogmatic statement of faith. Up till now we have reflected mostly (not only) on the difference between an original statement of faith and a theologico-dogmatic statement dependent on it and based on it. Naturally, within this category of derived, theologico-dogmatic statements, there is once more a distinction between the statement which professes and refers to the reality itself, entrusts itself to it and praises it—and the statement in which the first ray of reflection is directed onto one's own knowledge itself. And this distinction has its ultimate, ontological basis in the nature of human knowledge itself in as far as the latter is always *both* direct and reflex, in itself and in the other and in as far as we can never adequately overcome this dualism. Hence there are dogmatic statements which by first intention are directed to the reflex self-possession of knowledge about something—and dogmatic statements which regard the reality itself. And both these kinds of statement are never absolutely separable from each other, in spite of and with all their differences.

4

EXEGESIS AND DOGMATIC THEOLOGY

WHAT this essay is intended to convey, refers not only nor even primarily to the academic question about the relationship between the two sciences of exegesis (and biblical theology) and dogmatic theology. Rather, this essay has arisen from the impression that there exists a certain estrangement within Catholic theology between the representatives of these two disciplines. It seems to us that not a few of those engaged in either of these fields of Catholic theology regard each other with a certain distrust and indeed irritation. The dogmatic theologians seem here and there to be under the impression that the exegetes are very little concerned about that theology to which the dogmatic theologian knows himself in duty bound, that theology which deals also with those questions which form the object of exegesis (in the widest sense of that word). The exegetes, on their part, seem here and there to be of the opinion that dogmatic theologians want to tie them down to things which are not objectively justifiable, and this because these theologians do not take sufficient note of the advances made by Catholic exegesis in the last decades.

It is not our intention here to give a more detailed description of the tension we have just indicated or to give documentary proofs for it. After all, this is a matter which has not as yet been clearly expressed in books and other printed forms. Up until now, this tension has manifested itself more in conversation, talks and lectures—right down to clerical chit-chat (which of course also exists). If we were to go into these things, we would lose ourselves in the undergrowth of personal strifes, sensibilities and polemics. This is senseless and is of no use to anyone.

On the other hand, if this supposed tension is not merely the product of a frightened phantasy, and if it is not to grow gradually into something seriously harmful to scientific thought and to the Church, then it will be advisable to make a few basic reflections on the relationship between dogmatic theology and exegesis, and to do this quite soberly but also quite openly. For we do not improve things or remove them from the scene by hushing them up.

It is quite possible that some people might get the impression from this exposition—contrary to the author's intention and to the actual state of affairs—that Catholic theology in Germany is in a bad way either in an objective or personal sense, or that the author is merely forcing matters into the public eye. Yet even such possible misunderstandings are no valid reason for omitting these reflections. Even correct and important arguments can be misunderstood.

We also do not mean to comment by means of these reflections either directly or indirectly on the shameful article by A. Romeo against the professors of the Pontifical Biblical Institute[1] which has been so injurious to the dignity and esteem of Catholic scholarship. In so far as the article indulges in casting unworthy suspicions particularly on German exegetes, the 'brume nordiche' (the thick fog from the North) —a 'kind' reference to German Catholic exegesis which even amounts to an explicit castigation of German Catholic exegetes—we intend merely to state one thing here in passing. German Catholic exegesis when it is suspected of heresy and unecclesiastical sentiments, rightly feels it as an odious disparagement of its honest work and thought for the Church. One can be perfectly orthodox even at a distance of several hundred kilometres from Rome. We would think that even the Catholic dogmatic theologians and the bishops will show their solidarity with the German exegetes by decisively and clearly refusing to accept such unqualified and wholesale accusations. But as already stated, this somewhat shameful topic is not what we want to talk about here.

If we discuss difficulties soberly and without trying to be controversial but starting from what is basic, then this is not to be taken as a proof that Catholic exegesis is in an alarming state or that those who

---

[1] A. Romeo, 'L'Enciclica "Divino afflante Spiritu" e le "opiniones novae" ', *Divinitas* IV (1960), pp. 387–456 (cf. *Herder-Korrespondenz* XV [1961], p. 287); 'Pontificium Institutum Biblicum et recens libellus R.D. A. Romeo', *Verbum Domini* XXXIX (1961), pp. 1–17; J.-M. le Blond, 'L'Eglise et l'Histoire', *Etudes* CCCIX (1961), pp. 84 *sqq.*; cf. also L. Alonso-Schökel, 'Argument d'écriture et théologie biblique dans l'enseignement théologique', NRT LXXXI (1959), p. 337; *id., Probleme der biblischen Forschung in Vergangenheit und Gegenwart* (Welt und Bibel) (Düsseldorf 1961).

call for the Church's thunderbolt of excommunication are right after all. Conversely, of course, it does not mean either that one should act as if there were no problems or difficulties at all.

Strangely enough it will be found, however, that at the present time the underlying problems which give rise to these reflections lie in the New Testament field rather than in the Old Testament. Thirty years ago the situation was still quite the reverse. Our reflections are, therefore, concerned principally with those questions regarding the New Testament which should be discussed more explicitly and openly among exegetes and dogmatic theologians. Some of what will be said may give the impression that it is the talk of someone who thinks he knows better and who is appointing himself as arbitrator. If this be so, the kind reader should ask himself whether this impression could have been avoided other than by leaving the matter well alone. Should he be of the opinion that such a course would have been still worse, then he must simply try to put up with his unpleasant impressions as unavoidable side-effects of an otherwise necessary business.

When we declare our opinion to all interested parties without fear and quite freely, we claim nothing more, it would seem to us, than the right of any child in the house of its father. A child does not need to be afraid to express his humble and respectful opinion to his parents. We claim nothing more than the right which is involved in the necessity of a public opinion in the Church, the absence of which—as Pius XII has explicitly declared[2]—causes great harm to pastor and flock alike.

The arrangement of the present reflections is quite simple: we will turn our attention first to the exegetes, then to dogmatic theologians, and will conclude with a few additional considerations.

To the exegetes: a word from the dogmatic theologian

Dear confrères and honourable colleagues: permit me to express the opinion that you exegetes do not always have sufficient regard for us dogmatic theologians and our theology. If I make somewhat sweeping statements, please do not take this amiss. Anyone who is not in fact affected by this does not need to take it as meant for him.

[2] Allocution to the participants of the International Congress of the Catholic Press, 17th February 1950, AAS XLII (1950), pp. 251 *sqq.*; cf. Utz-Groner, *Soziale Summe Pius' XII*, 2151/2152.

Yet it does seem to me that you exegetes forget sometimes that you are Catholic theologians. Naturally you intend to be this and, of course, you are. Naturally, I do not have the slightest intention of expressing the unjust suspicion that you do not know—or do not intend to observe—the Catholic principles governing the relationship between exegesis and dogmatic theology, faith and research, scholarship and the Church's *magisterium*. Yet you are only human, and sinners, like all other men (even dogmatic theologians). Hence it may after all happen to you in the everyday practice of your science that you do not pay enough attention to these principles. This does in fact happen sometimes. You may forget—though not deny and exclude in principle—that you are engaged in a subject which is an integral part of Catholic theology as a whole and which must, therefore, observe all those principles which are in fact proper to Catholic theology.

For this reason, Catholic exegesis is a science of faith and not merely a science of language and of religion; there exists a positive relationship between your science and the Faith and *magisterium* of the Church. The teaching and directions given by the *magisterium* do not represent merely a negative norm for Catholic exegesis—a limit beyond which one may not go—if one wishes to remain a Catholic. They form much more an inner, positive principle of research for the work of exegesis itself. This is true, even though we must always distinguish clearly— and we will have something to say about this in our word to the dogmatic theologians—between those elements in the work of exegesis and in biblical theology which are the result of a philological and historical method as such and those which are not. However little it can be stated more exactly here what it means in practice when we say that exegesis is a properly theological science, with all that entails, what we have said remains true.

It is, however, quite easy to grasp all this in a few of its external manifestations, as also to grasp the fact that you are not always sufficiently conscious of it nor alive to it. I have the impression that you often work quite happily as pure philologists and ordinary historians. And then, when this leads to difficulties and problems in the field of dogmatic theology or in the consciousness of faith of your young theologians or the laity, you are quite content to declare:—this has nothing to do with 'us'—this is a matter for the dogmatic theologians, let them work out how to deal with it. No, dear confrères—dogmatic theologians ought not to complain if you make work for them nor should they be annoyed by this. But you yourselves have also the essential duty to show how, or respectively to positively ensure that—without forcing matters and in all honesty—the results of your work are really and truly compatible with Catholic dogma and also (at least in principle) with those parts of the teaching of the Church which have not been solemnly defined. For you are Catholic theologians. You have exactly the same responsibility with regard to the teaching of the Church and the faith of the simple believer as has the dogmatic theologian. Please be not offended when I say that one may sometimes get the impression that you are not always sufficiently conscious of this your responsibility and that it gives you almost a twinge of malicious joy when you can make real or apparent difficulties for us dogmatic theologians. One sometimes gets the sneaking suspicion that you consider it to be the height and hallmark of the genuineness and true scientific nature of your science to be able to discover difficulties.

You must be critical—inexorably critical. You must not 'arrange' dishonest reconciliations between the results of your researches and the Church's teaching. You may quite rightly announce and honestly express a problem where necessary, even when you cannot yet see—and with the best will in the world cannot yet see—any clear, positive solution to the problem of how the teaching of the Church's *magisterium* (or what is regarded as such) can be reconciled with the real or supposed results of your scientific inquiries. But you should regard this as the true summit of your science only once you have really fulfilled your whole task. It is part of this task—part of your exegetical Catholic duty—to make manifest the harmony between your results and the Church's teaching and to show how these results lead naturally and as its genuine expression to the Church's teaching. Of course, not every single exegete needs to do this every time (it is impossible nowadays to get along without 'division of labour' and specialization)—but you should be much clearer than sometimes you appear to be about the fact that this is basically part of the exegete's task.

What happens in practice? When you simply leave the work of bridging the gap between exegesis and dogmatic theology conveniently to us, and we poor dogmatic theologians want to take up this work (and have then to concern ourselves also with exegesis, since a bridge crosses from one bank to the other) then you are the first to shout—admit it—that we dogmatic theologians understand nothing about exegesis, and that it would be far better if we left it alone rather than dabbling in it in a clumsy sort of way! Who then is to do this job which must be done? You behave rather strangely sometimes in this matter. On the one hand, you complain that too little attention is being paid to the Scriptures, that there is too much scholastic theology and not enough biblical theology. But then, when it comes to the point where it would be necessary to show how and where in the Scriptures the Church's teaching finds its expression or at least its ultimate basis, you begin to excuse yourselves and declare that even with the best will in the world you cannot find anything in the Scriptures which would serve as a basis for the teaching of the Church—for example, the Church's teaching on certain sacraments or on certain Marian dogmas. This, you say, is simply something for which Tradition and the *magisterium* alone are responsible. Is it not often your own fault then that some theologians speculate up in the clouds, when you suddenly give up all claim to any biblical foundation for truths which also belong to your Catholic faith? What source has Tradition then for such truths? After all, you are the very ones who, as historians, have least of all believed in subterranean channels in Tradition when something in the first centuries could not in your judgement be proved to be contained either explicitly or implicitly in the Church's public consciousness of faith. The *magisterium* on the other hand is the bearer of a truth of faith— the bearer of a possible explication—but not a material source of a truth of revelation. In other words, if a proposition which the later *magisterium* has declared to be revealed is not explicitly taught during the first centuries by the Fathers of the Church (in documents still accessible to us)—and if it can be made clear historically that this proposition was also not explicitly taught by 'word of mouth' (since otherwise its absence in the literature handed down to us could not be explained)—then the proposition in question must be contained implicitly in the teaching of Holy Scripture. And in this case it is part of the exegetes' duty to make their contribution of biblical theology, so that the dogmatic theologian may be in a position to show in an exegetically unobjectionable manner, that, and how, the particular proposition is contained implicitly in Scripture. Do you not have a duty, therefore, to fulfil those tasks which are really yours and not to be too quick in palming them off on someone else? Do you not barricade yourselves too quickly in certain cases behind the declaration that an exegete has simply to discover the immediate meaning of the words of Scripture and that everything beyond that is no longer part of his job?

Furthermore—please do not be offended—but I sometimes get the impression that you are rather afraid to give a basic exposition of your exegetical principles themselves (i.e. those principles which are not purely dogmatic but which grow in their concreteness out of the work of exegesis) and that you are rather afraid to prove their agreement with the principles of the Church's *magisterium*. I am well aware of the fact that this is not easy. In certain circumstances one may even have to say quite simply in the course of such work that this or that declaration made by the Biblical Commission at the beginning of the present century appears either out-dated now or seems still valid only after making certain necessary, fine distinctions. But you must have the courage for such 'dangerous' work. For this work must be done. Only you can do it, since you do not really believe us 'systematic' and dogmatic theologians capable of the exact knowledge of individual problems of exegesis without which such principles remain too general, too equivocal, too inexact, and of too little value for practical application. You have such principles. Yet you submerge them in particular instances of exegesis. The layman in the exegetical field (including the dogmatic theologian) is rather puzzled when he looks at your particular examples of exegesis and their results. He asks himself how this or that interpretation (exegesis) tallies with the inerrancy of the Scriptures and the *canones* laid down by the *magisterium* regarding the meaning of certain scriptural texts. He wonders how the *genus historicum* of parts of Scripture can still be maintained, he wonders what is the position as regards the pseudonimity of parts of Scripture, whether anything like this can be admitted as possible in principle even in the New Testament, how one squares all this with the decrees of the Biblical Commission, etc.

I am beginning to be impolite. Permit me, however, to make a further, rather malicious remark (since I willingly concede that the converse could be said also about the dogmatic theologian). It would be much easier—and not harder—for your exegesis sometimes if only you had a more exact knowledge of scholastic theology and if this theology had not sometimes, as in the case of certain representatives of your noble and sacred science, sunk to the level of a half-forgotten science, long gone out of practice. It seems to me, for instance, that exegetes would be able to speak even more clearly and in an even more balanced way than they actually do about the scriptural teaching on merit, on the one hand, and on the gratuitous nature of beatitude, on the other, if they were even more clearly aware of the scholastic doctrine about the relationship between freedom and grace and understood that doctrine to the furthest limits to which it can be taken. Such a scholastic doctrine is simply another form of biblical theology using a different set of concepts. If one did not think in terms of a doctrine of the Trinity as being presumably very primitive (I hope I may be forgiven this example which is simply meant to allude to an outstanding recent work of exegesis[3]), one would have no cause to assert that no real doctrine of the Trinity is to be found in St Paul. (Where else, in any case, would we find this doctrine in the New Testament, if it is not even to be found in St Paul? Presumably always in that part of Scripture on which one is not working at the moment.) If one realized fully what is implied in the teaching of scholastic theology about the merely relative difference of the three persons—a distinction which it is almost no longer possible to grasp—then one would also be capable of finding this degree of distinction in St Paul's teaching (although of course in different words), since he too does not simply use 'kyrios' and 'pneuma' as two words meaning absolutely the same thing without even the hairbreadth of a distinction.

One may possibly have misgivings as a Catholic theologian about certain non-defining doctrinal pronouncements of the Church's magisterium. But in such cases one should state this explicitly and give explicit reasons for it. It is not right, however, to rid oneself of the problem by simply shrugging one's shoulders and passing on to the business of the day. In many cases, the apparent, greater or lesser contradictions in the light of the pronouncements of the magisterium which seem to appear almost incidentally in the course of the work of exegesis will in reality be purely a matter of terminology. This can happen even in quite unexpected circumstances where at first sight it might seem to be a most dangerous business. In such cases, however, the exegete should also make the effort to keep before his eyes the manner of speaking adopted by the magisterium of the Church and to explain why there is no real difference between these declarations and his conclusions. It is not at all easy to say, for instance, what is an 'error' and what is not—even merely considering the formal meaning of such a notion—what 'error' looks like and what meaning 'error' is normally presumed to have. Hence, when the exegete admits an 'error' somewhere in the New Testament, he may mean something which, expressed

[3] Ingo Hermann, *Kyrios und Pneuma* (Munich 1961).

differently, is objectively true and undeniable and which no dogmatic theologian may or will deny, just as he cannot deny those papal encyclicals which exclude every error from the Scriptures. Thus, the exegete maintains in such a qualified sense, for example, that a certain statement in Scripture—e.g. that Abiather was high priest when David ate the loaves of proposition (Mk 2.26)—is an 'error', if this statement is taken apart from the literary form of the Scriptures in which it is embedded and if it is separated from the frame of reference which gave rise to its expression and is read on its own: this the exegete has every right to do.

No true knowledge is really a 'retrenchment'—even though it may at first have a disillusioning effect and cause certain difficulties which must be overcome. Yet it is much better if even the layman recognizes that you are building up and not merely tearing down—that you are furthering the knowledge of the life of Christ and do not merely prove that, from a historical point of view, there is much which we do not know quite as exactly as had previously been supposed. It must be quite clear that you do not merely preserve those facts of the life of Jesus, of his self-consciousness and awareness of his mission, which cannot be abandoned for dogmatic reasons and which are quite indispensable to the dogmatic theologian in Christology and Soteriology —but that on the contrary you also use the methods of historical knowledge to throw more light on these facts and to defend them. For then dogmatic theologians will easily understand that you are right when you do not conceive every word of Jesus in the synoptics as if it were a sort of 'tape-recording' or shorthand report of the very words of the historical Jesus; they will easily understand that on the contrary you rightly reckon with the fact (and not only in general and theoretically) that the theological interpretation of apostolic times is already at work in the handing down of the words of Jesus, giving them its own precision and adapting them already to the special circumstances of the assembly.

I know, you are quite used to all this—for you there is absolutely no problem any more in this. But not everyone is in that position. You must make allowances also for the 'weak in faith', for those who are slow to understand. You must take pains to make even these understand that you are constructive and not destructive. You must teach your young theologians in such a way that they themselves do not suffer any harm to their faith and that, when they become curates, they do not imagine that their main task is to proclaim exegetical problems from the pulpit which they themselves have perhaps only half understood—and which they oversimplify and then proclaim to people even less prepared for such things who are then left amazed and upset.

There would also be no harm if you were to reflect here and there with greater accuracy than hitherto perhaps as to which *a-priori* principles of dogmatic and fundamental theology even you must observe in this 'inquiry into the life of Jesus' so that the Jesus of your synoptical studies bears some historically still verifiable relationship to the Christ of faith. (Of course these *a-priori* principles must be very carefully interpreted and conceived, and must already be given those nuances, both in their scope and binding force, which are required in view of the problems of your own exegesis.) You do not need to engage in any 'Chalcedonian' Christology in your work of exegesis itself. But those statements which the historical Jesus has made about himself must be objectively the same (at least together with the paschal experience) as what dogmatic Christology knows about Jesus. It is also absolutely permissible to determine the literary form of the synoptic and Johannine accounts of miracles more exactly and to maintain that the general declaration to the effect that these are historical accounts is still too vague (especially when this is applied to individual accounts). Even you might, however, find it useful and liberating in certain circumstances to reflect with greater theoretical exactitude on what a miracle is meant to be in view of its nature as a recognizable fact. You too should not give the impression that you are of the opinion that it is impossible to know historically from the Gospels that Jesus actually performed such miracles (and especially the miracle of the Resurrection) which even today are still of importance for the authentication of his mission. If you have any understanding of the principles of fundamental theology (and this can surely be taken for granted), then you will make it clear to your hearers that the Resurrection of Jesus is not merely the object but also the reason of faith in Our Lord. Nobody will reproach you with seriously overstepping your boundaries if you yourselves explain to your hearers why and how both are simultaneously possible and correct.

One last point: it is an unjust practice, wronging both you and Protestant theologians, to accuse you of having adopted this or that from Protestant exegesis. For what does this prove, if it is true? Nothing at all. For Protestant exegesis—there should really be no need to emphasize this fact—can arrive at true conclusions. If this is so, it is only right therefore to adopt these conclusions. And if they are false and so cannot be accepted? Then one must reject them by giving objective proofs of their falsehood—not by simply condemning them as being Protestant theology. Yet even though all this is true, should you not avoid giving the impression sometimes that a Protestant thesis is right away more probable in your eyes simply because it has sprung up on the soil of Protestant exegesis and not originally on Catholic soil? And should you not bear in mind also that Protestant theology often approaches Scripture with a philosophical bias and not with an objective method which has grown out of the work of exegesis itself?

To the dogmatic theologians: a word from a colleague

I do not want to tread on anyone's toes—I must speak in general terms, for only then can I speak objectively to the many very different individuals. Hence I will address myself. Any one of my highly esteemed colleagues in dogmatic theology may take from it whatever may rightly apply to himself. When this is not the case, let him pity me while I teach myself. Thus, dear friend, be honest—you know less about exegesis than you should. As a dogmatic theologian you rightly claim to be allowed to engage in the work of exegesis and biblical theology in your own right, and not just to accept the results of the exegetical work of the specialist. For it is your job as a dogmatic theologian to use all available means for listening to the word of God wherever it is pronounced—and where better than in Holy Scripture? But then you must perform the work of exegesis in the way it has to be done today and not in the way you used to do it in the good old days— or better, not only in the old way. Your exegesis in dogmatic theology must be convincing also to the specialist in exegesis. This is true even though he has to grant you the right to put certain questions to Scripture which he himself is not necessarily concerned with—even though you can be quite sure that this or that particular exegete will not agree with you in every detail and will put forward his rejection of your interpretation in the name of exegesis itself (instead of in the name of his exegesis). But if you want to be able to speak the language of the exegetes, then you must really know how to employ their tools and you must really have felt the weight of their reflections and problems. Otherwise you may find that you pass over their questions by making too simple a distinction. (An example of this would be when we talk about *'scientia non communicabilis'* in order to explain the statement made by Jesus that the Son of Man does 'not know' [Mt 13.32] the day or hour of the Last Judgement.) And if you are honest, you must admit that you really have no explanation for texts like Mk 8.39 (there are those standing here who will not taste of death before they have seen the kingdom of God in all its power) and Mt 10.23 (the Son of Man will come before your task with the cities of Israel is ended)—and that you will be only too glad if the exegetes find an explanation, even though it may perhaps seem too daring to you. And do not forget—in your case such a question emerges only very late on and only on the fringes of your 'system' and of your consciousness. Consequently, it cannot have the same weight for you as it has for the exegete. For him such a question arises very early on and hence with quite a different force for the intellectual organization of his consciousness.

Be patient with the exegetes. Since a modern science is so vast and its methods so complicated, it is extremely difficult nowadays to understand enough of another science to be able to join in its thought. Quite often we merely think we understand something about it. Yet one would have to have worked a long time on it even just to understand something about it. It is not enough to have taken cognizance of the question and the objection of the exegete in the form of a short *'objectio'* in a scholastic textbook—such a matter has to be studied carefully in the long monographs written on it by the exegete. How many dogmatic theologians are still able to do this today? It will be almost impossible purely on account of the time and energy required for it. So, be at least careful. Do not merely cite a number in Denzinger or a sentence from an encyclical, and do not say: that cannot be true!

You must not complain that the exegete pays too little attention to your criteria, norms and sources and leaves you to worry about establishing the connections with his field, as if this had nothing to do with him—if you yourself take up the same sort of attitude towards him. Remember, you are working with the Scriptures as the inspired and inerrant word of God. The exegete, however, even *qua* exegete, is—may and must be—concerned also with fundamental theology. Therefore, even though what we have said above about the theological nature of his exegesis is true, the exegete has the right and the duty to do the work of the historian of fundamental theology in connection with the New Testament, precisely if and because he should be a

Catholic theologian who may not simply start from the bare and un-proved act of faith. Hence, he does not always need to begin by simply presupposing the inspiration and inerrancy of Scripture in every case. If he did this, then he would be a bad theologian, since he would be denying that there can be fundamental theology in the Catholic sense. Thus, he must also examine his source, viz. the New Testament, in his role of historian. Even in this role he must admit that the synoptics are historically trustworthy sources in essentials at least. Of course, this statement about the synoptics being historically reliable sources of our historical knowledge of the life of Christ does not by any means give us a really exact definition of the literary form used by the synoptics. This statement alone is not sufficient to allow us to pass an unequivocal judgement on what is really expressed in each single sentence for, what we today take at first sight to be a historical memorandum may not perhaps be so in the sense of modern historical writing. The really important thing, however, is the fact that the exegete may and must work on questions concerning the handing-down of the New Testa-ment even prescinding (methodically) from the inspired and inerrant nature of the Scriptures. For then, even though he may already hold fast to the substantial historicity of the synoptics on the profane his-torical plane, he has not only the right but also the duty to refrain from judging from the very start that all statements in Scripture are equally certain historically. Were he to do this, he would by this method change over from fundamental theology to dogmatic theology. Such a procedure, far from being an advantage would be a mistake. Hence, even when the synoptic writer makes an individual statement which he himself expects to be understood as a historical statement (which pre-sumably is not at all always the case), the exegete and inquirer into the life of Jesus must not declare every such statement to be equally certain and true in the historical sense. Whenever it is unequivocally certain that the synoptic author wishes to state something as an his-torical event—meaning by that what we mean today—the exegete who works in terms of fundamental theology may not of course say that the synoptic author certainly errs in this case; yet as a fundamental theo-logian he need not say either that the synoptic author is certainly right in this. Not only may he—but he must—speak with greater nuances than we who are dogmatic theologians rightly do in our subject. If we dogmatic theologians are convinced that we must maintain Christ's direct vision of God during his earthly life (since this is the binding, though not defined, teaching of the Popes since Benedict XV), then you also have the duty to show the exegete how such a doctrine can be really and truly reconciled (and not just by playing with words) with the impression which the exegete gets about the historical Jesus in the synoptics. You would have to show more clearly than you usually manage to do that you are quite familiar with the difficulties besetting your friend the exegete, and that you have a fairly good idea of how to employ his methods and know how to value the results of his work.

You have an easier task than your colleague who works in terms of fundamental theology. You can use every word of Scripture right away as an equally inerrant and inspired word in your dogmatic proofs. You need not ask first about its origin, or whether it is, just the way it stands, an historically speaking absolutely certain word of Jesus or has already been co-formed by the theology of the primitive Church and the authors of the New Testament. You need not ask whether it belongs to the very first, original data of revelation or whether it is already theology derived from these original data by the Apostles (naturally in a correct and infallible way). You are quite entitled to proceed in this way, although it should be pointed out in passing that it is not quite the ideal method even in dogmatic theology—for the more exact interpretation of a text does seem after all to depend also on the answer to questions which must be the concern of the textual critic and of the exegete who takes the historical strata of tradition into account. Would it, for instance, do any harm if it were noticeable in your scriptural proofs for the dogma of the Trinity that you are familiar with the questions of the historians about the command 'to go out' (Mt 28.16–20) and that, since no absolute dogmatic impossibility forbids it, you are quite unprejudiced about the possibility that the trinitarian formula put into the mouth of Jesus was nevertheless co-formed by the theology of the primitive Church?

There are many problems belonging to dogmatic theology as such which the theologian could and should pose, since their solution could help to open up things and make them easier for the exegete. For example, one might ask in dogmatic theology how the apparitions of the risen Lord could be conceived more exactly from the very nature of the matter, since—this is the important point—he no longer belongs to our world of appearances and experience, and his experience must therefore be quite different from that of, let's say, the risen Lazarus. One would perhaps find in this case that the vacillations in the description of these apparitions in the accounts of the paschal events are to be expected from the very nature of things, and that they do not need to be 'touched up' artificially. Starting from the intrinsic problems of the doctrine of the Trinity and of Christology, we dogmatic theologians could express many things more clearly right from the very start and thus make it easier for the biblical theologian to understand that biblical theology and scholastic dogmatic theology are indeed talking about the same thing. It would presumably be possible, for instance, to express what is meant by the theology of the Trinity even without continually repeating merely the formulae about 'person' and 'nature'. It would no doubt be possible to show that the entitative Trinity and the Trinity of revelation are so connected that as soon as one gives correct expression to the Trinity of revelation (as the Scriptures do), one has already affirmed also the entitative Trinity. It would be quite possible to develop a 'Christology of ascent', of the encounter with the man Jesus, with a very existential and ontological basis. Such a Christology would be much more akin to the viewpoint of the synoptics and of the Acts of the Apostles in this matter than if one merely pictures a Christology of the assumption of a human nature by the descent of the Logos. In a really metaphysically understood doctrine of the direct vision of God possessed by the soul of Christ even during his life on earth, it would presumably be possible to render the nature of such a basic condition very well intelligible (although it is not of itself a theme of discussion), in such a way that the exegete could understand that this scholastic doctrine really does not deprive him of the right to look in the life of Jesus for a genuine development, a real dependence on the religious environment of his time and the unexpected turn of events. Would it not be worthwhile, for instance, to think about whether in certain circumstances a particular kind of nescience might not be more perfect than knowledge, since it is perfectly characteristic of the freedom of the creature (which Jesus too possessed and exercised as one who truly adored and who was obedient to the inscrutable will of the Father)? After all, when the creature makes a decision it launches itself into the openly unknown and it properly 'knows' something as it really is only when it accepts it lovingly as something unknown. Why do we dogmatic theologians not reckon more clearly with the psychologically and existentially or ontologically quite self-evident fact that 'knowledge' is not at all an unequivocal term but that a man may actually have essentially different kinds of 'knowledge' which are not in the least mutually interchangeable—so that one may really know something in one way and not know the same thing (even as far as oneself is concerned) in another sense? If one is radically united with God, then one knows 'everything' by this and knows it all in the depths where this reality is experienced, without necessarily knowing or even wishing to know it in that dimension of the human soul in which one has definite, individual knowledge expressed in properly coined propositions (knowledge which would in certain circumstances merely make the silent oneness with the real and one truth impossible or would at least disturb it). Why then should we dogmatic theologians restrain exegetes from saying in a true sense (without of course covering even then the totality of Christ's reality) that Jesus did not know certain things—since he himself has said so (Mk 13.32) and we do not have any real reason to try to explain such statements away by clever distinctions?

We frequently are in possession of very correct and, in a sense, metaphysical principles in theology. We do not take notice, however, of how wide and spacious they are and all the things which can be accommodated in them. We do not make it clear enough to the exegetes who work in an *a-posteriori* fashion that they need have no qualms about starting from the individual facts discovered by their researches into the life of Jesus; there is nothing wrong in their finding a real living human being with a history, and they must never pass him by—and yet they will realize that their hands have touched the Word become flesh. We tacitly assume that the Resurrection was indeed a great miracle which attests Christ's mission, but that—if God so wished—this miracle could have happened to any other man, quite independently of the 'first-born' Son of Man and his Resurrection, by a resurrection not to an earthly life (as in the case of Lazarus) but by a resurrection to a real, total consummation of life. Is this tacit supposition as clear as we assume it to be, and is it really true? Or could one not say, after reflecting more exactly and deeply on this matter, that the Son of God must necessarily be the beginning of absolute salvation (which is not merely a stage on the way but God's absolutely final and unsurpassable salvation in person, and which only exists and shows this through the Resurrection as such) in the sense of the Christology of Chalcedon? Could one surmise that a 'functional' Christology does after all contain the traditional ontological Christology, if only it is thought through radically enough to its proper conclusions? And yet, if such a 'Christology of function' were completed in this way while at the same time preserving what is proper to it, would it not help many a man of today by pointing the way to the Christian faith, a way which, for fear of what appears to him (quite unjustifiably) as 'mythological' in it, he would not find otherwise? Would it not be possible to eradicate in this way quite a few monophysite tendencies in Christology (not, of course, in the official dogmatic theology but only in that of individual Christians), which on closer examination see nothing more in the 'human nature' of the Logos than a sort of livery or puppet for God, something which is directed only towards us and not also in dialogic freedom towards God? Would this not help us to understand better that a 'Christology of Resurrection' is not necessarily absolutely false, even though it does not seem to bother much about referring itself to the self-expressions given by Jesus himself during his lifetime when trying to explain his being, and simply looks to the Resurrection by which Jesus becomes 'Lord'? Should this not give us a greater understanding of the tendency of present-day exegetes (including Catholics) to see everything in the light of the paschal experience and to conceive the words and deeds reported in the life of Jesus as already interpreted in this light? Of course, we will have to be careful about this: we cannot dispute—and in any case have no historical reasons for disputing— any self-testimony of Jesus to his being during his historical life which contains his ontological divine sonship, provided that we do not maintain that such a self-testimony must already have employed a more or less direct 'communicatio idiomatum' or have worked with almost Chalcedonian concepts.

If only we dogmatic theologians would always bring out the value of our good, established scholastic doctrine about the merely analogical nature of original 'sin' right at the beginning of our treatment of original sin, if only we made it clear in this way that man can as it were 'ratify' original sin by his own personal sin—then it would no doubt never have happened that our exegetes still thought even a few centuries after Erasmus that they had to defend the augustinian interpretation of the 'in quo' (= Adam) in Rom 5.12. They would then have been able to recognize sooner that it is quite possible to interpret Rom 5.12 as speaking—in accordance with the simple meaning of the words—about the guilt of each individual human being, without thereby having to hold that nothing at all is to be found in this chapter about original sin correctly understood.

Yet probably, if we are to do justice to the exegetes, the most important thing for us dogmatic theologians is to recognize that the qualification 'historical' as applied to an account, even when it is correct, is in many cases far too vague. The expression 'historical account', as applied to the New Testament and in particular to the synoptics, does not mean that Christ's discourses for instance, are more or less just 'tape-recordings' which have at most been shortened by 'editing'. As a dogmatic theologian, one is almost ashamed to have still to make an explicit statement of this attitude. Yet our work in dogmatic theology always gives rise again to such a mentality and to the tendency to think along those lines—even though we have long ago recognized its false-hood at least theoretically. We cite Christ's words as proofs, and so we always tend almost automatically to fall back into the opinion that these words of Jesus must have been spoken by him exactly as we quote them —exactly as if we had been there and had heard these words ourselves. And yet there is no literary form of the historical in the New Testament such as to guarantee this. While the dogmatic theologian concedes this fact in the abstract and in a rather off-hand way, it is the daily bread of the exegete who has to reckon seriously with it—for it is a fact which can be shown by many examples and which should also be taken systematically into account even when it is not immediately evident from a comparison of the synoptic accounts. No wonder that the exe-getes and we find it difficult to understand each other.

It would be wrong to suppose, however, that everything is crum-bling and that there is no historical certainty left when one proceeds soberly and courageously from the fact that historical criticism must reckon with the possibility that the accounts of the words of Jesus given by the synoptics contain changes made by oral tradition or clari-fications due to some specific theological angle and that even these accounts may contain glosses which are not explicitly indicated or may have been coloured by certain graphic and dramatic expressions, etc. More precisely—if the individual parts of the Gospels have had a normal history before becoming part of the Gospel (as the history of literary forms has rightly taught us), then we must be prepared to find, on comparison of the individual parts with each other, that they will not always have exactly the same historical literary form. We must reckon with the possibility, for instance, that it is not as certain from the historical point of view of fundamental theology that Jesus was ever in Egypt or that he was crucified in Jerusalem. None of this is in any way directed against the authority of the accounts—for these accounts themselves by their very nature admit of such a question. They do not claim in any way to be a kind of 'police-report' painfully recounting 'nothing but' the historical events observed by everyone.

Of course, the fact of being prepared to reckon with such a possibility does not yet answer the question as to where, when and to what extent it is actually realized in the case of the individual accounts of the words and deeds of Jesus. It is the task of a legitimate historical criticism of the New Testament to determine all the particulars actually existing within the framework of possibility. Although such criticism does make the work of the dogmatic theologian 'more difficult' on many occasions, it does also quite frequently facilitate it. If one can, for instance, interpret the proviso in Mt 5.32 (everyone who puts away his wife [setting aside the matter of unchastity] causes her to commit adultery) as being a gloss introduced into the text by the casuistry of the primitive Church, then this makes things much easier for the dogmatic theologian than would be the case if even this clause must be regarded as coming really and directly from the mouth of Jesus. It is absolutely possible to make it easier for the dogmatic theologian to bear such heavy 'crosses' as the already mentioned texts in Mk 8.39 or Mk 10.23 (even though it is impossible simply to eliminate them, on account of the inspiration and inerrancy of the whole of Scripture), if one uses historical criticism to point out that Jesus himself could not simply have spoken 'thus' (i.e. giving such at least apparent precisions of time). The work of the exegete as well as of the dogmatic theologian is made much more laborious as a result of such presuppositions regarding the possibility of historical criticism. But this does not yet prove that one could spare oneself this labour by means of simpler principles.

As already said, it is not as if one ended up no longer knowing what really happened historically speaking. One is left in doubt about many things. Yet one can still know enough to hold on to those facts in fundamental theology which are the basis of the Church's teaching on the person and the work of Jesus. Indeed, one can have a historical certainty of these facts which is real certitude. But such a certitude must not be confused with the absolute certitude of metaphysics or of faith (each in its own way). And, of course, an exact epistemological analysis of when and why such historical knowledge can be called 'certain' in spite of its multidimensionality and difficulty is not at all easy. It is the same when a layman in the science of history is faced with the laborious reflections of a historian about what exactly were the facts of Caesar's campaign in Gaul—his head will probably be reeling too. He gets the impression that in the end we really do not know any longer whether Caesar was ever in Gaul at all. Such historical 'dizziness' is understandable, even though it is not justifiable on that account alone. The same is true of the work of the exegetes, presupposing of course that they work conscientiously and do not imagine that their main job is to destroy what had been supposed to be certain; we presuppose also that even in their work of exegesis they remain believing theologians and that given this (although such a presupposition may not of course enter as a material premiss into fundamental theology itself), they have a better chance to work in a correct historical manner than someone who is blind to what is announced here, viz. the miracle of God's grace fulfilled in Jesus Christ. But what reason could we dogmatic theologians possibly have for denying that these presuppositions do exist in the case of our exegetes? We do not need to accept their individual conclusions simply by a blind trust in the wisdom of the specialists. We have the right and the duty to do the work of exegesis for ourselves as far as we can and wish to, and to check quite calmly the discoveries of the exegetes. But we do not have the right to succumb to the temptation, peculiarly our own, to act (in most cases only unconsciously) as if even their method itself must be flatly contradicted.

It is quite a different matter to ask what significance the correct and matured results of such an exegesis can or cannot have for the pulpit, for instruction purposes and for religious edification. In the pulpit one quite rightly proceeds from the presupposition of the sacred nature of the Bible (which is precisely what the exegete who works in terms of fundamental theology may not do, at least not in the same sense). A sermon from the pulpit has, therefore, a different basis than the professor's lecture to a class specializing in exegetical studies. Hence, much of what exegesis is concerned with from the point of view of fundamental theology does not belong in the pulpit even though the faithful have the right to expect that the proclamation of the Word does not contradict the certain conclusions of exegetical research. Age and level of education will determine in each case the extent to which lectures and articles (rather than sermons) should be used to introduce the faithful to the problems of fundamental theology in exegesis. It must always be remembered, however, that preaching is the proclamation of the Word of God and is meant to serve the edification of the faith.

Some additional considerations

Dogmatic theologians and exegetes must understand that they are not the masters but the servants of the *magisterium* which Christ has entrusted to Peter and the Apostles, and not to professors. Yet not only Hegel but even the professors know that God has so arranged things in this world that the master has also need of the servant and is dependent on him in spite of his being the master.

This servant of the Church's *magisterium* has need of the Church's trust. He requires that scope of trusted freedom without which the servant cannot fulfil his humble but necessary task.

Nowadays, ecclesiastical science and especially exegesis has not merely to carry out those scientific tasks which interest the scholar. It must fight side by side with everyone else in the front line of the Faith and the Church; it must enlighten modern man as to the possibilities of faith; it must teach, fortify and comfort the intellectuals of our time. The intellectual of today is the spiritual child of historicism and the natural sciences—a terribly sober, careful and disillusioned man—a man who suffers from God's remoteness and silence (as he does in fact experience this). This is the kind of man with whom the Church must concern herself. For this is the man of today and tomorrow. It is easy to confine one's proclamation of the Faith to other types of people— to people who come from other intellectual and sociological strata, who are more easily 'believing'—to simple, humble folk who have not really been affected yet by the intellectual atmosphere of today—people who still have strong social ties, who for whatever reason always push intellectual problems aside or perhaps solve them in their own, and in certain circumstances, very uncatholic way and yet do not allow themselves to be disturbed by this in their official 'attachment to the Church'. The Church must concern herself with the real intellectual of today— she must not abandon him in his characteristic distress and willingness to believe. Anyone who does not recognize this crisis of faith, does not understand the real problems of today. These problems do exist. And consequently ecclesiastical science has no right to work on the 'closed shop' principle, but must think of the people of today. If it does this, however, then it will not be able to bypass questions which are difficult and dangerous. It will have to look for solutions which are new and untried, since it simply is not enough just to repeat the good well-tried truths, or even to formulate them in a new didactic or psychological garb.

It may be that the ultimate problems of the faith are not decided on the plane of individual questions and problems in theology. But many of these questions, about which today's intellectual who has not been trained in theology gets the impression that they have not been answered—that theology has no honest and simple answer, is beating about the bush and forbids honest discussion—do create a situation and intellectual atmosphere which could be fatal for modern man's will to believe—especially when on top of everything else the ultimate and basic decisions of life weigh heavily upon him. He requires a clear and intelligible answer from ecclesiastical science on these individual questions. He wants to know what is the position as regards evolution, what the Church has to say about the whole question of the history of religion, what is the lot of the innumerable non-Christians, why we must have (allegedly) so few and then only problematic miracles today when we are told of so many more wonderful and convincing miracles in ancient writings, what is the exact nature of the immortality of the soul and its proof. Even when such and innumerable other questions are not formulated explicitly (out of lassitude and a fear of endangering even the little bit of faith one has still managed to salvage and wishes to keep), they do nevertheless form the mental situation in which the intellectuals of today—and their number is increasing every day—do in fact spend their life and from which they cannot escape. To this kind of question belong also the questions occupying exegesis and biblical theology, i.e. questions about the historical reliability of the Scriptures (including the New Testament), about the credibility of the miracles recorded in the New Testament, about the possibility of verifying the Resurrection of Jesus historically, about the apparent or real discrepancy between the different accounts of the Resurrection, about the relationship between the teaching of Jesus and the theology and practice of the world of his time, etc. If exegesis were to try to avoid such and many similar questions, it would be guilty of not doing its duty. Such questions are difficult and 'dangerous'.

The Church has always acknowledged the fact that there are, and indeed must be, schools and different trends of theology. From a purely logical point of view, the mutually contradictory propositions of these schools have been objectively dangerous to faith in certain circumstances, since both propositions of two schools contradicting each other cannot be true at the same time and under the same respect. But it has rightly been felt that this danger to faith was not subjectively dangerous; one knew that each of these schools really conserved, and intended to conserve, those basic principles in such questions which needed to be conserved. It was, therefore, quite right to let theologians dispute among themselves. The Church did not interfere, but left them freedom—to the greater benefit of theology.

In questions which impose themselves on theology today, one cannot really avoid thinking about and trying out solutions which are not immediately seen to be clearly reconcilable with the binding teaching of the Church. One cannot always give an answer to such questions which will be so 'certain' that there will be no doubt or argument whatsoever. It will often gradually become clear whether such an answer is unobjectionable from the Church's point of view. As far as possible such questions should be discussed first in specialist circles before they are thrown open to the general public. This is quite a good principle—only, even with the best will in the world, it cannot always be observed. For there are very many questions which have not yet been purified and settled by the specialist theologian and yet are already questions for the man of today and not merely for the specialist. In such cases one cannot simply console these people by telling them to wait until one has won through to a '*sententia communis*' in 'specialist circles' which will be acknowledged as such by all theologians and by the *magisterium* of the Church. It is necessary to give an answer now, and to give it in such a way that even the non-specialist can recognize it as an answer to his questions. In certain circumstances, such an answer may later on be seen to be absolutely false—perhaps because it was too brief or because, even with the best intentions of the theologian concerned, it may objectively contradict some principle laid down by the Church's *magisterium*. Such an answer may also be perfectly true and even mature, and yet it may not be clear that in this matter certain non-defining pronouncements made by the Church's *magisterium* are in some need of revision (which is not merely possible but has quite often happened in fact in the past). It may be that, seen from an ecclesiastico-sociological angle, even a true but novel view requires a certain 'period of incubation' until people have become used to it and have come to experience in practice and psychologically that it is perfectly reconcilable with the old faith of the Church. The Church's *magisterium* has undoubtedly the right and the duty to watch over such a process of searching and groping and of discussion (i.e. serious discussion on which something really depends); the *magisterium* has undoubtedly the right and duty to keep such processes and discussions within bounds and to halt tendencies which are certainly and clearly going in a heretical direction. All this is self-evident for every Catholic theologian. Certainly no Catholic theologian will hold that every measure taken by the Church's *magisterium* is wrong or unjust simply because it is hard and bitter for this or that theologian.

Nevertheless, this period of questioning, of discussing and of searching, must not simply be passed over and replaced from the very outset by decisions of the Church's *magisterium*. According to Catholic teaching the *magisterium* is the sole authority capable of giving a decision binding in conscience in matters of theology even on the specialist theologian. It is not, however, the only authority capable of explaining open questions. Such explanations require reflection and discussion by theologians. Theologians are not merely a necessary evil in the Church or a debating society for their own amusement. They fulfil an indispensable function which has its own value. This fact is not cancelled out by the possibility that the highest teaching authority and scientific competence may be united in one person. The theologians are necessary in the Church; they must discuss, and must discuss questions today in answer to which they may have to 'venture' untried, dangerous opinions—opinions which will perhaps eventually turn out to be unacceptable and un-Catholic.

We trust that it is unnecessary to spend time in emphasizing that this is no charter for foolish opinions or opinions which any theologian worth his salt can recognize immediately as theologically untenable. (It is of course also clear from the theoretical point of view of scientific method—and it should be stated quite plainly—that it is impossible to give a formal principle according to which one could determine immediately and beyond any doubt the boundary between matters which can rightly be left open to discussion and opinions which must be rejected of their very nature. Thus, taking a risk is never quite avoidable when deciding according to the best of one's knowledge and conscience for either side. The Church's teaching authority may stop or forbid something at first which later on turns out to be a view which can be discussed after all—and the individual theologian may represent some opinion as tenable when it is really untenable from the very start and is therefore contradicted immediately by the Church's *magisterium*. In the face of such limitations connected with the fact that man is a creature and therefore finite, there is only one remedy—humility, patience, love.)

Everything said so far is really quite obvious. It has been said not because one could seriously be of a different opinion but because we wish to tie it up with something following from it which is perhaps less obvious and yet seems important as well as true. Let us suppose that theologians are discussing some really ticklish problem in exegesis imposed on them by modern developments. It may be the duty of the exegete and of the dogmatic theologian in such cases to speak in such a way during the discussion as to declare the opinion of another theologian to be irreconcilable with this or that principle laid down by authoritatively taught Catholic theology. This declaration may be right or wrong—but it must be possible to express such an opinion. It is not sufficient to say simply that the other theologian has after all the necessary knowledge to recognize such a discrepancy himself and so, if such a discrepancy really existed, the other theologian (who after all is a Catholic) would not have expressed this opinion. No, it is quite possible for a theologian to say something with the best of intentions which, viewed theologically and from the Church's point of view, is in reality objectionable but which he does not always immediately see to be such.

It may happen, however, that a theologian is in a position to, should and wishes to take a stand against another theologian by using these weapons which he has every right to use and may even in certain circumstances be obliged to use—and yet he foresees that this would have the result of putting the other in immediate danger of ecclesiastical censure, of the prohibition of the book in question or of his removal from the Church's *magisterium*. In such a case he would probably decide—with harmful results for the whole matter—not to employ these quite legitimate and indeed necessary weapons against his colleague. He would probably remain silent, talk round about the matter and give utterance to his view only in lectures. Yet this would not serve the cause of truth, and great harm would be done to the fraternal candour which should reign among Catholic theologians. One cannot say in such a case that by expressing his opinion, the other has only himself to blame for exposing himself to the danger of measures being taken by the Church authorities. The colleague who thinks about combating the view of the other can quite honestly be of the opinion that his opponent is an outstanding theologian, that his expressing his own view, even though not accepted, will advance the matter under discussion, and that his opponent is an absolutely faithful son of the Church. He may, therefore, be seriously of the opinion that his opponent should be preserved from falling under the Church's censure, although he utterly rejects his view and would dearly wish to combat it. If he must now fear that by reason of his denial of his opponent's opinion the latter is exposed to the danger of censure by the Church, then he will naturally be careful not to express his view in the form indicated. He does not wish to be responsible for such a censure. Such an attitude is quite understandable and perfectly honourable.

Yet such a silence or toning-down can only be harmful to the cause of truth. For it prevents necessary discussion and even fails to protect Catholic teaching in certain cases—a function which does in part pertain to the duties of the theologian. It would force the Church authorities to take over a function which the theologians themselves should normally exercise—it would push theological discussion out of the public forum of periodicals and books into a sort of 'underground movement' of parties disputing with each other merely verbally.

What has been said is not meant to suggest that the Church authorities simply accept blindly the verdict of one theologian against the opinion of another—or that they are doing something unnecessary or unjust when they undertake such a censorship. Yet it will not be possible either to say that unnecessary and unjust measures are always and *a priori* excluded—that they have never been used in the past. If, however, it is not *a priori* impossible that rash, objectively unjust or too severe measures might be used—or merely measures detrimental to the greater good which all desire to serve—then the theologian may also fear that such measures might actually be used. If he were to get the impression that something like this could easily happen, then he would be careful that this should not happen to one of his colleagues. This would paralyse discussion, and problems would remain unsolved. For censorship can at best block a wrong road—it does not thereby open up the right road.

Given this situation, one may come to the conclusion that, although the Church's *magisterium* has every right (and sometimes is forced) to take such measures against theologians who express their opinion in free discussion out of an honest sense of responsibility as regards their duty as professors, this should happen only rarely and then with great care and only after all the circumstances and exonerating reasons have been examined. Otherwise such interference will impede the necessary function exercised by theological discussion in the Church—to the detriment and not to the advantage of the Church's teaching. Such measures must not tacitly proceed from the principle that every false doctrine which is not explicitly condemned by the Church's *magisterium* will keep on spreading unchecked and can never be overcome by a clarifying of the question by purely theological means. If such measures of ecclesiastical censure occurred too often and too hastily, this would quite unintentionally give rise to the opinion in theological circles that a view is already accepted as reconcilable with the Catholic faith simply because it has not been immediately objected to by the *magisterium*. If, on the other hand, the *magisterium* did not object at all in an individual case—since it cannot happen in each case—then the theologian would be all the more afraid to express a contrary opinion. He would be under the impression that his disagreement must be false since otherwise the Church authorities would already have had to condemn this opinion. This in its turn would force the Church authorities to act more quickly so as not to create the false impression that this or that view may be held by Catholics. The necessary function of Catholic theology would be paralysed. Under the tacit presupposition that a non-defining pronouncement of the *magisterium* can in the final analysis be improved upon, the situation would become even more confused: one theologian would not speak because he fears the Church's censure and the other would not speak because he does not wish to call down such a censure on a third; if the Church's *magisterium* were to speak in such a case, its teaching would be accepted as something binding merely on the plane of Church discipline and not on the plane of infallible teaching—and this would be silently circumvented whenever possible.

What has been said just now is not meant to describe an actually existing alarming state of affairs. It is simply meant to give an analysis of a possible psychological set-up which might operate if the Church authorities were to put too little store by the positive effects of discussion among theologians, and if they consequently imagined that they must take measures to intervene in discussions as quickly as possible.

PART II

QUESTIONS ON THE THEOLOGY OF HISTORY

5

HISTORY OF THE WORLD AND
SALVATION-HISTORY

THE subject I have been asked to deal with is: history of the world and salvation-history. So many questions and concerns can be covered by this heading, that I doubt whether I will manage to hit on the particular ones with which I am perhaps expected to deal. All that I can hope to do is to select, from the vast field covered by this subject, a few questions which seem to be of some importance to a Catholic theologian. We will formulate what can be said in this way in a few quite simple theses, and will then clarify these a little.

1. Salvation-history takes place within the history of this world. Salvation is indeed what finally brings the whole man to his perfection, salvation can ultimately be granted to him by God alone, and salvation is not yet achieved and at best must yet become. It is impossible simply to encounter this salvation somewhere in the world. Indeed, it would be an absolutely fundamental heresy for any already given condition in the world, or any condition which man himself can realize by his own planning and action, to be regarded by man as his salvation, i.e. as what is really meant by salvation—the final and the beatifying. Salvation, understood as an absolutely transcendent mystery—as that which comes from God and is outwith our control—is one of the most basic concepts of Christianity. Accomplished salvation is in no sense a moment in history but rather the culminating cessation of history. It is not an object of possession or a produced effect but rather an object of faith, hope and of prayer. By this fact alone, all utopian conceptions of salvation-in-this-world are to be rejected as doctrines meriting condemnation. History is by this fact declared to be the realm of the provisional, the unfinished, the ambiguous, the dialectical—and any attempt to seize salvation in this world and to find completion in the history of the world as such would itself remain a moment in history—

part of what is evil, godless and vain in history—and would itself give way to other history coming after it.

And yet a Catholic-Christian theology of history cannot but say that salvation-history takes place within the history of the world. This means several things. First of all, salvation for the Christian is not a future which is simply still to come and which has not yet started at all since, when it does come, it will absorb the history of the world into itself. No, salvation takes place now. Man receives God's grace in the sense that grace is something which is already given to him now, something which he accepts and something which changes him interiorly. And since this grace is basically God communicating himself to man, it is not merely something provisional, nor is it merely a means to salvation nor a substitute for salvation. Grace is really this salvation itself, for it is God himself in his forgiving and divinizing love. Salvation-history within the history of the world means furthermore that this self-communication of God—which is the communication of salvation as such—takes place in the form of that free acceptance of this communication which we call faith, hope and charity in the freedom of man. And this man's free surrender of himself to God who communicates himself to him is not merely an esoterically confined happening in the life of man. Of course, since faith is meant to include all human dimensions in this salvation—so that nothing in man may stand unrelated outside of salvation—this faith (by which salvation is accepted) may and must indeed render itself consciously and socially tangible in the very ground of man's existence in profession of faith, in worship and in the Church. Yet this acceptance of salvation in freedom, takes place just as much with reference to the material presuppositions of man's freedom in which that freedom is accomplished. Real freedom of the spirit, in this world of the God of grace and of Christ, is always freedom with regard to salvation or damnation and cannot be freedom in any other way. Yet, precisely this freedom of the corporeal, social and historical creature which is man is always and necessarily a freedom which is exercised through an encounter with the world—the community and environment in which man lives; its nature combines both that of transcendental freedom and of a particular category of freedom. Hence the freedom of acceptance or refusal of salvation occurs in all the dimensions of human existence, and it occurs always in an encounter with the world and not merely in the confined sector of the sacred or of worship and 'religion' in the narrow sense; it occurs in encounters with one's neighbour, with one's historical task, with the so-called world of every-day life, in and with what we call the history of the individual and of communities. Thus salvation-history takes place right in the midst of ordinary history. Man works out his salvation or damnation in everything he does and in everything which impels him. Everything in the history of the world is pregnant with eternity and eternal life or with eternal ruin.

There is yet a third factor to be brought out with regard to this inclusion of salvation-history within profane history—a factor which is more characteristic of the Catholic understanding of this relationship than the first two we have mentioned. As we will have to state at much greater length later, the content and reality proper to salvation-history do indeed lie hidden in profane history, since immediately tangible historical events and realities do not of themselves give us any clear clue, as they themselves can be of a saving or a damning nature. These events and realities do not of themselves betray whether here and now something saving or damning is taking place in them. *Yet* this conceal-ment of salvation-history in an ambiguous and undefined profane history, which cannot be simply interpreted or 'judged' as a saving history, does not mean that salvation-history is enacted solely in an individual, transempirical history of the individual existent, of con-science and of absolutely intangible faith. It does not mean that sal-vation-history takes place behind a profane history which goes its own quiet way and is quite indifferent to it, simply in the form of a supra-history or history of faith. It is true that profane history in *general* and on the *whole* is ambiguous and cannot of its nature be interpreted with absolute certainty in questions regarding what part of it is salvation and what damnation. Profane history will reveal itself clearly in this respect only in the Last Judgement, which itself is not a moment of history but rather the final unveiling of history. But all this does not mean that this profane history does not become transparent here and there and does not within its own sphere draw man's attention here and there by signs and references to the question of faith and salvation and orientate the answer to this question in a particular direction. Salvation-history, which of its nature is a hidden history, works itself out in the dimension of profane history in which it takes place. God, who grants salvation, addresses man within the profane dimension of history. He does this through the prophets who interpret the inward history of grace and revelation by their words giving it a socially tangible form and authenticating this by those empirical facts, called miracles, which precede faith and justify it in a this-worldly manner before reason and moral responsibility, even though they cannot and are not intended to produce this faith. But above all, the history of this world has become transparent in regard to salvation (in a way which cannot be surpassed in this world) through the Christ-event in Jesus of Nazareth—through his resurrection and by the proof of the Spirit bestowed by him. In other words, the same man who in his whole and entire being is faced with the decision regarding salvation in his historical existence has ultimately only one history, in the sense that there are no isolated sectors of his existence which are in no way co-determined by the history of grace and faith (or vice versa). And this one history is not so uniform and homogeneous as to make salvation and God's action always and universally so clearly present in it that a profane zone of history could no longer be experienced at all or that the genuine decision of faith would no longer be possible; for if this were the case, then, no matter where man turned in such a history, he could not avoid encountering God and his offer of salvation everywhere with equal inevitability. In all this it can be left an open question here as to whether the eyes of faith alone can see this salvation-history shining through profane history in such a way that it is also accepted. In any case, the whole of profane history is disturbing, reproachful and disappointed even in its own sphere, and anyone who asks for salvation and reckons with the possibility of a personal self-exposure will find that profane history contains hints and 'signs' telling him where this salvation has taken place in his own history and where it is to be found. Salvation-history takes place within profane history.

2. Salvation-history is distinct from profane history. We have already had to enunciate this second thesis in explanation of the first. We must now reflect more explicitly and exactly on it.

(a) Salvation-history is distinct from profane history, firstly, because profane history by and large does not permit of any unequivocal interpretation with regard to the salvation or damnation taking place within it. Salvation and damnation are events of profane history, for wherever men achieve themselves in freedom, they stand before God and decide their salvation. If this were not so, then their activity would not be free in the real metaphysical and theological sense. For, freedom means man's self-determination in the face of God, whether he actually understands it explicitly in this way or not. But this saving or damning characteristic of the historical free decisions of man remains hidden. It does not of itself become an historically tangible fact. For a free action becomes 'historical' in the strict sense only once it is objectified in such a way as to be explicitly expressed in words as an object of human inter-communication in the various forms of the objective spirit in science, art, society, etc. Of itself, however, the saving or damning character of a free human act cannot become objectified, and therefore historical, in this sense. This is impossible for several reasons. The ultimate quality of freedom cannot become the object of reflection. For the motives—adopted in freedom and accepted as effective motives—which determine the moral and religious quality of freedom are not simply identical with the conscious motives adopted in their conceptual explicitness. Man always acts from a knowing and self-possessed basis of his freedom, a basis which cannot be accounted for simply by representational and moral reflection. For, the content of consciousness is greater and wider, deeper and more original than the sum total of what is known. Even consequent reflection is itself again an act which —reflectively—cannot outstrip its own limits. By this token, therefore, every form of reflection itself is a merely provisional, inexact account which only approximates to the totality of the basis and motivation of freedom but never catches hold of it completely. If this is true of the moral reflection of the individual subject of freedom on himself, it is *a fortiori* true also of the objectifications of his moral decisions in words, purporting to communicate him to others, as well as in the various forms of the objective spirit. It is undoubtedly possible to recognize in many cases, with sufficient certainty, whether these objecti-fications are in accord with an objective moral norm or not. But it is impossible to derive any real certainty from them about the moral quality of the innermost free decision a person makes with regard to God. And hence it is also impossible to do this in respect of the question as to whether this or that historical act is an event of salvation or dam-nation. By looking at the reality of history as it offers itself to reflection and objectifies itself in word and deed and only thus becomes historical in the strictest sense, one can surmise, hope or fear—but one cannot judge. The history of the world is not itself the judgement of the world, no matter how true it is that this judgement really takes place in that history. Furthermore, salvation is not to be found in the finality of the free decision of man, if this is taken to mean that man simply creates this salvation himself by his free decision. Salvation is God communicating himself—it is his free act, which is God himself—since there is no salvation in the real order apart from God himself. This God, in his free communication of himself, in the grace-giving gift of his own eternal glory, must indeed be accepted in freedom, even though this acceptance is itself once more an act of that human freedom which in turn is a gift of God himself, granted to man by God's communication of himself. But the God who communicates himself can only be experienced in his own reality by a direct experience without the veil of faith covering up this reality. God's very own reality can only be experienced in the direct vision of God—in an event, in other words, which is the achievement and in that sense the cessation of history, and not a moment in history—which is the fruit and not merely the maturing of that fruit. For these two reasons—i.e. the freedom of man and the gift of salvation by God—the event of salvation is indeed contained and achieved in profane history and yet is not present historically in its quality of saving event as such but is rather believed or hoped for. By and large, profane history does not of itself offer us any certain interpretation regarding salvation or damnation. Man works out his history, and it pertains to the inscrutable counsels of God alone to judge this otherwise unjudged history. History carries its eternal content into the silent Mystery—it itself cannot enjoy that content. And this is the first aspect under which salvation-history and profane history are distinct.

(b) If we were to regard salvation-history only from the viewpoint emphasized up till now, it would still always be co-extensive with profane history, for the latter would then represent the undeciphered and indecipherable salvation-history. The only difference between salvation-history and profane history would then lie in the fact that the one is judged and the other is not. They would be formally but not materially distinct from each other. There is in fact a reality and concept of salvation-history and even revelation-history (and our first task now will have to be to work this out more clearly) which is not indeed formally identical in this sense, though materially co-extensive, with the reality and concept of the profane history of the world. And so, before we can work out a material difference between salvation- and revelation-history in the narrowest sense of the word and the history of the world, we must first of all consider—or rather emphasize more explicitly—this material identity of a general revelation- and salvation-history and the profane history of the world. It is part of the Catholic statement of Faith that the supernatural saving purpose of God extends to all men in all ages and places in history. Everyone is offered salvation, which means that everyone, in so far as he does not close himself to this offer by his own free and grave guilt, is offered divine grace—and is offered it again and again (even when he is guilty). Every man exists not only in an existential situation to which belongs the obligation of striving towards a supernatural goal of direct union with the absolute God in a direct vision, but he exists also in a situation which presents the genuine subjective possibility of reaching this goal by accepting God's self-communication in grace and in glory. Because of God's universal saving purpose, the offer and possibility of salvation extend as far as extends the history of human freedom. But furthermore, this offer of the supernatural elevation of the spiritual reality of man enabling him to move by his spiritual and personal dynamism towards the God of the supernatural beatifying life is not merely an objective state of being in man which could be thought of simply as something beyond consciousness. Grace, being supernaturally divinizing, must rather be thought of as a change in the structure of human consciousness. This does not necessarily nor always mean that consciousness is given new proper objects which were until then unknown to it. But the 'formal object' (as scholastic theology is in the habit of saying), the horizon within which the normal, empirically experienced realities of consciousness are grasped, and the ultimate orientation of consciousness are changed by grace. This supernatural horizon is not necessarily such that it could or ought to be made an object of reflection in itself or that it ought to be taken out of the context of and distinguished from the transcendental horizon (of the experience of being) natural to the intellectual consciousness of man. For there is no question here of an individual, changeable datum of consciousness, but rather of the *a-priori* horizon of consciousness— and this *a-priori* formal horizon, within which the intellectual life of man is enacted, is always present in everyone. This horizon is not as such an object, but an unobjectified horizon within which the spiritual existence of man takes place. Yet precisely as such, it is unsystematically and unreflectedly and indeed for the greater part 'unreflectably' conscious—conscious but not known. It is that inexpressible, nameless and—precisely as such—present ordination of man in knowledge and freedom to something which is beyond anything assignable, which does not declare itself after the manner of an individual object but is as it were silent and yet by that very fact all the more all-embracing and operative in everything. It is the dynamism of the spirit's transcendence into the infinity of the silent mystery which we call God—the dynamism which is really meant to arrive and to accept, and not merely to be the eternally approaching but never quite arriving movement towards the infinity of God; it is meant to reach the infinity of God, since God gives himself to it of his own accord and in such a way that he has already even now entered freely into this movement of infinite transcendence itself as its innermost moving-force and *raison d'être*. If this is so, then this supernatural elevation of man which is granted by God's universal saving purpose already has of itself the nature of a revelation. Of course, it is not of its own nature alone a revelation in the sense of a propositionally expressed communication about some particular, definite individual object. It is, however, a revelation in the sense of a change of consciousness (although not a change of knowledge), which originates from a free personal self-communication of God in grace. It is, therefore, absolutely legitimate to call it already a revelation, especially since it already communicates or offers in an ontologically real sense as 'grace' something which also ultimately constitutes the whole content of divine revelation contained in proper propositions and human concepts, viz. God and his eternal life itself which, as God's self-communication in grace and glory, is the salvation of men. If man accepts this his supernaturally elevated transcendence— this supernatural horizon and hence this divine revelation in the self-communication of the one revealed—then he exercises, even though as yet in a very unsystematic manner, what in a Christian sense can certainly be called faith. It follows then that there is a history of salvation, revelation and faith which co-exists with the general profane history. We have called his the general salvation- and revelation-history so as to distinguish it from that other salvation- and revelation-history with which we will have to deal more explicitly in a moment. Of course, as we have already indicated briefly above, the notion of 'history' contained in the concept of the general salvation- and revelation-history must be understood in a wide and (if you will) watered-down sense. We can call it a history of salvation and revelation because it is a matter of real decisions and free acts both on the part of God and on the part of man; it is a matter of mutual, personal communications which are performed concretely in and on the material of profane history. But we can apply the term 'history' to this general salvation- and revelation-history only in a wider sense. For strictly as such and by its *a-priori* transcendental tendency, it does not as yet appear in those objectifications in word and objective cultural values which make it possible to have direct intercommunication between men, to have a concrete community of men and to have reflexly apprehensible knowledge about the relation to empirically experienced and communicable realities—and which in short represent history in the fullest sense of the word. This does not mean, however, that the general salvation- and revelation-history belongs to an absolutely meta-empirical sphere which is in no way connected with the tangibility of normal history. The basic condition or horizon in the line of grace of which we have spoken and which is the foundation of the fact that there is a general salvation- and revelation-history at all times and even outside the Old and New Covenants will make itself felt in the concrete history of men. It will influence the concrete forms of religion, of man's self-knowledge, of his philosophy and morality, even when this horizon as such cannot (or at least not easily) be made the object of reflection in conceptual purity and sureness of truth. There is a unity in the dimensions of human existence—the whole man is called to salvation—and there is an inner dynamism of grace by which it becomes effective in a healing, sanctifying and divinizing way in all the dimensions of man. It is therefore to be expected, furthermore, that this divinized ground of man will everywhere and always (although with varying force and very differing success) try to become the object of reflection, driven to this by the very dynamism of grace under a supernatural, saving providence of God. It is to be expected that it will try to objectify itself in explicit expressions of religion, such as in the liturgy and religious associations, and in protests of a 'prophetic' kind against any natural attempt by man to shut himself up in the world of his own categories and against any (ultimately polytheistic) misinterpretations of this basic grace-full experience. We cannot in the present context go into the details of this inter-action between profane history and general salvation- and revelation-history. But if this were possible, we could no doubt show that a Christian understanding of the universal saving purpose of God, and of the nature of supernatural grace, would enable us to gain a far more positive understanding of the explicit, reflex and socially constituted general history of religion which after all co-exists with profane history.

This would show us that it is absolutely possible to conceive of a religion before Christianity even apart from the Old Covenant—a religion quite legitimate in the eyes of the saving providence of God, i.e. positively willed by providence even though it might inseparably contain certain elements not willed by God. Thus, the Old Testament (as against the New) might be conceived in many respects as a divinely interpreted model of pre-Christian religion rather than as an absolutely and in every respect unique and incomparable quantity. We must, however, pass over these considerations here, even though they would greatly contribute to the elucidation of the question about the relation between profane and saving history. We will therefore return now to the consideration of the question as to why and in what respect salvation-history and profane history must be distinguished.

(c) Salvation-history and profane history are distinct because God has interpreted a particular part of this profane and otherwise ambiguous history by his word (which is a constitutive element of salvation-history itself), by giving it a saving or damning character. Thus he has distinguished this particular part of the one history from the rest of history and has made it the actual, official and explicit history of salvation. This explanation of the difference between the two histories may seem rather surprising at first. It may be thought that surely salvation-history in the strictest sense is to be found in the Old Testament and at the moment when Jesus Christ, the Word become flesh, came onto this earth, and when miracles occur—in brief, wherever God acts within history and accomplishes his actions on man. Yet, our thesis becomes immediately understandable if we ask ourselves about the reason for the presence of God's deeds in the history of men, and about the reason why God's actions enter into the properly historical dimension. For we still have to answer that it is through the word. A miracle would be merely an extraordinary and inexplicable event which would tell us nothing— even where, and precisely where, it refers to an empirically tangible and verifiable state of affairs—if it did not occur in connection with a word-revelation which is authenticated by it and which, in its turn, gives the miracle its basic meaning; the word-revelation makes the miracle basically comprehensible and gives point to its role as a sign indicating something. To the extent in which the real historical content of the Old Testament is not uttered and does not consist in the Word itself, the Old Testament can quite properly be regarded as the natural saving providence of God or as God's saving providence intended for and accorded to all peoples. In other words, we can conceive God as Lord of a national history which becomes an event of salvation only once it is clearly interpreted by the word of the prophets as corresponding or contrary to the will of God. And with regard to Jesus Christ, his Incarnation or hypostatic union is naturally a fact which is more than a human word; but it finds its inner, necessary and co-constitutive continuation in the absolute human consciousness in Jesus of being the Son of God—and it would not be present for us in our historical dimension (precisely because of its peculiar characteristic as an absolute transcendent mystery) without the self-revelation of Jesus in his human words. Having said all this, we do not mean to maintain that salvation-history is nothing but the divine Word in human words. Such an assertion which would identify the history of salvation with that of faith and which would reduce the history of faith to a purely existential actualism is not intended by what we have said. What we do say, however, is that the saving acts of God as such become present in the dimension of human history—in other words, become themselves historical—only when the word which expresses and interprets them is added. This is therefore not a word added externally or subsequently, which is pronounced about something already tangibly present in the realm of human history even without it; rather, it is an inner constitutive element of God's saving activity considered as an event of human history as such. Hence, wherever profane history is clearly interpreted by the word of God in history as to its saving or damning character—wherever God's actions in general salvation- and revelation-history are clearly and certainly objectified by the word of God—and wherever the absolute, unsurpassable and indissoluble unity of God and the world, and its history in Jesus Christ, become historically manifest by Christ's testimony to himself in the form of words—there is found the special, official history of salvation and revelation, immediately differentiated and standing out in relief from profane history. For the interpreting and revealing word of God, which constitutes the official and special revelation- and salvation-history as distinct from the general salvation- and revelation-history, does not occur always and everywhere but has its special place in time and space within history. Nor does it clearly interpret the saving or damning character of all early history but leaves large tracts of it unexplained although it does provide rules of interpretation regarding this profane history (with which we will have to deal later on) to aid the believing and hopeful ventures of the historically existing man. This setting into relief of saving history from profane history has itself a history all its own. It has not been equally intense and clear in all ages. Nor could it be. For by the general history of grace, salvation and revelation, real salvific activity becomes co-existent with the history of the world and takes place within it at all times and everywhere. For this reason salvation-history is always also the hidden foundation of profane history which also manifests itself in the latter in ever new forms: the religious element is everywhere the meaning and root of history and is never merely the most sublime flower of a merely human culture which is the word of men; it is already propelled from within by God-effected grace and co-determined from within by the proper, general salvation-history. Wherever the latter reveals itself so clearly that it begins to become itself historically tangible in word and in the objectifications of the spirit of history, there the general salvation-history begins to pass over into special salvation-history: one does not know exactly whether this or that man is a religious thinker and a religiously creative man or already a prophet; one asks oneself whether this or that religious experience is the mystical expression of man's search for infinite transcendence or already the mysticism of the experience of grace which carries the dynamic urge of the soul into the divine life; one is not quite sure whether this or that element of worship, religious institutionalization or custom is merely permitted, encouraged, or positively willed by God so that it may be the historical embodiment of that orientation towards God which is characteristic of the deepest reality of man and without which no one finds his salvation. We know that the Old Testament as a whole, with its great men of God and with all that has objectified itself in the holy Scriptures of the Old Testament, has been acknowledged by God as something really willed by him and as his own preparation for salvation—in other words, we know that it was real salvation-history within and delimited from profane history. Yet in the Old Testament, too, the dividing line between saving and profane history is still very fluid: it was only with difficulty that men in Old Testament times could distinguish between authentic and false prophets. For the prophets appeared only sporadically, and there was as yet no institution which could act as a final court of appeal endowed with an absolute discernment of spirits which could have distinguished on every occasion between genuine prophets, legiti-

mate religious renewal and criticism, on the one hand, and false prophets
and developments perversive of religion, on the other. The Old Covenant, taken as a whole, could have fallen away from its mission, and
from being an authentic, official and historical tangible manifestation of
the saving purpose of God for the people of Israel: it could have become an empty sign, an illegitimate usurpation of the sign of God's
grace in the world. Nor do we maintain that God did not make arrangements for the historically tangible salvation of other peoples, analogous
to the arrangements of the Old Testament. Of course, it remains the
privilege of Israel that its tangible and to some extent distinct salvation-
history was the immediate historical prelude to the Incarnation of the
divine Word, and that this history of Israel alone was interpreted
authoritatively by the word of God in Scripture in such a way that
it was thereby distinguished from any other profane history (which
also always contains religious elements), and that only thus it became
the official and special salvation-history in distinction to profane history. Only in Jesus Christ did the divine and the human reach an
absolute and indissoluble unity; only in the self-revelation of Jesus
is this unity also historically present; only now is this saving history
clearly and permanently distinguished from all profane history, and
everything, such as the Church, the sacraments and the Scriptures,
which follows from this Christ-event and which participates in its own
way in this unsurpassable finality of the Christ-event, participates also
in its distinction from profane history. Here in Christ and in the Church,
saving history reaches its clearest and absolutely permanent distinction from profane history and becomes really an unequivocally distinct
manifestation within the history of the world, thus bringing the general
salvation-history to self-realization and to its historical reality in word
and social structures within the history of the world. By this very fact,
this distinct salvation-history of an explicitly verbal, social and sacramental kind is also something destined for all men of every future age.
It intends to gather into itself the whole general salvation- and revelation-history and to represent it historically within itself; it *strives*
therefore to coincide with the general salvation- and revelation-history and thus also with profane history, although it knows quite well
that these two can never be fully identified in history but only in
the culminating dissolution of history.

3. Salvation-history explains profane history. This is the third
point we wish to make here about the subject under discussion. This

statement means two things. Firstly, salvation-history is an explanation of profane history because, in the form of general salvation-history, it represents the most profound character and basis of profane history, and because, in the form of official and special salvation-history, it manifests this ultimate character of all history in the revelation in which salvation takes place and at the same time shows itself historically. Secondly, salvation-history presents us by its word with an interpretation of profane history. These two aspects of the above statement do not require separate consideration.

(a) Salvation-history sets itself into relief from the history of the world—it demythologizes, undeifies the history of the world. Creation and history are not yet salvation. Salvation is God and his grace, and God's grace is not simply identical with the reality which is engaged in evolving history. Just as Christianity strips the world of divine attributes firstly by showing that it has a created nature essentially distinct from God and secondly by prohibiting any conception of the world which regards it simply as the corporeal aspect of the gods, so it is also with history. History is not simply the history of God himself—a theogony—and so does not find its ultimate basis in itself and is not self-explanatory. History is not the judgement of the world but is something created, finite, temporal and essentially referred to the Mystery which is other than itself. The 'Kronos' and 'Ananke' of history are not gods. Man has been thrown out into this undeified world. He does not merely live in salvation-history. He is a Christian and works out his salvation and this precisely by taking upon himself the soberness of the profane which is not yet itself salvation. Salvation-history creates its own presupposition by the very fact of turning the profane, the ambiguous, the God-veiling—in a word, the world and profane history—into the climate of faith and probation. It is true that salvation-history is silent about profane history, leaves its questions open ones and lets the cockle grow with the wheat without trying to make any clear-cut distinction between them. There is a way in which Christianity declares itself incompetent as regards worldly matters, the State and politics, economic matters and all other cultural affairs. At first sight, all this may appear to anyone who thinks he can deal with the world on his own as an all too desirable modesty. Yet in reality, this dualism between State and Church, science and theology—in short, between Christianity and the world together with its history—has another quite different side to it. We refer to the fact that God leaves history to its own devices; he leaves it to journey into the indefinite, to make its own attempts, to be responsible for its own 'planning', and he leaves it the possibility of losing its way and of tragically destroying itself, etc., even where people are not disobedient to the word of God and his commandments. Salvation-history, therefore, tells anyone who is looking for salvation to go out into profane history too—this history which remains a dark, unexplained and incalculable task—and tells him to hold out there, to prove himself there, to believe that life has a meaning even though this remains unexplained and precisely in this sense to accept God as his salvation. In short, salvation-history, by bringing out the distinction between profane history and itself, sends man out into a demythologized world which is not so much the realm of the rule of the gods, but rather the raw material for the task imposed on man—for the task which indeed man, the *homo faber*, actually and legitimately imposes on himself—only to know that, when he has fulfilled this task, he has still not gained salvation for himself by his own powers, but receives it as a gift from God, since it is more than the world and history.

(b) Salvation-history interprets the history of the world as something antagonistic and veiled. Precisely because salvation is not simply the immanent fruit of profane history, Christianity is sceptical towards profane history. It lets man go out to his worldly task, because it is precisely in the obscurity and ambiguity of this earthly task that man must work out his salvation which is by faith. Yet for Christianity this very task in the world is something which will always remain unfinished and which will ultimately always again end in failure. For as far as the individual is concerned, this task always finds an absolute limit in death. In the same way Christianity also shows that death is to be found even in the midst of universal history. This implies a futility arising from the fact that what can always be planned only partially will always remain incalculable—a futility which always springs afresh out of man's evil heart, even over and above the inherent tragedy of everything finite. Christianity knows no history which would evolve of its own inner power into the kingdom of God itself and it does not really matter whether one conceives this kingdom as the realm of the enlightened mind, or of the fully civilized man, or of the classless society or in any other way whatsoever. The opposition between man and woman, the intelligent and the stupid, the rich and the poor, war and peace, rulers and subjects, and any other ineradicable antitheses of existence, may take different forms, may become more refined and more bearable; the effort to humanize these oppositions may even be a duty for the human race and one which is imposed on it and whose fulfilment is to a certain extent even forced upon it by the exigencies of history. Nevertheless, the oppositions will always remain, they will always weigh heavily on man and will always renew the pain and bitter melancholy of human existence. Indeed, in Christian eschatology, these terrestrial antitheses, this combat between light and darkness, good and evil, faith and unbelief, are known to take on ever acuter forms. Of course, this combat which is actually part and parcel of salvation-history will never be such that the human combatants engaged on either side of this fight would identify themselves or could be identified with absolute goodness or absolute evil. No one but God can ever distinguish these ultimate fronts of salvation-history adequately, for they will always cut through the parties engaged in these combats in the history of the world as well as the individuals concerned. Yet according to Christian eschatology, the decisions taken in salvation-history will be enacted in ever clearer forms and signs; they will fashion their own embodiments and expressions in the most profound depths of existence within the history of the world, even though the final judgement, which will make a clear distinction between the wheat and the cockle within these objectifications, belongs to God alone. Christianity denies that the history of the world is progressing towards eternal peace—although this does not mean that war, which will always be with us, must necessarily be one fought with halberds or atomic bombs. Christianity knows that all progress in profane history is also another step towards the possibility of greater dangers and ultimate ruin. History will never be the place for eternal peace and shadowless light—rather if this life is measured by the absolute demands which God has empowered man to make or, indeed, which man has a God-given duty to make, it will always be the land of death and darkness.

(c) The history of the world is an existentially devaluated (*depotenzierte*) history in its Christian interpretation. We must be careful in our evaluation of profane history. The Christian is certainly not such a one as has a merely private concern about his salvation that he can settle down in some dead corner of the history of the world and seek his salvation there—quite unconcerned about the passage of the history of the world—in a flight from the world which in the last analysis is quite impossible. It may be winter in the history of a people, or in some other kind of historical form. It may be impossible in some particular period of history to achieve anything lofty or great, things to which one would otherwise be in duty bound. A man may perhaps even recognize this and *hence* know himself to be released from such a duty. There may be quite legitimate withdrawals from public life, from politics and the market-place of an impoverished age; indeed, in certain periods this may be the only possible way of existing for a wise, honest and courageous person, for not even he is capable of everything, nor is he bound to consider himself capable of it. Yet all this does not mean that the Christian may in principle withdraw from history. He has a duty towards history, he must make and suffer history. He can only find the eternal in the temporal. Yet this again does not mean that the temporal and the eternal are simply the same. And to this extent the Christian has the right and duty to make history something relative and—in a true sense—to devaluate and disarm it existentially. Who shall separate us from the love of Christ? Shall tribulation, or distress, or persecution, or hunger or nakedness, or danger or the sword? ... I am sure that neither death, nor life, nor angels, nor principalities, nor powers, nor things present, nor things to come, nor height, nor depth, nor any other creature will be able to separate us from the love of God, which is in Christ Jesus Our Lord— says St Paul. But this means that every significance proper to the history of the world is always already outdated for us, not indeed on our account but on account of God in Christ—always presupposing that we have taken refuge by faith in this outmoding of history by God in Christ. Neither death nor life, neither things present nor future possibilities are the ultimate, the finally significant, that which is salvation. Hence the Christian is told over and over again with regard to the history of this world and its incalculable possibilities and tasks: what does it profit a man if he gain the whole world but suffer the loss of his own soul? *This* flight from the world, which sees the significance of empirical history as something relative, is part of what is meant by being a Christian. It is no stoic ataraxy, no cowardice or cynicism. It is the faith which knows that entry into God's eternity can be gained through all the exits of the history of the world and through every rise or fall, provided only that one accepts God's salvation in faith—which one can do under any of the forms of profane history. That which often seems to be a somewhat narrow-minded, self-centred anxiety about salvation in the life of the Christian—this attitude of someone trying to salvage his soul out of the chaos of the times—is in fact (wherever it is the action of a true Christian) the attitude of a magnificent superiority of the faith over the world, such as is given expression in the text of St Paul quoted above. It means that the true Christian can take history seriously because he knows it to be already overcome by Christ. The history of this world is devaluated in a Christian sense, because salvation can take place in all its most contradictory forms— and at the same time this history is increased in value since in it can truly take place the limitless salvation, the eternal and lasting salvation, which is God himself.

(d) For Christianity, the history of this world is a history interpreted in a Christo-centric sense. This is really just a summary of what we have been saying. The world is the world created for the eternal Logos —by him and for him. The world and its history has been designed from the very beginning with a view to the Word of God become flesh. Since God wished, because he is Love, to express himself in his eternal Word, the world exists, and exists complete with the difference between nature and grace, and thus between salvation-history and profane history. For this very reason this means that this difference is enveloped by Christ and by God's absolute self-expression which takes place in Christ. Hence the history of the world too—and precisely in its profane nature—is a part of the pre- and post-history of Christ. Natural history in its material content and in its living form is the sphere which God puts before the finite spirit as the condition of its possibility—as the presupposition which transcends itself into the realm of the finite spirit by the dynamism of the absolute Spirit. So also the totality of the history of the world is the presupposition God has provided for salvation-history as the condition of its possibility transcending itself into it. Thus the history of the world is the sphere and the pre-history of the history of Christ, which is, since he is engaged in history not indeed as someone who needs to be but as the Love who surrenders himself, the history of God himself. That, however, which embraces world- and salvation-history in their unity and diversity, is the most real history of all.

6

CHRISTIANITY AND THE NON-CHRISTIAN RELIGIONS[1]

'OPEN Catholicism' involves two things. It signifies the fact that the Catholic Church is opposed by historical forces which she herself cannot disregard as if they were purely 'worldly' forces and a matter of indifference to her but which, on the contrary, although they do not stand in a positive relationship of peace and mutual recognition to the Church, do have a significance for her. 'Open Catholicism' means also the task of becoming related to these forces in order to understand their existence (since this cannot be simply acknowledged), in order to bear with and overcome the annoyance of their opposition and in order to form the Church in such a way that she will be able to overcome as much of this pluralism as should not exist, by understanding herself as the higher unity of this opposition. Open Catholicism means therefore a certain attitude towards the present-day pluralism of powers with different outlooks on the world. We do not, of course, refer to pluralism merely as a fact which one simply acknowledges without explaining it. Pluralism is meant here as a fact which ought to be thought about and one which, without denying that—in part at least—it should not exist at all, should be incorporated once more from a more elevated viewpoint into the totality and unity of the Christian understanding of human existence. For Christianity, one of the gravest elements of this pluralism in which we live and with which we must come to terms, and indeed the element most difficult to incorporate, is the pluralism of religions. We do not refer by this to the pluralism of Christian denominations. This pluralism too is a fact, and a challenge and task for Christians. But we are

[1] The following expositions are the notes of a lecture given on the 28th April 1961 in Eichstätt (Bavaria) at a meeting of the 'Abendländische Akademie'. No attempt has been made to enlarge these notes here, although a great deal in them remains extremely fragmentary.

not concerned with it here. Our subject is the, at least in its ultimate and basic form, more serious problem of the different religions which still exist even in Christian times, and this after a history and mission of Christianity which has already lasted two thousand years. It is true, certainly, that all these religions together, including Christianity, are faced today with an enemy which did not exist for them in the past. We refer to the decided lack of religion and the denial of religion in general. This denial, in a sense, takes the stage with the ardour of a religion and of an absolute and sacred system which is the basis and the yard-stick of all further thought. This denial, organized on the basis of a State, represents itself as *the* religion of the future—as the decided, absolute secularization of human existence excluding all mystery. No matter how paradoxical this may sound, it does remain true that precisely this state of siege in which religion in general finds itself, finds one of its most important weapons and opportunities for success in the fact that humanity is so torn in its religious adherence. But quite apart from this, this pluralism is a greater threat and a reason for greater unrest for Christianity than for any other religion. For no other religion—not even Islam—maintains so absolutely that it is *the* religion, the one and only valid revelation of the one living God, as does the Christian religion. The fact of the pluralism of religions, which endures and still from time to time becomes virulent anew even after a history of two thousand years, must therefore be the greatest scandal and the greatest vexation for Christianity. And the threat of this vexation is also greater for the individual Christian today than ever before. For in the past, the other religion was in practice the religion of a completely different cultural environment. It belonged to a history with which the individual only communicated very much on the periphery of his own history; it was the religion of those who were even in every other respect alien to oneself. It is not surprising, therefore, that people did not wonder at the fact that these 'others' and 'strangers' had also a different religion. No wonder that in general people could not seriously consider these other religions as a challenge posed to themselves or even as a possibility for themselves. Today things have changed. The West is no longer shut up in itself; it can no longer regard itself simply as the centre of the history of this world and as the centre of culture, with a religion which even from this point of view (i.e. from a point of view which has really nothing to do with a decision of faith but which simply carries the weight of something quite self-evident) could appear as the obvious and indeed sole way of honouring God to be thought of for a European. Today everybody is the next-door neighbour and spiritual neighbour of every one else in the world. And so everybody today is determined by the intercommunication of all those situations of life which affect the whole world. Every religion which exists in the world is—just like all cultural possibilities and actualities of other people—a question posed, and a possibility offered, to every person. And just as one experiences someone else's culture in practice as something relative to one's own and as something existentially demanding, so it is also involuntarily with alien religions. They have become part of one's own existential situation—no longer merely theoretically but in the concrete—and we experience them therefore as something which puts the absolute claim of our own Christian faith into question. Hence, the question about the understanding of and the continuing existence of religious pluralism as a factor of our immediate Christian existence is an urgent one and part of the question as to how we are to deal with today's pluralism. This problem could be tackled from different angles. In the present context we simply wish to try to describe a few of those basic traits of a Catholic dogmatic interpretation of the non-Christian religions which may help us to come closer to a solution of the question about the Christian position in regard to the religious pluralism in the world of today. Since it cannot be said, unfortunately, that Catholic theology—as practised in more recent times—has really paid sufficient attention to the questions to be posed here, it will also be impossible to maintain that what we will have to say here can be taken as the common thought of Catholic theology. What we have to say carries, therefore, only as much weight as the reasons we can adduce, which reasons can again only be briefly indicated. Whenever the propositions to be mentioned carry a greater weight than this in theology, anyone trained in theology will realize it quite clearly from what is said. When we say that it is a question here of a *Catholic* dogmatic interpretation of the non-Christian religions, this is not meant to indicate that it is necessarily a question also of theories controverted among Christians themselves. It simply means that we will not be able to enter explicitly into the question as to whether the theses to be stated here can also hope to prove acceptable to Protestant theology. We say too that we are going to give a dogmatic interpretation, since we will pose our question not as empirical historians of religion but out of the self-understanding of Christianity itself, i.e. as dogmatic theologians.

1st Thesis: We must begin with the thesis which follows, because it certainly represents the basis in the Christian faith of the theological understanding of other religions. This thesis states that Christianity understands itself as the absolute religion, intended for all men, which cannot recognize any other religion beside itself as of equal right. This proposition is self-evident and basic for Christianity's understanding of itself. There is no need here to prove it or to develop its meaning. After all, Christianity does not take valid and lawful religion to mean primarily that relationship of man to God which man himself institutes on his own authority. Valid and lawful religion does not mean man's own interpretation of human existence. It is not the reflection and objectification of the experience which man has of himself and by himself. Valid and lawful religion for Christianity is rather God's action on men, God's free self-revelation by communicating himself to man. It is God's relationship to men, freely instituted by God himself and revealed by God in this institution. *This* relationship of God to man is basically the same for all men, because it rests on the Incarnation, death and resurrection of the one Word of God become flesh. Christianity is God's own interpretation in his Word of this relationship of God to man founded in Christ by God himself. And so Christianity can recognize itself as the true and lawful religion for all men only where and when it enters with existential power and demanding force into the realm of another religion and—judging it by itself—puts it in question. Since the time of Christ's coming—ever since he came in the flesh as the Word of God in absoluteness and reconciled, i.e. united the world with God by his death and resurrection, not merely theoretically but really—Christ and his continuing historical presence in the world (which we call 'Church') is *the* religion which binds man to God. Already we must, however, make one point clear as regards this first thesis (which cannot be further developed and proved here). It is true that the Christian religion itself has its own pre-history which traces this religion back to the beginning of the history of humanity—even though it does this by many basic steps. It is also true that this fact of having a pre-history is of much greater importance, according to the evidence of the New Testament, for the theoretical and practical proof of the claim to absolute truth made by the Christian religion than our current fundamental theology is aware of. Nevertheless, the Christian religion as such has a beginning in history; it did not always exist but began at some point in time. It has not always and everywhere been *the* way of salvation for men—at least not in its historically tangible ecclesio-sociological constitution and in the reflex fruition of God's saving activity in, and in view of, Christ. As a historical quantity Christianity has, therefore, a temporal and spatial starting point in Jesus of Nazareth and in the saving event of the unique Cross and the empty tomb in Jerusalem. It follows from this, however, that this absolute religion—even when it begins to be this for practically all men—must come in a historical way to men, facing them as the only legitimate and demanding religion for them. It is therefore a question of whether this moment, when the existentially real demand is made by the absolute religion in its historically tangible form, takes place really at the same chronological moment for all men, or whether the occurrence of this moment has itself a history and thus is not chronologically simultaneous for all men, cultures and spaces of history. (This is a question which up until now Catholic theology has not thought through with sufficient clarity and reflection by really confronting it with the length and intricacy of real human time and history.) Normally the beginning of the objective obligation of the Christian message for all men—in other words, the abolition of the validity of the Mosaic religion *and* of all other religions which (as we will see later) may also have a period of validity and of being-willed-by-God—is thought to occur in the apostolic age. Normally, therefore, one regards the time between this beginning and the actual acceptance or the personally guilty refusal of Christianity in a non-Jewish world and history as the span between the already given promulgation of the law and the moment when the one to whom the law refers takes cognizance of it. It is not just an idle academic question to ask whether such a conception is correct or whether, as we maintain, there could be a different opinion in this matter, i.e. whether one could hold that the beginning of Christianity for actual periods of history, for cultures and religions, could be postponed to those moments in time when Christianity became a real historical factor in an individual history and culture—a real historical moment in a particular culture. For instance, one concludes from the first, usual answer that *everywhere* in the world, since the first Pentecost, baptism of children dying before reaching the use of reason is necessary for their supernatural salvation, although this was not necessary before that time. For other questions, too, a correct and

considered solution of the present question could be of great importance, as for instance for the avoidance of immature conversions, for the
justification and importance of 'indirect' missionary work, etc. One
will have to ask oneself whether one can still agree today with the first
opinion mentioned above, in view of the history of the missions which
has already lasted two thousand years and yet is still to a great extent
in its beginnings—for even Suarez himself, for instance, had already
seen (at least with regard to the *Jews*) that the *promulgatio* and *obligatio*
of the Christian religion, and not merely the *divulgatio* and *notitia*
promulgationis, take place in historical sequence. We cannot really
answer this question here, but it may at least be pointed out as an
open question; in practice, the correctness of the second theory may
be presupposed since it alone corresponds to the real historicity of
Christianity and salvation-history. From this there follows a deli-
cately differentiated understanding of our first thesis: we maintain
positively only that, as regards destination, Christianity is the absolute
and hence the only religion for all men. We leave it, however, an open
question (at least in principle) at what exact point in time the absolute
obligation of the Christian religion has in fact come into effect for every
man and culture, even in the sense of the *objective* obligation of such
a demand. Nevertheless—and this leaves the thesis formulated still
sufficiently exciting—wherever in practice Christianity reaches man
in the real urgency and rigour of his actual existence, Christianity—
once understood—presents itself as the only still valid religion for
this man, a necessary means for his salvation and not merely an obligation with the necessity of a precept. It should be noted that this is a
question of the necessity of a *social* form for salvation. Even though
this is Christianity and not some other religion, it may surely still be
said without hesitation that this thesis contains implicitly another thesis
which states that in concrete human existence as such, the nature of
religion itself must include a social constitution—which means that
religion can exist only in a social form. This means, therefore, that man,
who is commanded to have a religion, is also commanded to seek and
accept a social form of religion. It will soon become clear what this
reflection implies for the estimation of non-Christian religions.

Finally, we may mention one further point in this connection. What
is vital in the *notion* of *paganism* and hence also of the non-Christian
pagan religions (taking 'pagan' here as a theological concept without
any disparaging intent) is not the actual refusal to accept the Christian

religion but the absence of any sufficient historical encounter with Christianity which would have enough historical power to render the Christian religion really present in this pagan society and in the history of the people concerned. If this is so, then paganism ceases to exist in this sense by reason of what is happening today. For the Western world is opening out into a universal world-history in which every people and every cultural sector becomes an inner factor of every other people and every other cultural sector. Or rather, paganism is slowly entering a new phase: there is *one* history of the world, and in this *one* history both the Christians and the non-Christians (i.e. the old and new pagans together) live in one and the same situation and face each other in dialogue, and thus the question of the theological meaning of the other religions arises once more and with even greater urgency.

2nd Thesis: Until the moment when the gospel really enters into the historical situation of an individual, a non-Christian religion (even outside the Mosaic religion) does not merely contain elements of a natural knowledge of God, elements, moreover, mixed up with human depravity which is the result of original sin and later aberrations. It contains also supernatural elements arising out of the grace which is given to men as a gratuitous gift on account of Christ. For this reason a non-Christian religion can be recognized as a *lawful* religion (although only in different degrees) without thereby denying the error and depravity contained in it. This thesis requires a more extensive explanation.

We must first of all note the point up to which this evaluation of the non-Christian religions is valid. This is the point in time when the Christian religion becomes a historically real factor for those who are of this religion. Whether this point is the same, theologically speaking, as the first Pentecost, or whether it is different in chronological time for individual peoples and religions, is something which even at this point will have to be left to a certain extent an open question. We have, however, chosen our formulation in such a way that it points more in the direction of the opinion which seems to us the more correct one in the matter although the *criteria* for a more exact determination of this moment in time must again be left an open question.

The thesis itself is divided into two parts. It means first of all that it is *a priori* quite possible to suppose that there are supernatural, grace-filled elements in non-Christian religions. Let us first of all deal with this statement. It does not mean, of course, that all the elements of a polytheistic conception of the divine, and all the other religious, ethical and metaphysical aberrations contained in the non-Christian religions, are to be or may be treated as harmless either in theory or in practice. There have been constant protests against such elements throughout the history of Christianity and throughout the history of the Christian interpretation of the non-Christian religions, starting with the Epistle to the Romans and following on the Old Testament polemics against the religion of the 'heathens'. Every one of these protests is still valid in what was really meant and expressed by them. Every such protest remains a part of the message which Christianity and the Church has to give to the peoples who profess such religions. Furthermore, we are not concerned here with an *a-posteriori* history of religions. Consequently, we also cannot describe empirically what should not exist and what is opposed to God's will in these non-Christian religions, nor can we represent these things in their many forms and degrees. We are here concerned with dogmatic theology and so can merely repeat the universal and unqualified verdict as to the unlawfulness of the non-Christian religions right from the moment when they came into real and historically powerful contact with Christianity (and at first only thus!). It is clear, however, that this condemnation does not mean to deny the very basic differences within the non-Christian religions especially since the pious, God-pleasing pagan was already a theme of the Old Testament, and especially since this God-pleasing pagan cannot simply be thought of as living absolutely outside the concrete socially constituted religion and constructing his own religion on his native foundations—just as St Paul in his speech on the Areopagus did not simply exclude a positive and basic view of the pagan religion. The decisive reason for the first part of our thesis is basically a theological consideration. This consideration (prescinding from certain more precise qualifications) rests ultimately on the fact that, if we wish to be Christians, we must profess belief in the universal and serious salvific purpose of God towards all men which is true even within the post-paradisean phase of salvation dominated by original sin. We know, to be sure, that this proposition of faith does not say anything certain about the *individual* salvation of man understood as something which has in fact been reached. But God desires the salvation of everyone. And this salvation willed by God is the salvation won by Christ, the salvation of supernatural grace which divinizes man, the salvation of the beatific vision. It is a salvation really intended for all those millions upon millions of men who lived perhaps a million years before Christ—and also for those who have lived after Christ—in nations, cultures and epochs of a very wide range which were still completely shut off from the viewpoint of those living in the light of the New Testament. If, on the one hand, we conceive salvation as something specifically *Christian*, if there is no salvation apart from Christ, if according to Catholic teaching the supernatural divinization of man can never be replaced merely by good will on the part of man but is necessary as something itself given in this earthly life; and if, on the other hand, God has really, truly and seriously intended this salvation for all men—then these two aspects cannot be reconciled in any other way then by stating that every human being is really and truly exposed to the influence of divine, supernatural grace which offers an interior union with God and by means of which God communicates himself whether the individual takes up an attitude of acceptance or of refusal towards this grace. It is senseless to suppose cruelly—and without any hope of acceptance by the man of today, in view of the enormous extent of the extra-Christian history of salvation and damnation—that nearly all men living outside the official and public Christianity are so evil and stubborn that the offer of supernatural grace ought not even to be made in fact in most cases, since these individuals have already rendered themselves unworthy of such an offer by previous, subjectively grave offences against the natural moral law. If one gives more exact theological thought to this matter, then one cannot regard nature and grace as two phases in the life of the individual which follow each other in time. It is furthermore impossible to think that this offer of supernatural, divinizing grace made to all men on account of the universal salvific purpose of God, should in general (prescinding from the relatively few exceptions) remain ineffective in most cases on account of the personal guilt of the individual. For, as far as the gospel is concerned, we have no really conclusive reason for thinking so pessimistically of men. On the other hand, and contrary to every merely human experience, we do have every reason for thinking optimistically of God and his salvific will which is more powerful than the extremely limited stupidity and evil-mindedness of men. However little we can say with certitude about the final lot of an individual inside or outside the officially constituted Christian religion, we have every reason to think optimistically—i.e. truly hopefully and confidently in a Christian sense—of God who has certainly the last word and who has revealed to us that he has spoken his powerful word of reconciliation and forgiveness into the world. If it is true that the eternal Word of God has become flesh and has died the death of sin for the sake of our salvation and in spite of our guilt, then the Christian has no right to suppose that the fate of the world—having regard to the whole of the world—takes the same course on account of man's refusal as it would have taken if Christ had not come. Christ and his salvation are not simply one of two possibilities offering themselves to man's free choice; they are the deed of God which bursts open and redeems the false choice of man by overtaking it. In Christ God not only gives the *possibility* of salvation, which in that case would still have to be effected by man himself, but the actual salvation itself, however much this includes also the right decision of human freedom which is itself a gift from God. Where sin already existed, grace came in superabundance. And hence we have every right to suppose that grace has not only been offered even outside the Christian Church (to deny this would be the error of Jansenism) but also that, in a great many cases at least, grace gains the victory in man's free acceptance of it, this being again the result of grace. Of course, we would have to show more explicitly than the shortness of time permits that the empirical picture of human beings, their life, their religion and their individual and universal history does not disprove this optimism of a faith which knows the whole world to be subjected to the salvation won by Christ. But we must remember that the theoretical and ritualistic factors in good and evil are only a very inadequate expression of what man actually accomplishes in practice. We must remember that the same transcendence of man (even the transcendence elevated and liberated by God's grace) can be exercised in many different ways and under the most varied labels. We must take into consideration that whenever the religious person acts really religiously, he makes use of, or omits unthinkingly, the manifold forms of religious institutions by making a consciously critical choice among and between them. We must consider the immeasurable difference—which it seems right to suppose to exist even in the Christian sphere—between what is objectively wrong in moral life and the extent to which this is really realized with subjectively grave guilt. Once we take all this into consideration, we will not hold it to be impossible that grace is at work, and is even being accepted, in the spiritual, personal life of the individual, no matter how primitive, unenlightened, apathetic and earth-bound such a life may at first sight appear to be. We can say quite simply that wherever, and in so far as, the individual makes a moral decision in his life (and where could this be declared to be in any way absolutely impossible—except in precisely 'pathological' cases?), this moral decision can also be thought to measure up to the character of a supernaturally elevated, believing and thus saving act, and hence to be more in actual fact than merely 'natural morality'. Hence, if one believes seriously in the universal salvific purpose of God towards all men in Christ, it need not and cannot really be doubted that gratuitous influences of properly Christian supernatural grace are conceivable in the life of all men (provided they are first of all regarded as individuals) and that these influences can be presumed to be accepted in spite of the sinful state of men and in spite of their apparent estrangement from God.

Our second thesis goes even further than this, however, and states in its second part that, from what has been said, the actual religions of 'pre-Christian' humanity too must not be regarded as simply illegitimate from the very start, but must be seen as quite capable of having a positive significance. This statement must naturally be taken in a very different sense which we cannot examine here for the various particular religions. This means that the different religions will be able to lay claim to being lawful religions only in very different senses and to very different degrees. But precisely this variability is not at all excluded by the notion of a 'lawful religion', as we will have to show in a moment. A lawful religion means here an institutional religion whose 'use' by man at a certain period can be regarded on the whole as a positive means of gaining the right relationship to God and thus for the attaining of salvation, a means which is therefore positively included in God's plan of salvation. That such a notion and the reality to which it refers can exist even where such a religion shows many theoretical and practical errors in its concrete form becomes clear in a theological analysis of the structure of the Old Covenant. We must first of all remember in this connection that only in the New Testament —in the Church of Christ understood as something which is eschatologically final and *hence* (and only for this reason) 'indefectible' and infallible—is there realized the notion of a Church which, because it is instituted by God in some way or other, already contains the permanent norm of differentiation between what is right (i.e. willed by God) and what is wrong in the religious sphere, and contains it both as a permanent institution and as an intrinsic element of this religion. There was nothing like this in the Old Testament, although it must undoubtedly be recognized as a lawful religion. The Old Covenant—understood as a concrete, historical and religious manifestation—contained what is right, willed by God, *and* what is false, erroneous, wrongly developed and depraved. But there was no permanent, continuing and institutional court of appeal in the Old Covenant which could have differentiated authoritatively, always and with certainty for the conscience of the individual between what was willed by God and what was due to human corruption in the actual religion. Of course, there were the prophets. They were not a permanent institution, however, but a conscience which had always to assert itself anew on behalf of the people in order to protest against the corruption of the religion as it existed at the time, thus—incidentally—confirming the existence of this corruption. The official, institutional forms known as the 'kingdom' and the priesthood were so little proof against this God-offending corruption that they could bring about the ruin of the Israelitic religion itself. And since there were also pseudo-prophets, and no infallible 'institutional' court of appeal for distinguishing genuine and false prophecy, it was—in the last analysis—left to the conscience of the individual Israelite himself to differentiate between what in the concrete appearance of the Israelitic religion was the true covenant with God and what was a humanly free, and so in certain cases falsifying, interpretation and corruption of this God-instituted religion. There might have been objective criteria for such a distinction of spirits, but their application could not simply be left to an 'ecclesiastical' court—not even in the most decisive questions—since official judgements could be wrong even about these questions and in fact were completely wrong about them. This and nothing more—complete with its distinction between what was willed by God and what was human, all too human, a distinction which was ultimately left to be decided by the individual—was the concrete Israelitic religion. The Holy Scriptures do indeed give us the official and valid deposit to help us differentiate among the spirits which moved the history of the Old Testament religion. But since the infallible delimitation of the canon of the Old Testament is again to be found only in the New Testament, the exact and final differentiation between the lawful and the unlawful in the Old Testament religion is again possible only by making use of the New Testament as something eschatologically final. The unity of the concrete religion of the Old Testament, which (ultimately) could be distinguished only gropingly and at one's own risk, was however the unity willed by God, providential for the Israelites in the order of salvation and indeed the lawful religion for them. In this connection it must furthermore be taken into consideration that it was meant to be this only for the Israelites and for no one else; the institution of those belonging to the Jewish religion without being of the Jewish race, (i.e. of the proselytes) was a very much later phenomenon. Hence it cannot be a part of the notion of a lawful religion in the above sense that it should be free from corruption, error and objective moral wrong in the concrete form of its appearance, or that it should contain a clear objective and permanent final court of appeal for the conscience of the individual to enable the individual to differentiate clearly and with certainty between the elements willed and instituted by God and those which are merely human and corrupt. We must therefore rid ourselves of the prejudice that we can face a non-Christian religion with the dilemma that it must either come from God in everything it contains and thus correspond to God's will and positive providence, or be simply a purely human construction. If man is under God's grace even in these religions—and to deny this is certainly absolutely wrong—then the possession of this supernatural grace cannot but show itself, and cannot but become a formative factor of life in the concrete, even where (though not only where) this life turns the relationship to the absolute into an explicit theme, viz. in religion. It would perhaps be possible to say in theory that where a certain religion is not only accompanied in its concrete appearance by something false and humanly corrupted but also makes this an explicitly and consciously adopted element—an explicitly declared condition of its *nature*—this religion is wrong in its deepest and most specific being and hence can no longer be regarded as a lawful religion—not even in the widest sense of the word. This may be quite correct in theory. But we must surely go on to ask whether there is any religion apart from the Christian religion (meaning here even only the Catholic religion) with an authority which could elevate falsehood into one of its really essential parts and which could thus face man with an alternative of either accepting this falsehood as the most real and decisive factor of the religion or leaving this religion. Even if one could perhaps say something like this of Islam as such, it would have to be denied of the majority of religions.

It would have to be asked in every case to what extent the followers of such religions would actually agree with such an interpretation of their particular religion. If one considers furthermore how easily a concrete, originally religious act can be always directed in its intention towards one and the same absolute, even when it manifests itself in the most varied forms, then it will not even be possible to say that theoretical polytheism, however deplorable and objectionable it may be objectively, must always and everywhere be an absolute obstacle to the performance in such a religion of genuinely religious acts directed to the one true God. This is particularly true since it cannot be proved that the practical religious life of the ancient Israelites, in so far as it manifested itself in popular theory, was always more than mere henotheism.

Furthermore, it must be borne in mind that the individual ought to and must have the possibility in his life of partaking in a genuine saving relationship to God, and this at all times and in all situations of the history of the human race. Otherwise there could be no question of a serious and also actually effective salvific design of God for all men, in all ages and places. In view of the social nature of man and the previously even more radical social solidarity of men, however, it is quite unthinkable that man, being what he is, could actually achieve this relationship to God—which he must have and which if he is to be saved, is and must be made possible for him by God—in an absolutely private interior reality and this outside of the actual religious bodies which offer themselves to him in the environment in which he lives. If man had to be and could always and everywhere be a *homo religiosus* in order to be able to save himself as such, then he was this *homo religiosus* in the concrete religion in which 'people' lived and had to live at that time. He could not escape this religion, however much he may have and did take up a critical and selective attitude towards this religion on individual matters, and however much he may have and did put different stresses in practice on certain things which were at variance with the official theory of this religion. If, however, man can always have a positive, saving relationship to God, and if he always had to have it, then he has always had it within *that* religion which in practice was at his disposal by being a factor in his sphere of existence. As already stated above, the inherence of the individual exercise of religion in a social religious order is one of the essential traits of true religion as it exists in practice. Hence, if one were to expect from someone who lives outside the Christian religion that he should have exercised his genuine, saving relationship to God absolutely outside the religion which society offered him, then such a conception would turn religion into something intangibly interior, into something which is always and everywhere performed only indirectly, a merely transcendental religion without anything which could become tangible in categories. Such a conception would annul the above-mentioned principle regarding the necessarily social nature of all religion in the concrete, so that even the Christian Church would then no longer have the necessary presupposition of general human and natural law as proof of her necessity. And since it does not at all belong to the notion of a lawful religion intended by God for man as something positively salvific that it should be pure and positively willed by God in all its elements, such a religion can be called an absolutely legitimate religion for the person concerned. That which God has intended as salvation for him reached him, in accordance with God's will and by his permission (no longer adequately separable in practice), in the *concrete* religion of his actual realm of existence and historical condition, but this fact did not deprive him of the right and the limited possibility to criticize and to heed impulses of religious reform which by God's providence kept on recurring within such a religion. For a still better and simpler understanding of this, one has only to think of the natural and socially constituted morality of a people and culture. Such a morality is never pure but is always also corrupted, as Jesus confirmed even in the case of the Old Testament. It can always be disputed and corrected, therefore, by the individual in accordance with his conscience. Yet, taken in its totality, it is *the* way in which the individual encounters the natural divine law according to God's will, and the way in which the natural law is given real, actual power in the life of the individual who cannot reconstruct these tablets of the divine law anew on his own responsibility and as a private metaphysician. The morality of a people and of an age, taken in its totality, is therefore the legitimate and concrete form of the divine law (even though, of course, it can and may have to be corrected), so that it was not until the New Testament that the institution guaranteeing the purity of this form became (with the necessary reservations) an element of this form itself. Hence, if there existed a divine moral law and religion in the life of man *before* this moment, then its absolute purity (i.e. its constitution by divinely willed elements alone) must not be made the condition of the lawfulness of its existence. In fact, if every man who comes into the world is pursued by God's grace—and if one of the effects of this grace, even in its supernatural and salvifically elevating form, is to cause changes in consciousness (as is maintained by the better theory in Catholic theology) even though it cannot be simply *as* such a direct object of certain reflection—then it cannot be true that the actually existing religions do not bear any trace of the fact that all men are in some way affected by grace. These traces may be difficult to distinguish even to the enlightened eye of the Christian. But they must be there. And perhaps we may only have looked too superficially and with too little love at the non-Christian religions and so have not really seen them. In any case it is certainly not right to regard them as new conglomerates of natural theistic metaphysics and as a humanly incorrect interpretation and institutionalization of this 'natural religion'. The religions existing in the concrete must contain supernatural, gratuitous elements, and in using *these* elements the pre-Christian was able to attain God's grace: presumably, too, the pre-Christian exists even to this day, even though the possibility is gradually disappearing *today*. If we say that there were lawful religions in pre-Christian ages even outside the realm of the Old Testament, this does not mean that these religions were lawful in *all* their elements—to maintain this would be absurd. Nor does it mean that *every* religion was lawful; for in certain cases several forms, systems and institutions of a religious kind offered themselves within the historically concrete situation of the particular member of a certain people, culture, period of history, etc., so that the person concerned had to decide as to *which* of them was here and now, and on the whole, the more correct way (and hence for him *in concreto* the only correct way) of finding God. This thesis is not meant to imply that the lawfulness of the Old Testament religion was of exactly the same kind as that which we are prepared to grant in a certain measure to the extra-Christian religions. For in the Old Testament the prophets saw to it (even though not by way of a permanent institution) that there existed a possibility of distinguishing in public salvation-history between what was lawful and what was unlawful in the history of the religion of the Israelites. This cannot be held to be true to the same extent outside this history, although this again does not mean that outside the Old Testament there could be no question of any kind of divinely guided salvation-history in the realm of public history and institutions. The main difference between such a salvation-history and that of the

Old Testament will presumably lie in the fact that the historical, factual nature of the New Testament has *its* immediate pre-history in the *Old Testament* (which pre-history, in parenthesis, is insignificantly brief in comparison with the general salvation-history which counts perhaps a million years—for the former can be known with any certainty only from the time of Abraham or of Moses). Hence, the New Testament unveils *this* short span of salvation-history distinguishing its divinely willed elements and those which are contrary to God's will. It does this by a distinction which we cannot make in the same way in the history of any other religion. The second part of this second thesis, however, states two things positively. It states that even religions other than the Christian and the Old Testament religions contain quite certainly elements of a supernatural influence by grace which must make itself felt even in these objectifications. And it also states that by the fact that in practice man as he really is can live his proffered relationship to God only in society, man must have had the right and indeed the duty to live this his relationship to God within the religious and social realities offered to him in his particular historical situation.

3rd Thesis: If the second thesis is correct, then Christianity does not simply confront the member of an extra-Christian religion as a mere non-Christian but as someone who can and must already be regarded in this or that respect as an anonymous Christian. It would be wrong to regard the pagan as someone who has not yet been touched in any way by God's grace and truth. If, however, he has experienced the grace of God—if, in certain circumstances, he has already accepted this grace as the ultimate, unfathomable entelechy of his existence by accepting the immeasurableness of his dying existence as opening out into infinity—then he has already been given revelation in a true sense even before he has been affected by missionary preaching from without. For this grace, understood as the *a-priori* horizon of all his spiritual acts, accompanies his consciousness subjectively, even though it is not known objectively. And the revelation which comes to him from without is not in such a case the proclamation of something as yet absolutely unknown, in the sense in which one tells a child here in Bavaria, for the first time in school, that there is a continent called Australia. Such a revelation is then the expression in objective concepts of something which this person has already attained or could already have attained in the depth of his rational existence. It is not possible here to prove more exactly that this *fides implicita* is something which dogmatically speaking can occur in a so-called pagan. We can do no more here than to state our thesis and to indicate the direction in which the proof of this thesis might be found. But if it is true that a person who becomes the object of the Church's missionary efforts is or may be already someone on the way towards his salvation, and someone who in certain circumstances finds it, without being reached by the proclamation of the Church's message—and if it is at the same time true that this salvation which reaches him in this way is Christ's salvation, since there is no other salvation—then it must be possible to be not only an anonymous theist but also an anonymous Christian. And then it is quite true that in the last analysis, the proclamation of the gospel does not simply turn someone absolutely abandoned by God and Christ into a Christian, but turns an anonymous Christian into someone who now also knows about his Christian belief in the depths of his grace-endowed being by objective reflection and in the profession of faith which is given a social form in the Church. It is not thereby denied, but on the contrary implied, that this explicit self-realization of his previously anonymous Christianity is itself part of the development of this Christianity itself—a higher stage of development of this Christianity demanded by his being—and that it is therefore intended by God in the same way as everything else about salvation. Hence, it will not be possible in any way to draw the conclusion from this conception that, since man is already an anonymous Christian even without it, this explicit preaching of Christianity is superfluous. Such a conclusion would be just as false (and for the same reasons) as to conclude that the sacraments of baptism and penance could be dispensed with because a person can be justified by his subjective acts of faith and contrition even before the reception of these sacraments. The reflex self-realization of a previously anonymous Christianity is demanded (1) by the incarnational and social structure of grace and of Christianity, and (2) because the individual who grasps Christianity in a clearer, purer and more reflective way has, other things being equal, a still greater chance of salvation than someone who is merely an anonymous Christian. If, however, the message of the Church is directed to someone who is a 'non-Christian' only in the sense of living by an anonymous Christianity not as yet fully conscious of itself, then her missionary work must take this fact into account and must draw the necessary conclusions when deciding on its missionary strategy and tactics. We may say at a guess that this is still not the case in sufficient measure.

The exact meaning of all this, however, cannot be developed further here.

4th Thesis: It is possibly too much to hope, on the one hand, that the religious pluralism which exists in the concrete situation of Christians will disappear in the foreseeable future. On the other hand, it is nevertheless absolutely permissible for the Christian himself to interpret this non-Christianity as Christianity of an anonymous kind which he does always still go out to meet as a missionary, seeing it as a world which is to be brought to the explicit consciousness of what already belongs to it as a divine offer or already pertains to it also over and above this as a divine gift of grace accepted unreflectedly and implicitly. If both these statements are true, then the Church will not so much regard herself today as the exclusive community of those who have a claim to salvation but rather as the historically tangible vanguard and the historically and socially constituted explicit expression of what the Christian hopes is present as a hidden reality even outside the visible Church. To begin with, however much we must always work, suffer and pray anew and indefatigably for the unification of the whole human race, in the one Church of Christ, we must nevertheless expect, for theological reasons and not merely by reason of a profane historical analysis, that the religious pluralism existing in the world and in our own historical sphere of existence will not disappear in the foreseeable future. We know from the gospel that the opposition to Christ and to the Church will not disappear until the end of time. If anything, we must even be prepared for a heightening of this antagonism to Christian existence. If, however, this opposition to the Church cannot confine itself merely to the purely private sphere of the individual but must also be of a public, historical character, and if this opposition is said to be present in a history which today, in contrast to previous ages, possesses a world-wide unity, then the continuing opposition to the Church can no longer exist merely locally and outside a certain limited sector of history such as that of the West. It must be found in our vicinity and everywhere else. And this is part of what the Christian must expect and must learn to endure. The Church which is at the same time the homogeneous characterization of an in itself homogeneous culture (i.e. the medieval Church) will no longer exist if history can no longer find any way to escape from or go back on the period of its planetary unity. In a unified world-history in which everything enters into the life of everyone, the 'necessary' public opposition to Christianity is a factor in the existential sphere of all Christianity. If this Christianity, thus always faced with opposition and unable to expect seriously that this will ever cease, nevertheless believes in God's universal salvific will— in other words, believes that God can be victorious by his secret grace even where the Church does not win the victory but is contradicted—then this Church cannot feel herself to be just *one* dialectic moment in the whole of history but has already overcome this opposition by her faith, hope and charity. In other words, the others who oppose her are merely those who have not yet recognized what they nevertheless really already are (or can be) even when, on the surface of existence, they are in opposition; they are already anonymous Christians, and the Church is not the communion of those who possess God's grace as opposed to those who lack it, but is the communion of those who can explicitly confess what they *and* the others hope to be. Non-Christians may think it presumption for the Christian to judge everything which is sound or restored (by being sanctified) to be the fruit in every man of the grace of his Christ, and to interpret it as anonymous Christianity; they may think it presumption for the Christian to regard the non-Christian as a Christian who has not yet come to himself reflectively. But the Christian cannot renounce this 'presumption' which is really the source of the greatest humility both for himself and for the Church. For it is a profound admission of the fact that God is greater than man and the Church. The Church will go out to meet the non-Christian of tomorrow with the attitude expressed by St Paul when he said: What therefore you do not know and yet worship (and yet *worship*!) that I proclaim to you (Ac 17.23). On such a basis one can be tolerant, humble and yet firm towards all non-Christian religions.

7

CHRISTIANITY AND THE 'NEW MAN'

The Christian Faith and utopian views about the future of this world

CHRISTIANITY is a religion with an eschatology; it looks into the future; it makes binding pronouncements about what is to come both by explaining what will come and by looking on these future events as the decisive guiding principle of action in the present. Indeed, Christianity declares that with the Incarnation of the eternal Word of God in Jesus Christ, the last age has already begun, that the future has already been decided as to its final sense and content and that now it only requires that what is already and remains be revealed. Christianity no longer knows any ultimately open salvation-history but declares that—since the coming of Jesus Christ who is today, yesterday and in all eternity—the end of the ages is really already present and that we live, therefore, in the last ages, in the fullness of time. One thing only remains for us and that is to await the coming of the Lord in glory, even though—reckoned in earthly measurements of time—this period of waiting may appear long to us and even though thousands upon thousands of years on this earth may pass through this one moment of the silence of the end of time before the real and ultimate end finally dawns. Christianity understands itself as the religion of the future, as the religion of the new and eternal man.

Christianity cannot be indifferent, therefore, in the face of an interpretation, planning and utopian ideal of the future which originates outside her and which tries to determine man's present attitude in view of his future. It cannot be doubted, however, that the spiritual situation of man today is essentially determined by the blue-print of the new man of the future. The man of today feels himself to a larger extent to be someone who must overcome himself in order to prepare himself for a new and quite different future. He feels himself to be someone whose present can be justified only as the condition of his future, though this future which justifies him is not conceived—eschato-logically—as the gift of God dissolving temporal history but as some-thing which man himself creates and conquers for himself. Hence, the question as to how these two conceptions of the future are related to each other is an unavoidable and, for the Christian, an absolutely decisive one.

Before tackling this question directly, we must make at least some attempt to give a clearer picture of modern, extra-Christian thought concerning the future, so that we may know with what we are really comparing the Christian eschatology. Naturally, the 'picture of the new man' can be sketched here only in its most formal traits. Yet this picture of the new man cannot be simply presupposed as known at least not from *those* points of view which must be our special concern here. We presuppose in this that this 'new man' is already present today in his beginnings, in the sense that, to some extent at least, his further developments and final form can already be divined. Further-more, in describing the new man, we are not concerned with laying down a binding, systematic view of the characteristics exposed.

The man of today, and even more so the man of tomorrow, is the man of a history unified the world over, the man of a global space for life and hence the man of a world in which everyone is dependent on absolutely everyone else. The 'United Nations' organization is a small indication of this. And the boundary lines drawn by the various 'cur-tains' today do not limit the meaning of what has just been said, for one's enemies are usually 'closer' to oneself—in the sense of being more decisive for one's own destiny—than one's friends. Whereas in the past (prescinding from the only hypothetically and approxi-mately ascertainable beginning of the human race) the history of indi-vidual peoples, and hence of individuals, was more or less clearly divided up by historical vacua—thus, for instance, what was happening at the time in the empire of the Incas was quite immaterial to the history of fourteenth-century Europe—today, all the histories of differ-ent peoples are part and parcel of the one, real world-history. The 'field' which determines the fate of the individual today is, not merely physically but also historically, the whole earth. The present and the history of individuals has become the present and the history of all, and vice versa.

The man of today and tomorrow is the man of technology, of auto-mation and cybernetics. This means, in our present context, that man

is no longer (or at least no longer to any large extent) the man who
simply lives out his existence according to the given pattern of nature
in an equally pre-existent environment, but someone who fashions
his own environment. Man now inserts an external world made by himself in between himself (eking out and asserting his existence both
physically and spiritually) and 'Nature', i.e. the physically and bio-
logically tangible environment which is the condition for man's own
existence. It is of course true that there has never been a man without
any culture, a man—in other words—who was able to live like an
animal in the sense that his struggle for existence (by procreation and
upbringing of offspring, protection against the dangers of his environment, etc.) was related immediately to a purely pre-established reality,
as in the case of the animal. But in the past, culture, understood as
something external, has on the whole consisted merely in such slight
modifications of man's natural environment as this environment itself
permitted: it consisted merely in the *utilization* of animals and plants
in a certain systematic way, without any deliberate transformation of
nature in the inorganic and organic world in the light of freely chosen
ends and under rational control. Life today, which has been thus transformed, always and everywhere manifests the reason why such a
transformed life in an environment determined by ourselves is possible:
the modern rationality of Western man, his calculated planning, the
disappearance of the feeling of awe which used to be inherent in the
experience of the world itself, and the 'profanation' of the world turning it into the raw material of human activity, an idea which—starting
with the Western world—has become the determining presupposition
of any consideration of the *raison d'être* of the whole world and of
humanity.

The man of today is not, however, merely the man of the rational
calculating creation of his own space of existence—the *homo faber*.
Unlike the man of previous ages (especially since the start of the
modern fashion of 'turning in on the subject') the man of today is not
merely the man given to that sort of rational reflection on himself in
which (at least at the first and important appearance) the object of
reflection is not altered by the fact of reflection. Rather, he is someone
who applies his technical, planning power of transformation even to
himself—someone who makes himself the object of his own manipu-
lations. He no longer simply takes stock of himself, but changes himself; he contents himself neither with steering by his own history

merely the alteration of his sphere of existence nor with the mere actualization of those possibilities which have always offered themselves to man in his commerce with his fellow men both in peace and in war. The subject is becoming its own most proper object; man is becoming his own creator. It does not matter in the meantime that for many different reasons and in many different respects these possibilities of a planned self-alteration and adaptation are as yet relatively few. The important thing is that man has thought of the idea of such a transformation, that he already sees possibilities of realizing this idea and indeed has already begun to realize it. Against this background must be seen the Freudian depth-psychology, birth-control, human eugenics, the transformations of man, based on Pavlov's psychology, which override the free judgements and decisions of man in the Communistic world and which are practised—in somewhat more careful doses—even in the West (one need only think here of the techniques of propaganda, advertising, etc.).

This man of the unified, planetary living-space which is to be extended even beyond the earth—the man who does not simply accept the world around him but creates it and who regards himself as merely the starting point and raw material for what he wants to make of himself in accordance with his own plans—has for these very reasons the impression of standing at a beginning, of being the beginning of the new man, conceived as a kind of superman who will show clearly for the first time what man really is. What comments are to be made on this ideology of the new man, if the situation and programme just described are looked at from the point of view of the Christian faith?

I

Christianity has no predictions to make, no programme and no clear-cut prescriptions for the future of man in this world; it knows from the very start that man does not have them either and that he (and hence also Christianity itself) must therefore go unprotected into the dark venture of his intramundane future. The eschatology of Christianity is no intramundane utopia, it sets no intramundane tasks and goals. As a consequence, the Christian is not given any concrete directions for his life in this world as such, which could relieve him of the anguish of planning the future and of the burden of his passage into the dark unknown. He has the moral law of nature and of the gospel. But he himself must convert these general principles into concrete imperatives which themselves are not merely applications of these principles to a static material of moral action with which he has to deal, but also represent decisions about some definite plan of action and about the choice of different possibilities—none of which can be clearly deduced from these general principles. By the fact that man changes himself and his environment—and by the fact that, since paradoxically but truly this planning does not make all this any the less unpredictable but rather increases the uncertainty in equal proportion to the extent of the planning, these alterations themselves have in their turn the character of something unpredictable, of trial and a wandering into the uncertain—ever new and surprising tasks are imposed by very reason of the principles advocated by Christianity, tasks which earlier Christianity could not have dreamt of and which require a long, laborious process of acclimatization for the Christian and the Church before they can be mastered at all.

Yet it is not as if this passage into the unpredictable future were unimportant for Christianity itself and of no significance for Christianity both as a Church and as the Christian life of individuals and nations. Truly realized Christianity is always the achieved synthesis on each occasion of the message of the gospel and of the grace of Christ, on the one hand, and of the concrete situation in which the gospel is to be lived, on the other. This situation is always new and surprising. Consequently the intramundane and Christian task of the Christian is really and truly a *problem* whose solution must be looked for laboriously amid surprises, pains, fruitless and false steps, false detachment and restoring, timidly conservative reserve and false fascinations with novelties. Thus the Christian too may stand frightened and fascinated before the future of intramundane tasks opening out before him. He too may feel himself called to action and to criticism, in brotherly union with all those others who salute this future and who know themselves called to bring it about. Since the mastering of the intramundane situation represents a task (in so far as this is possible for man) which is also really Christian—because eternal life must be effected in time—it is sadly perhaps possible to show that the Christians of this day and age occupy themselves far too little with the programming of man's future in this world, as if this did not present any problems or could safely be left to the non-Christians.

It is indeed true, and a fact of decisive importance, that the gospel does not offer or intend to offer any ready-made plan for the future and that the Church cannot give us any clear-cut and binding ideas about such programming. But this in no way means that *every* programming for the future—whatever it may be—can be reconciled with the Christian spirit and life and with the nature of man of which Christianity is the custodian. Hence, it does not mean that even in their practical life Christians have no duty or obligation with regard to such practical programming. It is absolutely possible for Christians to have a task as Christian individuals which the Church as such does not have. And it may seem that Christians do not have a clear, courageous and infectious enough conception and love of this planning of the future and of these demands—which go beyond the abstract principles of the unchanging gospel—and that they merely seek to defend the spirit of the gospel by a *defensive criticism* of the dangers of plans for the future and of intramundane ideologies.

Nevertheless it remains true to say that the Christian as such is not given any clear prescriptions by the gospel as to how the future is to look or will in fact look. He is a pilgrim on this earth, advancing into the uncertain and going out to venture in brotherly union with all those who plan the future of this world, and he may quite legitimately feel proud of being that creature who plans himself and of being the place (called 'spirit' and 'freedom') where the great world-machine not only runs its course in exalted clarity but also begins to steer itself.

II

Christianity draws man's attention to the fact that, while he is under the impression of standing on the threshold of a new and unheard-of future, this future too will constantly lead him back to himself as the finite creature he is. This future, planned by himself and to be built by himself, is inevitably finite for the Christian; he already recognizes, experiences and suffers it as something finite in advance. In other words, the future too is built out of materials with definite structures whose finite nature also sets internal limits to the possibilities of the future and renders them finite. Man does indeed over and over again express surprise at how he has underestimated his own possibilities, at how the world is greater than he had thought, at how new avenues open out to possibilities which he had up until now regarded as utopian. Certainly it is dangerous in many respects to declare something to be impossible; for many times in the past such declarations have been the beginnings of successful efforts to make the impossible come true. Nevertheless, man is not and will never be the Creator who creates omnipotently out of nothing—he is and will always be the creature who creates out of himself and out of the already existing realities of the world around him. And he and the reality surrounding him have structures and laws; these already existing realities, together with their determined structures, form the *a-priori* law of what they can become.

These essential structures are not—this modern man has learnt and this also differentiates him from the man of earlier ages, including the Christian Middle Ages—a static barrier which prevents any genuine process of becoming and change and being-changed. These essential structures are most certainly endowed with an inner dynamism towards development. But precisely in this way they also form the law according to which this development takes place and the horizon within which the history of this development runs its course. And no matter how much this course may take us into the boundless, there are twists and turns in it which betray the finite and created nature of this course of becoming, the becoming to which it remains necessarily subject. There are many such *a-priori*, inevitable elements in the finite nature of man. There is his spatio-temporality: even if man should conquer a new part of the world for himself outside his earth (and if we stop to think, are we not still very far from this being true?), he will always face the immensity of the universe as someone who begins his short span of existence from the earth and not from anywhere else. Then there is man's biological constitution together with all the limitations this entails: the different stages of life, his dependence on nourishment, the finite nature of his brain—the store-house of his activities—which provides the basis for what he can really experience and by which alone in the final analysis, all other (artificial) stores of usable content become really interesting for him, in the same way as someone finds interest only in *those* books of a library which he reads (and not in those which he can read) or at most in those which he could read *without* having to give up the reading of others. And finally there is the limited nature of his life which ends in death.

This brings us then to the most irrevocable and clearest limit of man: he dies, he has a beginning and an end, and this means that absolutely everything which lies within these 'brackets' is under the relentless sign of the finite. We are able to prolong human life and in fact have already done so. But what a laughable alteration would it really be if we were all to become 120 or 180 years old? Who has ever claimed or prophesied that he could do more? And who—even if he were to give but a little thought to such a utopian idea—could even merely hope or wish to live for ever in the kind of human existence which is the only one given to us? The *inner* finiteness of human existence would turn the *external* endlessness of life into utter madness— into the existence of the eternally wandering Jew—and into damnation, since what is unique in a finite sense is impressive and sweet only if, and because, it is not always available; a time which I could really have to infinity whenever I liked condemns the content of each moment to absolute indifference, since it is absolutely repeatable. And then: what significance does it have for *me*—*I* who will die—if I could help to make it possible that at some future date a man may be bred who will never die any more? None whatsoever! But we will have to come back to this point later on.

No, the message of Christianity about the finite and created nature of man remains true even today. And the more it might be possible to achieve what today lies still in a utopian future, the less could this achievement blind us to the finiteness of the achieved or deaden the pain of this finiteness. This is all the more true since it is an unproved supposition that the possibility and the pace of new developments experienced by us today could never be followed by a certain phase of stagnation, or that the time of pre-planned and self-directed development—once started—must unceasingly flow on in ever greater acceleration to ever new shores. It is just as possible that the development may, as it were, stagnate again (although this time on the higher level reached by then) just as it did in many earlier centuries as far as the progress of technology and the external style of living was concerned. And since society is always and inevitably composed of individuals (it being quite indifferent for this whether one adopts an individualist or Communist view of the exact relationship between the individual and society), the finiteness we have spoken of determines not only the existence of the individual as such but permeates right through the life of society.

Since society cannot pass on culture by biological heredity, it must to a great extent always begin again at the beginning. No matter how cunningly exact and comprehensive our planning may possibly be, it will never be adequate but will always produce surprises and failures, for a finite consciousness inevitably contains more objectively un-reflected elements than elements which have been fully reflected upon. This is so even simply because the act of reflection cannot itself be reflected and yet a great deal regarding its content depends on it and on its characteristics. Indeed, it may be that there is an absolutely finite optimum of what can be planned. All planning must work with un-planned factors; the proportion between the unplanned factors, which are of practical importance for the result of the plan, and the planned factors and their certainty for the planned result is variable; it can easily happen that the more complicated plan which is calculated to avoid more mistakes, works out worse in practice than the simple plan which works with less explicit factors. To put it more simply still: even the culture and civilization of society, which is seemingly growing into infinity, will always remain conditioned by the individual—in other words, by the finiteness of his consciousness, by the limited number of individuals and the finite nature of the life of individuals. And so this culture and civilization remain finite.

It can happen, of course, that this finiteness does not appear—at least not explicitly—in all its existential radicality in the consciousness of the individual and in the commonly expressed opinion of a group or of an age, etc. Perhaps the movement is experienced enthusiastically as a movement into infinity even on account of its very presence alone, for the simple reason that one has overlooked the fact that a move-ment—even though its limitation is not clearly experienced—never attains anything beyond what is finite, and because one has not adverted to the fact that an infinite potency does not by any means promise an infinite act. In any case, this intoxicating experience of infinity will always end up in cruel disillusionment—at the latest in death. And the pretension to infinity found in man—which according to the teaching of Christianity stems from the infinite promise of grace—will always weigh up again what has been, and what can be, achieved in this world and will always find it to be of too little weight.

III

Christianity knows an individual and existential notion of time which those who dream up a future paradise on this earth do not possess, and the lack of any such notion shows the latter conception to be insufficient. Let us take a closer look at this. It is said—and no doubt rightly—that the future has already begun. It is said, both in the West and in the East, that we are moving towards a glorious age: man will conquer outer space, there will be enough food for everyone, there will no longer be any underdeveloped and undernourished countries, everybody will have what is required to fulfil his needs, class-distinction will be abolished. The Christian must not indeed act as if all these plans for the future are proved wrong simply by his declaring sceptically that paradise is not to be found in this world. Anyone who simply counters such ardent dreams of the future with sober scepticism is—presumably—not experiencing hunger, is not at present in danger of cancer and hence is not particularly interested in finding the means by which medicine may at last conquer this disease. Yet the Christian is right in the long run when he points out that this happy future has not yet arrived, that he himself will not be alive to experience it and that he cannot agree that the question of *his* existence is solved by saying that it will be solved for others in the future.

The fight for a better future does consciously or unconsciously live on an evaluation of man, and even of the individual, which attributes an absolute value to man as a spiritual person. And this is quite right. For why should someone living today sacrifice himself for someone in the future if the future individual is just as insignificant as the present-day individual is thought to be, and if the present-day individual could be sacrificed precisely because he is insignificant? The Communist who today sacrifices himself in true freedom and quite unselfishly for those who will come after him, affirms by this very fact that he, as a person, and those future persons have an absolute value, whether he admits this explicitly to himself or not. Anyone who affirms someone else to be of absolute value does the same for himself. He does not consider himself to be necessary in his biological existence, but he does acknowledge himself to be necessary in the dimension in which he takes the decision of self-sacrificing affirmation, viz. as a free, personal spirit. Any conception which regards the future as something which does not simply come about by itself but must be conquered by sacrifice, acknowledges implicitly what Christianity affirms explicitly: the future of the human, spiritual person in no way only lies in *that* future which will be present at some later date but is the eternity which is brought about as the result of the spiritual act of the person.

Christianity is quite right in saying that there is a personal, existen-

tial time which is the coming to be of the unconditioned finality of
the free decision and of existence—and which works in time by overcoming merely continuous time. All ideologies concerned with the
future which declare that the future which is yet to come in a *temporal
way* is something absolutely inevitable and not something to be merely
overcome in the same way as the bare present must be overcome,
borrow this notion of the absolute nature of the future from that
future which is really absolute, viz. the future of the free person. This
future of the free person will not come later on but is present in
the spiritual person and his free act; it realizes itself in the sphere where
life—open to the unbounded in its linear temporal nature—is brought
to an end by biological processes. If every existing thing were completely subject to that time, whose every moment is indifferent since
it passes away into an equally indifferent later moment in time which
in turn unmasks its own insignificance by disappearing once more in
the next moment, then we would have no reason for preferring a future
to the present which is no longer the future of the one who has this
preference. The present is necessarily the only true and valid reality for
someone who is simply passing away, if indeed he ever becomes at all
conscious of himself and of his transitoriness. Only if there is a future
of the personal individual spirit is there any real sense in fighting for a
better future in this world for those who will come after us.

It is clear from these few cursory remarks that Christianity has a
notion of time in its teaching on the individual and freely achieved
finality of the person, which goes beyond the notion of time employed
by any ideology and utopian view which—concerned only with this
world and its future—thinks of time purely as a sort of line passing
into what is yet to come.' The Christian notion of time goes much
further, for it provides whatever is genuine and morally justified in
these ideologies about the future with the only foundation which will
really hold water, and opens up a supra-mundane and supra-historical
'future' for man which is above the eternal flux of time, viz. eternal life
which finds its temporal expression and proof in time and which is
the only future which has really already begun even now, in every
present moment of the free decision of believing love.

IV

Christianity has already surpassed all ideologies about the future and all utopias in a completely different way still, viz. by its teaching on the Incarnation of the eternal Word of God and the universal salvation already ushered in by this event. It is first of all very striking how pale and shallow everything becomes when those who believe in an intramundane future (conceived as a beatifying paradise and as the triumph of successful man thus bringing nature to its own proper completion) are asked to explain what this future they are striving for will really look like. We will be able to circumnavigate the moon and will perhaps be able to land on Mars; Russia will have surpassed America's meat production; no one will suffer want any more; there will be enough time and money to give everyone the best education possible and to offer him all the cultural goods he desires, etc.; everyone will have everything he needs. And so the catalogue goes on. But one gets the impression that all this is not very much different from what is already possible and in part already normal even today—in other words, that the 'new man' will look hopelessly like the old one.

In contrast to this (not in the sense of mere contradiction but of a message regarding a completely new and different dimension of human existence) Christianity proclaims that man can have a direct encounter with the Infinite and the Absolute—with the One who from the outset surpasses everything finite and who is not constituted piecemeal by finite moments of progression. Christianity proclaims that man's business is with God himself; it tells us that this unspeakable mystery we call God does not merely remain the ever-distant horizon of our experiences of the transcendent as well as of the finite, but that the Infinity as such can also descend into the heart of man which is 'finite' in such a way that it can nevertheless be given the grace of this unspeakable Infinity. Christianity proclaims that we will come face to face with the Infinity of absolute Reality, with the inaccessible Light and the Incomprehensible who is infinitely beatifying life. It proclaims that this personal Infinity has already begun to assume the finiteness of the spiritual, personal world of man into his eternal life by the fact that Jesus Christ, the eternal Word of God has already made this finite quest for the infinity of God (i.e. human nature) his own and has replied to it with the answer of the eternal Word.

Christianity teaches that God has already broken up the world and has already opened up an exit for it which leads into his own Infinity, even while the world still pursues its course along the interiorly crooked paths of its finite history—even while it is still subject to change by the fact that it can only replace *one* finite thing with another finite thing which, even though it may be better than what had gone before, will always remain both a promise and a disappointment and nothing more for that spirit who recognizes and suffers his finiteness. In the actual world, creation no longer means merely the bringing into existence of something out of an infinite foundation and the perpetual keeping of this originated reality distant from its incommunicable source, but means rather the production of the finite as something on which the Infinite lavishes himself in the form of Love.

This history of the infinite endowment of the creature with God's reality is indeed primarily the history of the personal spirit and certainly takes place primarily as the existential history of faith across the temporal progress of the history of the material cosmos. Yet this fulfilment of the finite by the infinity of God does nevertheless refer to the whole of created reality. Christianity knows no history of the spirit and of existence which could be conceived simply as overcoming and repulsing the material, and for which the history of the cosmos would at most offer the external stage on which the drama of the personal spirit and his divine endowment would enact itself in such a way that, when the play is over, the players would leave the stage and would leave it dead and empty and abandoned to itself. After all, the history in which God himself takes part by entering personally into it is the history of God's becoming *flesh* and not only the coming of a merely ideological spirit. Christianity professes belief in the resurrection of the body and means by this that in the last analysis there is only *one* history and *one* end of *everything*, and that everything reaches its end only once it has taken possession of God himself. Christianity, indeed, only conceives and knows a matter which is different from spirit and out of which the spirit cannot simply develop as the very product proper to that matter, as is taught by dialectical materialism. Yet Christianity knows only a matter which is created and exists from the very start *by* the Spirit who is called God and *for* the spirit called man, in order to make spiritual, personal life possible and to act as a basis for such a life. The spirit is not a stranger in a spiritless world which follows its own paths quite unconcerned about this spirit, but rather this material world is the corporeal presence of the spirit, the extended being of man, and has therefore ultimately the same end and destiny as man. Even in eternity—when the spirit will be fully achieved—the material world will be the expression of this achieved spirit and hence will participate in the final state of this spirit in—as we say—a 'glorified' manner. Hence we profess that the end will be a new earth and a new heaven.

We cannot say very much about this achieved, final state of the bodily, mundane spirit: and this precisely because every intramundane achievement could only be an achievement constituted of finite elements, and so not at all an absolute achievement. Precisely because God's message has given us the boldness to believe in an infinite achievement, the only way we can in principle describe this consummation in its material content is to say that God himself will be this consummation. And since God, the Infinite, is the mystery which can be named and called upon only by a *via negationis* and by pointing silently beyond anything which can be put into words, we can speak of this consummation only negatively in images and likenesses and in speechless reference to absolute Transcendence. Our consummation, therefore, is not fitted to become the subject of party tirades, of glowing imagery, of plastic description or utopian conceptions. And when the man of today reads the old descriptions of this consummation which were less burdened with the images of an apparently intramundane utopia but employed an apocalyptic rather than a properly eschatological imagery, he will feel less at ease in all this than the man of previous ages. He will 'demythologize' in a manner both justifiable and necessary if he is to be truly orthodox. This does not mean, however, that he has thereby in any real sense moved further away from an understanding of the reality itself. On the contrary, he knows that the truly infinite nature of his consummation is something unspeakable embracing all the dimensions of his being (but each of them in its own way) and that it—precisely *qua* achievement by God and in God himself—is something unattainable by man himself, something given to him as a gratuitous gift of pure grace.

By the fact that this coming of God himself is the true and the only infinite future of man, Christianity has always already infinitely surpassed all intramundane ideologies and utopias about the future. The infinity of this future which is already beginning embraces all intramundane futures: it does not exclude them, nor does it make them unlawful (as long as they are mindful of their limitations as created

forms). Again, it is not as if the man who believes in the coming
of God's future can no longer acknowledge himself to be called to
co-operate in working for these intramundane futures; and his supra-
mundane, eschatological outlook does not necessarily have to dampen
his inner urge for such co-operation. Even if we leave it an open
question whether God does not in fact realize certain things (which he
wishes to be achieved in the world) through the *guilt* of men and not
through the actions of those who love him, it must still be said in
principle that the Christian is absolutely justified and qualified—and
indeed to a certain extent obliged—to take an active part in working for
the progress of the human race and thus of the world, by developing
his own immanent powers and those of the world. For the consummation to be brought about by God does not, in the last analysis, expect
a dead but a living humanity which has gone to its very limits and so
is burst open by salvation from above by developing its own powers.
For man's finiteness and the essential tragedy and fruitlessness of all
human history, inherent in all finite development, becomes manifest
more relentlessly in this way than it would in a purely static world.

v

However much the Christian—the man of a divine future—is a
citizen of the world to come and not merely the child and supporter
of the present world, and however great the development of this world
into the unlimited may be thought to be, the Christian must nevertheless live at present in this world which is always a world of a future
already begun: a new world full of earthly goals, tasks and dangers.
It would be a complete misunderstanding of everything that has been
said so far, if one were to think that a Christian may withdraw into
some dead corner of world-history, as it were, or that he is someone
belonging historically or socially to that class of people to be found
in every history and development, i.e. the people of yesterday who
are no longer really attuned to the times—the adherents to what is
over and done with—the conservatives who weep for the good old
days.

It cannot be denied, of course, that the good Christian Christianity
often gives this impression. It is true that Christianity has not been
given any guarantee by God that it will be unable to sleep through the
present. Christianity can be old-fashioned, it can forget that the old

truths and the values of yesterday can be defended only if and when one conquers a new future. And it has actually to a great extent fallen into this error, so that today's Christianity often gives rise to the painful impression that it is running mopishly and in a disgusted, critical mood behind the carriage in which the human race drives into a new future. One gets the impression that God's immense revolution in his history, in which he lets the world burn up in his own infinite fire, rests on the shoulders of people who really put their trust in what has proved itself in the past, although this is ultimately also only of this world and hence brittle, ambiguous and transitory, just like what is still to come in this world. Why are Christians so often to be found only on the conservative side? They really would not be forced to subscribe to other people's plans for the future if these are Unchristian and inhuman. But then they ought also to have their own list of imperatives for the next couple of centuries and not just for eternity—and not merely general principles which they declare to be valid yesterday, tomorrow and always.

All these facts do not need to be covered up but can be admitted without any qualms. They do not alter the *principle*, however, that the Christian can truly achieve his own proper Christian being completely and fully only if he lives evidently and unconditionally in the present and in the future, and not merely in the past. This does not mean that someone who is going to build a new future in this world has already lived and proved his Christianity by this fact alone. But it is part of the convictions of a full Christian life that the Christian faith and morality are in fact, and of necessity, exercised by using the concrete raw materials of human existence and not in some other, extra-worldly sphere. It belongs to these convictions that these raw materials of Christian self-realization consist in the whole reality of the world created by God. This, however, makes the task of the Christian one which he does not freely choose himself but one which is pre-arranged for him—in short, the concrete existence, the historical hour, into which he is placed. He may and indeed ought to be able to master this task in a different way from the non-Christian. Yet he must fulfil this task and no other. Wherever and whenever one does not want to face up to one's own peculiar situation in one's own particular age but tries instead to take refuge in a world of yesterday—a dreamt-up world, a dead corner of history, a social set-up which was alive and powerful yesterday—one not only falls down on one's earthly task but in such a case Christianity itself suffers both from the artificiality of this existence and the false pretences of the fictitious.

The fact that being a Christian imposes a task within the world does not mean, of course, that 'official' Christianity (i.e. the Church herself) must therefore take it into her own hands to develop and advocate a concrete programme for an intramundane future derived solely from principles which Christianity alone must advocate. It is impossible to stress that intramundane cultural affairs are relatively autonomous in their own sphere (to stress, indeed, that the Church today must inevitably live in a pluralistic society and cannot under any consideration lay claim to any immediate and direct ruling power in 'mundane' matters) *and* at the same time to bemoan the fact that the Church has nothing very clear and stirring to say about the future now dawning and about the way it should be shaped. But Christians themselves must surrender themselves to the future and regard it as their most proper task, even though this may expose them to uncertainty and risks. Christian lay people, in particular, are not merely organs for carrying out the instructions given by the official hierarchy of the Church, but must themselves try to discover God's unique will for them and for their times.

This again does not mean, however, that the official Church in the most strict sense, i.e. the Church in her own inner life, does not have any tasks arising precisely out of this situation. On the contrary, the Church has many such tasks. She ought to think a lot more about how she can arrange her life and message so as to avoid creating *more* difficulties than is necessary for the man of today and tomorrow—for the men of tomorrow who already live today. The Church is still far from having accomplished this task, and this not only because this task is ever new and must always be solved anew. The Church has also a lot of ground to make up as regards what she has failed to do in the last one and a half centuries. For during the modern age which is now coming to an end, her thinking and feeling, and her familiarity with the situation, have not kept pace sufficiently with modern developments; during this period she has become more of a conservative power defending herself than was right.

By the fact that she is in arrears with her accomplishment of old tasks, the Church has naturally become overburdened in the fulfilment of her present tasks. There are many new tasks for her in Church life and worship, in the reform of the liturgy, in the adaptation of the way of life of the Religious Orders, in the courage to express the old truth in a new way in theology, in the reform of Canon Law. She ought to be reflecting on the problems posed for her by our modern pluralistic world and society, such as the problems arising out of the debate with other religions (or rather, out of the loving attempt to understand them), problems arising in connection with the formation of a type of Christian who can survive and endure the unavoidable and permanent secularization of the world of today, or in connection with the activation of a public influence suited to the society of today and tomorrow. She should be making her presence felt in this sense through organs which meet the demands of the present and the future, by stirring up courage for planning such as is taking place today (in contrast to previous ages) in all the other dimensions of human existence. She should be presenting the demands of Christian morality in such a way as to make it apparent that they are not incomprehensible imperatives imposed from outside but rather the expression of what is objectively right. She should be establishing a relationship between the clergy and the laity which corresponds to the present condition of lay people and which, while conserving the permanent structure of the Church, does not confuse it with an old-fashioned patriarchism and does not buttress it with taboos about authority which can be safely 'demythologized' even within the Church.

If, at the end of these reflections, we now take another look at the brief and formal portrait of the ideology concerning the future discussed at the beginning, it may be in place here to point out the following: the Christian is completely capable of regarding the planetary unification of world-history under a positively Christian aspect—indeed, from an aspect necessarily demanded by Christianity. In other words, if the universality of the Church is to be or become something real, and is not to be merely something belonging to the basic definition of Christianity, then this can be achieved by Christianity in the concrete only in, together with and by the creation of this globally unified history. The Christian will not be surprised to learn, therefore, that this fusion of the history of every nation into one had its real starting point in the very birth of Christianity and in the place where Christianity first took roots in the world and in history, viz. in the Western world. If this world and history of the future is a world of rational planning, a demythologized world, a world secularized by the creature in order that it may serve as the raw material for man's activity, then this whole modern attitude—no matter what particular elements in it we may be able and ought to criticize—is basically a Christian one.

For in the Christian outlook—and only in this outlook—man has become the subject which Western man has discovered himself to be; only in Christianity and by its teaching about the radically created nature of the world as something confided to man to serve as the raw material of *his* activity and as something which is not more important and powerful than man but is meant to serve and is created *for* man, could there spring up that attitude to the cosmos which demythologizes it and which legitimizes the will to control the world. In a metaphysical and theological (Christian) sense, man has always been for Christianity someone who has control over himself and over his own final destiny. If we consider the doctrine of freedom and of absolute responsibility for self—and the doctrine stating that the particular fate (and eternity) of each individual person is the result of his own free acts—then it becomes clear that the possibility gradually dawning on man today, viz. the possibility of making himself the object of his planning and formation, is merely the echo and particular application of that deeper self-responsibility which Christianity has always acknowledged man to possess and which it has always steadfastly refused to relieve him of, since it has always regarded it as his own—sometimes painful—burden.

In the last analysis, therefore, the spirit of the approaching future is not at all as unchristian as the pessimists and the timid often think. Christianity has always been the religion of an infinite future. When Christianity tells us that the future which it professes has always already surpassed all the ideologies concerning the intramundane future of the new man—and when, *even though* in a critical spirit, it examines and tones them down, demythologizing them also so to speak—then it does this out of a truly Christian, eschatological spirit and not out of a spirit of static conservatism. In this way, Christianity makes man morally responsible to God in his justified desire for an intramundane future—to be created by man himself in unlimited development—and opens this desire to the infinite life of God. This is the life of which it will always remain true (and of which it always becomes true anew) that it has been promised to us as our most proper future by grace.

PART III

CHRISTOLOGY

8

CHRISTOLOGY WITHIN AN EVOLUTIONARY VIEW OF THE WORLD

T HE subject to be discussed here is: 'Christology within an evolutionary view of the world'. This discussion will therefore be concerned with showing how one statement can be or is fitted into a complex of other statements; it will not be concerned with each of these statements themselves. This makes it clear right away that the problem posed here is neither the exposition of Christian and Catholic Christology itself nor the exposition of what is described— even though vaguely—as the evolutionary view of the world. It is here rather a question of the possibility of correlating these two views. For our present purposes, we will simply presuppose that there is such a thing as an evolutionary view of the world, even though this is neither self-evident objectively nor unobjectionable from a methodological point of view. Having boldly presupposed this, we will inquire as to whether Christology fits into such a view, and not vice versa, although the converse would also be a possible question—and indeed in itself the better and more radical one. Once more: we are not going to attempt to give an exposition of Christology itself and to unfold it theologically, nor will we try to prove that Jesus of Nazareth laid claim to what we subsequently explain in theological language as meta-physical sonship of God, Incarnation and Hypostatic Union, or that this claim of his can be made comprehensible as a legitimate (i.e. believable) claim. All this is presupposed here or will be treated from a different point of view. Furthermore, when we speak of the 'in-clusion' of a doctrine in a 'view of the world'—of Christology fitted or fitting into the evolutionary view of the world—we do not mean by this that the Christian doctrine of the Incarnation can be deduced as a necessary consequence and as a demanded extension of the evolutionary view of the world (this would be an extreme which we do not envisage) —nor do we mean by it that the doctrine of the Incarnation does not directly contradict, either simply in an objective sense or in a logical sense, any certain knowledge and scientific conclusion contained in this view of the world (which would be the other extreme, which it would be easy to prove but which would not be particularly significant and so is not sufficient for us).

If we did mean the former, then we would be making an attempt at constructing a theological rationalism—an attempt to transform faith, revelation and dogma into philosophy—which, of course, is not what is intended here. If, on the other hand, we were to aim simply at the other extreme, then we would be discussing something which is not really a problem at all and so would be achieving too little. For even if the doctrine of the Incarnation of the divine Logos is seen as a doctrine not directly denied by the present-day evolutionary view of the world —or is seen as a doctrine not invalidated by propositions contradicting it on purely logical grounds—it would still be experienced as something foreign in the mind of man. For a man disposed to think in terms of the evolutionary view of the world would in this case experience the doctrine of the Incarnation as something quite unrelated to his other thoughts and feelings; if such a man were or is nevertheless a Christian for some other reasons, he would then be forced to think along two completely unrelated lines of thought. Hence—while not attempting to make the Christian doctrine of the Incarnation a necessary and inner moment of the present-day view of the world, of its way of thinking and the present-day feeling of life—our task lies precisely in not only removing formal logical contradictions (or better: in showing that no such contradictions exist, particularly not where they seem to appear) but in bringing out clearly the inner affinity of these two doctrines—a sort of similarity of style—and in explaining the possibility of their being mutually related. Of course, in a short lecture like this, there cannot be any question of considering the *general* problem of a certain sameness of human perceptions in one period or in one individual—which is a problem concerning the possibility of a kind of common *style* of thinking or of one thought-form which gives a common pattern to many perceptions of quite different material content—although, of course, there would be many obscurities and important points to be considered even in this general problem. For the rest, what exactly we do and do not intend to do should become clearer as we actually proceed in our attempt to answer our question.

Given a certain previous understanding of the problem posed, however, the difficulty, laboriousness and breadth of this problem will also appear quite clearly. Everything with which the Society of St Paul[1] concerns itself seems to enter into this question: all the questions concerning the reconciliation of the Christian teaching and interpretation of existence with the present-day way of living, thinking and feeling, are necessarily concentrated in our problem; all the objective and historical difficulties brought to mind by the phrase 'Christianity and the contemporary spirit' enter also into our question. For our question concerns the most central and most mysterious assertion of Christianity but an assertion which at the same time refers to a reality said to belong precisely to that dimension with which the man of today is most familiar on the scientific, existential and affective plane, i.e. the dimension of the material world and of tangible history. In short, our question concerns an assertion of God's presence (i.e. God as he is meant in theology) in precisely *that* dimension where man feels himself at home and in which alone he feels himself competent, viz. in the world and not in heaven. This makes it again quite obvious that it cannot be our job here to speak of the most general questions and difficulties connected with the reconciliation of the Christian religion and modern thought (no matter how fundamental these questions may be). It is quite obvious that we must confine ourselves to dealing with the special questions posed by our subject, even though we are quite aware of the fact that modern man's sense of bewilderment and astonishment when faced with the doctrine of the Incarnation is perhaps due in great part to his feeling of strangeness in the face of metaphysical and religious statements in general. But enough of introduction.

We must, however, add a few preliminary remarks about the plan of our reflections. We will start with the present-day evolutionary view of the world, presupposing rather than describing it. We will ask first of all, therefore, about the connection made in this view between matter and spirit—in other words, about its view of the unity of the world, of natural history and the history of man. All this will of course be treated only very briefly, touching only on those connections which —if we may put it this way—are 'common to all Christian thought' and 'general theology'. To put it in another way: we will try to avoid those theorems with which you are familiar from your study of Teilhard de Chardin. If we arrive at some of the same conclusions as he

[1] To whom this whole Volume is dedicated.—*Tr.*

does, then that is all to the good. Yet we do not feel ourselves either dependent on him or obligated to him. We want to confine ourselves to those things which any theologian could say if he brings his theological reflection to bear on the questions posed by the modern evolutionary view of the world. This means, of course, that we must put up with a certain abstractness which will perhaps disappoint the natural scientist a little. For it would be quite understandable if the latter expected more exact details than we will actually give, about a certain homogeneity between matter and spirit. He would probably expect us to give details based on those findings of natural science or their evaluation to which he is accustomed. If (like Teilhard) we were to do this, however, our reflections would not only have to lay claim to such scientific knowledge—which we poor theologians can after all gather only very much at second hand—but we would also have to contend with all the drawbacks which are inevitably connected with such evaluations of the results of truly scientific inquiries, i.e. with evaluations which are not entirely undisputed. We have quite enough difficulties of our own, however, arising out of the philosophy and theology of these questions.

Following on this, we must then pass on to a second consideration and try to see man as the being in whom the basic tendency of matter to find itself in the spirit by self-transcendence arrives at the point where it definitely breaks through; thus in this way we may be in a position to regard man's being itself, from this view-point within the basic and total conception of the world. It is precisely this being of man, seen from *this* view-point, which—both by its highest, free and complete self-transcendence into God, made possible quite gratuitously by God, and by God's communication of himself—'awaits' its own consummation and that of the world in what in Christian terms we call 'grace' and 'glory'.

The first step and definitive beginning, and the absolute guarantee that this ultimate and basically unsurpassable self-transcendence will succeed and indeed has already begun, is to be found in what we call the Hypostatic Union. At a first approximation, this must not be seen so much as something which distinguishes Jesus Our Lord from us, but rather as something which must happen once, and once only, at the point where the world begins to enter into its final phase in which it is to realize its final concentration, its final climax and its radical nearness to the absolute mystery called God. Seen from this viewpoint, the Incarnation appears as the necessary and permanent beginning of the divinization of the world as a whole. In so far as this unsurpassable nearness by complete openness takes place precisely in relation to that absolute mystery which is and remains God—and in so far as this final phase of the history of the world has indeed already begun but is not yet consummated—the course of this phase and its end-result remain shrouded in mystery. Hence the clarity and finality of Christian truth consist in man's unflinching surrender to the Mystery: it is not clarity in the sense of a clear view over a certain partial element of the world and of man. These then, in preview, are the steps in our considerations which we want to embark on together as far as strength of mind and heart—and time—will allow. If these steps are fairly successful, then—it seems to me—we will have covered what was intended to be our subject here. The extent of our success will depend, of course, on how far the immensity of our subject, its unaccustomed nature, our lack of practice in this kind of subject and the ridiculously short time of one hour will permit us to succeed.

I

1. The Christian professes in his Faith that all things—heaven and earth, the material and the spiritual world—are the creation of one and the same God. This does not simply mean that everything *in* its variety stems from *one* cause, which—since infinite and omnipotent—can create the most varied things. It means also that this variety shows an inner similarity and community: that the contents of this variety must not be simply regarded as essentially different or even contradictory but rather that this variety and difference be seen to form a unity in origin, self-realization and determination, in short: *one* world. It follows from this that it would be quite wrong and unchristian to conceive matter and spirit as realities simply existing side by side in the actual order of things while being really quite unrelated to each other, the spirit in its human form having—unfortunately—to utilize the material world as a kind of exterior stage. A Christian theology and philosophy deems it self-evident that spirit and matter have more things in common (to put it this way) than things dividing them.

2. This 'community' shows itself first of all—and at its clearest—in the unity of man himself. According to Christian teaching, man is not an unnatural or merely temporary composite of spirit and matter but

is a unity which is logically and objectively prior to the diversity of his distinguishable elements, so that the properties of these elements are intelligible only when the elements are understood precisely *as* elements of the *one* man into which this originally one being of man necessarily spreads and unfolds itself. This helps us to understand that, ultimately, we know what matter and spirit are only by starting from the one man and hence from his one self-realization, and that we must therefore conceive of them from the outset as mutually related elements. To this corresponds also the Christian doctrine which tells us that the consummation of the finite spirit which is man must be thought of only in terms of the one (however 'unimaginable') consummation of his *whole* reality and that of the cosmos; yet the materiality of man and of the cosmos—however impossible we may find it to form any positive image of a perfect state of materiality, and however little this is required for being a true Christian—must not be simply eliminated from this consummation as if it were a merely temporary element.

3. Natural science, taken by itself as merely one element of man's one and complete knowledge, i.e. ultimately the knowledge of himself in his basic orientation to the unutterable Mystery, knows a lot 'about' matter, i.e. it defines ever more exact relationships of a 'functional' kind between the various phenomena of nature. Since, however, natural science does its work in methodical abstraction from man himself, while knowing a great deal *about* matter it cannot know matter *itself*, even though this knowledge about the functional and temporal relationships of its isolated object does in the end lead it back again to man himself in an *a-posteriori* manner. This is really quite obvious: the field, the whole as such, can*not* be determined by the same means as those used for the determination of its parts. Only in relation to man is it possible to say what matter is—and not vice versa, what spirit is in relation to matter. We have said in relation to '*man*' and not in relation to '*spirit*'. The latter would be something quite different—it would again simply be that platonism which is likewise contained in materialism. For materialism, like platonic spiritualism, believes that it has discovered a jumping-off point for its understanding of the whole and its parts: but this is done quite independently of the understanding of man as the one totality in which alone these two elements of spirit and matter can be experienced in their real nature. Starting from the original self-experience of the one man, however, it can be said that spirit is the one man in so far as he becomes conscious of himself in an

absolute consciousness of being-given-to-himself. This man does by the very fact that he is always already referred to the absoluteness of reality as such and to its one root (called God), and by the fact that this 'return to himself' and his 'being referred to the absolute totality of all possible reality and its root' mutually determine each other. This 'being referred to', however, is not like a possession of the known which has an emptying effect by its very power of penetration. It should be characterized rather as the process of being lifted out of oneself and being drawn into the infinite mystery. This process of being 'abducted from oneself' is therefore such that it can be genuinely undergone only in loving acceptance of this mystery and within the unpredictable designs God has for us—in that freedom which is necessarily given together with this transcendence over oneself and everything individual. To the extent in which man is *matter*, he grasps himself and the environment necessarily belonging to him in so far as the act of this return to himself—in the experience of his orientation to a mystery which must be accepted lovingly—always and primarily takes place only in an encounter with the individual, with what shows itself spontaneously and with the concrete which cannot be disposed of but is given unavoidably (though only to a limited extent). As matter, man experiences himself and the world he directly encounters precisely in so far as he is a fact, someone who is added to, someone who is pre-defined for himself and who as such is someone not yet fully penetrated; and precisely in so far as, in the midst of knowledge (understood as self-possession), there stands what is alien and each individual, something foreign and something unaccountable to himself. Matter is the condition of possibility for the objectively 'other' which the world and man are in their own eyes. Matter is the condition of what we experience directly as space and time (precisely when we cannot objectify this for ourselves); it is the condition of that otherness which estranges man from himself, which forms the requirement for the possibility of a direct intercommunication with other spiritual existents in space and time—i.e. in history. Matter is the basis for the pre-required existence of the 'other' considered as the material of freedom.

4. This condition of mutual relatedness between spirit and matter is not simply a static condition, but has itself a history. Man, considered as a spirit becoming conscious of himself, experiences his pre-established nature in otherness; he experiences his self-estrangement as something having temporal duration and as belonging to

natural history; he comes to himself as someone who has already existed in time both in himself and in his surroundings (which also belong to him and his constitution). And conversely, this temporal materiality understood as the pre-history of man considered as reflex freedom must be understood as being orientated to the history of the human spirit. This last point should be expressed a little more exactly. Without separating them from each other, we have tried to understand spirit and matter as two correlated elements of the one man, elements which are inseparable from each other and yet are not reducible to each other. This irreducible pluralism of elements in the one man can also be stated in such a way as to express a difference of nature between spirit and matter. To make this distinction is of paramount importance and significance, for only in this way do one's eyes remain open to all the dimensions of the one man in all their immense and indeed infinite extent. But, as we have already pointed out, this difference of nature must not be misunderstood to mean that these two elements are opposed in nature or absolutely different in nature or indifferent to each other. Starting from this inner interrelation between these two factors and concentrating on the *temporal* duration of this relationship between these two factors, it may be said without scruple that matter develops out of its inner being in the direction of the spirit. But we must not leave the question there—we must go on to make this state-ment a little clearer still and defend this way of speaking by making it intelligible. First of all, if there is any 'becoming' at all (and this is not merely a fact of experience but a basic axiom of theology itself, since man's freedom, responsibility and perfecting by his own respon-sible activity would otherwise have no real meaning at all), then 'becoming' in its true form cannot be conceived simply as a 'becoming *other*' in which a reality becomes different but does not become more. True 'becoming' must be conceived as something 'becoming *more*', as the coming into being of more reality, as an effective attainment of a greater fullness of being. This 'more' must not be imagined, however, as something simply added to what was there before, but, on the one hand, must be something really effected by what was there before and, on the other hand, must be the inner increase of being proper to the previously existing reality. This means, however, that if it is really to be taken seriously, 'becoming' must be understood as a real self-transcendence, a surpassing of self or active filling up of the empty. This notion of active self-transcendence—self-transcendence by which an existing and acting being actively approaches to the higher perfection still lacking to it—must not, however, turn non-being into the very ground of being and turn emptiness as such into the source of fullness—in other words, we must not violate the metaphysical principle of causality. Consequently (and I am merely summarizing very briefly all the extensive considerations which would be necessary here) this self-transcendence cannot be thought of in any other way than as an event which takes place by the power of the absolute fullness of being. On the one hand, this absolute fullness of being must be thought of as something so *interior* to the finite being moving towards its fulfilment that the finite being is empowered by it to achieve a really *active self*-transcendence and does not merely receive this new reality passively as something effected by God. On the other hand, this power of self-transcendence must at the same time be thought of as so distinct from finite, acting being that it is *not* permissible to conceive it as a constitutive principle of the *essence* of this finite being achieving itself. For otherwise, if the absoluteness of being—which gives efficacy to a being and empowers it to be effective—were to constitute the nature of the finite acting being, then this being would no longer be capable of any real becoming in time and history, since it would already possess the absolute fullness of being as something absolutely proper to it. These reflections cannot be developed further here; above all, it cannot be explained here how the experience of spiritual transcendence, understood as the movement of the evolving spirit, directly shows this dialectic as something experienced. In other words, it is impossible to explain here how being is both absolutely the most interior and yet the most foreign factor of this movement and how, in this dialectic of its relationship to the finite evolving spirit, it can support the whole of this movement and yet allow it to be the movement of this spirit itself. We must content ourselves with stating the thesis that the notion of an *active self-transcendence* (in which the 'self' and the 'transcendence' are to be taken equally seriously) is a necessary notion in our thought if the phenomenon of becoming—which is possible, since it exists—is to be saved. Let us simply remark in this connection that this notion of self-transcendence includes also transcendence into what is substantially new, i.e. the leap to a higher *nature*. To exclude the latter would mean emptying the notion of self-transcendence of its content; it would mean that one could no longer evaluate certain phenomena with an untroubled mind, e.g. such notions as the procreation of a new human being by the parents in what appears at first sight to be a merely biological event. An essential self-transcendence, however, is no more an intrinsic contradiction than (simple) self-transcendence, as soon as one allows it to occur in the dynamism of the power of the absolute being which is within the creature and yet is not proper to its nature—in other words, in what in theological language is called God's conservation of the creature and his concurrence with its activity, in the inner and permanent need of all finite reality to be held in being and in operation, in the being of becoming, in the being of self-becoming—in short, in the self-transcendence which belongs to the nature of every finite being. Given, however, that this notion is a metaphysically legitimate one, and that the world is one and thus has one history, and that in this one but not always already all-comprehensive world everything is not always already present from the very beginning—then there is no necessary reason for disputing the fact that matter has evolved in the direction of life and of man in that self-transcendence whose notional content we have just now been trying to bring out. This is, of course, a question of an *essential* self-transcendence, for we do not mean to deny or obscure in any way the fact that matter, life, consciousness and spirit are not the same thing. Quite the contrary. But precisely this difference, this essential difference, does not exclude development, if there is becoming and if becoming does or can mean a really active self-transcendence and if self-transcendence does or can mean at least *also* a self-transcendence of nature. And what is grasped in this way, as logically possible by an *a-priori* reflection, is also confirmed as real by better and more comprehensively observed facts. It is not merely a question here of an inner solidarity of spirit and matter. We must also take into consideration the known history of the cosmos as it has been investigated and described by the modern natural sciences: this history is seen more and more as one homogeneous history of matter, life and man. This one history does not exclude differences of nature but on the contrary includes them in its concept, since history is precisely not the permanence of the same but rather the becoming of something entirely new and not merely of something other. These differences of nature also do not exclude the fact of there being one history, since history itself results precisely from an essential self-transcendence in which what was previously, surpasses itself in order to dissolve and conserve itself in very truth in the new which it itself has effected.

In so far as the self-transcending always remains present in the parti-cular goal of its self-transcendence, and in so far as the higher order always embraces the lower as contained in it, it is clear that the lower always precedes the actual event of self-transcendence and prepares the way for it by the development of its own reality and order; it is clear that the lower always moves slowly towards the boundary line in its history which it then crosses in its actual self-transcendence—that boundary line which is only seen to have been clearly crossed from the vantage point of a clearer development of the new condition, without it being possible however to give an absolutely clear definition of this line itself. Of course, these are all very abstract and vague statements. Naturally, it would in itself be desirable to show more concretely what common traits are to be found in the evolution of material, living and spiritual beings—to show (more exactly) how the merely material is a prelude in its own dimensions to the higher dimension of life, and how the latter in its dimension is a prelude to the spirit in its ever greater advance towards the border line to be crossed by self-tran-scendence. Certainly, if we really postulate a unified history of all reality, it would be necessary to indicate which permanent formal structures of this total history pertain in common to the basic constitu-tion of matter, life and spirit, and how even the highest (even though it is *essentially* new) can still be understood as a change of something previously existing.

But all this would lead the theologian and philosopher too far afield from his own sphere and would necessitate his developing these basic structures of the one history by the more *a-posteriori* method proper to the natural sciences and with the aid of concepts such as are devel-oped by Teilhard, for instance. Obviously this cannot be the task of the theologian—and particularly not in the present context. It should be noted here, however, that the theologian not only can admit (even in the case of all material reality) an analogous notion of self-possession —which finds its fullest natural expression in consciousness—but also as a good thomistic philosopher he really *ought to* admit it. For what he as a thomist calls the 'form' in every being is for him also essentially the 'Idea'; and that reality which we call the 'unconscious' in the ordinary and—in its place—quite correct sense, is from the meta-physical point of view the kind of being which possesses only its own 'Idea'; it is something which, being caught up in itself, has only itself and its own 'Idea' and hence—is not conscious. Seen in this way, it becomes understandable even from the thomistic point of view that a really higher, more complex organization can appear also as a step towards consciousness, and finally towards self-consciousness, even though *self*-consciousness at least does include a real essential self-transcendence of the material as opposed to its previous condition.

5. If man is thus the self-transcendence of living matter, then the history of Nature and spirit forms an inner, graded unity in which natural history develops towards man, continues in him as *his* history, is conserved and surpassed in him and hence reaches its proper goal with and in the history of the human spirit. In so far as this history of Nature is dissolved in man into freedom, this natural history reaches its goal in the history of the free spirit. In so far as the history of man always still includes the natural history of living matter, it is always still supported—even in the midst of its freedom—by the structures and necessities of this material world. Hence, in so far as man is not *only* the spiritual *observer* of nature—since he is a part of it and must precisely continue its history too—his history is not only a history of culture (in the sense of an ideological history situated above natural history) but is also an active alteration of this material world itself. Thus, man and nature can reach their one common goal only by activity which is spiritual and by spirituality which is activity. It is true, of course, that precisely because this goal corresponds to the transcendence of man into the absolute reality of God who is the infinite mystery—and because it consists in the infinite fullness of God —this goal itself remains hidden and unattainable for the natural powers of man. It can be reached only by accepting the fact of its being hidden and withdrawn. In so far as this history of the cosmos is the history of the free spirit, this history—like that of man—is posed in freedom as guilt and trial. In so far as this history of freedom, however, always remains based on the pre-determined structures of the living world, and in so far as (as the Christian professes) the freedom-history of the spirit is enveloped by the grace of God which perseveres victoriously unto the good, the Christian knows that this history of the cosmos as a whole will find its real consummation despite, in and through the freedom of man, and that its finality as a whole will also be its consummation.

II

Before we can even think of connecting these initial assessments and basic conceptions with Christology, we must first try to state more exactly what stage the world has reached in man.

1. First of all, it must be stated that—despite the wonderful results and perspectives of his science—even the modern natural scientist still remains to a large extent confined within the limits of a pre-scientific as well as pre-philosophic and pre-theological outlook. For very often he still maintains even today that it is a peculiarly characteristic part of the spirit of the natural sciences to regard man as only a weak, fortuitous being exposed to a Nature quite indifferent to it and passing its existence in this world as a kind of day-fly until it is swallowed up again by a 'blind' Nature which had produced it quite by accident in one of her careless moods. This contradicts not only metaphysics and Christian thought but also natural science itself. If man exists, if he is the 'product' of Nature, if he does not come onto the scene just at any time at all but at the end of a development which, at least partially, only he can steer by going out to meet this his producer and by himself objectifying and transforming it—then Nature does become conscious of itself in *him*, then Nature is planned for him, since 'chance' is a word without any real meaning for the natural scientist who concludes from the result to a movement orientated towards it. If things are not regarded in this way, then there is right away no sense in seeing the history of the cosmos and that of man as *one* history. One would sooner or later fall back into a platonic dualism. For a spirit who is thus regarded as a chance stranger on earth, will not for long let himself be despised and reproached as being unimportant and powerless. If the spirit is not regarded as the goal of Nature—if it is not seen that Nature found herself in him, in spite of all the physical powerlessness of the individual man—then the spirit will after a while be regarded more and more as merely the opponent of Nature who exists quite apart from it.

2. The characteristic which becomes reality in man, which reaches finite reality in him and into which matter transcends itself, is first of all the fact of being present to oneself and of being referred to the absolute totality of reality and to its first ground as such. There then flows from this the possibility of a real objectification of individual experience and of the individual object, which thus becomes capable of being separated from any immediate reference to man in his vital sphere. If this is seen

to be the end of the history of the cosmos, then it can be said absolutely that the established world finds itself in man, and that in man it makes itself its own object and is no longer referred to its ground merely as presupposed behind it but rather as an imposed task before it. This assertion is not invalidated by the objection that such concentrations of the spatio-temporal dispersion of the world into itself and within its foundation are present in man only in very formal, almost empty beginnings, and that this could be conceived to be present in non-human spiritual persons (monads) which would be much better suited to accomplishing this, without being—like man—subjects of the totality and self-presence of the world in such a way that they have to be at the same time also a *part*-factor of this world. Such beings may exist. The Christian is even sure that they do exist, and calls them angels. But precisely this concentrating, synthesizing—even though still very much incipient—self-consciousness of the totality of the cosmos in the individual man is something which can occur many times over (and each time in an absolutely unique manner), particularly if it springs from a part-factor considered as a spatio-temporal individual magnitude of the cosmos. Hence one cannot say (especially when one bears in mind the uniqueness of each act of freedom) that this cosmic self-consciousness need not be given in man or can be given only once. It occurs each time, in its own unique way, in each individual man. The one material cosmos is, as it were, the *one* body of the *multifarious* self-presence of this self-same cosmos and of its orientation to its absolute and infinite foundation. Even though this cosmic bodily presence of the innumerable personal self-consciousnesses in which the cosmos can become conscious of itself begins to appear (like man's own bodily presence in the narrower sense) only very tentatively in the self-consciousness and freedom of the individual human being, it is nevertheless present in every man as something which is intended to be and can become actual. For in his corporeality, every man is an element of the cosmos which cannot really be delimited and cut off from it, and in this corporeality he communicates with the whole cosmos in *such* a way that through this corporeality of man taken as the other element of belonging to the spirit, the cosmos really presses forward to this self-presence in the spirit. This self-presence of the cosmos in the spirit of the individual man, which is still in the process of becoming and in its very initial stage, has its still-continuing history; this history is still taking place in the internal and external history both of the individual and of humanity as a whole, in the act of thought and in the self-present external act, both individually and collectively. We are certainly again and again under the impression that nothing final will ever come of this unnecessarily long and laborious process by which the cosmos finds itself in man. For this process seems always to dissipate itself again, and instead a kind of hidden contrariness against self-consciousness—a kind of will to the unconscious—seems always to assert itself again. But once we presuppose that evolution proceeds in the final analysis in a one-way direction and ordination (and that anything else makes the notion of evolution quite unthinkable from the outset since something which simply wants to return again to the beginning and has no other tendency at all, would not have left this beginning in the first place), then this process by which the cosmos gradually becomes conscious of itself in man—in the individual totality and freedom which each individual realizes—must also have a final result. The result seems to disappear and dissipate itself, it seems to fall back into the misty beginnings of the cosmos and of its dispersion, only because we who exist at this *present* determined moment in space and time are quite incapable of experiencing the final coming to itself of such a monadic unity of the world and the uniqueness of the fully grasped totality of the cosmos at our particular point in space and time. It must however exist. In Christian language we usually call it the immortality of the soul; it must, however, be clearly seen here that this immortality, if it is properly understood, is precisely a (formal, and of itself empty) finality and consummation of this very process by which the cosmos finds itself, and hence must not be confused with the escape of a spiritual soul—an alien in this cosmos—from the totality of that world which is always also material (and is so precisely in the service of the spirit) and has always had and still has also a material history.

3. According to Christian teaching, this self-transcendence of the cosmos in man towards its own totality and foundation, which has itself a history, has really reached its final consummation only when the cosmos in the spiritual creature, its goal and its height, is not merely something set apart from its foundation—something created—but something which receives the ultimate self-communication of its ultimate ground itself, in that moment when this direct self-communication of God is given to the spiritual creature in what we—looking at the historical pattern of this self-communication—call grace and glory (in its consummation). God does not merely create something other than

himself—he also gives himself to this other. The world receives God, the Infinite and the ineffable mystery, to such an extent that he himself becomes its innermost life. The concentrated, always unique self-possession of the cosmos in each individual spiritual person, and in his transcendence towards the absolute ground of his reality, takes place when this absolute ground itself becomes directly interior to that which is grounded by it. The end is the absolute beginning. This beginning is not infinite emptiness or nothingness, but the fullness which alone explains the divided and that which begins, which alone can support a becoming and which alone can give to that which begins the real power of movement towards something more developed and at the same time more intimate. But by the very fact that this movement of the development of the cosmos is thus carried along both from the outset and in all its phases by the urge towards ever greater fullness and intimacy and towards an ever closer and more conscious relationship to its ground, the message which says that there will be an absolutely direct contact with this infinite cause, is already given in this movement—not indeed as something which must necessarily be recognized from this movement in all its phases, but at least as something which can certainly be more and more approximately envisaged as the absolute goal of this development. If the history of the cosmos is always basically a spiritual history —the desire to become conscious of itself and of its cause—then the direct relationship to God in his self-communication to his spiritual creature, and in it to the cosmos in general as the goal which corresponds to the meaning of this development, is basically an indisputable fact, provided that this development is allowed to any degree at all to reach its own absolute goal and is not merely moved by it as something unattainable. We, as single and physically conditioned individuals, experience only the uttermost beginning of this movement towards this infinite goal. Yet we are after all beings who, even in that consciousness with which we engage in our physico-biological fight for existence and for our earthly dignity, live and act (in distinction to the brutes) out of a formal anticipation of the whole. We are those even who in the experience of grace experience the event of the promise of the absolute nearness of the all-founding mystery (even though this experience is an unobjectified one). And this fact gives us the right to that courage of faith in the fulfilment of the coming history of the cosmos and of each individual cosmic consciousness, which consists in the direct experience of God as he communicates himself in a most real and unveiled manner.

Such a statement also implies naturally and most radically in the very nature of things the preservation of the ineffable mystery which reigns over our existence. For if God himself, the inexpressible infinity of mystery, is and becomes the reality of our perfection—and if the world understands itself in its most proper truth only when it commits itself radically to this infinite mystery—then this message does not merely say this or that, sayings which stand as *one* content of expression *among* others, and fall under a common co-ordinated system of concepts. Rather, it states that before and behind every individual thing, which has to be incorporated into an over-all order and in view of which the sciences engage in their search, there always stands and is already presupposed the infinite mystery—and it states that in this abyss, the origin and the end are the beatifying end. Man may feel irritated by a seemingly excessive demand and may declare himself to be uninterested in this abyss of the beginning and the end—he may try to take refuge in the comprehensible clarity of science, regarding this as the only sphere of his existence suited to his powers . . . yet the question of the Infinite is one which envelops man and is one which alone answers itself. Even if he were capable of it on the surface of his objective consciousness, man may not and cannot leave this question unsolved in the all-supporting and all-nourishing depths of the really spiritual person. For this question exists: there is nothing which could answer it from outside but rather it is a question which answers itself when accepted in love. It is a question which moves man; only when he concerns himself with this movement which belongs to the world and to the spirit, does he become really conscious of himself, of God and of his goal in which the beginning is given directly.

III

Only in the light of all we have seen can we now determine the place of Christology in this evolutionary world-picture.

1. We presuppose, therefore, that the goal of the world consists in God's communicating himself to it. We presuppose that the whole dynamism which God has instituted in the very heart of the world's becoming by self-transcendence (and yet not as that which constitutes its nature) is really always meant already as the beginning and first step towards this self-communication and its acceptance by the world. In exactly what way are we then to conceive this self-communication of

God to the spiritual creature in general and to all those subjects in which the cosmos becomes conscious of itself, of its condition and of its basic cause? To understand this, it must first of all be pointed out that these spiritual subjectivities of the cosmos signify freedom. We can only state this baldly here and must abstain from going into the transcendental reasons for it. Once we presuppose this, however, we presuppose also that this history of the self-consciousness of the cosmos is always necessarily also a history of the inter-communication of these spiritual subjects. For the fact that the cosmos becomes conscious of itself in the spiritual subjects must mean above all and necessarily that these subjects—in which the whole is present to itself each time after the manner proper to that subject—become more closely associated with each other, as otherwise the 'becoming present to itself' would separate and not unite. God's self-communication is, therefore, communication of freedom and inter-communication between the many cosmic subjectivities. Hence this self-communication necessarily turns in the direction of a free history of the human race, and can only happen in *free* acceptance by these free subjects and in a *common* history. God's communication of himself does not suddenly become uncosmic—directed merely to an isolated, separate subjectivity—but is given to the human race and is historical. This event of self-communication must therefore be thought of as an event which takes place historically in a specifically spatio-temporal manner and which then turns to everyone and calls upon their freedom. In other words, this self-communication must have a permanent beginning and must find in this a permanent guarantee of its reality so that it can rightly demand a free decision for the acceptance of this divine self-communication. (In this connection it should be mentioned briefly that this free acceptance or refusal on the part of individual free beings does not really determine the actual event of self-communication but, more exactly, only determines the attitude adopted by the spiritual creature towards it; of course, normally only that is called self-communication which is accepted freely and hence beatifies, i.e. only the successful, accepted self-communication of God.)

2. From this there follows first of all the explanation of the notion of Saviour. We give the title of Saviour simply to that historical person who, coming in space and time, signifies that beginning of God's absolute communication of himself which inaugurates this self-communication for all men as something happening irrevocably and which

shows this to be happening. This notion does not imply that God's self-communication to the world in its spiritual subjectivity begins *in time* only with this person. This does not need to be the case at all; it can quite easily be conceived as beginning before the actual coming of the Saviour, indeed as co-existent with the whole spiritual history of humanity and of the world—as was actually the case according to Christian teaching. The historical person whom we call Saviour is that subjectivity in whom this process of God's absolute self-communication to the spiritual world is *irrevocably* present as a whole; through him this self-communication can be clearly recognized as something irrevocable, and in him it reaches its climax, in so far as this climax must be thought of as a moment in the total history of the human race and in so far as this climax is not simply identified with the totality of the spiritual world subject to God's communication of himself (which is a different, though absolutely legitimate notion of the climax of the divine self-communication). For, in so far as this self-communication must be conceived as free on the part of God and of the history of the human race which must accept it, it is quite legitimate to conceive of an event by which this self-communication and acceptance attains an irrevocable and irreversible character in history—an event in which the history of this self-communication realizes its proper nature and in which it breaks through—without it thereby becoming necessary that this history of God's self-communication to the human race has already simply found its end and conclusion both in its extension and in regard to the spatio-temporal plurality of the history of humanity. It must be noted in this connection that this moment in which the irreversible character of this historical self-communication of God becomes manifest refers equally to the communication itself and to its acceptance. Both these factors are included in the notion of the Saviour. In so far as a historical movement already lives in virtue of its end even in its beginnings—since the dynamism of its own being desires its end, carries its goal in itself as that towards which it is striving and really unveils itself in its own proper being only in this goal—it is absolutely legitimate, and indeed necessary, to think of the whole movement of God's communication of himself to the human race (even when it takes place during the time *before* the event which makes it irrevocable in the Saviour) as something based on this event—in other words, as something based on the Saviour. The whole movement of this history lives only for the moment of arrival at its goal and climax—it lives only for its entry into the event which makes it irreversible—in short, it lives for the one whom we call Saviour. This Saviour, who represents the climax of this self-communication, must therefore be at the same time God's absolute pledge by self-communication to the spiritual creature as a whole *and* the acceptance of this self-communication by this Saviour; only then is there an utterly irrevocable self-communication on both sides, and only thus is it present in the world in a historically communicative manner.

3. Seen in this light, it now becomes possible to understand what is really meant by the doctrine of the Hypostatic Union and of the Incarnation of the divine Logos and how, following quite naturally from what has been said, it fits into an evolutionist view of the world. In the first place, the Saviour is himself a historical moment in God's saving action exercised on the world. He is a moment of the history of God's communication of himself to the world—in the sense that he is a part of this history of the cosmos itself. He must not be merely God acting on the world but must be a part of the cosmos itself in its very climax. This is in fact stated in the Christian dogma: Jesus is true man; he is truly a part of the earth, truly a moment in the biological evolution of this world, a moment of human natural history, for he is born of woman; he is a man who in his spiritual, human and finite subjectivity is just like us, a receiver of that self-communication of God by grace which we affirm of all men—and hence of the cosmos—as the climax of development in which the world comes absolutely into its own presence and into the direct presence of God. Jesus is the one who— by what we call his obedience, his prayer and the freely accepted destiny of his death—has achieved also the acceptance of his divinely given grace and direct presence to God which he possesses as man. All this is Catholic Dogma. If one is not to fall into a false belief or heresy, one must not think of the God-man as if God or his Logos had put on a kind of livery for the purpose of his saving treatment of man, or as if he had disguised himself, as it were, and had given himself merely an external appearance to enable him to show himself in the world. No, Jesus is truly man. He has absolutely everything which belongs to the nature of man; he has (also) a finite subjective nature in which the world becomes present to itself and which has a radical directness to God which, like ours, rests on that self-communication by God in grace and glory which we too possess. It must also be underlined in this connection that the statement of God's *Incarnation*—of his becoming

material—is the most basic statement of Christology. This is not self-evident. This was not at all in keeping with the 'tendencies of the day' and the spirit of the age in which the dogma of the Incarnation was defined. If a God—who, as spiritual transcendence, is conceived as simply and absolutely superior to the material world—draws near to the world in order to save it, then he must be conceived as a God who, as a spirit, draws carefully nearer to the spirit of the world from outside, meets the *spirit* and finally, if at all, also takes effect in this way —psychotherapeutically as it were—for the salvation of the material world. And this was in fact the view adopted by the most dangerous heresy against which primitive Christianity had to fight, i.e. the view of Gnosticism. Christianity, however, teaches differently. According to Christian teaching, God takes hold of the world in the Incarnation and in the fact of the Logos becoming part of the material world—or better —precisely in that one point in which matter becomes present to itself and the spirit has its own being in the objectification of the material: in short, in the unity of a human nature. In Jesus, the Logos bears the matter just as much as the soul, and this matter is a part of the reality and the history of the cosmos. Theology even stresses the fact that in that phase of the human existence of Jesus during which, on account of his death, there existed a different relationship between his 'soul' and his 'body' than during the period of the biological life familiar to us, the relationship of the Logos to his body did not become any looser on account of this greater distance between body and soul. The divine Logos himself both really creates and accepts this corporeality—which is a part of the world—*as his* own reality; he brings it into existence as something other than himself in such a way, therefore, that this very materiality expresses *him*, the Logos himself, and lets him be present in his world. His taking hold of this part of the one material-spiritual world-reality may quite legitimately be thought of as the climax of that dynamism in which the Word of God who supports everything, supports the self-transcendence of the world as a whole. For we are quite entitled to conceive what we call creation as a part-moment in that process of God's coming-into-the-world by which God actually, even though freely, gives expression to himself in his Word become part of the world and of matter; we are perfectly entitled to think of the creation and of the Incarnation, not as two disparate, adjacent acts of God '*ad extram*' which in the actual world are due to two quite separate original acts of God, but as two moments and phases in the real world of the unique, even though internally differentiated, process of God's self-renunciation and self-expression into what is other than himself. For such a conception can certainly appeal to a most ancient Christian tradition of 'Christocentricity' as found in the history of Christian theology, and it does not deny in any way that God *could* have created a world without an Incarnation, i.e. that he could have denied the final climax of grace and Incarnation to the self-transcendence of the material in the spirit and towards God by His own dynamism inherent in the world (without thereby becoming constitutive of its being). For every such essential self-surpassing always stands in a relationship of grace— the unexpected and the gratuitous—to its lower stage, even though it is the 'goal' of this movement. But we have run ahead of the actual course of our reflections. At this stage we are merely concerned with understanding that the Saviour, whom we comprehend as the climax of the history of the cosmos, is indeed the climax of this history itself (but of course within that climax of history itself which allows the whole world of the spirit to transcend into God) and that the Christian dogma of the Incarnation tells us exactly this: Jesus is truly man with everything this implies, i.e. with man's finiteness, his being-in-the-world, his materiality and his participation in the history of this cosmos which leads him through the narrow gates of death.

That is one side of the question. Now we must look also at the other side. We have already said that the very event of salvation must take place in the world and in its history in such a way that God's self-communication to the spiritual creature becomes something definitive and irrevocable and becomes present in such a way that this self-communication of God to spiritual creation is seen to be given in the light of a unique, individual history. If we presuppose this, however, as the 'normal' consummation of the history of the cosmos and of the spirit, without implying that this development must *necessarily* go this far or has already done so, then we must say that this limit-notion of the Saviour implies that notion of the hypostatic unity of God and man which constitutes the real content of the Christian dogma of the Incarnation.

This is perhaps the point where we reach the real crux of the problem which runs through the whole of our reflections. And so we must not rush on but must exercise a little patience. We want first of all to clarify a little more what exactly we are *asking* now. It seems to me that we should have no particular difficulty in representing the history of

the world and of the spirit to ourselves as the history of a self-transcendence into the life of God—a self-transcendence which, in this its
final and highest phase, is identical with an absolute self-communication of God expressing the same process but now looked at from God's
side. This final and absolute self-transcendence of the spirit into God
must, however, be conceived as something which happens in all
spiritual subjects. In the nature of things, one could of course think
that a real self-transcendence does not take place in every 'specimen' of
the original state but only in a certain few, just as in the biological
evolution there survive, side by side with the new and higher forms,
certain specimens of the lower forms from which the higher are
derived. But in man's case this is not rationally conceivable, since man
is 'by nature' and by his very being the possibility of transcendence
become conscious of itself—the self-conscious reference to the absolute
and the knowledge about the infinite possibility. If the accomplishment
of this final self-transcendence is granted generally (i.e. to other similar
spiritual subjects), then it can hardly be refused to such beings in
individual cases. But be that as it may, the Christian revelation tells us
that all men are offered this self-transcendence as a real possibility of
their individual existence, one to which they can close themselves only
by guilt. Hence, in accordance with the characteristic of the spiritual
being, the end taken as the perfection of the spirit and of the world
must be regarded as something intended for *all* spiritual subjects. And
in so far as Christianity understands grace and glory as the direct self-
communication of God, it also professes this insurpassable consummation to belong to *all* men (and angels). How then does the doctrine
of the Hypostatic Union of a determined *single* human nature with
God's Logos fit into this basic conception? Is this to be conceived
merely as a *proper*, still higher stage of an essentially newer and higher
kind of divine self-communication to the creature, which this time is
given only in one single 'case'? Or is it possible to conceive that, even
though this Hypostatic Union is given only once in its essential characteristics, it is nevertheless precisely the way in which the divinization
of the spiritual creature is and *must* be carried out if it is to happen
at all? In other words, is the Hypostatic Union a higher stage in which
the gift of grace given to the spiritual creature is surpassed (even
though it is also 'conserved') or is it a peculiar moment in this process
of the granting of grace which cannot really be conceived without this
Hypostatic Union taking place on account of it?

We hope that the significance of this question for our subject as a whole is clear. For if the Incarnation is to be regarded as an absolutely proper and new rung in the hierarchy of world-realities which quite simply surpasses all the world-realities given so far or to be given in the future yet without being itself necessary for these lower stages themselves, i.e. without being the condition and possibility of the general granting of grace to the spiritual creature, then this could mean one of two things. Under this presupposition, either the Incarnation could still be seen as the climax surpassing all the other world-realities arranged in ascending layers, so that it could be positively fitted into an evolutionary world-view—or both thoughts must be abandoned, i.e. it could no longer be thought that the Incarnation of the Logos is the climax of the development of the world, towards which the whole world is orientated even though it remains free in grace—and it could also no longer be thought that the Incarnation fits into an evolutionary picture of the world. But it is almost impossible or even absolutely impossible to see how one could understand the Incarnation as a higher or even the highest stage in the reality or development of the world in *such* a way that it also appears as the goal and end of this world-reality, without the aid of the theory that the Incarnation is itself already an intrinsic element and condition of the general gift of grace by which God gives himself to the spiritual creature. The Incarnation would, of course, always appear as the highest stage in this world-reality because it is the hypostatic unity of God and a world-reality. But this does not yet make it intelligible as the goal and end, as the climax which can indeed be envisaged from below but always only as something unreachable. This seems possible only by presupposing that the Incarnation itself is to be made intelligible *in* its uniqueness and *in* the degree of reality given by it (in and not despite this uniqueness) as an intrinsic and necessary element in the process of God's giving himself in grace to the world as a whole and not only as an actually utilized means for this process (this no Christian can deny) which could quite easily have happened in some other way, a way in which it would not be shared in itself by the Incarnation as such.

The theologian who puts this question in this way can first of all take note of the fact that the Hypostatic Union takes effect interiorly *for* the human nature of the Logos precisely in what, and really only in what, the same theology prescribes for *all* men as their goal and consummation, viz. the direct vision of God enjoyed by Christ's created human soul. This same theology emphasizes the fact that the Incarnation occurred 'for the sake of our salvation', that it does not give any real increase in reality and life to the divine nature of the Logos, and that the prerogatives which accrued interiorly to the human reality of Jesus on account of the Hypostatic Union are of the same essential kind as those intended by grace also for other spiritual subjects. This fact alone should make us careful in answering the question posed. Theology has already tried to clarify this problem for itself by asking the in itself, of course, unreal question as to what, for instance, would have to be preferred if one had to choose: the Hypostatic Union without the direct vision of God or this vision of God—and decides for the second alternative. It can be clearly seen from this also how difficult it is to determine more exactly the relationship between the kind of consummation which the Christian faith professes to be common to all men and the unique consummation of human possibility (in the sense of *potentia obedientialis*) which we profess by the doctrine of the Hypostatic Union. And yet such a more exact definition of this relationship is demanded by the question we have posed ourselves, viz. whether we can, must or may think of what we call the Incarnation of the Logos as the manner in which the divinization of the spiritual creature in general is realized, so that we implicitly envisage this Hypostatic Union at the same time as we see the history of the cosmos and of the spirit arriving at the point at which are found both the absolute self-transcendence of the spirit into God and the absolute self-communication of God to all spiritual subjects by grace and glory. Hence the thesis towards which we are working purports to show that, even though the Hypostatic Union is in its proper nature a unique event and—when seen in itself—is certainly the highest conceivable event, it is nevertheless an intrinsic factor of the whole process of the bestowal of grace on the spiritual creature in general. Why is this so? We have already pointed out that, if this total event of the divinizing sanctification of humanity attains its consummation, it must be a concrete, tangible phenomenon in history (in other words, it must not suddenly become a-cosmic) and hence must be an event in such a way as to spread out spatio-temporally from one point (in other words, it must not destroy the unity of mankind and men's essential community and intercommunication but must on the contrary come into existence within these very factors); it must be an irrevocable reality in which

God's self-communication proves itself not merely as a temporary offer, but as an absolute offer accepted by man; it must (in accordance with the nature of the spirit) become conscious of itself. Whenever God—by his absolute self-communication—brings about man's self-transcendence into God, in such a way that both these factors form the irrevocable promise made to all men which has already reached its consummation in this man, there we have a hypostatic union. When we think of 'hypostatic union', we must not simply remain attached to the imagined model of any sort of 'unity' or connection. To grasp the proper nature of this particular unity, it is also not enough simply to say that, on account of this unity, the human reality must also be attributed in all truth to the divine subject of the Logos. For this is precisely the question:—*why* is this possible, and *how* are we to conceive this unity which justifies such a statement of the 'communication of idioms'? This 'assumption' and 'unification' has the nature of a self-communication; there is 'assumption' so that God's reality may be communicated to what is assumed, viz. the human nature (and in the first place the human nature of Christ). But this very communication which is aimed at by this 'assumption' is *the* communication by what we call grace and glory—and the latter are intended for all. It must not be objected that *this* (latter) communication is possible even without a hypostatic union, since it does in fact occur without it in our own case. For in us this communication is possible and effected precisely by this union and acceptance as it occurs in the Hypostatic Union. And, theologically speaking at least, there is nothing against the assumption that grace and hypostatic union can only be thought of together and that, as a unity, they signify one and the same *free* decision of God to institute the supernatural order of salvation. In Christ, God's self-communication takes place basically for all men, and there is 'hypostatic union' precisely in so far as this *unsurpassable* self-communication of God 'is there' irrevocably in a historically tangible and self-conscious manner. Once more we ask: why? Apart from the case of the Beatific Vision (and perhaps even this is no different in this respect from other cases, but we cannot deal with this here), every self-manifestation of God takes place through some finite reality— through a word, an event, etc., which belongs to the finite realm of creatures. As long as this finite mediation of the divine self-manifestation, however, is not in the strictest sense a divine reality itself, it is basically transitory and surpassable (since it is finite) and is not in this finiteness simply the reality of God itself; and thus can be surpassed by God himself simply by positing a new finite reality. Hence, if the reality in which God's absolute self-communication is pledged and accepted for the whole of humanity and thus becomes 'present' for us (i.e. Christ's reality) is to be really the final and unsurpassable divine self-communication, then it must be said that it is not only posited by God but is God himself. The pledge itself cannot be anything else than a human reality which has been absolutely sanctified by grace. For a mere word would not be the actual event of self-communication but would merely tell us about it: in other words, it would not be in any sense (since the event itself in its openness, and not a word *about* it, is the primary proclamation of itself) the *actual* and really primary communication addressed to us about this self-communication made to us. If this is so, and if this pledge must be truly and absolutely God himself, then it must be a human reality which belongs absolutely to God—in other words, exactly what we call 'Hypostatic Union'. Hence, if we may put it this way, the Hypostatic Union does not differ from our grace by what is pledged in it, for this is grace in both cases (even in the case of Jesus). But it differs from our grace by the fact that Jesus is our pledge, and we ourselves are not the pledge but the recipients of God's pledge to us. But the unity of the pledge, and the inseparability of this pledge from the one who pledges (indeed, pledges *himself to us*!) must be conceived in accordance with the peculiar nature of the pledge. If the real pledge made to us is precisely the very human reality itself which has been given grace and in which and through which God pledges himself to us in his grace, then the unity of the one who pledges and the pledge cannot be considered as a merely 'moral' one—as for instance the unity between a human 'word' (or something similar which is merely a sign) and God—but must be conceived as an *irrevocable* unity between this human reality and God making a separation between the proclamation and the giver of this proclamation impossible—which, in other words, makes of the really humanly proclaimed and the pledge given to us, a reality of God himself. And this is precisely what is meant by hypostatic union. It means this and, properly speaking, nothing else: in the human reality of Jesus, God's absolute saving purpose (the absolute event of God's self-communication to us) is simply, absolutely and irrevocably present; in it is present both the declaration made to us and its acceptance—something effected by God himself, a reality of God himself, unmixed and yet inseparable and hence irrevocable. This declaration, however, is the pledge of grace to us.

It is of course impossible here to pursue this initial consideration any further and to unfold the whole of Christology from this initial insight: an insight which would give us a much better understanding also of the rest of Christology. The time at our disposal is far too short for this. But such a study would show us that the genuine and properly understood doctrine of the Hypostatic Union has nothing in common with mythology. It would become clear that the monophysite interpretation of Christology adopted unconsciously and implicitly—and for that very reason all the more effectively—by many Christians, is really a misunderstanding.

IV

In conclusion, let us merely add a few remarks which will help us, at least to some extent, to round off our subject.

1. Up till now we have simply tried to fit Christology into the framework of an evolutionary world-view of a cosmos which evolves towards that spirit who attains absolute self-transcendence and perfection through and in an absolute self-communication given by God in grace and glory. Hence we have not so far spoken yet of guilt and redemption, i.e. liberation from sin. And yet the perspective of redemption and remission of sin is the perspective which would show us the Incarnation of the Logos in its clearest light. Does this mean that we have after all deviated in some unlawful way from the traditional Christology? We must at least make a few brief remarks concerning this question. It should be stated, first of all, that there is quite a long established school of thought among Catholic theologians (usually called the 'Scotist school') which has always stressed that the first and most basic motive for the Incarnation was not the blotting-out of sin but that the Incarnation was already the goal of the divine freedom even apart from any divine fore-knowledge of freely incurred guilt. This School holds therefore that—seen as the free climax of God's self-expression and self-effacement into the otherness of the creature—the Incarnation is the most original act of God anticipating the will to create and (presupposing sin) to redeem, by including them, as it were, as two of its moments. In the light of this conception—which has never been objected to by the Church's *magisterium*—it is therefore impos-

sible to say that the view of the Incarnation proposed by us could arouse some real misgivings on the part of the *magisterium*. In the Catholic Church it is freely permitted to see the Incarnation first of all, in God's primary intention, as the summit and height of the divine plan of creation, and not primarily and in the first place as the act of a mere restoration of a divine world-order destroyed by the sins of mankind, an order which God had conceived in itself without any Incarnation. It would be heretical, of course, to deny that the reality and the actual event of the Logos becoming a creature signify also the victory over sin. But this proposition itself does not determine its own 'place-value' (to put it this way) and it can be shown, as we will indicate in a moment, that the proposition concerning redemption from sin can be deduced quite freely, and without forcing things at all, from our own systematic starting-point. Secondly, the unity of the history of the spirit and of matter—of the one corporeal and spiritual cosmos— which was our starting-point, need not and must not be misunderstood to mean that freedom, guilt and the possibility of ultimate perdition by final, self-willed self-closure to the meaning of the world and of its history have no place in this unity. It need not and must not be misunderstood to mean that in such a conception of the world guilt could be nothing more than a kind of unavoidable difficulty which is all part of the development and is included dialectically from the outset as one of the factors of this process. It is also well-known that Teilhard has been reproached with rendering sin harmless in this way—a reproach which H. de Lubac has surely invalidated most lucidly in his most recent book about Teilhard. If such an evolutionary world-view is properly understood, there is no real need to reproach it with this. The cosmos evolves towards the spirit, transcendence and freedom, it evolves in a really essential self-transcendence towards the spirit, the person and freedom. In that moment in which spirit and freedom have been attained in the cosmos, the history of the cosmos receives its structures and its interpretation from the spirit and from freedom and not from matter, in so far as the latter is still in a pre-spiritual way the otherness of the spirit as such. (And this is then true also of the whole cosmos, including its material part, a fact which a purely idealist world-view is completely incapable of explaining; and so by this very fact it reveals its insufficiency for the requirements of Christian theology.) But wherever there is freedom in and before the reality of the cosmos as a whole, and in a transcendence towards God, there can also be a guilt and freedom which closes itself against God: there can also be sin and the possibility of perdition. Whether, and to what extent, this possibility and its actualization are once more conquered by the greater freedom of God in his grace, is a different question again. In any case, it may not be said that freedom and a genuine guilt which can no longer be blotted out by man can have no place in such a conception of the world. Once we have presupposed and emphasized this, it is possible to understand, precisely on the basis of our conception, that in a history which, through the free grace of God has its goal in an absolute and irrevocable self-communication of God to the spiritual creature—in a self-communication which is finally established through its goal and climax, i.e. through the Incarnation—the redeeming power which overcomes sin is necessarily found precisely in this climax of the Incarnation and in the realization of this divine-human reality. The world and its history are from the outset based on the absolute will of God to communicate himself radically to the world. In this self-communication and in its climax (i.e. in the Incarnation), the world becomes the history of God himself. And so if and in so far as it is found in the world, sin is from the outset embraced by the will to forgive and the offer of divine self-communication becomes necessary. For, since on account of Christ this offer is not conditioned by sin, it becomes necessarily an offer of forgiveness and of victory over guilt; indeed, sin is permitted merely because, being finite human guilt, God knew it to remain always imprisoned within his absolute will regarding the world and his offer of himself. This possibility of forgiveness does not originate from man—from 'Adam' as such or from the human stage of history as such—but comes from that power of God's self-communication on which, on the one hand, depends the development of the whole history of the cosmos and which, on the other hand, becomes historically tangible from the outset in its own identity and which, by establishing its own goal, becomes manifest in the existence and existential realization of Christ. And this is the meaning of the proposition which states that we have been redeemed by Christ from our sins. This already becomes clear by the fact that this very decision of God, to give existence to Christ and his saving work, is the basis of this saving work and is not dependent on it; properly speaking, it is not Christ's action which causes God's will to forgiveness, but vice versa, and this redemption in Christ (one might also say: in view of Christ) was already effective from the beginning of humanity. Added to this is the fact that according to Catholic teaching the 'redemption' and destruction of sin must not be understood as a merely moral or legal transaction, or as a mere acquittal from guilt, or as a mere non-reckoning of guilt. It is the communication of divine grace and takes place in the ontological reality of God's self-communication. It is, therefore, in any case the continuation and accomplishment of that existential process which consisted from the very beginning in the supernatural pardoning and divinization of humanity. If it is supposed that this original pardoning of humanity's sin existed and continued to exist not merely as a demand but as an effective force because, and in so far as, it was from the very beginning orientated towards the Incarnation and God's self-communication to the whole human race (and not because it had begun in 'Adam'), then we have formed the idea of the Christian redemption in such a way that it follows of itself from a Christological evolutionary conception of the world. For in this way the original pardoning became of itself also the victory over sin —the obstacle to this self-communication—as soon as this obstacle appeared by man's free choice during the history of the carrying out of this self-communication.

We do not mean to give the impression that we have sounded all the depths and breadth of a harmatology and soteriology by these brief pointers. All we have intended to indicate by our remarks is how redemption incorporates itself into the developed ground-scheme of a Christological evolutionary world-view.

2. We must touch here on a further question. We have, one might say, projected the idea of a possible Incarnation from the formal scheme of a world-evolution which reaches its climax in God's communication of himself. Naturally, the historical nature of human and also metaphysical knowledge permits us in actual fact to formulate such a formal scheme with such clarity only because we already know about the fact of the Incarnation, all of which is possible only *post Christum natum*. This is not however really very surprising. Even a metaphysical reflection always involves 'bringing in' an experience already had. The transcendental scheme of man as a free being, for instance, is transcendental in an *a-priori* way and yet is in fact dependent in its accomplishment on an actual experience of freedom. But there is one thing which cannot be accomplished even in this way, viz. the proof that this transcendental scheme of a possible Incarnation has in fact been actualized precisely in Jesus of Nazareth—in him and only in him. The *idea*

of the God-man and the acknowledgement of Jesus and of no one else as the one, unique and real God-man are two quite different perceptions. Only this second perception, which is one of faith, makes one a Christian. In other words, one is a Christian only once one has grasped the uniquely concrete fact of this particular man, and once it has been grasped as God's absolute expression of himself and as God's pledge of himself to you and me. The fact that the salvation of man does not depend merely on the idea but also on the contingent, concrete facts of real history—that belongs to Christianity. But this again shows the significance of all our considerations. Within our briefly outlined ground-scheme in which the spirit is not something alien in the material world but is the factor by which this bodily reality itself becomes present to itself, all that has really to be made clear is that only a concrete bodily reality—and not a universal idea—can really save and be eternally valid—and that Christianity cannot really be an 'Idealism' if it is properly understood. The act of grasping the concrete reality of this determined man and seeing that it is the reality of the saving God-man is other and more than the *a-priori* projection of the idea of a God-man conceived as the basic ground of a divinized humanity as a whole and as the basic ground in which the world reaches God himself. But it is no longer the task of our present reflections to show *how* by his historical experience and his faith man comes to the knowledge of faith that in the very person of Jesus of Nazareth the history of the world has reached—not indeed its full and absolute perfection—but its unsurpassable final phase of perfection. All we can do here is to draw attention to this further question.

3. A correctly understood incorporation of Christology into an evolutionary world-view must also stop to think about the *point in time* in this one, complete world-history at which the Incarnation took place. Even the theological reflection of the early ages of the Church already found difficulty in answering this question. On the one hand, it regarded the coming of Christ as the end, and as the arrival of the last ages of world-history, as the last hour pointing directly to the end of all history and to an early return of Christ—in short, it saw the coming of Christ as the beginning of the end. On the other hand, the Incarnation and Christ's victory appeared to this reflection as the beginning of a new epoch, as the foundation of a Church which is to expand only slowly in an unforeseeably long history, and as the beginning of a leavening process within the very matter of world-history,

a raw material which only this divinization of the world—which seems to begin in Christ—can change from an unformed material into the form God really intends it to have. Under both these aspects, however, the field of vision of early Christianity was very limited with regard to both the past and future temporal extent of the history it had to interpret in its theology of history. And in both cases this was due to the very limited spatio-temporal horizon of its own historical existence. Today we believe that we know a history of humanity which stretches several hundred times further back into the past than had been imagined in the old days, and we get the impression that, after a very long and up till now almost stagnant starting period, humanity has a history before it, a history whose future in this world has only just begun. Hence, whereas previously one had the impression that God had entered the world through the Incarnation of his Word in the evening of world-history, we now get the impression that (in terms of large periods) he came approximately at the moment when the history of man's active self-possession and of his knowing and active self-steering of history was just beginning. Someone recently estimated the total number of human beings who have lived on this earth up until now to be in the vicinity of seventy-seven milliards; this would mean, therefore, that in perhaps a thousand years from now (which is but a tiny fraction of the total time man has lived on this earth) more people will have lived *after* Christ than before him, and this proportion would then increase ever more rapidly so that Christ would recede further and further towards the beginning of humanity. The really important theological factors in this question may perhaps be expressed briefly as follows:

(a) It is certainly true that Christ is the beginning of the end (it being quite immaterial in this respect as to how long the history of the human race will last and as to what results it will still produce). This is true in so far as in Christ there has basically and irrevocably arrived the event of humanity's radical self-transcendence into God, and in so far as—understood as promise and task of humanity—this event cannot in the very nature of things be surpassed any longer by any further and higher self-transcendence of history. To this extent is the *telos* of all previous ages present in Christ (1 Cor 10.11), and in a way which is unsurpassable.

(b) On the other hand, nothing in this properly eschatological interpretation of the saving period of the New Testament which began definitely and finally with Christ prevents us from seeing this Incarnation also as the start of other, even intramundane ages of humanity, at the very beginning of this epoch. This means that—beginning with Christ and including also the modern age and the future planetary age, with its higher social organization, an age in which man will gain ever greater control over nature and regulate it more and more, instead of just serving it—the history of the West can be regarded as one which in certain not unessential aspects, and viewed from within the world and history without falling into a Communistic utopianism, is only beginning to be that epoch towards which the past life of humanity has been striving and in which humanity is discovering itself actively and not only contemplatively, really and not merely aesthetically— thereby also permitting the world to discover itself.

It is absolutely legitimate to regard this new period as one whose ultimate reason is to be found in the faith of Christianity. For only the demythologization and secularization of the world which not only actually takes place but is willed and carried out by Christianity has turned the world into a material which man himself can manipulate technologically: and only through the Christian message concerning the final self-transcendence of the spirit by grace into an absolute God who is totally distinct from the created world, has cosmocentricity been turned into an anthropocentricity. Viewed in this light, it is perfectly meaningful and understandable that the Incarnation stands at the beginning of this first really all-human period.

4. This leads us immediately to our final consideration. Christology both constricts and frees all intramundane ideological and utopian views of the future, in so far as the dogma of the Incarnation of the Logos does not contain any definite mention about the future course of intramundane history, in so far as it declines to accept any kind of chiliastic view, and in so far as it has already gone beyond the whole history of the world and its future (without wishing to imply that it has declared it to be futile or indifferent) no matter how man may shape it by his efforts in this world. For in the very nature of things, the being directly present to the absolute and infinite mystery of God has necessarily already surpassed any particular form of intramundane achievement of man, including the human achievements of the future, however great they may be expected to be. Christology frees these views, since it does not wish to enter into competition with, or become a substitute for, such intramundane planning of the future, but leaves the latter to

do its own work with regard to determining the duration and content, the planning and the incalculable challenge of the particular matters of man's future. It liberates it because this doctrine of the Incarnation does not deny, but includes the fact that man can realize his transcendental future, his attainment of God in himself, only by means of the material of this world and its history, i.e. also by exposing himself to, and either holding his own or failing in, this intramundane future with both the happiness and death necessarily attendant on it. To this extent, the promise of a supra-historical consummation in the absoluteness of God himself—a promise given together with Christology—does not diminish man's task in this world but provides it with its ultimate dignity, urgency and danger. Because man cannot effect his salvation apart from his worldly task but only through it, the latter attains its highest dignity, honour, danger-point and ultimate significance by this very fact. Through this task man also accepts the salvation which is God himself in his absoluteness and immediacy; time and space are the space of time in which the true eternity matures as their fruit and permanence. At the same time, however, Christology also binds all intramundane categorical projects and ideologies concerning the future. These are never salvation itself but are always only the material which man uses to exercise his openness in order to accept salvation from God's hand, since this salvation is God himself whom man does not create but always finds already there in the ground and abyss of his existence. Thus Christology sobers down and subdues man's own plan of action for the future. The future which man creates by his own action is never the only factor justifying man as he really is. For man is always already justified by God through the decree by which God in his holy, incomprehensible and unspeakable infinity pledges himself to man so that every action of man, right down to the last, consists in the acceptance of God's action on him. But in the long run, this sobered and subdued intramundane will for the future is the more fruitful for the future. In this way, man is not tempted to cruelly sacrifice the present for the future; he does not need to become brutal so as to take eternal peace by brute force; he does not need to let everyone be submerged in a sterile equality when he does not wish anyone to feel himself worse off than anyone else. If Christ is the decisive existential factor of man's life, then man will experience the unrest caused by the infinite extent of a divine future whose greatness overshadows every age and temporal deed; then is there peace, since the real, ultimate and infinite salvation is then already known and accepted as something present and as the gift given to man's action of faith, and does not require to be taken forcibly by the desperate and at the same time ridiculous over-exertion of man for the future; then is the dignity of the individual protected, since then he does not find the sole justification for his existence in using it up for the benefit of individuals of a future still to come, but also remains safe as an individual of eternal worth—safe in God and in his love; then is the community also justified and established with absolute validity in the face of this individual and his eternal dignity, for one cannot find the salvation of Christ unless one loves one's brothers and sisters—Christ's brothers and sisters; then is despair redeemed, for every fall into the abyss of the unspeakable and incomprehensible in spirit and life means falling into the hands of the one whom the Son addressed as his Father, when in death he commended his soul into his hands.

9

DOGMATIC REFLECTIONS ON THE KNOWLEDGE AND SELF-CONSCIOUSNESS OF CHRIST[1]

THE subject of this modest and brief guest-lecture is to consist of a few dogmatic reflections on the human self-consciousness and knowledge of Christ, and so it does not require any long explanations of the problem concerned.[2] Theological tradition attributes

[1] The following exposition forms the text of a guest-lecture given on the 9th December 1961 before the Theological Faculty of Trier. Cf. Karl Rahner, 'Current Problems in Christology' in *Theological Investigations* I (London 1961), esp. pp. 168–174, which corresponds to Karl Rahner, 'Chalkedon— Ende oder Anfang' in *Chalkedon* III (Würzburg 1954), pp. 3–49.

[2] Of the older literature, where it is not merely a case of the corresponding section in the Christologies, we would mention:

F. Brunetti, 'La science infuse du Christ', *Revue des sciences ecclésiastiques* I (1903), pp. 20 *sqq.*, 100 *sqq.*

B. M. Schwalm, 'Les controverses des pères grecs sur la science du Christ', RT XII (1904), pp. 12 *sqq.*, 257 *sqq.*

A. Chiquot, *La vision béatifique dans l'âme de Jesus-Christ* (Brignais 1909).

J. Maric, *De Agnoetarum doctrina* (Zagreb 1914).

E. Schulte, *Die Entwicklung der Lehre vom menschlichen Wissen Christi bis zum Beginn der Scholastik* (Paderborn 1914).

E. Schulte, 'Vom Kampf um das Wissen Christi', *Theologie und Glaube* VII (1915), pp. 392–398.

F. Diekamp, 'Über das Wissen der Seele Christi', *Theologische Revue* XIV (1915), p. 108.

J. Maric, *Das menschliche Nichtwissen Christi kein soteriologisches Postulat* (Zagreb 1916).

K. Weiss, *Exegetisches zur Irrtumlosigkeit und Eschatologie Jesu Christi* (Münster 1916).

O. Graber, *Die Gottesschauung Christi im irdischen Leben und ihre Bestreitung* (Graz 1920).

a knowledge to Jesus as man which embraces and exhausts all past, present and future reality, at least to the extent in which these realities are related in some way to Christ's soteriological task; thus the encyclical 'Mystici Corporis', for instance, attributes to Jesus an explicit knowledge about all men of all ages and places.[3] This theological tradition furthermore attributes to Jesus—from the very first moment of his human existence—the possession of the direct vision of God as it is experienced by the blessed in heaven. Such statements sound

B. Vigné, 'Quelques précisions concernant l'objet de la science acquise du Christ', RSR XVIII (1920), pp. 1–27.

P. Jérôme, 'S. Bonaventura et la science humaine du Christ', *Etudes Francisc.* XXXIII (1921), pp. 210 *sqq.*

F. Tillmann, *Das Selbstbewusstsein des Gottessohnes* (Münster 1921[3]).

V. Kwiatkowski, *De scientia beata in anima Christi* (Warsaw 1921).

P. J. Temple, *The Boyhood Consciousness of Christ* (Washington 1922).

J. Bittremieux, 'La science infuse du Christ d'après S. Bonaventure', *Etudes Francisc.* XXXIV (1922), pp. 308–326.

P. Galtier, 'L'enseignement des Pères sur la Vision béatifique dans le Christ', RSR XXIII (1925), pp. 54–68.

P. Szczygiel, 'Zur Parusierede Mt 24', *Theologie und Glaube* XVII (1925), pp. 379–390.

J. Szabó, 'De scientia beata Christi', *Xenia Thomistica* II (Rome 1925), pp. 349–491.

L. Lumini, 'La dottrina di Gesù e la sua coscienza messianica', *Scuola catt.* LVI (1928), pp. 345 *sqq.*, 421 *sqq.*

A. Carron, 'La science du Christ dans S. Augustin et S. Thomas', *Angelicum* VII (1930), pp. 487–514.

F. Segarra, 'Algunas observaciones sobre los principales textos escatologicos de Nuestro Señor', *Gregorianum* XVIII (1937), pp. 534–578; XIX (1938), pp. 58–87.

L. Ott, *Untersuchungen zur theologischen Briefliteratur der Frühscholastik* (Münster 1937), pp. 351–385.

A. M. Dubarle, 'L'ignorance du Christ chez S. Cyrille d'Alex.', *Eph. Theol. Lov.* XVI (1939), pp. 111–120.

G. de Gier, *La science infuse du Christ d'après S. Thomas d'Aquin* (Tilburg 1941).

A. M. Dubarle, 'La connaissance humaine du Christ d'après S. Augustin', *Eph. Theol. Lov.* XVIII (1941), pp. 6–14.

Cf. also the Blondel-Hügel discussion (January–April 1903) in: René Marlé, *Au cœur de la crise moderniste* (Paris 1960), pp. 114–139.

[3] AAS XXXV (1943), p. 230; Denz 2289.

almost mythological today when one first hears them; they seem to be contrary to the real humanity and historical nature of Our Lord. At first sight they seem to be in complete contradiction to statements in the Scriptures which speak of a developing consciousness in Jesus (Lk 2.52), of a Master who professes ignorance of decisive matters precisely in the soteriological field (Mt 24.36; Mk 13.32) and a Master who is stamped with the spirituality and religious spirit of his age (as is being shown ever more clearly by modern research), so that one almost gets the impression that the only original thing about Our Lord is himself together with the unique combination of environmental influences which, of course, are to be found in every human being. The usual dogmatic theology found in textbooks tells us that we must differentiate between infused knowledge and acquired knowledge (the latter not being contradicted by the former). It tells us that we must think of Our Lord voluntarily and intentionally lowering and adapting himself to his environment, and that we must distinguish between direct and indirect knowledge. But all the time one has the feeling that such information is artificial and improbable, indeed one gets the impression that these explanations achieve only a verbal harmony between the historical and dogmatic statements about the consciousness of Jesus. Our present subject belongs, therefore, to those questions about which one cannot deny that a certain tension exists between exegetes and dogmatic theologians, a tension which is for the most part 'resolved' by the exegete not 'bothering his head' about the dogmatic theologian,[4] and vice versa. Thus the controversy between them does not become manifest, simply because they try to formulate things in such a way that they do not come into open and formal conflict with the conception held by the other discipline, the net result being that one fails to do justice to the question itself. Nevertheless, discussions in the most recent literature on this question show that the desire for an honest exchange of views between the two disciplines, and for new solutions to this problem, is not universally lacking. As examples of this, I would refer the reader to the book written by my colleague Gutwenger[5]

---

[4] Cf. e.g. Otto Karrer, *Neues Testament, zu Mk* 13,32 note, p. 152: 'Even the Son does not yet have the Beatific Vision of God during the time of his pilgrim experience on earth in the way in which he has it sitting at the right hand of the Father.' Present-day exegetes like J. Schmid pass over the dogmatic question arising at this point.

[5] E. Gutwenger, *Bewusstsein und Wissen Christi* (Innsbruck 1960).

which contains the previously mentioned bibliography on this matter, and the Conference of French theologians held at the Dominican House in Eveux which was devoted to Christology and at which our subject was the main topic of discussion. It should also be mentioned at least in passing that there is also an internal dogmatic problem in the theology of recent years concerning the '*Io di Cristo*',[6] Christ's consciousness and his self-consciousness as a creature whether in the form

[6] Cf. on this question, and hence on the more recent literature about our whole subject:

Déodat de Basly, La Christiade française (Paris 1929), 'L'Assumptus Homo. L'emmêlement de trois conflits: Pélage, Nestorius, Apollinaire', *La France Franciscaine* XI (1928), pp. 285–314; 'La Moi de Jésus-Christ', *La France Franciscaine* XII (1929), pp. 125–160, 325–352; 'Scotus docens', *Suppl. à la France Franciscaine* XVII–XVIII (1934/35), p. 164; 'La structure philosophique de Jésus l'Homme-Dieu', *La France Franciscaine* XX–XXI (1937/38).

P. Galtier, *L'unité du Christ. Etre-Personne-Conscience* (Paris 1939²).

H. Diepen, 'La psychologie du Christ selon S. Thomas d'Aquin', RT L (1950), pp. 515–562; 'Note sur le baslisme et le dogme d'Ephèse', RT LI (1951), pp. 162–169.

P. Parente, *L'Io di Christo* (Brescia 1951) (2nd enlarged edition 1955).

P. Galtier, 'La conscience humaine du Christ à propos de quelques publications récentes', *Gregorianum* XXXII (1951), pp. 525–568.

B. Leeming, 'The Human Knowledge of Christ', *The Irish Theological Quarterly* XIX (1952), pp. 234–253.

M. Cé, 'La discussione sulla coscienza umana di Cristo nella teologia moderna', *Scuola Catt.* LXXX (1952), pp. 265–303.

F. Lakner, 'Rezension Parentes', ZKT LII (1952), pp. 339–348.

L. Ciappi, 'De unitate ontologica ac psychologica personae Christi', *Angelicum* XXIX (1952), pp. 186–189.

P. Parente, 'Unità ontologica e psicologica dell'Uomo-Dio', *Euntes docete* V (1952), pp. 337–401 (reprinted in the *Collectio Urbaniana*, Ser. III Text. ac Docum. [1953], pp. 1–68).

R. Garrigou-Lagrange, 'L'unique personnalité du Christ', *Angelicum* XXIX (1952), pp. 60–75.

H. Diepen, 'L'unique Seigneur Jésus Christ', RT LXXX (1953), pp. 62–80.

M. J. Nicolas, 'Chronique de théologie dogmatique', RT LXXX (1953), pp. 421–428.

P. Galtier, 'Nestorius mal compris, mal traduit', *Gregorianum* XXXIV (1953), pp. 427–433.

P. Parente, 'Echi della controversia sull'unità ontologica e psicologica di Christo', *Euntes docete* VI (1953), 312–322.

P. Galtier, 'La conscience humaine du Christ. Epilogue', *Gregorianum* XXXV (1954), pp. 225–246.

B. M. Xiberta, *El Yo de Jesucristo* (Barcelona 1954).

E. M. Bosco, *La scienza umana del Cristo in San Tommaso e San Bonaventura* (Naples 1954).

J. Ternus, *Das Seelen- und Bewusstseinsleben Jesu: Das Konzil von Chalkedon III* (Würzburg 1954), pp. 81–237.

E. M. Llopart, 'Una tesis de Dom. Diepen, O.S.B., sobre el Assumptus Homo oriental y el Concilio de Calcedonia', *Rev. Españ. Teol.* XIV (1954), pp. 59–78.

E. Gutwenger, 'Das menschliche Wissen des irdischen Christus', ZKT LXXVI (1954), pp. 170–186.

J. M. Delgado Varela, 'El tema del "yo de Christo" en la Teologia contemporanea española', *Rev. Españ. Teol.* XIV (1954), pp. 567–581.

P. Inchaurraga, 'La Unidad Psicologica de Cristo en la Controversia Galtier-Parente', *Lumen* III (1954), pp. 215–239.

K. Forster, *Die Verteidigung der Lehre des heiligen Thomas von der Gottesschau durch J. Capreolus* (Munich 1955).

F. Lakner, 'Eine neuantiochenische Christologie?', ZKT LXXVII (1955), pp. 212–228.

M. Cuervo, 'El Yo de Jesucristo', *La Ciencia Tomista* LXXXII (1955), pp. 105–123.

F. de P. Solâ, 'Una nueva explicación de Yo de Jesucristo', *Est. Ecl.* XXIX (1955), pp. 443–478.

A. Peregro, 'Il lumen gloriae e l'unità psicologica di Cristo', *Div. Thom.* LVIII (1955), pp. 90–110, 296–310.

B. M. Xiberta, 'In controversiam de conscientia humana Christi animadversiones', *Euntes docete* IX (1956), pp. 93–109; 'Observaciones al margen de la controversia sobre la consciencia humana de Jesucristo', *Rev. Españ. Teol.* XVI (1956), pp. 215–233.

B. Lonergan, *De constitutione Christi ontologica et psychologica* (Rome 1956).

R. Haubst, 'Probleme der jüngsten Christologie', *Theol. Rev.* LII (1956), pp. 146–162.

R. Haubst, 'Welches Ich spricht in Christus?', *Trierer Theol. Zeitschrift* LXVI (1957), pp. 1–20.

C. Molari, *De Christi ratione essendi et operandi* (Rome 1957).

A. Grillmeier, *Zum Christusbild der heutigen katholischen Theologie: Fragen der Theologie heute* (Einsiedeln 1957), pp. 286–296.

J. Galot, 'La psychologie du Christ', NRT XC (1958), pp. 337–358.

of neo-chalcedonism or a purer Chalcedonian Christology, or from
the view-point of an *Assumptus-Homo*-theology or a so-called 'Basly-
Christology'. A. Haubst gave us a good survey of all this a few years
ago,[7] so that we do not have to enter explicitly into this whole group
of questions occupying current theology. Finally, it should just be
emphasized at the beginning of our reflections that these reflections are
intended to be purely dogmatic. Hence we have neither the intention
nor the competence to carry out a work of exegesis. The only thing we
intend to do in this respect is to offer the exegete a dogmatic conception
of Christ's self-consciousness and knowledge which will perhaps make
it easier than it has been in the face of previous conceptions for him to
admit that this conception is compatible with his own historical findings. We say: that it is 'compatible'. For this is all that is required. It is
not demanded of the exegete that he himself, with his historical methods
or with a biblical theology based directly on the texts, should be able to
arrive at dogmatic statements about the knowledge and self-consciousness of Jesus. These dogmatic statements are indeed ultimately based
on what Jesus said about himself, in so far as what we call the Hypostatic Union of the Logos with a human nature in Jesus Christ is

J. Alfaro, 'Cristo glorioso, revelador del Padre: Christus victor mortis',
Gregorianum XXXIX (Rome 1958), pp. 222–270.

J. Mouroux, 'La conscience du Christ et le temps', RSR XLVII (1959),
pp. 321–344.

C. Molari, 'Aspetti metafisici e funzionali della conscienza umana di
Cristo', *Divinitas* IV (1960), pp. 261–288.

Philippe de la Trinité, 'A propos de la conscience du Christ; Un faux
problème théologique', *Ephem. Carmeliticae* XI (1960), pp. 1–52.

F. Malmberg, *Die sogenannte Logoshegomonie und Christi menschliches
Ich-Bewusstsein: Über den Gottmenschen* (Freiburg 1960), pp. 89–114.

E. Gutwenger, *Bewusstsein und Wissen Christi* (Innsbruck 1960).
Reviews of Gutwenger:

J. Ratzinger, 'Bewusstsein und Wissen Christi', *Münchner Theol. Zeitschrift* XII (1961), pp. 78–81.

A. Turrado, 'Un libro reciente de E. Gutwenger acerca de la Psicologia de
Cristo', *Augustianum* I (1961), pp. 136–145.

J. Pritz, *Zeit im Buch* XV (1961), pp. 18–20.

[7] R. Haubst, 'Probleme der jüngsten Christologie', *Theol. Rev.* LII
(1956), pp. 146–162; id., 'Welches Ich spricht in Christus?', *Trierer Theol.
Zeitschrift* (Pastor bonus) LXVI (1957), pp. 1–20.

ultimately based on Christ's own statements, at least in the light of the paschal experience: in other words, in so far as it has a foundation in the New Testament and in so far as this doctrine of the Hypostatic Union is the basis of the dogmatic statements about the self-consciousness and knowledge of Jesus. This very fact shows clearly, however, that these statements can no longer be *non*-mediate theses of the exegete himself. Hence, when we make a dogmatic statement about the knowledge and self-consciousness of Jesus, right away our only intention relative to the exegete is to arrive at a view compatible with his findings, and to do this as well as we possibly can—but nothing more. For to do more is neither necessary nor possible. Of course, this does not as yet settle the question as to whether the New Testament Christology— in so far as it is different from the statements made by the historical Jesus about himself – already contains statements about the knowledge and self-consciousness of Jesus, including the direct vision of God.

After these few preliminary remarks, we must try to get as directly and as quickly as possible to the very heart of our question, and this by refraining from reminiscing on the history of dogmas and of theology. Such reminiscences could not in any case be presented with the necessary accuracy in the brief space of one hour. What will be said in no way claims to be a binding theological doctrine. It is not intended to be anything more than a conceivable theological conception which is not opposed to the declarations made by the official *magisterium* about our question. It is simply meant to be a theological conception which seems to make sense because it seems to prove itself to be deducible from dogmatic presuppositions which are certain, a conception which without forcing things is compatible with the historical findings of the researches made into the life of Jesus. Since we are going to propose a positive solution which does not alter anything in the declarations made by the *magisterium* even where these have no absolutely binding authority (i.e. are not dogmatic definitions), this also saves us from discussing the question of the exact theological note given to this traditional doctrine in the declarations of the Church's *magisterium*.

In preparing for our reflections proper, it should be stated first of all that knowledge has a multi-layered structure: this means that it is absolutely possible that in relation to these different dimensions of consciousness and knowledge something may be known and not known at the same time. We state this because one gets the impression that the explanation of the knowledge of Christ usually starts with the tacit presupposition that man's knowing consciousness is the famous *tabula rasa* on which something is either written or not, so that this simple 'either-or' is the only possibility with regard to the question of something being written or not written on it. Yet this does not correspond to the facts. Human consciousness is an infinite, multi-dimensional sphere: there is reflex consciousness and things to which we attend explicitly; there is conceptual consciousness of objects and a transcendental, unreflected knowledge attached to the subjective pole of consciousness; there is attunement and propositional knowledge, permitted and suppressed knowledge; there are spiritual events in consciousness and their reflex interpretation; there is non-objectified knowledge of a formal horizon within which a determined comprehended object comes to be present, and this sort of knowledge is an objectified, conscious *a-priori* condition of the object comprehended *a-posteriori*; and finally there is the knowledge about this object itself. All this is really self-evident and yet has not been considered sufficiently when thinking about our present question. In the discussion of our problem, one has always known, of course, that there are different kinds of knowledge, and one has distinguished between infused and acquired knowledge with several sub-distinctions in each of them. Yet in this connection one has always more or less explicitly looked upon these different kinds of knowledge as different ways of gaining objective knowledge, rather than regarding them really as different ways of knowing a reality, i.e. one has considered them as different ways in which things come to be written on the *tabula rasa* of consciousness but not as totally different ways in which a reality can be present in the multi-dimensional space of consciousness. It cannot be our job to draw up an empirico-psychological or transcendental scheme of these different ways in which something may be present in consciousness. The point just touched on is merely meant to indicate the fact of this multiplicity of possible forms in which a reality can be present in consciousness. Our remarks were not intended to give an exact analysis of the mutually distinct ways of being conscious of something, of having knowledge or of being known—it was not our intention to analyse such basic states and conditions.

There are just two things to which we would draw further attention. Firstly there is among these forms of knowledge an *a-priori*, unobjectified knowledge about oneself, and this is a basic condition of the spiritual subject in which it is present to itself and in which it has at the same time its transcendental ordination to the totality of possible objects of knowledge and of free choice. This basic awareness is not knowledge of an object, and normally one does not concern oneself with it. Reflection can never quite lay hold of this basic condition even when it makes an express effort to do so. The conceptually reflex knowledge of it, even when it is present, is never this condition itself but is always supported by it in its turn and for this reason alone never gets an adequate grasp of this basic condition. Furthermore, it is not necessary that the reflection on this basic condition should succeed; it may perhaps even be impossible, and its never quite successful exercise may depend on the external, historically contingent data of external experience, on the conceptual material offered from elsewhere and on its historical character. Ideally, of course, the theses just formulated should be proved exactly and in detail, but this is quite impossible here. But we may get some understanding of their meaning and truth simply by reflecting on the fact that spirituality, transcendence, freedom, the ordination to absolute being found in every, even the most commonplace, act of man which is concerned with any indifferent matter of his biological self-assertion, are not indeed given as a theme or an object, and yet are nevertheless really conscious data. Indeed, they are the most primitive of the data of consciousness, possessing transcendental necessity, and of an all-embracing significance: a significance which nevertheless can only be caught hold of in themes or objects with the greatest effort and then only in a long history of the spirit, hidden beneath the extremely changeable history of terminology and only with very mixed success and the greatest differences of opinion as to their interpretation.

The second preparatory remark consists in a critique of the Greek ideal[8] of man in which knowledge is simply the yard-stick of human nature as such. In other words, a Greek anthropology cannot but think of any ignorance *merely* as a falling short of the perfection towards which man is orientated. Nescience is something which has simply to be overcome, it is not regarded as having any possible positive function. Anything which through nescience is not present is simply something which fails to take place, but this absence is not seen as an opening out of space for freedom and action, which can be more significant than the mere presence of a certain reality. Living at the

[8] Cf. on this Gutwenger, *op. cit.*, pp. 103–104.

present time, we cannot think as undialectically as that about knowledge and ignorance. And we have objective reasons for this. It is
impossible here to develop the positive nature of nescience—of the
'docta ignorantia'—in every direction. We would merely draw the
reader's attention to the following fact. A philosophy of the person and
of the freedom of a finite being, a philosophy of history and of decisions, could undoubtedly show with comparative ease that the fact
of challenge, of going into the open, of confiding oneself to the incalculable, of the obscurity of origin and the veiled nature of the end—
in short, of a certain kind of ignorance—are all necessary factors in the
very nature of the self-realization of the finite person in the historical
decision of freedom. It could be shown quite easily that freedom also
always demands the wisely unobstructed area of freedom and its willingly accepted emptiness, as the dark ground of freedom itself and as
the condition making it possible. In other words, there is certainly a
nescience which renders the finite person's exercise of freedom possible
within the still continuing drama of his history. This nescience is,
therefore, more perfect for this exercise of freedom than knowledge
which would suspend this exercise. There is, therefore, undoubtedly
a positive will for such a nescience. That there is a place for nescience
is always already affirmed and this precisely in the will for absolute
transcendence into the infinite and incomprehensible being as such.
And in so far as the nature of the spirit is directed towards the mystery
of God—in so far as all the clarity of the spirit is founded on the ordination to the eternally Incomprehensible as such, and this even still in the
visio beatifica, which does not consist in the disappearance of the
mystery but in the absolute nearness of this mystery as such and in its
final beatifying acceptance—it becomes once more manifest, from the
point of view of the final perfection of the spirit, that one must be very
careful when one is tempted to qualify nescience as something merely
negative in man's life. Whether this consideration has any contribution
to make to our subject—and if so, what contribution—is something
which will become clear only later on.

We come now very quickly to the very heart of our reflections.
These reflections are of a dogmatic kind. Hence we ask: for what
reasons must one, together with Catholic text-book theology and the
magisterium, ascribe to Jesus even during his life on earth the kind of
direct vision of God which is the basis and centre of the beatific vision
of God enjoyed by the blessed in heaven? If we put the question this

way, it is because we wish to indicate even in the way we put the question, that right from the beginning one ought not to speak here of a 'beatific vision'.[9] For one thing, it is far too easily taken for granted as self-evident that direct contact with God must always be beatific. Without necessarily adopting the Scotist view about the manner of beatitude, it may nevertheless be asked why absolute nearness and immediacy to God, understood as the direct presence to the judging and consuming holiness of the incomprehensible God, should necessarily and always have a beatific effect. Furthermore, is it certain that what is meant, in the tradition of theology, by the consciousness of Jesus is really intended to convey an idea of beatitude by direct union with God over and above this union itself? In view of the data provided by the historical sources regarding Christ's death-agony and feeling of being forsaken by God in his death on the Cross, can one seriously maintain—without applying an artificial layer-psychology—that Jesus enjoyed the beatitude of the blessed, thus making of him someone who no longer really and genuinely achieves his human existence as a 'viator'? If one may reply to these questions in the negative, then the problem occupying us at present is simply a question of determining what valid theological reasons could be brought forward to convince us that we are quite correct in attributing a direct union of his consciousness with God, a visio immediata, to Jesus during his earthly life, but this without qualifying or having to qualify it as 'beatific'.[10]

It will probably be possible to preface this more specific question with a preliminary reflection. We will be able to divide the possible answers basically and in accordance with the facts of the history of theology into two groups. The first group of answers (naturally of many different shades) will attribute this direct union to Jesus because, and in so far as, it starts from the principle that, even on earth, Jesus

[9] As I already emphasized in *Theological Investigations* I (London 1961), pp. 170 *sq.*, note 3. I am delighted to be able to refer the reader to Ratzinger who agrees about this in reference to the same reflection by Gutwenger (p. 90): cf. *Münchner Theol. Zeitschrift* LXXX (1961), p. 80.

[10] The '*beata*' in Denz 2289, or the '*beati*' in Denz 2183, may without question be understood as a specifying and not as a reduplicative qualification. For the fact that Jesus was not simply as blessed on earth as the Saints in heaven cannot really be denied. To maintain this would be the same as the heretical denial of his sufferings which were not merely physiological.

must have had all those perfections which are not absolutely incompatible with his earthly mission, especially if this perfection can be proved to be—or at least probably be—a help or a more or less necessary presupposition for his teaching authority. In this group of answers, therefore, this *visio immediata* is really an additional perfection and gift granted to Jesus, a perfection which is not ontologically bound up with the Hypostatic Union but which at the most is connected with it by a certain moral necessity, just as for similar reasons Christ is for instance credited with infused knowledge, etc. This group of answers to our question is then, of course, more dependent on an appeal to the testimony of the Scriptures and of Tradition than is our second group which will be discussed in a moment. For a *legatus divinus* claiming divine authority, a prophet, is absolutely conceivable even without a *visio immediata*. Furthermore, the principle that Jesus is to be credited with all those perfections and privileges which are not incompatible with his mission (for there are such, as e.g. freedom from suffering), finds itself faced with the question as to whether this *visio immediata*, which is practically always regarded as beatific, is not itself incompatible with the mission and life of Jesus on earth—a question which, in view of the historical evidence of the life of Jesus, could be answered in the negative only with many reservations and obscurities. Beyond this, however, one will have to say that the backing which must be found in Tradition for this sort of reply does not represent too solid a prop, especially when one takes into consideration the Greek concept of self-evidence of quite a few tacit presuppositions in this tradition, presuppositions which are human and not dogmatic. If one appeals simply to the teaching of the Church's *magisterium*, then the dogmatic theologian must be reminded of the fact that it is his very task to show how, and from where, the modern *magisterium* has taken its teaching, since it does not receive any new revelation but only guards and interprets the apostolic tradition and hence must itself have objective reasons for its interpretation of this apostolic tradition. Thus, recourse to the teaching of the Church's *magisterium* does not suffice, especially since this doctrine has never up until now been proposed as a defined and hence binding dogma, and since its content can still be given essentially different interpretations. Even seen in this light, the first group of answers—the extrinsicist theory (to call it that)—has not a great deal to recommend it.

The second group of answers regards the *visio immediata* as an intrinsic element of the Hypostatic Union and hence regards it as simply given bound up in this Union and as something which also cannot be abandoned. Thus in this view, it is not at all necessary to find a proper direct proof for this in the tradition of all ages. Furthermore —and this is a decisive point for our reflections —it follows in this view that this vision can be determined more exactly from the nature of the Hypostatic Union, in such a way that the consequences of this nature for the *visio beatifica* must also be affirmed, and whatever does not follow from it must also be denied theologically, whenever one cannot support it by any other certain and theologically binding additional tradition, which presumably will not be the case.

We must now explain the meaning of this second answer more fully and—for reasons of time —this will have to be done in as brief a speculative reflection as possible, without even attempting to find any confirmation of it in the history of theology. We start then from the axiom of the thomistic metaphysics of knowledge according to which being, and self-awareness, are elements of the one reality which condition each other immanently. Hence, something which exists is present to itself, to the extent in which it has or is being. This means that the intrinsically analogous and inflective nature of being and of the power of being, is in absolutely clear and equal proportion to the possibility of being present to oneself, to the possibility of self-possession in knowledge, and the possibility of consciousness. Let us presuppose this axiom—without being able to develop its meaning and justification more exactly here—and let us apply it now to the reality of the *Unio hypostatica*. The Hypostatic Union implies the self-communication of the absolute Being of God—such as it subsists in the Logos—to the human nature of Christ which thereby becomes a nature hypostatically supported by the Logos. The Hypostatic Union is the highest conceivable—the ontologically highest—actualization of the reality of a creature, in the sense that a higher actualization would be absolutely impossible. It is the absolutely highest manner of being there is apart from God's. The only other form of being which might be comparable with it, is the divine self-communication by uncreated grace in justification and in glory, in so far as both forms of being do not come under the notion of an efficient causality but rather of a quasi-formal causality, since it is not a created reality which is communicated to a creature but the uncreated being of God himself. In as much as the Hypostatic Union involves an ontological '*assumptio*' of the human nature by the

person of the Logos, it implies (whether formally or merely consequently need not be investigated here) a determination of the human
reality by the person of the Logos and is therefore at least also the
actualizing of the *potentia obedientialis*, i.e. of the radical capacity of
being 'assumed', and hence is also something on the part of the creature,
particularly since—as is stressed by scholastic theology—the Logos is
not changed through the Hypostatic Union, and anything happening
(which is the case here in the most radical way) takes place on the side
of the creature. But according to the previously stated axiom of the
thomistic metaphysics of knowledge, this highest ontological determination of the created reality of Christ (i.e. God himself in his hypostatic,
quasi-formal causality), must of necessity be conscious of itself. For,
according to this axiom, what is ontologically higher cannot be lower
on the plane of consciousness than what is ontologically lower. Thus,
given that this self-consciousness is a property of the human reality,
then this ontological self-communication of God is also—and, indeed,
specially and primarily—a factor in the self-consciousness of the human
subjectivity of Christ. In other words, a purely ontic *Unio hypostatica*
is metaphysically impossible to conceive. The *visio immediata* is an
intrinsic element of the Hypostatic Union itself. What has just been
stated is simply intended to indicate what is meant here and thus to
indicate the general direction which the second group of answers tends
to follow in solving the problem stated at the beginning. What we
have said is not meant to imply, however, that all this would not have
to be explained at much greater length and with far greater precision
than we have been able to do here.

We also do not mean to imply that the recognition of the fact of the
visio immediata as an intrinsic element of the Hypostatic Union could
not be reached in some completely different way. It would be possible
to arrive at the same conclusion, for instance, by basing oneself on the
profound reflections made by Bernhard Welte in the third volume of
the work on Chalcedon, under the title of '*homoousios hemin*', where he
shows how in an ontology of the finite spirit the Hypostatic Union is
the most radical (gratuitous) actualization of what is implied in the
nature of a finite spirit as such. After that, it is easy to see that such a
Hypostatic Union cannot be conceived as a merely ontic connection
between two realities conceived of as things, but that—as the absolute
perfection of the finite spirit as such—it must of absolute necessity
imply a (correctly understood) 'Christology of consciousness'; in other

words, it will then be easily seen that only in such a subjective, unique union of the human consciousness of Jesus with the Logos—which is of the most radical nearness, uniqueness and finality—is the Hypostatic Union really present in its fullest being. If one conceives of the relationship between the Hypostatic Union and the *visio immediata* in this way, it is not at all necessary that the latter should always have been attested explicitly by Tradition or Scripture, whereas the Church's teaching on this reality acquires nevertheless a necessity and binding force which is greater than if it were proved with the help of merely morally certain arguments of convenience.

Deriving this doctrine in this way will also give us an insight into *how* this direct union of Christ's human consciousness with God is to be conceived. When we hear about Christ's direct vision of God, we instinctively imagine this vision as a vision of the divine essence present before his mind's eye as an object, as if the divine essence were an object being looked at by an observer standing opposite it, and consequently as if this divine essence were brought into Christ's consciousness from without and occupied this consciousness from without and hence in all its dimensions and layers. Once we have adopted this imaginative scheme (naturally we do not do this reflectively, but for that very reason this schematic representation determines our notion of the vision of God all the more profoundly) then we pass equally unconsciously and naturally to the thought that this divine essence offering itself and viewed in this way as an object of vision from without, is like a book or mirror offering, and putting before Christ's consciousness, more or less naturally all other conceivable contents of knowledge in their distinct individuality and propositionally formulated possibility of expression.

But then we have arrived at the problem with which we started: can such a consciousness have been that of the historical Jesus as we know him from the Gospels—the consciousness of the one who questions, doubts, learns, is surprised, is deeply moved, the consciousness of the one who is overwhelmed by a deadly feeling of being forsaken by God? Precisely this schematic image requiring an immediate conscious union with God and forcing itself upon us as if it were self-evident is not only not demanded but is also proved to be false if we start (as we have tried to indicate briefly above) from the only dogmatic basis we have for the recognition of the fact of this conscious, direct vision of God. For it follows from this that the direct presence to God, considered as a basic

condition of Christ's soul, must be thought of as grounded in the substantial root of his created spiritual nature. For this direct presence to
God is the plain, simple self-awareness—the necessary self-realization
—of this substantial union with the person of the Logos himself . . .
this and nothing more. This means, however, that this really existing
direct vision of God is nothing other than the original unobjectified
consciousness of divine sonship, which is present by the mere fact that
there *is* a Hypostatic Union. For this consciousness of divine sonship
is nothing more than the inner, onto-logical illumination of this sonship—it is the subjectivity of this objective sonship necessarily present
as an intrinsic factor of the actual objective condition. But for this very
reason, this awareness of sonship, which is an intrinsic element of the
objective sonship, must not be conceived as a being-faced-with an
object-like God to which the intentionality of the human consciousness
of Jesus would then be referred as to the 'other', the 'object' facing it.
This consciousness of sonship and of direct presence to God (which is
not something merely known by starting from outside it, but consists
in a direct presence to God which is at once—and absolutely identi-
cally—both the reality itself and its inner illumination) is therefore
situated at the subjective pole of our Lord's consciousness. The best
and objectively most correct way of understanding it is to compare its
characteristic nature with the intellectually subjective basic condition
of human spirituality in general. This basic condition of man—his
spiritual nature, his transcendence and freedom, his unity of knowledge
and action, and his freely activated understanding of self—is consciously present in him not only when he thinks about it, when he
reflects on it, when he forms propositions about it, or weighs up
the various interpretations of this reality. Whenever and wherever he
is and acts as a spirit—in short, wherever he occupies himself intentionally with the most commonplace external realities—this 'looking away
from himself' towards external objectivity rests on this unformed, un-
reflective, perhaps never actually reflected knowledge about himself; it
rests on a simple self-awareness which does not 'reflect' or objectify
itself but which—looking away from itself—is always already present
to itself by way of this apparently colourless, basic condition of a
spiritual being and by way of the horizon within which all traffic with
the things and notions of daily life takes place. This inescapable, conscious and yet in a sense not-known state of being lit up to oneself, in
which reality and one's consciousness of reality are still unseparated

from each other, may never be reflected upon; it may be given a false conceptual interpretation; it may be—and indeed always is—attained only very inadequately and never completely; it may be interpreted from the most variant possible and impossible view-points, using the most assorted terminologies and systems of concepts, so that man may systematically tell himself what he has already always known ('known' in that unformed attunement which is the unembraceable ground of his whole knowledge, the permanent condition of the possibility of all other knowledge, its law and gauge, and its ultimate form). This all-pervading basic condition is present and is conscious even in a person who declares that he has never noticed it.

To this innermost, primitive and basic condition on which rests all other knowledge and activity, there belongs in Jesus that direct presence to God which is an intrinsic subjective element of the hypostatic 'assumption' of the human spiritual nature of Jesus by the Logos. And this conscious, direct presence to God shares in the characteristics of the spiritual, basic condition of a man, for it belongs to it as an ontic factor of that substantial basis whose self-presence constitutes this basic condition. This direct and conscious presence to God must not be understood in the sense of the vision of an object. This fact does not make this direct presence any the less ontically and ontologically fundamental and unsurpassable. But it means that this direct presence is the same kind of presence as is meant by the '*visio immediata*', except that it excludes the element of 'standing opposite' an object, an element which is usually associated with it as soon as one forms an image of 'vision'; we can quite rightly speak of a vision even in this case, as long as we exclude from our notion of vision this particular element of an objective, intentional counter-pole. A direct presence to God belongs to the nature of a spiritual person, in the sense of an unsystematic attunement and an unreflected horizon which determines everything else and within which the whole spiritual life of this spirit is lived. This direct presence to God belongs to the nature of a spiritual person as the ground which, though not allowing us to grasp it completely in a reflex manner, is nevertheless the permanent basis for all other spiritual activities and which, on this account, is always more 'there' and less objectively 'there' than everything else. This presence belongs to the nature of a spiritual person as the tacit factor in self-awareness which orders and explains everything but cannot be explained itself, since a basis is always the clear but inexplicable factor. To make all this still

more precise and more intelligible would require further development and proof of this doctrine of the spiritual, unformed and non-
conceptual and non-objectified basic condition of a spirit. It would
then be possible to say—and it would be more understandable—that
this is also precisely the way in which we must conceive the direct and
personal presence of the Logos to the human soul of Jesus. Since this
more general task cannot, however, be carried out any further here, we
must content ourselves with these modest pointers to a conceivable
understanding of the absolutely immediate nature of the fact that the
Logos is consciously communicated to the spiritual human nature of
our Lord.[11]

We must, however, explain briefly a few further conclusions to be
drawn from this at least briefly outlined theory, which will lead us back
to the series of problems with which we started these considerations.
If we take what has just been said above about the characteristic nature
of Christ's conscious, direct presence to God, and connect it up with
what was said in our first introductory remark, then we may say that
the basic condition of direct presence to God is not only reconcilable
with, but moreover demands, a genuinely human spiritual history and
development of the man Jesus. After all, this basic condition is itself of
such a nature as to demand a fixed form and a spiritual, conceptual
objectification, without it itself having such a form as yet, though
leaving all the necessary free room for it in the *a-posteriori*, objective
consciousness of Christ. In spite of man's always already-given basic
condition *as* a spiritual being, and in spite of the attunement (*Gestimmt-
heit*) which is always present in the very ground of his existence (but
which has nothing at all to do with a 'mood' or '*Stimmung*'), a man

---

[11] We must, therefore, also abstain from dealing explicitly with the controversy between Galtier and Parente (and hence also with the famous
emendation of the Encyclical '*Sempiternus Rex*', between the time of its
publication in the *Osservatore Romano* and its official publication in AAS
XLIII [1961] p. 638), and the literature connected with it. This controversy
refers to the unity and twofold nature of the Ego-consciousness of Christ and
the theory put forward by Galtier as to how the man Jesus knows about the
Hypostatic Union. It can merely be mentioned briefly that whereas in
Galtier's theory Christ knows about the Hypostatic Union because he has the
visio, in our theory Jesus has the *visio*, because he has the Hypostatic Union
and the intrinsic element of this Union, viz. the basic condition of direct
presence to God.

must first 'come to himself', i.e. only in the course of long experience can he learn to express to himself what he is and what indeed he has always already seen in the self-consciousness of his basic condition. In other words, just as there is this objectively reflexive process of becoming conscious of what has always been already understood consciously but without knowing it and in an unsystematic and unobjectified manner, so it is also in the case of Christ's consciousness of divine sonship and his basic condition of direct presence to God. This consciousness in Christ realized itself only gradually during his spiritual history, and this history does not consist only, or even first and foremost, in being occupied with this or that fact of external reality but consists rather in the never quite successful attaining of what and who one is oneself, and this precisely as what and whom one always already possessed oneself in the depths of one's existence. Hence it is absolutely meaningful, and no cheap trick of a paradoxical dialectic, to attribute to Jesus at the same time an absolute, basic state of being directly present to God from the very beginning and a development of this original self-consciousness of the created spiritual nature being absolutely handed over to the Logos. For this development does not refer to the establishment of the basic state of direct presence to God but to the objective, humanly and conceptually expressed articulation and objectification of this basic state; this basic condition is not a fully formed and propositionally differentiated knowledge, nor is it an *objective* vision.

These two notions are not merely not mutually contradictory—they demand each other of their very nature. For it is in accordance with the nature of spiritual, personal history itself, and its whole content, that a basic state should tend to communicate itself to itself, and in a spiritual being the explicit knowledge of its own constitution can always understand itself only in the form of an interpretation and articulation of a basic condition which always supports it again, which can never be fully attained by it, and which consists in the most secret and innermost self-illumination of a spiritual reality. We can, therefore, speak without qualms about a spiritual and indeed religious development in Jesus. Such a development, far from denying the fact of his absolute, conscious and direct presence to the Logos, is based on this fact and interprets and objectifies it. Such a history of the self-interpretation by a spirit of his own basic condition obviously always occurs in his encounter with the whole gamut of his own external history of self-discovery in his surroundings, and in the whole history of his associating himself with his own age. That which was always already present to itself, finds itself in this material. It is therefore absolutely legitimate to try to observe in what pre-established conceptual form and in what eventual development, to be built up without bias and *a-posteriori* historically, this systematizing self-realization of the God-man's basic condition—of Christ's direct presence to God and of his divine sonship—actually took place from the very beginning. It is absolutely legitimate to desire to see which of the notions prescribed by his religious environment Jesus actually used in order to express slowly what he had always already known about himself in the very depth of his being. In principle, at least, such a history of his self-declaration has in no way to be interpreted merely as a history of his pedagogical accommodation, but can quite legitimately be seen also as the history of his own personal *self*-interpretation of himself to himself. For this does not mean that Jesus 'discovered something' which he did not know in any way up until then, but it means rather that he grasped more and more what he already always is and basically also already knows. It is not the task of dogmatic theology (which in this question is to a certain extent *a-priori*) but of the *a-posteriori* research into the life of Jesus, to determine whether anything can be said in particular about this history and to determine the actual course of this history. If this research proceeds properly, it will not find anything—at least in its *a-posteriori* materials —which contradicts such an original basic condition of absolute, direct presence to God. Perhaps it would even arrive historically at the recognition that the unity of this history of Christ's self-consciousness—its inner uninterrupted, clear and unshakable nature—can be explained sufficiently only on the basis of this basic condition even when, historically speaking, the individual factors of the conceptual materials and of the general background of this self-consciousness can or could be derived to a larger extent from Our Lord's religious environment.

What has just been said may suitably be followed by a brief remark about Christ's 'infused knowledge'. Gutwenger has tried to show that there is no constraining theological reason for assuming such knowledge to exist side by side with the direct vision of God and acquired knowledge. Hence it will be quite permissible, for instance, to refuse to accept Ott's qualification of Christ's having such infused knowledge as being *sententia certa*. As far as I can see, the theological discussions of Gutwenger's work have not brought forward any objections against his opinion on this particular point. If one starts from the direct presence to God taken subjectively and understands it as the ultimate basic condition of Christ's consciousness in such a way that it must of its very nature and by a historical development seek to translate itself into an objective knowledge, then it is possible to see implicit in this circumstance the factual content of what is meant by the theory of an (at least habitual) infused knowledge in Christ, and it is then possible to let the whole question rest there. For it is not necessary to conceive of the infused nature of this knowledge as something constituted by an immense number of individual '*species infusae*', but it could be conceived as an *a-priori* basis for a knowledge developing through the encounter with the world of experience.

It might be objected against the theory just outlined, that it certainly asserts that Christ's self-consciousness was radically in the direct presence of God from the very beginning, but that it also teaches that there was a proper history and development at least in the dimension of the conceptual reflection and objectification of this original basic condition, and that this necessarily implies phases in which certain objectifications, developments and expressions of this basic condition were not yet present—in other words, that there was nescience in this sense and in this dimension. We would grant that this kind of initial nescience existed, but would absolutely deny that there are declarations by the Church's *magisterium* or theologically binding traditions which do not allow us to accept such a nescience. In fact, it must be said that— if the doctrine of the true, genuine human nature of the Son as essentially similar to our own is not to be degraded into a myth of a God disguised in a human appearance—such a historicity and 'coming from beginnings' in which what was yet to come (precisely because it was historical) was not always already present, must necessarily be attributed to Jesus. The Church's doctrinal pronouncements command us to hold fast to the direct vision of the Logos by the human soul of Jesus. They do not, however, give us any theological instructions as to what precise concept of this vision of God we must hold. It is perfectly permissible to say that this unsystematic, global basic condition of sonship and of direct presence to the Logos includes implicit knowledge of everything connected with the mission and soteriological task of Our Lord.[12] In this way one will also do full justice to the marginal

[12] We are of the opinion that in this way justice is done to the explanation of Denz 2184. For one will not be able to say that this text commands us to

and incidental declarations of the Church's *magisterium*[13] which point in this direction, without having to suppose for this reason that Jesus possessed a permanent, reflex and fully-formed propositional knowledge of everything after the manner of an encyclopedia or of a huge, actually completed world-history. These remarks will help us to understand what was really meant by our second introductory remark, viz. that not all or any knowledge at any moment of the history of existence is better than nescience. Thus, freedom in the open field of decisions is better than if this room for freedom were filled with knowledge of such a nature as to suffocate this freedom. It cannot simply be retorted against this consideration that the same reasoning would then have to be valid also for the proposed basic condition of direct presence to God, and that this proves our reasoning to be absolutely false, since it is impossible to show it to be valid in this dimension. For this basic condition is precisely that knowledge which, rather than cluttering up, opens up the room for freedom. For the transcendence into God's infinity (no matter how exactly it is to be conceived, i.e. whether it is as in our case or as in that of Christ) is precisely in its infinity the necessary condition for freedom; the transcendental anticipation of all the possible objects of freedom is the very basis for freedom, whereas the objective perception of every individual object right down to the last detail would be the end of freedom. In this connection it may perhaps be observed, finally, that this general conception would also enable us to give a clearer explanation of the eschatological consciousness of Christ.[14] This consciousness does not consist in the prophetic anticipation of the 'last things', but consists in projecting these 'last

---

be of the opinion that Jesus had the same kind of knowledge of everything which God knows by the *scientia visionis*. This is quite inconceivable and is already excluded by the impossibility of a *comprehensio* of God by the human soul of Christ (S. Th. III, q. 10, a.1), since the comprehension and non-comprehension of God is also of significance for the kind and depth of the knowledge of the rest of the possible objects. Once the difference of kind is clear, however, then it will also be clear that Denz 2184 must be interpreted carefully and with reticence.

[13] Cf. e.g. Denz 2289. It must always be remembered that the presence of a loved person in consciousness can be conceived in many different ways.

[14] Cf. Karl Rahner, 'Theologische Prinzipien der Hermeneutik eschatologischer Aussagen' in *Schriften zur Theologie* IV (Einsiedeln 1960), pp. 401–428. (*Theological Investigations* IV [London/Baltimore 1967].)

things' from what Christ knew in his basic condition of divine sonship and direct presence to God. He knows the 'last things' and knows them in so far as, because, by the fact that, and in the way that he knows himself to be the Son of God and to be in the direct presence of God: in this direct presence he knows them absolutely, and in the objective translation of his basic condition he knows them in the way and to the extent in which this condition can be given such a historically conditioned and *a-posteriori* expression with regard to this particular question.

Let us close this whole consideration by formulating a kind of thesis:

The dogmatic theologian and also the exegete are not permitted to doubt the binding, although not defined, doctrine of the Church's *magisterium* which states that the human soul of Jesus enjoyed the direct vision of God during his life on earth. But to begin with, this does not mean that the exegete engaged in the work of fundamental theology must or even can positively take this theological doctrine into account. Furthermore, it is a perfectly theologically correct interpretation of this direct vision of God to understand this vision, not as an extrinsic addition to the Hypostatic Union, but as an intrinsic and inalienable element of this Union, since—after all—it is held to be necessary to understand the Hypostatic Union itself ontologically and not merely ontically. It is then legitimate to be of the positive opinion that such an interpretation can understand the vision of God as a basic condition of the created spiritual nature of Jesus, a basic condition which is so original and unobjective, unsystematic and fundamental, that it is perfectly reconcilable with a genuine, human experience; there is no reason why it should not be perfectly reconcilable with a historical development, understood as an objectifying systematization of this original, always given, direct presence of God, both in the encounter with the spiritual and religious environment and in the experience of one's own life.

PART IV

ECCLESIOLOGICAL QUESTIONS

10

REFLECTION ON THE CONCEPT OF
'*IUS DIVINUM*' IN CATHOLIC THOUGHT

IN this brief investigation, we wish to try to suggest a conceptual 'variation' (to put it this way) on the theme of the concept of '*ius divinum*' in contrast to the '*ius ecclesiasticum*', a variation which may perhaps be found to be in itself conceivable without destroying the notion of a genuine 'divine law', while being at the same time applicable to the reality of historical development and indeed explaining the latter less artificially.

The significance of the 'divine law' for Catholic Canon law is well known; at many points the Catholic constitutional law of the Church and Catholic sacramental law declare a certain norm to be of divine positive law, a norm which is unalterable and which neither flows from natural law nor is simply a positive decree of the Church herself: as e.g. the Papacy, the episcopal monarchical constitution of the Church, the fact that the sacraments are seven in number, the obligation incumbent on the baptized person to submit his mortal sins to the Church's power of the keys, etc. Such and similar rights and duties in the Church—rights and duties which take many forms—are declared to be of divine law; they are traced back to a positive ordinance of the founder of the Church, an ordinance which—because it comes from him—is by this very fact declared to have been instituted as a permanent feature of the Church and to be an ordinance which even the highest authority of the Church cannot repeal. It is a well-known fact that the difficulty of this concept lies not so much in the concept itself but in the particular institution of the Church in which it is declared to be realized. The difficulty lies in the question as to whether the laying down of some particular 'divine law' can be proved historically. Protestant Church law has in many cases disputed that Christ instituted a particular divine law and has refused to accept the proofs brought forward by Catholic dogmatic theology and Canon law since they are inconclusive.[1] And even the more recent, less 'sectarian' historical studies, take up position largely on the side of those who dispute such a 'divine law' in the case of many of the ordinances of Catholic Canon law. Certainly, the fact of there being disputes does not of itself furnish a conclusive argument against the Catholic conception. This is especially true because no one could, seriously and as a matter of principle, be of the opinion that the fact alone of two views having opposed each other for a fairly long time, without one of them being able to dispatch the other from the scene, proves that neither view can bring forward any objective and compelling proofs in its own favour. For it does remain true, after all, that the objectively compelling proof is not necessarily also the psychologically successful one. Extremely optimistic defenders of the democratic principle may perhaps think so. Actual reality, however, seems to persuade us differently. Nevertheless, a profound difference of opinion over many centuries must itself have an objective reason, even though this may not necessarily be the whole reason. What this means is that —with regard to many of these ordinances—it will not be easy for Catholic theology and Canon law to prove the existence of the '*ius divinum*', since history does not readily provide absolutely compelling arguments in these matters. The formal, basic difficulty is always the same in all these cases: the current statement of the 'divine law' as verified in a certain regulation sees this regulation in a fully developed state in the concrete, and in the wide range of the applications and consequences of this statement which states this regulation to be of 'divine law', etc., so that it is quite true to say that in certain periods of the Church this regulation or statement of law is not tangible 'in this form'. And what is cited by Catholic dogmatic theology as being the original 'germ' and the earliest form of this regulation or of this consciousness of law (e.g. also corresponding statements in the Scriptures), is far too equivocal to allow us to identify it in any compelling way with the later institution or legal proposition in its clearness and significance. Even when it is possible to show a material historical continuity between the earlier and later form, it is always still questionable whether the earlier form (e.g. the position held for a time by Cephas in the church at Jerusalem) appeared in its day with the claim

[1] On the doctrine of the *ius divininum* (and of its renewal) in Protestant Church law, cf. above all Erik Wolf, *Ordnung der Kirche* (Frankfurt 1961), pp. 458–469, and Art. '*Jus divinum*', RGG³ III (1959), Sp. 1074 *sq.*

of being valid for all time and of being unchangeable law. One will often say in such cases that in the primitive Church and her life, the Catholic 'divine law' current today was perhaps a *possibility also* actually adopted but that it did not as yet appear there as a clear *reality* besides which there were even then no others equally valid; and thus this particular institution cannot be proved to have been one which did not merely appear as a fact (as, for example, the command that women must cover their heads during divine worship) but also as a fact with the claim of being final and unchangeable. The historian of dogma and of law, who has no 'confessional axe to grind', will perhaps get the impression that he can discover the beginnings of the most varied developments in the early and earliest times of the Church (developments towards a more collegial or more monarchic, more charismatic or more institutional, more local or more supra-regional form, etc.). He may perhaps form the impression that he can regard it as a matter of historical chance which of the many, originally projected possibilities actually gained acceptance, and that such a 'historical selection' can in no way claim to be of obligation—in the sense of being the will of the founder—for all future ages.

At this point, we may be permitted to introduce two subsidiary remarks. Firstly, even the Catholic dogmatic theologian and canonist knows that not *everything* relative to the concrete historical form in which such a *ius divinum* appears or appeared in its own time or in another age, is already of divine law simply because the divine law is only actually real and properly effective in this particular time-determined form in which it appears at its particular time. This is certainly a difficult epistemological problem; in accordance with good scholastic teaching, a metaphysical being or a notion can be known only by a '*conversio ad phantasmata*', by a return to the 'image'. The metaphysical structure is always grasped only by way of a concrete model. This is true even though both are not the same and even though the metaphysical being can also be real in a different concrete sphere. One may define the concept of 'private property' in an extremely metaphysically abstract way. One may try to purify this concept of all elements of historical conditioning and chance. Theoretical considerations in the field of the metaphysics of knowledge may lead one to say most generally and abstractly that the concept and the image do not coincide. And yet, in the concrete and in one's own historical situation, one can think of 'private property'—and use it as a blueprint for life in practice and in the reality of life—only if one thinks of it in the concrete, in an image which one can no longer adequately distinguish in the concrete case from what is meant by the concept proper. For this again would be possible only by the return to another schematic image. And a historical and metaphysical critique of a schematic image—by which the concept referred to is distinguished from this image as something different—again takes place only in a return to *another* schematic image which—when unreflected—again exposes and subjects to its historical conditioning even the critic of the particular historical form of a metaphysical nature. This is also true in our present case. The 'divine law' can never be 'imagined' other than in its historical form. Historical criticism compares one form with another and thus legitimately proves the historical conditioning of the one form, that one form which must be conceded precisely by someone who says that this 'divine law' has existed in the Church from the very beginning (since precisely he more than all others must maintain that this divine law still existed even though in a form which was doubtlessly different from its present-day form). Hence historical criticism must not maintain—at least not in principle—that such a law either must have existed even in earlier times in its present-day form or did not exist at all. This tacit presupposition is the basis of many historical proofs of the non-existence of a currently claimed divine law: according to this presupposition, nature and form are simply identical. Yet there can be identity of nature under different forms. Anyone who denies this in principle denies (at least in the questions which concern us here) the permanent nature of the Church (and this even the Protestant dogmatic theologian and canonist will not do, no matter how formalistic he may be in his reading and interpretation of the Scriptures) or he must affirm the sameness even of the form of this nature, an affirmation which is contradicted by experience. Furthermore, one could prove to him that in the latter case, he tacitly formalizes and 'typifies' the old form of the nature until it can be made identical with the current form. It is certainly true that one will only really be able to explain the phenomena of the Church and of her life in history if one is able to conceive at the same time of the identity of nature throughout the historical variation of its form and the difference of form in spite of the same nature (of the divine law). Of course, this statement merely poses the problem but does not solve it. For the question now is, how are we to conceive a change of form which, while leaving the nature untouched, yet can really be conceived in the way in which, according to the testimony of history, it obviously took place? It is precisely the object of this essay to make a little contribution to this question: but only a very small contribution which does not venture to solve the whole problem.

This brings us to our second subsidiary remark. When we said just now that it is quite impossible to make an *adequately* reflected and material distinction between the nature and the concrete form in which this nature realizes itself, this was in no way meant to imply, of course, that such a distinction cannot be made in any way whatsoever, or that it is not a task to be faced ever anew by theology and Canon law. On the contrary: the always new, always more clearly posed and answered question about the distinction between the nature and its historically conditioned form belongs even with regard to questions about the divine law in the Church to the most basic tasks of dogmatic and canonical Ecclesiology. One may perhaps be of the not too unreasonable opinion that more could be done than has in fact been done on the Catholic side to answer this question. How little, for example, is said nowadays about the question as to what should be the actual form today of the balance between the primatial and episcopal structure of the Church, both of which are declared to be of divine law by Catholic Ecclesiology. This can only be remedied by a really accurate description of the relationship existing today between these two structures, by an ecclesiologico-sociological analysis of those causes of this present-day form which are not to be found merely in the *ius divinum* of these two structures, and (because the problem cannot be solved without it) by an ever new, dispassionate comparison between the current form and the many earlier forms of this relationship. Such a comparison presupposes for the Catholic historian of dogmas and laws—*qua* Catholic—knowledge of what he has to expect and what it is not necessary for him to expect *a priori* with regard to the permanence in nature throughout the changes of history. (This applies to him even in so far as he proceeds methodically *as* a believer and does not regard this *a priori* as a check on, but rather as a sharpening of his capacity of gaining historical knowledge, since it gives him a greater inner sympathy with the object to be known—a sympathy which is a presupposition of all really objective knowledge—whereby the Catholic researcher is not only permitted but basically even offered an apologetic historical investigation, i.e. an investigation which does not already proceed from the *a priori* of faith.) This question cannot be simply dismissed by the statement that he must expect that the one and the same nature of the Church—a nature which Catholic Ecclesiology declares to be *iuris divini*—was always already present, and that he can (presumably) also discover this one nature *a posteriori* in history. This question cannot simply be dismissed by stating that he may dispassionately expect (since the Church is a historical immensity) that a not insignificant change of form will be connected with this permanence of nature. For the historian always meets the nature only in its actual form. Thus the question arises as to what in the concrete form he must recognize as 'essential', i.e. as '*iuris divini*', and what not. After all it is not as if the only answer to this question were:—anything which was recognized even in those days *as* being *iuris divini*. This is a very analogous situation to the history of dogmas in general.

It is rightly said in Catholic dogmatic theology that only what tradition has always handed down as divinely revealed—whether it be in an explicit statement or implicitly contained in another statement explicitly handed on by Tradition—can be defined as an absolutely binding statement of faith. The difficulty about this proposition is that, for instance, the statement to be defined here and now may indeed have been always or for a long time expressed in tradition but without any previous explicit qualification *as* a statement revealed by God and binding in faith, and that moreover it may have been stated among a great number of propositions without any clear distinction from other statements which certainly cannot claim to have been divinely revealed. How, then, can one recognize the revealed character of the earlier statement, if in the past it did not carry—at least in a clearly recognizable manner—the mark of revelation, and if this recognition as revealed must not nevertheless be the consequence of the present definition but rather the presupposition of the lawfulness of this definition, at least for the Church's *magisterium* itself?

This same question arises also with regard to the *ius divinum* in the Church. It is not fully answered by showing that such a statement of law or such an institution obtained previously. The question is: did this *divine* law, even in those days, make the binding claim to be the *divine* law—and if this was not the case or cannot be proved to have been the case as clearly as is to be desired—how, then, can one recognize that it is not merely a law in fact applied but was instituted by the founder of the Church as an unchangeable law binding on all later ages? Even if one can or could appeal to the fact that the Lord of the Church has commanded something like this, this does not mean that the question has been clearly answered. For one just cannot seriously maintain that all the ordinances given by Jesus or by one of the Apostles lay claim to being a binding law for all time. As they stand, the different regulations in Mt 18 about fraternal correction, for instance, are surely tacitly abrogated as outdated (even if one says that, in different circumstances, their spirit is preserved in new and different forms); the precept about women covering their heads is also not a norm of divine worship binding today. The division of the different kinds of authority belonging to the Church into *those* offices which exist today may reasonably be regarded as not simply binding for all times, even when this division goes right back to apostolic times. Could the Church, for instance, discontinue the diaconate as a sacramental step in the hierarchy which is *iuris divini*? If one feels that this must simply be denied, one could ask whether the Church has not long ago begun to discontinue it, as far as the thing itself is concerned and not merely the title and legal fiction, even though (in the Latin Church) she is perhaps thinking again today about reintroducing even the separate reality of the diaconate. In brief, one cannot simply maintain that every legal reality of apostolic times, or legal realities which can appeal to a declaration made by Jesus or the Apostles, are by this fact alone of divine law. If this cannot be presupposed, however, then a *ius divinum* does not so easily follow from an *a-posteriori observation* of the legal structures of the primitive Church, even when the change of the form in this particular structure since that time is said not to have been so very great. Hence the question remains: how does one recognize in such ancient legal structures the characteristics of a *ius divinum*, when they did not state this explicitly at the time? To what extent can the idea (nature) and the form be separate from one another without losing the real, historical existence and continuity of a legal reality *iuris divini* in all ages of the Church? In other words, what change of form can one expect at least without having to say right away, as a Catholic, on account of the permanence of the *ius divinum*: it cannot have been this way, because this or that must always have been so already since it is recognized as divine law by the present-day Church?

This is the question to which the following consideration tries to give a partial answer. We readily admit from the start that our consideration may be of interest only to Catholics since, at least to begin with, it simplifies and clarifies a problem which only the Catholic is faced with (in this particular way). Whenever it is denied right from the outset—by appealing to the facts of history—that this or that legal reality, which the Catholic declares to be of divine law, existed in the apostolic Church, it is of course at once superfluous to try to grasp the idea of a possibly very great change in form which nevertheless does not destroy the continuity of nature and so leaves open the possibility of maintaining a *ius divinum* with regard to the legal matter in question. But perhaps the notion we are going to develop will not be without some interest even to someone who disputes its application to the particular cases envisaged here. Space and competence do not permit us to make use of the historical materials themselves in developing the carefully defined concept of the divine law we are going to propose. It must also be emphasized very clearly that we are not particularly concerned with providing any real proof of the fact that this concept of a possible species of divine law is actually realized in a particular historical structure (for instance, in the papal primacy of jurisdiction or in the monarchic episcopate, etc.) or that the development of such determined institutions can certainly only be explained by applying this notion. Naturally we have definite historical facts in mind. The proposed concept, after all, is not meant to be merely a speculative possibility or a play on words. But a proof as to whether, where and how this concept is to be found in concrete historical structures and developments will nowhere be given by this investigation of the concept. If there are vague allusions to historical matters, this is meant in the sense of a clarifying illustration without maintaining at the same time that the illustration corresponds with certainty to historical reality. We will construct our proposed concept synthetically by a series of individual considerations.

1. The historical development of a historical structure is not necessarily reversible simply because the development in question is a state which did not always exist. There are one-way historical processes which are no longer reversible. This is true even if these processes were not necessary, i.e. even when the preceding state was neither a fact nor a necessity which was bound to lead to the state in question. If we take this statement in its most general sense, then it is no doubt a self-evident statement for any historical thinking which really considers something existing historically, i.e. something which has a history in the sense that this history is essential to it. We take the

liberty not to give any further proof for this statement in the present context. Yet this statement is not simply a self-evident truth for our consideration, a truth on which one need not waste words. For one can surely question whether the average Catholic jurisprudence does not overlook or tacitly deny it in the matters which concern us here. For one may get the impression that the dogmatic and canonistic ecclesiastical jurisprudence tacitly starts from the thought that what can be ascertained only as something which has developed at some point in the history of the Church—at a later point in time and not already in the apostolic age—shows itself, even by this fact alone, to be changeable and at least in principle to be reversible. If the general statement made above is correct, then this tacit presupposition is at least unproven and at least may not be presupposed as self-evident. For surely it is *a priori* absolutely conceivable that even juridical realities may belong to such historically developed and yet irreversible factors of a one-way history. The contrary would at least have to be proved first, since the above statement proceeds from the universal nature of historical reality and thus includes also juridical reality, at least until the contrary is proved. This is true especially since any structure with a real history is essentially (even though perhaps not exclusively) of a juridical nature. Such a structure—if it were always reversible—would have to be either unhistorical (or respectively its juridical nature would have to be untouched by its history) or this itself legal history could only be of a very peripheral kind. But a law which is 'historical' only in the sense of being reversible in any direction of its development one cares to choose, basically could not be anything really present in historical reality. For—no matter how paradoxical this may seem at first sight—a law, if it is to be the law of a real history and in a real history, does not become more valid and real by the fact that it knows of no history. The more unhistorical it is, the more unreal it will also be. (Nor is this contradicted by the properly understood doctrine of the 'natural law': for this doctrine takes for its basis the nature of man, a nature which has a true history, even though it always remains metaphysically the same. This metaphysical identity does not itself exclude but, on the contrary, includes a history which co-determines this nature as such, because the spiritual history of persons is not an accidental layer surrounding an unchanging nature but is the very history of this nature, especially since the nature of individual human beings receives an eternal determination from this history and will always exist only in this way—either saved or damned.) Hence we regard this proposition as at least meaningful and conceivable: even a genuine history of law can be one-way and irreversible within the history of man; basically, therefore, there can be legal creations which, although they come into being at some point in time, can nevertheless be valid for all time and can be a now inseparable element of a historical structure. Whether, where and how this statement can be shown to be verified in concrete reality is something which we cannot and need not investigate more closely here. Suffice that we have at least indicated a basic logical possibility.

2. There are processes within a historically existing reality which at least can be recognized as legitimate by the nature of this existing reality, even though they spring from a free decision and even though these processes and decisions cannot be proved to be the only possible ones, and hence cannot be proved to be the only obligatory means for the nature of the historically evolving reality. In order to get a clear idea of what this statement means, let us take the concrete example of an individual, spiritual and freely acting person. Such a person can make decisions. These decisions may determine this person's fate and history at least for a long time ahead. These decisions may be physically free and—measured by the moral norm binding this existing being—one can recognize them as not offending against this norm. For this they do not need to be such as to be simply binding in a determined historical situation of this individual by reason of his nature and its essential norms. It suffices that these decisions conform to the nature of this existent and to the norms to which such an existent is subject; in short, it is quite sufficient if they are *one* of the possible fulfilments and realizations of nature for this existent. No one who believes in the physical and (at least partially existing) moral freedom of a person, will be able to deny that there are such decisions: decisions, that is, which are in conformity with nature bu' ot of the necessity of nature (either physically or morally). Naturally non-necessary decisions can be such either in themselves or *quoad nos*, i.e. not recognizable by us as anything more than non-necessary decisions which nevertheless are in conformity with nature. Both of these are fundamentally possible, even though this does not permit us to deny that there is a very great objective difference between decisions which are merely in themselves in conformity with nature and those which we cannot see to be anything more than this. Yet we may lump

both of these in themselves quite different kinds of decision, under the one concept. This is quite legitimate for the following reason: it may quite easily happen that in most cases (indeed, in a strict metaphysics of knowledge, perhaps in almost all cases) it cannot be recognized whether (in itself) the fact that a certain decision is in conformity with nature, is such *only quoad nos* and in reality hides a necessity of nature (or respectively, announces it in this conformity to nature) or whether it is really merely a question of *de facto* conformity to nature. This concept of a 'decision in conformity with nature, even though not in itself or *quoad nos* of the necessity of nature', can also be applied—beyond the field of the individual, physically free person—to historical structures of a more complex nature. Even a society, a State, a Church, etc., can be the subject of such decisions of either kind. To the extent and in the way in which we can attribute a free decision to a moral person (we are not going to treat here how and to what extent we can attribute it)—since this is certainly possible in some meaningful way or other—we can also predicate the possibility of such acts of a moral person. Nobody can seriously doubt this. For it is undoubtedly possible to bring forward examples of decisions made by a State, etc., which are genuine expressions of the historical 'physiognomy' of this structure, and which correspond to or contradict its historical 'mission' and perhaps its right constitution, etc., without it being necessary to say in the former cases that such a collective structure could be or was able to decide only in this way in the situation concerned.

3. It is possible to conceive of such a historical decision—a decision in conformity with nature even though not necessary by nature—which is both of a juridical nature and itself creative of law (in the sense of proposition 1), and irreversible. Anyone who admits our first two propositions will not really be able to object to this third one. For there is no reason which could prevent the combination of the idea of the first proposition with that of the second. On the contrary, if and where a law is irreversibly established (and if the historical structure establishing it is not to annul itself or to become rigidly fixed and so tend to destroy itself by such an establishing of a law), the irreversible establishment of the law must be understood to be at least in conformity with nature, even though it need not always be of the necessity of nature. For otherwise it is impossible to make it intelligible *why* such a positive, irreversible institution of law should be irreversible. In itself, it is quite possible to conceive that such an

irreversible juridical decision and establishment is also of the necessity of nature. For it would be unhistorical to think that what is necessary by nature in an existent must therefore also have been actually present from the very start, and hence that the mere fact of something appearing at a later point in time by being (explicitly or implicitly) established as a law, already proves that it was not of the necessity of nature, and that in such a case it can therefore be at the most a question of whether this decision can be seen as something in conformity with nature or as something contrary to nature. Of course, whatever belongs necessarily to the nature of a spiritual, personal being in the physical or social order must always have been already present in some way or other as soon as the nature in question was present. The basic nature must contain within itself whatever belongs necessarily to that nature. But the question is how it must or also must not contain it. It is certainly possible, for instance, to characterize the faculty of sight, the capacity to laugh or the capacity to make contact with the surrounding world by free decisions, etc., as being of the necessity of nature, or as belonging with absolute necessity to the nature of man. And yet one will not be able to say that these necessities of nature are present in the embryonic stage of a human being in the same way as later on, nor will it be possible to say that what is added in this way later on must no longer be designated as being 'necessary to the nature'. A nature fulfils itself and evolves out of the basic condition in which what evolves and appears was undoubtedly already contained, but contained precisely after the manner of the basic condition and of possibility; what thus evolves is precisely its nature and not something added to this nature afterwards as something indifferent to the nature. If this is basically correct, then it must be said absolutely that something which appears later on can still be something necessarily belonging to the nature. Since, however, the sheer beginning and basis of a reality cannot be attained directly in itself (at least not in most cases or for the most part) and since what is contained in this basis appears only in the achieving of the nature, in the appearance of what evolves from that basis, it is not so easy to judge as to whether something which is historically established later on belongs necessarily to the nature or is merely in conformity with the nature and as such (for this or that reason) irreversible.

4. An irreversible, law-establishing decision of the Church which is in conformity with her nature (which corresponds legitimately to that

nature) can be regarded as '*ius divinum*' when it took place at the time
of the primitive Church. Much in this proposition requires explanation.
Thus, first of all, the notion of 'primitive Church' in its particularly
pregnant theological sense. We might also have called it perhaps the
'apostolic age'. In any case, it means that age during which—in the
Catholic understanding of faith—the time and history of New Testament revelation was still open. For, however much the Apostles and
the authors of the written New Testament are in the last analysis
ambassadors and witnesses of the word of Jesus and of *his* history,
the Catholic understanding of faith has never doubted for one moment
that we must basically count with the fact that the Apostles were not
merely the first generation of those who pass on revealed truth—the
first link of Tradition—but are also to be regarded as vessels of
revelation, in any case in the sense that we do not have first to question
critically what they say as to whether they transmit by this the teaching
of Jesus or merely communicate their own 'thoughts'. However much
one may ask oneself in the field of fundamental theology and in the
history of dogmas as to what, for instance, is the 'source' of St Paul's
knowledge of what he says—in other words, however much one may
try to understand his teaching as his 'theology' (i.e. as the legitimate
unfolding of the simple message of Christ himself)—it remains true
that the message of the Apostles is for us still an 'event of revelation'
and not merely the authoritative transmission of this message. In
accordance with this realization, the Catholic understanding of faith
is accustomed to express this fact by saying that with the death of the
last Apostle the official Christian revelation is closed, and that from
then onwards the task of the Church is merely to protect this completed revelation—to proclaim it, interpret it, guard it against error,
unfold it as required by the spiritual situation of a particular age—but
not in the proper sense to 'increase' it further. Conversely, however,
this means that the Church supposes that revelation still took place
during the apostolic age and that this era of the occurrence of revelation must not be simply regarded as already closed with the death or
Ascension of Jesus. We would prefer to speak of this period in a
theological sense as the age of the primitive Church. However much
it is true that the Apostles (the Twelve, with Peter and Paul standing
in a relationship difficult to define but one with which we are not concerned here) played a leading and unique role during this period, we
would prefer to call it the 'primitive Church' rather than the 'age of the

Apostles'. For, on the one hand—as is shown by the writings of a Luke and of a Mark or by an Epistle to the Hebrews—there are other vessels of such a revelation (and inspiration) besides the actual Apostles in the strict sense of the word, and the fact is not altered by saying that they are this as pupils of and as commissioned by the Apostles. It is true that—understood as a historically temporal process by which the full belief in Jesus as the Son of God, as the Christ and only Redeemer (together with everything this implies) becomes conscious of itself—the whole process of revelation is to be conceived as being already supervised and turned into norms by the actual Apostles in a 'magisterial', authoritative sense even during this period of the primitive Church, and as being valid and lawful only in conjunction with them. (In this sense, the old tradition that Mark wrote the Gospel according to St Peter, Luke the Gospel according to St Paul and that the author of the Epistle to the Hebrews wrote it in the name and by order of St Paul, has an absolutely true and real meaning.) Yet all this does not deny, but reaffirms, the fact that it was not simply the Apostles alone who were themselves the vessels of the process of revelation still going on in the primitive Church. This is particularly true since the opposite view would again leave us faced with the question as to what 'canonical' position St Paul holds in relation to the Twelve, and whether even he, as a vessel of revelation, does not himself prove the view we have just expressed, viz. that not only the Apostles are vessels of revelation, since he can no longer be called an Apostle in the strictest sense (realized only by the Twelve). Moreover, it is presumably indicated that one should not terminate the age of the primitive Church too absolutely with the physical death of the last Apostle. For if one understands this *terminus ad quem* too chronologically, then one will affirm implicitly that it is absolutely necessary and certain, for instance, that the Epistle to the Hebrews, the second Epistle of St Peter and the Gospel according to St Luke, were written before the death of the last Apostle. It will be much more prudent and objective not to declare this categorically but to leave it an open question. The meaning of the proposition that the New Testament revelation was concluded with the death of the last Apostle is thereby nevertheless retained: the first generation of the Church provided the authoritative 'beginning', the permanent norm, the all-supporting foundation and the unsurpassable law, for all subsequent Christianity. For it bore in its womb the one who is the absolute Word of God in the flesh, and this 'his' age—an age necessarily belonging to him and an age whose faith in his message and reality is still constitutive of this message itself—remains the kairos which will never be replaced. This, then, is what we mean by the primitive Church, when we say first of all that Law-establishing, irreversible decisions in conformity with the nature of things can have been made in her. This proposition is nothing more, to begin with, than an application of the thesis stating that the age of the primitive Church was still the age of active revelation, and not merely an age of the transmission of revelation. It is possible, of course, since even legal propositions can be part of the contents of such a revelation. This is primarily simply self-evident for the Catholic understanding of faith. For if there is any law at all in the Church which can be called divine law (i.e. legal propositions or at least—and this even a Protestant canonist will not deny absolutely— facts and perceptions which of themselves demand a law of a very special kind), then this means that such a law is 'revealed' since it is not intended to be merely natural law but the spiritual law of the Church herself historically instituted by Christ. If revelation only terminates at the end of the time of the primitive Church, at the end of the apostolic age—and if we must not terminate this time before that—then we have the right and duty to expect also to find revelation of juridical norms during this period, and this during the whole of this period. The above-mentioned first part of our proposition would still be a completely self-evident truth for the ecclesiologist to this extent. But it signifies more than what we have so far indicated.

Our proposition implies primarily a definite, possible conception of the nature of revelation as it appears on the basis of human experience. Revelation appears as 'decision'. In the Catholic theology of the schools, the word 'revelation' is only too easily and almost instinctively associated with the image of a kind of purely passive hearing of a proposition communicated word for word. Revelation may indeed be conceived in this way, but it does not need to be. The fact, for instance, that a gospel is inspired, depends also on the real decision to write it, a decision belonging to the particular evangelist who no doubt experienced the writing as his own spontaneous decision. Of course, it is quite correct to say that the quality of this decision must be known from elsewhere. But where the event can be known only from revelation itself with regard to its inner characteristics, its positing may also be thought of as a moment in the process of revelation itself.

For it proclaims itself by itself, it reveals *itself*, even though its most proper, intimate quality (as, for instance, its 'being inspired') cannot be recognized by this alone but can be grasped only in a wider context. This does not, however, detract from the fact that the process of writing a gospel belongs itself to the factors concerned with the revealing of its inspired character, especially since everything belonging to this revelation as its constitutive element must not be conceived as the simple communication of a proposition about its inspired nature. The process is far more complicated than that; it certainly contains elements which are in their turn processes and realities—and not directly propositions about such processes and realities[2]—in which we can read the fact of inspiration, presupposing certain other revealed propositions. For it is impossible to discover or postulate with historical probability anywhere in the apostolic age propositions testifying directly to the fact of something being inspired. If, as in the view of quite a few theologians, the primacy is indissolubly bound up with the office of the bishop of Rome, and if the primatial See cannot legally be transferred by a later holder of primacy to a different See (*de jure* and not merely *de facto*), then this circumstance (presupposing other more general propositions) is obviously brought about as well as revealed by St Peter's decision to go to stay permanently in Rome. Why should we not, on the one hand, regard the election of Matthias and his co-optation into the apostolic college—in short, his belonging to this college—as revealed and, on the other hand, regard it as brought about by the decision to choose him and indeed revealed *in* this very decision? Events can certainly have the character of a definite material revelation; this presupposes merely that they take place, as it were, in the field of men who already have a certain amount of knowledge of revelation and thus in the light of such knowledge are in a position to judge such an event, and the determined quality of the event which can be known only through revelation. It is not then possible to say that only the material principles are revealed and not the quality of the event which is known with the help of these principles. At least one will not be able to say this as far as the apostolic age is concerned. For if one regards the quality of the event concerned to be revealed, if it is realized (at least

[2] Cf. on this: K. Rahner, *Über die Schriftinspiration* (Freiburg 1959). (English translation: *Inspiration in the Bible*, Quaestiones Disputatæ I [Edinburgh/London 1961].)

by the Apostles) not on account of a completely new and proper initiative of revelation on the part of God but with the help of these universal principles, and if these principles alone—as merely universal propositions—do not in any way provide us with this insight into the quality of the event concerned, then the event itself must quite simply be regarded as playing a role in its own revelation. It reveals itself. Free events, therefore, can certainly have the character of revelation in the age of the primitive Church. They are human decisions, and in them precisely is accomplished God's will to reveal, a will which desires, brings about and reveals this event in all its characteristic nature in and through this freedom of decision pre-defined by this will. Hence, if it is said that this and that particular fact was realized by a free decision of the Apostles, then this does not deny the revealed character of this fact though it was brought about by a free decision, but it does give rise to an idea of the *way* in which this revelation took place in the particular case, at least if we presuppose this free decision to be desired by God in a free and formal pre-definition. This does not yet tell us *what* particular quality in a law-establishing decision taken in the primitive Church is revealed by this decision within the totality of the primitive Church (and within the totality of her knowledge about herself). We will have to treat of this later on. At the moment, it is important for us to see something else with regard to this decision, a decision to which we attribute the possibility (but not always and necessarily the fact) of being a process of revelation: we must see that such a law-establishing decision can quite easily take the form of a choice between *several* possibilities. The establishing of a law can quite easily have the character of a selective decision between several possibilities presenting themselves. The other possibilities neglected in favour of the one chosen, may be not merely physically but also ethically and juridically possible; the establishment of the law may be truly a decision. Hence, if it may or might be possible to prove that within the primitive Church there were different possibilities of constitutional and juridical concretization of the Church, possibilities which are still recognizable even to the regard of the historian—if it could be shown that certain absolutely different 'modes' of a possible evolution of the constitution and of the law offered themselves at that time—then this certainly does not mean that the actual decision (e.g. in the direction of a monarchical episcopate in distinction to a more collegial constitution) must be contrary to nature merely because it chooses *one* possibility instead of another. It is not necessary, therefore, to imagine the situation of the primitive Church either as if, right from the start and at every moment, the juridical decisions appearing during this period were present as the only *possibility*, or as if even after such decisions the different possibilities must necessarily still have remained rightful possibilities which could be realized later on. Hence if one should, for instance, get the impression as a historian that all the different 'constitutions' of the later Christian confessions were already in some way and to a certain degree present and prefigured in the primitive Church, then this is no argument (at least not one which is decisive by itself) for saying that this multi-potentiality of the primitive Church system must always remain even later on as a legitimate possibility. It is quite possible that the Church took an irreversible decision (since this is basically possible) and decided in favour of a certain possibility, and that this decision should then remain binding on all later ages. To begin with, all that this demands is that one can prove that such a decision was not contrary to but in conformity with the nature of things. This is true even if it is at least not immediately comprehensible that this actualization of one possibility before others, understood as an irreversible process, was necessary with a necessity of nature. Such a process is at least thinkable: the Church (within the period of the primitive Church, being the time of the still-occurring revelation) decides in a process of juridical concretization and by an irreversible decision establishing a law in which particular direction and manner, out of all the given possibilities, she wants to actualize her own juridical nature.

If, and in so far as, such a decision can be regarded as a process of revelation (as has already been shown to be the case) then there arises the question as to what exactly in this process of decision has been revealed by it (within the known, total situation of the Church). First of all—given the presupposition that such a selective, law-establishing process did occur in the primitive Church—it can certainly be said that the legitimacy of this decision, its conformity to nature, is revealed. So much may be said to start with in any case. The primitive Church was fully capable of being convinced in connection with such a process that she had properly fulfilled and developed her nature, or at least had not done anything contrary to it, even though other possibilities of decision might 'of themselves' also have been open to her. When the Catholic theologian of the later Church acknowledges the

Pope's basic right and authority to decide, and in certain circumstances even infallibly, about whether, for instance, the constitution of a particular religious Order is a legitimate way of genuinely following Christ—a way which substantially is in sufficient conformity with the Gospel—then we must *a fortiori* acknowledge the right and authority of the apostolic Church (under its legitimate ruling power, whatever this may have been at that time) to recognize that a certain constituted nature given by her to herself is in conformity with her original law, i.e. that this constitution is a legitimate mode of her realization of herself in conformity with her nature. She must be able to do this. For, on the one hand, she *must* act and fulfil her nature in a completely *determined* manner. And, on the other hand, being the Lord's saving community fulfilling itself in this way because it is eschatologically indestructible, she must have the consciousness of her substantial identity with the Church of Christ and with her own beginning. Hence she makes this decision *as* something legitimate, she makes it in her role of *primitive Church*, she makes it with the consciousness of being and remaining the norm and standard for all times, she therefore expects the recognition of this lawfulness even from her later generations, and she reveals the fact that this decision is in conformity with her true nature. To conceive the process of the law-establishing decision in the primitive Church as a process of the revelation of the lawfulness of this selective decision causes no theological difficulties. Is it possible to go further (a second step) and make it intelligible that in the occurrence of this process the irreversibility of this decision, and hence its permanently binding character for all later generations of the Church, is also revealed, notwithstanding the fact that this decision originated out of a multivalent situation of the concretizing self-realization of the primitive Church? This question may rightly be answered in the affirmative. To begin with, it must be emphasized (in conformity with what has been said previously) that the irreversibility of an action and decision is not something particularly strange and surprising, but rather is exactly what one should expect in the light of the nature of freedom. The primitive Church (as can be shown *a posteriori*) continued to take juridical decisions with the consciousness that these were final decisions binding on all later ages. A case in point would be when St Peter baptized without demanding of the pagan recipient of baptism that he pass through Judaism and its practice of circumcision in order to become a full member of the

Church. It is possible to say that such a decision was required by the nature of things and necessarily flows from the belief in the redemption by Christ alone. But it nevertheless had to be taken, and it was deduced from what the Apostles must always have known already about Jesus Christ and his significance for salvation. For, in the abstract, it would have been conceivable that, for example, circumcision could be kept as an element of the initiation rite and indeed could be just as obligatory as the continued use of the Old Testament, without thereby necessarily denying the pure redemption by Christ. This is clear from the fact that—if the abrogation of the law of the Old Testament followed necessarily simply from the nature of Christian Redemption—a continued observance of the Old Law by the Jewish Christians would have had to be contrary to the Christian law even during the period of the primitive Church. Hence, a decision to abrogate the practice of circumcision may be regarded as necessary by the nature of things, once this decision has been taken, but it need not necessarily have been so before this decision was taken, and at least need not have been recognizable as such *from* the previously given nature of Christianity. It will not be easy to find any sure support in the New Testament for simply presuming that there was a special revelation which not only contained a demand to renounce circumcision, but also contained an explicit revelation of the intrinsic necessity of such a renunciation. For St Peter and St Paul give much more the impression of arguing in favour of their decision from the conformity of this renunciation to the nature of things and from the superfluous nature of the imposition of a further burden, rather than basing themselves on the fact that, apart from these considerations, they had simply been forbidden by God himself to demand circumcision. Thus one may surely suppose that in this case it was a question of a decision of the primitive Church —a decision in conformity with the nature of things—which claimed to be irreversible, even though this may still not answer the question *as to how* exactly the Apostles and the apostolic Church recognized this irreversible character of their decision. One may say that they acted thus, and so declared by this action itself that they regard their decision—which has been proved to be in conformity with the nature of things—to be irreversible. And then (to begin with, in this example) even this factor can be regarded as revealed, using the same formal reasoning which we employed above with regard to the lawfulness of such a law-establishing decision.

Such a selective, historical decision of a juridical nature, which is made in conformity with the nature of the Church and which reveals itself as such and as an irreversible decision in the primitive Church by a proper revelation, may rightly be called 'iuris divini' in its creation of law. In other words, at least to begin with, ius divinum can be thought to come into existence in the primitive Church by the fact that there occurs in the primitive Church a decision (formally pre-defined by God) which is in conformity with her nature but which (at least quoad nos) is not a priori recognizable as being intrinsically necessary, a decision which selects one of the many possibilities offer-ing themselves in the nature of things (at least apparently) for shaping the constitution of the Church and of her law. This sort of thing can undoubtedly be more easily incorporated into the totality of the historical development of the primitive Church. For it does not pre-suppose that such a creation of law, as it were, simply falls from heaven without finding any support in the milieu and in the juridical ideas and possibilities of this environment of the primitive Church. And even it can still be regarded absolutely as divine law. For nothing more is necessary for this than the divine revelation of a juridical reality belong-ing to the Church which remains obligatory for all succeeding ages of the Church and which is withdrawn from any change by the later Church. Our conception of a decision made by the primitive Church in conformity with her nature and made irreversibly—a decision which is revealed in both of these respects—satisfies these demands made on a ius divinum positivum in the Church, even if it is conceived as having originated out of a greater number of juridical possibilities which were in themselves present and 'available' and thus are still historically tangible. The revealed character of such a ius divinum does not exclude the observable nature of its development from empirically verifiable tendencies and causes which were in a kind of competitive combat with other existing tendencies of development. Even the divine law of the Church is a divine-human law. Even the life of the law, and hence also of the divine-human law, is a one-way history in which (similar to the phylogenesis and ontogenesis of the living being) the concrete form of the law develops out of a necessarily multi-potential system by progressively determining what is to be realized out of the great abundance of the potential. As long as this process takes place within the primitive Church in the strictly theological sense of the word, it can perfectly well (which does not mean that it absolutely must in every detail of development) belong in its individual elements to the constitution of the Church in conformity with revelation—to the constitution of her nature itself—although, of course, it can be this only as a consequence of the basic nature given by Christ and his salvation. The freedom and contingency of these steps of development—which, being (physically and morally) free steps, presuppose the plurality of other possibilities and which, therefore, not only permit us to see such a plurality but almost demand that we dig for them —are no argument against their being willed by God or against the *ius divinum* resulting from this development.

As we stressed already at the beginning of these considerations, it has not been our concern to prove the real existence in the primitive Church of a divine law understood in the way suggested but, in spite of references to examples from this period, our intention has merely been to give plausibility to the fact of such a concept of divine law understood in an evolutionary sense. It will be the task of the exegete, of the biblical theologian, of the historian of dogmas and of the historian of Canon law, to judge whether the suggested concept will help them in any way when—on the basis of the fundamental Catholic conviction about the continuity of nature of the present-day Catholic Church with that founded by Christ and with the primitive Church— they attempt to make it historically clear how the nature of the present-day Church was already contained in that community of Jesus existing after his Ascension, and when they attempt to make it clear that it was contained there as the form we must preserve in the community of Christ's faithful founded by himself. If they do not need such a concept, and if there are 'easier' ways of proving the binding continuity of the present-day Catholic Church with the primitive Church—a proof which, it must be remembered, has to be developed in a historical way by a Catholic understanding of an ecclesiology conceived from the point of view of fundamental theology, and not merely presupposed by belief in the self-evident character of the Catholic Church —then the notion offered may be reproached with being a superfluous subtlety. But perhaps one or two Catholic historians of Canon law may nevertheless get the impression that in this way the dictates of his historical and his dogmatic conscience can be more easily reconciled with each other than in the case of a notion of divine law in which this law is indeed established by God at a certain point in time but has no history itself in any way.

5. It must not be said that it is *a priori* and certainly impossible to ask the question as to whether there can be a *ius divinum* which is decided on by the *post*-apostolic Church by an irreversible decision in conformity with her nature. This is the final proposition which we wish to put forward here. By it we simply mean to invite further reflection. Nothing more. This proposition merely states that one ought not to be too hasty in refusing to consider from the very start the question of the development of a post-apostolic *ius divinum*. It states no more than that. It in no way decides the question as to whether such a law is conceivable, much less whether there has ever actually been such a law. It is easy to understand why there is perhaps more sense in at least putting this question, no matter how it may finally be answered. There are undoubtedly constitutional and legal 'crystallizations' (understanding this term in a completely positive sense) which can be conceived as having still taken place in the age of the primitive Church (e.g. the development of the monarchic episcopate as distinct from a collegial government of the individual congregation, which cannot easily be demonstrated to have been impossible at the moment when Christ left his Church or to have been made impossible by anything Christ said about his Church). Can this, however, be said with certainty and in a historically verifiable way about all factors which according to Catholic conviction belong to the divine law of the Church? This question is not in any way meant to be answered in the negative, nor is such an answer even 'tentatively suggested' here. After all, there is again a big difference between whether someone speaks as a believer and says that all the elements of the divine law must have been established at least formally (explicitly or at least implicitly) during the apostolic age (as otherwise they could not be *ius divinum*) or whether someone speaks historically and says that the presence of all these elements in the primitive Church cannot be proved historically. And the individual Catholic historian is certainly not bound by his faith to maintain that he personally has fully succeeded in giving a historical proof for each of these elements. At least in this sense, a Catholic historian can also say: I cannot discover all the elements of the *ius divinum* (e.g. St Peter's absolute primacy of jurisdiction over the whole Church in the full clarity and comprehension of the Vatican definition) to be already present in the primitive Church. (One will surely be unable to doubt that, for instance, the consciousness of faith with regard to the primacy of the Roman Pontiff was still very

indistinct and to a certain extent 'fluid' in the Church at the time of Cyprian.) In view of these facts, one cannot esteem it an *a priori* super-fluous question to ask whether one could perhaps expect there to have been a development of constitution and of law even in the early Church which, on the one hand, took place *after* the time of the primitive Church (in the manner indicated briefly above) but which, on the other hand, can nevertheless still be called divine law. No doubt, this question is more difficult to answer, and has more reasons against it, than the thesis relating to the primitive Church. For in the primitive Church there still occurred revelation even after the Ascension of Our Lord; precisely this, however, can no longer be affirmed of the post-apostolic era. The new question posed seems by this fact to have already been decided in the negative: divine law requires to be re-vealed, no matter how one may envisage this revelation taking place. Revelation was closed at the end of the era of the primitive Church. Ergo. . . . But let us be careful. The theological doctrine of the schools clearly supposes that there are decisions taken by the *magisterium* of the Church which relate to facts of post-apostolic times and yet are infallible. Are these doctrinal decisions the revealed word of God in the proper sense? Most modern theologians deny this and—in order to explain why such a doctrinal decision made by the Church can nevertheless be infallible (e.g. regarding the correctness of a canoniza-tion, or the morally unimpeachable nature of a certain constitution of a Religious Order, the fact of a modern philosophical system being irreconcilable with the Christian faith, the meaning of a proposition in a theological treatise, etc.)—they introduce the concept of 'ecclesi-astical faith' in contra-distinction to 'divine faith' in the actual word of God which He himself has spoken and directly attested to be true by His own authority. By 'ecclesiastical faith' one believes in an infallible word which is not formally the word of God itself but which one believes in view of the (of course divinely guaranteed) authority of the Church, so that this word, even though infallible, is not to be regarded as divine revelation. Even today there are, however, quite a few Catholic theologians who, without outside objection, reject the concept of a *fides ecclesiastica* as a wrong notion which has no basis in older tradition. These theologians must, therefore, by this very fact think of all those propositions, which they regard as infallible declara-tions by the Church's *magisterium*, as also divinely revealed proposi-tions. And they must see *how* they can explain the fact that something which in its historical existence appears only after the time of the primitive Church, may be revealed by God (e.g. that Eugenio Pacelli was a rightful Pope, on which proposition depends, for instance, the binding power of any infallible definition given by him). How they explain this can no longer detain us here. All that we will say is that, if one presupposes the possibility of this theory and perhaps even confirms it by facts which no theologian can deny, then it is not necessary to regard a historically later, post-apostolic event as being certainly and simply outside the object of revealed faith. Once we presuppose this, and once we suppose furthermore that there could be irreversible juridical decisions in conformity with the Church's nature even in the later history of the Church (and this fact does not of itself require to be disputed *a priori*, since even the history of the Church after the primitive Church is still law-establishing, historical and irreversible, with the result that such a possibility of an irreversible decision does not of itself need to be disputed from the very outset), then it is perhaps not quite so self-evident as it would appear at first sight that no *ius divinum* can be established by a later decision of the Church since it can no longer have the character of a divinely guaranteed revelation. If in certain circumstances the completion of revelation with the death of the last Apostle does not prevent the possibility of recognizing with revealed certainty the character of a later, post-apostolic event as something which is revealed by God, then something similar could perhaps also be supposed to be the case with regard to an irreversible establishment of law by the Church selecting and deciding from a plurality of possibilities in conformity with her nature even if this decision only occurred later on in history. But as has already been said, we do not mean to answer this question here. All we have said and meant to say about the question here was merely to note that one should not decide too quickly and unreflectingly on a negative answer.

II

ON THE THEOLOGY OF THE COUNCIL

THE Pope has announced a Council of the Church for this year, an ecumenical Council of the holy, Catholic, apostolic and Roman Church. It is therefore right for us Catholic Christians to focus our attention on, and prepare our hearts for, this Council; for it is our Council, and its resolutions will in certain cases have profound effects on our own lives and certainly on the life of the Church.

This Council could be envisaged from many different points of view. We could ask ourselves to begin with (and this would seem to be the most obvious view-point at first sight) as to what problems this Council will be concerned with, and turn our attention to these. But in practice this is not a question which those of us who have not been intimately associated with the preparations for the Council can answer. It is probably no exaggeration to say that never before has there been a Council whose theme has been as veiled and unknown, at least for the outsider, as the theme of the present Council. For up till now there has practically always been a quite definite, external occasion which had clearly brought about the calling of a Council: a dogmatic controversy, or a question of ecclesiastical politics.

Today we know merely that the Council has been called and that it is going to be concerned with the renewal of the Church, a task so broad and indeterminate as to belong to every Council, and hence it does not really tell the outsider anything. The ecumenical intention which was in the foreground when the Council was first announced has since been made more precise by our being told that this intention is to be achieved by a renewal of the Catholic Church herself and not really by direct discussions with the Christians of other denominations. Hence this ecumenical determination of the Council cannot tell us very much about the objective theme of the Council either. Thus, all one can really say is that the Council's theme will, on the one hand, consist of all those problems which are experienced sufficiently universally in the Church and, on the other hand, in all those problems which, in the mind of both those who have called the Council and those who will take part in it, are to be tackled precisely by a Council and not in some other way; this description of the theme of the Council, of course, does not get us very far.

The above remarks are not meant to be anything more than . . . remarks. For the nature of a Council does not give us the right to demand that it should always have a very concrete and urgent cause. This cannot even be deduced and demanded by the 'extraordinary nature' of a Council. For we will see that a Council, if regarded from the point of view of the nature of the Church, is not such an extraordinary thing as might appear at first, and indeed could be conceived almost like a constituent assembly as distinct from an ordinary parliament. Yet it follows immediately from the simple fact of the subject matter of this Council being unknown to us that we must adopt a different course if we are to get some ideas about this Council. Hence the title of our reflections: On the *theology* of the Council. We are going to ask ourselves exactly what a Council is when seen in the light of Catholic doctrine. This and nothing more is our question. We will see, however, that this will result in insights which are of the greatest importance precisely for this particular Council and for our attitude towards it, insights which are of greater importance than an attempt to be as 'topical' as possible in our reflections.

THE STRUCTURE OF THE CHURCH

If we really want to understand the nature and task of a Council, then we must concern ourselves more particularly with the nature of the Church and with what the Church is according to the Catholic understanding of faith. Starting from the motive which inspires us here, we can make the following statement in this regard: the Church is at once constituted and ruled by the college of bishops with the person of the Pope at their head. This institutional, hierarchical constitution of the Church in *official functions* does not, however, exhaust the nature of the Church, since this nature includes also a truly charismatic, non-institutional and juridically not clearly controllable element.

The Church as an official institution

The twofold statement just made must be explained a little further. The Catholic Church does not simply understand herself as a democratic or charismatic association formed from below, an association of people in whom the faith in the message of Jesus has become actual and who, subsequent on this individual event of faith, can form an association and hence can both determine the structures and forms of this association according to their own personal likes and dislikes and change them in accordance with the absolutely free changes of history. Rather, the Church is a society instituted authoritatively from above by Christ himself by the appointment of the episcopal college with Peter at its head, a society which has a divinely given title to man's obedience, faith and incorporation, and a society whose basic traits of constitution, law and division of powers, in spite of many changes of detail, are determined by Christ's instituting will. According to Catholic teaching, therefore, the bishops as successors of the Apostles —with the Pope as successor of St Peter at their head—are those invested and authorized by Christ to preach the gospel in a way demanding obedience, to dispense the sacraments in a proper and effective manner and to sustain the visibly constituted unity of the Christian life; in short, they are the vessels whom Christ has given the teaching, priestly and pastoral powers since (and in so far as) they derive their powers in a legitimate and juridical manner from the apostolic college and Peter, its head, by a real—both formal and material—uninterrupted apostolic succession.

The collegial structure of the official institution

In this connection we must note the following: the episcopal college must not be regarded as the subsequent summation and only secondary union of the individual bishops seen as the individual successors of individual Apostles. As against the Church as a whole, the episcopal college and its powers in its collegial but true unity precedes the individual bishop and his rights. The individual bishop is a bishop in so far as he is a member of the collegial unity and thus shares in its functions in and towards the whole Church. The fact that a certain man is a member of this college may indeed be recognizable by the fact that he has been legally assigned to administer and rule a well-defined diocese in the Church as its local Ordinary. Prescinding from subordinate questions of detail, this assignment may indeed be the normal, concrete way in which someone is admitted into this college. But this does not in any way alter the more basic fact that the collegial unity of the whole episcopate under the one successor of St Peter (i.e. the Pope) is an objectively and juridically superior entity as compared with the territorial limitation of the rights of the individual bishop and his territorial function. Hence, the nature, meaning and right of the whole episcopate is not the subsequent adding together of the nature, rights and meaning of the individual episcopate of each individual bishop. Only in this way, for instance, does it become intelligible why —according to Catholic teaching—the total episcopate may have absolute infallibility of teaching under certain presuppositions, a fact which could never be explained by the mere adding together of each individual bishop's teaching authority as such which is something fallible. This shows, therefore, that a bishop possesses rights and duties towards the *whole* Church not merely subsequent on and consequent to his territorially limited, individual authority, but prior to it, even though always only as a member of the collegially formed total episcopate.

Conviction about this fact—a fact which has not yet been thought out in theology right down to its last detail—finds its most tangible expression in the doctrine of the ordinary teaching authority of the episcopate as a whole, an authority exercised under and together with the Pope. According to Catholic teaching, the teaching authority and power of the total episcopate does not merely exist when the latter joins together in a Council and thus forms a corporate unity, nor is it merely the ordinary teaching authority of the Pope during the periods when there is no Council, but there is always and at all times an ordinary *magisterium* of the episcopal body, even outside a Council, an ordinary teaching authority exercised with and under the Pope. This fact shows (especially keeping in mind the infallibility of this teaching authority—the same quality of infallibility as that of the Roman Pontiff) that the episcopal body always already possesses a real unity, that it is always already a unified subject of rights and duties and that it does not merely become this by gathering together for a Council. The episcopal body as a whole, together with and under the Pope, is already a true, juridical subject by divine law and institution even before it comes together at a Council. Even outside the Council, the episcopal body has the duty, right and capacity to act as a collegial unity, especially when—and because—(as in most cases) it uses this its possibility, given to it by its nature and by its unity in the Pope, through the personal summit and representation of this permanent unity, i.e. through the Roman Pontiff. This fact, understood correctly, does not destroy the active unity of the episcopal body—a unity which the latter always possesses—but emphasizes this unity and permits it to remain permanently actual. This does not imply, of course, that this capacity for action of the one episcopal body is actualized and manifested only in the actions of the Bishop of Rome. We cannot give a closer analysis here of the thousand different ways in which the episcopal body has acted in the history of the Church both in the actually united teaching, direction and ruling undertaken by the individual bishops throughout the world, and in the effecting of this unity through a continual 'give and take' between the individual bishops and the Roman Primate. But these different ways do show that—however little the details of its juridical reality, unity and the juridical structures of its action had been thought out by theology—the episcopal body has always existed and acted in the Church as a real and truly collegial unity.

Primacy and Episcopate

In such short expositions as ours it is impossible to describe the exact relationship of the episcopal body to the Pope. It can be said right away, however, that it is a Catholic dogma that this universal episcopal body possesses the highest powers in the Church only in so far as it itself forms a unity under and with the Pope. Hence the universal episcopal body is not the collegial governing body of the Church independently of or in opposition to the Pope, but only in so far as it itself is given its unity by the Pope as its own personal head. It is true that in this way, as indicated by the doctrine concerning the highest teaching authority of the episcopal body, the episcopate as a whole possesses the highest power in the Church and is responsible to no one else but God, even though it does not possess it as an authority in distinction or in opposition to the Papacy. There is no authority on the same or on a higher level which, after thorough investigation of some matter, could give a decision on its formal or material lawfulness; there is no other authority where the only safeguard against misuse

of its power lies in the promised assistance of the Holy Spirit and no
other which is no longer subject to any canonically tangible restrictions
or courts of appeal. According to Catholic teaching, it must be said
furthermore that the Roman Pontiff can personally exercise (in so far
as he is Pope, it is true) those rights which belong to the episcopate as
a whole with the Pope at their head, i.e. the highest jurisdictional and
teaching power in the Church, and that he therefore also possesses
these rights over the individual members of the episcopal body.
Thus the Pope is the supreme head of this collegial depositary of the
highest authority in the Church—one who can act by himself—and
he does not require any special, legally controllable delegation for
this from the college of bishops, since the college of bishops itself is only a subject of rights, capable of exercising authority in
and over the Church, in as much as it is formed into a unity in the
Pope.

    However true it is, therefore, that the Roman Pontiff really possesses
in his person the highest power in the Church, this does not mean
that the episcopal body as such could be abolished by the Pope, or
that this body is merely the executive organ of the papal power and
this merely by participation in the papal power. In fact, it will be
possible to go further than the above-stated proposition expressing the
Catholic conviction of faith about the existence of an episcopate by
divine right in the Church. It will be possible to say that even where
the Pope acts in his own person and out of the fullness of powers
belonging to him in person, he acts *as* the head of the episcopate as
a whole. For the above proposition does not mean that the Pope
requires a legally verifiable commission from the body of bishops
understood as a legal subject distinguishable from him and his power.
We may therefore say that in the Church there is *one* supreme holder
of the fullness of powers communicated to the Church by Christ, viz.
the episcopate as a whole (under and together with the Pope) which is
a collegial entity and which from the very outset cannot be separated
into two different holders of powers, one of which could be opposed
to the other as a delegating, controlling and limiting power. The Pope,
however, is the head of this subject of collegial unity, a head capable of
acting by itself, without this subject itself being a separate reality distinct from the Pope. The Pope, even when he acts '*ex sese*', does not on
this account cease to be the summit of the college in this action, even
though he has a further episcopal jurisdiction over every individual

bishop (taken as an individual member of this college) and even though he himself can determine the exact form of his action for it to become the action of the head of the episcopate as a whole, and is not bound by any determined, juridically examinable form for his action to be that of the head of the Church and of the episcopate as a whole.

The one ruling power in the Church

Once the relationship between the episcopate as a whole and the Pope is conceived in this way, there is no longer any question about whether there is one bearer or two inadequately distinguishable bearers of supreme power in the Church, when we understand this question in this connection to concern both the relationship of the Primacy to the episcopate as a whole and the relationship of the Pope to the Council (which is usually taken to be the only question). We need not say that there is only *one* such bearer in the sense that the Pope communicates his power or some other power to the episcopate as a whole. Nor need we say (and this would in any case have to remain very obscure) that there are two inadequately distinguishable holders of supreme power in the Church, viz. the Pope by himself and the episcopate as a whole together with and subject to the Pope. It is logically quite inconceivable that in one and the same society there could be two supreme authorities, each endowed with absolutely all the rights and full powers of this society. This becomes no less impossible by thinking of these two authorities as merely inadequately distinct from each other. In so far as they would nevertheless be distinct in such an explanation, the problem would still remain. Hence, theologians like Salverri, for instance, say quite rightly that it is logically much clearer and simpler to hold that there is only one supreme authority in the Church, viz. the authority of the Pope and that a Council derives its authority from him (whatever may be the more exact explanation of this derivation). Should one, however, really make the Pope in this way the sole bearer of supreme power—without seeing him in this precisely *as* the head of the college of bishops— then (as Salverri himself admits) it would no longer be really possible to account clearly for the completely universal and traditional doctrine, expressed also in canon law, which states that a Council possesses the highest power in the Church. For by definition, a power communicated by one office bearer to another in a society cannot be the highest power in this society but must be a derived and hence not the supreme power.

We can avoid all these difficulties by stating that there is *one* supreme and highest bearer of the supreme and highest power in the Church, and that this is the collegial body of bishops formed into a unity in and under the Pope, and that this one supreme holder of authority is capable, in accordance with the nature of a college, of adopting *different* ways of acting without thereby destroying the unity of the acting subject. Thus it can exercise its authority either in the Pope acting as the head of the college or in some other way in which the collegiality of the one college becomes more directly and tangibly apparent, i.e. by a way of acting which is directly composed of the action of individual bishops. But the *a-priori* unifying function of the Pope is still operative even in this second way (viz. in so far as these bishops are in themselves and in their action 'at peace and in communion with the Apostolic See') and even this way does not produce a merely subsequent adding together of the actions of individual bishops.

The charismatic element in the Church

Before we apply these considerations of constitutional law to the Council, we must go on to consider the second part of our initial proposition. Only when we have done justice to this part, too, can we safely understand the nature of a Council and evaluate it correctly, both positively and negatively, in the light of what we have just said. We said at the beginning that the institutionally hierarchical constitution (i.e. the episcopate as a whole united in Peter) does not exhaust the nature of the Church understood as the divinely directed government of the faithful, but that the charismatic element, which is to be distinguished from this institutional element, also belongs to the nature of the Church. The great fullness and permanent finality of the powers instituted by Christ in the offices of the Church—powers which are to be handed on in a juridical manner by apostolic succession—might lead the student of the nature and constitution of the Church into the error of thinking that the whole life of the Church exhausts itself in the exercise of these powers of teaching, of dispensing the effective signs of grace and of ruling, on the one hand, and the exercise of faith, reception of the sacraments and their grace and obedience to these powers, on the other hand. Or at least he might think that everything else which perhaps exists in the Church does not properly concern the Church as such but remains in the private sphere and forms part of the personal history of salvation of each individual.

One might get the impression that every guiding influence, every impulse of God and of his saving activity relative to the Church must always and exclusively be given through these hierarchical powers, through their possessors and their activity, as if every divine influence were exercised through the Church's hierarchy and as if *only* the particular divine influence exercised on *it* (the hierarchy) were a direct, and essentially always direct influence. Yet this is a totalitarian, bureaucratic conception of the Church, which, though it will find an echo even in the minds of many superiors and subjects within the Church herself, does not correspond to the Catholic truth. There is also a free, charismatic element in the Church and this also belongs to the Church herself. Not only are God's influence by grace, God's giving of grace to the individual and the sacramental communication of grace all clearly distinguished one from the other in Catholic teaching: not only is it true that certain extremely important saving or damning influences exercised by God on the individual both within the Church and outside her extend far beyond the sphere of the sacramental communication of grace through the Church in her *potestas ordinis*: but it would moreover be nothing less than heretical to subscribe to the view that God exercises his action on the Church in Christ only through the medium of the hierarchy and no one else, so that the hierarchy alone possesses an (all-round) direct relationship to God. God has not abdicated in the Church in favour of the hierarchy. The divine Spirit blows through the Church in other ways besides the beginning of the activity which rests in the highest authorities of the Church.

There are the charismatic effects of the Spirit in the form of new insights, new forms of the Christian life for new decisions, on which depend the fate of the kingdom of God—effects of the Spirit which take root in the Church wherever the Spirit himself desires it. He can give even the poor and the little ones, the women and children, the non-officials—in short, every member of the Church and not merely the members of the hierarchy—a great or small task in God's kingdom, a task given for the Church and to the Church. The nature and existence of the Church is bound up with the existence of the free charismatics—an existence guaranteed just as necessarily and to the same extent by the Spirit promised to the Church as is the existence of the hierarchy—and thus these free charismatics must live in peace with those who hold office, and the latter must use the charism of the distinction of spirits in order to test, regulate and make use of the powerful action of the Spirit for the benefit of the whole Church. But the official element in the Church must never think that everything depends on it alone and that it is in autonomous and sole possession of the Spirit in the Church. It must never regard those members of the Church who have no official function as members whose sole function is merely to carry out those commands and impulses which can alone be given by the officials in the Church. The Church is not a kind of totalitarian State on the religious plane. The Church must not imagine that everything functions best in her when everything is as far as possible directed in an institutionalized manner and this from the very summit of the Church, when obedience has become the virtue which completely replaces everything else, including all individual initiative and any questioning about the urgings of the Spirit and individual responsibility—in brief, the virtue which replaces completely any idea of an independent charism coming directly from God. No, there are things in the Church which cannot be planned, which cannot be institutionalized and which are unexpected, and hence there is a genuine history in the Church which is more than merely the carrying out of an always already known plan of God's house. There is a charismatic element in the Church, as part of the Church, and only complete with this element is the Church what God wants her to be and what she also always will be through His Spirit.

The official and the charismatic element

It is of course clear that not only is it difficult to distinguish between the official function with its charism (we can call it a charism quite correctly) and the free charism, but that even an office-bearer can be the bearer not only of the existentially fully received fullness of the charism of his office but also of very essential, free charisms most important for the salvation of the Church and for the accomplishment of her task. The office-bearer and the free charismatic can in a sense be united in one person. This has often been the case in the past and is something most desirable even though it is sometimes not without its dangers. But in spite of this frequently existing union in the one person, such a union cannot be brought about forcibly and cannot be established by official action (at least not to any great extent and then only in a particular way made obvious in the history of the Church). To try to establish an absolute personal union of both these charisms in the *one* bearer, and to do this always and everywhere, would be a foolhardy attempt and one doomed to failure. God does not desire that the office-bearer in his Church should always and everywhere be also the highest bearer of the Spirit, or that the highly endowed charismatic should always and on this account alone be entrusted also with the highest official functions in the Church. Again, the union and fusion of these two elements is not to be found either in the official function as such or in the free charism as such, but in God alone and in that guidance of the Church which in the last analysis He does not share even with those who are charged with the direction of the Church. For even the latter are led by God without being asked and without possibility of appeal, and even they cannot *a priori* and into the bargain universally determine the course of their directing activity.

If this is so, however, then the Christian must neither expect nor demand that the charismatic element, necessarily found in the Church, should be adequately represented by the official element in the Church. It would be an unjust accusation against the official element in the Church, and would betray a fundamental misunderstanding of the nature of the Church, if one were to presuppose tacitly in one's actions and judgements that the official element in the Church has fulfilled its duty once it has, as it were, absorbed all the charismatic elements into itself and then radiates and realizes them in its own decisions. The Church is seen correctly only when she is seen as the unity of official and charismatic functions adequately administered by God alone; what belongs to and is the task of either of these two kinds of function cannot be demanded completely of the other function.

All this has to be stated if we really want to understand what a Council is and what we may or may not expect from it.

THE COUNCIL AS AN EXPRESSION OF THE STRUCTURE OF THE CHURCH

The Episcopate as a whole

To start with, what was stated in the first place above permits us to understand the nature of a Council. According to the declaration of the Code of Canon Law, a Council possesses the highest authority in the

Church. This states a fact of divine law in the Church and is not merely a constitutional paragraph of an ecclesiastico-human law from which the Church or the Pope himself could dispense. A Council (presupposing it has been legitimately convoked and properly constituted) is not a new and previously non-existent corporate association of individual bishops, a corporate body whose rights and powers must first be newly created, either by new legislation, or by papal investiture, or by a combination of the rights of each individual bishop as such. Rather, a Council represents a meeting together of the highest collegial subject of that fullness of authority which always already exists in the Church; a coming together of a collegial subject of the highest power in the Church, a subject which was already in existence before and indeed has already always exercised this power. Hence it is not a matter of a new subject of powers coming into existence, but merely of an old subject exercising its old and permanent power in a different way. This enables us to understand why the calling of a Council is purely a question of whether it is deemed necessary, why there is no necessity to hold Councils regularly and why there have been, and there presumably will also be in future, long periods when no Council was or will be held; as well as why *once* it does meet, a Council has the highest authority in the Church. For what emerges and acts in a Council already exists and acts at other times, i.e. the one episcopal body which is the one collegial seat of government in the Church, in unity with and under the direction of the Pope.

The episcopate as a whole, complete with its permanent fullness of authority, can act in a conciliar manner, but does not need to do so, since it can also exist and act in other ways. If it does act as a Council, then in acting in this way it has the same powers and rights which it has at other times, viz. the power of infallible teaching (under certain presuppositions and conditions which we will not go into here), the powers of a supreme law-giver, and the supreme power of government. It means, therefore, that in this case the ordinary *magisterium* acts in an extraordinary manner, and that it can in this sense be called the extraordinary *magisterium*—but in both cases the subject is the same. And when the episcopal body meets in a Council, it can appeal only to those powers which it always possesses. The new *manner* of acting does not give it any new powers.

Representation of all the faithful

Naturally, the official element in the Church, instituted by Christ, is also the representative of the Church in general in such a meeting in Council, i.e. a meeting of the majority of the whole episcopate in one place with the purpose of acting in common in the *particular* manner determined and made possible by direct contact in one place. In other words, it represents *all* the faithful in the way in which the official element in the Church does this also at other times; not as the representative of the whole people of the Church democractically commissioned by the totality of the faithful, but representing this people as the pastors of the faithful who have been given their mandate and powers by Christ. Yet this does not make these pastors forming the episcopal body any less but rather even more truly the real representatives of the people of the Church. We abstain here from going more deeply into the question as to whether, in what sense and in what way the pastors of the Church meeting together in a Council have such a 'materially democratic' duty even at a Council as would oblige them to act in such a way as to be capable of representing by their actions the cause of all the members of the one Church and to act in a true sense in the name of the people of the Church; also whether they have the duty to attend—as it were—to the common good of the Church and hence to the legitimate wishes and tendencies of the people of the Church. In any case, there exists so close a bond between the pastors and the people of the Church—a bond of union created by God himself and one which is objective and guaranteed in its effects by the Spirit in the Church—that the pastors assembled in Council are in a true sense also the representatives of the whole Church and of all her members. After all, it is not as if the Church, understood as the people of the redeemed and of those who believe in Christ, only begins to exist through the effort of its official representatives, as in the case of the adherents of an ideology or the members of an association who are recruited only by those officially appointed for this task and who are formed into an association by the free decision to recruit made by the founder-members. Both the office-holder and the individual believer are preceded in the same way by God's absolute, pre-ordaining decision to establish the Church as the community of believers; they are both preceded by the redemption, thus also by the objective sanctification of humanity in Jesus Christ and his redemptive act, and by humanity consecrated as the people of God.

God's saving action, which is the real basis of the Church and which precedes man's will to community and the existence of an official institution, creates both faith (at least in the office-bearers themselves) and the official institution equally originally and correlates both these realities in an ultimately inseparable unity. This is seen both by the fact that faith is directed towards the common and ordered profession of this faith and originates from hearing the accredited message from the mouth of those authorized to proclaim the gospel, and by the fact that this ecclesiastical office can only be found in someone who first of all (even though he himself be the Pope) professes the true faith at least in the public juridical dimension; for these reasons faith and office can never exist absolutely apart (even though for understandable reasons of juridical stability the authority of the individual office-bearer in the Church is not dependent on his *inner* state of faith). This means, however, that the office-bearers are themselves necessarily believers, at least in the social dimension of the external profession of faith; they themselves, to be capable of being office-bearers, must belong to the believers, to those who listen and obey; they and the people of the Church are not simply opposed to each other as the ruling body and the subjects, or as those who give commands and those who receive them. Both stand before God as believers *and* obedient subjects, as those who are grounded on the one basis which is Jesus Christ and his redeeming act; they are already united as brothers and sisters and possess Christ's grace even before this unity of the redemption and of faith is organized, in accordance with the will of Christ, into the individual functions of the one body of Christ; there are, therefore, also charisms of the office of teaching and of governing which do not belong to everyone in the same measure. Hence, even without any democratic authorization from below but precisely because they are given their office by Christ within the one already existing Church to which all Christians belong as members of the one Body of Christ and this not merely as subjects, the rulers of the Church are always, and especially at a Council the representatives of the Church and of all her members. Even though we maintain that the hierarchy naturally represents the whole people of the Church, this does not yet mean, of course, that this basic representation cannot appear in many different ways and cannot be carried out in the most diverse manners . . . better *and* also less good ways. Much less do we deny that one can rightly have opinions today about how and in what way even the influence of the people of the Church could and should make itself felt at a Council— a way absolutely reconcilable with the divine constitution of the Church and with the power of ruling which belongs to the episcopate alone. In this respect it is not necessarily true that every actual practice of the Church's hierarchy must necessarily be equally ideal and suited to the circumstances of the times.

The Council and the charismatic element in the Church

But the important thing for the purpose of our reflections is to see that a Council is of its very nature the concrete way in which the whole, always existing *official* element of the Church (i.e. the whole Episcopate) can exercise its functions. We say: the Episcopate as a whole. For a Council is nothing other than the coming together in one place of the whole episcopate with the intention of acting as the whole episcopate in the exercise of the powers always belonging to the episcopate as such. It follows from this, however, that a Council does indeed represent the episcopate as a whole, together with the Pope as its head, and also the Church as a whole both in so far as she is always and permanently represented by the episcopal body and in so far as she is united in this body into one, acting social subject but that it does so only in so far as all this is the case. This also means, however, that it cannot be demanded and expected of a Council that it should be, as it were, the acting subject and representative of all the charismatic elements in the Church. Anyone who expects or demands this, acts stupidly and is unjust to the Council. This may appear to be a very abstract and far-fetched principle. But in reality it is a very practical and concrete maxim.

Thousand upon thousand of demands are made on the Council and many things are expected of it. If one examines the majority of these demands and expectations, it will become clear that people expect a Council to deal with an enormous number of desires and debatable matters, so that it would take a monster Council of unforeseeable length to discuss and decide on them all. But not only that; it also becomes clear that very often these wishes and demands contradict each other and are very often desires which have grown out of typically Central European conditions and mentalities, and are not at all suitable for the other parts of the universal Church, but at best should be dealt with by particular laws (for which, it is true, there should be more room in the Church than there is at present). Finally, it becomes clear also—and this is decisive for our reflections—that at least at the present moment in the history of the Church and of her development, many of these wishes are the object of charismatic efforts, of the movement from below supported by the divine Spirit, of projects as yet unofficial and of enterprise which has still to prove that it comes from the divine Spirit, but not things that the Church as an official and juridical institution (i.e. the episcopate as a whole) can reasonably be expected to consider in a Council in general or at any time or even just at the present time.

This affirmation does not in any way decide either positively or negatively the question as to whether—on account of the partial failure of the charismatic element in the Church, or on account of a partial 'extinction' of the Spirit in the Church by the official element, by suspicion, overmuch timidity, excessive enslavement by what is common tradition in life and doctrine, quite possibly by culpable 'false developments'—there might be a state of affairs in the Church of which we cannot absolutely approve, a state of affairs which, absolutely speaking, should not exist (anyone who would simply deny the possibility of such a state of affairs would dispute the very meaning and reason for a Council), a state of affairs which cannot simply be made to disappear from the face of the earth by a Council and conciliar decrees and which while it persists simply does not as yet permit the Council to use certain, in themselves quite conceivable, possibilities of conciliar self-reflection and decision. As to whether earlier charismatic movements and developments, if sufficiently present, could have created sufficient presuppositions for a Council to take official, juridical decisions at the present time—presuppositions which are not present —is quite a different question again and one which we cannot answer here. One certainly should not regard the whole history of the Church —as some do today—as constituted only of false decisions and developments, of mistakes, missed opportunities, suffocated charismatic outbreaks, lazy compromises with the world, or dour self-closure to modern times. For such judgements misunderstand and overrate the possibilities and value of historical knowledge; such judgements are often unjust and foolish, and confuse the inevitable tragedy of every historical development with guilt the Church could and should have avoided. Nevertheless, there can be false developments leading to relatively static conditions in the state of the Church at any particular time, at her mental and spiritual level and in her charismatic energy, or leading to atrophy, false developments which are presuppositions at present unalterable by a Council while being the *a-priori* limits of its possibilities. But quite apart from all this, it is in any case true that a Council represents the official element of the Church—and only to this extent does it represent also the Church—and hence its possibilities and task concern what belongs to the official element and not what belongs to free charisms in the Church.

This does not mean, of course, that the official elements do not need to or may not pay attention to the charismatic elements in the Church and should not take them into consideration, and that—even in this limited sense—a Council has nothing to do with the free charisms in the Church. Just as there always exists a close, inner order and a mutual relationship of dependence between the institutional and the charismatic structures in the Church, so a Council is naturally required to give due consideration also to the charismatic element in the Church, to presuppose it, encourage it, respond to any stimuli which may have matured from it, etc. But a Council cannot replace the charismatic in the Church, nor can this be demanded of it. At a Council, the official element can also try by every legal endeavour—by decrees, ordinances, doctrinal decisions, etc.—to elevate and clarify the doctrinal, disciplinary and spiritual state of the Church, but in no sphere of the Church's thought and life can it replace the living government by the Spirit in the Church; the Spirit does not necessarily govern her in such a way that the real initial ignition of new charismatic impulses must or even simply could come from the official element in the Church. The following considerations must now be understood in the light of these fundamental reflections.

Expectations from the Council

It would be impossible to expect from the Council that it will proclaim basically new insights into the doctrines of faith. This statement is naturally not meant in the sense that anyone would think or wish that a Council could proclaim anything else but the truth of the revelation of Jesus Christ as it has always been proclaimed by the Church. But in view of the present state of the world and of history, of the problems which have already come to the fore and all the new problems which are still appearing—in view of the mentality of positivistic, scientific and industrial man, a changing mentality and one which is affecting the whole world with enormous rapidity—it is surely conceivable and desirable that the gospel be preached in a new way. It is surely conceivable and desirable that the truth might be expressed in such a way that as a result of a thinking through anew of the old eternally valid truth of the Christian revelation, the truth would come to be formulated in the light of the mentality of the man of today, in a manner which from the very outset would take both modern man's initial understanding and his difficulties in understanding into consideration as something obvious, so that the eternal truth of Christ is put before man in such a way as to present no more difficulties and obstacles than is absolutely unavoidable when the lofty truth of God seeks entry into narrow-minded, prejudiced and sinful man. Yet one must recognize quite soberly here that one cannot expect very much in this respect from a Council in the situation in which we find ourselves today. In keeping with its nature, the official element of the Church, even when it is the *magisterium*, must adhere to what is commonly taught, to what has been tried and what has already found universal acceptance. The *magisterium* as such can only employ formulae to which we have become accustomed and which have been proved to be lawful by the tried tradition of recent decades or centuries.

Any wishes one might have concerning a modern proclamation of the gospel and of the faith of the Church should have been addressed to the theology of the last few decades or centuries. This theology has of course made quite considerable efforts to express the revealed word in a manner adapted to the times and in a manner which is existentially 'acceptable'. But we would be indulging in an unjustified optimism and mutual flattery (not uncommon although unintentional, even among theologians) if we were seriously to maintain that, by and large, modern theology is possessed of that strictly scientific yet equally charismatic verve which would make its declarations as truly actual and convincing as they should or might be in light of the truth that God's word and Christ's truth are the salvation yearned for by every age.

Many people undoubtedly will not be pleased to hear this, and our having stated it does not mean that we think that we have done better ourselves and so can afford to criticize. The fact, however, that Christianity all over the world is today for the greater part on the

defensive, must at least be partially due to the fact that the preachers
of the Christian message do not proclaim it as it ought to be and could
be proclaimed. This does not necessarily imply guilt on the part of the
preachers of the gospel, even though this should not be excluded (for
why should the office-bearers in the Church be allowed to imagine that
they are anything else but poor sinners and indolent servants of God?).
But if, as the Church teaches, God's gospel is clear and radiant in itself,
and suited to the intelligence of every man in all ages, and if we do not
have any right to regard the majority of men as either exceedingly
stupid or malevolent, then there is nothing left for us preachers and
theologians of the Church but to admit that obviously we have not
yet learned to proclaim God's gospel in such a way as not to obscure
it in its radiant brilliance by our manner of proclaiming it. Whether or
not we feel this ourselves does not change the fact of the matter. It must
be so, and this especially when we do not experience it so ourselves and
are of the opinion that it is impossible to pass on God's message in any
better way than we are doing.

Theology and the average proclamation from our pulpits and in the
schools being what they are, it cannot seriously be expected—without
becoming unjust to a Council and its possibilities—that there will be
any essential difference in the Council's theological decrees from what
is true of present-day theology in the schools, in the pulpit and in
theological books. (This is true especially if a Council is to be of short
duration and if the main work has to be done by the self-same theologians who represent that theology of the Schools of which no one
can say that it could not be much more in keeping with the times.)
We must expect good, carefully thought out, thoroughly debated
doctrinal decrees. But it will be as well to say without any false
optimism and quite soberly that we cannot expect any doctrinal decrees
which will make the non-Christian sit up and take notice to any
particular extent and which will fill the minds and hearts of Christians
with a completely new and unusual light. To demand this would be
quite out of keeping with the nature of a Council in present-day
circumstances. The *magisterium* cannot replace the charism of theology
and it is not its job to do so. If this charism is weak today, then this will
manifest itself also in the doctrinal decrees of a present-day Council.
Indeed, in accordance with what is reported to be one of the intentions
of the Holy Father, one may perhaps even hope that there will not
be too many definitions. When a Council does not meet with some

definite, already currently discussed question of a doctrinal kind in view (and this is obviously not the case today, since this Council has not been called to settle newly arisen and disputed questions which are giving rise to the danger of a new, not yet condemned heresy) then there is the danger (humanly speaking, for who can tell?) that one may, as it were, *search* for an object of a doctrinal kind for the Council, an object worthy of such a Synod, and that one may suggest certain doctrinal definitions for voting solely in order that the Council may show itself to be important and great in this sphere.

Such a temptation is humanly too natural for it to be held to be impossible from the very start. I suspect that not only Luther but even Catholic Christians have sometimes thought that the fifth Lateran Council had much more important issues to settle (issues which it left unsolved, however) than the definition of the natural immortality of the human soul, however true this proposition is. The few neo-aristotelians condemned as a result of this definition were not the real danger threatening the Church at that time. The prelates at that Council should have looked for that danger much nearer home. The heresies which threaten the real substance of Christianity today are not those basically harmless, even though perhaps really erroneous and (regarded purely logically) very substantial errors to be found here and there perhaps even among Catholic theologians. Real positivism; latent and cryptogamic materialism; the inability to realize that the non-empirical is real; the feeling that the mystery which we call God is present only by its 'absence' and is too great to be honoured by anything but an anxious silence; sentiments deeply rooted in the spirit, which cannot be attained by the purely logical, about the relativity of everything human and hence also of everything religious, sentiments which arise in view of the unconquerable pluralism of present-day cultures and in view of the territorially and historically immeasurable variety of religious appearances and the unforeseeable nature of future developments, in the conviction that we have still great new phases of development in front of us—all these real or partial 'heresies' have not yet been sufficiently systematized in theology and have not yet been sufficiently 'worked out' (theoretically and existentially) as to enable the Church's *magisterium* to formulate the truth against them so as to lighten the mind and heart of the Christian in a way the usual teaching has not managed to do up till now.

Precisely because this cannot and must not be demanded of the

Council, one would hope that the Council will not try by a lot of (obviously true) definitions to create the impression that it nevertheless wants to do this job. May we say quite frankly that—always speaking humanly, and answering to human and (before the final decision of the Council) lawful and indeed demanded considerations—it would be highly inopportune if some particular theological controversies were to be decided conciliarly in this Council, controversies which came up for discussion under Pius XII, such as those about monogenism, the fate of infants dying without baptism, the evaluation of psycho-analysis, or this or that other question which has been quite sufficiently evaluated by Pius XII in '*Humani generis*'?

With regard to matters concerning more directly Church discipline, the Council will undoubtedly be able to and probably will take certain quite important decisions. In this field there are many questions which have been broached from many quarters and for a long time now, questions which fall directly under the competence of the official func-tions of the Church even in their conciliar form of action and which (since they directly concern the law of the Church) can be solved by them alone and this even at this date. We have in mind questions about the relationship between religious associations and the bishops, ques-tions about a certain decentralization of the Church into greater territorial units (not simply into small individual dioceses as such which today are after all no longer viable structures with regard to many ecclesiastical questions), a decentralization which in no way con-tradicts the fact that it is in many respects imperative for the Church in this age of world-unity that there should be an increased unity and responsibility of each part, each diocese, etc., with the Church as a whole. We refer also to questions of a greater openness towards the non-uniate oriental Churches and the Protestant Christians, questions of the possibility that ecclesiastical structures which desire to unite with the Catholic Church may be able to preserve the genuine tradition of their past in a kind of 'rite'. We are thinking of questions concerning a more courageous simplification of the Church's penal laws and of her other canonical forms. We envisage questions concerning the recogni-tion of many things which have already been set in motion by the liturgical movement but which have not yet been completely carried through by the liturgical reforms of the last two Popes: questions such as those concerning the restoration of the diaconate in keeping with the times, questions of adapting the laws of the Eucharistic fast and of fasting and abstinence in general to life as it is today (if indeed it is still thought possible to deal with this by universal legislation). Such and similar questions have presumably a much greater chance of being solved by this Council, partly because they are simpler, partly because they have no special, already present 'charismatic' presuppositions and partly because the understanding required for a definite solution can be presupposed to exist already in the whole Church.

No doubt one can suppose also that among such solutions which lie within the direct competence of the official function of the Church and which are possible solutions for that function even at the present stage, there will be or may be those which at first sight appear to be very harmless, self-evident and not very far-reaching solutions but which in reality can have an as yet incalculable effect on the future and on the outlook of men within the Church, an effect which perhaps cannot even be estimated by the very authors of any such decrees concerned with Church discipline, the liturgy, educational discipline or pastoral matters. What consequences, for instance, could the decrees about the oriental Churches have in the long run, decrees which will do justice to the wishes of the Uniates, if they are to be capable of serving at some future date as the model for other great sections of the Catholic Church in Africa, Asia, etc., sections which have a cultural character all their own and which in the long run it will no longer be possible to subsume under the Western-Occidental and Latin Church?

But even in this sphere one will have to guard against expectations which cannot but do injustice to the Council. Even the best and wisest decrees are no real substitute for the Spirit. Even a well-meaning decree about the reading of the Scriptures and the use of Scripture in the Liturgy, in theology and in Christian life cannot produce a love for the Scriptures or a 'biblical movement' such as still remains to be desired in the Church since it does not yet exist. With regard to the adaptation of religious communities to the present day and age (which may also include a more tangible opposition to the 'spirit of the world' than is usually the case at present) a Council cannot really express much more than a few wishes and recommendations and a few skeleton rules, without conveying directly either the spirit or the *concrete* ideal which will produce results. Who has not experienced at some time that some legislation about studies remains a dead letter which is carried out externally so that one can dispense oneself from the spirit of the law? Hence, we must not expect miracles from a Council even with regard to Church discipline in the widest sense. The man of today who has learned to distinguish even an ideal law from reality can precisely on this account become unjust and bitter in the face of a legislating assembly. He immediately expects from it the ideal reality which it cannot provide, and he condemns the law or disparages it because, to begin with, he does not even always believe it unreservedly possible that the legislators take the ideal words of the law as seriously as they sound.

We have perhaps strayed too far from a theology of the Council in general into the practical details of the coming Council. Perhaps we have ventured rather too pessimistic or sober prognoses which, if at all, can be substantiated only very vaguely. The brief outlines just given are not intended in any way to state or even suggest that the coming Council has no great and realized tasks to perform. On the contrary. This Council has great tasks before it, tasks indeed which it can fulfil and which we are absolutely confident will be fulfilled. The purpose of our whole reflection has simply been to ask ourselves quite soberly and on the basis of a dogmatic consideration of the nature of a Council in general as to what can be expected from a Council and what it would be dogmatically unjustified and unjust to expect from a Council. Anyone who regards the task which thus remains for a Council as something unimportant cannot appeal to these reflections; he underestimates this realizable and real task of a Council, and will not find any support for his judgement here.

How many Councils there have been which apparently were not able to master their task. The disturbances caused by Arianism, which the first ecumenical Council was intended to overcome, really came into their own only after the Council was over. After the Council of Chalcedon, the monophysite heresy began to flourish all the more. Neither of the Union-Councils of Lyons and of Florence effected any real union. Neither Constance (nor Basle) nor the Fifth Lateran Council brought about the necessary reform of the Church in head and members which would have helped to prevent the Reformation before it became acute. Hence no Christian is bound to expect a heaven on earth from a Council. Even after the Council, the Church will still be the Church of sinners, of pilgrims and of those who must search laboriously, the Church which always obscures God's light again by the shadows cast by her children. All this is no reason for not having a Council or for expecting nothing or too little from it. Here too God's power will become mighty in our weakness. Much may be decided which God will then change in his own way into grace and blessings for the Church and humanity. Man and the Church must do all that lies within their power. They must sow and plant in patience. It is wonderful that even in the Church and for the Church all increase comes nevertheless from the hands of God and that we can hope for this without any merit on our part.

12

THE THEOLOGY OF THE RESTORATION
OF THE DIACONATE

THE following systematic exposition of the doctrine of the diaconate in the Church—its meaning, its justification and the reasons for advocating the restoration of the diaconate, including the manner in which this restoration might roughly be conceived —presupposes certain investigations on the diaconate from the point of view of biblical theology, history and the *magisterium*, and does not intend to repeat these here. It is nevertheless obvious (in the light of the essential methodology of Catholic theology) that systematic investigations in Catholic theology cannot be anything else but the systematization of what is known from historical revelation and therefore by means of the historical studies of theology and the doctrinal definitions of the Church's *magisterium*. Should the reader, therefore, ask for proofs in the course of our explanation—proofs which are not explicitly given here—then we would refer him tacitly but emphatically to the other chapters of this book.

I. CONCERNING THE LEGITIMACY OF THE QUESTION ABOUT THE RESTORATION OF THE DIACONATE

(a) The problem of the legitimacy of the question about the restoration of the diaconate refers to the question as to whether it is in any way justifiable and has any sense in practice to make the possibility of the restoration of the diaconate in the Latin Church the subject of an investigation which is not purely theoretical and has some practical significance. For one might be of the opinion that the prevailing practice in the Latin Church today, and what the Church does and avoids as a result of it, is itself already a compelling argument for the view that this practice is not merely one among many possibles but is also the best possible one, since it has been formed by the experience of many centuries and since its untroubled acceptance over many centuries has been considered something self-evident by the Church. It might seem, therefore, that it is no longer possible right from the start to pose any serious practical question regarding some other, opposed practice. This is the reason why this first Section will attempt to give a systematic explanation on this point of the legitimacy of posing our question at all.

(b) Presuppositions for the answer of this first question.

(i) The diaconate is a part of that office or '*ordo*' which Christ gave to the Church when he founded her; the diaconate as an ordination, or transmission of an office, belongs to those rites for the transmission of office which Christ instituted in and for the Church by a proper *sacrament*, no matter how we may conceive this institution more exactly.[1] The sacramental nature of Orders in general, and also the sacramental nature of the Order of the diaconate in particular, can be presupposed here as proved from the positive sources and the doctrinal pronouncements made by the Church's *magisterium*. As far as the sacramental nature of the diaconate is concerned, the present thesis is at least '*sententia certa et communis*'.

(ii) The proposition concerning the sacramental nature of the diaconate refers to the ordination-rite for this office (together with its powers and duties), an office which has been called the diaconate and has existed and been exercised under this name from the very beginning in the Church, i.e. from apostolic times right up to the present time. It is indeed true that the more exact conception of the office going under this name, with its duties and its rights, shows quite considerable differences in various periods and regions of the Church. Yet anyone desirous of affirming not merely verbally but in very truth that the diaconate is a sacrament given to the Church by Christ will have to concede that all those who possessed this office in apostolic times and this for longer periods and in wider regions of the Church were real deacons, in spite of and with the greater or lesser differences in the office actually exercised by them; he will have to concede furthermore that those who held office under the name of deacons received their powers by a real sacramental ordination. The quite considerable differences in their official duties do not pose any real difficulty even as far as

[1] Cf. K. Rahner, *Kirche und Sakramente* (Freiburg 1960), pp. 85–95. (English translation: *The Church and the Sacraments*, Quaestiones Disputatae IX [Edinburgh/London 1963].)

the unity and sacramental nature of this office and of its rite of transmission are concerned. For in spite of their differences, all these official
duties coincide in the fact that, on the negative side, they do not include
any rights pertaining to the real power of ruling in the Church and
consequently also do not include the proper function of the priestly
office which consists in the offering of the eucharistic sacrifice, while
on the positive side they signify all those activities which assist the
actual leaders of the Church in the fulfilment of their *own* office as such.
In other words, the historically speaking very different functions of
deacons are nevertheless of the one nature, viz. to help those who
direct the Church, an assistance which does not usurp or replace the
function of these leaders but supports its exercise by those who
actually direct the Church herself. All assistance of this kind can
basically be a factor in the office belonging to deacons and can, therefore, be rendered possible by that grace which is or can be given by the
sacramental ordination of deacons. Even though in this way all such
assistance falls both in the nature of things and as a matter of principle
into the sphere of the diaconate, the Church can (as she actually did)
lay special emphasis on one or other of these ways of assisting as the
needs of the times may demand or take it out of the sphere of the
powers of the diaconate given by the sacrament or leave it in that
sphere—as it were—but keep it dormant (as she in fact did, for instance, in the case of certain powers of other grades of Orders, such as
a simple priest's power to confirm). All this leaves the nature of the
diaconate intact, on the following three conditions:

There must remain the one function of assisting those who direct
the Church in a task proper to these 'directors': a task which consequently belongs to the office-holders in the Church in contrast to
the layman.

This office of assisting must basically and in itself be intended as a
permanent task, since it would not be reasonable that a diaconate,
whose sacramental nature and whose character cannot be lost, should
of itself be given as a function conceived from the very start as something merely transitory.

This office of service and assistance must in fact be of fairly great
importance since, according to the testimony of the history and
practice of the Church in all ages, lesser degrees of such assistance have
always been given in the Church, either permanently or in passing,
by men who were neither called deacons in the strict sense of the word

nor were appointed and equipped for such an assisting function by sacramental ordination.

(iii) The diaconate *can* indeed be a 'step' by which someone ascends to the priesthood, at least in the *particular* sense that, as is proved especially by the teaching and practice of the Latin Church, the Church transmits a higher office to someone only after she has given him the lower office of the diaconate. This practice, however, is not essential but rather accidental to the diaconate; it is in principle based rather on the common human circumstance that the good exercise of a lower function often shows that the office-holder concerned is suitable for a higher function and thus can be called to this higher office. For the practice of the ancient Church proves that the diaconate was in no way merely regarded as a step on the way to the priesthood but rather that it was looked upon as a positively permanent office in the Church. This can also be seen from the very nature of things. If their characteristic function is properly understood, an office and a task which are necessary for a society and which are differentiated in this society from other offices are not just a step towards a higher office but can certainly be given to someone without thereby also transmitting to this office-bearer the capacity and the right of passing on to a higher office. Indeed, it may be that the nature of such an office is so different from that of another that the efficient exercise of the one does not yet prove to any appreciable extent that the holder is suitable for another higher office. It is in this light that we must interpret the proposition stating that the diaconate is the step by which one proceeds to the priesthood. If all this proposition is meant to state is that the Latin Church does not in fact ordain anyone to the priesthood unless she has first ordained him deacon, then this is a self-evident proposition. It would be an absolutely false proposition, however, if it is meant to imply that in the very nature of things the Church can ordain someone to the priesthood only after his ordination to the diaconate, as if the latter were a necessary presupposition for ordination to the priesthood (just as Confirmation presupposes Baptism), or that the diaconate is of its very essence the human testing of the moral and religious suitability of a candidate for the priesthood, or that someone can be suited for the diaconate only if he is also suited for and called to the priesthood. For the office of presbyter can be given validly even without previous ordination to the diaconate. This affirmation does not, of course, say anything against the present-day practice of the Church—a practice established in law—of only ordaining deacons to the priesthood. The hitherto existing practice of leaving only a very short interval of time between ordination to the diaconate and ordination to the priesthood does not give the impression that the diaconate is a means for testing the suitability of a candidate for the priesthood. The official duties of a deacon, properly and fully understood, are so different from those of a priest that suitability for the diaconate does not of itself signify any suitability for the priesthood, and thus this also need not be demanded of the deacon as such. To this extent the diaconate does not have of its very nature the character of a step to the priesthood, except in the sense that (for reasons to be given later) the priesthood includes the powers of the diaconate '*eminenter*' and that, in fact, only those who are already deacons are ordained to the priesthood.

(c) The question about the restoration of the diaconate understood in this way (i.e. the question as to whether it is possible and advisable to restore the office and the transmission of the office of deacon in the Latin Church without the persons so ordained being ordained from the outset precisely as candidates for a later ordination to the priesthood) is a legitimate question for the following reasons:

(i) First of all, it would be wrong to maintain that the Church's present-day practice and legislation concerning the diaconate conceived merely as a step to the priesthood are absolutely universal. For the practice and legislation of the Latin Church does not by itself constitute the practice of the universal Church. In the Uniate Oriental churches there has been up to this day a diaconate which is more than merely a step to the priesthood. If one keeps this fact in mind and does full justice to it, then the practice of the Latin Church can at the most be taken as an argument for maintaining that at certain times in certain circumstances a diaconate considered merely as a step towards the priesthood was a possibility and perhaps also opportune. The Latin practice, however, proves neither that it is the only possible or lawful one, nor that it is and will remain the most opportune practice for all future ages and circumstances.

(ii) The fact that this practice endured for centuries likewise does not prove that it is to be advocated for the present age and for all future ages. As we know from Church history, there have been many practices and customs in the Church which were fairly universal and of quite long duration without it being possible to conclude from this fact to their observance also in other and later ages and circumstances.

The practice of admitting the laity only rarely to the Eucharist, and only under conditions unnecessarily difficult to fulfil, existed for centuries. For centuries during the patristic age, there was a practice and precept in the Latin Church by which certain sinners were admitted only once to sacramental ecclesiastical penance. For centuries there was a practice of granting indulgences for gifts of money to pious purposes. For many centuries it was not necessary for the validity of a marriage that it should be contracted in the presence of a priest. Furthermore, it must be borne in mind that the present-day practice concerning the diaconate has developed, without much thought and without any really explicit decisions, from historical conditions which no longer necessarily apply today. Basically, even within the present-day legislation of the Latin Church, a deacon need not be *ipso facto* debarred from the exercise of the powers and rights of his diaconate, if, after his ordination, he does not allow himself to be ordained to the priesthood; this fact is further proof that at best the present-day practice can be put forward only with extreme caution and many reservations when one is arguing about the best and most recommendable practice and legislation for the Church of today. Hence, even in practice it is really possible and legitimate to pose the question about the restoration of the diaconate in all seriousness.

2. REMARKS ABOUT THE MUTUAL RELATIONSHIP BETWEEN THE INDIVIDUAL OFFICES IN THE CHURCH

(a) As has already been said, we presuppose that positive theology has proved with regard to the diaconate that the ordination to the diaconate is a sacrament in the sense of being part of the sacrament of Orders in the Church. This, however, does not as yet provide a sufficiently clear explanation of the relationship between the diaconate and the priesthood, a clarification which however is the necessary presupposition for any really adequate answer to many questions necessarily connected with the problem of the restoration of the diaconate. It is impossible, therefore, to avoid this question about the exact relationship between the priesthood and the diaconate completely, however much in this answer will remain uncertain and debatable for lack of magisterial pronouncements and on account of the obscurity of the history of the primitive Church.

(b) In view of the account of the election and constitution of the

Seven (even if we want to or must understand them as deacons), and in order to do full justice to the considerable differences in structure of the 'churches' in apostolic times, as well as for other reasons which cannot be explained here, it will be impossible to suppose that the tripartition of this office in the Church (i.e. the episcopal office, the sacerdotal office and the office of deacon) goes back directly to the explicit will of the historical Jesus before or after the Resurrection. This does not deny the *ius divinum* of these three kinds or steps of this office. We will be perfectly free to suppose that Jesus instituted this office in the Church and gave it to her even with regard to these three steps *in the sense* that he gave the apostolic college with St Peter at its head all those powers and faculties, duties and rights, which are either given necessarily (even without explicit declaration) together with the nature of the Church founded by him or which have also been explicitly declared to be such by him (e.g. with regard to the power of constituting certain sacraments); we will be quite free to suppose that with this institution of the Church as a perfect society, this office has also been given the right to transmit the power of office, to other later bearers of this office, in accordance with the practical needs of various places and times, either completely or merely to a certain limited degree.

The Apostles obviously already made use of this possibility in the primitive Church, at least in the commission they gave to the Seven (who clearly were not given all the powers and responsibilities of the Apostles themselves), in the commissioning of deacons who clearly did not possess all the powers proper to those who in this connection are called ἐπίσκοποι, and in the commissioning of a supreme collegial or monarchic authority in the individual 'congregations' during the lifetime of the Apostles, which supreme authority was obviously not given the fullness of the powers of an Apostle in the proper sense. The variability of such partial transmissions of offices in the primitive Church surely shows that the Apostles were conscious of the fact that they were not bound by any fixed stipulations made by Jesus regarding this distribution of the one total office present in and given to the Church by Christ in accordance with her nature, at least not by any stipulations beyond the appointment of the apostolic college with Peter at its head and the continued existence of this college through the authoritative transmission of its permanent powers. The same thing will then apply also to the official transmission rite of such an office. Basically the transmission of an office in the Church is a sacrament at least where it concerns that office in its innermost being as sanctifying rather than sovereign power, and it remains sacramental, even if only part of this one office in the Church is transmitted, as long as the Church does not have a contrary intention in transmitting such a part-office of lesser extent (always under the general presuppositions, of course, which must necessarily be present for the existence of a sacrament, presuppositions arising either out of its own nature or out of the presuppositions of the intention in sacramental distribution as laid down by the Church herself). It is easy to see from this that, to start with, the consecration of a bishop must be regarded absolutely as a sacrament (in spite of the medieval attack on this proposition), presupposing of course that it is not to be supposed that all the *potestates ordinis* are already given by ordination to the priesthood but in a 'tied up' form which is 'untied' in a liturgical manner only by the sacramental of an episcopal consecration. It also becomes clear from the above consideration that the transmission of that part of the Church's office which is certainly the office of the priest communicates such an important part of that office in the Church that even this partial transmission of an office preserves the fundamental character of the Church's transmission of office in general, viz. its sacramental nature. This explains also why Tradition has always credited the ordination of a deacon with a sacramental nature. It makes us realize that the medieval theory of the sacramental nature of the subdiaconate and of the Minor Orders is not necessarily false, and that conversely the currently almost common conception of these Orders can nevertheless be also correct, since it ultimately depends simply on the will of the Church whether or not she only associates a very modest part of her universal office, and the official rite of its transmission, with her will to administer a sacrament.

(c) What we have seen so far already enables us to make certain important statements with regard to the diaconate. In our apologetics concerning the restoration of the diaconate, we must first of all be careful (if what has just been said is true) not to proceed too simply and without sufficient qualifications from the fact that the diaconate as found in the Church is a sacrament. This thesis is indeed correct, in so far as the actually administered ordination to the diaconate is undoubtedly a sacrament. The diaconate is also certainly a sacrament willed by God *in so far as* the Church can give a separate transmission of the limited part of her office given in the diaconate and can transmit this part also by a sacrament. It is probably not absolutely certain, however, that the Church *must* always adopt such a tripartition of this office for all times, and so could not simply abolish the diaconate, i.e. could not transmit these official functions in such a way that they would always be given to a determined subject only together with the priestly powers. It is of course quite conceivable (and we have no intention of denying it here) that the tripartition of this office which was made by the Apostles themselves during the apostolic age (even if it was not explicitly prescribed by Christ himself) nevertheless binds the later Church absolutely and that in this sense the diaconate is therefore *iuris divini* not only in content and possibility but also in its separate existence from the priesthood.[2] But since this cannot be maintained with absolute certainty, it is also impossible to state absolutely and categorically that the separate existence of the rights and duties of the diaconate in a separate office was laid down by Christ and thus binds the Church for always. It cannot be demanded categorically by this fact alone that the real diaconate should be restored, simply because the Latin Church is thought to be only fulfilling this obligation in appearances, as it were, by its particular form of diaconate as merely a fleeting step leading to the priesthood and not an office which endures and is really exercised in its own right. We will see later on that one can still appeal for the restoration of a really exercised and sacramentally administered diaconate even without using this over-simplified argument. Furthermore, we have already touched above on the fact that it is quite conceivable that at one time the official powers of the Minor Orders and of the subdiaconate used to be transmitted by a sacramental ordination, without it being necessary to hold for this reason alone that the constitution of these offices should still be a sacrament in the Church even today. It is impossible at least in principle clearly to exclude that possibility since there are also other similar cases which at least may be interpreted in this sense. For instance, the possibility of the Apostolic See giving a simple priest the faculty of confirming and perhaps even the faculty of ordaining priests can at least be interpreted in this way, without anything being essentially altered by the fact that in both cases it is presupposed at the very least that the subject invested extra-sacramentally with this new faculty must

[2] Cf. on this difficult question, my Essay in the jubilee volume for Erik Wolf (Frankfurt 1962): 'Über das ius divinum in der Kirche' (p. 277 in this volume).

be an ordained priest. For it could equally well be conceived in other cases that baptism (or Confirmation) are sufficient presuppositions for the possibility of a similar extra-sacramental transmission of the official powers of the Minor Orders and the subdiaconate, even though these can be given also by a sacramental rite; in short, it is quite conceivable that the manner of transmission depends to a certain extent on the will of the Church. We do in actual fact see that, particularly in the case of the diaconate, such a possibility must be taken into account. For it will hardly be possible to point to any function of the diaconate which the Church could not in any way bestow by an extra-sacramental authorization, and yet no one can dispute the fact that the ordination to the diaconate, by which such powers are actually conferred, is a sacrament. We must, therefore, basically recognize the fact that there can be offices in the Church which can indeed be conferred by a sacramental rite but which do not necessarily need to be conferred in this way, so that the exact manner of conferring them (whether it be sacramental or non-sacramental) depends on the will and the (implicit or explicit) intention of the Church. The recognition of this fact is not merely negatively significant for the question of the restoration of the diaconate by pointing out that one must not be *too* quick to conclude immediately from the possibility of a sacramental conferring of an office to an absolutely strict obligation on the Church to transmit the office concerned in a sacramental manner. Such an immediate inference is valid only for the totality of such transmissions of this office in the Church, in as much as one can certainly say with absolute certainty that the Church does not have the right to abolish altogether the sacramental transmission of an office, i.e. the sacrament of Orders. But this is surely all we can conclude from the above. There is, however, also a positive side to this recognition which gives us an argument for the restoration of the diaconate. For if the above recognition is correct, then the way is absolutely open to us to reckon with the possibility that the office of deacon can exist also in a form in which it is not conferred in a sacramental manner. It is, in other words, the duty of theologians to have a look around the Church to see whether this office does not already actually exist and is not already actually exercised there as an office distinct from the priesthood, without it being also conferred for this reason alone by a sacramental rite. This is a genuine possibility especially because, according to what has been said previously, it cannot be postulated *a priori* that such an, as it were, anonymous deacon must already possess absolutely *all* those faculties which the Church grants at present to her already sacramentally ordained deacons (e.g. the right to administer solemn baptism and the right to distribute Holy Communion). For if, as we have said, the Church has the fundamental right to use her own discretion in giving someone a certain share in her universal office, then such a determinate participation can in certain circumstances still fulfil the nature of the diaconate even if certain particular powers are not included in this participation. It will soon become clear what exact significance these reflections have for our question concerning the restoration of the diaconate.

3. QUESTIONS CONCERNING THE OPPORTUNENESS OF THE RESTORATION OF THE DIACONATE

(a) A more exact definition of the question.

It will be useful to make the question of the opportuneness of the diaconate more precise, since it can be posed in different ways and since the precision given to this question here does not in any way suppose that it can be posed meaningfully *only* in the way it is posed *here*. It would be quite possible, for instance, to pose this question also with regard to the restoration of an independent but exclusively celibate diaconate, or with regard to the restoration of a diaconate with a predominantly liturgical task, or with regard to the restoration of a diaconate which equally refers from the outset to the whole Church. It is not our intention, however, to pose this question in any of these ways, since the point at which this whole problem touches most closely on life today demands that we pose the precise question we are going to ask here. This will become still clearer in the course of our later reflections about the opportuneness of the restoration of the diaconate. We are speaking, therefore, about a diaconate which:

(i) is transmitted by the already familiar sacramental rite, i.e. the sacramental ordination to the diaconate, and

(ii) is not merely a step to the priesthood.

The question about the restoration of the diaconate is posed in this respect in a positive but not exclusive sense. This means: we do not maintain that a permanent diaconate distinct from the priesthood is *alone* to be recommended and *alone* makes any sense, and that consequently any form of diaconate intended as a step towards the priesthood should be rejected. We therefore exclude right away the question as to whether or not the Church should also (even though not exclusively) keep to the present-day practice in her education and sacramental commissioning of her priests of the Latin rite. It is reasonable to expect that the Latin Church will continue even in the future to ordain only deacons to the priesthood, and that she will also continue to maintain the previous canonical norms and obligations of the diaconate in those cases where the diaconate is conceived and accepted right from the start as a step to the priesthood. The question about the restoration of the diaconate does not at all concern itself with this other question, since we presuppose here from the very start that, side by side with a permanent office of deacon which is not to be thought of as a passage to the priesthood, there can also be—and it is sensible and advisable that there should be—a sacramental diaconate which serves as a step to the priesthood. For in this way it will be impressed on the future priest that his office is not merely the office of the 'elders' or of the director of a congregation, but also the office of the deacon, since the higher office in the Church also includes at least the obligation to do all in one's power to see to it that the office in the Church is given and exercised in all its fullness and in its fullest sense. Understood in this way, however, it includes also all those functions which are proper to the deacon. The point of the diaconate conceived as a stepping stone to the priesthood would also become clearer in such a case if the future priest were to exercise his diaconate for a longer period and in a really practical way, as a catechist, as a helper in the Caritas organization, etc., thus giving assistance to the ordinary care of souls and being really tested (at least to some extent) as to his suitability for the priesthood. But as stated, our question here concerns the restoration of a permanent diaconate which does not act as a step to the priesthood, and takes this question in a positive yet not in an exclusive sense.

(iii) We are going to pose our question primarily as a question about a diaconate without any obligation of celibacy. In this respect, too, our limited but practical problem is meant in a positive and not in an exclusive sense. This means that we do not dispute the fact that the question of a sacramental and permanent diaconate can itself be posed meaningfully even if such a deacon were to be given the obligation of celibacy. It is also obvious that, if there can be and indeed should be married deacons in the Church, this does not exclude the possibility of deacons who have a proper obligation to celibacy and who are ordained deacons on this presumption; this refers not only to those deacons who receive the diaconate as a stage on the way to the priesthood but also to other cases. Why, for instance, should it not be just as possible for a member of a religious Order or of a secular institute to be ordained deacon, as it is for a married man: given, of course, that the usual presuppositions for the reception of sacramental ordination to a permanent diaconate are fulfilled? If we pose the question about the restoration of a diaconate without obligation to celibacy, this not only leaves these questions quite open (or better, given an affirmative answer to the question of the possibility of a married diaconate, these other questions will *eo ipso* and *a fortiori* be answered in the affirmative), but also leaves it an open question under what precise conditions and presuppositions the Church may wish to and should confer the sacramental diaconate on a married man. It would also be conceivable, for instance, that the Latin Church might adopt a similar practice in this respect to the custom already existing in the Eastern churches, with regard to the ordination of a secular priest; in other words, it is quite conceivable that she might be prepared to confer the diaconate on someone already married, but permit marriage to someone who was ordained deacon while still unmarried only on condition of his returning to the lay state, thus ensuring (if, for instance, a longer period is laid down between marriage and ordination to the diaconate) that only those will be admitted to the sacramental diaconate who have been sufficiently tried while still in the married state. All these questions are left open here. The basic question concerns married deacons, however, since this is the only real way today of giving a sufficiently real meaning to this whole question. For it cannot be expected that the number of deacons would increase sufficiently for the accomplishment of the present-day mission of the Church, if the question about the restoration of the diaconate is not posed and positively solved as a question about the possibility of married ordained deacons.

(iv) When we pose the question about the opportuneness of restoring the diaconate, this does not implicitly presuppose that this opportuneness must necessarily be equally great in all parts of the Church, and that if this question of opportuneness is answered in the affirmative in principle the diaconate must therefore be restored in an equally real manner in every part of the Church. Even if we do affirm in principle that it is opportune, it still remains absolutely possible that in certain parts of the Church, where the social and pastoral conditions are simpler than elsewhere and where there is a sufficient number of priests, the old practice will continue. Such a difference in practice in the different parts of the Church is quite conceivable since such a difference actually already exists if one does not simply identify the Catholic Church with the Latin part of the Church, and since there follows from the basic considerations already given the conclusion that the segmentation of the one office in the Church may be determined in its concrete realization by those concrete circumstances of the Church which in fact are not the same in the individual parts of the Church. Even supposing that the basic question is answered in the affirmative, it can easily be seen that the details of such a restoration in individual parts of the Church will have to be worked out by Canon law, leaving it to the larger individual parts of the Church (such as, for instance, an ecclesiastical Province or a national episcopal conference of larger countries) to decide whether or not (and to what extent) such a permanent diaconate should be restored in their part of the Church.

(b) The basic starting point for a correct answer of the question.

If one wishes to pose this question correctly both in theory and in practice, and if one wishes to establish the presuppositions for a legitimate answer, then it must be borne in mind that as a matter of fact the office of deacon already exists in the Church. This is true even though in the Latin Church of the last few centuries this real and permanent office has not actually been conferred by a sacramental rite and perhaps does not contain all those powers which, according to current Canon law, belong to a sacramentally ordained deacon and which would really be desirable for the actual office of a deacon. If we are to pose this question correctly, we must always remember the distinction and right relationship between the office and the sacramental transmission of this office. These are not identical entities, nor are they —as we have seen above—absolutely inseparable entities, at least in the case of the diaconate. They are mutually related realities in the sense that the sacramental rite of the transmission of the office receives its ultimate justification from the office and not vice versa. As stated above, no matter how true it may be that in certain circumstances there may be an office in the Church which can be, but is not necessarily, transmitted sacramentally, the ultimate reason for the opportuneness of a sacramental transmission of office will always be the opportuneness of the office itself. For a rite for the transmission of an office—a rite which is a sacrament—is not intended to be anything else than the sacramental conferring of the office itself and the sacramental distribution of the grace required for this office. Hence, of its very nature, the transmission of office finds its ultimate significance and reason for its opportuneness in the office itself. If, however, the question about the restoration of the sacramental ordination to the diaconate is to be posed legitimately and with any meaning at all, then it becomes necessary to consider the opportuneness of the office of the diaconate, since we must first of all clarify this question before there can be any real sense in posing the question about the opportuneness of a sacramental transmission of this office.

The question of the opportuneness of the office of the diaconate itself, however, can be posed in two ways. Either we ask about the opportuneness of an office which does not exist, or we answer the question about the opportuneness of the office by showing explicitly that this office does already exist, and that it exists precisely because it is useful and necessary in the Church. After that we can then proceed from this fact to bring out more clearly the special significance of a sacramental transmission of office. We can in fact adopt the second course. In other words, we proceed from the fact that the office of deacon actually exists to a sufficiently large extent in the Church or at least in many larger parts of the Church and thus shows itself to be meaningful, useful and indeed necessary. It is quite easy to substantiate this statement in the light of the basic description of the nature of the office of deacon just given above (and as seen also in its history). It is certainly true that in the Latin Church only sacramentally ordained deacons possess the powers of administering solemn baptism and of distributing Holy Communion in the ordinary course of events. But it would be arbitrary and objectively unjustified to conceive these two powers as the real nature of the diaconate: as if this nature were present only when these powers are present. These two powers do not have any essential superiority over any others, if only because no one can dispute the fact that the Church could, if she wished, confer these two powers even without the sacramental ordination. The remaining duties of proclaiming God's word, of fulfilling important administrative functions as auxiliary organs of the bishop, of teaching Christian doctrine to the rising generation, duties of catechesis of adults, marriage instructions, even—in exceptional cases—of looking after a parish which is without a priest, duties of directing Christian organizations and clubs, etc., all these are certainly factors just as important in extent and depth for the total office and commission of the Church as are the specifically liturgical functions which one may not indeed exclude from the basic elements of the office of deacon and yet must not raise either to the exaggerated position of the universal and most central essential element (even though the objective order and connection of the individual functions in the ideal nature of the diaconate may still remain completely open, and even though there can be no objection to the view that this ideal and full nature of the diaconate may in a certain respect be centred on the deacon's function at the altar).[3] The false emphasis laid on the liturgical functions of the deacon, which gives the impression that one can be a real deacon only by those functions and by them alone, probably stems from that strange and subconscious dread of a certain physical contact with the Eucharist, a dread which forgets that the ordinary Christian's contact with the Eucharist by his reception of it is no less in reality than the contact permitted to the deacon.

Keeping these considerations in mind, we need have no hesitation in making the following quite definite statements:

The office of the diaconate exists in the Church, and this even (if not almost exclusively in reality) outside the ranks of ordained deacons. For there are full-time, professional catechists, full-time and professional 'welfare-workers' (in the widest sense of the word), who have taken on the full-time job of fulfilling the Church's mission of charity, who give lifelong service to the hierarchy and who certainly think of the job for which they have been explicitly commissioned by the hierarchy as fulfilling an essential task for the Church. This is a task which belongs not only to the Church in general (so that it can be fulfilled from the outset and quite obviously even by lay people) but belongs quite

---

[3] Cf. my Essay 'Priesterliche Existenz' in: *Schriften zur Theologie* III (Einsiedeln 1960[4]), pp. 285–312. This Essay works out the connection between the priesthood and the sacramental, liturgical function and shows also the function of the prophetic as a factor on which the existence of the priesthood is founded. This could be applied analogously to the connection and difference of the functions of the diaconate. No matter how much the liturgical function, properly and fully understood, may be the starting point and source for the whole nature of the diaconate, the charitable and kerygmatic task of the deacon too, in their unfolding of the total content of the Mystery of the Altar, are not merely secondary consequences of this essential basis but are themselves essential factors of the diaconate on which its existence is based. (*Theological Investigations* III [London/Baltimore 1966]).

peculiarly and specially to the office-bearers of the Church, to the hierarchy as such, so that this charitable work really possesses the formal nature of a real diaconate. There is in the Church a full-time and professional administration which represents a real auxiliary function for the fulfilment of the task of the hierarchy as such. We can speak of an office of deacon at least where these functions are exercised, to a fuller extent, by an explicit commission received from the hierarchy, under the immediate direction of the hierarchy and as a direct assistance to the task of the hierarchy, as a permanent and enduring function— even in those cases where this office has not been transmitted by sacramental ordination. This is true especially because this assertion does not deny that the determination, limitation and exact organization of such offices could be undertaken in a more ideal fashion—in other words, that it would be quite consistent with the nature and meaning of such actually existing offices—if the Church, by her decrees, were to give them this or that further power which would clarify the significance and, for instance, the ultimate source of the already existing powers, i.e. their relationship to and ultimate connection with the altar. The starting point of our reflections on the opportuneness of the restoration of the diaconate is therefore to be found in the thesis that the concrete office of deacon which is to be restored already exists in the Church, even though only anonymously and without any exact canonical delimitation. This gives rise to the following conclusions:

Firstly, all that remains now to be asked concerns the opportuneness of a *sacramental* determination of these already existing offices, and secondly, this question is to be posed only where these offices exist or should exist in view of the requirements of the pastoral situation in a particular part of the Church. If we pose our question in this way, then it will be clear from the outset that the desire for the restoration of the diaconate is concerned only with those parts of the Church where, by reason of pastoral needs, this office exists or ought to exist; this desire does not demand a diaconate simply for the sake of having ordinations to the diaconate. Hence we are not really concerned with introducing any new office, but only with the restoration of the sacramental conferring of an office which basically already exists though in an anonymous way.

The precision thus given to our question is obviously not meant to dispute the fact that, by restoring the sacramental transmission of this office, the office itself can be made clearer and more permanent, and

that the faithful can thereby be given an increased appreciation of this office and that the determination of the functions and powers of this office can thereby be widened. It is particularly important to stress this, since the reasons for the opportuneness of the sacramental conferring of the office can quite correctly be based on the needs discovered in pastoral theology (such as the lack of priests, the significance of this office, etc.) although these reasons do not directly prove the opportuneness and importance of the transmission of office but rather the opportuneness and importance of the office itself. Nevertheless, these pastoral reasons for the office, even where the office itself already exists, are also reasons for the opportuneness of the restoration of the sacramental transmission of the office, and this precisely because a sacramental transmission of office (as distinct from a non-sacramental transmission) can make the faithful more aware of the significance of the office itself, and can increase the attraction, propagation and appreciation of the office itself for and among the faithful.

(c) The reasons for the opportuneness of the thus understood restoration of the diaconate.

(i) As already said above, there are many reasons which can be put forward for the restoration of the diaconate even in the sense defined here, and even though they prove directly the opportuneness of the office and only indirectly the opportuneness of the sacramental conferring of the office. Everything has really been said already about these reasons in many different ways and at different places in this book. Hence, all we really need to do here is just to say a few words about these reasons: the lack of priests which forces us to transfer many of the functions previously exercised by priests to others who should nevertheless belong to the clergy; certain new needs of the care of souls growing out of the social and cultural situation which cannot be supplied by the priests alone, even with the assistance of the specific apostolate of the laity (Apostolate of Catholics) and of Catholic Action in the strict sense; the dignity of certain offices existing in the Church which are not specifically sacerdotal offices but should nevertheless be recognized and honoured by being given sacred Orders; the possibility of winning a considerable number of men through a sacramental diaconate for the specific tasks of the Church's hierarchical office, men who do not feel themselves called to a celibacy based on spiritual reasons, without it being necessary to abolish the obligation of celibacy for priests; the possibility of relieving priests of many of the tasks of the hierarchical (and not properly lay) apostolate which do indeed belong to the hierarchy as such and hence both theoretically and in practice cannot simply be delegated to lay people, and yet are of such a nature as to distract priests from a specifically priestly spiritual life and from a specifically priestly care of souls. As has been said, we do not intend to develop these various reasons further here since this has already been done elsewhere and also since they are not the real, ultimate dogmatic proof for the opportuneness of the restoration of the sacramental diaconate.

(ii) The decisive reason consists in the fact that (1) the office already exists, (2) a sacramental transmission of this office is possible and (3) such a transmission, at least where the office exists, must be regarded basically and from the outset, if not as something necessary yet as something fitting and opportune. After what has already been said, the only point in this fundamental argument which really requires further explanation is the third one. God can certainly give the holder of an office the grace undoubtedly required for the carrying out of an existing office—a grace which in such a case is salvific not only for the office-bearer concerned but also for the Church herself—even if this office was not transmitted to the holder by a sacramental ordination. So much is self-evident, especially since according to the common opinion the highest office in the Church—the primacy of the Pope—does not require any new sacramental ordination and yet undoubtedly requires the highest and most comprehensive grace of office which in this case is not a sacramental grace even though it has sacramental roots, if you like, in the episcopal office of the Pope. Whenever there exists an office in the Church which is necessary or useful to the Church, such an office necessarily participates in its own way, and of course to a different extent and in different degrees of urgency, in the assistance by grace which God has promised to the Church for her continued existence and life. The assistance of grace must also take sufficient effect, by reason of the eschatologically indestructible character of the Church, even though this fact alone does not provide any absolute guarantee that this grace intended for the Church will become effective in a particular individual office-bearer. To this extent, the office in the Church—quite apart from whether or not it is conferred sacramentally—is itself already a tangible way in which God promises a grace of office even if this office is not conferred sacramentally; the office itself is an element (if we may put it this way) of that proto-sacrament which is the Church herself, in so far as she herself is in her nature and existence the eschatologically final tangible form of God's salvific purpose for the world. Seen from this point of view, it is certainly true that we must not exaggerate the importance of a sacramental transmission of office (e.g. of the diaconate) for the holders of such an (explicit or anonymous) office of deacon. Seen in this light, it is also possible to find a certain justification for the Church's present practice in this matter which in the light of what has just been said need no longer be condemned as a totally regrettable and almost no longer explicable false development.

Yet it remains true to say that when the office and the divine assurance of the grace necessary for fulfilling the office can be given in a sacramental manner (and if this is meaningful and practicable) then they should be given in this way. This is certainly a governing principle of the Church's practical attitude in her sacramental practice in other respects. Theologians do not maintain, for instance, that Confirmation or Extreme Unction, Confession of devotion or frequent reception of the Eucharist, are based on any absolute divine obligation for such sacramental actions. This implies, therefore, that absolutely speaking, the graces which can be received by such a reception of the sacraments can be received also in a non-sacramental way, since neither the increase of sanctifying grace nor the specifically sacramental graces must be conceived as if they could be obtained only by receiving the sacraments, and yet can be not merely very beneficial for salvation but in certain circumstances may even be necessary for salvation. Yet the practice and teaching of the Church in such cases is directed towards encouraging such a reception of the sacraments as something most salutary. It would be contrary to the Church's outlook, for instance, to discourage so-called Confession of devotion on the basis that the graces given by it can be obtained just as well by some other means (such as prayer, examination of conscience, mortification, etc.). As far as is humanly possible and genuinely practicable, it is obvious that even those graces are to be given a sacramentally tangible form and presence in the life of the individual and of the Church which are not bound up with a sacrament either by the nature of the grace concerned or by a divine ordinance (as in the case of baptism by water and of sacramental confession in the case of mortal sins) which imposes a positive obligation to receive the sacrament. All this follows simply from the basic structure of the Christian order of grace. This order is the order of the Word of God *become man*, the order of the Church, and of the eschatologically indissoluble union of the pneuma and the ecclesiological corporeality of the Spirit. The office and the grace of office belong together in the eschatological situation of the Church, in which the tangibility of the Church and of her possession of the Spirit in its totality can never be again torn apart; the grace of office, since it is the grace of God become man and the grace of the visible Church, always presses of its very nature towards some concrete tangible form and sign. Consequently it can be said just as fundamentally that whenever the sacramental communication of grace is within the bounds of human possibilities and of what can reasonably be done, then it should be permitted to take place; in these circumstances, such a sacramental communication of grace is basically to be recommended and is opportune, and such a statement of its opportuneness cannot then be countered with the objection that one could after all receive these graces even without the sacrament.[4] Even though this statement regarding the possibility of obtaining the grace concerned may be perfectly correct, it simply cannot be used as an argument against the sensibleness and opportuneness of a sacramental communication of this grace. Otherwise the *only* counter-argument against the arguments purporting to show that baptism by water is superfluous would be to appeal to an arbitrary, positive decree of God. We do not attribute any special force in this argumentation to the fact that the sacrament of the diaconate imparts an indelible sacramental character which cannot be received in any other way; after all, the significance and desirability of such a character *qua 'sacramentum et res'* ultimately depends entirely on the significance and desirability both of the full power belonging to the office and of the grace of office, for which the character is a (positive but in our case not absolutely necessary) title.

Such an argumentation based on the nature of an office, of a grace of office and the possibility of the promise of such a grace by a sacrament, includes also the assertion that considerable existential effects will accrue from the facts and associations aimed at in this argumentation. This means that it is to be expected that someone who is given an office and God's promise of the grace of office in a sacramental manner will accept this office and grace of office in a much more radically existential manner, on account of the solemnity, uniqueness and in-

[4] Cf. on this my Essay 'Personal and sacramental piety', in: *Theological Investigations II* (London 1963), pp. 109–133, where what has been said here in thesis form is developed more in detail.

destructible effects of such a sacramental transmission of office, than if he were given more or less the same office and grace in a different way. This is true especially because the grace of the sacrament is as such and of its very nature capable also of bringing about or deepening the personal acceptance of it in those who do not close themselves to it; in other words, given the necessary presuppositions, the sacramental grace itself extends and deepens the dispositions which are required for it.

In summary, it can be said quite simply that there exists in the Church a sacramental, grace-effecting rite of transmitting the office of the diaconate, at least as a possibility *iuris divini* in the Church; the office to which this sacramental rite of transmission is objectively adapted already exists in the Church to a sufficient extent and in a sufficient manner; there is a general law of the nature of the sacramental order of grace which states that a sacramental rite which is possible should also be really applied to the communication of grace signified by it, wherever and whenever this communication is demanded; an office existing in the Church (even though to some extent only anonymously) requires the help of God's grace for its exercise, for the salvation of its holder and for the benefit of the Church. It makes sense, therefore, to recommend that this existing office should also receive the grace necessary for it through the existing, sacramentally effective rite, and that the rite should not be employed simply for someone who either does not exercise this office or who (in so far as he does exercise it) receives the necessary grace for it from the Order of the priesthood or who, as the holder of this office, tries to gain the necessary grace for his office in an exclusively extra-sacramental way. Hence, if a certain sacrament is possible in the Church, and perhaps even necessary (in the common opinion) then basically speaking all objections against the opportuneness of its existence on the basis that it has to be realized by ever new ordinations must be rejected as false and deceptive from the very start. Whether we presuppose that the Church must or merely can, according to Christ's will, establish the diaconate as an office separate from the combined office in the Church alters nothing as far as the stringency of this consideration is concerned. For if the diaconate taken as a 'grade' of the combined office is a reality which must exist in the Church *iure divino*, then it is self-evident that the obligatory existence of this Order is not fulfilled merely by the diaconate as it exists in the Latin Church today, where it is not very far removed from being a legal fiction, since in this part of the Church there is an ordination administered for an office which as such is almost never exercised in virtue of this ordination and which in this form has in any case no real significance in the Church. If the necessity and meaning of the sacramental transmission of an office must be justified by the office itself, then the office itself must have a significance in the Church which can really justify a sacramental rite; the diaconate which exists through the ordination actually administered in the Church today does not have this significance, and the actually existing and significant office of deacon in the Church lacks this ordination. Supposing, however, that the Church has the legal possibility but not the obligation *iuris divini* to give this sacramental ordination to the diaconate, then the right of not making use of this possibility can be explained and justified only if it can be proved that in present-day circumstances the Church can and does do without this separate office, and that she therefore is also quite right to omit the sacramental rite of the transmission of this office. But there is no possible proof for this. For the Church has actually got this (albeit un-ordained) office and this demonstrates its necessity. The real non-existence of the diaconate in the Latin Church also cannot be remedied by simply obliging the future priests to exercise their diaconate for a somewhat longer period and in a more concrete manner before their ordination to the priesthood by helping as catechists, for instance, or as assistants in the parishes (by a 'diaconate year' or 'holiday diaconate'). For even so the Order of the diaconate would still be regarded as a mere step to the priesthood—and this is objectively false. Even under these circumstances, those who are actually engaged professionally and full-time in genuinely fulfilling the real tasks of the diaconate would still be deprived of the sacramental communication of the necessary grace of office; in other words, they would be deprived of a sacrament which of its nature is intended for them and does not really signify the sacramental communication of grace for the period during which someone is being tested as to his suitability for the priesthood. The simultaneous existence of a currently existing office and of the sacrament giving the grace primarily destined for this office (and which at the most is only secondarily intended also as a step to the priesthood) provides a basic argument for the opportuneness of the restoration of the diaconate as a sacrament. Fundamentally, therefore, it is not a question of comparing and weighing reasons for and against opportuneness; rather, as a result of a more profound theological insight into the nature of the diaconate both as an office and as a sacrament and into the historical conditions of the development which has led to an actual emptying-out of the sacrament of the diaconate, it is simply a question of squaring this with the basic fact that a possible and actually existing sacrament of ordination to an office must be given to those who have this office.

(iii) In any case, there are no serious objections to the opportuneness of such a restoration. After all, any fears of serious unsuitability will not arise on the grounds of the sacramental rite of the transmission of office but will at most be due to the office thus transmitted and existing in certain persons. This is really obvious and needs no further proof. The office of deacon does, however, already actually exist in the Church (even though without ordination) and its existence and the growth of its scope and of the numbers of those exercising it shows that the inconvenience, the harm and danger which might give grounds for maintaining that the restoration of the diaconate is inopportune are not any greater in this case than is usual with any office administered by men. If such a good and useful office which has not caused any inconveniences through its holders hitherto comes now to be conferred by a sacramental rite of transmission of office, then this cannot bring about any hitherto unknown harm and dangers. One thing, of course, is true; a sacramental ordination to the diaconate makes the ordained officebearer a member of the clergy, both from a dogmatic and a canonical point of view. But someone thus ordained is a cleric precisely to the extent of the function and power which he already possesses even now (prescinding from a few liturgical powers which do not make any essential difference here). Hence, if these powers and functions did not cause any inconvenience when invested in a non-cleric, why should it be otherwise when they are invested in a cleric?

The question as to whether the existence of *married* clerics would give rise to difficulties and dangers in the Church will be treated separately.

(iv) Our basic argumentation proceeded from the fact that the office of deacon already exists in the Church and that the ordination to this office should be given precisely to this already existing office (or one which should be created by reason of the necessity of the office itself) since this also already existing ordination rite exists for this very purpose. This argumentation does not mean, however, that the opportuneness of such a restoration can be proved *only* under the presuppositions laid down by us. Even someone who is not prepared to admit that the office of a professional, lifelong catechist, or of a social welfare worker, etc., is basically already the office of a deacon, can still prove that the restoration of the diaconate is justifiable. For even he can appreciate that, if the significance of one of Christ's sacraments in the Church is properly evaluated, it will be seen quite clearly that it was not instituted nor does it exist simply as a (very unreal) prelude for those who will be ordained priests a few months later and who after that do not exercise this office as such any longer (an office for which they received a sacred Order) to any great extent and in any explicitly realized way. If one presupposes the existence of this sacrament in this way (as we have also done, of course, in our basic argument) then it also becomes clear that we can confine ourselves in all our considerations here regarding the restoration of the diaconate to the question of the male holders of such offices which we regard as belonging fundamentally to the diaconate. The question as to whether and why sacramental orders are reserved to the male sex—and this even in their lowest 'grades' and in spite of the existence of an institution of deaconesses in the early Church—does not need to occupy us here, since the only problem concerning us here is to determine to whom in the Church it makes any sense to give that sacrament which already exists at the present time and which as such is given to men only.

4. DIACONATE AND CELIBACY[5]

We have already stated above that the question about the restoration of the diaconate is really practical and significant only if it also at least includes the question of the restoration of a sacramental diaconate for married men. For many, the latter question contains the strongest emotional and practical difficulties against the desire for such a restoration. In order to get a clear idea of this question, it must first of all be pointed out once more that the question of celibacy or non-celibacy must not be regarded in view of the sacramental ordination to the office, but in view of the office itself. Wherever celibacy is thought to be necessary or most desirable, the demand for celibacy must be deduced either from its intrinsic significance for the Church or from a considera-

---

[5] It is not our intention here to treat of all the aspects of this question. This question is discussed more fully in A. Auer's contribution to the collective work *Diaconia in Christo*, edited by K. Rahner and H. Vorgrimler (Freiburg 1962), pp. 325-339.

tion of the office as such with which celibacy is to be associated. That celibacy has an intrinsic significance for the Church, is neither disputable nor does it require any further explanation and proof here. A celibacy which is immediately and of itself alone significant for the celibate and for the Church (as lived in the communities which practise the Evangelical Counsels) is from the very outset excluded from our discussion. In our present context it can only be a question of determining whether the office of the deacon, like the priestly office, has such an inner affinity with celibacy that, as in the case of the Latin priestly and episcopal office, the Church deems it advisable and feels it justifiable to demand celibacy also of the deacons (no matter how precisely this mutual affinity is to be interpreted: whether it be by the nature of celibacy itself or by pastoral consideration, or in view of the service of the altar, etc.). If one bears the distinction of office and of the rite of the transmission of office clearly in mind—and if one is quite clear in one's mind about the fact that in the very nature of things a rite of the transmission of office can 'demand' celibacy only if the office to be transmitted demands it—then it will be easy to answer the question with which we are now concerned. For the Church shows by her practice that she does not see any very close and necessary connection between the office of deacon and celibacy. For this office exists and is transmitted in the Church without celibacy being demanded. For, those men and office-bearers in the Church in whose case the desirability of a sacramental transmission of office is indicated here are *de facto* for the most part married men, and neither the official Church nor people in the Church have ever maintained or felt any incompatibility or inconvenience in the co-existence of this office and marriage in recent centuries or at the present time.

Thus, if properly posed, this question does not inquire whether, in contrast to previous practice, one should from now on stop imposing the obligation of celibacy on anyone who is to be ordained a deacon. For the candidate for ordination with whom we are concerned here is not someone who wants to become a priest and someone on whom— basically for this and no other reason—the Church already imposes the obligation of celibacy at the time of his ordination to the Sub-diaconate; he is a candidate to whom the Church is to give the sacramental ordination for an office which he already has as a married person, which has been transmitted to him and which he exercises as a married person. Hence, from an objective and not merely verbal point of view, there is no question here of annulling any previous law existing in the Church today; for, the deacon who exercises his own particular office as a permanent job in the Church no longer exists, and has not existed for a long time now, in the Church (or at the most exists only '*per accidens*', viz. when someone, in accordance with can. 973 §2, advances no further than the diaconate on his way to the priesthood, and yet is not laicized). The answer to the question as to the fundamental necessity of imposing the obligation of celibacy must be sought by asking whether these deacons, who exist in as far as the nature and the office of the diaconate are concerned even though they are not ordained deacons, should have the obligation of celibacy newly imposed on them, contrary to the previous practice of the Church who up till now has given what in fact is the office of the diaconate to married people. Once this question is put properly in this way, it immediately becomes evident that it must be answered in the negative. Marriage has a greater inner affinity with the office of deacon than has celibacy, since the deacon in his specific, official function is quite clearly the link between the clergy and the altar, on the one hand, and the world with its Christian task, on the other; up till now the Church has not demanded celibacy for this office, and such a demand also does not follow from ordination. Why should there then be a demand for it now, a demand which in practice would to a large extent prevent the new realization of the diaconate, since in this case most of those who are deacons in fact would, and would have to, give up any claim to the official ordination which is due to them, and the few among them who already live a celibate life for other reasons (especially in religious communities) would not be able to supply that additional number of real deacons which the present-day pastoral situation of the Church demands? It must always be borne in mind in this connection that in a true theology of marriage, marriage must really and truly not be regarded as a mere concession to human weakness (a conception attempted over and over again by an almost manichaean intellectual undercurrent in the Church) but must be seen to have an absolutely positive and essential function, not only in the private Christian life of certain individuals but also in the Church. Marriage, understood as a sacramentally consecrated union, is both in and for the Church the concrete and real representation and living example of the mystery of Christ's union with the Church. Hence, marriage fulfils an absolutely necessary function in the Church and for the Church herself. How, then, should marriage be less advisable for the office of deacon? A deacon may see his marriage rather as an essential factor for his duties as a deacon, since a Christian marriage has precisely this function of testifying to the powerful influences of grace for the Church. Since, in the case of the ordained diaconate being retained also as a step to the office of the priesthood, the formation and task of the deacons going on to the priesthood and of those who remain deacons will be different and separate from the outset, and since both these different kinds of deacon and the faithful will be clearly conscious of this very difference, it cannot seriously be feared that we might arouse opposition to the celibacy of the diaconate as leading to the priesthood by appealing for married deacons. Nor need we be afraid that the position of these married deacons might be used to relax or attack priestly celibacy. If there were any danger of this happening, then the existence of married priests in the Eastern Uniate Churches should also be a danger to the celibacy of the priests in the Latin Church, or serious difficulties should arise from the co-existence of celibate bishops and married priests in the Eastern Churches. Furthermore, none of the faithful in the Latin Church have any difficulty in seeing that celibacy has a special affinity with the priesthood as such, and they certainly distinguish the duty and dignity of deacons so clearly from the duties and the dignity of the priest that they will neither get the feeling that if deacons married, then the priest should also be allowed to marry, nor that deacons should be celibate because the priest is celibate. Certain emotional restraints and difficulties (as, for instance, in the case of receiving Communion from a married deacon) have no real objective basis and will quickly disappear when people get used to things, just as certain emotional qualms about a reception of Communion not preceded by a longer period of eucharistic fast have disappeared.

That the Church's feelings too have always made a distinction in this question between the priest and the deacon is shown by the fact that the right to marry has been restored in many cases and with comparatively little difficulty to deacons who have been laicized, whereas the laicized priest is usually refused this permission. Although the permission to marry will certainly avoid considerable difficulties and burdens for the deacon, difficulties and burdens which would occur if celibacy were demanded of him, it need not be denied that marriage also presents certain difficulties and dangers for the exercise of a diaconate worthy of this office. Nevertheless, in view of the specific function of the deacon which directs him to go out into the world, these difficulties and dangers are certainly considerably less than if celibacy were demanded. These difficulties and the danger of harmful results for the Church could be lessened even further if canon law were to offer a fairly wide and practicable possibility of laicization for deacons, to be given either at the request of the deacon himself or at the instigation of the bishop. As has already been emphasized, the recommendation of a diaconate together with marriage is naturally not meant to suggest that *only* married deacons should be bearers of an independent and permanent office. There is nothing to stop the Church from ordaining to the diaconate even those who either have already taken the obligation of religious celibacy upon themselves for some other reason (as, for instance, in religious communities) or who undertake this obligation in connection with their ordination to the diaconate and by an explicit declaration before the Church. It has also been stated already that one might consider the possibility of combining ordination to the diaconate with marriage only in the case of those who are already married and who have already proved themselves by their Christian married life and their previously exercised functions of the diaconate to be suitable candidates for the reception of this ordination. Only, in such a case, one ought not to drag out this testing period for too long; considering the professional character of the diaconate, this period could no doubt be fixed approximately in accordance with what is demanded in this respect from candidates for the priesthood. For even the ordination to the diaconate is not, after all, a reward for a diaconate already exercised for almost a whole lifetime, but is the communicating of grace for the exercise of an office which is still to be carried out.

5. OFFICE AND GRACE OF OFFICE

It will be useful to give a few further systematic reflections about the office and the grace attached to the office, both separately and in their relations to one another.

(a) It is clear from history and also from the declarations of the Church's *magisterium* and Canon law how widespread and intrinsically diversified the office of deacon is. It has also become clear from history that the conception of what actually is the very heart of the essence of the diaconate has been, and has remained to this day, comparatively fluctuating and contradictory. It is probably not to be expected that the

Church herself will make any real declarations in the coming Council about the question of a basic, unified essential structure of the office of deacon. This question will presumably always remain a disputed question among theologians. Nevertheless, it will surely be possible to base oneself on the fact that, judging by the declarations of current canon law, the liturgical function will not be lacking even in the essential picture of the future deacon, however much it must be left an open question to what extent in individual cases and details the regulations (which perhaps will not necessarily be uniform in all parts of the Church) will or will not draw on the future holders of a permanent diaconate for the carrying out of liturgical functions (e.g. for assisting at marriages, distributing Holy Communion, etc.). In the same way, one will have to hold it to be an indisputable fact that this future ordained diaconate will not be limited to these liturgical functions but will have wider and important tasks and powers in the Church and in her pastoral practice. Given these two presuppositions, there then arises the speculative question about the mutual relationships between these many different liturgical and extra-liturgical functions which are all part of the one diaconate.

To begin with, it is (naturally) obvious from the history of the diaconate, from the similar practice of the Church with regard to the priesthood and from the basic possibility (explained above) of dividing and accentuating the different parts of the collective office in the Church, that there can be different types or distinct forms of the one complete diaconate. This means in practice that, without prejudice to the unity and uniformity of the office of the diaconate, the focal point of the task of a deacon may at different times lie in different directions, and that on this account the candidates for such an ordained diaconate may also be able to approach this one office and calling in the Church from comparatively very different directions. In other words, even in any future practice and legislation of the Church, there will presumably be no deacons who would—in principle and permanently—want to exclude the liturgical commission and obligation, although it can be left an open question as to whether or not such an intention and legal determination on the part of the Church would nevertheless be in itself possible. This does not, however, exclude the possibility that the focal point of the life of such a deacon might lie in the work of the Church's Caritas movement, or in the administrative sphere of the Church. And in principle there are many other conceivable functions

apart from those just mentioned, functions which determine the concrete form of the diaconate (without it being necessary or possible to
enumerate them here) provided only that these functions are part of the
Church's official functions as such, and that in the service and diaconia
of the episcopal and sacerdotal office there is fulfilled the task belonging
to the hierarchy as distinct from the laity in the Church. It will moreover be possible to say that one can quite properly centre all these
different tasks on the Altar, if we may express the referred-to connection and inner unity of these many-sided tasks of the diaconate in this
way. It will not be necessary to say that the liturgical function of the
deacon is the real, proper function of his office, whereas all his other
functions are just secondary, 'part-time' functions. Such a statement
surely contradicts the early history of the diaconate; it would surely
bring us back again to that conception which has led to reducing the
scope of this office, the very thing we should be trying to overcome
today; it would also be wrong for the very reason that these liturgical
functions do not in practice and in the concrete presuppose ordination
with any greater necessity than do the rest of the deacon's functions (or
do so at most only *iure humano* in Canon law).

On the other hand, the equally necessary character of the kerygmatic,
charitable and administrative functions of the deacon for the essence of
the diaconate does not prevent us from regarding them as functions
which basically are really already given together with his duties connected with the central mystery of the Church which is the Eucharist.
For the Eucharist is not only the sacrifice of Christ offered to God and
the sacrament of the individual encounter with Christ and of private
satisfaction; rather it is the event in which the nature of the Church
itself comes to be actually realized in the most intensive way, the event
in which the Church becomes herself and comes to be present in her
most profound actuality at a certain point in space and time.[6] Here in
the anamnesis of the death of Christ is the effective pronouncement of
the Word of God which at best can really only be interpreted when
proclaimed and taught.[7] Here the unity of the Church is achieved in its
most intensive way in the sacramental symbol and the love of Christ.
Hence, if the deacon shares in a special way in the Eucharist understood

[6] Cf. K. Rahner, 'Zur Theologie der Pfarre', in: H. Rahner, *Die Pfarre*[2]
(Freiburg 1960), pp. 27–39.

[7] A more detailed exposition of this will be found in my Essay 'Wort und
Eucharistie', in: *Schriften zur Theologie* IV (Einsiedeln 1960), pp. 315–355.

as the central self-realization of the Church, and if he does this as the helper of the episcopal or priestly representative of Christ Who is the Head of the Church, and as the representative of the people and as the interpreter of the sacred mystery for the people—and all this as a permanent function—then the deacon cannot in principle withdraw from those functions of the Church by which she gives an exposition, in her sacred teaching, of the anamnesis of the Redemption and by which her unity in faith, hope and charity, celebrated in the Eucharist, is spread by her—through the direction of the faithful and through Christian charity—over the whole of man's life. Seen in this light, it becomes understandable how these different basic functions of the deacon, however distinct they may appear at first, form a unity among themselves, and proceed from and return to the central mystery of the Eucharist. This also makes it understandable that the old controversy about whether the diaconate is a more spiritual or a more profane office in the Church is really due to a misunderstanding. The proclamation of the word and the realization of love which are sacramentally present in the Eucharist are not profane realities in life, but are a self-realization and an actualization of the holy Church, in so far as she is holy in the actual reality of life in which man's salvation must be effected.

(b) It is not easy to delimit the task of the deacon from the tasks and possibilities a layman possesses in the Church by his lay apostolate and his participation in Catholic Action.[8] This is difficult even from a purely extrinsic point of view, since it is really impossible—from a purely material point of view—to mention any function of the deacon which even an 'unordained' layman could not fulfil, provided merely that he has been given the necessary authorization by the Church. This is true even of the deacon's liturgical functions. Yet this fact is not really surprising and does not represent any real problem peculiar to the diaconate as such; it is a question already raised by the Church's official functions as a whole. One can, of course, say that there are certain individual powers and tasks belonging *iure divino* only to ordained office-bearers (the power of consecrating in the celebration of the Eucharist, the power to ordain priests, the power to administer Confirmation and the Anointing of the Sick, the giving of priestly absolution).

[8] This question is taken up once more in P. Winninger's chapter, with special reference to the situation in France and the very active Catholic Action in that country: *Diaconia in Christo* (Freiburg 1962), pp. 380-388.

It would be completely wrong, however, to try to say in principle that these tasks and powers alone characterize the Church's office and that everything else (prescinding perhaps from strictly jurisdictional acts) is *eo ipso* a merely lay task and power. Rather, the hierarchical office includes the power of proclaiming the gospel and also the exercise of Christian *Caritas* in a way specific to this office as such, even though—on a superficial viewing—the material realization of such hierarchical tasks may not appear to be very much different from the words and deeds of a layman witnessing to Christ's gospel and love. Even though this formal distinction may not be immediately clear, it nevertheless exists. The layman's task as such, for instance, will be to bear witness to the truth and love of Christ by his words and deeds only in *that* situation of his life which is proper to him by reason of his human natural existence. The holder of hierarchic powers and tasks, on the other hand, will have to bear witness to and proclaim the gospel even outside his proper 'place' determined by his human and natural existence. He will in a real sense be an 'ambassador', an 'ἀπόστολος', who by his divine mission is sent out of his own personal situation in order to carry the gospel 'in season and out of season' into strange places (which is just as possible and necessary in the 'home missions' as it is in the 'foreign missions'). Similarly, the attestation of the *Caritas Christi* will be a task of the Church's official function in the measure, urgency and concrete manner by which this *caritas* appears as the direct act of the 'visible Church' as such and no longer merely as the fulfilment of the general Christian duty of Christian love of neighbour. We do not claim that by these few allusions we have made a sufficiently clear and exhaustive distinction between the characteristics of these tasks of the official element of the Church and those of the laity in the Church which may—materially speaking—appear to be almost identical. But this difference does exist, because there is a difference *iure divino* between the hierarchy and the people of the Church (in spite of the universal priesthood of all believers) and because this difference cannot be confined to the few powers of the *potestas ordinis* which we have actually mentioned or to the *potestas iurisdictionis* in the strictest sense.

If this difference exists then this means, however, that all the tasks and powers of a deacon are characterized by the general characteristics of the tasks and powers of the Church's hierarchical office as distinct from the tasks and powers of lay people. That this fact is not very evident in the practical administration and consciousness of the Church today, is due to the fact that nowadays certain tasks and powers are fulfilled by lay people as a lifelong profession (and not merely as a spare-time job and by reason of a passing, accidental need), tasks and powers which basically belong to the hierarchy as such and as a whole and which in the past, if they had been performed professionally and permanently, would have stamped those performing them as members of the clergy, so that the Church would also have confirmed this membership by ordination. Hence, the circumstance that—to the superficial observer—most of what this future 'absolute' deacon will be doing, could also be done by laymen, does not, on closer analysis of this activity, speak for its truly lay character, but rather for the demand that such an office-bearer ought to be given that ecclesiastical and, in certain circumstances, sacramental ordination which exists or existed in the Church precisely for these offices. The fact that the boundary between a lay task and a hierarchical one is somewhat vague (in the 'downward' direction) is due to the nature of things and merely proves the inner unity of the official element and the people in the Church relative to the task of the Church which after all is one and the same in its concern for the Kingdom of God. Empirically speaking and in practice it can always be said, however, that whenever someone performs a task permanently and professionally, and whenever this is a task which the higher office (i.e. the bishop and the priests) recognizes and exercises as an intrinsic element of its own task or as an indispensable, direct and in itself significant auxiliary function of that task, this person is in principle performing a clerical office.[9]

On this basis, it is absolutely feasible to draw a basic distinction between the office of the deacon and the task of the lay apostle, and to prove the demand for the restoration of the ordination to the diaconate.

(c) In this connection, we must also say a word about the relationship of the diaconate to the priesthood and consequently of the deacon to the priest. Here too there are certain obscurities in the traditional conception. It sometimes looks as if the diaconate and the simple priesthood are two co-existing extensions of the one episcopal office (even though they are not simply of the same rank and of equal dignity), so that the deacon cannot really appear as an auxiliary to the

[9] Cf. for this my Essays on the subject of the layman in the Church, indicated by the Chapter 'Laie und Ordensleben', in: *Sendung und Gnade* (Innsbruck 1961[3]), pp. 364–396.

simple priest; at other times—and this is probably the clearer and more widespread view—there appears the conception that the deacon is simply the helper of the priest, and this in such a way that even the simple priesthood possesses *eminenter* all the rights and powers of the diaconate and the diaconate can only be regarded as an extension and auxiliary organ of the simple priesthood. If our reflections in No. 2 above were correct, then the question as to which of these two conceptions is in fact the right one (which is sometimes more than a purely theoretical question) can really be decided only by an actual decision of the Church, in the knowledge that the Church could in certain circumstances have decided differently. For if the Church can, under the necessary presuppositions, divide her collective office according to the concrete pastoral needs in the Church at any particular time, then she can in principle do this by separating two co-existing offices from her collective office, so that then neither of these offices would possess the powers of the other, or she can separate a higher and a lower office in such a way that the higher would include the powers of the lower. It is sometimes not so easy to tell which of these two possibilities has in fact been realized in the consciousness and intention of the Church. We have already pointed out, for instance, that one may possibly suppose that even the simple priesthood may of itself include the powers of confirming and of ordaining priests in its *potestas ordinis* (although these will in most cases be present only in a 'dormant' state), powers which are certainly contained in the episcopal office. One should also consider the question as to whether a deacon, who is consecrated a bishop '*per saltum*' without previous ordination to the priesthood, also receives the priestly powers solely by this episcopal consecration. On the basis of these and similar reflections it should be possible to draw the conclusion that many, if not all, things regarding the constitution of the scope of an office depend on the actual will of the Church. Hence, given that certain powers are different of their very nature, they may indeed be conferred separately, but they need not be. Consequently, the answer to the real question about the relationship of the diaconate to the priesthood cannot be simply deduced from the abstract nature of these two realities but only from the question as to which powers the Church in fact wishes to confer by this or that ordination and which not. If, however, the question is posed in this way, then it will be impossible to doubt that in her ordination to the priesthood the Church does not presuppose the ordained to possess the powers of the diaconate in such a way that, if he did not already possess them on account of his ordination to the diaconate then he would not receive them by this ordination to the priesthood. This follows, as has been said, not only because it is not easy to see from what has just been shown under (a), why a priest should not already be commissioned and obliged to the self-realization of the Church in teaching and in charity by his duties at the altar, since these tasks seem to result of themselves from the full nature of the Eucharistic celebration, but it follows also from the Church's own free intention which, in the case of an ordination to the priesthood *per saltum*, has never yet maintained that such a priest is incapable of exercising the powers of the diaconate. Even so, such a consideration may not be absolutely compelling on the purely speculative level, for one cannot assert that the powers of the diaconate can be conferred only by a sacramental ordination; yet, when looked at in the whole setting of real life, the above fact nevertheless shows the intention of the Church outlined above, since the Church has never appealed to her right to transmit the diaconate extra-sacramentally when it was a question of the possibility of a priest's exercise of the functions of the diaconate without actual ordination to the diaconate; instead, the Church has always explained her conception and intention regarding this fact by maintaining that the priest can do *eminenter* what the deacon is capable of doing. Hence, it will have to be said that by the priestly ordination actually dispensed by her, the Church intends to constitute a priest who is always also, at least *eminenter*, a deacon, whether or not he has been specially ordained deacon beforehand.

This, however, does not yet provide a clear explanation of the relationship between priest and deacon which is in question here. All that it tells us is that every priest is also a deacon, but this does not as yet really tell us anything clearly about the intrinsic relationship between the specific powers of the deacon and the specifically priestly powers. We also cannot simply presume with regard to this question that the different functions and powers of the diaconate must all have the same relationship to the specific nature of the priesthood. It may be true, for example, that the priest *qua* priest, and hence *qua* mystagogue of the celebration of the mysteries of the Church, has a more essential and a closer relationship to the task of teaching than to the charitable task. This would be true particularly if it were conceivable in the nature of things that the Church either confers priestly powers on a priest without thereby obliging him to a different form of *caritas* than that to which any Christian is obliged, or entrusts a deacon with the performance of charitable works which as such are an obligation of the hierarchical Church; in other words, even when such a separation is not undertaken, the emphasis within a commission which in itself embraces several powers, may nevertheless be very different. Consequently, and in spite of what has been said up till now, it is not absolutely impossible that a deacon may, for instance, be the organ of the collective episcopal power with regard to the charitable works of the Church with an emphasis and explicitness which are not present in the actual office of an individual priest in the service of the bishop. For the rest, it will in practice depend on the actual will of the bishop whether he associates a deacon and his task more directly with himself or whether he wishes to see the task of the deacon as a direct help for the simple priest (the parish priest). The fact that the ordaining Church recognizes that the powers of the deacon are also contained in the priesthood as such and intends to confer them by the priesthood does not in practice exclude the possibility of associating the deacon directly to the bishop as his helper.

(d) There is not much to be said here about the grace of office of the diaconate. The powers given by an office and the grace attached to an office for the exercise of the office—an exercise which sanctifies the office-bearer himself—are certainly realities distinct from each other yet mutually related to one another. The ordination itself naturally cannot directly—by the very act of ordination—give the grace of office demanded by a lifelong exercise of this office. The ordination must be understood rather as the divine (sacramentally tangible) promise of the help of grace which, by reason of this promise, God is ready to give in the course of the life of the office-bearer, and which he will give to the extent in which the office-bearer opens his soul more and more to this grace by trying to do justice to his office with the help of divine grace. As regards the grace of office itself, everything to be said about the effect of divine grace in general applies also to this grace in particular. Furthermore, whatever applies to all the sacraments which have in any way a constituting character (i.e. Baptism, Confirmation, Holy Orders and Matrimony) applies also in this case: it is possible to allow for their graces to revive, and it is possible to deepen these graces.

6. FULL-TIME AND PART-TIME DIACONATE

Any discussion of the restoration of the diaconate will have to consider also the question as to whether these deacons (especially the married ones) would be meant to practise their diaconate as a full-time occupation—in other words, as priests and bishops do in normal circumstances—or whether this ordained diaconate should be a kind of part-time job for men who for the rest of the time follow a normal secular occupation and, as it were, conceive their diaconate as an intensified activity of the lay apostolate or of Catholic Action which has been given a special character by ordination. If we are to expect any kind of clear answer to this question which undoubtedly is also of practical importance, then we must first of all distinguish our concepts. For, as far as the concept of 'vocation' is concerned, we must distinguish between a vocation in a metaphysical and theological sense and a vocation in the ordinary economic sense. St Paul, for instance, was a tentmaker in the ordinary economic sense, i.e. he was forced to devote a great deal of his time to this trade in order to give himself an economic basis for existence. By his inner attitude, however, he was an apostle and nothing else, i.e. his apostolic vocation and task was the only real, personal motive force of his whole life; it formed his life, it was the only guiding line of his actions, everything else was subordinated to it, and even his economic vocation, by which he earned his bread, served this other vocation and nothing else, no matter how time-consuming it may have been. His apostolate, if we may put it this way, was not a spare-time job, it was not merely a hobby or just an additional though extremely ideal occupation transforming his life, but the real existential, formative principle of his life, even though it may of necessity have taken up less of his time sometimes than his trade of tentmaking. A religious task and purpose does not *eo ipso* become the life-giving formative principle of a vocation in the metaphysico-theological sense, simply because it is objectively on a higher level than what constitutes a secular, economic vocation. Someone who, for example, is a research chemist by the whole inner inclination of his personality, can nevertheless be an extremely zealous worker in Catholic Action as a lay apostle; he can in certain cases play an important role in a parish; he may indeed recognize and acknowledge the purely-objectively higher value of his religious purpose as compared with the ideals of his vocation as a chemist; nevertheless, he will be a chemist by profession even in a metaphysico-theological sense, and not an apostle. For, in spite of everything and having regard to the whole of his personal life, his job as a chemist is the essential law of his life (understanding, of course, that this does not refer to the general formative principles valid for every human being and every Christian, but to his professionally specifying formative principles). Conversely, a member of a secular institute, for instance, if he understands his life according to the Evangelical Counsels properly, will have to interpret his secular occupation as a means of realizing those specifically religious and apostolic purposes which are proper to such a secular institute; in a metaphysico-theological sense, such a member (even if he is a research worker) will, therefore, have a spiritual and not a worldly vocation, even when—in a secular, sociological sense—he does a secular job. Of course, it also follows from what has been said, that the transition from one of these notions to the other will be quite vague in the hard realities of life. It is clear that in the individual concrete case, it will perhaps be difficult to determine the boundary. Indeed, in the history of a particular life, a part-time occupation may become a real vocation in the theological and existential sense, and what was previously a vocation in the metaphysico-theological sense may deteriorate to being a job in a merely economic or perhaps secular sense, i.e. to being a 'job by which one gains one's living'.

If one makes this fundamental distinction, then one will presumably be able to say: only where the diaconate is a vocation in the theological and existential sense in the life of a certain person should the Church ordain that person by the sacrament of the diaconate; where, on the other hand, in spite of the inner understanding and serious idealism with which they are exercised, the functions of the diaconate are merely something like an idealistic spare-time occupation which does not really constitute the inner structural principle of a person's life, such a person performing the activities of the diaconate should not be ordained deacon by the Church. This principle surely follows from the fact that an ordination, especially by the character given by it, is meant to stamp a person permanently and completely and should claim the whole person, with all his internal and external powers, for such a permanent commission and authorization of service in the Church. If this principle were to be basically disputed, then it would also be no longer possible to explain why the Church does not normally want the priest to be burdened with some other civil job but wants him to live

by the altar. In view of this fact, the ordained deacon must fundamentally be someone who normally receives his livelihood from the Church
in basically the same way and with basically the same 'titles' as Canon
law envisages for the priest. Of course this does not tell us anything
about the extent to which this normal case will be realized at a particular
time and in a particular country. It does not determine whether the
exceptional cases (as was already true at the time of St Paul) will not
sometimes become the 'normal' practice, i.e. whether ordained deacons,
as well as priests, must not in certain conditions work for their living
by a bread-winning job. Yet even in this case they would be, and would
have to be, men whose personal life is completely formed by their
vocation as deacons, their vocation in the theological sense. In other
words, ordination to the diaconate cannot be given as a kind of reward
or decoration for a zealous apostolate. This again does not mean, however, that it is inconceivable that in certain economic and social conditions, where those who are anxious to do creative work can and do
leave their bread-earning jobs in good time, there will be a noticeable
increase in the number of those who regard and choose the diaconate
as a genuine vocation in the theological sense. The mere fact of more
advanced age is no real obstacle to this.

7. REMARKS ABOUT CERTAIN PRACTICAL NORMS FOR THE RESTORATION OF THE DIACONATE

We intend merely to indicate these norms here in so far as they more
or less represent self-evident conclusions from our previous fundamental reflections; in this way we should be in a position to show to
some extent that even in practice such a restoration of the diaconate is
not really as revolutionary a measure as might be thought at first. It
must be understood, of course, that such norms can have legal validity
only if they are laid down by the ecclesiastical authorities.

(a) The canonical and liturgical laws regarding those deacons who
accept their office and ordination with the declared intention of becoming priests can quite easily remain as they have been up till now.
It is not the task of these reflections to examine whether a practical,
longer interval between the time of ordination to the diaconate and
ordination to the priesthood would be advisable and practicable for the
training and testing of candidates for the priesthood. Since in the Latin
Church the candidate for the priestly office makes a sworn declaration

before reception of the subdiaconate, to the effect that he knows the obligation of celibacy and wishes to take it freely upon himself, there can be no doubt about which of the two classes of deacon someone belongs to, especially since the candidates for the priesthood who become deacons receive a religious and theological training which is completely different in content, place, etc., from the training of the 'absolute' deacons (to coin a phrase). If one leaves the diaconate as a step in Orders towards the priesthood, then nothing at all needs to be changed in the canonical legislation for the priesthood, and the candidate for the priesthood is made to realize with sacramental clearness that his office, too, since it includes the diaconate, is a service and not a lording it over others. It becomes clear to him in this way also that he must regard the 'absolute' deacons as his true brothers in the spirit, appointed for the same unique task of the Church as his.

(b) All our previous reflections started from and were directed to the fact that the sacramental transmission of the office of the diaconate should be used whenever this office already exists more or less explicitly (even though perhaps not in all its functions and powers) and that we should not create more or less artificial offices which are not demanded by the needs of the care of souls but are created simply in order to be able to confer an ordination to the diaconate. It cannot be doubted, however, that the offices presupposed for the restoration of the ordination of deacons do not exist to the same extent, with equal significance and in equal numbers in different parts of the Church. And furthermore where they do not exist, they are presumably non-existent partly because they are not really required (since there are, for instance, sufficient priests who can easily and without special difficulty fulfil the tasks of the diaconate together with their own); on the other hand, these offices may indeed be absent partly also on account of a certain atrophy in the Church's pastoral care which really requires these offices but simply has not yet developed them to a sufficient extent. Such a situation certainly makes it desirable that the centralized, universal ecclesiastical legislation concerning the restoration of the diaconate should be merely a skeleton legislation making it possible to administer such ordinations where the actual existence of these offices would make such a procedure reasonable and desirable. Such a legislation should advise and facilitate the establishment of such offices where the situation of the care of souls demands it and where the possibility of an ordination to an office would make it easier to give these offices to suitable candidates. It should be legislation, finally, which does not make the restoration of the diaconate an obligation for regions where the situation does not warrant it and where this restoration would have no real meaning if it were carried through. A merely skeleton legislation, which would leave room for a genuine differentiation in the Church in accordance with the religious, pastoral, cultural and historical situation, would reasonably and homogeneously fit into that general tendency in the Church (in accordance with the principle of subsidiary functions valid also for the Church) which desires to introduce a certain decentralization in the Church wherever the objectively existing or desirable difference of the individual parts of the Church obviously calls for such decentralization. The most suitable subjects for such differentiated and independent practices with regard to the ordination and utilization of deacons presumably would not be so much individual dioceses but rather certain wider ecclesiastical configurations, such as an Ecclesiastical Province or the totality of dioceses in a country, so that a Metropolitan or a National Conference of bishops would be the proper legislator (with the approval of the Apostolic See) for such particular regulations.

(c) Such a skeleton legislation issued by Rome could give the holders of particular rights in the Church (perhaps with certain conditions to be worked out in more detail) the right to ordain men to the diaconate without obligation to celibacy, provided they have proved themselves by a Christian life put to the test and by a 'professional' exercise (cf. No. 6) of an important part of those tasks which, according to the Church's tradition, constitute the office of deacon (i.e. liturgical, teaching, charitable, administrative functions, in which connection it should be noted that such a candidate of an ordained diaconate need not have exercised all these functions in actual fact, but may have specialized in one of them as his main task). Before ordaining anyone, the bishop must be convinced that the candidate for ordination to the diaconate has the desire and firm purpose to exercise this office for life, as a member of the clergy but without a desire to become a priest, and that he has the necessary physical, mental and religious qualifications for this. If the candidate is already married, then the bishop must of course also take his Christian conduct of marriage into consideration when judging his suitability. It will probably also have to be part of this skeleton legislation to decide whether the ordination of an 'absolute' deacon should be administered to someone already married (if he has not accepted the obligation of celibacy by ordination or by membership of a religious institute) or whether ordination to the diaconate can be given even to a suitable candidate who is still unmarried but does not wish to renounce the right to marry. Perhaps the question is not so urgent in practice because it can be expected in general that a candidate for ordination to the diaconate who has already been tested for a longer period (which is necessary) and who is likely to think about getting married, will be already married by the time the longer trial period of his training and testing in the exercise of his vocation is over, a period which must be demanded in any case. Certainly, it has been said elsewhere that this trial period should also not be stretched out *too* long, if we are not to contradict the whole meaning of such an ordination. No matter what may be the exact details of this skeleton legislation, a certain elasticity in its application to territorial and personal circumstances will be advisable, in the same way as it has already been done in the case of the legislation regarding the priesthood (dispensation from the statutory age for ordination, etc.). This skeleton legislation will have to incorporate also some general rules about the possibility and manner of laicization of such ordained deacons. It will be advisable, for various practical reasons, not to make withdrawal from *this* clerical station too difficult, whether the first move be made by the deacon himself or by the bishop (both of which must be open possibilities). This outline-legislation must naturally also occupy itself with the celibate 'absolute' deacon, since he too is a possibility. With regard to the obligation to celibacy in this case, the legislation will either have to state what is already (or perhaps will be) the canonical rule with regard to the celibacy of deacons going on to the priesthood, or what is right where there is some other reason for the celibacy of such a deacon, viz. on the grounds of his obligation as a member of a religious society or secular institute. To this extent it will be quite easy to lay down rules for the celibacy of such a deacon.

(d) The deacon thus ordained will surely also have the right, at least basically, to exercise those liturgical functions which belong to him according to can. 741, 845 §2, 1147 §4, 1342 §1 of the CIC, and will have this explicit and unreserved right even if he is married. It must be left to the Church's legislative activity and presumably to her universal legislation to decide whether these liturgical powers should be extended still further and should be made more precise by a universal ecclesiastical legislation (whether they should be extended, for instance, to the right of assisting at marriages, to wider powers for blessings for all things permitted to the priest, to the power of giving Benediction). The diaconate will, however, gain in significance, in estimation and pastoral usefulness, if the legislation is magnanimous and broad-minded in this respect. After all, even this skeleton legislation can make provision for the individual Ordinary to promulgate more exact regulations regarding the use of these liturgical powers, even though in certain cases this may mean limiting these powers to some extent in practice. It is taken for granted that in these liturgical functions the deacons will be bound by the liturgical laws (e.g. with regard to liturgical dress) just as the rest of the clergy.

(e) An elastic, general legislation of universal canon law will probably not be able to go further in its decrees about the exercise of the office, about dress and about the married deacons' way of life, than stating that they must in all these respects follow the directions of their Ordinary. But with regard to these directions to be given by the Ordinary, we will once more have to remind ourselves of the fundamental principle that it is the *office* and not the ordination to the office which must be the basic norm for all these directives. Hence, the manner of life which up till now has been recognized and encouraged by the Church authorities as corresponding to the office must also correspond to this office even after ordination. This applies also, for instance, to the question of lay dress of such an office-holder according to the customs of the particular country. These ordinances must therefore not be an external and mechanical transference of the laws applicable to the conduct of the bearers of higher Orders.

(f) The canonical obedience towards his bishop, to which the ordained deacon is obliged as a member of the clergy, embraces:

(i) The obligation to exercise his office as perfectly as possible on the lines laid down by the bishop, i.e. that office which the person concerned exercised in the service of the Church even before his ordination to the diaconate and which was meant to be sanctified and perfected by this ordination. This canonical obedience at least need not contain the obligation to exercise a totally different kind of diaconate from the one for which the person concerned was trained and in which and for which he was ordained;

(ii) The obligation to exercise the liturgical functions of a deacon, when and in the measure to which the bishop deems this necessary for an ordered and fruitful care of souls;

(iii) The obligation to lead a life in keeping with his ecclesiastical office and ordination. For the rest, the norms of this canonical obedience will have to be conceived analogously to those of the canonical obedience of the priest, with obvious modifications which will be necessary in the nature of things.

(g) The livelihood of a deacon in the service of the Church (again in accordance with our basic reflections) will first of all be that which the Church (the bishop or the parish) had already given and was obliged to give to such a deacon on account of the office he exercised even before his ordination. It is clear that the Church's obligation to see to the deacon's maintenance is increased by ordination and by the fact that the ordained belongs to the clergy. The formally juridical part of the Church's obligation to look after the maintenance of the deacon can be carried out in accordance with the '*titulus canonicus*' of the other Orders. It is understood that this maintenance which the Church owes to her ordained deacons within the limits of her possibilities includes also the maintenance of the deacon's family in accordance with what is fitting for the station and purpose of his vocation.

(h) The training of an 'absolute' deacon.

The general, skeleton legislation will no doubt have to lay down certain guiding lines also for the training of 'absolute' deacons, without thereby doing violence to the great difference of conditions in different countries and hence of the actual characteristics of the deacon's service in these different countries. In this sense it would have to be demanded that the formation of such deacons correspond to the following principles:

(α) The deacon must receive a general religious education corresponding to what is customary and possible in the case of an educated Christian layman in a particular region.

(β) He must receive the schooling and formation demanded by the needs and possibilities of the particular region for the carrying out of the office he exercises or should exercise even apart from ordination to the diaconate (e.g. the office of welfare worker, social worker, catechist, ecclesiastical administrator, etc.). It is not necessary, therefore, that this professional training should be the same for all deacons. On the contrary, it will be desirable that this formation should be very specialized but thorough so that as a result of this formation the later professional activity of such a deacon will vindicate itself on its own merits and not merely by the ordained character of the person concerned. It follows from this that at least this part of the general formation of a deacon will demand different training schools and cannot be given uniformly to all deacons. This will not necessitate the establishment of a very complicated, new training machinery, since no new offices and hence no new training institutes need be created; it will be quite sufficient to utilize and eventually adapt to one's higher purpose those training facilities which even now serve the purpose of preparing candidates for their different occupations. If the future ordained deacon is to engage mostly in catechetical tasks in the Church, then he must of course be given a thorough theological training, a training which must more or less correspond to the training demanded of a priest engaged in the care of souls (according to the rules and customs of the particular country). A more detailed treatment of this question will be found elsewhere in this book. The general schooling (secondary school, etc.), demanded and sufficient in the institutions concerned with this vocational training, should also be demanded and suffice for ordination to the diaconate.

(γ) This formation of the deacon will also have to include a fairly long period of exercising his particular office in the service of the Church before ordination. It would perhaps be more desirable to determine the age for ordination of the absolute deacon on this basis, rather than simply demanding systematically a certain fixed age for this. If, for instance, someone has exercised his diaconate outstandingly well for three to five years after thorough training (and has thereby automatically reached the age at which the Church confers even ordination to the priesthood) then there should be no reason for not conferring ordination to the diaconate.

(δ) Finally, there should be an additional, brief but thorough period of instruction and practice in the liturgical functions which are part of the deacon's duty. The question as to whether it would be possible and desirable to train all the different categories of deacons in common as far as this part of their training is concerned is something which will have to be decided in accordance with the different conditions in different countries. During the whole training (i.e. both the more vocational and the liturgical training) the corresponding religious and spiritual instruction and formation of the candidates for the diaconate must also be looked after. This part of the training could be conceived analogously to the formation given to candidates for the priesthood by the Spiritual Director.

(i) Since presumably any skeleton legislation issued by Rome could say very little about the actual life of ordained deacons both 'on duty' and privately, it will be the task of the bishop to help the ordained deacons by suitable norms and recommendations to ensure that their personal, human and religious life will correspond to their spiritual station and their office in the Church, that marriage may harmoniously fit into, and positively advance, the mission given to them by the Church and that they may foster that unity and co-operation among deacons and with the priestly pastors of souls which are so necessary both for the fulfilment of their task, and to ensure that the unity and co-operation between deacons and priests are made evident and the characteristics of the office of the deacon come to be clearly distinguished from the priestly office. Above all, it will have to be recommended that the deacon should assist at the daily celebration of the Eucharistic sacrifice and that he should make a regular habit of meditative reading of the Scriptures.

(j) In accordance with the proper nature of the different Orders in the Church, it seems less suitable—and indeed superfluous—to demand reception of the Minor Orders as a condition for ordination to the diaconate in the case of 'absolute' deacons.

13
SOME REMARKS ON THE QUESTION OF
CONVERSIONS

THE question of individual conversions is one of the problems connected with the ecumenical movement. We are simply going to make a few remarks about this question here, remarks which in no way claim to give an adequate treatment of this difficult subject. The selection of these remarks has been fairly arbitrary, and the apparent one-sidedness of their perspectives must not be misinterpreted as a basic outlook.

The Catholic Church claims to be the true Church of Jesus Christ to the exclusion of all others. Since, in the case of adults, conversions to Christianity as a religion of personal faith cannot ultimately come about except by the free decision of each individual, the Church—being the true Church of Jesus Christ—cannot give up her claim that she can and must oblige the individual to join her by his free decision. In principle, even the fact that such a decision would have to go against the whole outlook of his people, his generation, his relatives, the trends of the situation of his own mental development, etc., would not be sufficient to release the individual from the obligation of this free decision. Nor does the fact that the individual concerned is already a Christian excuse him. All these factors may indeed affect the practical application of the general principle in different ways, but they can never annul the principle as such. Ecumenically speaking, it is, of course, particularly important that the claim of the Catholic Church is seen to refer fundamentally also to the other Christians and does not excuse them because they are already Christians. The ecumenical movement as such, in so far as it tries to bring about a *rapprochement* and ultimately a union between the Christian communions as such, can and indeed must—in trying to serve this important and legitimate goal—give up trying to canvass in its work for individual conversions. For no individual effort, and no organization serving an individual goal, can dispute the right or obligation of some other effort or some other goal just because it is not included in its own aims. It is also quite possible that in the person of her official representatives who are responsible for the totality of her tasks and obligations and who plan accordingly, the Catholic Church may give less encouragement to certain tasks in favour of a legitimate general aim. In view of man's finite nature and the plurality of his tasks, such preferences are essentially and indeed physically quite unavoidable and hence also quite legitimate in the moral sense. To this extent, even the official leadership of the Church (and not merely the ecumenical movement) could give somewhat less attention to the demand made on the individual non-Catholic Christian to become a Catholic (i.e. to the efforts for conversions) than it does to more general ecumenical endeavours. But fundamentally, the Catholic Church must claim not only the right but also the duty to concern herself with individuals as such, and hence also with the individual non-Catholic Christian, with a view to making them members of the Catholic Church. This is particularly true since the Catholic Church regards herself not as an important promoting agency for salvation but as necessary for salvation. This is not the place to try to explain the meaning and limits of this notion of the necessity of the Church for salvation. But the notion itself must be mentioned here, since presumably many other Christian communions and individual non-Catholic Christians today no longer attribute this necessity-for-salvation to their own communion as such (i.e. in so far as it is distinguished from any other Christian communion). The old Reformation communions did indeed profess themselves to be necessary for salvation (and this not only with regard to the essential, universal Christian truths and sacraments); they thus transferred the inherited teaching of the old Church about her necessity for salvation to themselves and hence proclaimed their teaching within a Catholic ethos of a claim to absoluteness. Many of the present-day non-Catholic communities of belief, however, would presumably no longer make this claim either in theory or, at least, in practice. To this extent they should really have a fundamentally different attitude to the work of winning converts for their own communion from the attitude found in the Catholic Church. If one regards the individual Christian denominations merely as different manifestations of the one Christianity —manifestations which all have basically the same right to man's adherence, even though they are not all equally successful manifestations—then there is no intrinsic reason why they should assume an absolute right and a heavy responsibility for the gaining of converts, a reason which does, however, exist in a Church which fundamentally and in line with her own proper conviction of faith does not recognize such equal rights in other Christian communions. Such Christian denominations could and indeed should perhaps renounce their endeavours to make converts in this age of the ecumenical spirit. For they could and indeed should concentrate all their efforts on the winning of converts among the pagans as well as on general ecumenical endeavours. In any case, the different attitude of the individual Christian communions towards convert work is based on this deeper difference. Sometimes this difference may surprise other Christians and they may feel it as an obstacle to the ecumenical dialogue; they may be tempted to interpret the Catholic Church's desire for converts as something un-ecumenical. Whenever this happens, non-Catholic Christians must try to understand that this desire for 'proselytes' is based on the Catholic Church's claim to be absolute and that they will just have to accept this as a fact, just as they must accept everything else which separates them from the Catholic Church. (Of course, this leaves untouched the question of the actual manner of such efforts to make converts. These may still be loveless, intolerant, unfavourable to the higher aim of the ecumenical movement as such and hence may appear to be unjustifiable even from a Catholic point of view.)

In so far as this very general principle signifies an objective obligation on the part of the individual non-Christian to become a Catholic (i.e. to be 'converted') it should be interpreted in the light of all the principles of Catholic ethics concerning the gravity of an obligation: the difference between the objective obligation and the subjective 'realization' of such an obligation, the different way in which one is obliged by a prescriptive and a prohibitive commandment or by a commandment of natural law and one of divine positive law, the reasons and causes which hinder the subjective recognition of an objective obligation and which excuse the non-fulfilment of a commandment, and other similar part-principles.

In this respect, the scientific insights and the experience of Christendom with regard to what causes the lack of such a recognition of the obligation of conversion have undoubtedly increased a great deal as compared with the first centuries after the Reformation. We living today have come to realize the immeasurable subjective conditioning of the knowledge of the individual, especially in questions concerning his view of the world—in other words, especially in existentially radical questions concerning the whole man. This understanding authorizes us and our duty obliges us, on the one hand, to presume 'good faith' in our fellow men unless we have strict proof of the contrary. Thus we are no longer inclined today to deny good faith to all 'educated' non-Catholics who, although they do in some ways come into actual contact with Catholics and the Catholic Church, nevertheless do not become Catholics. This may seem an obvious platitude to most of our contemporaries—even to Catholics and present-day theologians—a truth which even the Pope himself practises by the unaffectedly friendly reception he gives to non-Catholic Christians (which was probably not the case in this particular way in earlier centuries): but this now self-evident truth was not by any means self-evident even only 150 years ago, and even today is still not so in Latin countries. The present author himself can still remember vividly a conversation with an old parish priest in Lower Bavaria who took it for granted that a Protestant theologian cannot possibly adhere to his beliefs in good faith, since he is surely in a position to recognize the truth of the Catholic Church. In Boswell's 'Great tour through Germany and Switzerland', an Englishman describes a meeting with a Jesuit in the year 1764 at Mannheim. To the Anglican, the Jesuit appears very well educated, very charming and open-minded. But when the Englishman tells him that he is a non-Catholic and adds that he hopes the Jesuit would not count him among the damned on this account, the latter declared: 'It may sound hard, but it is absolutely necessary for me to believe this to be the case. The extenuating circumstances present in the case of a poor country yokel are not valid in your case. You are educated.' We today can no longer think in such a naïve way. For in the face of the great number of non-Catholics and their close contact with the Catholic reality, we would either have to doubt the good faith of so many people (for which—if we do not think jansenistically of man—we have no reason and no indications from experience) or we would have to doubt the universal salvific will of God and think, again jansenistically, that God would refuse these people the grace of salvation (i.e. even merely sufficient grace) without any guilt on their part, a grace necessary for the fulfilment of an obligation present not only objectively but also subjectively. But if we can no longer say this today after the manner of post-Reformation polemics, then there naturally arises the question—a question which to date has probably received only a very general and formal skeleton answer—as to how the concession of *bona fides* (at least fundamentally) even in the case of non-'*rudes*' (to use the theological terminology of Vatican I) can be reconciled with the doctrine that the truth and the binding claim of the Catholic Church are recognizable by clear rational and historical arguments as *signa certissima et omnium intelligentiae accommodata* (Denz 1790), since this quality of the perceptibility of Christian revelation is also explicitly referred to the Catholic Church as such (Denz 1794). This question is a particularly difficult one because the judgement of the objective knowability of the Christian revelation and of the claim of the Church refers not only to the quality of the arguments '*in se*' but also to their suitability and their effectiveness in relation to actual people. This really gives rise to the following question: How could these arguments be regarded as *omnium intelligentiae accommodata* if in actual fact they have so little success even in cases where they seem to be present to the judgement and conscience of non-Catholics (since the latter do come into contact with the Church who is herself declared to be an argument of her own credibility [Denz 1794])—unless we presume that there is bad faith on the other side?

We have not posed this question here in order to answer it, for this is not our present task. We have posed it for another reason which is of importance for the question of conversions itself. For this whole problem at least shows that there are a great number of psychological influences which can obscure the knowability of the Church's claim in the concrete case. These influences must not be conceived as being effective merely on the individual, for they are also of a general kind and they concern and essentially constitute the concrete milieu of whole ages and peoples. We may even go on to add a twofold observation in this regard.

Firstly, the period (taken very loosely) between the time when the denominational boundaries began to become increasingly blurred in Central Europe (i.e. since the beginning of the nineteenth century) and the present-day era of mass population movements and massive changes in political structure is identical with the period which saw the spirit of the age growing more and more anti-Christian and threatening all Christian denominations without distinction. This is not self-evident but, once realized, it does give us a partial explanation as to why the historically and existentially tangible presence of the Catholic Church in the concrete environment of the non-Catholics does not really have the effect one might expect when one thinks of the Catholic Church as the *signum levatum in nationes*—as the witness to her own divine institution—and hence expects that in the nature of things she will have little proselytizing effect only where she is not present with sufficient historical concreteness in the environment of a people. Ultimately the same cause (viz. modern society) has given rise to two effects which practically cancel each other out in terms of the Church's power of attraction for prospective converts and which leave the actual state of affairs the same as it was at the time of the denominationally committed individual States: a far-reaching, firmly established situation of inter-denominational relationships altered only by the common losses of all denominations to this 'neo-paganism'. The greater contact between different denominations has not itself altered anything.

Secondly, this common situation of all Christian denominations *vis-à-vis* 'neo-paganism' also signifies in actual fact a weakening in one's sense of the religious existential urgency in the question of which denomination one ought to belong to: one experiences one's own Christianity as a secure and personally won possession of immeasurable significance, compared with which the denominational differences are subjectively (and objectively) of lesser importance, all of which can be said even if one does not falsely reduce these differences to nothing. A person may be subject to many situational factors and other elements of psychological motivation: these influence his personal decisions by determining the number of existential possibilities worthy of serious consideration in such a way that the possibility of conversion, for instance, is no longer a serious possibility worthy of one's consideration, and this even before it comes to a moral decision and without any question of moral fault (and we must suppose this to be the case, if we do not wish to deny today that the majority of Christians in our parts who do not become Catholics, are in good faith). If this is so, then it is naturally also true that a great number of such subconscious motivations enter also into the process of actual conversions. We must be clear about this fact: the sum total of the factors actually affecting a person in a free decision is certainly not identical with the sum total of the explicitly and consciously grasped, and as such freely willed, motives. Just as a person cannot reflectively exhaust something he perceives—since every reflection requires another new series of perceptions, reasons and logical operations which themselves (since otherwise we would have to postulate a regression to infinity) are not reflex—so it is also and even much more so, in the case of free decisions. This applies, of course, also to the decision of conversion. It can happen—in this case just as much as in others—that in certain circumstances a third party has a much clearer idea of some part of the unreflected background and motivation of a conversion than the person concerned himself: the subjective soil, the emotional basis, on which such a decision is actually built up, can be much more tangible to the external observer than to the convert himself. The soil in which a conversion grows may be a strong aesthetic need (among other things, of course) which certainly is also normally present; a person may get the stimulus leading to conversion because he experiences a strong personal tie to a proselytizing Catholic; he may be someone whose strong critical tendency gives the impetus to his adopting a critical attitude towards the actual condition of his previous church; it may be that someone would never have got the idea of conversion if he had not suffered very great personal disappointments in his own communion, even though these themselves have objectively nothing or only very little to do with the question of truth. Such and innumerable other motivations which are not all systematically thought out by the convert may form the impetus for a conversion (just as they may also impede it, and this as equally unsystematic limitations of the existentially really present question). This does not, of course, argue in any way against the objective foundation of a conversion. A person may perfectly well understand the theorem of Pythagoras, for instance, even though he or others say to themselves that he would never have comprehended it if he had not got the urge—for quite different reasons than interest in matters of geometry—to become absorbed in the objective proof of this theorem. Yet even from this point of view, the question as to the moral correctness and obligation of a conversion in a concrete case is a much more difficult question than is commonly supposed, even when the convert is not conscious of any reprehensible motivation (such as worldly motives of honour, consideration for one's marriage partner, one's career, etc.) and when the objective reasons for the conversion seem to be grasped purely in their doctrinal, reflex conceptuality. We know that no Christian can say *with certitude* that he has really acted for *those* particular motives—and that *those* motives were certainly the interior and moral form-giving factors—which he has consciously represented to himself and which he has tried to aim at, for otherwise he would know with certitude that he is in the state of grace when he makes an act of faith, hope and charity in accordance with their perfectly exact and objectively correct formulation by the theologians. In the same way, a convert can never tell with absolute certitude whether the explicit motives of his conversion—about whose correctness there can be no doubt—are in his actual case also the real, actual underlying factors of his act, the factors which determine the moral quality of his act, or whether the latter are not really contained in those subconscious motivations on which he cannot adequately reflect. But what about the case where another person—for example, the one who is giving the instructions—has reasons to doubt whether the prospective convert's motives are really pure? It cannot be said that such a case is impossible. It also cannot be said that such a case can always be solved by appealing to the prospective convert himself. Even when an embittered, dogmatic kind of person, who has had a rough time in his previous religious communion, is made aware of the peculiarities of his disposition and is shown that they may possibly influence him very strongly, he will naturally declare that all this does not make any difference to his intentions. Must the other person believe him in every case? In many cases, like the priest who often has to assist at marriages whose motivation and future stability he has reason to doubt, he will have to endorse the conversion. But there can also be cases where a person who is in a position to encourage a conversion, if he *wishes*, can ask himself whether he should not rather refrain from doing so, or at least be free to refrain, when he has reason to suppose such underlying motivations. In a marriage, for instance, it is in certain circumstances easy for one of the partners to stimulate the other to conversion. Should he do this, if he has on the whole the impression that the whole mental and religious make-up of the other is simply not suited or prepared for a real, existentially religious conversion (even though there would never be any question of a dishonest conversion)? Can one really say that in the concrete conditions of man's life, such a change of outlook and such a preparation and cultivation of the conditions of soul necessary for a conversion are always really possible in the limited time available and in the given circumstances? If they are not, must one nevertheless still encourage such a conversion? To answer this question, we must first of all make a further distinction.

A conversion has a twofold meaning. The objective belonging to the Church has a meaning in itself. And the belonging to the Church means both in itself, and in view of the Church's truth and means of grace, the objectively greater possibility of salvation for men, which gives conversion its subjective meaning, i.e. its meaning in view of the salvation of this individual. Both these 'values' are at the root of the divine command of belonging to the Church. Even the first-mentioned value. For in the order of the Incarnation, and hence of the historical and eschatological tangibility of the salvific will and of grace (which we call the Church), God wills the Church as a visible society even before the question arises as to whether the chances of salvation for a determined individual are thereby increased in the concrete or not. If one did not affirm this, then it would be rather difficult to give any clear explanation of the theological reasons for the Church's missionary mandate, right and duty. For it would then always be possible to say that in view of God's universal salvific will, every person—even if he is not a member of the visible Church—is given a chance of salvation, and this chance is not any smaller essentially than it would be within the Church, for perhaps the greater chance of salvation which in itself is given within the Church is balanced out by the greater responsibility one then has by the fact that a subjectively greater burden rests on those who are better instructed and who recognize stricter moral demands. Hence, if the missionary mandate is not to be based on a purely positive divine command without any intrinsic justification, then it will be necessary to find the reason for this missionary mandate in a meaning and value to be found in what is historically tangible and hence in the growing Church. But, of course, even the second above-mentioned value of a conversion is of essential importance to it. It is quite clear that the value of a conversion based on the first point of view is not such that it could in no case take second place in favour of some other value as a result of a (here possible and meaningful) weighing of values. For example, the baptism of a child would certainly not be a moral duty if it were bound up with grave danger to the life of the baptizer. Such a baptism could be postponed in this case (taking the case of a child not actually dying). The objective belonging to the Church, which represents a value in itself, is not in every case a value which cannot be displaced by some other value. But as far as the other, more subjective aspect of a conversion and of belonging to the Church is concerned, the following point must be borne in mind. With regard to this aspect, the value concerned is essentially determined in the concrete by the question as to what extent a certain person is reasonably judged to be actually in a position of accepting and subjectively realizing the saving goods offered to him by membership of the Church. In this regard there are, however, very great differences between individuals, social groups and particular ages. We must not have any illusions about this: the average man in the Church 'realizes' subjectively only a very small part of the actual possibilities and realities of salvation at his disposal within the Church. If we take a realistic view, we will see that his knowledge is very limited (at least concerning those religious truths which he has managed to salvage for his actual life from what he was taught at school). He will not know much more than a few basic truths: that God exists, that He is the guardian of the moral order, that we have been redeemed by Christ, that there is a Judgement and eternal life. Nobody can doubt that, if these 'basic truths' of the Faith are to some extent seriously realized in practice, then we have a 'good Christian'. No one can seriously doubt that in very many individual and social situations it can be said with sufficient moral certitude that, as far as one can judge from the empirical appearances of life, this or that person is in fact unable to rise above this level (which, of course, does not give us any grounds for an adequate judgement about the ultimate state of a man before God). The same is true of the use of the 'means of grace' offered by the Church. It is indeed true that the Catholic Christian, who does not oppose himself explicitly to the Church, will make use of these means of grace to a certain extent; he will assist at Sunday Mass and he will receive the sacraments now and then. But if one inquires into the results of the sacramental life in the light of the experience of a dispassionate pedagogy of popular religion, one will find it difficult to maintain that it is certain that they are greater on the whole than the results which would be achieved by a religious education for ordinary people relying more on the subjective means of grace; the latter, after all, are undoubtedly also important and indispensable occurrences of the process by which divine grace becomes effective and is acquired, and not merely subjective human events: prayer, listening to the Word of God, repentance for sins, keeping the Christian commandments, trying to achieve a spiritual 'awakening' and conversion, the impression made by the good example of the Christian life of others, etc. Thus, all things considered, there arises the question as to whether, with regard to the subjective aspect of conversion, the real Christian 'success' is actually very great in many cases. This is not meant to pass judgement on any particular conversion. In this question, one must not refer oneself to any conversions with which one is familiar. Whenever these conversions take place with an extraordinary religious seriousness (as in the case of many of the conversions we are used to, which take place very spontaneously and very little through any special 'propaganda') even the 'subjective success' of the Church membership of such converts is, of course, very great and no doubt clearly justifies such conversions on this account alone. But given the case that a priest, thinking about a non-Catholic with whom he is in close contact, says to himself: If I wanted to, I could win this person for the Church; I could presumably influence him in the given circumstances in such a way that he would become a Catholic, of course with all the seriousness possible in such a case. But I would have to say to myself that the individual concerned—by his natural dispositions, by his mental and spiritual past (in so far as the actually possible religious instruction of the prospective convert probably would not be able to alter the influences of the past to any considerable extent), by his occupation, his possible interests, etc.—is in such a condition that in practice he could at best 'realize' as much, but not more, of the Christian possibilities of the Catholic Church as he is already doing in his present Christian situation. In other words, even after conversion, he could probably realize only those 'basic truths' of Christianity which are already known to him even now and which even now he puts into practice; he could live only as much of the inner life of grace through reception of the sacraments and by his subjective religious life as he has actually already realized even now (though by more subjective means). In such a case one must surely ask oneself: does the subjective side of such an actually possible Catholic Christianity surpass a non-Catholic Christian life so decisively that this consideration demands going to great pains for the conversion of a Christian, or is this not the case? If one does not think in too much of a purely objective and almost magic manner—in other words, if one is quite clear about the fact that the significance of a conversion has its limits even in its objective aspects, and if one understands clearly that it cannot be taken for granted that in the case of many Christians their properly realized Christianity

would be realized any differently in the subjective sense by a conversion—then it will be absolutely possible to ask: are there situations
in which the Church does not indeed renounce her fundamental rights
to conversions (and does not intentionally keep the universal, and
hence Catholic, gospel from anyone) but in which, in view of the
limited powers and means at her disposal, she may say to herself that
it is not a very urgent matter to direct her efforts towards making
converts among other Christians? Fundamentally it will be possible
to answer this question quite soberly with a yes. There *can* be such
situations. But this is in no way meant to insinuate that the Church
must, on account of these considerations, change her strategy and
tactics with regard to her missionary work among non-Catholic
Christians, either in our own or in other countries. On the contrary:
here at home, those who become converts will in general be people
to whom these considerations do not apply. And yet it would seem
that these considerations are of some practical significance. If we are
quite honest and dispassionate about this and see things as they are,
then we will have to admit that in Central Europe the efforts directed
towards making converts among Protestant Christians are practically
nil. It is indeed one of the particularly emphasized official duties of a
bishop to encourage efforts in this direction. But, if we may put it
quite bluntly: We do not believe that mid-European bishops in general
expend a great deal of time and effort in the fulfilment of this duty.
But precisely this sober statement of the facts now no longer shocks
and scandalizes in view of the above considerations. This attitude is
quite right on the whole, no matter how much it may perhaps surprise
and dismay a Spanish Catholic, for instance. For he will probably
be of the opinion that the Catholics of Central Europe should go to
battle against the Protestants (at least) with the sword of the Spirit,
in order to spread the Church, and that they ought to gain very swift
and important victories if they are at all zealous, in view of the convincing evidence of Catholic truth, especially since today—with the
disappearance of the Protestant State—the external obstacles to such a
re-Catholicization have also to a great extent disappeared. In view of
the forces actually at the disposal of the Church, the actual tactics of
the Church with regard to the encouraging of conversions in our
countries will however have to be justified on the whole in the light
of our considerations.

It also follows from these considerations that we Catholic Christians cannot rightly and with a good conscience hope for substantial losses within Protestant Christianity. We do not refer here to *numerical* losses of members of non-Catholic denominations, even though we should deplore even these as a very painful injury to ourselves also, if they are losses to present-day neo-paganism. For from whatever quarter modern non-Christianity may draw its adherents, its growth is always a threat even to Catholic Christianity, an injury done to the name of Christ and to the power of the gospel. How could we Catholics experience this with anything but deepest sorrow and pain? But we refer here to the *inner* loss of substance, loss of the clear profession of the traditional Truth which is really common to all Christianity. For centuries it was part of the stock-in-trade of Catholic polemics with regard to Protestant Christianity to prophesy that it would soon be 'sold out'; it was usual to develop the consequences of the basic principles of heresy so logically as to show that these logical consequences must very soon be clearly, completely and finally realized in the reality of life. These prophecies have still not been fulfilled, however, even after four hundred years. And it does not look as if they will be fulfilled in the near future. Periods of 'liberalistic' and 'enlightened' thought causing substantial losses in Protestant Christianity have been followed by quite powerful movements in the opposite direction. It is moreover true that the Catholic Church, in her official nature, has indeed resisted the attacks of the anti-Christian modern spirit most staunchly and impressively, and yet it cannot be said that Catholic Christianity as such has suffered less substantial losses during the last one hundred and fifty years than Protestant Christianity. Even in Latin countries, which have a more Catholic set-up, the number of really believing Catholics is just a small minority. And Catholic countries are, if anything, in greater danger from the organized godlessness of Bolshevism than Protestant countries. We may try to explain this fact by reasons lying outside the denominational sphere . . . the fact nevertheless remains. Communism was almost victorious in Spain. Today, Italy and South America are special hopes of Communism. We mention all this here merely to point out that, in view of this state of affairs, we do not have the least reason for regarding the loss of substance within Protestant Christianity with the feeling that all this is merely something inevitable and something we have long foretold, or even to regard it with a kind of malicious joy at other people's misfortune. The gain does not belong to the Catholic Church but to neo-paganism. It would be insane ecclesiastical politics to think that the others' loss in this matter is our gain. According to human estimation (in the supposition that one could do anything else ultimately than to hope for God's victory in Christ even when this seems beyond hope in human estimation), one would have to say that the whole of Christianity will either live or die together. Whether, how and when the unity of Christendom will come, we do not know. But one thing we do know, to hope for its coming through the external or internal bankruptcy of a part of Christendom would be engaging in stupid and shameful politics, building on the catastrophies of others. This means in its turn, however, that we ought to help each other to extend our common ecumenical efforts in an attempt to preserve each other from internal and external losses of substance. Why could we not help and instruct each other in the question as to how one can speak effectively and convincingly today to those who think they cannot be Christians? Why could we not instruct each other as to ways and means of proving Christianity to them, a Christianity which after all is common to us all in its most essential points? Why should not Catholic exegesis, here and there, be able to help its Protestant counterpart to be critical without 'demythologizing' everything to such an extent that Christianity simply disappears? Could not Protestant exegesis perhaps preserve some of our Catholic exegetes from making mistakes in Catholic exegesis due to their exuberance in making up for the lack of scientific research in the past, the same mistakes which Protestant exegesis made in the past and which it has since then overcome? Could we not exchange our pastoral experiences in missionary work in the present-day technological mass society? One does not get the impression that Catholic pastoral theology takes much notice of its Protestant counterpart. And the converse is probably just as true. Yet it cannot be said that we could not learn anything from each other. Here and there we have already done so, as, for example, with regard to the 'academies'. We could learn something from each other even in dogmatic theology. For there are already common viewpoints in Scripture studies regarding truths which do not in any way belong to controverted theological points. The language of each theology could learn from the other: for quite frequently each of them has in its own way certain traditional forms of expression which make it seem dead and out of date and which thus increase the difficulty of preaching the gospel to the present age. All these reflections may seem to have nothing to do with our present subject. Is it not a fact that the realistic possibility of gaining converts from Protestant Christianity, correctly understood, is such that it is actually secondary as compared with other tasks, and that both sides should agree on the slogan: Let us help each other to win the fight against this new paganism and let us look for 'converts' among those who today no longer have any real, actual connection with the Christian churches. Here is a wide field for missionary work, big enough for all denominations; here it could then show itself which is the stronger force. Such an orientation of one's efforts could perhaps have another effect as well: without prejudice to the actual question of truth, a great deal of what separates the Christian denominations, and keeps them separated, is not so much the theological differences but the whole way of life, the historically conditioned form of piety, the contradiction in the *ius humanum* of the respective systems of Canon law, etc. Even the dogmatic differences are, after all, seen subconsciously against the background of *these* other separating differences. One knows (on the basis of this 'lived' difference which one finds obvious and indisputable) that one is separated, and so one's theological endeavours are subconsciously aimed at also discovering this lived and seemingly indisputable separation in theology, so as to justify it from that point of view. So it happens that the theological controversies sometimes give the impression that one is actually *looking* for a difference by ever more subtle distinctions so that one may not need to unite. Of course, this is not done on purpose, but it is nevertheless a real thought mechanism and instinct: conclusions are proved of whose correctness one is already certain, viz. by the very fact of separation; this is an existential correctness which is 'evident' from the difference of life and not really from the difference of theology. If only Christians of all denominations would make intense efforts to rechristianize neo-paganism, all the different denominations would perhaps have to develop a style of Christian life, of theological language, etc., in dealing with the same 'material' of men, a style which on account of the sameness of 'material' would be largely the same (in spite of the different denominational starting points) and which therefore would lead to closer contact between the denominations themselves in the actuality of their real life, feeling and thought. This could then be extended to the theological talks which would then have more hope of success. If, for instance (to take just one example; one could of course also develop useful applications for the other side), the Catholic Church in Latin countries would really actively and successfully concern herself about the industrial mass society and its neo-paganism, both of which exist in an ever-increasing measure even in these countries, this presumably would automatically give rise to an image of the Catholic Church in these countries which would make it easier for a mid-European Protestant Christian to rediscover his own Christianity in this Christian and ecclesiastical life.

The question of the religious obligation of a conversion is quite frequently tied up with the question of the time interval permissible in conscience between the time of realizing one's obligation to become a Catholic and the actual fulfilling of this obligation. After all, there may be various reasons for wanting to be permitted to postpone one's conversion for a while, even after one has seen it to be one's duty. In accordance with what was stated at the beginning, it will have to be said first of all that the recognition of the truth of the Catholic Church and of her institution by Christ basically brings with it also the obligation to join the Church. This obligation of the individual does not in itself cease on account of the advantages one may hope for from one's ecumenical activity within one's previous religious communion—advantages, that is, for the unity of Christianity as a whole. This is true, not merely because these advantages will in most cases be extremely problematic and because such hopes can very easily be just wishful thinking, especially since such crypto-Catholics are usually listened to less than those who are clearly professed Catholics. But the fundamental reason why the individual obligation of conversion remains even in such a case is because any basic recognition of the justification of such tactics of deferment would objectively have to end up in a denial of the obligation to conversion of the individual *qua* individual in favour of the sole obligation of seeking a social union of the Christian groups among themselves. Such a thesis would, however, turn the individual as such into an absolutely and exclusively dependent functionary of the Christian community; it would make the communities the sole bearers of religious decisions, all of which constitutes a conception which must be absolutely rejected. On closer reflection, there are certainly very difficult problems in this connection, at least with regard to those Christian communions which from a Catholic point of view must be regarded as schisms, and not as real heresies, and this merely in so far as they are schisms—or, respectively, take effect as schisms—in the consciousness of faith of each individual.

Will it not have to be said in this case that the practice of the Catholic Church has up till now presupposed that, if the leaders of the Eastern churches were to unite with Rome, the members of their flocks would also, by that very fact, be united with Rome? Does this not mean, however, that we recognize these pastors to have a certain authority over their flocks by right? Under *this* presupposition, can an individual Christian leave the question of the removal of the schism to the head of his church and acknowledge him to be solely responsible in this matter? Or is every schism also at least an implicit heresy, so that the general principles concerning the individual's obligation of faith and of profession of faith also apply here in some way? But why, in this case, does tradition distinguish between schism and heresy even to this very day? No matter what may be the answer to this question which must remain unanswered here, it is clear in any case that, as far as heresy is concerned, we cannot accept the sole principle of a communal solution to the split in Christianity, nor therefore any other principles and practices which implicitly come to the same thing as this other principle. A postponement of one's conversion, until the moment of Union, as a matter of principle, is to be rejected. Yet this provides us only with a very external framework for the question about the timing of a conversion. For the Christian, even once he recognizes the necessity of the Church, has undoubtedly quite a considerable interval to play with as far as the fulfilment of his obligation to join the Church is concerned. For there is a long time given even for the catechumenate of the unbaptized, where things are really more urgent than in our case since then it is a question of receiving baptism which is necessary for salvation, whereas in our case it is a question of a Christian who is baptized and who already to large extent has those means of salvation at his disposal which will also help to support his later life. It is no good pointing out that the catechumen is not yet sufficiently instructed. For the reception of baptism at least would not require instruction lasting several years. And to point out the other reasons for such a catechumenate lasting for years proves exactly that there can be reasons for a relatively long postponement of the actual entry into the Church. Hence, it would have to be proved that a prospective convert could not have any such reasons. That his reasons are different from those of someone seeking baptism does not make it impossible for him to have legitimate reasons. Since the objective importance of belonging to the Church probably does not carry much weight in certain individual cases, it will be necessary in such cases to evaluate, as best one can, the concrete subjective importance of full membership of the Church (for, after all, the non-Catholic Christian already belongs to the Church in certain respects). If there can be no question of any serious threat to his personal salvation in the actual case, one will no doubt be able to make a fairly broad judgement as to the moment when his obligation to full membership of the Church becomes acute 'here and now'. This is especially true when the fact that someone postpones his decision and waits before taking the final step cannot be taken as a sign of any basic denial of his obligation to join the Church. In the case where a prospective convert, although officially belonging to a Protestant denomination, really comes rather from neo-paganism, it may happen that his getting used to a really lived Christianity in general—a stage which can already be combined with a great deal of Catholic 'practice' (assistance at Holy Mass, participation in Catholic life, etc.)—may take quite a lot of time, and in such a case this may be justified in the same way as a long catechumenate. It is difficult to see in itself why the Church could not treat such a Christian, who is on the way to conversion, in the same way canonically speaking (i.e. as regards ecclesiastical burial, etc.) as she treats a candidate for baptism.

There is still another question which can profitably be posed today with regard to the possibility and moral lawfulness of conversions, viz. the question about the subjective capability of grasping the objectively sound reasons for a conversion, or respectively for the legitimate claim of the Catholic Church to being the only true Church of Jesus Christ.

This question has already been touched on above. But we wish to reflect on it once more for its own sake. Everyone engaged in controversial theology today knows how difficult it is to give the non-Catholic a clear rational and historical understanding of the reasons for the obligation of conversion, in such a way that they convince those who have not already decided (for whatever reasons) to become Catholics. The question of the history of religion, of biblical theology, of Church history and Church law, which have to be explained and answered in the course of such a task (or which would have to be explained and answered in the case where one is encouraging a conversion which has not already taken place 'existentially' for non-scientific and non-theological reasons) are objectively so difficult (as is shown by theological controversies among specialist theologians on both sides) that one might ask oneself whether the normal non-specialist in this field can in the average case come to an objectively well-founded and unequivocal judgement, presupposing that such a non-specialist has only a limited amount of time and capacity-for-learning to give to such questions. If this is doubtful, then we have here a further justification for holding back in our zeal to make converts in this manner, in cases where the individuals concerned have not already decided to become Catholics for some other kind of reason. This question shows the necessity and justification for proper ecumenical efforts: a goodly section of Christians can, as it were, come to a reasoned judgement about where the true Church of Christ is to be found only with the help of the collective reflection of a whole church and not as individuals. We need not be surprised at this statement. For St Thomas Aquinas this is valid even with regard to the simple knowledge of God, which is certainly easier than forming an opinion in controverted theological questions. One would have to go even further, and ask whether in one's teaching of converts (i.e. converts of one kind or another) one ought not to prove the moral and theological lawfulness of their decision by considerations of an *indirect* and *global* kind, considerations which can to a large extent and quite legitimately avoid the series of problems connected with individual controverted questions of theology. Let us explain a little further what is meant by this. Is it being too daring or sceptical to maintain that (while admitting that the Primacy can be objectively proved by means of an exact biblical theology) it is not really quite honest to pretend to a simple convert that this proof is simple and easy to grasp, that all one needs to do is to quote Mt 16.18, give a few easily understandable explanations of this text, and then the matter will be quite clear? Surely, one must say quite honestly that such a method of controversial theology cannot really be permissible when dealing with a prospective convert (even when it eventually has its intended effect), since it does not provide him with a real, objectively justified (and in itself possible) insight into the solution of the question (nor one which is capable of being this in the time available and under the given presuppositions) and yet pretends to give such knowledge. Thus there arises the question as to how we might solve such individual theological questions in an *indirect* but lawful manner and so be able to create the fundamental theological presuppositions for an acceptance of the Catholic Church. To do this is surely possible. We might, for instance, develop the thought that in accordance with the whole incarnational structure of the salvation brought by Christ, the Church founded by Him must be a historical reality and hence a reality possessing historical continuity, and that it cannot be a merely ideological structure which, as it were, would always come to exist anew and thus, as something new, would simply replace the previous ecclesiastical structure by a *generatio aequivoca*. We might stress furthermore that, under this presupposition, the Catholic Church with her properly tangible apostolic succession, must be presumed to be the legitimate Church of Jesus Christ, at least as long as it has not been proved without any shadow of doubt that she has betrayed and abandoned the Spirit of Christ and the fundamental doctrines of the primitive Christian Church: in other words, that on account of the continuity of the Catholic Church, a continuity which is historically clearer than that of the Reformation churches, the burden of proof for the idea of a 'renewed foundation' must lie with the representatives of the Reformation which was a new foundation of the church. These proofs, it might be said, will obviously not be forthcoming, however, especially since at least the possibility of a basic denial of fundamental Christian doctrines can be clearly seen in the Protestant communions. Such an approach would make it possible to give objectively legitimate reasons of fundamental theology for the obligation of conversion, without having to go into individual theological questions of controversial theology, questions which are quite beyond the normal convert and which we could treat only in an unobjective and superficial manner. If this can be said, however, then it shows once more what we have already observed implicitly: to be psychologically effective, such argumentation presupposes the Catholic Church to have an empirical form which 'makes it difficult' for the non-Catholic Christian (if we may put it this way) to have involuntary and subconscious inhibitions against the alternative that 'one' could actually be a Catholic. He may, however, associate the image he gets from experience with a certain clericalism, with an uncomprehended liturgy and with many other things comprehensible to someone of a Latin culture, but not to a Central European . . . with a centralization difficult to put up with, etc. If this image offers him right from the start so many unreflected, in themselves, quite inconclusive and yet psychologically effective grounds which already suppress any really practical question of the possibility of becoming a Catholic, then of course even the just suggested, indirect and presumptive argument for a Christian to become a Catholic cannot unfold its effectiveness. We can only hope and pray that those in authority in the Church will learn to understand even more how great a responsibility they have as regards the picture presented by the Church to the world, even in those respects where it is no longer a question of something morally bad by the standards of theoretical ethics. For something can be good or possible in itself and yet it ought not, in certain circumstances, to be imposed on someone else as an unnecessary burden. If one examines the image presented by the Church in this light, then there arise serious questions.

14

DOGMATIC NOTES ON 'ECCLESIOLOGICAL PIETY'

IF the dogmatic theologian were merely to develop an all-round view of his ecclesiology then he should really have a great deal to say about the subject of an 'ecclesiological piety' (whatever exactly may or should be understood by this notion). Although this is not immediately evident, there are real statements of *faith* about the Church and not merely about God and *His* relationship to us, a relationship which remains hidden and intangible within him; there are realities, in other words, which only faith can grasp but which nevertheless are not the reality of God (anyone who cannot feel any surprise at this fact has not really understood very much about the radical nature of faith as something incommensurable with any other kind of information). The Church is one of those believed and believable realities, i.e. realities to which is related the most absolute form of 'taking something seriously' and of total engagement, that act of grasping the measure without measure, that act of being circumscribed by a horizon which is not surrounded by anything else as *its* dimension; in short, what we call faith. And so there is an ecclesiology in dogmatic theology as such. Hence all the dogmatic theologian really needs to do, if he wants to treat of our subject, is to unfold his ecclesiology and to examine its content with a view to discovering at once its significance for our piety and the way in which these truths must be 'realized' subjectively. And which of the truths of ecclesiology could be insignificant in this respect if they are believed and believable, i.e. if they are the object of that mysteriously unique act which we call faith, without which all piety would necessarily become mere empty and worthless show, just a pious atmosphere of self-indulgence which is not worth talking about?

But before we can even go on from here to think things out, the dogmatic theologian contradicts himself (and contradicts perhaps even more the feeling of post-Tridentine Catholics and above all the feeling of the nineteenth century which is still very much alive today) by pointing out that the Church is indeed an object of one's faith, but that one does not believe in the Church, a most important distinction already made by the Apostles' Creed and yet one which is not always quite obviously and clearly respected in the practice of piety.

Once more: before we can reflect on *this* distinction, we must first of all reflect on something which concerns the Christian even more immediately in his relationship to his Church than the question as to whether and to what extent he (rightly or wrongly) as it were 'personifies' and 'hypostasizes' the Church and thus behaves towards her in a way which destroys the difference between the belief *in* God and the Church as an object of belief. The dogmatic theologian should indeed stick to his last and not play the historian of the spirit and the philosopher of culture. But perhaps he does after all observe correctly that the Church has become a kind of collective person for the modern Catholic (especially in the nineteenth century), a moral person which he honours, loves, trusts, defends, of which he is proud, in which he feels safe, and which appears incomparably nobler, purer, mightier and more indestructible to him than any other reality in this world: which appears to him, in other words, as the real Incarnation of everything that is true, good and promising. It might be said, of course— and quite rightly at first—that it has always been like this, that this has been an essential element in the attitude of Catholics from the very first days of Christianity when (even more than now, and in an almost gnostic sense) people were inclined to conceive the Church as one of the primeval heavenly powers and aeons and when they certainly spoke of 'Mother' Church without whom one could not have God for Father, the one Ark of salvation, the Bride of Christ, the new Eden and the Queen who stands by the side of the Saviour. All this is perfectly true. Yet there are overtones in the modern awareness of the Church which are neither dogmatically self-evident nor present in all past ages (and it must be remembered in this connection that the dogmatic theologian has also the right to address his critical questions to the actual, unreflected, uncritical awareness of the Church in past ages, and that consequently this question addressed to the present-day awareness will not be made to appear unjustified by the mere fact that one could pose the same question to previous ages). In order to see this it need only be borne in mind that the Catholic of to-day still thinks of himself primarily as someone who professes himself to belong *to* the Church, as someone who defends her, who feels himself her 'child', but who does not really see himself as her member. It is true that a lot has been said in the past few decades (and this is praiseworthy and good) about the Mystical Body of Christ, and in this connection there naturally appears also the doctrine that every Christian is a member of the Church. Yet as soon as this truth goes beyond the fact that every Christian shares in the blessings of the Church and has also the responsibility to stand up for her in his life and apostolate (all of which can be understood even by the 'child of the Church'), then the membership of the Church becomes an abstract, and no longer a religiously realized notion. For how many Christians are there today who feel themselves to be members of the Church in *such* a way that they experience themselves in the concrete—with all they are, do and suffer—as an element of the Church herself? Who, after all (except perhaps with regard to external persecutions), experiences the Church as the pilgrim, as the one who searches laboriously and who is often restless, or as the sinful Church of sinners; who has any clear experience of the difference between the Church and the looked for, yearned for, prayed for Kingdom, awaited with almost despairing patience, this kingdom of God which the Church simply does not yet constitute but for which she is the beginning, the genuine promise, the sacrament and not the clearly manifested reality itself? Yet the Church ought to appear also (and not only) as all these things to someone who recognizes *himself* as her *member* and who at the same time undergoes the bitter experience of being himself a pilgrim far from home, someone who gropes restlessly in the dark, a sinner. Of course, not every attribute of the individual Christian can be predicated of the Church as such, simply because this Christian is her member. But is this a sufficient reason for thinking that the Church is no longer also the sinful Church[1] (in spite of her permanent holiness on account

---

[1] Cf. K. Rahner, *Die Kirche der Sünder* (Freiburg–Vienna 1948) and the famous address by Hugo Rahner at the Cologne *'Katholikentag'* in 1956: *Die Kirche, Gottes Kraft in menschlicher Schwachheit* (Freiburg 1957). Without being indiscreet, we may recount a small anecdote in connection with *this* address, since it is typical of what we are talking about here. Pius XII read the above-mentioned address afterwards without any objection and yet also without being particularly affected by it, so that one of his closest collaborators told the author: 'Yes, he is indeed much closer to the Church triumphant.'

of her saving possessions and the 'subjective', existentially lived holiness of many of her members who, without being distinguishable from the rest, do not allow the eschatologically victorious grace of Christ to escape them)? Does the fact that the Church can never end up outside the truth of Christ mean also that she proclaims this truth with that power, in that topical and always freshly assimilated form one might hope for and which would make it truly salutary? Is it really always and clearly the case that—by transforming this truth, by opening it out into the infinity of God, by applying it comfortingly and in a redeeming way—she allows this truth to become most intimately united with that immeasurable, impetuous, entangled and yet so glorious chaos of perceptions, questions, conjectures, intellectual conquests, abysmal perplexities, which we call the 'world picture', the world outlook of modern man? Do we not frequently (contrary to the meaning of the gospel truth) purchase the permanence of the gospel message in the Church at the price of guarding scrupulously against exposing ourselves to this 'chaos' (out of which the world of tomorrow will be born) or, at best, by meeting it purely defensively, trying merely to preserve what we have? Is there not also this side to the Church? Can we say all this complainingly only of the *human beings* in the Church, when the Church is not an other-worldly aeon but the 'mass of believers' and hence also of the weak in faith? Is it not part of the correct picture of the Church to recognize this too, to take this scandal into consideration and to believe that it is permitted and 'must' be endured because things are not really meant to be so glorious in the Church? The fact that the Church recognizes herself as the guardian of the natural law and of the law of Christ does not by a long way mean that her faithful may not to a large extent be groping in the dark and disagree with each other about *how* these correct principles may and must be translated into those concrete, clear and practicable imperatives which are required over and above the correct principles themselves if one is to pass from thought to powerful action. The fact that the Church is always the Church of Saints does not yet ensure that these Saints will always exist, work and witness in the forum where the history of the world is being made, or that they are in the right place even only to a limited extent which God might permit even though His Church is not to be the Church of the mighty ones of this world. Hence, to a large extent, it would be absolutely conceivable for the individual Christian—precisely because he sees himself as a *member* of the Church—to experience his own lot as that of the Church. By thus transferring the existential factors of his own existence to the Church, he would not need to lose sight of the fact that the Church is . . . the Church of Christ. On the contrary: she is the Church of Christ, precisely by reason of the fact that God's incarnate, forgiving grace has taken hold of human beings like ourselves—and precisely as we experience ourselves to be, with all our constantly mortally-threatened burden of existence—and has fashioned them into the Church. Would it then involve even the slightest dogmatic falsehood if the individual Christian were to see the Church precisely in the light of the experience of his own existence, viz. as the community of those who, although sinful, do not deny their guilt but hasten with it to the grace of God? Would it be dogmatically false for the individual to see the Church as the community of those who acknowledge that they are indeed nailed to the *cross* of their existence, but nailed there together with their crucified Lord . . . to see her as the community of the perplexed who nevertheless by faith redeem their darkness by advancing into the mystery of God . . . to see her as the community of those who have the courage to confess: my God, why hast thou forsaken me, and who, having said this, nevertheless commend their souls into the hands of the Father, even though it is a terrible thing to fall into the hands of the living God? Why, then, should not the Christian feel himself to be a member of the Church in the sense that he experiences his own experience and fate as the experience of the Church and as the fate endured in her by faith, so that precisely this experience characterizes his Church for him? For precisely *by the fact that* death is accepted in obedience, that the light of God is believed in darkness, that uncertainty is simply entrusted to the mystery, there comes into existence that community of believers which is and, by the grace of God, will always remain the Church. For she is never merely the external society organized and guaranteed by God in Christ; rather, this external society is always merely the social appearance and the sacrament of that mysterious community of those who truly believe and whom God's unrestrainable action of grace has made into true believers. But will it be possible to say that the Christian of today sees the Church though not entirely yet at least 'also' from *this* side? He sees her as the teaching Church and not as the Church which needs to believe; he sees her as the Church who stands in the light and dispels darkness, but not as the Church which patiently endures darkness; he sees her as the goal of the works of God and not as the means to the future achievement of the purposes of God; in short, he sees her as the Queen and Mother, but not as the multitude of those who are like himself and who precisely in *this* way (and in no other) know themselves to be safe in God's grace. There are probably few Christians who would formulate all this as Bernhard Martin has done and who would experience it directly as an absolutely legitimate awareness of the Church: 'I am certainly grateful for having found my way into the Church or (which deep down comes to the same thing) for having been led into her, but I did not then nor do I now intend to feel "at home" on earth, not even within the Church.' How could such an experience of 'having here no lasting city' (even within the Church) be uncatholic, when the Church to which we belong is the Church *on pilgrimage* and we—the members of this Church—are suffering, erring, searching members, still hoping for what shall be, which alone is the finally valid reality?

It will perhaps be possible to make the meaning of all this a little clearer by expressing it in terms of dogmatic theology. The modern Catholic lives, one might say, according to the awareness of the Church expressed in the first Vatican Council. The characteristic quality of this awareness lies in the fact that the particular emphasis of this awareness (and not, of course, its exclusive content) is on the Church regarded as an empirical motive of credibility and not on the Church as an (in itself hidden) object of faith. We do not mean to say that there is no such thing as the Church understood as a motive of credibility for the fact that God has spoken in and through her, or that this aspect had been completely outside the religious consciousness of Christians in earlier ages (the 'see how these Christians love one another', and the ecclesiological, triumphal self-consciousness that the new generation of men has become tangible, as found in the writings of Minucius Felix, in the Epistle to Diognetus, in Tertullian, etc., are very old indeed). But to the religious consciousness of the Christians who are 'still' modern the Church is nevertheless to a marked degree a Church whose empirical appearance convinces people of her nature, and only to a very small extent a Church whose nature is believed 'in spite of' her appearance. The concept of the Church as a motive of credibility and the concept of the Church as the object of a necessarily difficult faith which consumes the whole power of one's heart and which is possible only by the miracle of grace, are strangely intermingled. Nowadays one almost gets the impression that she—the Church—is the point at which one can almost physically lay hold of what one believes: 'Behold a house full of glory . . . '. One is very little aware of the fact that her empirically identifiable 'properties' and 'notes', and her believed and known properties (even though both are in part called by the same names) are not absolutely identical. What, for instance, would an *empirical* Catholicity mean (especially today, when for the first time there are also other organizationally constituted world- and life-systems of world-wide nature and power even apart from the Church), if one were not permitted to *believe* that really and truly all men have their place in her great variety, since her space is not her own but that of God? What would the unity of teaching and organization mean to us ultimately, if we could not *believe* (which does not mean 'experience') that in and beyond this (i.e. beyond the formulae and every form of organization) the very truth and reality are possessed in common in the faith which follows on the Spirit, and that in and beyond this all hearts are one, hearts which seem to be so unspeakably lonely? What would be the value of any empirical moral achievement in the Church (even to the extent of martyrdom) if one were not permitted the courage to *believe* that in the midst of all this, God's Holy Spirit achieves *his* work and pours out his love i.e. (himself) into these hearts, so that when one really gets down to analysing this moral achievement in its very depth, one really falls, not into the emptiness of man, but into the abyss of God? What would be the use of an empirically identifiable 'apostolicity' of the Church and of every uninterrupted hierarchic succession if we did not have the *belief* that this two-thousand-year-old Church has preserved the intangible fullness of her beginning, and has preserved it against every deadly expression of historical transitoriness? Yet does not modern awareness of the Church see the (genuine) visible 'glitter' of the Church and her believed glory too much as one and the same thing and does it not almost overlook the 'ontological difference' (based on the fact that the one—even though God-effected—is something finite and the other is God's absolute nature itself)? But might we not perhaps venture the paradox that, the more the Church is the community of those who *believe contra spem in spem* that God has done great things in them (i.e. of those who believe precisely because they accept the servant-form of the Church and help to endure it patiently to the end), the more (and really only thus) the Church will also become—

precisely in this way—that *signum elevatum in nationes* of which the first Vatican Council speaks so triumphantly? It will be difficult to maintain, however, that such dogmatically absolutely possible—indeed latently always also lived—aspects of the Church and of ecclesiological piety are very much to the fore in the modern awareness or that they have been made the subject of a great deal of systematic theological thinking.

We must now return to the beginning of this reflection. What import does it have for ecclesiological piety that one believes *in* God but not *in* the Church, and that the Church is merely an object of one's belief? This circumstance must mean something for ecclesiological piety, for after all, Christian piety is nothing other than belief becoming active in love. When we say that God is not merely the object of our belief but that we moreover believe in God, we mean by this that the act of faith does not stop at a proposition which is held to be true (because it 'agrees' with reality—a reality, however, which one possesses only in so far as one masters the proposition concerning it, which is a finite and inadequate expression of it) but that it encounters and possesses what is believed or, more correctly, the one who is believed. And it does this in a twofold respect: firstly, in so far as in the act of faith (seen from our side) there occurs that peculiarly *personal* act of relatedness in which the knower and the one who affirms is not aware of *himself* by knowledge 'about something' but which is a relatedness in which he really reaches beyond himself, bursts open and transcends himself, and so passes beyond reflection and 'mediation' and finds the courage to hold on to the 'reality' itself (which is a person), a relatedness in which the knower does not, in order to make sure, return to himself with consequent suffocation within himself in the interior business of reflection. Secondly (and this is more important) in so far as the act of faith is an act of grace (and grasps itself precisely as such and *thus* gets away from itself), it is supported and effected by the reality of the one who is the object of the act of faith. For 'grace' (understood as 'supernatural', 'infused' virtue) is not just any 'assistance' for some other, intrinsically still purely human act. In spite of all its 'createdness' (i.e. in spite of God's real transforming arrival in man himself) grace is in ultimate truth God himself communicating his own reality (although as the infinite mystery) to his creature; in this way and by this fact, God makes the act of faith possible and supports it, so that *that* which is believed is in very truth the ground of being for the act of faith. Hence, one believes in very truth . . . 'into God'. And this certainly can be said of faith only in relation to God and not of any other reality which is believed: not even of the Church. Only further reflection will show the exact meaning of this difference, although this will require patience.

It is, of course, theologically speaking absolutely possible to say that the Church is in a certain respect the *ground* of faith and that she supports the faith of the individual. In a certain sense this is even easier to understand today than ever before. For precisely *if* faith goes 'into God'—because it becomes faith precisely and, properly speaking, only by the fact that the absolute, limitless Mystery who embraces our being from all eternity, communicates himself to the finite creature in an unspeakable nearness of forgiveness and beatitude and does not remain in the frightening splendour of unapproachable light which unmasks us as pure darkness and expels us from his sight —would we today have the courage to believe this on our own account, if we could not believe and hope it also for *everyone?* We today (even though we let God . . . be God and adore his decrees as both incomprehensible and irreversible) cannot feel so 'aristocratic' (or naïvely egotistic?) as to be able to hope or fear less for others than for ourselves. Hence, we can only hear the message telling us that the incomprehensibly remote, infinite Mystery wishes to be absolutely near to us for our beatitude, and realize that it is said to each one of us, if we hear it as the message addressed to *everyone*, if we really believe in the 'universal salvific will' of God and if we have no more fears for others regarding its 'conditional nature' than we have for ourselves. Because this message is addressed to everyone, we (each individual ego) dare to hear it as addressed to 'me' and are not afraid that it might be the most terrible misunderstanding with which my crazy self-delusion has ever deceived me about myself. I may and must think only the best of others, I must hope for the Infinite for them, I may not have a low opinion of *them*, for then I look down on them and fall into the deadly state of hatred (since hatred is already present whenever there is not infinite love). Thus, when we believe today, it always happens in the midst of that unnumbered and truly all-embracing throng of those to whom we firmly believe the same word is addressed and for whom we firmly hope that they may hear this word unto salvation. We always believe in communion with all those who are addressed by God, who listen and who believe, and hence also we always believe in the Church. For we understand the Church, when we believe, *in this way*, viz. as the historically and socially constituted assembly of those who have the courage to believe, who as it were confess to one another the secret enormity of the faith living in the ground of their being, and who—by professing, praying, celebrating and rendering present the very basis of their courage, viz. the Death and Resurrection of Jesus—give one another courage to make this daring, absolute claim to infinite grace. Thus faith comes through the Church, and the Church through faith. *To this extent*, the Church is also the ever-supporting ground of faith, a ground which faith—being the grace of God and thus the Original, the Ultimate which presupposes nothing—prepares for itself. This does not, of course, by any means say everything that should be said if we are to get a completely clear idea of why and to what extent the Church is the ground of faith. She is this also because she passes on the message of Christ, and this from Christ, by her teaching and in her faith and thus (and thus alone) brings together the whole fullness of what is believed, which alone makes faith to be faith. For faith must never be understood as a merely formal 'attitude' (no matter towards whom); it is the laying hold of a reality whose truth depends entirely on the fact that this very reality itself (and ultimately this is God's grace) is grasped in a knowing-believing way. In and by this the Church is the ground of faith even in her teaching authority. This is true not merely with regard to what is explicitly and authoritatively taught by her or what is obediently accepted (this factor is already constituted by the Church understood as the authorized messenger of Christ's word), but also in another respect which is most frequently overlooked. Faith is really faith in something certainly taught, only by the fact that in and through this, faith is the overcoming of self by entering into the unspeakable mystery of God. To this extent, the explicit faith (strange as this may sound) lives by the *fides implicita* and not merely vice versa. This process of bursting through what is grasped by faith in word and proposition and of thereby passing beyond it into the Incomprehensible (which is greater than our comprehension in faith) and into the Mystery to which our 'mysteries of faith' point (i.e. the Mystery contained in them only in so far as they point to it and away from themselves) and with which they wish to put us into contact, is not the regrettable 'deficiency' of propositions which 'really' and in their 'positive content' should not have this obscurity. The Mystery

is precisely what matters, the real 'positive content' of these propositions, the permanent and unsurpassable element. For when one day
these propositions will give way to the direct vision of God, the
Mystery will not disappear but will then appear for the first time and
for ever, and will then become completely immeasurable: the incomprehensible God who, precisely in the *visio beata*, remains the Incomprehensible and Who is seen as *such*. If the knowledge of faith is not
ultimately a possession but a 'being possessed', not a disposing but a
being disposed, if it is a surrender to the Mystery in itself and not
merely a holding-on-to certain not fully penetrable propositions in
which one could at least hold on to what is comprehensible in them
... then it is a fact that the knowledge of faith is as it must be here, but
conviction of that fact cannot be achieved simply by a formally empty
leap away from the propositions into the Mystery (which would again
be simply the enjoyment of one's own power of self-transcendence);
this conviction can be achieved only by surrendering one's faith into
the faith of believers in general and taking this as the norm of one's
faith, and this particularly if the individual has not yet in any way
made this faith explicitly or consciously his own. Explicit faith is always
also faith which from the outset inserts itself with silent obedience into
the faith of the Church—the greater, far more comprehensive and
manifold faith of the Church—the faith which, to be itself, has been
given the scope of the whole time of salvation (and this right up to
the final consummation) for its history, experience and development.
We can certainly expect modern man to show understanding for this
'ecclesiological character' of faith.

It is certainly true that the almost deadly feeling of the relative
character of all knowledge and of all religious convictions, the feeling
that it all depends on one's perspective and historical development (a
feeling encouraged by the present-day *reflex* consciousness of the great
number of religions, Christian denominations, religious convictions
and theological schools) must not be allowed to turn modern man
into a relativistic sceptic or agnostic, who simply falls silent, turns
away his face and lets the unexplorable have the mastery over him.
But one thing will become vividly clear to the man who has this experience, and this is the realization that the real communication between men in the truth—a truth which must exist if the desire for
truth is not to be a completely idle claim doomed to failure—cannot
be present only where and because men agree with one another on

certain formulated principles, even though such an agreement is necessary as a manifestation, confirmation and means of another, deeper communication. There must be a deeper more realistic union in truth which however is not merely something postulated ideologically: the union which takes place when man's knowledge—by willingly and obediently passing beyond itself—reaches its ultimate reality by surrendering itself to the greater mystery called God, the union which is achieved in a historically *real* way and also manifests itself in this way, whenever man surrenders himself to the universal belief in its historical and concrete form, i.e. the faith of the Church. The believer realizes that he *really* believes (i.e. that he bursts through his knowledge and passes into the uncomprehended Comprehending Being) by believing with the faith of the Church and by surrendering himself to the faith of all the witnesses beginning with Abel the Just right up to the last believer at the end of time. Thus, modern man in particular—in his sober, painful experience of the historical and conditional nature of his own knowledge and of the knowledge of each individual—experiences the Church as the community of believers; this is a community in which each individual (even the one who is actually teaching, since even the correct teaching he proclaims at any particular moment is never an adequate expression of the faith of all believers in all ages) is both humbled and liberated by the faith of all those with whose exercise of faith he communicates mysteriously and yet (in his obedience to the Church) soberly and firmly, both by his obedience in faith towards the faith of the Church and by the one, common possession of what he believes by the grace of faith which is itself a matter of faith. He is humbled, because no one can achieve the fullness of the whole faith by himself and merely as an individual. He is liberated, because—in spite of his very 'subjective' knowledge of faith—the fullness of faith and the full reality of what is believed are his in the Church of believers. In *this* way the believer may also hear the actual official proclamation of doctrine as embraced by the whole faith of the Church (for these two are not identical) and, over and above this, of all true believers (in so far as they are not yet members of the visible Church) and hence also as introduced into the believed reality itself, which is the infinite mystery of God. This is not surprising, for the believing Church (a concept presupposed by the right distinction between the teaching and the listening Church, and one which must not be shortsightedly identified with the 'listening

Church') always believes 'more' (not in a quantitative sense but in intensive nearness to the reality accepted by faith) than the teaching Church. If this were not so, then either there could be no progress in the development of dogma in respect of what is defined by the *magisterium*, or there would have to be a further public revelation after the close of the apostolic age from which such new decisions of the *magisterium* could be drawn. The content of such new definitions was, therefore, already present before the definition, and this precisely in the greater faith of the believing Church. Yet we must not imagine all this as if every and each element thus present in this exercised faith of the believing Church—a faith which embraces the faith of the individual and the teaching of the extraordinary *magisterium* as well— urgently requires formulation in a doctrinal proposition issued by the *magisterium* and that in this way the juridical, official teaching reflection will gradually catch up with this all-embracing faith of the Church. This is not so, for the simple reason that this all-embracing faith of the believing Church is itself still growing in a certain respect and manner (without thereby contradicting the fact that revelation 'closed' with the death of the last Apostle). For the 'closing' of revelation with the 'death of the last Apostle' does not imply an arbitrary fixing of the boundary for what is revealed, as if there were a further field of possible but not actually realized divine communications. It means rather that this is the completion of divine revelation, because it is the absolute and unsurpassable self-communication in grace and glory and *hence* cannot be surpassed to any essential degree (unless it be when the present condition passes into the vision of glory). But precisely this self-communication of God can be accepted ever more radically in a 'subjective' sense. If this were not so, then the grace of faith could not grow (which no theologian would dare to affirm) or at least this growth would have no significance for the appropriation in faith of what is believed (which is equally unthinkable). This genuine and continuous growth in faith is conceivable and is an increase in 'knowledge' quite apart from whether or not one thinks it possible that the teaching of faith formulated in propositions by the *magisterium* grows by ever new propositions. There is not only growth by articulate increase of analysis (and this is practically the only way in which one almost involuntarily understands the development of dogma) but also growth by silent synthesis. It can be seen from this that faith today—precisely where the 'credere *in* Deum' becomes clear to it over and above the *'credere Deum'* and the *'credere Deo'*—makes the believer aware in particular of the presence of the Church as the wider congregation of believers, not merely as the messenger and guarantor of an (always again only individual) faith, but as the subject to whom the *'individuum'* who experiences his historical finiteness even in his faith, entrusts his faith.

Yet, according to dogmatic theology (going back now to the beginning of this reflection for which the last few pages have been merely a limiting digression) this faith is not a *'credere in Ecclesiam'* but only a *'credere Ecclesiam'*. This fact is of the greatest importance for the 'ecclesiological piety' of today (or perhaps only of tomorrow?). The personal entrusting of each other to each other, which is included in the *'credere in Deum'*, cannot be applied to the Church. However much we may and must 'personify' the Church, however much she may be more than just the numerical sum of individual Christians, however much she is a reality which is not only a juridical reality or fiction, an ideological structure, or a 'moral unity'—the Church as such is not a person, i.e. the Church, in so far as she must be distinguished from real individual persons, cannot be conscious of herself, cannot justify herself, cannot decide, nor is she eternal.

The Church, therefore, cannot give herself in that personal surrender of which a real, self-disposing person is capable, and as such she also cannot receive such a surrender. If love, respect, loyalty, etc., mean first and foremost a relationship between real persons, then man and Christ can have love, respect and loyalty towards the Church only in a derived, secondary sense. Or, alternatively these attitudes towards the Church are ultimately (in so far as they are not directed to God himself) attitudes towards the persons who form this Church. *These* are loved in the Church because, and in so far as, they are such in God's supernatural providence that they form the Church. This does not mean, however, that 'ecclesiological piety' dissolves itself in a nominalistic way into a merely ideal collective sum of attitudes of one Christian towards other individual Christians. For these individual Christians are 'individuals', 'single ones' and, each one of them, uniquely individual persons, precisely in the absolutely irreplaceable and inalienable uniqueness of their spiritual existence *in so far as* they love and accept one another, and in so far as they open themselves toward one another and are one with each other in the one truth and love (through the real self-communication of God in grace and Vision).

Spiritual 'individuality' and spiritual 'community' are realities which grow in direct and not in inverse proportion to each other; they are realities which mutually condition each other. Hence, someone who loves the individuals in their irreplaceable uniqueness, loves them also in their mutual unity, and hence also in the ultimate depth and radicality of this unity, and thus in the ground of *this* unity which is the Spirit of God, and he consequently loves them also as the Church. Added to this there is the fact that even these attitudes which are directed first and foremost to persons, and only *thus* also to the Church, are a '*credere in*' only in so far as they are supported and exploited to their ultimate depth by the personal faith and love towards the personal nature of *God*. Hence, even though one may say quite truly to someone: 'I believe *in* you' as a child of God, as someone redeemed, as someone called to salvation—and imply that in this movement of faith one attains the Church as well—yet even this 'I believe in you' which —within the Church—one person can, and indeed must, say to another in a certain sense, must be based on the still more original 'I believe in you' which God and man say to each other in the grace of 'divine' faith (in quite a different way, of course, since the dialogue of the supernatural saving event does not take place between two equal partners; but there is a possible analogy here, since there is an absolute and personal self-communication and surrender to the other person on both sides). Hence this faith is even more truly a faith of the Church rather than a faith 'in the Church'.

This does not merely provide us with a useless and somewhat subtle distinction, although it may appear so especially to someone whose analysis of faith usually overlooks the depth of the augustinian distinction between '*credere Deum—Deo—in Deum*'. This distinction is presumably of greater significance for present-day 'ecclesiological piety' than it ever was before. The man of today (or tomorrow) has the experience of having the Church as an object of his faith but not of believing *in* the Church, i.e. he experiences her as the object but not as that ultimate ground of faith which for faith considered as a personal act (which completely engages the whole person of the believer) can only be the person 'in whom' one believes. The fact that this experience is pressing and oppressing, really follows already from what has been said before. Whenever the qualitative difference between the empirical experience of the Church as an extrinsic motive of credi*bility* and the *supernatural* experience of God's testimony to himself as an inner motive of faith becomes radically clear to the Christian—and how could this not be actual to the Christian today with his empirical experience of that Church which is his destiny, i.e. with his experience in which he (also) experiences the Church just as he experiences himself in his frailty, as someone exposed and threatened—then the Christian can no longer subjectively overlook the objective difference between the Church as a motive of credibility and the Church as an object of faith. The Church is an object of his *faith* because he believes *in* God. The Church thus becomes 'for him' also an object sustained by his faith, something which he upholds with the last ounce of strength in his heart and by the pure power of grace, even though he does not see in her what he believes of her. We are merely repeating a truth here which has been stated many times before, but it is a truth which must be repeated in this connection: in modern society which is in every respect a pluralistic society, the Church is no longer a sociologically obvious reality, something which supports everything from without, or something which, as a dimension of existence independent of the individual and his decision, is simply a quite obvious, pre-established reality. Of course, the Church exists and remains even if 'I' do not believe, for God's effective and eschatologically victorious grace will always see to it that there are men who believe in Jesus Christ and who profess this faith in unity, order and love. But in contrast to previous ages, the Church today remains *for* '*me*' *in particular* only when I believe. She really shows herself again more clearly, more painfully, more challengingly than ever before since the time of Constantine's Empire Church as what she always was and will be: the Church of believers, the Church which exists because she is the object of faith, and is the object of faith by the fact that one believes in God through Jesus Christ. One should not be shocked by this way of putting it: the Church exists because she is the object of faith. Naturally, she remains even if an individual, even if many individuals do not believe. But she would no longer exist if she were not believed at all. By the very fact that this faith is always effected anew by God's grace—by the fact that it is effected absolutely by pre-defining, effective grace and that therefore there is not merely (in the Old Testament sense, one might say) the organization and the sign but also the animated body of Christ and effective, fulfilled sign—by and through *this* very fact God 'preserves' the Church, and not merely by the sociological continuance of the juridical Church organization (which is certainly also absolutely willed and effectively caused by God's providence). All this is really quite self-evident. But the Christian of today experiences this obvious truth more clearly than in the old days. And this is an essential part of his ecclesiological piety today: the Church is the object of his faith; in his faith, and in the faith of many, the Church herself (in her inner pneumatic being) really becomes a reality. And this Church-forming faith of the Church takes place in the faith *in* God (*in Christo*), in the total self-surrender of man to the personal Mystery which—infinitely distant and yet having come unspeakably near through grace—reigns over and right through man's existence.

It is perhaps possible to clarify from a different point of view what we mean here by this self-evident, always valid and yet surprisingly new trait of modern ecclesiological piety. Who has not heard of St Augustine's saying (and perhaps even repeated it) that he would not believe the gospels if the authority of the Church did not move him to do so. Now, we do not mean to dispute the fact that one can give a correct meaning to this statement: the Church herself can be an extrinsic motive of credibility for faith in general (but not an internal motive of faith) in the case of many individuals, as has already been said; the Church, by her teaching authority—once she has become an object of faith in her authority as a divine institution—can and will be for everyone the mediatrix of divine revelation and an argument for the event of revelation, in the case of many particular propositions of faith which without her would not be attained in their exact content; all faith, as has already been said, acknowledges itself to be faith in the Church and of the Church. But speaking purely in terms of fundamental theology, i.e. theoretically—and today no doubt also existentially in the case of most people—it is a fact that the Church is not the first object of faith; belief in her rests on a faith (and its motives of credibility) which does not refer to the Church but to Christ and to God. Since the Church is also attained by means of this latter faith, she is also an object of faith. Hence it cannot be said either in theory or in practice (at least in most cases) that one believes in the Gospel simply because the Church is the object of one's faith. Rather (in spite of what St Augustine says) the Church is an object of one's faith because one believes the Gospel. Thus, every fundamental theology develops first the doctrine of Christ in his function as *'legatus divinus'* before going on to the treatise on the Church. Man entrusts himself to the Church because Christ, the One sent by God, has founded the

Church and has passed on his authority and power to her office-bearers. The ethos of augustinian ecclesiological piety—which conceived things as if the Church were simply and by direct 'grasp' the object first grasped and understood by Christian faith and that in this grasp everything else is attained—is therefore only partially true objectively speaking, but not only this, it is also not (any longer) subjectively characteristic of present-day ecclesiological piety. The Church is an object of our faith, we might say, but we do not believe (so much) on account of the Church.

The dogmatic theologian of today can envisage ecclesiological piety from still another, quite different point of view. Putting it very pointedly and perhaps exaggeratedly, one might say that the Christian of today experiences the Church not so much as the society of the heirs of salvation but rather as the historically and sociologically tangible vanguard of the heirs of salvation. Naturally, the Church is the Ark of salvation, the people of the redeemed, the community of those called to salvation. Obviously, it is just as valid today as it was in the days of the Fathers to state that 'outside' the Church there is no salvation, that the Church as well as baptism is an intrinsically necessary means for salvation and not merely necessary for salvation on account of an extrinsic precept. But with regard to this dogma stating that the Church is necessary for salvation *necessitate medii*, the consciousness of faith possessed by this very Church has passed through a very long and significant development the result of which is of most practical significance today. The Christian has a clear understanding today of the universal salvific will of God. He has grasped the fact that grace does not become grace simply because it will be given only to a few, and that it remains the miracle of an unfathomable favour even if it is offered to everyone, and even if it were to or does (who can say?) become operative in everyone. He knows that baptism attains an elementary, though very indistinct, visibleness even in the desire for baptism and thus can become effective (as faith and love) even before this freely accepted dynamism of grace has taken on a concrete form in the social, public structure of the Church as sacramental baptism of water. He knows that that innermost attitude and act of faith which becomes the whole basis of one's existence—in other words, the attitude and act by which a person opens himself up in the very depth of knowledge, hope and loving acceptance towards the 'revelation' which takes place as an event in the act of divine self-communication and which by this act of grace also changes the consciousness of man, albeit perhaps only in a very unobjectified way—can in certain circumstances take place also in a way in which the conceptually objectified content of this consciousness draws very little or almost nothing (or even nothing at all?) from the explicit or anonymous stream of divine verbal communications within the official history of salvation, without such an attitude thereby necessarily ceasing to be 'faith' in the theological sense. The man of today knows that he may hope courageously that very many people may find salvation through such faith, even if they have never during their whole life become members of the Church understood as the external juridical structure of the Church (which nevertheless belongs also to the nature of the Church in her role of providing the 'dimension for salvation'). However much he must fear for himself, and hence also for everyone else, that he may be lost—and must fear this with all the seriousness of his existence openly submitted to the hidden judgement of God—he is nevertheless confident that he may be permitted to hope for the victory of grace for everyone; he hopes this particularly since, as a Catholic Christian, he knows through the doctrine of 'Purgatory' (however much it may need to be interpreted more exactly) that the history of the world tangible *here* below is not simply and absolutely identical with what (as a basis and cause of finality) precedes eternity finalized in God's judgement. And this attitude, this hope is indispensable for the Christian of today. Unlike the Christian of earlier times (unlike even the great heart of a St Augustine, not to mention the puny, the self-righteous and the egotistical), he can no longer simply think that *he* himself has the good will, the faithfulness towards conscience and the readiness to obey God's call unconditionally, and that the others, who do not belong visibly to the Ark of the Church, do not have this attitude. He can no longer think in this way, even if he were to add the thought that his faith and good will are a gift of grace given to him without any merit on his part (and that God has obviously refused this 'effective' grace to the others, in the mysterious ways of predestination). He is not naively convinced of the good will of others, but the reason for this is the fact that he takes a most critical view of his own good will. He cannot do anything else but allow others just as much chance of good will and obedience to conscience and to the Word of God speaking through it; he cannot do anything else but grant them this chance even if up till now or right up to their death this presupposed, presumed and hoped for good will has not in their case led to official membership of the Church. He cannot act differently even for the simple reason that he knows that this official membership of the Church—even when it is supported by a 'good will' whose truth and existential genuineness, however, will always remain uncertain even in one's own mind—is not yet a guarantee for what it actually means and announces (like the sacramental sign which may be a fruitful sacrament or—who knows— a merely valid and sacrilegiously received sacrament); in other words, he knows that official membership of the Church is no guarantee that such a member belongs to the hidden multitude of those whom God alone knows and to whom God has given the gift of believing in Him and of loving Him in obedience to his word promising to give himself to them in his whole reality and glory.

The man of today can no longer think differently, and this even for a very simple reason which was not present previously. In previous ages, the different groups of 'world views' were on the whole at that time distinct groups even from national, cultural and geographical, sociological and historical points of view. And each of these groups, thus distinguished from one another in this 'intramundane' sense, had its own common world-view or soon settled down to such a common view after a short, critical period of combat. Consequently faith was also a simple sociological phenomenon, and so someone of a 'different Creed' or the unbeliever was also looked upon simply as the stranger who was already incomprehensible even by reason of all his other peculiarities of life, and often even as someone culturally inferior to oneself. Thus one would not be surprised that he did not have the right faith and one was quite prepared to assume without any qualms that he lacked the true faith on account of some guilt on his part and . . . that he would be lost through a just judgement. If one went to battle against the unbeliever not simply with the weapons of the spirit and of love, but also with physical force then the opponents were clearly the enemies of God, the 'unbelievers', the arch-enemies of Christianity, of truth and morality, and one could not really 'realize' that these others were also human beings who loved, were kind and faithful, who 'meant well' just as much as anyone else, who felt themselves unjustly attacked by the Christians, and who really thought that they were serving God when they said 'no' to Christianity. Today, the 'unbeliever' is the neighbour, the relative, the human person on whose honesty, reliability and decency one must rely just as much as on the corresponding qualities of one's fellow believers (in which process one sometimes gets the staggering impression that one can rely much more on the former than the latter). Today every Christian experiences how only too often people persevere in the religious convictions into which they were born, and that they do this with utter peace of conscience and inner peace of mind—almost as a foregone conclusion—even though they live in close proximity to Catholics and the Church, at least in their ordinary life. Indeed, must this not be said to be the normal case, if one understands by 'normal' the greatest number of actual cases, and if one hopes optimistically, on account of the universal and serious salvific will, that these appearances are not simply deceptive, and that most people do not live contrary to the dictates of their conscience during the whole of their life? We are not going to argue about the point here as to how this fact can be reconciled with the truth that the Church, with her truth and grace, is the path to salvation intended by God basically for all men, one to which they are also obliged and which in itself is possible for them. The only question here is how the Catholic, who believes the Church to be the universal path to salvation for everyone and who at the same time holds fast both in theory *and* in his practical hope to the certainty of God's *universal* salvific will, can come to terms with what he experiences in the above sense, viz. the existence of the pluralism of world-views, a pluralism which cannot be overcome in the foreseeable future, and which exists even precisely where people of different outlooks meet one another peaceably in the same sector of human existence and where they are no longer historically and sociologically separated from one another from the very outset, to such an extent that this does indeed explain their disagreements and yet does not give rise to any practical problem for each particular group.

The answer to this question can surely lie only in the following fact: the Catholic must experience and see the Church as the 'vanguard', as the sacramental sign, the historical tangibility of a saving grace which goes beyond the sociologically tangible and the 'visible' Church, i.e. the grace of an anonymous Christianity which 'outside' the Church has not yet come to itself but which 'within' the Church is 'present to itself', not because it is simply not present outside but because, objectively speaking, it has not yet reached full maturity there and hence does not as yet understand itself in that explicit way and reflex objectivity of the formulated profession of faith, of the sacramental objectification and of the sociological organization which are found within the Church herself. The Christian, in other words, will not regard the non-Christian (to facilitate matters, we leave the problem of the non-Catholic Christian out of consideration) as the non-Christian who, because he is not a Christian, finds himself outside the stream of salvation. Rather (if it is true that Christianity is salvation and that in the matter of salvation, God does not suddenly allow 'good will' to substitute for the real thing, for basically this would destroy the doctrine that the Church and grace are necessary means for salvation and not merely necessary by precept), the Christian will regard the non-Christians as anonymous Christians who do not know what they really are deep down in conscience, by grace and by a possibly very implicit yet true realization of what the Christian too realizes, even though the Christian knows what he is doing in this regard even in the objective reflex form of his consciousness. There can be no doubt about it: even this knowledge—this explicit, propositional, 'confessionally' formulated faith which also makes it possible and obligatory that there should be a sociological institutionalization of those who believe in this way —is a part of full Christianity; it is a grace which in its turn facilitates and ensures that what is professed in this way, is really present in the depth of human existence and of conscience. There can be no doubt about the fact that the Catholic feels and praises his explicit membership of the Church as an unmerited grace, as his good fortune, and as the promise of salvation (and indeed rightly so); but he also knows at the same time, in great fear and trembling, that the greater grace brings with it also greater dangers, that more is demanded of those to whom more is given, and that he does not know whether he is reaching the standard required of him and not of others, and that even here it may be true what Our Lord said: viz. that many will come from the East and from the West, and will feast with Abraham and Isaac and Jacob in the kingdom of heaven, but the children of the kingdom will be put forth into the darkness outside (Mt 8.11 *sq.*). But because the Christian hopes also for the salvation of the others, because he knows enough theology today to be able to see that he *can* hope for this since he can understand how one can be a Christian (i.e. a person living by the grace of God and of His Christ) even when one does not know the name of Christ or thinks one has to reject it—because of all this, the Christian can see himself and those who are Christians by name, i.e. the Church, only as the vanguard of those who are marching along the roads of history into God's salvation and into His eternity. The Church is for him, as it were, the uniformed part of God's soldiers; she is for him that point at which the inner being of the human-divine existence appears also historically and sociologically (or better: where it appears most clearly, since for the enlightened view of faith, God's grace does not lack all visible presence even outside the Church). He knows that the morning light on the hills is the beginning of the day in the valleys, and not the day above which judges the night below. In view of the Christian doctrine that there is no absolute principle of evil—that evil is the perishable, that the unique God is good and wills also the good of the world, that the real is also the good and hence a true realism must think well of reality—the Christian knows that it would be blasphemy to think that ultimately it is easier to do evil than to do good, that evil and not the good is installed at the very roots of 'dispassionately' and realistically fathomed reality, and that evil enjoys a longer life than the good. He knows that it is the creature's pride and not his humility which thinks in this way . . . which thinks that it can emancipate itself from God at least in doing evil, which in reality is just a stupid lie. The Christian knows that it is precisely the achievement of his existence which is demanded of him, to believe in the light while still in darkness, to believe in beatitude while still in pain, to believe in the absoluteness of God while in our state of relativity. He knows that in its history revelation has unmasked our sin for us merely in order that we may believe in the forgiveness of God (for guilt by itself we could have experienced already in our pain, our death and our desperate state). When St Paul (Rom 9–11) sees the disbelief of the Jews as something transitory, this is not yet sufficiently explained by holding that only the Jews living later on will come to believe but that those living earlier on have remained unbelieving (for only an unchristian collectivist could have such a naïve conception). The faith of the people of Israel which is to appear later on in history (which for us is—even later on—no tangible, certain predestination to salvation for the individual) must be a sign of the fact that God has had mercy on this people even earlier on but in an intangible manner (again without implying anything certain about any particular individual). For otherwise why should Israel as a whole be called by the faith of its later period and not by the unbelief of its earlier period? How could it otherwise be preferable to say that Israel as such will be found by God's grace, than that Israel has closed herself against God?

Hence, the Christian looks calmly and fearlessly into the world, into the world of a thousand opinions and views of the world. He does not need anxiously to consult statistics to see whether the Church is the greatest world-view organization or whether her numbers are keeping pace with the growth of the world population. He will indeed look into the world with missionary zeal. He will bear witness to the name of Christ. He will wish to share his grace with others, for he possesses a grace which these others lack . . . *still* lack. But he knows that if he remains calm and patiently zealous, then his zeal will have the greatest chance of success. He knows that he may imitate God's patience (which, according to St Paul, has a positive salvific character and not the character of a judgement). He knows that God has willed this world just as it is, because otherwise it would not be. He knows that even the merely 'permitted' is permitted only as an element of what is divinely willed (and not merely permitted) and that this willed reality may and must be hoped for not only as the revelation of the justice of God, but also as the revelation of God's infinite goodness to men. He goes out boldly and full of hope to meet as brothers even those who by their 'world-view' do not wish to be his brother. Yet he sees in them those who do not know what they really are, those who have not yet seen clearly what presumably they nevertheless accomplish already in the deepest dimension of their existence (to such an extent that one has the duty to presume this hopefully and that it would be loveless to take them for less . . . for, may I as a Christian simply presuppose, without any reason whatsoever, that the other is without grace?). The Christian sees anonymous Christianity at work in the other in a thousand different ways. When he sees him to be a kind, loving person who is faithful to his conscience, then he will no longer say today: these are merely 'natural virtues'. After all, such virtues exist ultimately only in the abstract. He will no longer say that these are certainly only the 'glittering vices of the pagans', as St Augustine said. Rather he will think: there is the grace of Christ at work even in someone who has never yet explicitly called upon it, but who nevertheless has already yearned for it in the inexpressible and nameless longing of his heart; there is someone else in whom the inexpressible groanings of the Spirit have already called upon and prayed for that silent but all-governing secret of existence which we Christians know to be the Father of Our Lord Jesus Christ. Take a Christian seeing the 'pagan' dying with resignation. He notices how the other lets himself fall resignedly in death into the bottomless abyss which he has never yet fathomed (since he would have to be infinite to be able to grasp God), and this as if it could not be otherwise (and yet it could be different, since one can use the last remaining ounce of the energy of one's whole clenched existence for one last, absolute protest and in one absolute, cynical doubt). He notices how the other professes in this no longer articulate willingness that this abyss is the abyss of the meaningful secret and not of damning emptiness. In this case the Christian sees in such a dying 'pagan' the one who has been nailed to the saving cross of existence at the right hand of Christ, and this reality—the personally accomplished and accepted reality of this dying person—speaks without words: Lord, remember me when thou shalt enter into thy kingdom. Why should it not be so? The pure transcendence of man which is no longer used as a means to assert his earthly existence, but which is accepted and endured, can surely be elevated by grace so that, having been freed from its deviation into the infinite, it becomes a dynamic urge directed towards the God of eternal life, in so far as God is in his very own, communicable and communicated reality, the goal and end of the supernatural destiny of man. Into the bargain, since—according to good thomistic teaching—this all-surpassing and liberating orientation of the spiritual transcendence of man by grace also changes the horizon (the 'formal object') of spiritual realization, even though it does not represent any objectively new object, it is also materially a 'revelation' and hence, if accepted, is also faith. Why then should not the fact of a person's obedient and loving entrance into the uncontrollable infinity of his transcendence—into which one does not enter in the measure of one's comprehension of it but in the measure in which one is uncontrollably comprehended by it—be more possible than *merely* a spiritual and natural transcendence? Why should it not be in fact the dynamic force which, by God's action within us, carries us into the life of God? And why should it not suffice that man accepts this dynamic urge by the fact that he willingly lets the Incomprehensible, in His incomprehensible way, do with him what He wills? (Must it be specially emphasized that this acceptance must be conceived as naturally containing all the demands of natural and supernatural ethics? Of course, this must be conceived in such a way that—as the experience of pagans and also of Christians shows—the right orientation towards God can be 'subjectively' achieved in practice even where there are most important errors with regard to individual material norms of morality.)

Hence, in his preaching of Christianity to the 'non-Christian', the Christian will not proceed so much from the idea of wanting to convert someone else into something which up till now he has not been at all, but rather he will try to make him more conscious of what he is. Naturally, he will do this, not because Christianity is—in a modernistic sense—merely the conscious realization of a natural religious need, but because God in his grace and on account of his salvific will has long ago offered the reality of Christianity to man, and because it is absolutely possible and probable that man has already accepted this reality, without being conscious of that fact. These, therefore, are the presuppositions under which the Christian of today and tomorrow will see and experience the Church. Not indeed as the exceptional, and as something which asserts itself only with difficulty, not as one of the many 'Sects' into which humanity is divided, not as one of the many factors of a pluralistic society and of a pluralistic mental outlook of humanity. He will rather see and experience it as the tangibility of something which already unites men internally as the historical constitution of what is universal and what (in spite of being quite freely established by God, yet being established precisely by *God* and not by some particular finite being) is really quite self-evident. The Christian of today and tomorrow will see and experience the Church as the genuine representation of the nature of man as planned by God (the 'historical' nature of man, to which belongs also his supernatural calling), as the sacrament of a grace which—precisely because it is offered to everyone —presses towards its sacramental, historical appearance even where the sacrament is not yet present, and which precisely in this way is never absolutely identical with its effective constitutive sign but rather promises—precisely by the sign which it renders present and by which it is rendered present (both are to be affirmed)—that it is powerfully at work *everywhere*. If the history of mankind is one in which everyone from Abel right down to the last man is connected and in which everyone means something for everyone else throughout all ages and not merely for those living at the same time and place on earth, then the Church is the leaven not only when we can see with our own eyes that she has taken hold of part of the rest of the flour and thus has herself made it part of the fermenting mass, but always and for each and every age, and especially also where the flour has not (yet) changed into the leavened dough in a way tangible to us. The Church will appear to such a Christian precisely as the promise made to the non-Christian world, and this not merely to the extent and only when this world itself has already become the Church. The promise is not merely the promise of the growing conversion of this world into the Church, but it is the promise of a possibility for the world to be saved by the Church even where it does not itself already become that Church which can be experienced historically.

All this is true even for the simple reason that the Church is after all also the promise of salvation for that world which lived and died before her time. For if Christ, in and through his historically tangible nature (and not merely as the eternal Logos of the world) is the salvation of all men—even of those who lived before his time (and lived for hundred thousands of years in an unpredictable, laborious and dark history quite incomprehensible to itself)—then this is valid in due proportion also for the Church. When we ask: what reveals the fact, and whereby it is promised to the world of all ages in a historically clear way and with accomplished objectivity that the world is subject to the mercy and not the angry judgement of God, the only answer we can give is that this is due to Christ alone and to his Body which is the Church. If, however, we accept and agree without difficulty that the Church was the effective sign set up for the salvation of earlier ages— a salvation belonging to these times before Christ and the Church without manifesting itself as (even though it was) a salvation coming through the Church—then it should not be surprising for someone who knows this, that the times after Christ lie in the dimension of the Christian and ecclesiastical salvation even when they have not yet become part of the Church in a tangible, sociological sense. After all, if it is true that the Church will always remain the sign of contradiction right to the very end, then this means, in a different terminology, that the Church seen sociologically will always be one single entity within a world which itself will always remain pluralistic in its world-views. Knowing this, therefore, the Christian works for the 'victory' of the Church in the knowledge that the Church will in truth never be absolutely victorious during the age of this world (which he knows, not from scientific forecasts of world-history but from the Word of God himself). If he nevertheless does not stop hoping that the whole world might one day be consumed into the pure flame of the love of God since ultimately the world itself is driven on by God's overpowering love for it in Christ, then he cannot see this Church otherwise than as the promise that, in the midst of the contradiction of the world against God, her deeper 'yes' to God will nevertheless be achieved by the superior force of God's grace. He will not see the Church as one camp to which is opposed the camp of evil on an equal footing, equally powerful and absolute (and both of them merely embraced by the non-revealed purpose of God who has basically kept the ultimate meaning of this drama an absolute secret). He will see the Church as the perceptible form of that 'yes' which he hopes God too has spoken in answer to, and through, the 'no' of the world, a 'yes' which remains victorious and which has long ago surpassed the 'no' of the world. Ultimately (it is different in the meantime) he will always refuse to consider the Church as a proposition which is in contradiction to what is really and most profoundly meant by the propositions of the others, so that he would ultimately have to choose between the two. He will frequently and patiently, modestly and self-critically (since even the knowledge of the Church must always grow further) say 'no' to the propositions of the others, but simply in order to say 'yes' to what they really mean by them. He will understand the Church in her true nature as that comprehensive 'yes' of God to the world in which God (i.e. the One apart from whom there can only be . . . nothing) promises Himself victoriously to this world. He will understand more and more that one can really only oppose an empty 'no' to this 'yes' of God, a 'no' whose emptiness manifests itself ever more clearly, and that even this 'no' finds its source of life and power in the partial or complete 'yes' to be found within it or at the back of it and which belongs within that 'yes' which is the Church. Does all this take the sting out of sin, error, darkness and the danger of eternal damnation in the world? Let no one assert this. It is simply not true for the man of today. After all, it is not as if this optimism of faith (which is not the optimism of middle-class security or an 'enlightened' optimism) comes easy to modern man. He does after all experience darkness, he does after all suffer to the very point of physical dangers to his very life from the pluralism of this world. There has probably never been a man who has been as little convinced of his own goodness than is modern man. Everywhere modern man feels his brittleness, his threatened existence, the possibility and probability that his most sacred idealism might one day be unmasked (and rightly so) as being simply fear, a vital need for security, cowardice, lack of vitality. He experiences his finite nature and his poverty, his threatened nature and unfathomable doubt. If he is nevertheless obedient to God's word and sees the best and the holy in man—if he believes (and how difficult this is) that man is a child of God, beloved of God and worthy of an eternal life which already acts and grows within him even now—then he will not get above himself and adopt an 'enlightened' attitude by regarding what has been promised as if it were his own secure, self-evident nobility. And if he finds it easier to think more optimistically of others than of himself, then this optimism will always find its limit and correction in this endured pessimism about himself, as well as finding there the means for making sure that his optimism will never go too far. The man of today may safely think optimistically of others. This is almost the only means which helps him not to despair of himself. He almost finds it easier to think highly of himself simply because he regards it as a moral duty and a deliverance of his existence to think well of man in general, and hence cannot do otherwise than to include himself, almost contrary to his experience, in this estimate. If, however, he must think in this way of man in general because it is the liberation of his own existence and the way in which he can find hope for himself (which, after all, is his Christian duty), then he cannot possibly see the Church as the exclusive host of those who are alone predestined. He must in this case experience the Church as the promise given to the others, as the manifestation of what these others are (and if this is not 'certain' with regard to these others—well, it is also not certain that those who are inside the Church belong to the camp of the chosen). In this way, it also becomes less of a vexation that so few in the world belong to the number of the Christians of this Church: the symbol of the mystery of the light shining in the darkness may be only a very modest one which may almost be overlooked; the message of what is to come (and this is the Church) cannot be the reality of what is to come; the Church in time is not as great as the eternal kingdom of God.

We do not claim that what has been said here raises *all* those points regarding 'ecclesiological piety' which, on the one hand, belong to the enduring elements of dogmatic Ecclesiology and which, on the other hand, are the most apparent ones in the ecclesiological piety of today or tomorrow. But it would seem nevertheless that the points we have mentioned do belong to those we are looking for: the Church of those who, as sinners, accept by faith everyone's existence in its ordinariness and burdensomeness, so that we experience our own fate as the fate of the Church and experience ourselves in *this* way as her members; the

Church who is an object of faith because we believe *in* God, and whose actual condition must not be identified with what she believes; the Church who is the promise of salvation even for that world which has not yet recognized itself explicitly as a part of the Church.

15

LATIN AS A CHURCH LANGUAGE

POPE JOHN XXIII's *Constitutio Apostolica 'Veterum Sapientia'* has once more focussed the attention of theologians on the question of Latin as a Church language. We will try in the pages that follow to look at the whole question of Church Latin under all its different aspects *sine ira et studio*. It is not our intention to write a commentary on the above-mentioned Apostolic Constitution. The brevity of this document alone makes it impossible to regard it as an adequate basis for a treatment of this problem. There are far too many questions, only touched on or even completely bypassed by this document, which must be posed explicitly in our present context. Hence, since there is no question here of a commentary on the papal document, our exposition must not be taken as a criticism of this document. Of course, it is also true that the question we have posed ourselves cannot be treated objectively without taking this Apostolic Constitution into consideration. Hence—with all the respect and frankness which must be shown towards such a Church document—we will inevitably have to point out any possible misunderstandings concerning this Constitution or any too strict interpretations of such a text. Our exposition divides itself quite naturally into four parts. The first part offers certain reflections on Latin as a Church language in general. The three subsequent parts treat of Church Latin as the language of the Liturgy, as the language of Church authorities and administration, and as the language of the ecclesiastical sciences.

Since we will be speaking exclusively of Latin as a Church language, the question of the value of a classical education based on knowledge of Greek and Latin and the question of the possibility or practical impossibility of using Latin as a common international language in the secular sphere (as in earlier centuries) will not fall within the actual scope of these reflections, and will be only very briefly touched on in

1.4.

1. On the Theology of a Church language

If one wishes to say anything really valid about a language in the Church and about the unity of language in and for the Church, then one would really have to base oneself both on a theology of language in general and on a theology of the Church. In other words, one should not in such a case plunge immediately into a consideration of the dignity of Latin, its significance in the history of culture, and the practical necessity of a unified language in the Church. While we are on this subject, we wish to state right from the start that obviously it is not one of the charisms of the Church's *magisterium* as such to be able to give a correct estimate of the cultural values of Latin, since these advantages of Latin are neither explicitly nor implicitly an object of revelation. Hence, declarations of the Church which argue for the particular suitability of Latin as a Church language by bringing out the intrinsic advantages of Latin, carry as much weight as belongs to the high human authority of the Church's powers and are an expression of the pastoral power which thereby explains and justifies the rightness of its decrees about Church Latin. It is clear that the fact of its being based on the pastoral power certainly permits us to draw the conclusion that Latin must be suitable as a Church language even as to its objective quality, but not really that it must of its nature be more suitable than any other language; for the ordinances of the Church's pastoral office can indeed under the necessary presuppositions (their universality, the seriousness of their obligation, etc.) claim to be good thanks to the assistance of the Holy Spirit, but cannot necessarily and to the same extent demand to be regarded as theoretically better than some other possible ordinance.

Let us return to the beginning of our reflection: the dignity and usefulness of Latin do not provide us with a sufficient starting point for a theological statement about a Church language. To find such a starting point, one would have to start with certain theological sources and try to determine from the standpoint of salvation history and of revelation the real function of human language and the multiplicity of human languages in the Church. It goes without saying that we can give only a few modest indications of all this here. Even according to what we know from revelation, language as such is associated exclusively with the nature of man. Because he is what he is, man speaks and he alone is capable of speaking. Indeed, it is precisely by speaking that he fulfils his human nature, for this nature consists in more than an interior and free self-consciousness; furthermore it does not merely consist in the experiencing of a world with which he comes into contact and in whose possession he possesses himself, but also signifies the possession and realization of his surroundings in an I-Thou communication which can be had and realized only by the use of a real language. This shows right away that language is not so much a supplementary means of human inter-communication, a means which can be replaced by something else, but that, even though it must be realized in a historical manner, it is a constitutive element of human nature to such an extent that we cannot really conceive man without it. Hence, the question about the language of man in the concrete touches directly on his existence and is, therefore, also governed by the norms of the natural law, so that there is, for instance, a right to one's mother tongue which does not come under the competence of any civil or even ecclesiastical decrees. According to the Scriptures, the multiplicity of languages is a given factor along with the multiplicity of peoples and with the separation and historical interrelation of individual national histories. To this extent, the pluralism of languages in the world has the same properties as the pluralism of peoples: the multiplicity of peoples and languages is the manifestation of God's positive will giving expression to the glory of his creatorship by this multiplicity of peoples, and yet at the same time it is also an expression of the sinful cleavage of man and of the salvific providence of God who, by this antagonistic pluralism of peoples, prevents any total rebellion of the one human race against God. Two consequences immediately follow from the fact that the human race, thus constituted in multiplicity and torn apart by guilt (both of which is given objective expression by the plurality of languages), is to be reunited by the one redemption of Christ and in the one Church. On the one hand, it cannot be the task of the Church to destroy the plurality of peoples and languages, as it were, by becoming an earthly City of God and by adopting a unified language which suppresses every other language, for this would be a denial of that order of creation in which the multiplicity of peoples and languages has certainly a positive function to fulfil. On the other hand, the Church in her nature as a saving force for a world fallen into sin and discord, certainly has the task of manifesting by what she is and through her life the unity of the human race split up into different peoples, and of manifesting it in the one Christ and in the one salvation He offers to all. How this, as it were, dialectic task of the Church must and can be accomplished anew, is shown by the example of the first Pentecost where the nature of the Church was historically manifested for the first time. In the event of Pentecost, according to the testimony of the Scriptures, the united representatives of the Church (i.e. the Apostles) speak in their ecclesiastical unity about the same unique salvation in Christ but in the different national languages. The pentecostal miracle of tongues is to begin with what is truly a charism given to the representatives of the Church and not merely something which takes place in the listeners to the sermon of Pentecost preached by the Apostles.[1] The actively proclaiming Church is the Church which speaks the many languages of many peoples and which, without losing her unity in the object and exercise of that word, is also sent out by a divine charism into the pluralism of languages without being permitted or forced to fear that she will thereby lose the oneness of her message either in its object or exercise. The permanent unity of the kerygma of the Church embraces and affirms the permanent plurality of the many languages and peoples. The fact that the power of the Spirit overcomes the dividing plurality of languages while at the same time preserving that plurality, provides us with the ultimate theological explanation of the nature of the language of the Church.[2] People of different nations do not receive the charism of all understanding any one language of the Church in a phonetic and historical sense, but rather the Church is given the commission and the ability of telling everyone of the one salvation of Christ in her capacity as the one channel for the salvation of all, without being ultimately dependent on a single human or sacred language.

[1] Cf. A. Stolz, 'Theologie der Sprache', *Benediktin. Monatschrift* XVII (1935), pp. 121–135; French translation: 'Théologie des langues', *Vie spirit.* LI (1937), pp. 86–107.

[2] Cf. H. Schmidt, *Liturgie et langue vulgaire* (Rome 1950), who concludes his exposition of the discussions at the Council of Trent about the language of the Liturgy with the affirmation: 'Ce qu'on appelle "unité de langue" dans l'Eglise n'est au fond qu'une uniformité. La vraie unité se compose de beaucoup d'éléments, tenue ensemble par un lien surnaturel d'esprit et de matière dans le Christ ... L'uniformité ne serait qu'un signe de la faiblesse humaine qui ne permet pas de maintenir l'unité dans la diversité' (p. 192).

Consequently, the Church of the Apostles entered into the *koine* without worrying anxiously about preserving the language of Jesus and of the Old Testament, but spoke Greek so that the Word of God found in the New Testament is not rendered in the sacred tongue of the Old Testament (although the Church was quite well aware of the essential importance of her origin from the Old Testament as a criterion for the lawfulness of her mission). She spoke in the language spoken wherever she carried the message of Jesus, and this not only inevitably during the first period of missionary work among the various peoples, but always and everywhere and thus even where it might have been possible in given circumstances to impose one sacred language of worship. This too is why we do not find any desire in St Paul to justify the use of a language in divine worship which would not be understood by the participants (cf. 1 Cor 14.1–25). He refuses to accept ecstatic speaking in tongues during divine service, at least when there is no interpreter present, by pointing out firstly that the listeners will not understand anything and so will be forced into the role of an uninitiated barbarian and secondly that it is better to speak 'five' comprehensible words in the assembly of the whole Church than ten thousand words inspired charismatically by the Holy Ghost but not understandable by others. Yet this sober realism does not make him a purist either: The people say 'Amen', 'Alleluia' and 'Maran atha'.

In view of this attitude of the growing Church towards the pluralism of languages—an attitude which stems from a simplicity ultimately based on theology—one will have to be careful not to go too far in one's desire to attribute a providential significance to Latin and its particular characteristics. The Church does not take up the languages of the peoples in whose region she comes into existence because she discovers in them any particular property and preferable suitability different from any other language, but only because she is immediately convinced of the necessity of speaking in the tongues of the peoples to whom she is sent, because she knows that she can proclaim the one salvation in all these languages and because she realizes that she can and must speak in the language of the Parthians, Medes, Phrygians and Arabians, just as much as in the language of the *advenae Romani* (cf. Ac 2.9 *sq.*). Undoubtedly, every language has its special advantages as compared with others, even presupposing that they are compared with each other on the same historical level of development. But each language, in comparison with others, has also its disadvantages. To deny either of these facts—in other words, to try to ascribe only advantages or disadvantages to one language as compared with others (always presupposing, of course, the same stage of development, which is not always true of every language at every moment of its historical existence)—would simply be a naïve nationalism. Just as there is no people which in its historically concrete nature and of itself is simply *the* people or to be preferred before all others as 'God's own country', so the same must also be said of every language.

One can, therefore, quite legitimately point out certain advantages of Latin which, other things being equal (and only then), make this language particularly suitable for use by the Church and suitable for what she wants to say. One can also regard these advantages as grounds for the providential nature of the practical utilization of this language in the mouth of the Church (as the *Constitutio Apostolica* and many earlier papal documents rightly do). But such advantages do not signify any absolute prerogative of one language over others, since the other languages do not indeed possess these particular advantages but do possess other advantages which in the ultimate analysis could make them equally, though differently, suitable as a language of the Church. Should anyone seriously want to dispute this simple reflection, then we would have to ask him what reason he could possibly have for disputing the equally great suitability of Hebrew or Greek, since God, after all, spoke his own Word to us in these languages and not in Latin.

Thus it can be completely denied that Latin possesses any really unique and special quality which, more than any other language, makes it of its very nature suitable to be the language of the Church. This is especially true since (just as in the case of the special qualities of individual peoples) any language, and hence also Latin, could be shown to have special characteristics which would be an obstacle to the proclamation of the Word in such a language. The fact that Latin has actually come to be preferred as the common language of the Church, is not ultimately due to any special intrinsic superiority of Latin, but is due to the historical factors of the Church's origin. For in God's providence, the Church began in certain cultural surroundings, and this fact must be understood and accepted as simply a free act of God's will, since even in such matters God's choice is a grace which ultimately needs no reason on man's part.[3]

[3] Fr. Lepargneur, 'L'universalité de l'Eglise romaine', *Eglise vivante* XIII (1961), pp. 403–416.

It may undoubtedly also be said that injudicious talk about Latin as the language of the Church would, not without reason, leave itself wide open to the reproach that it presupposes a clerical notion of the Church in which the Church becomes identified with the clergy, and the mass of the faithful are regarded simply as the object of the Church's saving care. If, however, all baptized Christians are members of the Church and together form the Church, then a language which at best is spoken only by the clerics of the Church, can be labelled as the language of the Church only if one takes great care not to lend even involuntary support to a concept of the Church which should really have been surpassed by now as a result of Pius XII's Encyclical '*Mystici Corporis*'. Even paying all due respect to the lasting core of truth in particular declarations made by certain synods during the nineteenth century,[4] it will be possible to say that such declarations

----

[4] Austria:

Vienna 1849 (*Collectio Lacensis* V 1363a);

Vienna 1856, Conv. Epp. Austr. a. 1856 (*Ibid.*, V 1261c);

Vienna 1858, Decr. Conc. prov. Viennensis a. 1858 tit. VI cap. 2 (*Ibid.*, V 202a);

Gran 1858, Decr. Conc. Strigonien. a. 1858 tit. VI 5 (*Ibid.*, V 61a);

Prague 1860, Decr. Conc. prov. Pragen. a. 1860 tit. I cap. 9 (*Ibid.*, V 431c);

Kolocza 1863, Decr. Conc. prov. Colocen. a. 1863 tit. IV cap. 3 (*Ibid.*, V 664d).

Germany:

Cologne 1860, Decr. Conc. prov. Colon. a. 1860 tit. II cap. 26 (*Ibid.*, V 368a).

Holland:

Utrecht 1865, Conc. Ultraiect. a. 1865 tit. IX cap. 2 (*Ibid.*, V 915b).

England:

Westminster 1859, Conc. Westmonaster. tit. II decr. 14, 7 (*Ibid.*, III 1018d–1019a).

USA:

Baltimore 1886, Acta et Decreta Conc. plenarii Baltimorensis III a. 1886 (Baltim. typis J. Murphey et Soc. 1886) Decr. tit. V cap. 2, 167s.

France:

Paris 1844, Litterae synodal. IV (*Coll. Lac.* IV 86d);

Paris 1849, Conc. prov. Paris a. 1849 tit. IV cap. 1 (*Ibid.*, IV 29d);

Rheims 1849, Conc. Rhemens. a. 1849 tit. 18 cap. 2 (*Ibid.*, IV 152d–153a);

Avignon 1849, Conc. prov. Avenion. a. 1849 tit. X cap. 1 (*Ibid.*, 360d–361a);

are merely further evidence (although not exclusively so) of the Restoration politics which were manifesting themselves at that period in the attempts to encourage the neo-gothic and 'nazarene' tendencies and a certain type of neo-scholasticism conditioned by the spirit of that age, in the defence of the monarchies, in too great a conservatism in the face of newly awakening social movements, in hypersensitive reactions against the efforts of pastoral reform during the period of

Lyon 1850, Conc. prov. Lugdun. a. 1850 Decr. 26, 7.8 (*Ibid.*, IV 485d–486a);

Aix 1850, Conc. prov. Aquens. a. 1850 tit. IX, cap. 4, 13 (*Ibid.*, 1000c);

Bourges 1850, Conc. prov. Bituricens. a. 1850 tit. III (*Ibid.*, IV 1108c);

Bordeaux 1850, Conc. prov. Burdigal. a. 1850 tit. V cap. 4, 3.6 (*Ibid.*, IV 595b; 596a);

Sens 1850, Conc. prov. Senonens. a. 1850 tit. IV cap. 5 (*Ibid.*, IV 906c);

Auch 1851, Conc. prov. Auscitan. a. 1851 tit. III, cap. 3, 186 (*Ibid.*, IV 1208b);

Bordeaux 1868, Conc. prov. Burdigal. a. 1868 cap. 10, 6.7 (*Ibid.*, IV 846b; 847a).

Italy:

Meeting of the Bishops of Umbria 1849, Consess. Epp. Umbr. a. 1849 tit. IX (*Ibid.*, VI 761b);

Meeting of the Bishops of Sicily 1850, Congreg. Epp. Sicil. a. 1850 tit. I cap. 2 (*Ibid.*, VI 813c);

Pisa 1850, Act. Synod. Conv. Pis. sess. IV cap. 1, 4 (*Ibid.*, VI 230c);

Loreto 1850, Conv. Epp. Lauret. a. 1850 art. 3 (*Ibid.*, VI 793a);

Ravenna 1855, Conc. prov. Ravennatis a. 1855 pars IV cap. 6, 3 (*Ibid.*, VI 201c–202a);

Urbino 1859, Conc. prov. Urbinatens. a. 1859 Adlig. IV, 1 (*Ibid.*, VI 99a–d);

Venice 1959, Decr. Conc. prov. Venet. a. 1859 pars II cap. 16 (*Ibid.*, VI 315c).

This collection of references is taken from the Essay by R. Herkenrath, 'Die Sprache der Theologie', ZKT XIII (1889), pp. 597–630, which provides a good description of the state of the problem at the end of the nineteenth century (with valuable references to the older literature).

The study of the Provincial Synods shows that, besides the predominance of Latin countries (France alone has more entries in this list than all the non-Latin countries taken together), there is also a corresponding decrease in the demands and the justifying reasons for the use of Latin (cf. R. Herkenrath, *loc. cit.*, pp. 601–605).

Enlightenment, and in too high an estimate of a historically conditioned form of the Roman Liturgy.[5]

2. Latin as the common language of the one Church—in general

Even though, in a theological sense, the only language of the Church
is the unity of the proclamation of the one salvation by the one, and
permanently one, Church—and this precisely in the multiplicity of
languages—this in no way denies the fact that it is extremely useful
and right, and indeed almost inevitable, that there should be one and
the same common language in the one Church. It is of course true that
all languages are languages of the Church when they serve the profession of the faith of the Church, when they manifest the inexplorable
calling of the Spirit in the hearts of Christians and help the worship
of a Christian church in a particular locality. For these languages are
then used legitimately for the self-realization of the Church by the
members of the Church and by her official representatives, and no
discussion about the language of the Church should ever forget or
obscure this fact. But in spite of the plurality of local churches, and
within that very plurality of peoples and their languages, the Church
is one in origin and of her very nature even in the historical sphere.
The churches in particular localities and in individual situations of
history always combine to form the one Church. This unity is not
merely the unity of the same, all-governing divine Spirit, nor merely
a unity of the same 'ideology' (or better, of the Faith), but is also a
unity of a historically tangible perfect society, the unity of the Church's
authority in the one supreme Pastor of the Church and in the unity
of the college of bishops indissolubly united with him, also a unity of
active love among all the members of the Church scattered all over the
world and finally a unity of mutual participation in worship. Such a
unity in the historical, social and liturgical dimensions can hardly do
without one common language. It may be that—to begin with—this
unity, which can never be achieved in all these dimensions except
with the help of human speech, is achieved by the very fact that the
same person who accomplishes and mediates such a unity speaks
several languages. But with the spread of the Church into many
lands and languages, it will become almost self-evident that the realiza-

[5] Cf. J. A. Jungmann, 'Liturgische Erneuerung zwischen Barock und
Gegenwart', *Lit. Jahrbuch* XII (1962), pp. 1–15.

tion of this unity will also require a gradual formation of a common language.

It is not the task of the present investigation to determine the many *a-priori* conceivable ways in which such a common language can overcome the continuing plurality of languages in the Church in order to realize more clearly the unity of the Church. Here we need merely establish the historical fact that such a common language was formed in the Church, that this language is Latin and that consequently this language is suited for the afore-named purpose. The fact that this common language was actually developed—since it was the only language of cultured Western society on that cultural level required for the life of the Church—and the fact that, since the Eastern Schism, the realm of the Roman Catholic Church did actually (though regrettably) coincide with the Western and thus the Latin cultural sphere, explain indeed why and how Latin, and not some other language, became almost inevitably the one common language of the one Church, yet these are not the decisive factors. The fact that this language of the Western sphere of culture which is also the realm of the Church of Christ, has rightly remained the common language of the one Church right up to our own day, finds its justification in the simple fact that the Church as such requires a common language, even though—and especially when—Latin is no longer the language of the one culture of a unified Western world and when, even in practice, the Church is no longer identified with the geographic boundaries of the Western world. Only if things are seen in this light, will it be possible to give a really pertinent answer to the question as to why the Church can in a true sense regard Latin as the language of the whole Church, even though historically speaking, the separated and Uniate Eastern churches have never known Latin as the language of their own cultural environment and yet are, or at least can be, equally rightful members of this one Catholic Church. Even for them Latin can be regarded as practically the only suitable common language in the universal Church, since Latin must be looked upon as the only possible common language in practice—not, ultimately, because of its history in the earlier Church but on account of the necessity for a currently practicable single common language. This does not deny, of course, that as far as the relationship of the Latin Western Church to the Latin language is concerned, the dignity and historical significance of Latin for Western culture as such is an added factor, over and above the other aspect of the necessity of a unified common language in the whole Church.

The Western, Latin Catholic has therefore a twofold relationship to the Latin language: for him, as for all Christians of the one Church, Latin is both the present-day common language and also the language of his historical past in a more restricted sense, and hence a language he will love and cultivate even on this account as the living ground of his own history. This second circumstance is almost completely absent in the case of the Eastern churches, and even in the age of the world-Church just beginning, this circumstance will not be present for the peoples of the Far East and of Africa to the same extent as it is for the Westerner. Yet Latin can and will remain the most suitable common language for everyone, for one cannot in practice imagine any better one. For the Church has no plausible reason for creating or using an artificial language such as Esperanto; there is also no reason why she should adopt one of the major living universal languages, such as English, as her own common language for international communication. Neither of these possibilities is indicated, since an artificial language could not serve the Church's purposes better than the old language of her past, a language already adapted to the Church's needs, and since a modern universal language has less prospect today of being gladly and successfully employed as the common means of communication by all nationalities in the Church than for instance French or English had one hundred years ago.

If the one Church requires a common language of communication more or less in all ages and for very practical reasons, then this is even more necessary today than ever before. For the multiplicity of nationalities and of cultures in the one Church, which is now preparing to be a really universal Church, is greater today than ever before in her history. It is more than ever necessary today that the whole Church should act as one in a concrete and historical manner, that she should have one global plan of action for the missions, that each of her members should help the other in a really practical way, etc. It might be objected against this, that the history of individual nations is becoming more and more intertwined into one world-history, no matter how great the inner conflicts of this history may be; yet at least up till now, this fact has not produced any really effective, unified language of communication. Instead, the understanding between people of different languages has been effected in different ways: either by utilizing the possibilities of easier and quicker translation from one language into another, or by using the language of a few world powers as international languages of communication. But such aids used in the concrete situation of a world-history becoming more and more unified, are stopgaps and nothing more; as against this, there already exists one common language in the Church and this language does not offend any sense of national equality nor the sensitivity of any people:—a language which has developed historically, a common language which does not have to be invented or discovered first but which requires only to be preserved, fostered and developed. What reason could one give, therefore, for renouncing this already existing common language?

While remaining quite calm and sober about it, it will certainly be necessary to be quite clear and precise about whether Latin is and will be such a common language of communication in the Church of the present and of the future. But that is all. The arguments brought forward by the humanists of the Renaissance and later on, and even during the nineteenth century—arguments by which they sought to show that Latin has an indispensable formative value for Western man (and perhaps this is still valid even today for a man of Western culture) —cannot be made to apply to those of other cultures who will enter into the Church in the present or some future age. Should one try to apply these arguments for theological reasons (and other reasons are right away questionable) then one would have to draw the logical conclusion and demand Hebrew and Greek just as much as Latin for Western Christians, for they too are essential languages of the Church's past. Latin does not have an indispensable and irreplaceable value for those in the Church who belong to other cultures; for them it is not a formative value pertaining to their own immediate historical past, but is rather (*sit venia verbo*) an ecclesiastical Esperanto which they will learn gladly and willingly out of love for the Church and her unity. For them, however, Latin has then only the limited, albeit genuine, significance belonging to such a common language, but it cannot be expected to fulfil the function of a spiritual foundation out of which grows one's own, permanent culture.

It might be objected that both by the entry of new peoples into the one Church and by the intertwining of all national histories into the unity of present-day world-history, the Western past has become an important element even in the history of these new peoples in the Church and that therefore Latin too should mean more to them than just some kind of Church Esperanto. In answer to this objection it must be said that we can to a certain extent agree with what this objection states, but that all this does not involve any very great practical effect even for the majority of the educated in these new nations, since the same argument could also be used to prove the opposite, viz. that the non-Western cultures too have today become a factor in the Church and in the present-day situation of the Western world and yet the great majority of educated Westerners do not conclude from this that they should on this account start studying Sanscrit, for instance, or classical Chinese.

There is one more point which should be noted with reference to this reduction of Latin to a mere, albeit practically indispensable, language of communication in the Church, something which brings out this reduction even more clearly. In the history of the Western world, Latin was for centuries the only language sufficiently developed to be able to serve all the religious and ecclesiastical needs of Christianity, even within the confines of one single nation. Even for each individual nation, Latin was the living language of education and of the educated, and other languages had not yet attained the same level of historical development. Today all this is quite different.[6] As we will show in detail later, the languages of modern cultures—at least of Western culture—are all in a position to be in every respect the languages of present-day science, culture, poetry and education, and also of the Christian religion in each of the nations concerned. Whether one likes it or not, this means that Latin has thereby lost some part of the significance it once had. The Western man of today—even if he is a very emancipated, educated person—will in the concrete exercise and live his Christianity through the medium of his mother tongue, and moreover he can do this without conflict, which was not yet possible for such a person a few centuries ago. Thus, even from this point of view, Latin has necessarily and unavoidably become a secondary language of communication, a kind of Church Esperanto. But the necessity for Western man to remain rooted in his own history —this anamnesis of his Latin past imposed as an obligation on Western

[6] This is overlooked when it is pointed out that Latin has undergone a Renaissance three times already (as is done also in the 'Ordinationes', AAS LIV [1962] p. 340). Furthermore, it can be said that the revival of 'classical' Latin in the Renaissance itself was the beginning of the death of Latin as a really living, developing language.

man—is a factor of his cultural life and not directly of the life of the Church as a whole and of the Christian as such. Yet it will always be necessary for the Church and theology to remain rooted in their past, and this fact does not imply any different kind of relationship for the Western Christian, as well as for the other Christians of the East and those of the future Church, than the relationship which the Church has towards her Hebrew and Greek past. Even a highly educated African theologian of the twenty-first century will have to understand something about Greek and Hebrew, since otherwise he will not be able to return to the very sources of the original revelation, and as a theologian he will also have to have the same relationship to Latin. Yet all these necessary requirements are basically no different and of no greater urgency and extent than those which present-day Western theologians acknowledge with regard to Hebrew and Greek. Taken as a whole, this changes nothing about the fact that in the Church of the present and—even more so—of the future, Latin has and will continue to have merely the function of a secondary language of communication, i.e. the function of a kind of Church Esperanto. In this way, and to the extent of this function, however, Latin has ever new and responsible tasks imposed on it, tasks which must receive ever new solutions.

3. Latin as a 'secondary' ('dead') language

There is yet another fact to be considered before we can apply our previous reflections about Church Latin to the different spheres of the life of the Church in which Latin serves, and should continue to serve, as the language of communication within the Church. We mean the fact that Latin has become a 'dead language'. We might perhaps avoid using this particular expression, and perhaps we even should avoid it, since it seems to have a pejorative or reproachful ring about it. But the question of terminology does not affect the fact of what is actually meant by this expression. The Latin which is spoken—and must continue to be spoken—in the Church, is no longer the spoken language of any people anywhere in the world; it is no longer a language in which a people lives its ordinary life and develops its culture. If the latter is said to be a 'living' language, then Latin is a 'dead' language, which is in no way meant to deny that even the dying of this language or (if you prefer) its transformation into the modern

Romance languages, took a long time and did not happen everywhere at the same time and, in particular, happened much later in certain educated circles than in the life and everyday routine of the masses, so that, e.g., in the Middle Ages Latin could still be regarded as the living language of the clergy, who alone were educated. Be that as it may, today Latin in its strictly defined sense is everywhere and on all cultural levels a dead language. Let us nevertheless avoid this word and say rather that Latin has become a 'secondary' language today. Of course, in so far as it can still be adapted to modern needs and in so far as it is still of practical use as a language of communication in the Church— even though perhaps this cannot always be achieved easily and even then only in a secondary sense, given its dependence on modern languages (which dependence we will have to define more exactly)— there is really no reason why we should not call Latin the *lingua ecclesiae viva* (Veterum sapientia n. 6).

Whether we call it dead or secondary, clearly neither of these expressions means that Latin cannot develop any further. The defenders of Latin often praise it as an unchangeable language, as is the case also in the afore-mentioned Apostolic Constitution. This immutability is regarded as rendering Latin particularly suitable for use in the Church, and is usually explained by the very fact that Latin is no longer a living language; since it is no longer subject to the historical changes of a people, being a dead language, it is also unchangeable. It will certainly have to be conceded that the suppleness of Latin has certainly greatly decreased in comparison with modern living languages. But it cannot be seriously maintained that this language has become strictly and fully immutable. Indeed, it must not be maintained:—for as soon as this language becomes really and completely unchangeable and no longer changes in its linguistic material, it will become largely unsuitable precisely for its intended function in the Church. After all, it will always be necessary to express new realities of thought, of religious achievement, of the encounter with a changing secular world, realities which did not exist in the old days or at least which man never consciously and systematically reflected on in the past. A language which has to cater for all this, must change and develop. It must form new words, and the mentality of those who use it will inevitably influence the whole character of this language, even far beyond the mere formation of new words, just as the Latin of the Church (particularly in the Middle Ages) was inevitably and quite rightly different from the Latin used at the time of Cicero and even of Leo the Great (and this not only with regard to the growth of its store of words).

John XXIII's Apostolic Constitution shows also that the Church does not seriously regard the language she wants to speak today as absolutely immutable. For one of the things demanded by this Apostolic Constitution is precisely a kind of Academy of Church Latin, in order to develop the Latin language and make it as suitable as possible for its use in the Church today. But—and this is the decisive point—this praiseworthy and necessary development of Latin which might make it look like a living 'language', and to a certain extent does indeed achieve this, is a secondary development, i.e. a development which will always and inevitably be dependent on the historical development of a modern language. No matter how highly one may esteem Latin and no matter how confidently one presupposes that Latin will be fostered and utilized to the fullest extent desired by the Church, it will not be possible to banish the fact that modern languages are at the basis of the intellectual, cultural and social life of present-day humanity. No matter how ideally Latin may be fostered, modern philosophy, the legal and political sciences, the social sciences, natural sciences, historical sciences and poetry—in brief, the whole intellectual life of modern man—will be carried on almost entirely through the medium of modern languages. The man of today will take hold of the reality of his existence, in all its encounters and historical changes, through the medium of his mother tongue. Even at best, Latin will always be a translation from those languages in which man's direct and original relationship to the world occurs today and will continue to occur in the future.[7] For this reason and to this extent, present-day Latin as distinct from the Latin of earlier times and perhaps as late as the eighteenth century (though this in a different sense) is a secondary language. Its present and future history and development depends on the extent in which the vocabulary of modern languages develops. There is and in practice never will be anyone who, for instance, makes progress in the modern natural sciences by first thinking things out in Latin. No one will any longer start by posing the burning social and economic questions, or questions of technology and of the mental mastery of the deeper problems of human existence, in Latin or really

[7] All attempts to form new Latin words prove this indirectly. Cf. e.g. A. Bacci, *Lexicon eorum vocabulorum, quae difficilius Latine redduntur*[3] (Rome 1955).

independently of some modern language. At best one will still be able to express in a Latin translation what has already been experienced, thought and grasped and communicated to others through the medium of one's mother tongue. In actual practice, there will no longer be anyone who, apart from the official liturgy, will speak to his God in prayers coming from the heart and yet couched in Latin terms; there will be no one who will say the words of love, of enthusiasm and of poetic praise of existence in anything else but in a modern language.

We may regret the fate of the great Latin language, but no one can alter it. The Christian who believes in the workings of divine providence in the history of nations and who knows that in God's positive plan there are meant to be many peoples speaking many different languages will have the least cause of all to want to turn back the clock of history in this respect. Latin has become a secondary language, and only if this fact is clearly presupposed can one seriously think about the role Latin can still play in the Church. Yet if one presupposes this fact unflinchingly, then two things will become clear. On the one hand, Latin cannot be called the language of the Church if this is to be understood in its ultimate and fullest sense, for the language of the Church is the fullness of the living languages of the nations united together in the unity of the Church and the power of the Holy Spirit, languages in which these nations originally fulfil their life even before God. On the other hand, there must be a common international language in the Church for practical reasons, a language which, as long as there are several original languages, cannot be anything but secondary. Given this, however, and in so far as Latin is such a secondary language, Latin is absolutely suitable for being this international language particularly of the Church and has no really serious rivals for this function, so that we simply have to see to it that, since this common language is necessary in practice, it is properly mastered within the framework and for the uses which apply to a common language.

4. Latin as an essential part of a classical education[8]

There is not very much we can say about this subject here, not because this question is unimportant or outdated, but precisely because

---

[8] This question is hotly disputed within the framework of the general

it is in itself so important, extensive and widespread that it would require a whole chapter for itself. This subject has frequently[9] been treated of in the declarations of the Popes during the last hundred years or so, right up to John XXIII, especially in connection with the question as to the form a classical education should take in the curriculum of our Junior Seminaries. In this connection it has been emphasized over and

---

problem of present-day humanism. We offer a very modest selection from the numerous publications of the last few years.

W. Rüegg, *Humanismus, studium generale und studia humanitatis in Deutschland* (Genf/Darmstadt 1954);

L. Kneissler, *Das humanistische Gymnasium im Zeitalter der Technik* (Vienna 1954);

J. M. Hoek, *Grieks—romeinse cultuur in de moderne samenleving* (Antwerp 1955);

R. Meister, 'Von der Wiedergeburt des klassischen Altertums zur Konstanz des Humanismusproblems', *Anzeiger der Österr. Akademie der Wissenschaften*, phil.-hist. Klasse XCII (1955), pp. 209–220;

F. Else, 'The classics in the twentieth century', *The Classical Journal* LII (1956); pp. 1–9;

W. Schadewaldt, *Sinn und Wert der humanistischen Bildung im Leben unserer Zeit* (Göttingen 1956);

C. Schmid, *Das humanistische Bildungsideal* (Frankfurt o. Main 1956);

F. Schnabel, *Das humanistische Bildungsgut im Wandel von Staat und Gesellschaft* (Munich 1956);

W. Richter, *Die alten Sprachen in der neuen Welt* (Göttingen 1957);

H. Kanz, 'Der Bildungswert des Lateinischen und die moderne Pädagogik', *Gymnasium* LXIV (1957), pp. 424–444;

J. Ferguson, *Roma aeterna. The value of classical studies for the twentieth century* (Ibadan [Nigeria] 1957);

Ch. O. Brink, *Latin Studies and the Humanities* (London 1957);

Bildungsauftrag und Bildungspläne der Gymnasien (Berlin-Göttingen-Heidelberg 1958);

A. Willot, 'Humanisme et langues vivantes', *Les Etudes Classiques* XXVII (1959), pp. 174–186;

W. Kaegi, *Humanismus der Gegenwart* (Zurich 1959);

W. Jaeger, *Humanistische Reden und Vorträge*[2] (Berlin 1960);

H. Becher, *Das Ringen der Gegenwart um den Humanismus* (Frankfurt/M. 1960);

S. Sinanoglu, *L'Humanisme à venir* (Ankara 1960);

K. J. Vourveris, ὁ Ἑλληνικὸς ἀνθρωπισμὸς σήμερον (Athens 1960).

[9] Cf. e.g. *Enchiridion clericorum* n. 461–465; n. 594 *sq.*

over again how extremely important Latin is for that general education which is an indispensable preparation even for the future cleric. Not only have these declarations stressed the usefulness of Latin for clerical studies as such, but they have also emphasized its purely formative value in itself. According to the most recent Apostolic Constitution, these declarations made by the highest teaching office of the Church and again underlined by this Apostolic Constitution itself—by reference to CIC can 1364 and to an Apostolic Letter by Pius XI dated 1.8.1922 (AAS XIV [1922] 453)—are applicable also to the training of so-called 'late vocations'; Latin, seen as part of the classical education of the future cleric, will certainly be of special importance for late vocations. For later on these students are to have a special relationship to the sciences of the spirit and above all they will have to be able to think historically, since this is a mental attitude of such importance that nothing else can replace it for an educated Christian and especially for a theologian. Thus the Church quite rightly is courageous enough even today—in this age of the natural sciences, of technology and of polytechnic education—to demand and provide an all-round training, especially for her future clerics, which will make them familiar with the works of the real history of the spirit. Apart from Greek (cf. Veterum sapientia n.7), however, Latin is still of the highest value and usefulness for this purpose.

Of course, even in this respect, one will have to see things as they really are,[10] and this in a twofold sense. First of all, even clerics belonging to the Western European and American culture cannot do without a formation which will make them educated men of *their* own time and culture and in the way education is understood at the moment. They must be capable of conversing on an equal footing with those academically qualified in their particular cultural surroundings and so

[10] In 1959, the FIEC (Fédération Internationale des Associations d'Etudes Classiques) submitted a report (which had been in preparation since 1956 as a result of many enquiries) to UNESCO. This report, dealing with the significance of the classical languages for present-day culture (*Le rôle de la culture classique et humaniste dans la vie culturelle d'aujourd'hui*), showed a retrogressive movement. Cf. references in the following periodicals: *Estudios Clàsicos* III (1956), pp. 485–490; *L'Antiquité Classique* XXVII (1958), pp. 395–398; *Siculorum Gymnasium* XII (1959), pp. 216–220; *Anzeiger für die Alterstumswissenschaft* XIII (1960), p. 189. UNESCO has announced a comprehensive publication of this report.

must have attained their level of education. Hence, the education of these clerics must not be confined to a 'classical education' in the strict sense (as was the case until towards the end of the nineteenth century) for otherwise they would be traitors to their own calling. Thus, even strictly ecclesiastical institutions which are meant to provide a general secondary education in order to prepare future clerics or other students for higher studies on a university level must of necessity and to a large extent take into consideration the normal curriculum followed in State schools (which does not mean that they must follow it slavishly) while at the same time fulfilling the creative and only rarely accepted task of giving a lead in the further development of these teaching plans in the spirit of a true humanism. Thus, since the normal education of man today includes also a formation in the natural sciences and in technical subjects (however the ideal balance between natural science —and technical subjects—and the classical subjects may be conceived), the intensity and success of the encouragement given to the study of Latin will quite simply have to be less for the average secondary school pupil than in previous ages. For there comes a point beyond which one cannot prolong the secondary school period; one can only get so much material into a certain period of training, and the study of natural science cannot be postponed entirely until after the secondary school period; and in any case even these subjects—if they are properly done—can be of great significance for the formation of man as such.

In the second place, we must here consider the fact that the Church has entered into the age of a world-wide Church within the one world-history. Certainly, this means that the history of Western culture, with all its educational values, has also become a factor in the history of the nations. Furthermore, it certainly means also that the history of revelation and of the Church, together with their various languages, becomes a task for those non-Western nations who are now slowly coming into the Church, bringing their own history with them. Nevertheless, it remains true to say that in future it will not be seriously possible to expect the peoples of Asia and Africa to have exactly the same relationship to Latin as the peoples of a Western culture. The hellenistic-roman culture need not, and cannot, be regarded by them as the real soil out of which their own culture has grown in the same direct way as it is regarded by the peoples of the Christian West. For them Latin will on the whole remain something like a Church

'Esperanto', and the educational values of hellenistic-roman antiquity will form a permanent reality in their cultures at about the same remove as the cultures of the Near East (including Israel and the Hebrew language) are from our Western culture.

II. LATIN IN THE LITURGY

We will speak only very briefly here about the question indicated by this sub-title, for enough has been said about it in the field of pastoral theology and of liturgical studies during the last few decades;[11] moreover, the afore-mentioned *Constitutio Apostolica* does not concern itself very closely with this special question, as no doubt it did not wish to anticipate the discussions and decisions of the coming Council on this matter. When this Apostolic Constitution lays down (in n.2 of the practical ordinances at the end) that the bishops must watch that in their part of the world nothing will be written against the Latin language either as a scholastic language or as a liturgical language, this ordinance obviously refers only to attacks on Latin made by *novarum rerum studiosi, praeiudicata opinione*. Hence, this ordinance obviously does not wish to forbid the objective and dispassionate discussion of a question which after all is subject to changing times and to the development of the historical situation . . . as long as this discussion is engaged in with the necessary respect towards the decrees of the Apostolic See; this cannot be the intention of the above ordinance, particularly since such a subject belongs undoubtedly to those matters of public opinion in the Church whose absence, in Pius XII's words, would be harmful both for the pastors and for the flock.[12] Furthermore, it must undoubtedly be admitted without discussion that the modern languages cannot be completely excluded from the official liturgy of the Church. There are many obvious reasons for this, such as the fact that the proclamation of the Word of God must be an integral part of the liturgy in its fullest sense, that the sacrament of Penance, for instance, cannot be properly administered without the use of modern languages, the fact that the Church has already in many respects permitted the in-

[11] For the older literature cf. H. Schmidt, *Liturgie et langue vulgaire* (Rome 1950), p. 12 note 3. For the most recent literature cf. A.-G. Martimort, *L'Eglise en Prière* (Paris 1961), p. 142.
[12] *Osservatore Romano* of 18.2.1950.

clusion of modern languages at least in the modern rituals,[13] and the fact that ultimately even those people's services, processions, etc., carried out with at least episcopal authorization, can properly be included under the concept of the liturgy—even in the strict sense—and yet are quite inconceivable in practice if they had to be carried out exclusively in Latin.

Once one is clear in one's mind about the fact that at a closer view the liturgy of the Church has never been, nor can ever be, carried out purely in Latin, then the only serious problem can be that concerning the proper proportion of Latin and modern languages in the liturgy. This presupposes, of course, that there are no good reasons for wanting to exclude the use of Latin from the Liturgy of the Latin Church, although it is to be freely admitted (as can be seen from the practice and law of the Uniate Eastern Churches) that the principle of celebrating the whole liturgy in a modern language must not be decried from the very outset as a basically uncatholic principle. Thus, since within the radius of the Latin sector of the Roman Catholic Church it is simply a question of the correct distribution of Latin and the vernacular in the Latin liturgy (a distribution corresponding to the demands of the times), this question appears immediately as a question of prudent evaluation based on considerations springing from pastoral theology. Basically, however, such questions are not of the kind which admit from the outset of only one solution; rather, they are questions which, after very prudent and exact weighing of all the reasons for and against a certain solution, demand a freely voluntary solution, since in the realm of the contingent and of the historical, free choice and decision must find their rightful place. Such a decision which chooses from among several basically lawful possibilities is, of course, in this case a matter for ecclesiastical authority. Hence we have no intention here of going into the details of the question of Latin as a liturgical language. These details, belonging mainly to the sphere of pastoral theology, are

[13] Cf. esp. the letter of the Internuncio to the bishops of India of 8.7.1949 (A. Bugnini, *Documenta pontificia ad instaurationem liturgicam spectantia 1903–1953* [Rome 1953], pp. 173 *sq.*).

Also: Card. P.-M. Gerlier, 'Les rituels bilingues et l'efficacité pastorale des sacrements', *Maison-Dieu* XLVII/XLVIII (1956), pp. 81–97. (This is a report of the Congress of Assisi, Sept. 1956); H. Schmidt, *Introductio in liturgiam occidentalem* (Rome 1960), pp. 159–164.

far too many-sided to allow of an objective treatment here.[14] All we mean to do in this Section is merely to make a few modest remarks on this whole complex question.

First of all, it must be pointed out that even in this connection there neither is nor can be a sacred language for Christianity in any absolute sense. The notion that a certain language has an advantage—for whatever reason—over any other, as to its power of intercession, its power of entering into communication with the divinity and of making God listen to our petitions, or its having some sort of magic effect which makes it preferable to others, is a false notion and something quite unchristian and, if taken seriously, leads to the same thing as what is called superstition in Christian morality. This is not meant to dispute the fact that different ways of saying things cannot vary as to their psychological suitability for appealing to man as *homo religiosus* even on the deeper levels of his being, and that in this sense not every way of saying things must be equally suitable as a liturgical language. Yet fundamentally all languages are equal before God, just as in the new dispensation different peoples do not have any special rights before God above any others. This principle is indeed something quite self-evident and cannot really be disputed within a Christian framework. But one may sometimes get the impression that the defenders of a sacred language start from the tacit presupposition that this or that people has a privileged position before God, so that the use of its language is to be preferred before any other when it comes to choosing a liturgical language.

It follows furthermore from this that, within the realm of highly developed national cultures, we may quite rightly include the use of Latin as a liturgical language under the question of the use of an international language. This may seem rather strange at first sight and may provoke opposition, yet it is perfectly true. Latin is indeed often advocated as a liturgical language on account of its unchangeable nature and its clarity. But when we examine the matter more closely, we will find that this is not really a conclusive reason. After all, for the greater part of its history as a liturgical language in the Church, Latin was still a living language and indeed a primary and not merely a

[14] Cf. e.g. H. Schmidt, *Liturgie et langue vulgaire. Le problème de la langue liturgique chez les premiers Reformateurs et au Concile de Trente* (Rome 1950); P. Winninger, 'Langues vivantes et liturgie', (*Rencontres* LIX) (Paris 1961).

secondary language. It was, therefore, in no sense an unchangeable language. On the contrary, the meaning of its concepts has undergone very profound changes, and has been shown quite clearly by recent investigations into the linguistic history of liturgical languages.[15] *Refrigerium, sacramentum, consortium, commercium, oblatio, gratia, devotio, pietas,* etc., have passed through great changes in the history of words, and these historical periods have left their mark, almost like significant fossils, on the actual language of the Latin rite, so that the terminology of the Latin liturgy is not at all as unchangeable and clear as some apologists of liturgical Latin have tried to make out.

Conversely, it must be added furthermore that, fundamentally speaking, it is not really true that modern languages seriously endanger that clarity which should certainly be aimed at, as far as possible, in a liturgical language. The clarity of the language of religion is much more necessary for man and for his religious instruction than it is for God, who easily understands the really intended meaning of what is said. If we were seriously to deny modern languages the possibility of theological exactitude, since supposedly they are not sufficiently unchangeable, then we would really be maintaining that it is impossible

---

[15] Cf. (*inter alia*) the works of the Nijmegen school, esp. those of Christine Mohrmann:

J. Schrijnen, *Charakteristik des altchristlichen Lateins* (Nijmegen 1932); H. Rheinfelder, *Kultursprache und Profansprache in den romanischen Ländern* (Florence 1933); H. Janssen, *Kultur und Sprache* (Nijmegen 1938); M. A. Sainio, *Semasiologische Untersuchungen über die Entstehung der christlichen Latinität* (Helsinki 1940); M. M. Müller, *Der Übergang von der griechischen ʒur Lateinischen Sprache in der abendländischen Kirche* (Rome 1943); Th. Klauser, 'Der Übergang der römischen Kirche von der griechischen zur lateinischen Liturgiesprache', *Miscellanea Giovanni Mercati* (Studi e Testi CXXI) (Vatican City 1946), I, pp. 467–482.

G. Bardy, *La question des langues dans L'Eglise ancienne* I (Paris 1948); Chr. Mohrmann, *Latin vulgaire. Latin des chrétiens, Latin médiéval* (Paris 1955); *idem.,* 'Die Rolle des Latein in der Kirche des Westens', *Theologische Revue* LII (1956), pp. 1–18; *id.,* 'Le latin médiéval', *Cahiers de Civilisation médiéval* (Poitiers 1958), pp. 265–295; *id., Liturgical Latin* (London 1959); *id., Etudes sur le latin des chrétiens* I (Rome[2] 1961), II (Rome 1961) (with a detailed bibliography); A. Quacquarelli, *Retorica et liturgia antenicena* (Rome 1960); W. Dürig, *Imago. Ein Beitrag ʒur Terminologie und Theologie der römischen Liturgie* (Munich 1952); *id., Pietas liturgica. Studien ʒum Frömmigkeitsbegriff* ... *der abendländischen Liturgie* (Regensburg 1958).

for the *magisterium*—which has been given the authority for this—
to make any sufficiently clear pronouncements about the Church's
dogmas of faith in a modern language. But this is absurd. And so, when
Pius XII declared in '*Mediator Dei*' that the Latin language of the
liturgy is an effective protection against any corruption of the primitive
teaching,[16] this is indeed quite correct when understood in a positive
sense. But it neither signifies that such a means has an absolutely
guaranteed effect in this direction, nor that such a means is absolutely
indispensable for the desired purpose; in other words, even a modern
liturgical language will not necessarily lead to a corruption of the
Church's teaching, as long as she watches with sufficient care over it.[17]
For if Pius XII's words meant anything else, then there could be no case
at all in which the Church could permit the use of a modern language
in her liturgy. Yet, immediately after the above-mentioned statement,
Pius XII says that she can do this if she considers it a good thing.

Added to this there is the fact, as had been said, that both within and
outside the liturgy, the Latin language has had a very chequered career
during its long history (one need only think of words like *persona*,
*natura, transubstantiatio, naturalis, supernaturalis, sacramentum, char-
acter, mysterium, attritio, peccatum*, etc.), and that it obviously cannot
be expected (a point to be treated in greater detail later on in Section
IV) that this history of the Latin Church language has now come to an
absolutely final stop. Yet all this is no reason for maintaining that Latin
does not have any advantages in respect of its 'unchangeableness' and
clarity as compared with modern languages. But such advantages
cannot be a really decisive reason for choosing Latin as a liturgical
language, since it is relatively easy to compensate for these advantages
by the Church's *magisterium* keeping a close watch over the liturgical
texts (just as the *magisterium* watches over Catechisms and other
official religious publications in the vernacular). No doubt these
advantages are also offset by certain disadvantages of considerable
weight in the sphere of pastoral theology, such as for instance the fact
that the majority of those taking part in the liturgy do not understand
the liturgical texts, and this at a time when the efforts not only of the

[16] AAS XXXIX (1947), p. 545.

[17] This is after all no less inapplicable to translations of the Bible into
modern languages, theological publications and catechisms. Cf. furthermore
P. Winninger, *Volkssprache und Liturgie* (Trier 1961), 2nd Chapter: 'Die
Reinheit des Glaubens' (pp. 87–103).

liturgical movement but also of the official Church authorities them-selves are pressing for a *participatio actuosa* of all the faithful in the Church's worship.

If one takes all these points into consideration, it will be seen that the real reason to be seriously adduced in favour of keeping Latin as the language of the liturgy must be the unity of the language of wor-ship for the many linguistically differentiated peoples; in other words, the real reason must be that a common spoken language proves itself meaningful and useful even in this sphere, by providing a language which, although not indeed the basis of the unity of the faithful of different languages, nevertheless manifests, encourages and to a certain extent preserves this unity from the dangers of national tensions. It also follows from this, finally, that the viewpoint justifying the use of Latin as a liturgical language is not of such absolute and exclusive weight that it must necessarily exclude every use of modern languages in the liturgy. After all, an international language such as we under-stand it here, presupposes the plurality of living languages and intends merely to overcome their unavoidable disadvantages and difficulties without destroying this plurality itself. If the voice of the Church by the power of the Holy Spirit is a sacred language in every tongue, since it penetrates right into the heart of God, then it will also be possible to use a modern language for the Church's worship (always presuppos-ing that the Church has given her official approval for this) wherever the meaning and purpose of a common language of communication are no longer applicable or are clearly not as great as the spiritual profit to be derived from the use of the vernacular. This, however, is the case in the liturgy (analogously to the sermon in the vernacular) when the Church's divine service of the Word addresses itself directly to the understanding of the faithful participating in the divine worship and when this is the whole purpose of some part of the service. Thus, when the Church reads the Holy Scriptures to the people, and when this is precisely part of the divine service itself, then—being a constitu-tive part of the service—it should be done in the vernacular of the faithful. This means, however, that those who officially carry out the liturgy, should read the Holy Scriptures as part of their liturgical function itself and not merely afterwards by an activity which already no longer belongs to the liturgical action as such. The desire for the Church's authorization of this principle is so universal today among liturgists, pastoral theologians and those engaged in pastoral work, that we may surely be allowed to expect that the recommendations of the Liturgical Commission and the decrees of the Council based on these, may bring about such authorization. This seems to be the least one might expect at the present time when we have reached the stage of culturally fully developed modern languages and when we are in an age when every believer is required to make ever new, personal decisions of faith and to participate most intensely—*participatio actuosa* —in divine worship. This moreover does not offend against the general principles of Latin as the universal common language even in divine worship. For the desired principle is but a practical application to the Scripture readings of the principle by which the sermon is delivered in the vernacular, since both of them together form a unity and are addressed to the very same audience and for the same purpose, viz. the believing, personal realization of what is celebrated in the liturgy. If one were to object that this could give rise to the question as to which of the languages spoken by a linguistically mixed congregation are to be chosen for these vernacular readings, or that all this might cause dissensions among those belonging to different language groups, then it must be pointed out in answer to this objection that the readings should be given in exactly the same language as the sermon in the service concerned, and that this need not cause any more fear of serious difficulties than arises from having the sermon in a particular modern language in such a divine service.

What has just been said about the Scripture readings will no doubt be applicable also to certain appeals and exhortations addressed as part of the liturgical function to the faithful in general (e.g. during the Ordination to Major Orders) as well as to certain chants which, in the original intention of the liturgy, were expressly meant to be chants of the whole people.[18] It is surely also correct to think that the exact proportional distribution between Latin and vernacular in the liturgy should correspond to the concrete situation in the various greater regions of the Church and that it should be the task of the episcopal conferences concerned to determine the actual demarcation between

[18] Cf. the conclusions of the Missionary liturgical Congress of Nijmegen which are even more drastic with regard to chants; cf. the report 'Mission und Liturgie', edited by J. Hofinger (Mainz 1960), p. 17. These conclusions were accepted without change by the Missionary Catechetical Congress of Eichstätt in 1960. (cf. *Teaching All Nations*, ed. J. Hofinger [London 1961], pp. 392 *sq-tr.*)

the two with the permission of the Holy See and in accordance with the general norms of the universal Church.

III. LATIN AS AN ADMINISTRATIVE LANGUAGE OF THE UNIVERSAL CHURCH

The necessity and utility of Latin is seen most directly in the administrative field of the universal Church as such, which for our purposes here must be taken to include also the exercise of the Church's teaching office by the Pope over the universal Church. Accordingly, the practical use of Latin as the universal language of communication is an actual and indisputed fact in this field. The papal or conciliar doctrinal decisions of the Church's *magisterium* addressed to the whole Church, the universal canon law of the Latin Church as found in the CIC, papal Encyclicals to the whole Church, decrees of Roman Congregations which are not indeed addressed to the whole Church but are more or less based on the universal law itself formulated in Latin, such and similar declarations will be given in Latin (as one would expect) even today and in the future just as in the past. Any other procedure is inconceivable in practice. Here then is the most obvious field for a common universal language in the Church, which in the concrete means Latin.

All this is really quite self-evident, but in view of the modern conditions, problems, etc., envisaged by these decrees, it does involve the necessity of quite considerable care and development[19] of Latin, both on the part of those who issue such decrees and especially on the part of those who are meant to understand them properly. Viewed in this light, this self-evident principle is seen to be extremely important, a fact which also makes the intention of the new Apostolic Constitution perfectly understandable. All priests, at least of the Latin part of the Church, should surely understand at least as much Latin as is required for an exact and evident understanding of the Latin words used by the

[19] Classical scholars are most intensively occupied with this question, especially after the two congresses on living Latin (1956 and 1959, cf. note 23 below). The same purpose is served by the *Certamen Capitolinum* (*Concorso internazionale di prosa latina*) which was issued for the 13th time in 1961 by the *Istituto Romani-Ufficio Latino*, Rome. Information about periodicals appearing in Latin will be found, e.g., in a discussion in the *Anzeiger für die Altertumswissenschaften* XI (1958), pp. 233–238.

central authorities of the Church. Yet it has to be admitted with regret that this is no longer everywhere the case. For, if one takes a sober look at the conditions in practically all European countries (not to mention non-European countries), it will be impossible to guarantee today that every parish priest finds it really easy, for instance, to read the Latin text of a papal Encyclical and to understand every word of it. This fact is actually very regrettable, since a knowledge of this official international language used by the ecclesiastical administration is not merely desirable but could also be achieved (even in the most realistic view of the limited possibilities) as long as there is good will. Just as one may say quite truthfully that the Protestant churches certainly achieve a sufficient standard in the training of their ministers as to enable their bearers of ecclesiastical offices to read the New Testament in Greek with a certain fluency, so one may just as truthfully say that a Catholic priest must be able to understand the Latin pronouncements of his universal ecclesiastical authorities and that this ability is attainable without other, even more important and essential tasks in the training of the future priest necessarily having to suffer thereby.

Of course, we should perhaps add right away that the carrying out of the young theologian's obligation and training in speaking Latin is obviously a good way of ensuring that he will be able to understand the Latin decrees of the official Church authorities without much difficulty. Yet this itself is still not a strict proof that such fluency in speaking Latin must be necessary and indispensable for this reason alone. A well-educated Protestant theologian will certainly be able to understand New Testament Greek and the Latin of St Augustine's 'Confessions' without too much bother, and yet normally in our part of the world he will not be able to speak either Greek or Latin. Whether there are other reasons for encouraging and training the whole clergy to become proficient Latin speakers, will have to be considered in a different context. Yet even the usefulness and necessity of Latin as an international administrative language of the Church has its limits. While as late as the nineteenth century, the decrees of diocesan, provincial and national synods and similar declarations of local law were still given in Latin, this is quite rightly no longer the case today. Today, for instance, directions concerning particular laws, and pastoral instructions, in German dioceses are given in German both in the codes of such laws and in diocesan instruction sheets, and the same is true also in France, to mention but one other example. No one will seriously wish or expect that such a development should be reversed again. For there can be no sensible reason for such a course. These norms are addressed only to people who speak one and the same language. They are in any case originally thought out and conceived in the mother tongue and not in the secondary language of Latin, and they are much more comprehensible in the modern tongue to the people to whom alone they are addressed. Hence, there can be no reason whatsoever for saying these things in Latin. On the contrary, such cases should provide good opportunities for perfecting the modern languages with a view to a more dignified and powerful way of expressing religious matters and a greater exactitude of theological and legal concept.

The case just mentioned is not the only one which throws light on the limits of Latin as a common ecclesiastical language. A missionary in the mission field, for instance, or a native priest living outside the Western cultural sphere, must develop his mother tongue as well as having (even purely as an educated person) a good knowledge of at least one of the international languages in common use. Even with the best intenitons in the world, it will be impossible to consider imposing an obligation on such a missionary or native priest to explain a complicated marriage case, or socio-political case, etc., to a Roman Congregation in Latin. In such cases, even with all the good will in the world and considerable knowledge of Latin, he will surely find it much easier and will express himself more clearly in the modern language he knows and uses as the normal means of communication, and he will surely be able to expect that such international modern languages are sufficiently understood in Rome to make it possible to understand him in such a language. Furthermore, a case like the Encyclical '*Mit brennender Sorge*' shows that in very important cases, when he is addressing himself to a single nation, the Pope can speak to them directly in a modern language, without subtracting from the weightiness of such a declaration.[20] Again, no one will regret the fact that Pius XII used one of the modern languages for a great many of his Allocutions concerning important matters of moral theology and certainly aimed ultimately at teaching the whole Church. In spite of the universal purpose envisaged by such Allocutions, the audience to whom he had to speak in a modern language was not merely an accidental decor or back-cloth which could just as well have been done without.

[20] Pius XI even wrote an Encyclical addressed to the Universal Church in Italian: *Non abbiamo bisogno* (AAS XXIII [1931], pp. 285-312).

Even in other respects, we may quite soberly recognize limits to the use of Latin as an ecclesiastical administrative language, limits which can hardly be expected to be changed today in favour of Latin. Even in future, unless it concerns a particularly important matter, communications between different Roman ecclesiastical administrative authorities will to a great extent be carried on in Italian, just as it already is today. As is shown, for instance, by '*Mater et Magistra*', it will be impossible (at least for certain subjects even in the case of solemn papal declarations in Latin) to dispense completely with a first draft in a modern language. In such cases it will then perhaps be also quite legitimate to return to this first draft in a modern language when looking for an objective interpretation of such a Latin document. One can even imagine ecclesiastical assemblies of very high authority —including even an ecumenical Council and its preparation—in which Latin will not necessarily and in every case be the universal language of the proceedings,[21] but in which the difficulty of conducting one's deliberations in several languages will be overcome by some other means, as in similar secular proceedings (such as by simultaneous translation into modern languages, etc.).

IV. LATIN AS THE LANGUAGE OF THE ECCLESIASTICAL SCIENCES

The consideration of Latin as the language of the ecclesiastical sciences is logically divided into the question about Latin as the language of research in the field of theology as a whole and the question of the use of Latin in the teaching of theology in the training of future priests. Our question can be logically divided in this way, even though it is quite clear that the dividing line between research and teaching is quite vague, since, e.g., in certain circumstances new lines in even scientific research can find their first expression in theological textbooks intended for teaching purposes. Nevertheless, research and teaching are distinct from each other (even though mutually dependent) to such an extent that the question about Latin is not quite the same in each case.

[21] Ximenez spoke in five languages besides Latin at the IVth Lateran Council so as to be understood by everyone. Cf. Hefele, *Conciliengeschichte* V, p. 875.

1. Latin as the language of present-day theological research

The question as to whether present-day theological research can or should continue to use Latin as its language, is not easy to answer. If we first of all take a look at the actual situation, we will find that everything points rather to a negative answer to this question. Not only in Protestant theology but even in Catholic theology, Latin has almost completely disappeared as the language of research. There are still one or two theological periodicals which, side by side with theological research articles written in modern languages, include also an occasional article in Latin (but even then not as a regular practice), an article which can be qualified as a scientific contribution to research. But by far the greater part of the almost innumerable scientific periodicals in the field of theology appear practically exclusively in modern languages. It is impossible to furnish statistics here for the present-day proportion regarding the use of Latin and of modern languages in the field of properly scientific research. Yet the fact just stated cannot really be seriously disputed.

The same holds good also in the realm of the publication of scientific theological books. We prescind here from scholastic textbooks, for they are not included in our question here, although we are quite willing to concede that even such schools books are not always merely for the exposition of traditional teaching but may sometimes also put forward new scientific conclusions and this for the first time, all of which could happen even in school books written in Latin. Thus we can state without hesitation that in the field of Catholic theology at the present time (i.e. at least during the present generation), the production of books which, on the one hand, put forward new scientific conclusions for the first time and, on the other hand, are written in Latin, has for all practical purposes ceased completely. It might be possible to point to one or two exceptions, but in this case the exceptions really prove the rule. If I were asked which theological work written in Latin within the past generation ought to have been read by every theologian in the field of the new and actively researching theology, then I know of only one really indisputable example, viz. '*Mysterium fidei*' by M. de la Taille.[22] There may be one or other Compendium in the field of Canon law (something more, therefore,

[22] Paris 1921; 3rd enlarged edition Paris 1931.

than what is required for the first elementary classes in theology) which
has been written in Latin even during the past decade or so; it may still
be possible to name a few books in Dogmatic and Moral theology
similarly written in Latin (e.g., Vermeersch, Dieckman, Lange, etc.);
there may be a few books which still use Latin in a way similar to
certain classical scholars who even today still sometimes write in Latin
in the Introductions to their publications of the texts (e.g. Stegmüller's
'*Repertorien*'). Yet all this does not alter the fact that modern theological research published in books, uses modern languages and no
longer Latin.

This is true in all sectors of theology, and not only in those sectors
in which this is tolerated without contradiction even by the enthusiastic
advocates of Latin as an academic language—as in the field of pastoral
theology, Church history and patrology. It is true also in those fields
of theology which traditionally are regarded as the most central. With
ever-decreasing exceptions, only modern languages are used nowadays
in proper dogmatic monographs and in monographs in the field of the
history of dogmas of any scientific standing and written in book form.
The '*Cursus Sacrae Scripturae*' is a thing of the past, and even the great
works of Catholic exegesis—in the vanguard of modern research—are
written in French or some other living language. The living liturgical
sciences no longer write in Latin. Modern languages have the mono-
poly whenever Moral theology rises above the level of a scholastic
textbook, as in the case of Häring or Tillmann, and even more so in
the case of proper monographs in moral theology. Obviously the
same applies, but only more so, in such fields of theology as pastoral
medicine (cf. e.g. Niedermeyer), psychology of the moral life, archæo-
logy, the history of ecclesiastical art, hagiography and ecumenical
theology (Christian philosophy will have to be treated separately in a
moment). There can be no doubt about the fact that, as a language of
theological research, Latin has disappeared for all practical purposes.

Of course, not every actually existing fact is also justified, although
—particularly in the sphere of the Christian life, just as elsewhere—one
must have a certain respect even for mere facts and must presume that
they are also legitimate. Hence, even with regard to the present fact,
it is basically a question of whether this represents a state of affairs
in the ecclesiastical sciences which can and ought to be abolished, or
whether we may regard this state of affairs as unchangeable and legitimate. Even a brief reflection will show that it would be wrong to try

to reverse this stage in the development of the ecclesiastical sciences within the realm of research.

We have shown in the first Section of our present considerations that, on account of the historical development of the present-day life of the spirit, Latin has become a secondary language. This precisely applies also to Latin understood as the language of the theological sciences, and it means that today Latin can no longer be considered to any great extent as a language for proper theological research.

We say that Latin has become a secondary language in the field of the theological sciences. What is the reason for this? In confirmation of this thesis, one might first of all point out that even scientific research—in spite of its sober objectivity—is an essential factor in the whole intellectual realization of man's existence but that this realization originates in the very heart of man and this can be reached originally and primarily only in the mother tongue. We should have to point out that even science, if it is to be properly integrated into this realization of existence by the spirit of man, must be thought out originally and primarily in the mother tongue, and this especially where it develops in a living manner, i.e. in the sphere of research. Yet if it were to be carried through with precision, such a reflection would lead us too far into the field of the philosophy of language, of the relationship of language to actual knowledge and of the relationship of the sciences to man's existence. Hence we refrain here from giving this more profound proof for the original relationship of scientific research in general—and hence also of scientific theology—to the living mother tongue, and will confine ourselves to a simple and practical reflection. All the present-day theological sciences have to rely so much on the closest contact with the profane sciences and on the most intensive encouragement given to them, that without these modern sciences— both in themselves and in their function—the theological sciences could not be what objectively they should be for the Church's proclamation of faith.

Anyone doing research into the history of the Church and of her dogmas is absolutely dependent on the closest contact with the history of lay life, the history of the spirit and history of philosophy. A moralist and canonist cannot do without modern jurisprudence, psychology of the moral life and the social sciences. The historian of dogmas must know something of the history of natural religion. The fundamental theologian, more than anyone else, must be in touch with the history of religion, with modern philosophy, current natural sciences, the methodology of the historical sciences, etc. Present-day exegesis is no longer conceivable without modern philology and Protestant exegesis. Pastoral theology would be an impossibility nowadays without knowledge of the modern social sciences. In these and many other ways not mentioned here, theology is dependent on a great number of modern sciences, their methods and their results.

This fact does not mean a degrading or erroneous dependence of theology on these sciences, in the sense of being subordinated to them. Theology as a whole, especially in its central disciplines, cannot and does not intend to be anything other than scientific reflection on the proclamation and life of the Church as they always are and must be in all their elements especially today in the present spiritual situation. Yet if theology, even in its scientific research, has the task of serving the self-realization of the Church both in her teaching and in her life, then theology cannot really fulfil this task if it refuses to face up to the present-day situation of the Church in all the spheres of the spirit and of life. Yet such contact of one science, called theology, with the present-day living reality of the spirit, can take place only by means of the other sciences which reflect the same current spiritual situation as that of the Church. These sciences, however, are human realizations of existence which take place in fact and also legitimately through modern languages, so that an artificial scientific language can never be the original means for the exercise of these sciences.

In any case, the Christian and the Church of today are faced with the fact that, with the relative autonomy of the various fields of profane culture, the profane sciences as such on the one hand are being carried on outside the sphere of theology and on the other hand are acting as factors in the mental life of the present-day world, in the characteristic situation of this world differentiating it into peoples and languages. Hence it is unavoidable that even the theologian of today, precisely if he wishes to serve the living research of his own science, must always live also in the realms and by the spirit of these profane sciences; in other words, it is unavoidable that he should live, think and research through the medium of modern languages.

In addition, it would be a naïve and clerical conception if theological science intended to address itself exclusively to the clergy . . . even though this were only when it poses new questions, when it researches and forms itself ever anew in the men of today. It would be naïve and would underestimate the intellectual vitality of the educated laity in our day and age, if it were seriously thought that theology is an object of interest for the educated laity only in its popularized form or when it simplifies matters as in the catechism. In an age when philosophy as a proper science is no longer merely a science for clerics, scientific theology as such must also be a matter for the educated Catholic and hence must be capable of being this. Thus, theology will only be what it should be when it comes to live in direct dialogue with the man of today and with his sciences, sciences which man works out in his present-day language. This dialogue is so essential for a living theology that, without injury to their relative independence, these naturally profane sciences are also inner, subordinate elements of theology itself.

This will also explain the fact with which we started. Modern theology in her research speaks the languages of the present, not because it has suddenly become too lazy to speak Latin, but because today even thinking in theology is no longer possible except in modern languages. This theology which inevitably lives and thinks in the dimension of the present-day spirit, may then be translated into Latin, and such a translation may succeed, although only with difficulty. Yet such a Latin theology (i.e. research theology) can only be secondary, since Latin even on this level can only be a secondary language which survives and develops only by contact with the history of modern languages and their developing terminology.

At this point, it may prove useful to take up once more the assertion that Latin is unchangeable and therefore desirable as the language of theology. Let us ask first of all: can theology be unchangeable? The only possible answer to this question is surely that theology should and can always be to the highest conceivable degree in possession of that truth with which it is concerned, i.e. the truth of divine revelation, which has indeed its own history (and even for this reason alone is not simply unchangeable), but which proclaims God's truth without deception, a truth which is always valid. But this is no reason why theology should be absolutely unchangeable, in the sense that it must always repeat the very same propositions. If every science, including metaphysics, has a history, and if this history is even today no more closed than it was in the past, then man's searching spirit will necessarily be faced with ever new questions, new realities will open themselves to his reflex and systematic understanding, and there will inevitably be new concepts and also a continuous, unavoidable and legitimate development of vocabulary. All this applies therefore also to theology, as is proved also by the history of this science. This being so, theology cannot make do with a store of concepts and with a vocabulary acquired once and for all and closed thereafter. Hence, it would be naïve to think that the conceptual tasks of theology did indeed develop slowly in the past (which cannot be denied except by someone completely ignorant of the history of dogmas) but that they have now arrived at an absolutely unsurpassable peak, so that from now on they will no longer have any real history but must now persevere unchanged in the perfection they have now attained. This is not true. The terminology and hence the vocabulary of theology are part of history and will remain so even in the future, as has also been proved over and over again by the pronouncements of the Church's *magisterium* right up to this very day, since they too must reach for new concepts, and hence new words which as such did not exist previously, in order to be able to say what has to be said.

This certainly does not mean that the history of the language of theology must have the same rhythm of development as the profane sciences. Theology may quite legitimately be more conservative and may—in accordance with the characteristic property of its object— change and perfect itself more slowly. But to deny its historical character would be to declare it dead. Hence, to expect theology to make do with a now utterly unchangeable language would imply a declaration of its unhistorical character and thus of its death. It is after all quite obvious that theology, even when it is and means to be absolutely orthodox, always keeps step with the rest of the history of the spirit and hence also with the history of the language of this historical spirit. It picks up concepts and hence also words from the terminology of present-day history of religion, the philosophy of existence, psychology, the philosophy of history and the social sciences, and uses them to express its ever-present object in new ways (although always within the limits of the old truth). Theology uses these concepts and this terminology to bring to light certain new relationships existing among these objects themselves and also between them and profane reality, in order to make this object assimilable for someone who can grasp this object by faith only if it is first of all brought into a reasonably adequate spiritual association with those realities of man's spiritual existence which constitute this existence before he hears and accepts the message of faith. All this however can be thought and spoken of originally only in modern languages.

The fact that the new research theology uses modern languages in contrast to the Latin of the theological sciences of the Middle Ages and the baroque period is not simply an evil whim of modern theologians but arises from the nature of things. Since during the Middle Ages and right up to modern times, Latin was a living language for the educated even in profane subjects—a language which established the contact with the reality to be examined, and this originally and not merely in a secondary manner—Latin was also the language of theology, but as a living and hence changing language and not as an unchangeable language. Latin also had, therefore, to cease being the language of research theology at the same time (or perhaps somewhat later) as it ceased to be the original and primary language of the new successful sciences in general.

It must be emphasized once more that even these reflections do not give rise to any objections against the possibility that, even today, at least in the sphere of theology,[23] Latin could or even should still be a secondary language of communication between theological scholars. Of course, the procedure at scientific theological congresses will presumably begin and continue to be the same on the whole as is normal at other scientific congresses: every scholar speaks in one of the current international, modern languages and is understood by his learned listeners in that language. Yet nevertheless, it would certainly be desirable if Latin, at least in the sphere of theology, could remain one of these international means of communication or even—within certain limits—were to become so again to a greater extent. Anyone who has taken part in international theological congresses and conversations

[23] Even among classical scholars efforts are being made to obtain a unified language for scholars by a revival of Latin. This has led to a discussion about the principles of the introduction of new words into Latin with a view to adapting this language to the needs of our times, the simplification of Latin grammar without falsifying it, the unification of the pronunciation and also questions of teaching Latin. Two 'Congrès pour le latin vivant' (Avignon 1956 and Lyon-Villeurbanne 1959) have concerned themselves with these problems. Yet even here it was impossible to do without modern languages, as will be seen from a reading of the acts of these congresses (*Premier Congrès pour le latin vivant*, Avignon 1956; *Actes du Deuxième Congrès pour le latin vivant*, Avignon 1960).

will confirm the fact that even in this sphere Latin an still play a useful role and can still facilitate the exchange of ideas between theologians of different languages.

2. *The use of Latin as a teaching language for theology*

This presents a somewhat different problem from the one we have just discussed. To begin with, it cannot be doubted that Latin offers certain positive advantages as a language for teaching theology, at least in certain subjects such as dogmatic theology, exegesis, moral theology and Canon law. After all, the budding theologian should be brought into close contact with the history of theology. He is supposed to acquire a real understanding of the pronouncements of the Church's *magisterium*, i.e. an exact, certain and easy understanding; he ought to learn to read the pronouncements of the Church's *magisterium* on doctrinal matters and on ecclesiastical discipline with ease and quite independently of any translation. In accordance with the particular office and task which he will have to exercise and perform later on by his own personal activity, he should be able to understand and to speak Latin as the common language of communication within the Church. All this will no doubt be achieved in very great measure by the fact that Latin is the language of theological teaching during the time of training of the young theologian. Indeed, one may quite rightly be of the opinion that no other means can serve equally well for reaching this goal. Furthermore, no one will deny that to a certain extent Latin as a teaching language serves to clarify concepts, to avoid idle chatter, to school oneself in abstract and precise thinking and to have the courage of sober objectivity.

Of course, one will also have to be careful not to overestimate these advantages. It is possible to blether even in Latin. The preciseness of Latin tags can quite often be merely apparent and may simply be a result of having become used to them; translation of Latin theological treatises into a modern language can sometimes show that the apparent clarity and precision has to be paid for by formalistic emptiness. Conversely, if one really takes the trouble, a modern language can be just as strict, clear and unbending, as can be seen for instance from the clear expression given to the present-day sciences or jurisprudence in modern languages. There are quite sufficient instances in all sciences where a modern language shows itself more pliable and exact than

Latin (how, for instance, could we express the quite considerable difference between community and society as adequately and with the same precise conciseness in Latin? Or the difference between 'existential' (*existential*) and 'ontological' (*existentiell*), and so on?).

Be that as it may, Latin undeniably has considerable advantages as a scholastic language over modern languages for teaching purposes. We should not find it too difficult to admit this and should leave those who defend Latin as a scholastic language every right and freedom to point out these advantages and to name still more advantages. Yet this does not solve the problem of Latin as a scholastic language. The way life is, not every possible and conceivable advantage worthwhile aiming at, can be achieved in the one concrete reality together with all the others. Every concrete decision in human affairs has its advantages and disadvantages. And no discussion as to which of several possible decisions is the right one or at least the better one in the concrete case should quietly pass over the disadvantages of a choice by a one-sided extolling of its advantages. Such a discussion can take place only if one looks soberly at the advantages and the disadvantages of a certain decision, all the while admitting that certain advantages can necessarily be obtained only by means of certain disadvantages. So it is also in this case.

Latin as a scholastic language would have very great disadvantages particularly if it were the sole scholastic language used in theology or in certain subjects of theology to the complete exclusion of all other languages. Those who champion Latin as the scholastic language among the Latin peoples may perhaps feel the weight of these disadvantages less than the Christians and theologians of the German, English and Slavonic nations and, even more so, of those outside Western culture. This is even more true if, and in so far as, the religious and ecclesiastical life in these Latin countries takes place in a certain clerical isolation, on account of a certain autarchy and distrustful withdrawal from the rest of the cultural life of these peoples. Yet these disadvantages do exist and must not be overlooked. The truths with which theology is vitally concerned must not be taught and thus passed on to the future priest as a merely indifferent series of concepts which is merely aimed at his mind and rational intelligence. While preserving their completely scientific objectivity, these truths—even more so in theology than in any other science, and precisely to make it possible for theology to be a distinctive science—must be taught to the listener in such a way that the whole being of man is called upon, in such a way that this teaching goes to the heart and reaches the deepest strata of the human person and becomes most intimately fused with the whole existence of the listener with all its religious and profane dimensions and experiences. There can be no doubt about the fact that this will happen more easily and effectively if theology is presented in the mother tongue of the listener, presupposing certainly that such a presentation is not merely a kind of colourless translation from the Latin (as was the case in quite a few of the theology textbooks of the nineteenth century, even though they appeared on the surface to be written in a modern language). The mother tongue establishes a much closer contact of mind, temperament and manner of experience between the theological material taught and the rest of the internal and external world of experience of the listener, since he always already encounters this world through the medium of his modern mother tongue.

I have frequently asked priests who had been saying their breviary in Latin for many long years (and had understood perfectly well what they were reading), whether the language, the usages, the thought processes and associations of the psalms really had had any noticeable effect on them in their sermons in the vernacular or in their personal, informal prayers. I have asked them whether certain phrases from the psalms had sprung to their lips as spontaneously as, e.g., certain phrases of the New Testament which they had already read many times in their own mother tongue (under the regrettable presupposition, for this experiment, that even in the vernacular the psalms are read very much less than the New Testament). Every time I received the honest answer that, in spite of the long hours spent in saying the breviary in Latin, the psalms had had practically no effect on their own spirituality and religious language. Who will not readily admit that for someone who does not live alone in a ghetto and exactly like a monk in the world of the Latin liturgy, a Gelineau psalm sung in French will reach far deeper strata of his being than if he simply recites the Latin psalm? Anyone who would fundamentally deny such an observation would also logically have to assert that—even presupposing a knowledge of Latin— man's most personal and spontaneous prayer even in a most critical existential situation—could be said in Latin without his experiencing any abatement in existential intensity. How many would be seriously prepared to assert this?

Furthermore, theology should be taught to the young theologian in such a way that he will be able to preach it later on, that his proclamation adapts itself quite naturally, genuinely and easily to the spiritual situation of his audience, and that his proclamation awakens, as it were automatically, all the associations of ideas in the mind of the listener who is to be addressed, so that the message of the preacher really 'reaches' his hearers. Can one leave this translation from the Latin scholastic language (if this is presupposed as normal) into the language of his own present to the listener to theology lectures himself? Would not such a translation be very clumsy and barren, just like the German, the French or the English of those nineteenth-century school books which pretended to be written in a 'modern language'? Would it still be really possible to avoid the danger of the listener shelving his Latin scholastic theology in his later priestly activity and looking for his theological 'provender' exclusively in the literature of *'haute vulgarisation'* which appear in his own mother tongue? It cannot be denied that the Latin language of the schools also has its disadvantages in the religious and apostolic field, disadvantages which are all the greater, the more it is true that the present-day religious and pastoral situation demands the most personal assimilation and proclamation of the truths of the faith, since today without them the environment itself no longer sustains the priest sufficiently in a personal and missionary sense.

The difficulties and hence the disadvantages of Latin as a scholastic language become all the greater, the closer the relationship and contact in the nature of things between the theological subject-matter and the immediate day-to-day reality that is grasped by means of modern languages alone. It may be that for practical reasons one is forced to give the lectures in all disciplines in Latin (as, for instance, in the Roman theological colleges). This, however, is certainly no reason for trying to prove, even in theological colleges where the audience all speak the same language—and prove it even in subjects closest to present-day life—that ultimately even these subject-matters can be expressed in Latin, viz. by forming Latin expressions which can be understood exactly only when one adds the modern counter-expressions in brackets. Hence, right away it can only be a question of whether or not dogmatic theology (together with fundamental theology), exegesis, moral theology and Canon law should be taught in Latin.

Before attempting to answer this question, it will be well to round off the statement of the problem itself by saying something about

Latin in philosophy as part of the training of the clergy. This too is not a simple question.[24] There is, of course, the study of philosophy intended as an introduction to theology. Such a study clearly is not really intended to be, nor can it be, anything more than a modest preparation for theology itself, i.e. a study, as it were, providing the formal tools with which theology works, together with a few, basically popular philosophical expositions on the existence of God and a few fundamental theses of anthropology and of ethics. One should also not be under any delusion about the fact that a great number of our clerical students are not at all capable of more than such a philosophical introduction to theology, bearing in mind the time allotted for its study and all the other subjects which must necessarily be taught even during the period intended for philosophy, as well as their intellectual capacity of comprehension. This is not derogatory of the dignity and depth of theological studies. It is just that the individual disciplines of human knowledge have taken on such proportions nowadays and each of them has become so difficult that only a few minds can still even as much as approach to an exact and independent knowledge of more than a single science. After all, one does not reproach the representatives of the individual natural or human sciences today (even though they certainly have an affinity to philosophy) with not being professional philosophers as well.

This is not the place to explain how the curriculum should be arranged so as to satisfy the distinction, connection and simultaneous existence both of such a philosophical introduction to theology and of a proper training in philosophy as a specialized subject for certain students within the whole framework of the study of theology. We would simply express the opinion in passing here that this could presumably be arranged in such a way that the introductory philosophy course could even serve at the same time also as the basis for the specialized philosophical training of the theologian who is to be fully trained as a proper philosopher. As we will see in a moment this has its advantages also for the solution of the question we have asked ourselves here.

[24] One should recall, for instance, the grave crisis caused at the *Institut supérieur de Philosophie* at Louvain when in 1895 Latin was prescribed as the language for lectures. Cf. L. de Raeymaeker, *Le Cardinal Mercier et L'Institut Supérieur de Philosophie de Louvain* (Louvain 1952) and the title-word 'Mercier': LThK² VII, p. 306.

The same principle as that still to be established for dogmatic and moral theology will naturally also apply to the language of this introductory philosophy course. This is quite obvious from the very purpose of this introductory course, for this is the very place where the student can and should gain practice in the specialized scientific terminology required for the study of theology. Within the limits and with the precautions in and with which the afore-mentioned theological subjects should be taught in Latin (as we will show later on), the same is true also of the basic course of philosophy. This itself immediately provides also a very useful introduction to and practice in the understanding of the Latin of ancient and medieval philosophy as well as of the theological sources and of the pronouncements of the Church's *magisterium*.

This fact undoubtedly accounts also for the regulation laid down by the Sacred Congregation of Seminaries in the appendix to Pius XI's Apostolic Constitution '*Deus scientiarum Dominus*', art. 21 (AAS XXIII [1931] n. 268), viz. that, in the institutions referred to by this Constitution, the *philosophia scholastica* must be taught in Latin. The word '*scholastica*' clearly shows that it is not demanded that philosophy and the history of philosophy as such must be taught in Latin. Even the form of Christian philosophy developed as part of modern philosophy can, of course, still be called 'scholastic' in so far as it keeps alive what is valuable in medieval and baroque scholastic philosophy as an essential part of its inheritance, but it would be more correct to call this 'Christian philosophy'. For a philosophy formed, for example, in a positive encounter with modern philosophy by philosophers like Sertillanges, Maritain, Maréchal, Mercier, Blondel, Gilson, Geyser, G. Marcel, Marc, Siewerth, M. Müller, Olgiati, Söhngen, Hayen, de Finance, de Waelhens, A. Dondeyne, de Raeymaeker, etc., has quite rightly assimilated so many elements of modern philosophy and this in such a positive way that it cannot be given the same label as the medieval philosophy of Christians without danger of misunderstandings.

Hence, when the above-mentioned ordinance demands Latin for the '*philosophia scholastica*', this term may quite objectively be reserved to that philosophy which serves as an introduction to theology, or respectively to the simultaneous basic course of the specialist Christian philosophy of today. As far as the language of the formation in the actual specialized philosophy is concerned, however, it will be perfectly possible to be of the opinion that it must take place in modern languages. Genuine, living and independent philosophizing is one of those basic intellectual human fulfilments which man, as already mentioned above, can accomplish originally and genuinely only in his mother tongue. The same thing as applies to the historical sciences in general applies also to the history of philosophy: they are nowadays taught through the medium of modern languages alone and there is no real possibility of changing this state of affairs. Furthermore, in spite of the irreplaceable significance of medieval philosophy, the greater part of philosophical writings in classical and modern times, and at present, is such that the philosophical literature in Latin represents only a very small fraction of all the philosophical documents of humanity with which the young specialist philosopher must establish a living and personal contact.

We Christians above all must not regard the modern philosophers simply as our enemies, whose works—like explosives—must be touched only very carefully and with great distrust. We must enter into open and brotherly dialogue with them and must learn and discover ever more from them that, since the birth of Christ, it is no longer possible to philosophize except under the star of the incarnate Word of God. The specialist philosopher must learn during his training period to speak the language of the philosophy of our age; he must learn to converse with the philosophers of our day in such a way as to be understood by them and in a way which does not make his own philosophy appear as the product of the spirit of a clerical ghetto. All this is possible only if the specialist philosophy proper is taught in a modern language. We see in actual fact that the Christian philosophers of today—even those among them who are clerics—write at least their really scientific works in their modern mother tongue. During the time of his training, the budding specialist philosopher as such must not simply be confronted with a Latin textbook *ad usum Delphini*, but must also become acquainted with those works which directly manifest the living force of present-day Christian philosophy. These works (like the technical language of any science) call for special efforts and cannot be understood simply by knowledge of everyday language, just as a Greek shoemaker could not understand the language of Aristotle without some training. Such an initiation into the philosophical terminology of the present, however, can be offered only in living teaching through the medium of the same language.

We must now return to our real problem, viz. the question as to which language should be used for the teaching of dogmatic theology (including fundamental theology), exegesis, moral theology and Canon law. All other subjects are already excluded from this question by reason of our earlier reflections, since these other subjects are from the very outset too close to the reality which can be genuinely and originally presented only through the medium of modern languages, and since (this fact must not be overlooked) they have not generally had a Latin history of their own during the Middle Ages and in the baroque period, so that in their case there is no question of betraying the past if they are taught in a modern language.

In the preceding reflections we have already outlined the advantages and disadvantages of teaching the above-mentioned subjects in Latin. There are indeed advantages and disadvantages. This is not likely to be denied either by the advocates of Latin as a teaching language or by the advocates of a modern teaching language. If we consider this fact soberly and honestly, then it will be seen that, on the one hand, the solution to our problem involves a decision which ultimately must be taken by the supreme authority of the Church and, on the other hand, that it does not provide us with definite proof that any particular measure is clearly and in every respect the ideal one. Such a decision should be taken or, if already taken, should be carried out with careful consideration of all the advantages and disadvantages which argue in favour of one or other solution; in other words, even the attempt at an honest compromise should be considered, for this may in such cases be really the best solution since after all it will usually be quite possible to find ways and means to combine the advantages of several 'uncompromising' solutions while at the same time avoiding the opposite disadvantages as far as possible. If, to begin with, we take a look at the already actually promulgated Church legislation on this question, then the following will have to be said:

In the CIC, Latin is laid down as a subject to be taught as part of the curriculum of the Junior Seminary, over and above the mother tongue (can 1364, n.2); hence, the normal curriculum of secondary education of anyone wanting to study theology later on contains Latin as one of the subjects to be taught. The same is stressed also in other declarations made by the Church's *magisterium*. This norm is, of course, still in force even today, so that all over the Catholic world the student starting the study of theology will have to make up this part of a classical education if Latin has not been taught sufficiently in the secondary school preparing for university studies. This is obvious: a theological training, such as is necessary for the priest, is quite unthinkable without a knowledge of Latin.

This does not yet, however, answer the question about Latin as a language for the teaching of theology. The CIC does not give any norm for this question. Such a norm for the teaching of theology in universities and proper theological faculties is provided in the rules for implementing the *Constitutio Apostolica 'Deus scientiarum Dominum'* laid down by the Sacred Congregation of Seminaries in article 21 of these rules (AAS XXIII [1931] 268); this article demands that . . . *Sacra Scriptura, Theologia dogmatica, Theologia moralis . . . CIC . . . tradantur lingua latina.* It can be seen from this ordinance that the Church certainly does not demand the use of Latin for the teaching of every subject included in the academic course of theology. Even though exegesis falls within the demand for Latin here, yet while the ordinance is naturally still legally binding (in so far as it has not been abrogated by a lawful contrary custom or by an implicit or explicit dispensation), this fact does not prohibit our drawing attention to a certain change in the situation of scriptural exegesis during the last generation and pointing out the desirability of dispensing exegesis from this obligation. The fact that John XXIII's Apostolic Constitution formulates this norm about Latin as the teaching language for theology in quite general terms may be taken as an indication that it is to be interpreted as a general repetition of the already existing ordinances on this question and not as a stricter application of them, since otherwise such a change of earlier laws would surely have been explicitly stated.[25]

There are, of course, a few other although comparatively old decrees on the use of the Latin language, which refer above all to the teaching of theology in a more non-academic form in the ordinary seminaries throughout the world. Thus, e.g., in a Letter of the Sacred Congregation of Seminaries, dated 1.7.1908 and addressed to the universal episcopate (Enchiridion Clericorum [Rome 1938] n.821); in a circular of the Consistorial Congregation sent to the bishops of Italy and dated

---

[25] The same is also no doubt true of the *'Ordinationes'* appended to this Constitution, at least as far as the Latin school-language in theological subjects is concerned. One might at most point out that these *'Ordinationes'* demand, besides Latin for lectures, also Latin exercises, examinations and textbooks (III Art. II §3, §5; IV Art. II §4, §5).

26.4.1920, which demands Latin as the teaching language for dogmatic theology (Enchiridion Clericorum, n.1107), for exegesis (*loc. cit.*, n.1109) and moral theology (*loc. cit.*, n.1110); in a note of the Congregation of Seminaries, dated 9.10.1921, which describes the use of Latin in the philosophical formation of clerics as 'fitting' (*loc. cit.*, n.1128) and which makes the same careful statement about dogmatic theology (*loc. cit.*, n.1134); then in a Letter of Pius XI to the Prefect of the Sacred Congregation of Seminaries, Cardinal Bisleti, dated 1.8.1922 (*loc. cit.*, n.1154) in which it is stated, without making it any more precise, that the *maiores disciplinae* must be taught and studied in Latin, including also *scholasticae disputationes*; in a Letter of the Sacred Congregation of Seminaries to the North American bishops, dated 26.5.1928, which demands Latin as the teaching language for philosophy, theology (no doubt meaning dogmatic and moral theology) and Canon law (*loc. cit.*, n.1235). It can be seen from these proclamations that, whenever they are given to individual countries, the normal ruling is adapted in view of different conditions. It will also be noted that these ordinances are already comparatively old for the settling of a question whose solution must necessarily be strongly influenced by the changing times, and that nowhere in these ordinances is it demanded that Latin should be used as the teaching language for the whole of theology and in all its subjects.

As already mentioned, we must—in interpreting this legislation— observe the general principles of such interpretation, just as in any other case. There may be a legitimate contrary custom;[26] human laws, even those of the Church, do not oblige in the case of grave disadvantages arising from various circumstances unforeseen by the legislator, which can quite easily be the case in our question here; there may be explicit or implicit dispensations or particular decrees of the Church to the contrary. Thus, for instance, it can be pointed out that, in view of the fact that German is the teaching language in the German universities and that in Germany the theological faculties belong to these universities, all subjects are taught in German there and this practice is legitimate, if only because it has been implicitly permitted by the Church's permitting these theological faculties to belong to the State universities, a practice which has been sanctioned by a long and

[26] CIC can. 5 can presumably be used as a norm for interpreting certain expressions used in the '*Ordinationes*' (*quavis contraria reprobata consuetudine*; III Art. II §3).

indeed many centuries old custom without objection from the Church authorities.

In view of this legal position, a compromise will no doubt be the best solution for the Church in general even from a purely objective point of view, in the sense that dogmatic theology, exegesis, moral theology and Canon law should be taught basically in Latin, and the other subjects in the mother tongue. These particular subjects have such a long Latin past, and are so directly related to the Latin pronouncements of the Church's *magisterium*, that it is completely and indeed objectively defensible to demand Latin as the language in which they are to be taught. Yet one must also see the disadvantages of such a ruling quite soberly and try to counter them by various suitable measures. Hence, even with regard to these subjects, it will be legitimate to hold that a partial employment of the mother tongue is not only quite permissible but even necessary, even though the 'substance' of the teaching in these subjects is to be done in Latin. Introductions to these subjects and excursions within these subjects by means of the history of dogmas and of laws, ethical psychology, pastoral theology, ascetic theology, etc., will best be given directly in the mother tongue. Thus, the Sacred Congregation of Seminaries declared explicitly under Benedict XV (Enchiridion Clericorum, n.1102) that the demand of Latin as the teaching language need not prevent the professor from following up his Latin exposition by a recapitulation of his thoughts in Italian in order to increase the understanding of what has been taught; the same Note (*loc. cit.*, n.1107) also provides explicitly, as far as dogmatic theology is concerned, for the interpretation and translation of scholastic concepts and formulae into the modern idiom. Similarly, norms of the Holy Office sent to the bishops (16.5.1943) demand that professors of moral theology must inform their students of the vernacular expressions, concepts and principles of sexual ethics (*Periodica de Re Morali, Canonica, Liturgica* XXIII [1944] 133). Accordingly, at least in France, there are here and there scientific works in which the method of such a double language is employed.[27]

The question about the scholastic language in exegesis is a particularly difficult one. On the one hand, wherever present-day exegesis is to be carried out and taught in a really scientific manner (which should

[27] As, for instance, Pedro Descoqs, *Institutiones metaphysicae generalis*, tom. 1 (Paris 1925); *id., Praelectiones theologiae naturalis* I. II (Paris 1932/35).

really be always the case), it has become a very complicated and typically modern science with a philological basis. Thus exegesis has become a science with so many technical terms—a science in such close and unavoidable contact with Protestant exegesis and its modern literature and moreover with such a very desirable orientation to real life, towards the witnessing of the Gospel in preaching and the utilization of Scripture in one's own spiritual life—that it is very difficult indeed to imagine a Scripture lecture which (unless it is absolutely necessary) is given only in Latin and yet still satisfies the demands of present-day exegetical work. On the other hand, the Church's decrees right down to the *Ordinationes* demand Latin as the teaching language in exegesis (wherever there is no special law to the contrary). In support of this one can adduce all those reflections which argue in favour of Latin as the teaching language in theology in general, if one regards exegesis mainly as biblical theology and if, in spite of its independence, one does not wish it to be cut off entirely from scholastic dogmatic theology (which unfortunately has sometimes been desired as a reaction against a biblical theology which simply furnishes dogmatic theology with the *dicta probanda*). Thus one will have to strive for a sensible balance. The Church's decrees about Latin in exegesis will have to be respected. But one will not necessarily have to extend these decrees to the side-subjects of exegesis, such as biblical grammar, semantics or any other purely philological systematization, archaeology, history of biblical times, etc., quite apart from whether these subjects are given as an independent course of lectures or whether they must for practical purposes be taught within the main course of lectures. For the rest, the same as has been said with regard to theology in general will have to be said also regarding the task of the professor towards his students in view of having to give them a really vital and completely human assimilation of the matter of the particular subject with which he is concerned.

The disadvantages of Latin as a teaching language can furthermore be counteracted by making provisions for free discussion between teacher and students, by the composition of little practice essays, the holding of actual seminars, etc., all in the mother tongue. If, in addition, the students are given guidance in familiarizing themselves with essays and books of current theology written in modern languages, then it may surely be hoped that this will compensate so largely for the disadvantages of teaching these subjects in Latin that the quite considerable advantages will prevent any harm coming from the disadvantages and will have a beneficial effect. Thus, the theologian trained in this way will have a direct and genuine relationship to the great works of the past in these theological subjects, to the present-day pronouncements of the Church on doctrine and discipline, as well as being able to use Latin sufficiently in the international commerce of the Church; he will be able to understand and speak the common language of the Church.

Everything which has been said about Latin as the language of oral teaching, applies *mutatis mutandis* also to the textbooks used in this teaching. It is desirable that there should continue to be such textbooks either written purely in Latin or written in several languages (in the sense indicated above). This does not exclude the possibility, however, that there may also be theological textbooks exclusively in modern languages. Even when such a modern textbook is, or is going to be, introduced as the official textbook for the teaching of clerical students, such a book must not contradict the meaning of the principle which demands Latin as the teaching language in these subjects. But such a modern textbook could—precisely in this way—supply the desirable completion and translation of the Latin lectures. It need not necessarily be regarded as excluding the simultaneous use of a Latin textbook, especially since even today the Latin text of St Thomas' *Summa* must still be regarded as the class text for the speculative part of dogmatic theology (at least for the formal academic lectures), and hence no modern dogmatic textbook can completely supplant the Latin textbook.

PART V

THE CHRISTIAN LIFE

16

SOME THESES ON PRAYER 'IN THE NAME OF THE CHURCH'

1. *The nature of prayer in general*

PRAYER is an act of the virtue of religion, i.e. an act of an intellectually endowed creature by which the creature turns towards God by acknowledging and praising His limitless superiority explicitly or implicitly and by subjecting itself to that superiority (in faith, hope and charity). Hence, prayer is an act by which (a) man as a whole 'actualizes' himself and (b) by which this thus actualized human reality is subjected and, as it were, surrendered to God.[1]

2. *The value of prayer in general*

As a consequence of the above, this act of prayer depends in its nature and value on two factors: firstly, it depends on the nature and dignity of this actualized and, as it were, God-surrendered human reality, and secondly, it depends on the intensity and existential deep-rootedness with which the one who prays can 'hang on' to God by such a surrender of himself. Even though this intensity itself depends again on the grace of God—who draws the one who prays to Himself in different ways and to a different extent—this drawing-near-to-God of the one who prays is actually effected by God by the fact that God allows man this greater or lesser *active* possibility of coming to Him precisely through the greater or lesser actualization of himself and of his surrender (for grace is precisely grace of *acting*, as a more remote or proximate active potency by which the creature depends on God). Hence, the nature and dignity of prayer depend on the particular way and measure in which the individual is able to come nearer to God.

[1] LThK I², pp. 256–259: 'Akt, religiöser' (J. B. Metz).

3. *The increase of the (external) glory of God*

To make what follows later on intelligible, we will preface what will follow with a few remarks about the *gloria Dei externa formalis.* Scholastic theology rightly distinguishes between objective (i.e. material) and formal giving of glory to God. Every creature gives objective glory to God in so far as it *is* and thus reflects something of the perfection of God. God is given formal glory when the rational and free creature acknowledges the infinite superiority of God in loving freedom. This formal and 'subjective' glory can be given to God only by human, and indeed morally good, acts (i.e. *actus honesti*). For, these alone acknowledge the infinite holiness of God and honour God in the way He necessarily wishes to be honoured by creatures. Every other perfection, and hence the whole external objective (i.e. material) giving of glory, is directed solely as a means and presupposition to this external formal glorification. Objective glory may indeed be given without giving any such formal glory (as it is in fact given both by the world which does not obey God as it should and by the damned); yet even in this case it subserves those beings who truly give formal glory to God, since there has never been and never will be a world in which there are no creatures who give formal glory to God, and since the actually existing world is such (i.e. a world in which formal glory is given to God) not merely by reason of the *voluntas Dei consequens* but also of the *voluntas Dei antecedens.* Furthermore—and above all—a rational creature cannot lawfully strive to give merely objective glory to God without directing it to the giving of formal glory, since this creature itself has been created and is ordained to give formal glory to God and thus would deny its own end if it intended to give merely objective glory to God.

This results in a principle which is most important for our whole question: all those acts of man (no matter which ones) which are not absolutely good in the natural and the supernatural sense (morally and —at least implicitly—religiously good), must be counted among those things which give only objective and material glory to God and thus are subject to the principle established previously regarding the giving of purely objective glory to God.

It follows from this that acts by which a sinner or unbeliever *either* administers sacraments *or* says prayers—as prescribed by the Church— purely objectively (i.e. without any real devotion, even though with external attention) *or* exercises some authority given in the Church, do indeed give objective glory to God, in as much as (precisely as acts, i.e. prescinding from the sinfulness of the act) they are willed by God just like anything else either directly created by God or brought about by God with the aid of some other creature; yet it cannot be said that such acts give formal glory to God or even increase God's formal glory, or that the spiritual creature should strive for these acts as such or that they are willed by God for their own sake. Such acts may nevertheless be signs objectively manifesting the effective will of God (as happens, for instance, both when a sinner performs acts of ecclesiastical power and also in the case of the positing of sacramental signs). They are thus acts which are effective instrumentally by virtue of a cause which already exists independently of them; this cause manifested by these signs—viz. the created will of Christ which instituted the powers of the Church and the sacraments—gives formal glory to God, but these acts themselves do not of themselves constitute a new value affecting God, for *such* a value is given only in acts which give formal glory to God.

All this indicates[2] what has to be said about the effectiveness of prayers which are said (and to the extent in which they are said) 'in the name of the Church' and to which some theologians[3] ascribe effectiveness by reason of this ecclesiastical commission *alone*. Of course, if and in so far as such a prayer is said without any inner devotion at all, it may still be regarded *quoad substantiam* as fulfilling the obligation of saying the breviary or as accomplishing a blessing prescribed in the Ritual or some other sacramental or liturgical function. Hence, even such a prayer is, in this sense, said 'in the name of the Church' and so is also an objective sign of those pious prayers which by formal divine predefinition will always and infallibly exist in the Church in the sense of prayers which are holy even subjectively. In so far as there is such a sign, the disposition of a pious person to whom, for example, such a sacramental is administered by an impious priest, can therefore be directed by this sign to the attainment of the fruits of *this* pious request made by the Church (since his disposition has been increased by this

[2] What follows immediately after this has been added merely to throw more light on the principle just stated, and will in part be explained again and applied further at the appropriate place later on.

[3] Cf. e.g. B. H. Noldin/G. Heinzel, *Summa Theologiae Moralis* II[31] (Innsbruck 1957), n. 754.

sacramental). Only in this sense can it be said that even the impious liturgical action of a priest bears fruit. Yet even though this prayer itself is said in the name of the Church, it does not produce any new 'supplicatory value' before God, since this could be produced only by acts which give formal glory to God and since even the Church herself, in so far as she is the cause of such a value, does this through these acts of *real* prayer, which prayer is in fact never lacking to the Church. Hence, on the supposition that *neither* the priest (who, for instance, administers a sacramental) recites the appropriate prayers with real devotion *nor* the believer (to whom this sacramental is administered) hears these prayers devoutly, then this 'prayer' is simply an insult to God, even though it can still be called a prayer 'in the name of the Church' in the above-mentioned sense.

4. *The nature of prayer, in so far as it takes place by supernatural sanctifying grace*

As can be seen from what was said in the introduction, the dignity of Christian prayer is measured by the dignity of man who has been elevated to the supernatural order and has been divinized by sanctifying grace. This nature of man divinized by grace is actualized by the acts of the theological virtues which are exercised in prayer and is, as it were, surrendered to God and actually (and not merely habitually) united with Him in this way. Thus it follows that in the present order of salvation in which man must and can strive towards a supernatural goal, only *such* a prayer merits eternal life *de condigno* and only a prayer aroused and animated by supernatural—sanctifying or at least actual—grace can be called a salvific act.[4] We cannot conceive of any greater dignity than this or even comparable with this *ex aequo* (apart from the Hypostatic Union), this dignity arises out of man's sharing in the divine life, and nothing greater than that can be conceived in the realm of creatures. This divinization consists ultimately in God's communication of himself through uncreated grace and it actualizes itself—in the one who prays—by those unutterable groanings (Rom 8.26) with

---

[4] From now on we will consider only the prayer of the justified, i.e. the prayer of the child of God in the state of grace, a prayer which is therefore a meritorious work *de condigno*. We prescind, therefore, from the prayer of the sinner which is said while in the habitual grace of faith and of hope or by actual grace, and is meritorious *de congruo*.

which the Holy Ghost himself divinizes this prayer in the hearts of the justified. There may indeed be ontological realities and hence values which, on the one hand, when regarded in themselves, must be called *true* values and which, on the other hand, are different from this value of divinizing (i.e. supernatural grace as such) and divinized being, since they are separable from this value of an absolutely and substantially supernatural reality and yet can be added to this value. These propositions, however, arise from a purely theoretical and speculative way of looking at things. For, if someone intentionally and freely strives for that value which surpasses every other value in dignity[5]—i.e. the value of grace in the strict sense—then he must not indeed deny or exclude any lesser values which may be added to this dignity of being a child of God; he may even be helped by what is of lesser value, as a secondary aid, in striving towards that most sublime good.[6] But he cannot, in his practical and 'existential' evaluation, strive for that lesser value as an 'end in itself'; for it is impossible to attain two *fines principales* (i.e. main or primary ends) with the same act; moreover, it would be blasphemous to have less regard for the dignity of prayer arising from grace than for the dignity given to prayer, for instance, by some ecclesiastical mandate.

What has been said about the dignity of prayer is equally applicable to its *efficacy*, since the latter is measured by the former, prescinding from that inscrutable divine providence by which God remains absolutely free in his gifts and hence even doubly so in the granting of prayers as such, i.e. in so far as prayer calls upon the free mercy of God and does not appear before God as a demand for a reward. Hence God is not under any obligation towards man or the Church.

5. *Increase in the value of prayer*

Since the grace which divinizes man is capable of increasing, the dignity, merit and pleading power of prayer increase in the same measure as grace. Hence, if (conversely) the dignity and efficacy of

[5] Even true 'values', such as the value of a commission or of delegation by the Church authorities, are—as such—values surpassed absolutely by the dignity of divinizing grace, of divine childhood, etc.

[6] So that indirectly, for example, this delegation given by the Church authorities influences the intensity with which someone realizes the dignity of his divine childhood in prayer.

prayer are to be increased, this can be achieved only through an increase in sanctifying grace. The latter can also be brought about by prayer itself (apart from the reception of the sacraments and the performance of meritorious acts). In the case of zealous and intensive prayer, the increase of grace and of the value of the prayer itself are in reciprocal proportion of causality, for any potency is itself increased by act, and when the potency increases the act itself also increases. Among the aids and impulses by which the zeal and intensity of prayer can be increased, there is to be counted (*suppositis supponendis*) the consciousness of being commissioned and juridically obliged by the Church to say a certain prayer. But the mere fulfilment of the obligation of the breviary by someone who is not in the state of sanctifying grace and who performs no *inner* act of *religio* by some (actual) grace does not have any value *before God*, even though the commandment of the Church is perhaps still fulfilled by this merely external recitation and hence this prayer can still be said to have been said 'in the name of the Church'.[7] Should it be objected that the Church's law about the recitation of the breviary demands that it be carried out meritoriously and in the state of grace, then this would merely reinforce and certainly not alter our statement. It must not be forgotten in this connection that by reason of the formal predefinition by which God wills his Church to be always holy even subjectively, there will always and everywhere be a sufficient number of those who in fact perform the Church-imposed duty of prayer in the state of grace, and so the outcome of this commission given by the Church will in general also be able to exist before God. Yet all this does not dispute but rather confirms the fact that the dignity of the prayer commissioned by the Church is ultimately based on the dignity of grace and does not have any other, different source.

6. The prayer of the just, in so far as it takes place in and through the Church

Man's divinization by the created and uncreated grace of Christ at the same time—and in equal proportion and measure—brings about a union with Christ as the Head of his Mystical Body which is the Church. The sharing in the divine nature and the union with Christ are simply two inseparable aspects of the same process of justification. One of these concepts can be replaced directly by the other. Hence,

[7] Cf. note 4 above; note 9 below.

what has been said about the nature and value of supernatural prayer can also be deduced from the union with Christ of the praying believer. In so far as this union with Christ by grace includes a union with the Mystical Body of Christ which is the Church, this value of prayer can rightly be called a consequence of the union of the praying person with the Church.

This raises a difficulty which, even though it is for the most part a terminological and not an objective difficulty, must nevertheless not be underestimated but must rather be carefully examined. In more recent pronouncements made by the *magisterium*, we are commanded to identify the terms 'Mystical Body of Christ' and 'Catholic Church'.[8] If we keep to this terminology, then only those people can be said to 'say prayers' in and with the 'Mystical Body of Christ' who are also 'visibly' members of the Church (i.e. by baptism, external profession of the true faith and subjection to the authority of the Church), but not those who do not belong to the visible structure of the Church, even though they are justified (and perhaps even baptized).[9] Nevertheless even such justified pagans and baptized non-Catholic Christians of good will (who for this reason may be regarded as justified) belong in *some* true sense to the Church. For if it is ecclesiastical Nestorianism to enumerate only those marks within the total concept of the 'Church' which belong to the social and external structure of the Church and to leave the inner 'animation' of the Church by the Holy Spirit out of this concept, then it cannot be said that those are absolutely outside the Church who possess this Spirit and hence are governed by that supernatural 'formative principle' which—if it attains its full effect—forms members of the visible Church. In this way, what has perhaps already been effected by this formative principle in the heart, viz. the union with Christ and hence also with his Mystical Body, is allowed to become 'historically' tangible, i.e. to become visible in the spatial and temporal order and in human society. This applies even more truly to

[8] Denz 2319; Encyclical '*Mystici Corporis*', AAS XXXV (1943), pp. 193 *sq.*

[9] Such a case is obviously possible. For there are those who are justified by the (even implicit) *votum* of baptism (Denz 413; 796; 807; 849; 898; 1031; 1677; Letter of the Holy Office to Cardinal Cushing, *American Ecclesiastical Review* LXXVII [1952], pp. 307–311). Cf. also: A. Card. Bea, 'Il cattolico di fronte al problema dell'unione dei cristiani', *La Civiltà Cattolica* CXII, 1 (1961), pp. 113–129.

the justified non-Catholics who have received valid and fruitful baptism. Hence, although they are not simply visible members of the visible Church, their prayers (in the absolute sense, i.e. judging prayer by its *ultimate* measure of dignity and worth which is grace) also possess the same dignity and the same value as the prayer of those who are members in the strict sense. For the prayer of the *latter* receives its highest and most important dignity from *that* grace and that union with Christ and his Mystical Body with which even these justified non-Catholics are gifted, and does not receive its dignity precisely from their juridical and external union with the Church. Hence we must not deny that even the prayer of those who are justified but 'outside' the Church has that dignity and value which we ascribe to the prayer of Catholics. In any case, the following must be noted with regard to their prayers: if their interior prayer (which in itself is supernatural and must be activated by grace if it is to be such a supernatural prayer) becomes visible externally (even in a cult which in itself is erroneous), then this prayer bears witness—in so far as it is supernatural—not to a false religion but basically to the Catholic Church; just as in the case of that valid and fruitful baptism which is administered outside the Church and yet is administered only apparently within the non-Catholic religious communion as such.

The unity of the person who prays and of the visible Church as such does not of itself and directly give this person's prayer any higher supernatural value over and above the value belonging to every prayer said by someone in the state of grace (and who *ex supposito* possesses the same measure of sanctifying grace). But the visible Church membership as such for many reasons bring a positive influence to bear on the value of prayer. For there can be no doubt about the fact that the visible and hierarchical Church as such contributes in many ways to the transmission and increase of the divinizing grace of man: by guidance, admonition, prescriptions, communal prayer, the sacraments, good example, the visible and hierarchical Church influences the granting and increase of grace (both as part of and outside of prayer itself) and in this way influences also the value prayer has before God.

7. *Prayer in common*

(a) *Firstly*, the *communal* prayer of the faithful of its very nature realizes and makes explicitly visible one of the essential traits of *all*

Christian prayer, viz. the fact that the one who prays must necessarily be united with Christ and the Church, and hence with everyone animated by the same Holy Spirit. For this reason, and on account of Christ's promise (Mt 18.19 *sq.*), communal prayer possesses a special efficacy. In practice, such a prayer has this special efficacy because—of its very nature and on account of the special actual graces granted to it by reason of Christ's promise—such a prayer is likely to be performed with much greater zeal and hence out of the increased sanctifying grace of each person praying (with that reciprocal causality of prayer as an act of grace and grace as the power constituting the measure of this act: cf. n. 5 above). Since—on the one hand—the community as such is not a physical subject capable of receiving sanctifying grace, and since—on the other hand—the real value of prayer is measured exclusively by sanctifying grace and the intensity of the realization of this grace, it is impossible to find any other explanation for the special dignity of community prayer, if one is not to elevate social structures arbitrarily to the status of hypostases.

(b) *Secondly*, there is another reason why the *communal* prayer of the faithful receives a special efficacy from the Mystical Body of Christ. God pursues individuals with his desire for their salvation, by regarding, willing and achieving their salvation in so far as they are members of the congregation of those who are to be saved and whom He has chosen, by eternal pre-election, to form his eternal Kingdom and the Mystical Body of Christ (i.e. the Church triumphant) in the unity and harmony of this community and in the diversity and mutual dependence of its members. In so far as these individuals are members of this Kingdom of God, which has already begun here on earth in the form of the pilgrim Church and which nevertheless embraces all the elect, God grants them actual (efficacious) graces for prayer (naturally always according to His pleasure whereby He himself establishes this eternal Kingdom in its manifold variety). Hence, every individual depends on *everyone* else in his prayer (which, when it takes place, always takes place by reason of efficacious graces). This is indeed true of every prayer. But, since this dependence becomes particularly perceptible and manifest in *communal* prayer, and since precisely for this reason Christ promised special graces to this kind of prayer, communal prayer receives many graces from the Mystical Body of Christ from the very fact that it itself is realized and manifested by the praying community. What we have said here applies in the very nature of things to *every* prayer of those who believe in Christ which is performed lawfully in common, and does not apply only to that prayer which takes place by a special commission given by the hierarchical Church.

8. *Prayer as an act of the Church*

There are two extremes in this question which must be carefully avoided: on the one hand, there is the danger of hypostasizing the Church herself in her nature as a community of many substantial beings, as if she herself were a substantial existent; on the other hand, there is the danger that this unity of the Church and her members might be underestimated, as if this one Church were not a true reality but merely a fiction.

(a) There are several ways of speaking of an act of the Church.

(i) We may rightly call it an act of the Church when a person exercises either the *potestas iurisdictionis* or the *potestas ordinis* in the visible Church. The greater the particular power and the more absolutely it is exercised, the more truly can we call an act flowing from the *potestas iurisdictionis* or *ordinis*, an act of the Church herself. The act, formally taken and as such, does not proceed from sanctifying grace, since even a sinner who possesses this power in the Church can exercise it. Such an act is an act of the Church as a visible and hierarchical institution. For even though it is physically the act of a single person, the act of this person is rightly called an act of the Church herself, since he does this act precisely *in so far as* he is one of the bearers of those powers which Christ has given to His Church as such. Derived from this, as it were, even those acts may in a secondary sense be called acts of the Church which are done by a simple member of the Church in so far as he is carrying out a commission given to him by the ecclesiastical hierarchy, for by such a commission the Church becomes in a sense the source of this act and so the act can in some way be ascribed to the Church herself.

(ii) Yet it is not only the act of a person who has such a sacramental or juridical power in the Church which can be called an act of the Church. Any saving act of any member of the Church can be called an act of the Church in a true sense; for, such an act springs from grace, grace which always has an ecclesiological character; such an act too has always a positive effect on the whole Mystical Body of Christ and (by its, albeit humble, contribution) transforms the visible Church into that sign set over the nations (Denz 1794) in which form the Church herself is also a witness to her own divine origin. For every saving act is in its own way a contribution to that inexhaustible sanctity and fruitfulness in everything good[10] whereby the Church becomes that sign. It is clear from this declaration of the first Vatican Council that the Church ascribes to *herself* all the supernatural meritorious actions of individual Christians as testimonies to her holiness. The same follows from the doctrine of the so-called 'treasury of the Church' (Denz 550–52; 740a; 757; 1541) which is formed by the merits and atoning acts of Christ and of all the just. For if these acts were not in a true sense acts of the Church, the combined meritorious and atoning value of them all could not constitute a 'treasury' over which the Church herself can dispose, since in this matter she disposes not over something which does not belong to her but precisely over something which is *her own*. Hence, all acts of Christians performed in the state of grace must undeniably and in a true sense be, and be called, acts of the Mystical Body of Christ. For all Christians, and not only those who direct the Church, are members of the Church understood as the Mystical Body of Christ. Since, however, the acts of the members are fundamentally acts of the body itself, and since in general there are no other acts of the Mystical Body apart from the good works and prayers of the faithful, these acts are rightly called acts of the Mystical Body. And since the Body of Christ and the Church signify the same thing, the meritorious acts of the faithful in the state of grace must be regarded as acts of the *Church* herself. This applies *a fortiori* to those acts which explicitly exhibit a social character. But this distinction between merely 'private' and explicitly 'social' acts is not an essential one. For in the Kingdom of God there are no acts which are simply 'private' or merely 'individual' before God. If this were not so, then the Church would either have to be identified with the hierarchy—despite the fact that in reality even lay people are members of the Church and not merely objects of the pastoral care exercised by the clergy—or we would have to deny this Church every act in so far as she is also made up of lay people. Yet both of these conceptions are false.

(iii) If we now compare the two kinds of acts of the Church enumerated under (i) and (ii), then the following has to be said: the acts of the hierarchy (of the clergy) are in different ways but totally orientated towards calling forth, directing and intensifying those acts which are

[10] Denz 1794.

performed by the members of the Church out of the divinizing grace of Christ. These hierarchical acts are indeed performed in the name of the Church (and of Christ) but are intended for the purpose of preserving and furthering the supernatural life of Christ in the members of the Church. This is seen most clearly in the case of the sacraments: the administration of the sacraments undoubtedly stands out most clearly among those acts performed by the Church's hierarchy in the name of the Church and of Christ, and performed precisely as acts of this hierarchy of the Church. But this whole administration of the sacraments attains its goal only in the faith and love of the individual members of the Church to whom the grace for this their divine life is given through the sacraments. With regard to the value of both kinds of acts [cf. (i) and (ii)] both in themselves and in comparison with each other, we would remind the reader of what has already been said above.

(b) Thus it follows that:

(i) Every supernatural *prayer* which has its source in the grace of Christ and hence takes place within his Mystical Body (even when it appears externally as a 'private' prayer) can rightly be called an act of the Church. It is not necessary for this that the prayer should be explicitly and concretely commissioned by the Church's hierarchy. As the Church has declared that all holy activity and suffering of her members (who believe in Christ) must be ascribed to her and is a manifestation of her own holiness and fruitfulness, so the same must be said in particular of the prayer of the faithful.

(ii) The same (in a greater measure but not of a specifically different kind) must be said *a fortiori* of the *communal* prayer of the faithful and even of that prayer which, according to the strictest concept of the liturgy commonly accepted today, can be called 'non-liturgical'.[11] For in every such communal prayer there appears visibly what belongs to the nature of every prayer, viz. the fact that it is performed by the grace of the Mystical Body, that in it—effective in the nature of things—the real basis of this prayer gathers strength and grows, i.e. the union between the person who prays and Christ and the Church, on account of

[11] Cf. CIC can. 1257; Denz 2298; Encyclical *'Mediator Dei'*; cf. on this: A. Stenzel, 'Cultus publicus: Ein Beitrag zum Begriff und ekklesiologischen Ort der Liturgie', ZKT LXXV (1953), pp. 174–214; C. Vagaggini, *Theologie der Liturgie* (Einsiedeln 1959), pp. 28 *sqq.*; J. A. Jungmann, *Der Gottesdienst der Kirche* (Innsbruck 1955), pp. 1–8; J. H. Miller, *Fundamentals of the Liturgy* (Notre Dame, Indiana 1960), pp. 24 *sq.*

the grace of Christ, and that the common fruit of this prayer, which strengthens this union with Christ and the Church, necessarily also accrues to the whole Church. Hence, communal prayer is rightly considered as the act of the *Church* beneficial to the Church. Since this follows from the very nature of things, it is not required that this communal (and also lawfully performed) prayer should be expressly commissioned by the Church's hierarchy. Hence if (we need not speak about this here) only that communal worship of God by the faithful which has been explicitly ordered and juridically regulated by the highest authority is called 'Liturgy',[12] then it may be maintained quite simply that even the 'extra-liturgical' communal prayer of the faithful can and must be called an act of the Church.

This act of the Church is not given any *higher* dignity before God by an explicit liturgical commission from the Church, for there is no greater dignity than the one given to prayer by the Holy Ghost with his unutterable groanings. In the regulation of the liturgy, the explicit commission by the Church is ultimately meant to ensure that this communal prayer of the faithful takes place *actually*, in a *dignified* manner and *frequently*. Hence, liturgical prayer is not really a greater and more intensive act of the Church as such, in so far as the Church is the Body of Christ animated by the Holy Spirit, but is over and above this an act of the Church, in so far as she is a visible and hierarchical society; the act of a subject which is performed by order of some social authority, is rightly attributed to this authority and thus to the society which is based on this authority, and so becomes *its* act. This does not question but, on the contrary, confirms the fact that *those* acts performed by the members of a society which can be exercised only under the explicit direction and guidance of the authority of that society (as, e.g., the sacrifice of the Mass understood as the highest act of worship of the whole Church) are *necessarily* regulated by the laws of the society concerned, e.g. by the liturgical laws of the Church and of her highest authority. But there is even in this case a *twofold* reason why this worship can be called an act of the *Church* herself: the ultimate, deepest and most sublime reason is to be found in the fact that the sacrifice of the Mass is celebrated (naturally under the necessary direction of the priest) by the faithful who are united by the grace of Christ in the one Body of Christ and who, on the basis of this union, offer this sacrifice of Christ as their own; the other, extrinsic and secondary reason lies in

---

[12] Denz 2298.

the explicit (and in this case necessary) liturgical authorization of the Church. The first reason goes right back to the invisible unity of all the faithful (which unity is also one of the constitutive elements of the Church herself), the second reason regards the external and 'visible' (social) unity of the faithful. The latter is to the former as the sacramental sign (*sacramentum*) is to the sacramental grace (*res sacramenti*). Furthermore, if the Church herself commands and orders certain prayers by her commission and her laws, then one can know *more certainly* with regard to them than in the case of so-called 'privately' arranged prayers that, even in their 'objectivity' (i.e. in so far as one prescinds from the good subjective intention of the one who prays), they are 'objectively' pleasing to God. Just as, for instance, an unworthily performed or received sacramental rite remains an objectively valid promise of grace on the part of God, so the external act of prayer commanded by the Church remains objectively lawful and is recognized as such, all of which cannot be affirmed with the same certitude of private prayer even regarding it merely from its objective aspect. But the whole of this objective lawfulness is ordained to the subjective act of the one who truly ('interiorly') prays by the grace of God and this lawfulness attains its real goal only in such a prayer 'in spirit and in truth'. This *objective* value of strictly liturgical prayer can never, purely as such, replace that value of prayer which God ultimately intends, viz. the value springing from a pure and humble heart. This objective value does not in itself alone constitute a legitimate goal for a human act.

We know indeed that the Church's *magisterium* has on several occasions in recent times attributed 'a greater force and power'[13] to liturgical prayer than to private prayer, and has said: 'It is true that liturgical prayer, being the public prayer of the august Bride of Christ, is superior to private prayers'.[14] Our statements do not dispute this fact. We have already pointed out above that it is possible to distinguish a twofold value in prayer. Furthermore, it must be noted that the comparison made by the *magisterium* between 'private' and 'liturgical' prayer refers to that 'liturgical' prayer which is in fact carried out by those members who are in the state of grace; this means, however, a liturgical prayer which also possesses *that* most sublime value which

[13] AAS XXVIII (1936), p. 19: Pius XI in the Encyclical '*Ad catholici sacerdotii*'.

[14] AAS XXXIX (1947), p. 537: Pius XII in the Encyclical '*Mediator Dei*'.

we have ascribed to prayer on account of supernatural grace. To *this* both supernatural and liturgical prayer is rightly ascribed a greater dignity than to private prayer which, being 'private', does not have that additional value belonging to liturgical prayer by reason of the Church's commission and liturgical law. But this *added* value possessed by liturgical prayer, when regarded by itself alone, is incomparably less than the value belonging to prayer which (and in so far as it) takes place in the Holy Spirit. We have already emphasized above that the 'existential' (if we may put it this way) power and efficacy of this ecclesiastical delegation as such must not be overestimated in the case of prayer. For if someone prays in the Holy Spirit, he prays from a motive of love, i.e. on account of the in itself lovable goodness of God, and orientating himself entirely to the glorification of God he places himself before the infinite majesty of God himself. All this takes place in every act of someone who prays and hence necessarily orders and, as it were, 'hierarchizes' also the orientation and motives of this prayer, since someone who prays is a member of the Church in *every* prayer and not merely in liturgical prayer, for only as such a member may he approach the throne of grace. Thus, in comparison with the ultimate reason giving prayer its dignity—viz. the Holy Ghost Himself, Who is the gift given to the just and Who in His prayer intercedes for him with God—the value of the *juridical* mandate given by the Church must be regarded as absolutely subordinate and secondary in the midst of the full light of the purposes and motives of supernatural prayer, motives which are nevertheless present on some level of consciousness or other to the one who prays.

9. *The notion of* 'opus operantis Ecclesiae', *as applied to prayer*

What has been said up till now will also explain the correct meaning of the notion *'opus operantis Ecclesiae'*[15] which is said to be only verified in prayer said in accordance with the liturgical laws laid down by the Church.

(a) Any prayer can (*firstly*) be called *opus operantis Ecclesiae* if, and in so far as, it takes place at the command and in accordance with the liturgical norms of the hierarchical Church, even though—when it is

[15] C. Vagaggini, *Theologie der Liturgie* (Einsiedeln 1959), pp. 86–91; J. H. Miller, *Fundamentals of the Liturgy* (Notre Dame, Indiana 1960); cf. against this: J. A. Jungmann, ZKT LXXXIII (1961), pp. 96–99.

said by an impenitent sinner—it does not possess any meritorious power and none of the value of formal glory given to God. In the eyes of God, this prayer as *such* has no value over and above the value of formal glory given to God which, as a necessary holy value, is always already present in the Church, even though it is an *opus operantis Ecclesiae* in the sense just mentioned. Of course, even such a prayer can be and remain an *objective* sign of that continuous intercession (and can be called, precisely as such, an *opus operantis Ecclesiae*) by which the Church, in the person of her just and her Saints, always intercedes for all her members by the meritorious prayers that are said in the state of grace; all the members of the Church can always appeal to this intercession even in their private prayers. But this sign as such does not increase the power of this uninterrupted prayer of petition, as would happen if this official liturgical prayer were performed by someone justified. The intercession of the Church which is always present in the Church by reason of divine predefinition and divine efficacious grace, is always available to everyone (properly disposed) for whom such a prayer is said even if said by a priest who is without grace or has absolutely no religious interest in what he is doing (when, e.g., he recites a blessing from the Ritual without any devotion), but this intercessory power of the Church does not come *from* this performance of prayer by this impious priest. If, and in so far as, a person to whom, for instance, a sacramental is administered by such a priest, is in fact (which is easily possible) brought to greater devotion than before, and hence to better dispositions by this objective sign of the continuous and unfailing intercession of the Church (which in no way takes place only through strictly liturgical prayers), then *this* person gets more benefit from the unfailing intercession of the Church, to which he appeals at least tacitly by the sacramental thus received, than if he, for instance, had appealed to this intercession of the Church merely in his private prayer before God, although this too, as has been said, is always open to him as an effective means. If we were to ascribe any efficacy to these prayers taking place as an *opus operantis Ecclesiae* independently of the devotion of the one who prays *and* of the one for whom they are performed, then this would be the same as maintaining (even though perhaps not in so many words) that this is an *opus operatum*,[16] and

---

[16] Especially since a prayer, taken formally as such, can be a sacramental sign (e.g. in the case of the anointing of the sick).

indeed even more than a sacrament[17] (since it would mean maintaining an effect of grace without any presupposed disposition—in short, a 'magic' effect) both of which are false.

(b) If (*secondly*) the prayer actually takes place in the state of grace, then it can be called an *opus operantis Ecclesiae in so far as* (although this cannot be determined with absolute certainty in any particular concrete case of prayer) this prayer (which always—at least implicitly —intercedes for everyone in the Church) springs from that formal, predefined and efficacious grace by which God achieves his will, that will which absolutely and efficaciously desires the Church as a whole to be infallibly holy even in the subjective sense—and *in so far as such* a pious prayer increases the so-called 'treasury of the Church' which must not be limited to acts of satisfaction for temporal punishment. One must, therefore, be careful not to ascribe to prayer—by appealing to the term '*opus operantis Ecclesiae*'—a true and proper value before God on account of the Church's commission alone, a value which in reality belongs to prayer only if it is performed in grace. For even in this case we must not mistake the sign of the reality (i.e. the impious prayer, even though it may in part be called *opus operantis Ecclesiae*) for the reality itself (i.e. the prayer performed in the state of grace) whether it be performed 'in the name of the hierarchical Church' which commands it, or whether it be performed as a 'private prayer'.

10. The prayer of the Breviary in particular

What we have said applies also to the recitation of the breviary. If, and in so far as, someone who believes in Christ says the breviary piously while in the state of grace, then he prays—even without any special commission—in, with and for the Church and performs an act which can rightly be called an act of the Church (understood as the Mystical Body of Christ). This applies *a fortiori* also to the breviary

[17] For the sacrament itself depends in its actual effect on the disposition of the recipient which is its condition and material cause. To overlook this fact, makes it all sound like 'magic' and would lead quite rightly to justified objections by the Protestants, objections which were already taken into consideration by the Council of Trent (Denz 741; 797; 799; 849). This would apply even more so if one were to ascribe power and efficacy to liturgical prayer independently of the disposition of the person who prays.

said in common, even without any special commission from the hierarchical Church. The Church's explicit authorization qualifies such recitation in addition as an 'act of the Church' even in the dimension of the *visible society* of the Church; but this additional qualification neither constitutes this prayer in the first place as an act of the Church nor gives it a higher value than that already belonging to it by the union with Christ through grace. Hence, the mandate given by the Church authorities to say the breviary—a delegation which exists in the case of those in Major Orders and of (many) Religious—adds an obligation to this prayer but does not in any real sense alter or increase the innermost nature of this prayer. Hence it is unnecessary that any such explicit delegation should be added whenever it is in fact impossible to impose a new obligation or when this is inadvisable in a case where no increase in frequency or intensity of prayer could be hoped for from this.

11. *The Mass celebrated in the name of the whole Church*

There has always been a dogma of faith in the Church to the effect that every Mass (even a so-called 'private Mass') is an act of worship by the *Church* and not merely by some private person (e.g. the priest himself as an individual and private person). It is, however, doubtful as to what is the exact sense in which this is to be understood. First of all, it is obvious that every act of worship offered by any member of the Church in the state of grace is a meritorious work full of blessing (by increase of grace) for the one who performs this act, and so on this account contributes also at the same time to the good of the whole Mystical Body. It is clear, furthermore, that those who assist at Mass receive *ex opere operato*, by the fact of their assistance, certain actual graces by which the very act of worship of the participant is increased both with regard to its dignity and with regard to its supernatural merit. This applies all the more truly to the acts of worship performed by those who are at the same time united for the celebration of the same sacrifice and who offer a particular sacrifice of the Mass by these acts. If, and in so far as, we prescind from this value and effect of every Mass (including even its 'social' effect), then it cannot be said that the individual Masses bring about a *new* 'value' distinct from that infinite value of the one bloody sacrifice of Calvary which is rendered present here and now by the Mass, i.e. of that one bloody sacrifice of Calvary which is contained in the Mass, and which is, as it were, put before God by the Church in the sacrifice offered by the faithful celebrating it, that sacrifice whose power is offered by God as a grace to those of the faithful who celebrate the Mass—a power which causes its actual effects in them *in actu secundo*, when and to the extent in which the faithful are capable of these effects by their (growing) dispositions. For, although the individual Masses are so many acts of Christ himself[18] in so far as He, the High Priest, commissioned the Church at the Last Supper to offer up Christ in His (Christ's) own name to the Father by a liturgical act, the glorified Christ in heaven does not perform any physically new acts in the Mass, acts which would be multiplied by the many liturgical sacrifices of the Church. Thus, in view of the meritorious and redeeming act of Christ which glorifies God, the value of the Mass is not added to the value of the bloody sacrifice, but rather the Mass offers this unique and infinite value to God and channels it to men. If, and in so far as, there is any additional *new* value in the Mass which benefits the whole Church, then this arises from the acts of sacrifice in so far as they are acts both of the priest who celebrates the Mass meritoriously and also of those who are present at the Mass. For these are acts which glorify God in so far as, on the one hand, they originate in the power of Christ's sacrifice on Calvary and, on the other hand, are distinct from Christ's act on the Cross which was offered to God the Father for all eternity; and so, these acts are really increased by the number of Masses. In so far as they are supernaturally meritorious acts of several people, viz. of those who celebrate the Mass, they benefit the whole Mystical Body of Christ. Hence, every Mass benefits the whole Church. This is the only basic way in which the individual Mass benefits the whole Church. For one must not imagine that every Mass is offered 'in the name of the Church' in the sense that the *whole* Church is the *immediate* subject which offers by this act or receives by it the fruits of the Mass. The eternal and infinite value of the *Sacrifice of the Cross* concerns *directly* and permanently *all* men, but most of all those who have been baptized and hence the *whole* Church; but precisely this value is, as it were, offered *sacramentally* by, and applied to, *those* who are present when this efficacious *sign* of that bloody sacrifice is constituted, i.e. the sign which takes up a certain limited place in space and time.

[18] Cf. e.g. the Allocutions by Pius XII, 31.5.1954 and 2.11.1954, AAS XLIX (1954), pp. 313–317; 668–670. On the interpretation of these texts, cf. K. Rahner, 'Die vielen Messen als die vielen Opfer Christi', ZKT LXXVII (1955), pp. 94–101.

Just as a sacrament as such (in so far as it is distinct from the *res sacramenti*, i.e. grace) can be directly applied only to someone who coexists with this sign in space and time, so it must also be conceived in the case of the sacrifice of the Mass as such, i.e. in so far as it is to be distinguished as a sign from the reality signified, viz. the value of the sacrifice of the Cross itself. When it is said in certain older sources that the Mass is offered in the name of the Church and that the Church celebrates the sacrificial meal, this is to be understood as referring to the local 'church', as is often the case even in St Paul. For precisely that 'multitude of the faithful' who celebrate a certain liturgical sacrifice, or that 'holy people' of whom the Canon of the Mass speaks as really and liturgically present, are rightly called a 'church' since this multitude performs the highest act of sacred worship which God has bestowed on the *whole* Church.[19] Hence, the whole Church appears 'here and now' in the action of a particular congregation which celebrates the Mass, and so takes on a concrete and historically tangible form. In this sense alone (apart from that other sense of which we have already spoken) is it true to say that the 'whole' Church celebrates each Mass, but this must not be understood as if the whole Church were the direct subject offering the concrete liturgical sacrifice or as if *all* the members of the Church were just as directly beneficiaries of the fruits of the Mass as are those actually present at the celebration of a particular Mass.

[19] Cf. K. Rahner, 'Zur Theologie der Pfarre', in H. Rahner, *Die Pfarr* [2] (Freiburg 1960).

17

THE 'COMMANDMENT' OF LOVE IN RELATION TO THE OTHER COMMANDMENTS

No one will dispute the fact that the commandment of love has a special position among the other commandments. It is called a 'commandment' in the New Testament and is thereby seemingly treated as one among many other commandments. Yet the New Testament also states that it is *the* ('first') commandment, that on it depend the whole Law and the Prophets (Mt 22.40) and that anyone who observes this commandment has fulfilled the whole law (Rom 13.10). Consequently, this commandment while remaining one particular commandment yet also must sum up all that is meant by all the commandments. It will not be possible to say that this commandment is simply a collective name for all the other commandments, in the sense—which is true—that one already loves God when one simply observes the other commandments, and that the love of God is merely another name for one's readiness to do the will of God expressed in different particular ways in materially distinct commandments. It cannot be correct to say that the other commandments are merely partial formulations of the one commandment of love of God and of neighbour. If this were the case, then Fénelon and Quietism would have been right in maintaining, or at least seeming to maintain, that there is only one really moral attitude, viz. the attitude of pure love of God, and that every action whose intention is directed to some other 'value'—to the salvation of one's own soul, the avoidance of punishment, the unfolding of one's own personality, etc.—is in effect already immoral. Thus we are faced with a peculiar dilemma: love is everything and yet not everything; where there is love, there is everything, and yet there are other values besides love which must not be excluded from the realm of what is moral. One cannot solve this dilemma by saying that love is the virtue which one can possess (according to any one of its essential characteristics) only if one also possesses the others, although conversely one can have the other virtues (as moral attitudes and even—at least in the case of faith and hope—as 'infused' supernatural faculties) without possessing love. It is indeed clear that it can be said that real love is present only if one is prepared to do the will of God in everything, and to fulfil the whole of his commandments. Yet this once again turns love (even though in different words) into the collective formula for all moral attitudes; one simply decrees that there is no love where one is not ready to do the will of the beloved in everything. But is this so obvious? It will, of course, be said in defence of this doctrine that while it is possible to have the feeling of love even without this decided readiness to do God's will in every respect, this feeling quite simply is not genuine or effective love. One may say this, but could not the same be said also of every other virtue? Could one not say also that purity without love of neighbour is not genuine purity but simply a proud fear of opening oneself in love to the other? Could it not be said also that truthfulness without love is merely an arrogance which believes that it is above such things as being considerate to oneself and others, or that it is merely self-assurance which, therefore, is in a position to be 'brutally' honest? Could one not say that justice which is not love, misses the whole point of what justice really is, viz. not a balance within a world of objective goods, but a real respect of man, and might it not be said that such respect can after all be shown in the true and real sense only through love, since anything else would not be the value-response due to the *person*? Could one not say even more generally and fundamentally that every moral value is ultimately a personal value, for only the person can be the basis for absolute values, since the *bonum honestum* is that value which is primarily and solely founded in the person (according to the axiom: *ens et bonum convertuntur*), and since each higher value can only be based on an *ontologically* higher being? The value-response due to the person, however, is simply love and nothing else, since every other evaluation lowers the value of the person. One might try to counter this argument by pointing out that the person is after all a multidimensional being and hence can be viewed from different and quite distinguishable points of view and can be responded to in its multiple forms of value, and that it is therefore also possible to take up different moral attitudes towards the person, without all of these attitudes being that of love. Yet this in its turn could be countered by asking whether these different partial aspects of man, precisely as *such*, can still represent *moral* values, since one or two of these aspects certainly do not. If one says that these partial aspects are moral values in so far as they remain orientated towards the *whole* of the person (i.e. 'human nature' considered as the proximate basis of moral values), then it would have to be replied that this may be quite correct but seems to prove exactly the opposite from what it is intended to prove. For if a human part-value is a moral value only when it remains referred to the whole of the human person and only when it is affirmed as a value thus referred, then this obviously means that a value-response to a human part-value (i.e. an individual virtue) is a virtue only if it is based on a moral affirmation of the whole human person, in the form such an answer should take in relation to this person as a whole. It would then have to be asked: is this response to the human person—a response corresponding to the person as a whole—anything else but love? Hence, after all, is not then a value-response and therefore a virtue conceivable only as a part-factor of the one love? Does it not seem, therefore, as if love not only includes every other virtue but also that every virtue includes love? Thus, are we not still in the same position we are trying to avoid, viz. being faced with the proposition that there is no real plurality of virtues?

If we are to get any further in this question, we must take a wider view and start from a different point altogether. For, as long as we regard the virtues only statically in their 'nature', they do in fact implicitly contain each other, always presupposing that we see their *full* nature in its *adequate realization*. But precisely this realization of nature has its own history—it 'becomes'—and is not always fully given; a virtue realizes itself only gradually and thereby, it is true, realizes also—love. Morality is the free personal acceptance of one's own pre-established nature, confidently coming to grips with one's own dynamic reality in all its united though multiple dimensions and precisely coming to grips also with that nature which realizes itself only when it turns lovingly to another person and when it accepts its own nature as the nature of the mystery of love. This acceptance does, however, have its history; it is not present all at once (as in the case of the angels), but is temporal and becomes. This means, however, that something already 'is' at a particular moment in time and can already be described in its nature; it means that there already is 'something realized' which nevertheless comes to its *proper* completion only in the completed whole of which it is but an element. We must not overlook the mystery of the temporal moment in the history of a temporal being: in order to be a moment in a whole history, it must itself be 'something' . . . it cannot be nothing, but must have a 'nature' (in the widest sense of the word). Yet again precisely the same moment must not exist simply for itself, cannot be adequately intelligible by itself, must point away from itself, must transcend itself, must be such that it only attains its own full and final nature (although it already has one) when it enters as a moment into a greater whole and thus becomes once more different in *itself* as a moment of this greater whole: this is the mystery and the dialectic of the individual temporal moment in a history which is one, and the dialectic mystery of the part in the whole. (If, however, one were to rely merely on this last viewpoint of the part in the whole, then it would have to be investigated *to what extent* the individual virtues can be regarded as part-factors of the one virtue of love considered as a whole, and to what extent they can nevertheless appear even outside this whole.)

If we now apply this, in itself obvious, insight to our present question, then it must be said that man's existential acceptance of his own nature has a history; man always discovers new dimensions of his own personal nature (and in the same way and at the same time necessarily discovers such different dimensions of the personal reality of others). Whether the 'route' for this journey of discovery of one's own reality is necessarily in all cases and for every individual of the same and recurring kind, or whether it is different for each individual, or whether there are certain basic avenues in the historic-temporal succession of the existential comprehension of such human values— all this is outside of our present investigation. In so far as such comprehensions of these multiple human values follow on one another, a person may already have come to a self-realization with regard to *one* virtue and may already have acquired this one virtue before he possesses another one. But in so far as this kind of acquisition by man of a *moral* value is as such conceivable and possible only *as* it is carried out and understood as a temporal moment in a movement tending towards the total acceptance of the whole personal being of man, this 'already' acquired individual virtue becomes perfect only once it is really integrated into the totality of the acceptance of one's own nature, i.e. love. Hence, every virtue which is not love may be regarded—in so far as it tends towards love—as a moment in the movement towards it, and only in this way can we speak of it as a *moral* virtue; or it may be regarded as a moment in and of love, and only to this extent is it complete in its own nature. Yet love is not, on this account, the collective formula for the individual moments of man's historical self-realization, i.e. of those individual moments preceding love and integrated into it. Love indeed necessarily absorbs all the preceding moments into itself because—as moments of such a self-realization—they are necessarily present in the one total attitude of which this self-realization consists, since the temporal nature of a personal spirit does not consist of moments which pass away and fall back into the emptiness of what has been; but are rather moments which become in order to exist and remain in the one unified total attitude of the person. But love is not the end of the integration of these partial moments of man's self-realization; rather, love is this self-realization itself as such and as a whole, without this wholeness being merely the sum-total of moments. Where the person completely possesses itself, completely pledges itself and engages itself totally in its freedom, there is found love, for all this can be done only through love. In love, the person realizes itself completely, and by love, everything which had already happened previously in the spiritual history of the person's gradual self-discovery is accomplished and integrated in this one act; but this totality is more than just the sum of the preceding moments: it is simply love and nothing else, an act, therefore, which cannot be described by any other reality, because by definition it is the sole complete self-realization of the one person in its very unity; this one person in its turn must not be conceived as being built up from individual moments, and so love has nothing by which it could be explained except the one person who himself, however, only learns who and what he is (as a whole person) when he loves.

Of course, this does not mean that love, considered from a temporal point of view, can be thought of merely as coming at the temporal end of the history of the whole person. There is an '*engagement*' which is present totally and yet can have a subsequent history. Love may already be present and yet may still have the task of realizing itself. The temporal nature of man necessitates not only a gradual temporal approach to love in successive stages, but necessitates also the kind of historical nature of love itself to be in successive stages. Love may already be present—it may, in other words, already be man's 'commitment in freedom' in the very core of the person—and yet the integration of all the dimensions and capacities of man, his love of God with his whole heart and might, may still be a task not yet completed by this man. The objection put forward above against the possibility of any other virtue being really a moral virtue without already being love was a basic realization of the necessary connection between the historical nature of man (and hence also of his virtue) and the self-transcendence of the individual virtues into the whole of man's self-realization (called love). To this extent it was quite right: the full nature of any virtue even as such exists only once it has fulfilled and lost itself in love. The concept of the 'fulfilled nature' of a virtue is certainly somewhat obscure and vague. Yet, if we do not wish to do harm to the fitting description of reality as it really is in its becoming, then we must be careful not to face this concept with the dilemma that a being either is or is not, and that there is no third possibility. An embryo is also already a human being, human nature is already 'present' in the three-day-old human embryo; a beginning has been made which is irrevocably the beginning of a human being, and is this and nothing else. Yet man is nevertheless a being having eyes and capable of singing, a being which loves, and it cannot be said that these possibilities have nothing to do with the nature of man. The nature of the embryo is intelligible—even though it is a reality by itself—only in and in view of what it is yet to become. Potency is not only prior to act but is an active potency only in its active intentness towards act, and this dynamism of the full development of nature is something without which potency itself cannot be understood. This dynamism itself, however, can be grasped only from the point of view of full act and the full realization of the nature. Hence, the notion of a full realization of nature (which must not be understood in a quantitative and additive sense) is a necessary one. Hence it can also be said that it is possible to find human self-realization in a stage in which it is not yet fully present (although the real movement towards full self-realization has already begun and we therefore find ourselves already in the moral sphere), and then we are dealing with man's individual virtues which are not the same as love. This human self-realization can also be viewed as full self-realization (even though still continuing historically) which indeed 'engages' man completely, and then we have love.

What has been said can be clarified further under different aspects. It is possible to *object* against the Catholic teaching that there can be mere 'attrition', by pointing out that even merely 'imperfect contrition'

requires a serious and unconditional will to observe God's commandments in future. Without this 'resolution', there cannot even be mere
attrition. God's commandments, however, include also that of the
love of God. Hence, anyone 'arousing' imperfect contrition, must
have the desire to love God. It follows then that the actual decision
to love God ('in future') is already love. For it is indeed possible to
distinguish between the real readiness to do something and the actual
doing of it in the case of material production, but not in the case of an
inner attitude. The desire for such an attitude and the attitude itself
are one and the same thing. It might be added furthermore: how often
do not confessors and spiritual directors tell their penitents and dis-
ciples that anyone *wishing* to love God, loves Him already. If the
above reflection were perfectly correct, then it would follow that there
cannot be any imperfect contrition which is not also necessarily perfect
contrition by love, and the opposite impression would be created
merely by the fact that the love which has not yet been accomplished
in attrition (i.e. accomplished in an explicitly 'awakened' act of love)
is confused with love itself, although one is quick to emphasize in
other cases that what matters ultimately is not such 'aroused' acts of
the three theological virtues formulated in a certain way, but rather
the genuine attitude of these virtues themselves which may quite
easily be present even in a less explicit manner, as the inner formative
principle of the concrete actions of life, i.e. as accomplished in the
concrete material of existence. It is surely essential to dispose of this
difficulty, for the presupposition that there really is such a thing as
attrition in the concrete is surely quite correct, even though the transition from imperfect contrition (which is nevertheless true contrition)
is probably much easier and more obvious than has been supposed in
the theological controversies between contritionism and attritionism.
It would seem that the only way to dispose of this difficulty is to
concede that faith, imperfect contrition and other preparatory acts
for justification, are really a beginning of love—the beginning of love
itself—and a process which by its inner dynamism itself tends towards
actual and achieved love (and which in real life is frequently this
accomplished love already) but that for the very same reason, such a
beginning and such a dynamism need not necessarily have reached
their goal to such an extent that this beginning itself can always and
in every case already be called after this its natural goal. Contrition
understood as an unconditional acknowledgement of the holy God

and of His will (and this belongs also already to attrition, no matter what may be the reason or motive for which the act is done) already means taking up position towards a value and—if it reaches its latent goal—is precisely an acknowledgement of the absolute goodness of God (understood as the goodness of a person) and thus becomes love, if it reaches the goal towards which such an act is already tending. Hence, the only possible answer to the above objection will be to point out that wanting to love God can certainly already be love and in fact will be this in many cases, and in any case is always on the way to being it, but that it need not necessarily have already arrived at actual love. For, given the historical nature of man and the plurality of his values (each of which points beyond itself to the totality of these values, but each of which—unlike the value of God—is not already the totality of all values) such a process of development makes a beginning possible, a beginning which is not yet formally the same as the end of which it is the beginning. It is imperative to conceive the virtues from the very start as an internally connected history of a realization of nature, not overlooking the fact, of course, that in a spiritual history the earlier phase remains 'preserved' and actualizes itself ever anew with regard to the object corresponding to it. Only in this way can we do justice to what is valuable in the difficulty discussed here and, at the same time, understand that nevertheless it does not prove what at first sight it seems to prove, viz. that there can be no moral attitudes (in this case, attrition) which are not already love.

If we pursue these reflections a little further, it will also become possible to uncover the deepest reason for this unity of the history of moral values. Scholastic theology rightly stresses the fact that the individual virtues are differentiated by their different 'formal objects'. But the 'formal object' of love is not merely one differentiated *alongside* the other formal objects of the other virtues. The formal object of love is of a peculiar nature; it is at the same time identical with the *a priori* horizon of the will and with that of freedom in general. For it is the *absolute* being in its nature of absolute value (and this as a person) and this precisely is not a specific value *alongside* other such specific values, but is the real basis and source of all values, embracing all other values. Thus, all other values in their specific categories are included within the dynamism of that movement which is directed to the transcendental ground of all values, i.e. the absolute value as such. This absolute value—considered in this sense as a 'horizon' and as the *terminus ad quem* of the intellectual and voluntary anticipation in which every object and thus every single value is grasped—is not always already the 'formal object', especially since even as such it must be freely willed if it is to constitute a moral act qualified by it. But it is precisely the same value as that towards which love as such also tends. One may say quite correctly that love is not just any particular intentional tendency, specified in any kind of way, towards some object or person; rather, the love with which we are concerned here, i.e. the love of God, is the free and (in some way or other) explicit acceptance of that basic movement of freedom as such which is at the root of everything else. If, and *in so far as*, the free acceptance of a specific, morally lawful individual object is already also an implicit acceptance of the transcendental basic movement towards the foundation of all freedom, then every moral decision is already love. If, and in so far as, freedom is possible as an affirmation of a particular value by registering an ultimate 'no' to this transcendental basic movement of the spirit which, as the 'nature' of the spirit and of its freedom, is always present (and without such a contradiction there would be no possibility of sin at all), then it becomes clear that the affirmation of a particular value by virtue of the transcendental movement towards the absolute value, is not always already (and we may add: not always already from the very beginning of the movement) necessarily a free affirmation of this absolute value, i.e. is not always already a love of God. The simultaneous presence of both can be understood only if it is presupposed that this dialectic (i.e. 'already love' and 'not yet necessarily love') which is present in the peculiar relationship between a specific formal object and the transcendental horizon, is the description of the historical nature of moral freedom and of the *development* of love.

At this point we may be permitted to add a note on the history of theology, even though space does not allow of a more precise proof from the historical sources. It seems to us that Thomas Aquinas placed that total 'commitment' which we call 'love' at the very *beginning* of human self-realization. His reason for this seems to be that he cannot conceive a spiritual movement of freedom except in virtue of an original orientation to the goal as such, which original choice of the goal—in distinction to the means and the step by step movement towards the goal—is simply the love (or the refusal) of the absolute Good and Being which supports the whole movement of the Spirit.

This probably explains the noticeable lack of interest in St Thomas for a more exact psychological description of the various stages of the process of justification. This would also explain the presupposition on which his whole theology of justification is based, viz. that the acceptance of justification is exercised by virtue of the grace of justification and so is fundamentally a momentary event which itself does not admit of a temporal duration. St Thomas is certainly also aware of acts preceding justification in time. But can it be said that the acceptance takes place *contrary* to the basic conception underlying his theology of justification? How can it otherwise be explained that he succeeds only with difficulty to find even the grace for these saving acts preceding justification to exist in a temporal sense, that grace which sustains the saving act and permits us to interpret it in an anti-pelagian sense? Modern theology, since the later Middle Ages, has in this connection quietly and—it would seem to us—rather too self-evidently presupposed a temporal succession of acts in the process of justification, and has presupposed for this a strictly supernatural, *merely* actual grace which turns these acts into saving acts, without demanding that these acts themselves must already proceed from the grace of justification and thus be already love. Whenever one regards love as just another particular task *beside* others—a task which is perhaps more difficult and can be undertaken only on condition of being ready to fulfil all other obligations—it naturally represents no difficulty to think of this virtue as one which is fulfilled *after* a whole series of other fulfilled obligations and tasks, since the most difficult task is usually left to the end of the total achievement (and one involuntarily thinks of justification as having its place in the series of divine virtues even in a temporal sense, without worrying too much about whether this objective series must necessarily always be also a temporal series). If love, however, is seen simply as the total act of self-realization and commitment, then the question becomes more difficult: must not such an act be necessarily exercised—at least in the form of an *'engagement fondamental'*—at the very *beginning*? Must it not be the first total act of man's taking possession of himself by his freedom, even though it will perhaps still be a somewhat formal act and will have to be filled in content in the course of history? Must it not be man's original attitude which then determines the ultimate direction and quality of individual part-acts performed in the course of existence? This original attitude may indeed be changed by these acts, since every later act can always be another such *engagement global et fonda-mental*, but it does nevertheless stand at the beginning of the history of each individual man, just as original sin also was not merely the first act of the history of humanity but was that 'beginning' which, as the all-determining horizon of the history of the freedom of the human race and as the 'setting out' point, belongs at the temporal beginning of history. In such a conception, the individual virtues in their very individuality can no longer be understood as anything more than particular interpretations and expressions of the one basic virtue of love (the *mater et radix* of all virtues, as St Thomas puts it), the other virtues being individual virtues in so far as they do not fulfil the whole of the ground on which they all necessarily stand from the very start. Of course, if this were so, how could it still be possible to think seriously of a faith which is no longer love, the possibility of which is nevertheless presupposed as quite self-evident by the Council of Trent (Denz 800, 808, 838)? Does not the doctrine of the essential distinction between mortal and venial sin mean also that a man not only does not always commit himself totally but also that he can exercise the act of freedom involved even in venial sin (or in a good act of the same peripheral personal nature as venial sin) even *before* the free decision by which the person commits himself wholly, although not necessarily totally (since both the good and the evil act—in the sense of a real personal self-commitment—are 'difficult' to attain)? For why should it be unthinkable that an 'easy' act, which surely exists, is exercised before every 'difficult' decision, since man is certainly an historical temporal being? Why should there not be such a groping 'preliminary practice' for the real total self-realization, a 'training period' in which man already has certain moral experiences which are a necessary pre-supposition for his realizing sufficient matter to make it seriously possible to speak of a real self-commitment? Certainly, such a concep-tion would still mean that such a total commitment of himself would still have to be conceived as taking place comparatively early on in the history of the individual; it would still mean that this global commit-ment—in its role of the 'form' of further decisions—would also co-determine the moral quality of those acts which, since less total, would have to be referred to as the act of an individual virtue or even merely as an 'easy' act. This would mean that, before justification by love, it may be presumed that a virtue need not indeed be necessarily qualified as a morally 'easy' act. Yet this act would nevertheless have to be existentially less radical in some sense (and not merely in the sense that before love it has not yet matured to the real essential fullness of its nature) than if it had already to be somehow thought of as co-informed by that existential radicality which obviously can be realized only in love, since the quality of the act and its existentially radical nature—or the kind and density of the existence of the act—are certainly not simply mutually independent entities. It would seem to us, therefore, that contemporary theology, by dispassionately making room for a temporal series of moral acts which only gradually lead to love, has made real progress. Modern theology has thereby reached a really much more serious consideration of the historical dimension than was the case with St Thomas. Yet, on the other hand, St Thomas in particular has every right to warn us in this question against conceiving this successive nature in too primitive a way (and the average moral theology today urgently requires correction on this point by St Thomas). While holding fast to the now normal representation of the '*processus justificationis*', it is also very important to realize that the basic decision of love is not just something which is also due at some time or other ('*saepius in vita*') but that, by the very nature of personal reality, it characterizes rather that beginning of man's spiritual history which, as a genuine source, continues to govern the development of this historical life of the spirit into the individual virtues. This fundamental decision of love alone gives these virtues their whole, otherwise impossible, deep-rootedness in the core of the spiritual person and thus helps them to perfect their own essential nature, a perfection aimed at by them of their own, already given nature.

It remains nevertheless true even in this explanation that the individual virtues can exist as other virtues besides the virtue of love, not only because there is a plurality of moral values based on the many-sided nature of man, but also because man—in his free realization of himself as a person—can realize and accept these individual values in temporal succession and can already recognize and affirm their particular nature without having already realized himself completely in the one love. This does not dispute but rather includes the fact that these individual virtues themselves attain the fullness of their nature in love; in other words, they are really informed by love when it is present and thus are changed within themselves and only thus become 'living', as pointed out by the Council of Trent (Denz 800, 838).

The mutual relationship between love and the other virtues can be regarded from quite a different aspect still. If we disregard certain of the other virtues (such as the virtues of religion and reverence) which have a particularly close relationship to love, then it must certainly be said that the other virtues and commandments demand certain tangible achievements or the omission of certain actions, concrete realities which therefore can be accomplished to the full and whose accomplishment can be checked. The fulfilment of a real obligation of justice, the obligation of being truthful, the observance of certain norms of sexual behaviour, even the fulfilment of an external obligation of worshipping God, are all (even though in very different ways) *concrete* achievements whose fulfilment can really and obviously be achieved, proved and checked. In these cases it is a question of commandments which primarily and of their very nature (i.e. precisely in so far as it does not dissolve itself into personal love in the full realization of the nature) do not demand man himself but rather demand certain achievements from him. There is only one 'virtue' which asks man for himself—really himself wholly and completely—and this is the virtue of love and it alone; all other virtues only 'participate' in this nature of the one love, in so far as they are destined, even though out of their own nature itself, to be more than just themselves.

This, however, brings to light a most fundamental difference between love and the other virtues. For love cannot be performed or negotiated. It is never simply present but is always on the way to itself. Whereas the other virtues, as it were, transcend themselves, love is always present only in its transcendence into its own nature. For it is absolutely false to reduce love to the mere fulfilment of the other commandments. Such a fulfilment may, under certain pre-suppositions, be a very good criterion as to whether love is present, but it is not love itself. Moreover, love itself is of its very nature measureless. It must be love with all one's might, with all one's heart and spirit. As long as we are pilgrims here below, we never 'have' *this* love. For who can honestly say that he loves God and his neighbour with *all* his heart? Moralists make subtle distinctions about this in order to bring out the fact that one can love even now, in a determined moment of one's still temporally unfolding existence, just as the Gospel demands it: with all one's heart. But whatever may be said about these distinctions, ultimately this whole ethical system trying so desperately to be absolutely objective cannot avoid admitting that if someone were to refuse point blank any willingness and any attempt to love God more than he does now, then in such a case there would no longer be any love at all. Moralists today usually express this admission by saying almost unanimously that the striving after perfection is a duty imposed under pain of grave sin on every man and not just on certain categories of people, even though the manner of realizing this obligation (for instance, by fully determined means, such as the Evangelical Counsels, or by other forms of radical renunciation) does not simply thereby fall under this duty itself. Yet what else is this obligation to strive after perfection but the duty of a greater love then one actually possesses? What else is it but an admission that one only achieves the love one ought to have by admitting that one has not yet attained that love to which one is obliged? This unique characteristic of love is not destroyed or 'dulled' by admitting with the moralists that one also has a duty for the future which one has actually to admit now; but precisely as a duty for later on this commandment of greater love is always valid but not 'for always', i.e. for every moment. For the readiness of really becoming freely involved in a development and a dynamism towards a later condition is surely something quite different from someone admitting today that he must pay his tailor bill tomorrow, which today he is still able to leave quite unpaid. He must start out *today* on the adventure of a love which not until tomorrow will be what it should be tomorrow because, and if, he has really opened himself to it *today* in an inner readiness which he could refuse, in which latter case love would not become tomorrow what it ought to become then, because it was not today what it ought to have been today. Love today is, therefore, what it should be today only if it acknowledges today that it is something of which more will be demanded tomorrow. It is true love even for today only to the extent in which it reaches out to become more than it is today, only if it is really on the way and forgets what it is now, reaching out for what lies ahead of it (cf. Phlp 3.13).

If this is the nature of love, however, and if this love alone—as the full and unsurpassable realization of nature—brings the other virtues to their own final achievement, then this introduces a characteristic into Christian ethics which we half or completely overlook both in our scientific ethics and in our average sermons: it is really quite impossible to say exactly what is really demanded by the Christian moral law. It can indeed be said that what is demanded is love. But this love itself does not represent some assignable performance which could be accurately determined; rather, it is that which every man becomes in the irreplaceable, characteristic way of his own unique realization of nature, something which is known only when it has been accomplished. This is not meant to imply that there is no universal notion of love at all, no notion whose content could be based on the proposition stating that man has an obligation to love God, and that therein consists the real fulfilment of the whole divine law and of all the commandments. Yet man is nevertheless obliged to love God with his *whole* heart. This one heart which man has to engage— the innermost centre of his person (and on this basis also everything else found in the individual)—is something unique: what it contains within its uniqueness, what is engaged and given gratuitously in this love, is known only once it has been done, when the person has really caught up with himself and hence begins to know what is in him and *who* he is in the concrete. By this love, therefore, man embarks on the adventure of his own reality, all of which is at first veiled from him. He cannot comprehend and evaluate from the very start what is actually demanded of him. He is demanded, he himself is staked in the concreteness of his heart and of his life lying still before him as an unknown future and revealing—once it has been accomplished and only then—what is this heart which had to wager and expend itself during this life. With regard to every other achievement we can know what is actually demanded of us. In all such cases it is possible to make estimative and comparative judgements to ask oneself whether the stakes and the gain are worthwhile. In these cases one can find something else to justify the effort demanded, viz. a result distinct from the effort, a result which proves the effort to be sensible and justifies it. This is impossible in the case of love. In this case, love itself is its own justification, but really only once it has been accomplished to the very end and with one's whole heart and with all one's might. For only then does it make sense. If it were not done radically and *completely*, then it would be senseless, since a carefully checked and measured love which basically closes itself to any greater love simply ceases to be love. And when love is not itself, then it becomes senseless, because it no longer has any true nature; in such an event it becomes more senseless than the other moral efforts and virtues which after all are still meaningful when measured by the particular reality out of which they arise and to which they answer, even though they have not yet been integrated, together with their particular dimension of human existence, into the totality of the human person and its total act which is love.

It follows from all this that this strange, incomprehensible love—which can be experienced only in the movement of an unconditional and trusting surrender of oneself to the unknown—is the real concern of Christian morality, seeing that all the commandments find their ultimate meaning in love alone and that love only is itself once it encompasses the whole man with its generosity and enabling him to love with all his might. Would not many a casuistic judgement, when applied to the concrete circumstances of the human life of the individual, take on quite a different appearance from what many a moralist would conceive, if we did not simply ask (in accordance with the formal axioms of the individual moral systems) whether and to what extent one is bound by a definite, certain or merely probable law, but if we asked (which perhaps cannot be asked by a universal ethics but could be asked by the individual in the decision of his actual conscience) whether this or that is not necessary or obligatory by the very fact that in such a case this concrete person would be basically refusing to obey the greater demand which is an essential part of love, if he were to close himself to this or that determined demand either of freedom or of the law (both of which are possible)? Would this not clarify what—without falling into a heretical situation ethics—has been called 'individual ethics'? For, could it not be that this love, demanded of everyone *without limits and reservations*, does not indeed demand this or that definite effort in the abstract (i.e. by reason of a universal morality of nature) but that a particular realization is absolutely necessary, not indeed by reason of the extremely abstract notion of love in general but in view of a determined love belonging to the individual nature of a concrete person? Could it not be that one should on this account be even more careful before declaring this or that manner of life and particular attitude towards another human person as offending against prudence, custom or what is normal? Should this not make us more careful before refusing to accept this manner of life and attitude as the concrete manner of realization of this person's own existence, if one were always to ask oneself whether this or that manner of acting, which might perhaps seem strange and unusual at first sight, might not be the only manner in which the person concerned can exercise his immeasurable love? It has always been recognized that the aristotelian theory of virtue as the happy mean can be applied to the Christian doctrine of virtue only by greatly forcing it and by giving it a different interpretation. Does this not become still clearer if one clearly understands the boundlessness of love that ultimately is the only measure of the Christian doctrine of love? Perhaps this is also the point where the Christian doctrine of law is most clearly seen to merge into the Christian doctrine of grace, the point at which it becomes clear that the teaching of the Synoptics on love as the perfection to be achieved by man, is identical with the Pauline teaching on morality and sanctity, given gratuitously by grace in the holy *pneuma* of God? After all, this love which consists in venturing into the boundless, is (to be still more precise) not merely a readiness for the boundless, in so far as the depth of one's heart can be sounded only by the venture itself and in so far as in it must be accepted the unforeseeable nature of any future situation in which this love will have to be exercised and which itself will enter into this love. The immeasurable nature of love and of its situation includes as an essential element also the unforeseeable character (as far as they are concerned) of the admission to the love of God and of one's neighbour, which itself is again an essential element of the depth and radical nature of one's own love. Love of God and of the other man is determined by the degree of depth and absoluteness to which the love of God and of the other person admits us. Of itself, all love is ready in its immeasurable nature to accept all love offered by the other, and to perfect itself in this acceptance. Consequently, morality and the fulfilment of the law always consist in one's readiness to allow oneself to be loved by God in the full measure and with all the demands on one's own love that is determined by God's love, and to enter into the experience of the radical and profound nature of this love which comes out to meet us. To this extent, all love of God is a readiness for the supernatural community of life, while this in its turn means nothing else than the most radical intimacy of God's love for us in which his most absolute divinity is communicated to us. If, therefore, we are asked in the 'synoptic' sense to achieve a love which in its own boundlessness is to accept the boundlessness of God's love for us and thus is to be so radical as to claim in very deed every last ounce of its unreserved energy, then this means that this love really demanded of us as a response to God's absolute love, is love sustained by God's love itself, i.e. a love made possible by God's self-communication. This means nothing other, however, than that this our love of God has its real ontological basis in God's love for us, i.e. in His communication of Himself in grace. Because of its radical nature which really lays absolute claim to all its willingness, the love demanded of us in the Synoptics is *per definitionem* the love which *realissime* comes about through God's love, i.e. the love which communicates God himself by grace. This, however, is precisely what St Paul says. His idea of morality as compared with the morality of the pharisees is the pneumatic morality of the pure reception of what is demanded of us, since it is the morality of boundless love as an answer to that absolute and irrevocable love in which God's innermost *Pneuma* gives himself gratuitously to us. Since we must give ourselves and not something else, and must give ourselves as a response to God's own giving of Himself to us, it follows that what we have to give is a pure gift from God.

The basic meaning of the Christian ethos is not that we must respect objective material norms which God has imposed on reality. For all these material norms become real norms only once they become the expression of the very structure of the person. All other structures of things are placed *below* man. He may alter them, he may twist them as far as he possibly can, he is their master and not their servant. The only ultimate structure of the person which expresses it perfectly is the person's basic capacity for love, and this capacity is boundless. Hence man too is boundless, every sin is ultimately merely the refusal to trust in this boundlessness; sin is the lesser love which, because it refuses to wish to become greater love, is no longer love at all. Naturally, in order to know what is really meant by this, man requires objectifications and these he meets in the form of the plurality of commandments. But everything which thus comes to light in this plurality of commandments, is an objectification or part-realization or preliminary onset of love, love which itself has no norms by which it could be measured. One may speak of a commandment of love as long as one does not forget that this law does not command man to do something or other but simply commands him to fulfil himself, and charges man with himself, i.e. himself as the possibility of love in the acceptance of the love in which God does not give something but gives Himself. Can this commission still be called a commandment? Whatever may be the answer to this question, the commission of love is a commandment which can be called this only analogously when compared with the other commandments. If the other commandments command something, then one becomes free *of* them by fulfilling them. This commandment commands the freedom *to* love. Hence, this commandment can really exist only because God is prepared to give what he commands and because he has always already given what he commands. The grace of love is not a power given for the fulfilment of a law which precedes this fulfilment; rather, the law is given because love is already there as a possibility to be liberated and to be aroused in order to fulfil itself, and because the will of God is already present in the world, that will which presents this possibility with its realization.

All this will perhaps help us to reach some kind of conciliatory understanding of the Catholic-Protestant doctrinal disagreement about the nature of the justifying act as such. The teaching of the Council of Trent declares that faith (of course, in the sense of the word as understood by the Council) does not justify by itself, although it is recognized as the beginning and root of justification. Protestant teaching declares that faith (naturally understood in *their* sense of the word) is the sole act by which God's justifying grace is accepted. Even prescinding from the explicit question of whether there is no real disagreement—as seems to be the case—on this point because the same word 'faith' is used in different senses, the following can be said in the light of our present considerations: Faith *as* a 'different' 'virtue' from love is not indeed the whole of man's grace-supported attitude towards God and hence cannot by itself constitute the process of justification. For, since man is free in his actions, the acceptance of justifying grace can undoubtedly occur only by an act which is the actualization of the possibilities given by the grace of justification. In other words, this acceptance can take place only in an act which in its nature corresponds wholly to the accepted divine life (even though it does not necessarily correspond totally to it, since this accepted life is to develop further). But clearly—and this the Protestant theologian will certainly not be able to dispute—love of God and neighbour also belongs to that possibility for which man is liberated by God's justifying grace. If this possibility is accepted, then this can happen only in and subject to the totality of the process of justification. To this extent, the teaching of the Council is absolutely correct. Yet we may pose the question: when is there that supernatural moral attitude which signifies justification once it has fully realized its own nature, and what name are we to give to that beginning which, as long as it is not suffocated contrary to its own nature in the realization of its nature, already signifies justification?—and then we can answer this question unhesitatingly (even after the Council of Trent) by saying: faith. For it may be said without hesitation that no other beginning (than faith) can be named by Tradition, i.e. no other beginning which lies *before* this beginning and yet already contains the whole of what is called justification within it as a beginning (and only thus), and this is a fact about which Catholic and Protestant theologians are agreed. Furthermore, no Catholic need dispute the fact that faith, if it is really what it should be and confides itself to the spiritual dynamism of freedom thus begun (and this it must do if it is to be true faith), can be destroyed only by a process of suffocation directed against the full realization of faith's own nature. In this sense, a Catholic need not hesitate to concede that we are justified by faith. Finally, it must be remembered also that evidently individual men cannot do anything else than characterize on their own account the whole of their natural and supernatural realization of existence in accordance with *that* factor which they experience most intensely for some personal or general historical reason, that factor which this particular individual or age experiences most clearly and most radically as the deciding factor of the whole Christian existence. It is quite possible, however, that in one case this factor may be love, while in another it may be faith and in yet another it may perhaps be hope or may have to be described in some other way altogether. Particular periods and individuals have different 'catch-words' which express for them the whole characteristic of their existence, even though this catch-word determines and clarifies the whole only in a certain direction. Such a characterization becomes false only when it really identifies this isolated factor with the totality of this one realization of man's nature in which every factor should overcome itself by entering into the whole.

This last statement is still valid (although not in exactly the same sense) even in the case of love. For even love—if it is to achieve itself completely in the multidimensional creature—must 'humble itself' and once more divide itself and enter into the different moments of moral existence which as such are not love. For, otherwise, love itself would not be what it must be, even though it is the whole of human and Christian existence, according to the terminology used by Jesus and Tradition, a terminology not absolutely alien to St Paul either. In a language which, in accordance with the style of a particular period, proclaims the summons to this total realization in such a way that the particular age understands what is 'really' meant by it, this totality may also be called upon by a different name when using an existential terminology, as long as this other language can make itself comprehensible to the universal Church. If someone preaches that everything is faith, he is not necessarily saying anything wrong. He may mean by this that anyone who has found the real beginning in faith, will also find completion. He may wish to say that faith is the clearest characteristic and the most difficult element of the whole of Christian existence. He may say that even love is really love only when it is a believing love. When in the Church the imitation of Christ is characterized as poverty, or renunciation or service, etc., it is just one further example of the same, basically possible freedom of an existential terminology. This is not surprising, for the totality called love means the fullness of God and of man. This fullness, however, is infinite and hence almost nameless. It will always be called love right to the end. But it itself demands the other names and is demanded by them.

18

THE SAVING FORCE AND HEALING POWER
OF FAITH

THE question to be treated here could be called even more simply: 'Faith and illness'. That this subject is an objectively real one will be seen from a brief look into the New Testament. Again and again we are told in its pages of miraculous cures performed by Jesus and the Apostles, and very often faith is even explicitly associated with this healing as its condition: If you have faith, all things are possible (Mk 9.19 *sqq*); Great is thy faith, let your wish—for a cure— be fulfilled (Mt 15.28); Your faith has helped you (Lk 17.19); Do you believe that I can do this? (Mt 9.28); Let it be done to you according to your faith (Mt 9.29). In these and similar ways, the New Testament over and over again sees a connection between faith and the healing of illness. After all, this attitude led to the sceptical expressions about 'faith that heals'.

What then is the truth about this healing power of faith? Even among those who call themselves Christians, there are widely different opinions on this point. They range from the opinion that faith has no more to do with the cure of illness than any other form of psychological sugges- tion, to the opinion of that Christian sect (called 'Christian Science') for whom the healing power of faith has more or less become the real centre of their belief. Consequently, we want to try here to work out an answer to this obscure question, an answer which is based on the *whole* of the Faith.

To begin with, the Christian faith is not indifferent towards illness, as if it were of no importance or had no meaning within the context of Christian existence as such. Rather, faith looks on illness, clarifies and incorporates it into its interpretation of the whole of existence. Illness in its concrete happening—as it is experienced by a particular person— does not necessarily arise out of the individual guilt of this particular sick person himself. Jesus expressed himself explicitly against such an interpretation if taken as a general one valid in every case (Jn 9.2 *sq.*), even though he is not at all blind to such a connection in certain concrete individual cases (Mk 2.5; Jn 5.14). In this way, he has really already defended himself against the tendency to be met with in modern medicine—at least in certain of its aspects, viz. that illness is always and everywhere, or at least to a great extent, merely a sign and expression of psychic conflicts or even of guilt deep down in the core of the person. There are such illnesses. But not every illness is the expression of the individual guilt of the sick person. Hence, illness in the concrete—in the form in which it is actually experienced—can have something of both. Illness thus becomes a puzzle for which there is no complete solution. There are two factors which always appear in illness in the concrete, and both of them in a unity which can never be adequately dissolved: the fate imposed on man and which falls upon him suddenly and unasked, and man's original act by which he understands himself and by which he affirms himself as the deed of his own freedom. In the latter case, man creates illness or accepts the imposed illness into himself in an absolutely definitive manner, takes up position towards it and thus transfigures it by what he himself is in freedom, i.e. in guilt or in obedience, towards God. Hence, faith will first of all see in illness that which constitutes the being of man in general, viz. his exposed condition, his freedom and his ultimate indeterminability by anyone else but God. Faith knows furthermore, however, that all illness—even that illness which is not due to any individual guilt and which is borne in a holy manner—is a sign of the sin in the world in general. In the last analysis, there is illness in the world only because there is sin in the world; illness is the bodily presence and appearance of guilt; sin is the ultimate reason for illness, in so far as 'guilt' does not refer to the particular decision of the individual but to the supra-personal power— the existential—under which we all begin our existence, even though this existential originally arose out of the free decision taken at the very beginning of the history of humanity.

But the same faith also knows something else about illness: as we experience daily, illness is a stage in that continuous dying in which man lives and which reaches its climax and end in death. Gregory the Great calls illness ˌne 'prolongation of death'. Yet death is not merely the wages of sin but also the manner in which we were redeemed, the manner in which the person who dies in obedience, accepts and finally makes his own the death of the Lord which is redemption. Thus, the suffering of illness also has this function in man's life. Whenever this suffering is undergone in faith, obedience and the willingness proper to the creature (and this, properly viewed, is a factor within illness itself and not merely an external attitude towards it), then it is a life-long practice for that readiness for death in which the Christian believingly accepts his liberating death. Thus in the Christian view, in so far as illness precedes even man's taking up of position (analogously to death), illness is of a most profoundly dialectic nature; it can be both a manifestation of *sin* and a manifestation of *redemption*; it can be the visible sign of an unbelieving despair in which the person of man slowly disintegrates, as well as the tangible sign of faith which, by its obedient acceptance of death as it announces itself, turns this fate of the 'body of sin' (Rom 6.6) into the carrying out of redemption and into a dying with the Redeemer. From a medical point of view, i.e. in an already particular viewpoint, human beings get indeed the same illnesses. From a more personal point of view which considers the whole man and bears in mind his supernatural salvation, illnesses which seem the same, are quite different in reality, according to whether they are suffered in faith or in unbelief, taking faith here not merely as the intellectual assent to propositions, but as the real acceptance of that love of God which communicates itself in a mysterious way in the inalienable form of the fate of one's own body and soul.

Only seen in this light, is it possible to understand what is the real and ultimate nature of the saving power of faith. In the Christian understanding, faith is always and in every case a saving power. The reason for this is that faith changes illness—understood as a happening in the whole man and not merely on the biological level as such—from being an occurrence by which the guilty degradation in unbelief becomes visible, into an occurrence of suffering and of overcoming sin by dying with Christ. By believing obedience towards the God who disposes of everything, the prolongation of the 'first death', the forerunner and onset of the second and eternal death (to use biblical language: Ap 2.11; 20.6–14; 21.8), is changed into a prolongation and maturing of *that* death by which one surrenders oneself into the eternal life of God. It is merely a secondary question as to whether or not the external appearance of illness, with which the art of medicine is or can be generally concerned, is changed by this determination of illness. Of course, anyone who as a sick person desires absolutely nothing else but that health with which he is quite rightly solely concerned cannot understand that the

illness of the believer and the illness of someone who is truly unbelieving (for many only think they are) are really intriniscally different. The
inability to understand this (to put it in another way, which will show
quite clearly the stupidity of this attitude) is to be found in those sick
people who never want to die, and hence simply suffer death under
absolute protest, i.e. in the unbelief that death is absolutely senseless: in those who in sickness never and in no way take into account
that by illness God offers them the acceptance of death as their
manner of accepting the gift of eternal life. Only someone who
unreservedly accepts God the Creator and the Redeemer knows that
faith is in any case a saving force for the, utterly human, reality of
illness.

This saving power of faith can manifest itself only by converting the
sick person's (unbelieving) protest against death as something senseless,
into the readiness for death as a redeeming gift of God who by it grants
him the real and perfect life. After all, we have already seen that death,
and hence illness understood as the threat of death, is a manifestation
of sin and guilt, i.e. of the guilt of the race or, in addition, also of the
guilt of the individual. Hence, when faith encounters illness, its transforming power can in certain circumstances have an effect also on the
restoration of bodily health since, and in so far as, the apparently
merely natural, earthly health is nevertheless a sign, a pledge and a
prelude of the absolute health of eternal life. After all, according to the
New Testament, we must not think of the present and of the eschatological state of existence as absolutely and completely separated and
successive states. The powers of the future aeon already penetrate the
present aeon: everything belonging to this world which is in any respect
healthy, alive, good and true, ultimately—according to the Christian
understanding—flows from that source which brings forth eternal life
and which creates in those apparently profane matters the presuppositions for the communication of the eternal divine life, so that the things
of this world carry within them the reflection of the eternal world. This
is why Jesus himself regarded his cures of the sick as a sign of the
arrival and the beginning of the visible dawning of God's reign. He did
not regard the miracles he performed merely and primarily as formal
testimonies to the validity of his mission. Rather, he saw in *what* thus
happened—in the recovery of health itself—the resplendence of the
Kingdom of God in which God really makes everything whole and
brings it to completion: the *one* whole man, body and soul. Thus,

whenever the faith, by which God's reign comes and is accepted, meets illness, it corresponds absolutely to the inner relationship of both, that this meeting can lead to an overcoming of illness experienced already here and now, i.e. to a cure in the medical sense. This does not mean that faith can conquer illness only in this way. If faith were to be understood as present only if the illness is fully overcome by it, then it would no longer be that unconditional surrender of man to God's absolute providence by which every single providential act—whether it kills or restores life—is accepted as the coming of eternal love. Hence, healing power (in certain cases even in a medical sense) belongs only to *that* faith which does not merely strive for an earthly bodily cure but intends to adopt a point of view by which man rises absolutely above any ideas of illness or bodily health as absolute values. But the *possibility* of manifesting itself in a special way also in bodily health pertains to the nature of saving faith.

It is not easy to determine exactly *how*, in an empirical sense, the saving power of faith has an effect on illness. It does not always have to be in the same way, if we look at this matter from the point of view of its immediate appearances. There is certainly a way which may be qualified as 'psychological' (at least at first sight) for which one may adduce certain analogies from outside (or sometimes even merely apparently outside) the proper field of faith. Faith can have a calming effect, it can make a person feel quite cool and collected, internally free and relaxed. The believer knows himself to be safe and secure in God's hands; he is no longer faced with the absolute dilemma of conquering illness in an absolutely definite way or of succumbing to it; as a result, he becomes relaxed in his desires and is freed from inhibitions; the cramp of efforts and the fear of absolute defeat in his attempts to maintain existence disappear. All this can undoubtedly have a healing effect, if there is such a thing as psychosomatic medicine, wherever this kind of medicine can be effective and to the extent in which it can be effective. We know indeed that even saints can be ill and that even the process of becoming a saint can endanger health, just like *any other* very great spiritual and personal effort endangers the unimpaired, harmlessly vital state of man. But whenever the believer is someone who believes completely—in other words, whenever he has let go of himself from the innermost centre of his being and freedom and fearlessly handed himself over and entrusted himself—and thereby also his fears and cares and thus his illness—to God, his illness, even when it remains, loses its inescapable senselessness and thus is provided with the best presupposition for overcoming it.

This 'psychological' explanation of the *manner* in which faith can have an effect on illness does not explain very much and certainly not everything. This is true even simply because the word 'psychology' covers in this case a great variety of intrinsically different factors. For: peace, ease of mind, resignation, confidence and similar psychological states are themselves again of the most different kinds and themselves extend once more through the most different sectors of man's being, beginning with the realm of the most primitive psycho-somatic mechanism right up to that inner depth of the spiritual person where freedom, transcendence into the Absolute, grace and decision and thus faith are really situated. Hence ease of mind, confidence and similar terms mean very different things in these different spheres, and the somatic effect exercised by such psychic processes is not really explained by saying that faith gives rise to an attitude of calmness, confidence, etc., and that this has a healing effect or at least an effect conducive to healing. For precisely this faith and the attitudes associated with it are not at all such an undifferentiated happening as the simple words used for them might seem to suggest. In so far as psychological happenings and attitudes, taken as the concrete events of each particular man, in spite of all their 'explicability' always retain precisely as such and here and now a final irreducible element, any psychological explanation of these happenings within the soul and of their effect on the somatic element does not mean any exclusion of grace. For, apart from everything else, the fact that this psychological attitude may have succeeded here and now even though, in spite of all our extremely clever psychology, it could also always fail, and even though even the cleverest psychology can never grasp or control the totality of all the factors involved really adequately and clearly—this very fact makes it quite legitimate for the believer to regard the success of his spiritual attitude as a divine grace, no matter how well planned and organized that successful attitude may have been. Thus, in the case of faith, even this saving effect of faith—no matter how psychological an explanation may be given—remains nevertheless the always incomprehensible grace of God.

When we speak of the ways in which faith can become empirically health-giving, there is one way which must not remain unmentioned, a way which has played quite an important part in the Christian tradition and in the life of the Church, i.e. miracles. Jesus himself, as we said at the beginning, associates healing, miracle and faith. It is of course impossible in as short an exposition as ours to show at length the problems, the nature and meaning, possibility and intelligibility of what in the New Testament and in Christian language is called a miracle and a sign. We can merely give a few indications of all this here.

First of all, it can be seen from what has been said up till now, why the authentic Christian miracles consist for the most part of cures. After all, miracles are meant to be signs, not merely of the power and authorized mission of the miracle worker but also of the content and the nature of his mission, i.e. signs which make free faith possible without making it necessary. For both these purposes, however, spectacular physical events (the 'signs from heaven' refused by Jesus in Mk 8.11 *sq.*) are unsuitable. The miracles of healing, on the other hand, allow the meaning of the divine act to appear clearly within experience: the salvation of the whole man, right from the innermost centre of his being and hence starting from faith; they do not necessitate but call upon the free decision of man, so that the best miracles (if we may put it this way) are not the 'most massive' but those with the greatest intensity of meaning. Of course, their recognition and acknowledgement presuppose that man approaches them with a synthetic outlook which seeks their meaning and which perceives a meaningfulness, in the concreteness of this event in relation to himself and to his total question of existence, a meaningfulness which he, if correct, must then interpret as the word of God addressed to him and not merely as a coincidence. Seen in this light, it is not particularly good if right from the start we remove these miracles of healing effected by faith from the total context of human history into the isolation of the selective approach of such natural sciences as physics and medicine and then ask from within this artificial state of isolation whether or not the laws of nature are 'suspended' in the case of these miracles. The gospels and Christian history do indeed record a sufficient number of exactly observed and authenticated miracles of bodily healing which even the natural scientist ought to recognize as inexplicable by his laws, i.e. if he does not from the outset deny all miracles on the basis of some philosophical prejudice or by going beyond the principles of his method. Yet ultimately it is not really the most important thing about a miracle and its acceptance whether the natural scientist can or cannot positively show that in the case of a particular miracle a law of nature has been suspended, or at least what is meant by such a law here, or whether he simply leaves the matter as something he cannot explain and then regards this inexplicability as something merely temporary from his methodological standpoint as *such*. For, in the first place, one need not necessarily speak of a suspension of the laws of nature and yet may accept the miracle, viz. if one presupposes (what is really self-evident) that every determined level and order of being is from the very start open towards a higher level and order and can be incorporated into it, without its own laws thereby having to be suspended. The laws of two-dimensional space are valid also in three-dimensional space, even though they are given quite a different meaning there. It is true that biology, for instance, is a sphere of a higher order in which there are phenomena which do not exist in physics and chemistry, without it following from this that the laws of inorganic matter must necessarily be suspended in biology. Similarly, the world in its material content must be conceived as open from the outset to the reality of the spirit and of faith seen as the total act of the innermost core of the spiritual person, and must be conceived as open to the reality of God. Hence the higher dimensions of the whole of reality come to appear in the lower dimensions of this reality by transforming them, but in such a way that the lower dimensions are preserved at the same time as the meaning and nature of the higher reality become visible within them.

What then is the truth about the saving and healing power of faith? This power does exist because, and in so far as, faith lays hold of the whole man. The faith which places the whole of reality obediently at the absolute disposal of God, becomes in this readiness for life and death the truth and the deed which lays hold of the healing salvation of God. God's grace promises its power to the whole man, in his body and soul, and if it here and now heals in passing, it is essentially intended to make it credible for man that it will heal and transfigure him finally when his consummation dawns in the passing of life through death. Thus, when Our Lord said to the Samaritan who alone among the ten who had been cured, came back to thank Him: Arise, go thy way, for thy faith has saved thee' (Lk 17.19), this contains the twofold and, in the last analysis, the only meaning of: your faith has healed *and* has saved you; it has granted you both the cure and salvation. Is there any greater healing power than the saving force of faith?

19
WHAT IS HERESY?

THE history of Christianity is also a history of heresies and hence also a history of the attitude towards heresy taken up by Christianity and the Church, a history which consequently also includes a history of the concept of heresy itself. All religions which have anything like a well-defined doctrine (i.e. all religions of higher cultures) experience differences of opinion about their teaching and about the religious sociological structures supporting these different doctrinal opinions. To this extent it might be said that the *eidos* of heresy is to be found in all of the more highly developed religions. Yet one will have to be careful: for it has been maintained that religious wars are to be observed only within the realm of Christianity. No matter how much this affirmation may have to be distinguished and in whatever way this asserted fact may have to be explained more exactly (and much about it may have very little to do with Christianity as such), this questionable statement nevertheless does make us take note of something: Christianity alone provides the presupposition for a perfectly specific understanding of heresy, viz. a radical, quite definite ethos of truth, and so the real nature of heresy is really to be found only within this framework.

Two factors probably specify the ethos of truth referred to here: the consciousness that there has been a divine revelation of truth at a perfectly determined point in space and time and that it has taken place as an event in perfectly determined people and through them alone—and the consciousness that this truth is itself significant for salvation. Combining these two factors, it may be said to be the historical form of an absolute truth of itself significant for salvation. To make it clearer why and how this leads to a definite concept of heresy and correspondingly to a definite relationship to heresy—both of which belong specifically to Christianity (seen as a whole)—we still have to give a more exact explanation of what we have just stated.

We must first of all reflect on revelation understood as an event by Christian understanding. We prescind here from the question (however important and even decisive it may be in other respects) as to whether and how the substance of the Christian message comes from within (i.e. by the offer of grace as a result of the universal salvific will of God) but in an unreflected manner, without being clearly expressed in propositions, and thus comes really close to *all* men even where they are only attained by a historical revelation which is not clearly determinable. Even when this is the case, it nevertheless remains true to say that, according to Christian understanding, this hypothetically accepted and admitted communication of truth 'from within' finds its explicit expression and clearly authentic conceptualization (which makes it once again more unmistakably applicable in the concrete forms of life) in absolutely definite points of space and time in history: through the prophets, through Jesus Christ, through the Apostles, through authorized and accredited announcers and interpreters of God's truth proclaiming God to man in the free self-opening of His being and will themselves unattainable by men through their own efforts.[1] The fact that, here and now, in the name of God, the word of *God* issued forth clearly and with a demand of obedience, and then always still goes forth yet further while always remaining new, this is already—even before any consideration of the actual content of the message—the basic factor in the understanding of the Christian truth. The referring back to this event as such and to the authority announcing itself in that event belongs, therefore, to the nature of Christian truth. Christians may fight among each other as to *who* exactly is the bearer of this eventful witnessing to the truth, but as soon as the referring back is overlooked, there no longer is any Christian understanding of truth. Whenever differences are seen as merely different opinions about mere 'content', any one opinion can never experience the other as a 'heresy' in the

---

[1] When one remembers that this self-opening and communication of God takes place just as essentially in what Christian theology calls the 'participation in the divine nature' by the grace of justification, then it would perhaps be safer and more exact to formulate the above statement as follows: . . . proclaiming God to men in the divinely authorized, humanly communicated side of His free self-opening of His being and will, themselves unattainable by men through their own efforts.

proper sense of the word. Only where there is on both sides the basic desire to refer back to this event and to the authority manifesting itself in it, is it possible for both sides to regard each other as 'heretics', i.e. as those who—against their will—break off the genuine and clear relationship to this authoritative event (which they still hold on to in itself) in their difference of opinion about objective content.

Thus, heresy is always a doctrine which, contrary to intention, threatens the whole of one's spiritual existence, in so far as this existence is based on the reference to the one complete event of revelation which even the heretic affirms. Where this affirmation no longer exists, it is also no longer a question of heresy. Such an opinion (from the Christian point of view) would be apostasy from Christianity itself. Because, and in so far as, this kind of point of reference, from which the many propositions were received and towards which they remain referred, hardly exists outside of Christianity as something essential to a particular religion, this means that there cannot be any real heresy in these other religions, nor any real feeling against the heretical, such as there is in the Christian religion. Heresy is possible only among brothers in the Spirit. These are possible, however, only where there is some real common basis within the religious sphere explicitly binding them together. Among such brothers, however, heresy (i.e. something more than just differences of opinion on unimportant matters) can be present only when one or both parties holding different opinions objectively destroy and thus (at least) subjectively endanger the ultimate basis of Christianity and of its unity. We will have to take a closer look later on at what follows from this for the nature of heresy and for one's attitude towards it.

Before doing so, we must reflect on the other point already mentioned. As we said, if there is to be any question of heresy, then it must be a matter of a *truth* which, precisely *as* truth, is significant for salvation. If we are to realize that this proposition is not at all self-evident, we must reflect here on one of the most profound changes in the spirit of the last three centuries, a change whose advent is perhaps only now becoming quite clear at the very time when it is already on the way out. What does the average contemporary European feel about truth, especially religious truth and the truth expressed in the form of a 'world view'? His attitude might be defined in the following terms: Outside the field of the simple, brute facts of direct sense experience which can be observed anew at any time by experiment, there are only theories and opinions . . . nothing else. These opinions may be correct in different degrees; one opinion may have a greater chance than the other of 'coming closer' to reality and hence to the real truth, but more than this sort of approximation is never possible. The mode of this 'outlook on the world' is radically, individually, socially and historically conditioned, and hence relative. In any case (and this is the decisive point), the particular *content* of such an opinion is of no importance (i.e. of no importance before the judgement seat of God, if there is such a thing) for the absolute 'moral' evaluation of the one who holds this opinion, since it may be supposed that everyone has formed his opinion with the best will and conscience. Certain people will indeed concede that it is in itself and in principle conceivable that someone may be *guilty* of a false opinion (because he has been guilty of not informing himself sufficiently, and of stubbornly shutting his mind to what is more correct and adequate). But even in such a case they would hold that what endangers salvation and characterizes man *absolutely* is not so much the missing of the truth and thus of reality in their determinate content, but the immoral cause of this failure; the ultimate qualification of a person, it would be held, can never be made to depend on *what* is the content of his opinions. This, it is held, is surely an immediately evident fact: men (even the most decent among them) hold the most different opinions and this even on the (in themselves) most important questions. Hence—so they would say—it is obviously absurd to regard someone else as a scoundrel simply because he is of a certain, i.e. different opinion.

Thus, the recognition of truth as such, in so far as it is determined by its definite content, has moved from the centre of human existence to the periphery of man's concern, and has come to be counted among such things as one's colour of hair, one's tastes and one's race, on which man's absolute qualification cannot be made to depend. People would concede (as far as one reflects on it) that certain errors, even though they are adhered to without guilt, can nevertheless have fatal *consequences*; it will be conceded, for instance, that an innocent error about the right of way on the road may cost one's life. But precisely this is what is different in the absolute, final accounting for everything; for this, the only thing that really counts is surely 'how well one has meant it' and not *what* one meant. Since (this is the basis tacitly presupposed as self-evident) one can have good reasons and hence a good conscience for any opinion, it is not necessary either for us or for God to judge as to *what* opinion one has held, when it comes to the full judgement, 'as long as one has been a decent fellow'. The fact that one might possibly be able to judge this precisely on the basis of *what* opinion one has held, is a possibility to a large extent excluded from modern consciousness. Democratically speaking, every opinion has to begin with the same right to be held as any other. (Why this proposition, considered as a 'rule of the game', must not in its turn be disputed is something about which 'one' does not usually think very much). The cognoscitive content (to express all this a bit more theologically) is no longer important '*de necessitate medii*' for salvation; only the moral quality of gaining it, i.e. its '*necessitas praecepti*', is of universal importance.

Thus according to this opinion, God sees to it (even though not for this earth, yet for the whole course of the world and for eternity) that nothing can ultimately go wrong through error as such. This opinion is based on a strange subjectivist idea of 'interiority': reality is 'outside', 'thoughts' are only 'inside' and are not the real thing; only reality can be harmful; yet thoughts 'about reality' do not produce a real and essential contact with reality for, after all, reality is not changed by this: such contact can be effected only by what reality does to one apart from one's own thoughts about it. The fact that in the nature of things one enters into quite a definite relationship with realities precisely by what one 'thinks' about them, and that they themselves thus become different for oneself according to how one thinks 'about them', is a fundamental truth about the real nature of one's knowledge which has largely been lost to present-day consciousness. It is precisely this present-day opinion about the ultimate indifference of truth that is rejected by Christianity, and this rejection is the second reason for the Christian attitude of rejecting an error only *as* an error. It is a *fundamental* fact for the Christian understanding of existence that there is truth which can be missed only in a culpable manner. This proposition (it seems to us) has become so obscured even among Catholics (for reasons to be mentioned later) that we must start by giving at least some proof to them and this under their presuppositions. Only once this has been done, can we try, on the one hand, to dispel as far as possible modern scandal over this proposition and, on the other hand, to understand on this basis the anti-heretical attitude of Christianity (and thus the nature of heresy itself). Catholic Christianity teaches that no one who has reached the use of normal reason, can find his true and real salvation without a correct faith in the true revelation of God. This statement refers to proper theological faith in the real truth of God's revelation. It is not our intention here either to make this proposition more precise or to prove it more exactly. We presuppose it as something incontrovertible for a Catholic Christian. What is important here is that this proposition implies the above-mentioned basic principle regarding the essential significance for salvation of the knowledge of truth as such; for this proposition states that finally and decisively (also, although not exclusively)—with the deadly earnestness of any question of man's ultimate destiny—what we are concerned with is *what* one believes, whether one has grasped the true fact, by recognizing the genuine reality in truth, that what matters is not merely good will, a noble effort and a decent attitude, but whether one has in fact recognized and grasped the absolute reality itself, since salvation itself consists in this grasp which is essentially also (although not merely) a recognition.

Before getting up in arms against this thesis with a protest against 'Greek intellectualism', it would be well to reflect on whether if one thinks it so imperative to reject this Christian doctrine one only proves by such protests that one has not yet really understood what recognition means. Naturally, this thesis presupposes that there is a basic fulfilment of human existence, a depth of human existence (which is not always or everywhere attained), in which knowledge and decision, truth and goodness are no longer separable, but where only the true possesses goodness and where only the good cannot land outside of truth. Yet precisely this original basic act (in which knowledge achieves its full nature by saving itself, and thus preserving itself, within the decision of love, just as the converse is also true) is still an act of the knowledge of truth and significant for salvation, in so far as this act is (also) precisely this because the truth itself belongs to the highest moral goods and hence morality (if it is not to empty itself out into a pure formalism, or merely a search into the manner of 'how' one does something, it being quite indifferent *what* one does) fails itself if it does not find the real truth (and not merely a well-intentioned opinion).

Naturally, Christianity has always already asked itself during its reflection on theology about how this basic conception of the decisive salvific significance of the truth as such is reconcilable with the observation that people seem to be disagreed about the most important questions of truth, at least if one does not have the courage to regard all those who do not explicitly recognize the official Christian truth as being already lost on this account alone. It is not to be denied, first of all, that many Christians, starting from this Christian concept of truth, have had the 'courage' to maintain precisely this; even as St Francis Xavier still told the Japanese whom he wished to convert that obviously all their ancestors were damned in hell. Even St Augustine ought to have given this answer according to his theology, and right up to our own day this attitude was part of the fundamental outlook of Christian missionary work among the heathens. But it must not be disputed that one need not have this 'courage', indeed one may say that a Christian today, in the present state of the development of dogmas and of the Christian consciousness of faith, is no longer *allowed* to have this absolute courage from a Christian point of view. Theology has reflected a great deal on the question about why and how one can defend the above proposition about the salvific nature of truth as such, without having to demand this courage for a cruel pessimism about the salvation of the majority of people. Usually theologians used the information (by appealing, for example, to Heb 11.6) that this absolute seriousness of decision regarding the (revealed) truth is present only when we come to the ultimate and most fundamental truths. Thus, anyone who denies or does not know that God exists as the guardian of the moral order, was held to be certainly deprived of that faith, understood as the possession of truth deciding one's salvation. Yet, it was held, it is quite obvious that this primitive truth can easily be discovered and that it can be missed (at least in the long run) only by one's own fault (and thus, after all, the only thing that matters ultimately would be the moral factor as such). Other truths, however, can be missed or remain unknown (without moral fault) without this fact alone making all saving faith impossible. No matter how important and true this information may be, it alone will no longer be sufficient today to reconcile modern man with the thesis stated above. For, on the one hand, the experience of the most radical differences of opinions among men has become still more pronounced and widespread (even the enlightened monotheist can no longer be thought of as someone not seriously threatened by a wider reduction of faith) and, on the other hand, the man of today— no matter how egoistic he may be in actual life—experiences an almost irrepressible feeling of solidarity with all men; he does not believe in, and does not desire for himself, a heaven from which he sees others excluded, others whom he does not seriously regard as worse than himself and who nevertheless are not given more or less the same chance of gaining salvation as himself. Hence, it will undoubtedly be necessary today to add to the previous information that in certain cases someone may be perfectly capable of attaining and affirming a truth even as such in the depth of his realization of existence, even though he thinks that he must deny it in the explicit form of his concepts or does not know anything about it explicitly. In other words, there may be those who think they are atheists while in actual fact they affirm God (for instance, in the unconditional decision to look honestly for the truth, or in being faithful to the absolute declarations of conscience), just as, conversely, there are Christians who on the plane of theoretical concepts affirm God's existence and yet deny Him in the core of their freely understood existence.

Whatever may be the truth of all this, and however we may solve the inevitable questions arising out of the above thesis (which is not part of our subject here), the basic Christian conception mentioned must not be denied or endangered: truth as such is—even here on earth—so fundamental for existence and for salvation that it must be attained and accepted here below, if man is to find salvation at all. If we make an ultimate distinction between the possession of truth and morality (religiosity)—in other words, ethicize truth and intellectualize the ethical, then this will make the statement under consideration more understandable to the man of today but will not and must not deny it. One can say to a man of today that someone who truly affirms the good does not basically miss the truth, since he affirms the decisive truth at least implicitly together with his affirmation of the good. But this also means conversely that anyone who is really indifferent towards the truth as such and hence does not attain it at all fails absolutely to attain the good.

All this had to be said here (and had to be defended against contradiction) so that the Christian attitude towards heresy might become intelligible. This attitude is sustained by the basic conviction that truth as such is significant for salvation and (we may add right away, since it comes to the same thing) by the conviction that the discovery of the truth or the failure to find it has a fundamental moral quality, all of which is a basic conception difficult to grasp for the man of today. Of course, when we say 'the man of today', we would probably be better to say 'the man who still belongs to the present age because he is really the man of yesterday'; for there is obviously no danger of splitting

truth and morality in this way within the Eastern Communist understanding of human existence: anyone who theoretically does not toe
the party line and who does not keep to the truth of the collectivity
adopted by the leaders of the State shows himself by this very fact to be
morally decadent and consequently is treated on account of his 'views'
in exactly the same way as a thief or a murderer is treated in the West.
(The Christian ought to be very careful not to protest against the false
and primitive application of this basically true insight attained in the
East by adopting an outlook which is Western and false).

Only in this way can we understand—which does not necessarily
mean justify or regard as justifiable even in the future—the manner in
which Christianity has reacted against heresy in the course of her
history. Certainly, the history of the persecutions of heretics, of the
Inquisition and of the internal Christian 'wars of religion', is a terrible
chapter in the history of Christianity, full of horrible events which must
not be defended, least of all in the name of Christianity. Yet one can get
an objectively and historically just and understanding (although not
approving) comprehension of this history of the Christian attitude towards heresy only if one recognizes and adapts to oneself even in this
matter the outlook permanently and basically essential to Christianity
and one which can never be relinquished; the falsehood of heresy is a
much more absolute threat to human existence than all other happenings against which the use of force will be felt to be justified even by
modern man (unless he advocates absolute non-violence which even
Gandhi and Nehru never defended or at least never actually realized).
For the Christian of earlier periods, the person who professed heresy
was not the holder of a different opinion about which one could have a
quiet chat, as if the character of real human existence which is possible
for all in common and only in common, were not in any way seriously
affected by these opinions; for him the heretic was someone who by his
views was mortally dangerous to more than physical life and earthly
welfare, viz, directly to eternal salvation.

Anyone who has no understanding of this ethos of truth—anyone
who has no sense of the deadly earnestness of a decision about whether
this or that proposition is true—will also not be able to understand the
Christian evaluation of heresy. The Christian judgement of heresy does
not deny that in certain circumstances a person who explicitly rejects a
particular truth may possess this truth implicitly (just as the converse is
also possible), nor does it maintain that the question whether there can

in principle be any Christian and moral use of force against a false doctrine and—if yes, when and within what limits—is already fundamentally and exactly answered. But in this Christian attitude towards truth it is realized that in the matter of truth as such (not merely and not even primarly with regard to its possible consequences distinct from it, as e.g. in the case of wrongly or correctly diagnosed illness) it is a matter of life and death here below and in eternity, and not merely a question of opinions which one could discuss in the course of a pleasant conversation. Moreover, since Christianity is of the conviction that this absolute truth which is salvation has communicated itself in a final concrete way wherever there is Christianity (in Jesus Christ, in Scripture, in the Church, in the faith of this Church which can be brought to a definitive self-consciousness in the final pronouncements of the *magisterium* of this Church), Christianity—it may quite rightly be said—is most sensitive towards any heresy raising its ugly head among Christians. For here is lost that absolute truth which already existed in a historically clear manner of expression. Here it is not merely a question of endangering what is provisional, what is as yet undetermined or what has not yet reached its goal, but of endangering again or of having already lost what had actually been finalized. Paganism may be seen as a possibility and preliminary of Christianity, as the advent of Christianity, and consequently one may be inclined to judge it lightly; seen as something provisional and as the lesser, it does not indeed involve any danger for the Christian (as long as it does not itself employ force), for in this case the Christian can simply regard himself as someone who has gone further, as superior and as being on a higher level of religious 'development'. But all this is quite different in the case of the heretic: he has not merely not yet arrived; he leaves the goal and pretends that by doing this he alone possesses it. Christianity therefore finds it more difficult to credit *him* with good faith than to grant it to an unbeliever who has not yet been a Christian. The unbeliever shows himself to be a victim of a generally sinful history of humanity which has not yet reached its goal. The heretic, on the other hand, has enjoyed the gift of the promised truth. In view of this experience, how could the heretic be guiltless in being incapable of distinguishing true from false Christianity? He is the most dangerous person of all: he combats the real and final truth of Christianity in the name of Christian truth itself.

As can be seen, Christianity has its own proper relationship to error when it arises in its own midst, a relationship peculiar to Christianity alone. Furthermore, this error itself has a nature which cannot simply be reduced to the common denominator of all opinions on religious matters which are rejected as false by some other religious communion. Heresy is rather the (objective) self-failure in existence precisely where it is already absolutely 'present' as a divinely effected existence, under the proselytizing and misleading appearance of its exercise. Naturally, all this would be much simpler and more proof against the misunderstanding of heresy as a merely indifferent, incorrect and un-ecclesiastical opinion on religious questions, if the same Christianity could at the same time maintain that every objective heretical error is always and in every case also subjectively culpable in the actual individual professing it and that it therefore is also really a subjective lapse from the absolute truth involving as a consequence the loss of salvation. The anti-heretical ethos of Christianity is primarily directed against the case when error as such has also been subjectively realized, grasped and welcomed into the very core of existence; in other words, it is directed against the religious error which represents a danger to salvation (and means the destruction of salvation). We cannot even at this point treat systematically of the long over-due question as to whether and how this kind of error can actually exist at all, i.e. how an act of real knowledge can be free in itself and thus can itself come under a moral qualification. For this seems at first sight to be an impossibility: conscious error—one might think—is uncovered, overcome and no longer acceptable error, while unnoticed error *as such* cannot be so freely accepted that it can make the act of acceptance morally worse. Yet we will have to stick to the fact that the true and the good, knowledge and freedom, are so closely connected at the very roots of their existence that one can find their one meaning only by taking both of them together, i.e. a truth which is accepted as a value, and conversely: knowledge which is gained only as a free decision and which can precisely in this way reach its true objectivity. Yet Christianity can never basically start from and take for granted the tacit and unspoken yet widespread opinion that all agree it to be something immediately obvious that anyone making a statement which is false in its objective wording, 'deep down' means the right thing and the same as oneself, and that differences of opinion are right away and always simply differences in terminology due to difficulties in understanding each other which do not really in any way affect one's real convictions in their profoundest nature. No, the attitude of Christianity (whenever it is realized in the proper way) is of the same dialectic nature as the matter itself to which it refers: the affirmed proposition (the proposed theory) and what is really meant by it, and the basic conviction which really grasps the real meaning, are not simply identical; it may happen that the person who expresses a false proposition has nevertheless grasped the truth in the depth of his morally purer understanding of truth. Hence, such a person is to be tolerated as someone innocently in error, and his error should also be gently tolerated as a bad formulation of a realized truth.

But this difference is not a complete separation and certainly does not mean a relationship of mutual indifference and independence between the formulated proposition and what is 'actually meant' deep down in the person, between the value of the expressed opinion and the value of man himself. The ultimate judgement on the relationship between these two factors in the concrete case—as to whether, since they are not simply identical, they stand in a contradictory or synonymous relationship to each other—belongs neither to the outsider nor to one's own self-reflection (the so-called 'good' conscience and 'honest conviction') but principally to God alone. Yet (if we may put it this way) the proclaimed proposition is nevertheless the 'sacrament' of the inner attitude, of the actual encounter with that truth which does not merely have some loose connection with salvation but *is* this salvation itself. Hence, the erroneously expressed proposition is indeed the most terrifying possibility of that threat and temptation of the evil realizing of error in the very depths of man's being by which man accepts the unreality and the lying appearance as his truth and reality and thus becomes corrupted. Hence, one cannot simply tolerate the bald erroneous proposition with mildness; one cannot simply regard it as one of the possible starting points of a calculated approach (in an eternally open dispute) in which it is ultimately indifferent for the infinitely distant final result, which (more or less distant) approach-value one has used as one's starting point. No, for Christianity, even that error is hideous which does not yet ring out clearly like the last judgement for the person in error himself; for Christianity, even such a proposition is separated by an (objectively) infinite distance from the truth and is not merely a somewhat more badly formulated truth than the propositions of authentic Christianity. Even though it may be very difficult to decide in the case of particular propositions, propositions which do not

T I—Q*

deal with simply verifiable empirical matters, when and why they are not merely inadequate and misleading formulations and one-sided illuminations of the matter, but are simply so erroneous that all the force of anti-heretical hatred must be brought to bear upon them. Yet the fundamental difference must remain, if life is not to become a harmless game and an endlessly babbling chatter.

There is still another aspect of this anti-heretical attitude of Christianity to be considered: the Christian does not deem himself to be more intelligent than others; rather, he regards himself as a sinner and believes that, just like the first, this second self-evaluation also extends into and has an effect on the dimension of knowledge, especially since stupidity and sin are not without very essential mutual relations. Yet because of this the Christian looks upon heresy as an actual temptation, seduction and delusion, from which he does not feel himself immediately immune. He knows, therefore, that his instinct for the real truth can become blurred and confused; he knows the temptation of the modern, of the (too) sweeping and handy solution, the allurement of novelty; he feels in himself the enemy within, which will treacherously meet half-way the untruth coming from without. Hence, he cannot simply adopt a superior and mild attitude and go out in sovereign impartiality to encounter those theses which, when proposed to him, endanger his conviction of faith. Or—to put the same thing more psychologically— precisely because he knows that his actual conviction, since it is that of a corporeal creature, is exposed to thousands of non-logical influences and is not by any means built up exclusively by habit, mass instinct, subconscious imperatives, etc., he cannot treat heresy as he would treat a scientific theorem which one discusses in the friendly neutrality of a scientific debate. Naturally this distrust of oneself and of the powers of darkness, which hold secret sway in error, can also lead to wrong reactions: it may lead to narrow-mindedness, witch-hunting, to the rejection of insights which are right and important. Such mistaken reactions may achieve the very opposite of what was intended; they may further error without wanting to, because they lend it the appearance of narrow-mindedly persecuted truth or because they prevent or delay the solution of questions without which error cannot in the long run be held in check. Yet basically this mistrust is justified because it corresponds to the legitimate Christian self-evaluation of the person who knows that, just like any other sin, error possesses a seductive power in this world. In this sinful world, the 'defence instinct' has a certain priority (for man's reaction) over the respect and regard for the 'unqualified objectivity' of thought (although this too is a Christian virtue).

II. THE TRADITIONAL NOTION OF HERESY AND OF THE HERETIC
AND THE PROBLEMATIC NATURE OF THIS NOTION

We are now in a position to understand and critically evaluate the traditional notion of heresy. This intermediate consideration will form a transition to the last section of our present investigation which deals with the change in form undergone by heresy and with cryptogamic heresy[2] within the Church herself.

In the juridical realm of the Church, a heretic is defined as someone who, after baptism and while retaining the name of Christian, pertinaciously denies or doubts any one of the truths of divine and Catholic faith (CIC can. 1325, § 2).

Hence, to be a heretic in the sense of the terminology used by the *magisterium*, one must first of all be baptized. Even by this fact alone, heresy manifests itself as an event within Christianity itself; it manifests itself as an opposition not from without, on the part of those who have never yet accepted the message of Christianity in profession of faith and sacrament, but as an opposition from within, from the very midst of Christianity itself. Even here there already appear certain questionable elements. Is the heretic who has never been a Catholic, even though he has been baptized—in other words, someone who has never belonged to the true Church and her common faith in the unity of the consciousness of faith in its social constitution—really a heretic in the same sense as the Catholic who becomes heretical? Can his heresy ever call forth the same protest by the Church, the same attitude of radical opposition and defence against the inner danger to her own existence, as is pronounced against those who themselves and of their *own* original initiative left the Church by separating themselves from her? Certainly, formal (i.e. subjectively culpable) and material heretics (i.e. those who are guiltlessly caught up in error) are distinguished and one could say that those described above are material heretics, while the latter are formal heretics, and that by this conceptual distinction the difference

[2] We have translated '*kryptogame*' by 'cryptogamic' throughout this Chapter, since this botanical term seems to render most accurately the meaning intended by the author. The term is used of a plant having no stamens or pistils and therefore no proper flowers. *Tr.*

we have just pointed out is fitted into neat categories. Yet basically this is not true. For it is quite possible (even in spite of the true statement made by the 1st Vatican Council, Denz 1794[3]) that in the sphere of Church statistics, some of those who belong to the Catholic Church in the 'visible' dimension and who profess the true faith, *innocently* err from the Church and hence are also merely material heretics, with the result that the two distinctions do not coincide in actual fact. Hence, in practice, it will not be permissible to regard the just mentioned difference as unimportant (and we should also try to determine it terminologically): heresy, as it now arises within the Catholic Church and thus separates itself from her, is something different from the (now historical) heresy of those who have never belonged to the Church and hence cannot really reject the Church and her possession of truth in the same way as those who at one time experienced it in the concrete (or could have experienced it).[4]

Nevertheless, these two kinds of heresy agree in the fact that the name of Christian is retained by both ('*nomen retinens christianum*'), in contrast to apostasy.[5] This is a peculiar factor within the definition of

[3] Cf. on this J. Trütsch, Art. 'Glaubensabfall', LThK[2] IV, pp. 931 *sqq.*

[4] Of course, if one supposes that there are also Catholics whose relationship to the Church and to the truth proclaimed and lived in her is or was as unexistential and external as the relationship of born non-Catholics to the Catholic Church—as a result of bad instruction, excess of various other environmental influences, mediocrity and superficiality of Church life surrounding them—(and this case cannot be thought *a priori* as impossible) then the difference worked out above becomes untenable in these cases. It is then a case of Catholics of whom one can indeed say with regard to their official registered status that they are Catholics, but not that they have certainly accepted this status '*sub Ecclesiae* (*as* a grace-giving and salvific institution) *magisterio*' (Denz 1794). In this case the referred to difference between non-Catholics by birth and 'Catholics' who have become heretical will certainly be at least insignificant.

[5] It may help the reader to understand what follows if we preface it with a short explanation. Moralists emphasize (and quite rightly, judged by their standards and criteria) that there is no specific, but at most a gradual, difference between the sin of apostasy and that of heresy, since both cases represent a denial of a truth revealed by God. Yet there are very basic differences, as will be shown by the reflections which follow. The problems arising from these differences makes it necessary to get a better grasp of the nature of heresy.

heresy and of heretics. Further, the presupposition implied by this is not immediately self-evident. For this factor seems to presuppose that one does not necessarily either fall away '*totaliter*' (like the apostate) from Christianity nor possess it to the fullest extent. For the *attitude* of faith (and thus the virtue of faith as a divinely effected, habitual faculty given by grace) is indivisible: one cannot possess only half of it as far as its proper nature is concerned. Why and how can there then nevertheless be men who are still Christians and yet no longer have this one indivisible faith? Can there really be such men when it is a question of a *culpable* denial or doubt of a truth of faith, or is this impossible in such a case, i.e. is a formal heretic always necessarily more than a heretic and hence an apostate? Does the definition of a heretic therefore refer after all merely to material heretics, i.e. to those who inculpably (even though decisively, '*pertinaciter*') dispute a certain truth of faith and who, since they do this without guilt, retain the basic attitude of faith and hence do not reject the Christian faith deep down where it is merely a question of a simple Either-Or? Or does the '*nomen retinere christianum*' refer to the purely external state of affairs, in other words to the question of whether or not the heretic concerned still wishes to call himself a Christian and of whether or not he still holds one or other of the doctrines which are usually regarded as specifically 'Christian' in the normal sense of the term? Yet where, under this presupposition, are we to draw the line between specifically Christian and non-Christian truths? (One will not, for instance, want to call everyone who is barely a theist and no more, a mere heretic even if he would still like to call himself a Christian, since in his opinion the 'essence of Christianity, consists merely in a mild belief in God.)

The vagueness of this essential characteristic of heresy does not indicate the question to be one of mere theological subtlety. This is not so even for the simple reason that this is the basis for the dilemma as to whether the Church can refuse the name of Christian to someone in certain circumstances even when the person himself calls himself a Christian and lays great store in this designation. This question will find an objectively correct solution only when and by the fact that the criterion for this distinction between the 'partial' and the 'total' is seen neither exclusively in the realm of the inner attitude of faith nor exclusively in the deposit of specifically Christian doctrines. If the question of the inner attitude were to be completely excluded from the criterion, then it really could no longer be understood why the greater or lesser amount of Christian propositions still conserved could decide such an important distinction as that between heretical Christians who are still Christians and apostates who no longer are Christians; for it is difficult to indicate exactly when the residue of convictions still shared with Christianity—a residue regarded and evaluated purely in itself— is no longer enough for the 'Christian name'. Yet if one were to make the criterion to consist in the inner attitude alone, then it would no longer be possible to make a distinction between a heretic and an apostate in every case, since there are undoubtedly cases when, in spite of just as complete a loss of a true attitude of faith (as in the case of the apostate, i.e. as a formal heretic), a particular person is nevertheless generally regarded as a mere heretic and not as an apostate. Hence, the correct interpretation of the obscure definition will have to say that heresy (in contrast to apostasy) is to be found wherever, on account of the greater amount of still professed Christian truths (which possibly are also still believed with at least human faith), there is a good deal of probability and (to a certain extent even legally important) presump- tion that such a person still attains also the one salvific reality in truth (signified both by what is still adhered to and by what is denied) in the truths to which he still adheres.

Of course, this still leaves us with a rather vague boundary line between heresy and apostasy and with a very great uncertainty about the result of the material adherence to the (relatively still) great number of Christian truths. The distinction between heresy and apostasy is indistinct because no one can really say *exactly* what degree of adher- ence to certain truths of faith still entitles one to use the name of Chris- tian.[6] Indeed, it would be possible to show that such a dividing line,

[6] If one wanted to answer this question very systematically and funda- mentally—i.e. if one wanted to draw a (theoretically) clear line of demarca- tion—then it would be necessary to say that a person is still a Christian if he affirms those truths which one must believe either *necessitate medii* and/ or *necessitate praecepti*, in order to be able to 'believe' at all. Yet, no matter how true this answer may be in itself, it can again be disputed whether one is still a heretic or already an apostate if one also rejects truths which must certainly be believed explicitly *necessitate praecepti*, what kind of explicitness is demanded (this again is by no means a clear concept), and above all what truths are essentially required for Christian faith, i.e. are to be believed explicitly *necessitate medii*, which is a well-known point of disagreement in scholastic theology.

making a clear-cut material distinction in both directions, presumably just does not exist.[7] Conversely, with regard to the outcome of real faith, even an adherence to a great number of Christian truths is uncertain, since even in such a case there may be an inner negation of the whole signified *reality* of faith; for otherwise it would not be possible to lose faith and justification through negation of one single (and thus, in certain circumstances, one sole) truth of faith. Yet one will nevertheless be able to say that, if the unfolded fullness of articulated truths of faith is to have any significance at all for a successful inner attitude of faith—a possibility which cannot reasonably be denied (although faith, grace, justification and thus the whole reality of faith referred to, may already be present even when there is merely belief in the existence of God: Heb 11.6)—then it cannot be denied that basically and *ceteris paribus* one must give a greater chance of real existential belief and thus of attaining the *whole* reality of salvation (in grace) to someone who adheres more explicitly, more clearly and in a more articulate way to the greater part of the Christian propositions of faith and who still aims explicitly at the Christian reality which he has encountered historically and which he calls 'by name' (whereby he has a real relationship to it which is still—in part—independent of the fact as to how he interprets this reality). Such a person must be called a heretic in distinction to an apostate for whom such a chance is indeed possible but at least is no longer present in a measure clearly perceptible to us.

These problems of the '*retinere nomen christianum*' give rise to two further considerations: one about the possibility of apostasy or mere heresy in an existential environment influenced by the Christian tradition, and the other about the inner essential ambiguity of heresy and of the heretic.

First of all: if the distinction between an apostate and a heretic consists properly speaking in the (even though) fluid and not absolutely

[7] For anyone who is of the perfectly defensible opinion that an act of Christian, supernatural and hence (presupposing love of God) justifying faith is possible in certain circumstances even if this act of faith includes only the existence of God as the guarantor and ultimate explanation of the moral order (whereby it is in certain circumstances possible also to make very mild, and thus optimistic, demands on the necessary explicitness of such an act), cannot, properly speaking, indicate any real limit of faith which, if transgressed, would make one cease to be justified, apart from a real (and existentially realized) denial of God itself.

clear, yet important, distinction within the 'continued adherence' as
regards the question as to how much chance and hope there is of
awakening and exercising the *whole* faith (with the cryptogamic re-
gaining of the whole reality of salvation under the contrary appearance
of heresy)—and if one does not think in a too obviously individualistic manner in this matter, but sees the sociological components in
every man's fulfilment of existence—then we may pose the question as
to whether (not thinking here in the sense of the terminology of Canon
law but in a theological sense) there can be anyone in a historical environment formed by Christianity who is more than a heretic—in other
words, an apostate. It should be noted that in the case of a heretic, it
does not matter whether or not he possesses justifying faith and hence
that contact with the reality of salvation which brings salvation. He
may be as far away from the faith in this respect as the apostate, since
he may be unbelieving in the personal and supernatural sense even
though, in the purely human formation of his theological conviction,
he still shares many propositions of faith (as such, i.e. as individual
propositions) with the Christian. The criterion for the distinction
between the heretic and the apostate, therefore, does not consist in the
kind of existential effect the adherence to propositions actually has on
grace and faith, but the kind of effect thay *can* have in the nature of
things. If this is remembered, then it will become clear that one of the
differences between heresy and apostasy—a difference which is perhaps
still quite important in practice but which theologically speaking is not
an essential one—consists in whether a person accepts certain (specifically Christian) propositions by an in itself purely *human* conviction,[8]
or whether these propositions are present for him only as co-determining factors of the spiritual situation in which he inevitably finds himself. Where, when and as long as someone lives unavoidably in an
environment which in a thousand ways (even though perhaps quite
anonymously and unsystematically) is co-formed by Christianity and
by the reality manifesting itself in the (rejected or still accepted)
Christian propositions of faith, such a person has always still a chance
of coming perhaps quite unconsciously into contact with this reality

[8] To which these propositions are not of themselves ordained, since of
their nature they are meant to be heard by the properly supernatural faith
in which the whole reality of faith and hence (at least implicitly) the objectively inseparable totality of the propositions of faith must and is always
accepted indivisibly.

and of (perhaps quite unsystematically) becoming a Christian. This process is not essentially different in the theological sense from the one in which someone takes hold of the full nature of faith and of the reality of salvation by surrendering himself to the inner dynamism of certain Christian propositions to which he had previously adhered in a merely human formation of opinion. In the one case he surrenders himself to the force of the propositions of his environment—to the external, 'public' opinion—and in the other case, to the force of the propositions of his inner, private opinion.

Hence, only where the defection can take place in such a way that the person who defects leaves the historical environment of Christianity altogether—and no longer (as far as the historical dimension is concerned) has to be in a dialogue of 'yes' or 'no' with Christianity—only then would there be a *pure* case of apostasy. Whether there *can* be such a case in those cultures which were at one time Christian, is a question of fact *and* of basic principles of theology; moreover, it is inevitably perhaps a question which today is already outdated by events. For if there is today anything like a unified planetary civilization, i.e. if today the elements and structures of every culture with their history have become—even though up till now still in different degrees of intensity —co-determining factors of this unified planetary civilization and thus of all individual cultures of the world, and if Christianity continues to exist in the world at all, then no one at all in the world today (although of course, in different but on the whole growing degrees) can withdraw himself from the outset from the dialogue with Christianity (no matter what may be the outcome). To this extent, therefore, no one can any longer live in a purely withdrawn, apo-static relationship to Christianity, but is forced to contradict it by explicitly separating himself from it by heresy. In a theological understanding, everything non-Christian and all non-Christians are somehow moving into a permanent and unavoidable role of explicit opposition towards Christianity and thus precisely of being orientated towards it. For gradually Christianity is coming to belong everywhere in the world to the roots of that (universal) history in which one still remains rooted even while in opposition. Seen in this light, we are completely justified in preferring to call the present-day world—terminologically—heretical rather than apostatical. The modern world remains compelled to carry on a dialogue with Christianity and cannot avoid the fact that in its self-realization the 'Christian name' always comes into the picture again, even when this world avoids reflecting on how much of the material of its historical form (with which it necessarily always has to come to terms again) is Christain. This of course presupposes conversely that present-day Christianity begins to have no longer any real 'paganism'[9] outside it, as something simply unrelated and completely separated, but that it must find in it a partner for dialogue in the common historical situation and existence, a partner who more or less has the characteristics of a heretic.[10]

More important still, however, is the second consideration, viz. the ambiguity of heresy and of heretics resulting from the 'retention of the Christian name'. Before we explain what is meant by this, it will be necessary to refer to a phenomenon which is of basic importance for what follows, viz. the unity of the reality of salvation and hence the unity of the doctrines of faith. The doctrines of faith understood as propositions are not merely kept together by the formal authority of a God who reveals them all and who proposes them all to man with a demand for his faith: they have an inner objective unity; they belong together and they describe one and the same reality of salvation under different aspects. Certainly, this one reality of salvation is not a uniformity; it is certainly the unity of a personally, spatio-temporally, etc., multi-dimensional plurality, so that the connection between these different realities (God, Christ, grace, saints, sacraments, Church, ages, places, etc.) is partly a necessary one and partly a freely established

[9] It must not be forgotten that since Old Testament times 'peoples', the 'pagans', were not separated and defined merely by a religious but by a cultural and sociological difference. Medieval, like modern Christianity (right up to our own day), always encountered the 'pagan' also as someone living in a different historical and cultural sphere, i.e. as someone who rejected Christianity 'from outside', and not 'from within', by a being and action which Christianity also could not help experiencing as something 'alien' and outside its sphere of existence. Precisely this fact, however, is now undergoing an ever accelerating change: the historical spheres of existence are overlapping, and this changes also essentially the character of the encounter between Christianity and the non-Christians. The latter, even though they remain non-Christians, cease to be simply those who up till now have not been touched by Christianity. They become—if one may formulate it in this way—unbaptized heretics.

[10] This is connected with the fact that the differences between 'foreign' and 'home' mission, 'paganism' and 'neo-paganism' are becoming more and more blurred.

connection. Yet they nevertheless have a real unity; they belong together, refer to each other, depend on each other, explain each other and form a unified meaningful whole.

It follows from this that anyone who really grasps one of these many realities in knowledge and in love, will also be drawn by this knowledge into the dynamism connected with the objective unity of this many-sided and yet one reality of salvation: one perception points to another, provides practice in the understanding of another, teaches the understanding of the meaning and of the spirit of the whole and thus prepares for the understanding of another part; every question which is imposed by some perception leads inevitably beyond the individual reality into the whole of reality. Furthermore, there is the fact that in each individual recognition of faith there is at work (at least in the sense of an offered saving grace) the one grace of God which as one and the same grace signifies the essence of the whole reality of salvation (since it is the self-communication of the divine Trinity in Christ) and thus has an inner relationship of nature to all saving realities and their knowledge. If this is right, however, then it must be said that everyone who picks and chooses heretically and thus does not accept the whole reality of salvation and yet (*'retento christiano nomine'*) adheres to an important part of it, is in an indefinable, undecided ambiguity of existence, which really can exist only if, and in so far as, this existence is still in an unfinished process of becoming. In so far as someone refuses heretically, he offends objectively (and possibly also subjectively) against the faith as a whole, not only because he contradicts the formal authority of the revealing God who guarantees the revelation as a whole, but even more essentially by the fact that in denying a truth he surrenders himself to an immanent logic of knowledge attached solely to the state of things which must eventually lead to the denial of the whole of revelation. Even though he does so explicitly to begin with only when confronted with a certain truth which he uses as the material for the exercising of his attitude, he nevertheless adopts an attitude which in its final and fully matured realization (even though he does not know and notice it as yet) must necessarily lead to the denial of the whole truth of revelation. Yet the converse is also true: in so far as he adheres to essential truths of Christian revelation, the opposite process is also operative in him; he is set on a course leading towards the whole of Christian truth. Hence his situation is ambiguous.

It may be that the heretic arrives by this grace at a really super-natural affirmation of faith in those Christian truths to which he adheres, and in this way (i.e. by the objective logic of these truths and by the *grace* of this act) he may grasp implicitly the *whole* reality and truth of Christianity theoretically and in practice; his heretical convictions, on the other hand, may only be 'opinions' (i.e. *'opinio'* in the thomistic sense) which he indeed holds and which he does not see to be irreconcilable with the act of his knowing, appropriating and existentially much deeper personal faith, but which are existentially much more peripheral, uncertain and temporary than the person concerned may realize. If such is the case, two things must always be remembered.

Firstly: The understanding of and adherence to all these many propositions which a person thinks he sees to be true, does not have exactly the same nature logically and existentially with regard to each particular proposition. Man (ultimately by reason of the bodily, physiological and sense conditioning of his knowledge) is that being which can adhere to the contradictory and to the opposed. Yet this does not mean in its turn that these contradictory propositions could be affirmed simultaneously in strictly the same kind of acts. Rather, the truth of the matter is that such propositions have a different position and rank in the structural reality of the logical and existential 'system' of a man, and this must be so, for otherwise this logical and existential 'schizophrenia' of the normal person would be quite impossible (this does not mean, however, that these different value levels of the different propositions must be consciously grasped by the person). One proposition will be a proposition affirmed with utter determination as a strict 'judgement' and will be made the real fixed point from which all one's other propositions (in so far as they can be surveyed) take their focus; other propositions will simply be mere 'opinions', hypotheses and speculations, as long as there is nothing better, and always ready to be corrected and to be abandoned. Between these propositions there exists the same effective logical and existential relationship as there can be between a man's moral acts: he loves God from the very core of his free being ('from the heart') and yet commits peripherally a venial sin which contradicts his basic decision but this only because it is after all in the objective, intentional sense (*i.e. quoad materiam*) and existentially (in the centrality of the act) of less qualitative weight than the basic act which it contradicts.

Secondly: Even heresy itself includes once more a dynamism towards the whole Christian truth, although not of course in so far as heresy is simply and formally error and nothing else. But error never exists in this abstract pure form in concrete heresies, in the actual way in which they are affirmed. Heresies which become historically effective and powerful are not simply mere propositions arising from stupidity, obstinacy and bad information; rather, they are supported by a genuine original experience formed by some reality and truth. It can easily be the case—and even will be the case in most instances—that this reality and the truth contained in it (even though it is not denied and is always also seen and expressed in some way) has not yet been seen and experienced in orthodox Christianity in the same explicit and passionate manner and with the same depth and power of vision as the historical error imposed on and demanded of someone who subsequently realizes this genuine experience in the form of error. Just as evil lives by the power of the good and can always be willed only by force of the desire for that good which is the permanent residue in evil and without which it could not even be evil but would simply be nothing (which cannot be willed at all), so it is also in the relationship between the affirmed and experienced truth and the really achieved error. Even error lives by truth. Great, complete error has inevitably a great content and a powerful internal driving force, both of which urge it on towards the *one* truth, to the truth which the heretic has perhaps already actually attained in that Christian truth which he explicitly professes by his retention of the Christian name.

Yet the opposite may also be true: error may be the real, central and basic act of the heretic and the real systematizing principle of his total mental system, while the still retained Christian truths ('*nomen christianum*') are still present merely as peripheral 'opinions', continually in danger of being recognized as contradictions to the basic theoretical and practical tendency and hence in danger of being 'revised' and excluded. In spite of the truths of Christianity still adhered to as 'opinions', the intended reality is lost completely and the person is left without grace; it is pushed out by the heretical error introduced existentially and radically into the very centre of the person.

This ambiguity can never be overcome by *reflection*. If this were not so, then the person would know with absolute certainty whether he really believes or not. To know this, however, is never granted to reflection, just as one can never have absolute certainty about whether one is justified. Reflection (i.e. the objectifying, propositional self-expression) never adequately attains the person as what he is and what he realizes of himself by his immediate outward-directed actions. This cannot happen by the very fact that the act of reflection is itself once more an act which forms and alters the person and which alters the system by attempting to objectify and determine it. Hence this ambiguity itself is part of a constant process (in the individual as well as in the social history of heresy): the deciding centre of the person can constantly be shifted and gradually stray away from the true Christian propositions, held on to as its real truth, to the heretical errors, and equally vice versa. One can never say with *absolute* certainty whether a heretic exists within the truth in spite of his heresy, on account of the Christian truths to which he adheres, or whether in spite of these truths, he actually is in error on account of his adhered to heretical propositions. This ambiguity cannot be resolved; one cannot say what is the actual position, for this historical process itself never stops but is always on the move, and every determinable moment of this history may already be surpassed by the next, if it is fixed in a pronouncement. An error can already be paralysed for a long time and be excluded from the basis of the spiritual person, even though it is still adhered to and defended in its propositional, theoretical formulations with a great deal of verbal subtlety. And conversely, a seemingly small error (small, that is, in comparison with the great mass of true propositions adhered to) can already have infiltrated mortally into the core of the spiritual person and hence have become the true, all-embracing, although still not fully effective norm of the relationship of the person to the whole of reality. This can be the case even though the person still adheres to a great many truths basically and objectively irreconcilable with this error and even though this collection of truths has the necessary appearance of being correct and all-embracing with the result that the deadliness and the heretical isolation of error remains hidden to the reflection of both the heretic and of others.

III. THE CHANGE IN FORM OF HERESY

Our reflections about the problems arising out of the traditional notion of heresy and of the heretic have provided us with certain preliminaries to help us with our understanding of a phenomenon which we want to call the change in form of heresy.

Before going on to develop these preliminary aids to an understanding of this change in the form of heresy, we must first reflect on a certain characteristic of our present-day intellectual situation which in its present-day manner and extent was unknown to previous ages, viz. the great amount and variety of experiences, of knowledge and of sciences, which can no longer be comprehended or mastered by any one individual and which precisely *in* this unmastered state (however paradoxical this may sound) co-determine the spiritual situation of the individual. Of course, man has never lived simply on the basis of what he knew or even of what he had systematized by reflection. To *this* extent the spiritual situation of the man of today is not really different from what it was in previous ages: the space of his spiritual existence and its structures (understood as pre-established *a priori* elements of his thought, decisions and actions) are co-determined by what he does not know and hence also cannot and need not be responsible for, but which nevertheless belong to the forces of his spiritual existence. But in the past, these powers were not perceptions, theories, opinions and postulates of *men* themselves, but objective data: soil, race, talents and so on, things therefore which on the whole still possessed the innocence of having been created by God. Whenever, in the past, certain spiritual human realities belonged to these powers of existence, they were fundamentally comprehensible to the individual; everyone could learn and know them for himself, could take up a position towards them, could balance them among themselves and could bring them together into a system for which he himself was responsible. Anything he was unable to learn in this way, did not affect him essentially in his spiritual existential situation. Whatever he did not know, even though it was something knowable, did not take place in his life considered as a whole.

Today all this is different. We live in an age where everyone's knowledge has concrete consequences for everyone else—in other words, is 'present' as a power of his own existential sphere for everyone else—and yet can no longer be known by each individual. Have we adverted sufficiently to this peculiarity of the situation of every person? The known world, the world of knowledge, of experiences or theorems, hypotheses and claims on one's attention, has become pluralistic[11] in a

---

[11] We must refrain here from reflecting more exactly on the existential, ontological and always already present basis of the *possibility* of this plurality: on the circumstance that man never possesses a knowledge which originates from *one* original source and from *one* original systematic design alone;

way which was not the case in the past. Naturally, even in the past not everyone knew everything which 'was known', i.e. by others. But it was basically possible for him to learn it; the amount of material to be known could still be comprehended; it was possible to learn more or less everything during a few years of study at the 'University' (where the *universum of* knowledge was really available), at least all that was of basic importance for the whole world of the known and did not merely signify some detailed knowledge necessary only for some special professional function within society but not for the construction of the 'world-view' as a whole. For anyone who could not learn in this way, the things to be learnt which he did not learn, simply did not exist for him in his own world: any anthropological reality which really occurred in the world of a shoemaker during the Middle Ages was also understood by him; and whatever he did not understand, did not happen in *his* world.

Today the reality of man has become pluralistic. No one can hold his 'system' to be even approximately identical (even only materially) with everything that is to be known about it. We come to a limit: the sum total of what an individual has the time and is physically capable of knowing and assimilating, and the whole field of what is known, can no longer be even approximately equated to each other. Naturally, one tries to overcome this difficulty: intermediaries are introduced and teams are formed; every science in fact always succeeds anew in achieving a break-through to some sort of systematic knowledge which simplifies the whole of the knowledge of a science again and makes it more manageable. Yet all this does not fundamentally alter the fact that the individual himself can no longer administer the whole of the knowledge which supports him and which helps to determine his existence (and this even as a spiritual person and not merely in his physical, biological and external social reality). As has been said, if this knowledge—possessed by others but which can no longer be mastered by

---

rather he has from the very outset a plurality of experiences which encounter each other only *a posteriori* in a historical process of reflection and which must first of all be synthesized in a never finished process. This has always been the case. But what is new is the fact that the plurality of possible experiences has increased to such an extent that today no single individual can any longer even come near to having personally and fully even merely the experiences of those with whom he comes into direct contact in the biological, sociological and (which is decisive) spiritual sense.

the individual—did not play any part in his own existence, then everyone could just forget about it, just as it was quite indifferent for the life
of a Bavarian farmer in the year 1400 (as far as *his* life was concerned)
whether or not he knew to what dynasty Thutmosis II of Egypt belonged. If this unknown and unknowable knowledge were simply of an
innocent factual nature like the (equally unknown) functioning, for
instance, of the peristalsis of the intestines, then one could surrender
oneself to it with childlike trust and just let it go on in its natural way.
But this knowledge is not knowledge of indisputable facts and of so-
called results of scientific investigations (which the man of the nineteenth century trusted much more naïvely than the thirteenth-century
theologian trusted the Bible). This unaccounted, unmastered knowledge is an amorphous (and yet immensely efficacious) mass of real
results of scientific investigations, of theorems, hypotheses, postulates,
wishful thinking and utopias, of one-sided tendencies, dark inclinations,
in which are involved good sense and simplicity, every human dimension, guilt, the powers of darkness and divine inspiration from above.
The whole of this world of the spirit created by man himself takes on
concrete form in technology, discoveries, sociological institutions, influences brought to bear on people's attention by advertising and a
thousand similar realities which have become again physical, and this
world is present everywhere 'in the atmosphere' of the spiritual situation of every person. Of course, within this amorphous mass of the
'objective mind' there are always again beginnings of certain structures—islands of meaning—just as at the commencement of a process
of crystallization, the first crystalline systems shoot through the mother-
lye like a shaft of lightning. But such formations remain islands of
meaning within an amorphous mass to which new materials are added
faster than their organization can progress.

It is no real comfort (and a false sedative, current among Christians)
to say about this situation that we do at least know the 'principles' and
general norms of the mental penetration, mastering and synthesis of the
whole of this formless *materia prima* of the spirit: the principles of logic,
ontology, the natural law, social teaching, etc. This information could
be a *complete* comfort only for a rationalist, i.e. for someone who thinks
that the universal, *a priori* principles are really presented to him in their
unchangeable purity in the face of the world of an always incomprehensible experience. In reality, the adequate understanding of these principles themselves becomes conscious only at the end of a slow process,

in the encounter with the material of historical experience which is to be structured and mastered by these principles. The incomprehensible immensity and growing pluralism of experiences, which are no longer possible for any single person, obscures even these principles and makes them more difficult to manage. No matter how great their permanent, *a priori* validity may be, they reveal their *absolutely exact* meaning— what they imply, exclude, forbid, etc. (and it is the exact meaning which matters)—only by being brought into contact with experience. Experience, however, is pluralistic, and so pluralism is insurmountable. The new situation referred to here can be seen in the frequently deplored fact that there no longer is any unified terminology, that there is a babel of languages, and so on.

The cause of this confusion of languages is found in the experiences of the many[12] which are simply no longer reconcilable in one individual. These experiences explain also how one cannot expect any basic improvement in this state of affairs, no matter how useful, worthy of pursuit and even practicable partial improvements may be. In the past there used to be a fairly unified terminology in the realm of the sciences of the spirit, since the contemplated material, the imaginative models and the examples could be and were the same for all, and because their distribution of weight, impressiveness, etc., were approximately equally great or at least showed only individual differences (or belonged to social structures which from the outset and for other reasons—as, for instance, because of separated cultural spheres—never even entered 'into dialogue' with one another and hence could not cause any linguistic confusion). It must always be remembered in this connection that this insurmountable pluralism of our experiences of the world is not

[12] The pluralism of experiences does not exist merely (to state this explicitly) in the physical, biological world—i.e. in the natural sciences whose results can no longer be surveyed by a single individual—but equally in the experiences of the sciences of the spirit. No one, for instance, can any longer have a living contact at first hand with the whole extent and breadth of the history of philosophy or with the whole of the wide-open history of cultures, of the political life of nations, of music, of law or of other human realities. Each person knows merely different sections of all this. The difference of experiences creates human beings who find it much more difficult than before to make themselves understood and to communicate with each other. Basically, this state of affairs cannot be overcome, no matter how much it may be possible to improve it.

one whose individual moments are separated by a mental and cultural no-man s-land wedging itself in between individual social levels, cultures and peoples, but that it is a pluralism in *one* and the same spiritual world in which live the many members of the one planetary world-civilization, of the classless society and of all possible technological and sociological concretizations of these structures of the pluralistic, objective mind. Hence, everyone is embraced, sustained and co-formed by a spiritual world of man for which he himself can no longer be responsible in his own knowledge and decision in the way in which in the past a person could make his spiritual world his own 'possession'.

The basic characteristic of the situation of the man of today must now be related to the ambiguity of Christian existence which we discovered when thinking about the classical notion of heresy. To enable us to do this, it will be necessary to point out yet another circumstance which up till now has not been mentioned explicitly. The ambiguity of the situation of the heretic is indeed particularly pronounced and disturbing (in his case) when measured by the critical standard of the true Christian believer and when seen from his point of view. But it is really something which is also found in the case of the orthodox Christian. As has been said already, no one can know with absolute and reflex certitude whether he really believes. For no one can give a final account as to whether the propositions of faith which he is certainly willing to accept as his own, are also accepted by him in his free theoretical consciousness with such depth and existential power of free decision (and without such a free 'agreement' there can be no faith, but at the most a sympathizing with recognized propositions) that these propositions have a sure theoretical and practical validity governing all those other norms and ideals which everyone also inevitably possesses.[13] The undoubtedly existing subjective system of values which one freely constitutes for oneself, is not fully subject to absolutely certain reflection. Yet if one were to objectify everything which is present in a person and even in the most orthodox—all his judgements, prejudices, attitudes, preferences and opinions (and all this *also* always and ultimately not something which can be analysed and seen to be the

---

[13] There is not and cannot be any life of the spirit which, in a purely 'fideistic' way, is nourished and sustained *merely* by the motives of revelation and their continuance. The experience of the individual—even considering him as an individual—is pluralistic both from the direction of revelation and of the world.

consequence of free decisions and not merely something independent of them and preceding them)—then there would also appear 'propositions' (side by side with the propositions of objective faith) which are objectively heretical (even though they are never explicitly pronounced by this person in this objectified way). Even in the case of the orthodox Christian, neither he himself nor anyone else could decide with absolute certainty whether these 'heresies' are for him merely 'opinions' incapable of destroying his existentially radical decision in favour of the truths of faith, i.e. his real 'assent of faith' (as an existentially 'weighty' act), or whether on the contrary these convictions of faith remaining untouched *qua* 'opinions' (and no matter how much they coincide objectively with the whole of Christian doctrine) are nevertheless merely residues and a façade, behind which lurks quite a different (equally theoretical although not as clearly reflex and formulated) world of freely accepted convictions.

After these preliminary reflections, we are now in a position to state and explain our theses about the change in form of heresy. We can formulate this as follows: there is far more 'cryptogamic' heresy today than ever before. This cryptogamic heresy exists also in the Church, alongside her explicit orthodoxy. This kind of heresy has an essential tendency to remain unsystematized, and this fact constitutes its peculiarly and extraordinarily dangerous nature. Christianity's attitude of anxiety, watchfulness and touchiness with regard to heresy—an attitude essential to Christianity—ought nowadays to be directed above all against this cryptogamic heresy. This is extremely difficult especially because this kind of heresy is to be found also in the members of the Church, and because it is very difficult to distinguish it from legitimate tendencies, from the justified spirit of the age, etc.

One might start with the fact that cryptogamic heresy exists today to a far greater extent than ever before, and try to deduce this thesis in an *a priori* theological manner. One could say, to begin with, that there 'must' always be heresy (in the sense of a 'must' of salvation history, where it exists in spite of the fact that it 'should not' exist), and this as a possibility which cannot be so foreign to the Church from the very outset as to ensure that the Church Christian as such could not even be seriously threatened by it. One could next point out that the development of the Church's consciousness of faith has gradually made the norm of faith itself—in all its formal, juridically clear structures—an object of faith, that this development has come to a certain completion in the definition of the Pope's infallible teaching primacy, and that therefore there can no longer be any doubt or uncertainty (as there was in earlier ages) as to whether or not an *explicit* doctrine belongs to the Christian Church. Then, combining both these considerations, it would follow that the kind of heresy which even today is a danger for the Christian in the Church and yet 'must' exist, must and does in fact take on a less explicit form, i.e. takes on the form of cryptogamic heresy, whereby it presents a smaller surface for attack by the *magisterium*, and so has a greater chance of being dangerous within the Church. Even on this basis, one could already point to certain manifestations within the most recent history of the Church since the time of Modernism, manifestations which could clarify this understanding of the existence and nature of cryptogamic heresy that we have gained in an *a priori* way.[14]

But we can also use an *a posteriori* approach to come to an understanding of the nature and existence of cryptogamic heresy. For this we must combine what we said about the pluralism of the uncontrolled powers of the spiritual existence of each individual (a pluralism which the individual can no longer catch up with or overcome in any adequate and full sense) and what we saw about the ambiguity of each individual's existence in faith (the possibility of being a latent unbeliever). The man of today lives in a spiritual existential environment which, as an individual, he is unable to measure fully and for which he cannot take complete responsibility. This existential environment, however, is undoubtedly also co-formed by attitudes, doctrines and tendencies which must be qualified as heretical and as contradicting the teaching of the gospel. All these heretical elements which thus co-determine the existential environment of each individual, do not necessarily need to objectify themselves in theoretical propositions. This will indeed happen quite frequently, but is neither necessary nor decisive. Actual behaviour, concrete measures, etc., can be determined by a heretical attitude, without this attitude formulating itself reflexly in abstract doctrinal propositions. It is sufficient if it realizes itself in the concrete material of life. It must be noted in this connection that these material objectifications (in the practical sphere of one's life, of one's style of life, of morals, customs, actions and omissions, of emphases, of stressing some aspects and of playing others down) are particularly and equally

[14] Cf. K. Rahner, *Gefahren im heutigen Katholizismus* (Einsiedeln³ 1955), pp. 63–80.

suitable both for objectifying and for hiding the basic heretical attitude. For often, viewed purely in the abstract, they are not clearly conceivable *only* as objectifications of the heretical spirit, if we prescind from their (often difficult to measure) intensity, their place within the totality of spiritual existence, and so on. The reverence shown to the human body, for instance, and the idolization of the body are difficult to distinguish one from the other in their tangible manifestations, especially in situations where there is a certain 'need to make up for' a lack of realization in the Christian evaluation of the human body in the past. Hence it becomes doubly difficult both to decide whether such an evaluation of the body is still Christian or already heretical, and also whether the seemingly Christian protest against such tangible manifestations is really an anti-heretical Christian attitude or whether it arises out of an old, historically conditioned understanding of human existence which, because of its long association with real Christianity, appears as something Christian itself though in actual fact it has perhaps been very much influenced by latent heresies of previous ages. Yet if—on the one hand —a heresy although very latent nevertheless exists, and if—on the other hand—it co-determines modern man by reason of the insurmountable pluralism of his spiritual existential environment, and does this precisely in such a way that one does not take up any reflex and systematic position towards it, and indeed is not even capable of doing so (explicitly), then we have the phenomenon which we refer to as cryptogamic heresy.

It must be noted in this regard that this notion—like the traditional notion of heresy—may well leave it a completely open and abstract question as to whether this heresy is present in a 'formally' or merely 'materially' reflex manner (even though naturally not in a reflection on its heretical content as such) or merely in an unreflected exercise; in other words, whether it is present as a dangerous peripheral 'opinion' or as the basic existential act in the very centre of the person. We may say for the time being that everybody today is infected with the bacteria and virus of cryptogamic heresy, even though he does not on this account have to be qualified as having become diseased with it. Everyone conforms at least unconsciously, and at least in the form of peripheral 'opinions', to the peripheral existential attitudes of his surroundings, attitudes which originate from a basic heretical attitude and in which there is sufficient *'materia gravis'* to constitute actual heretical attitudes. We can all only hope (but not know with absolute, reflex certitude) that these heretical or pseudo-heretical attitudes, practices, motivations, etc., present within us, have not already become part of the structure of our basic decisions (in a reflex, theoretical manner) but that these decisions also correspond in fact to the systematically and explicitly approved norms of the gospel.

This cryptogamic heresy lives also in the Church. After all, the Church is not a substantial entity over and above the community of Christians but is 'the throng of the faithful' themselves, without prejudice to the fact that this 'people of God' is constituted socially in a sacred society, is governed by its office-holders and is led by the Holy Spirit. The Church understood thus as the mass of the faithful lives on in this even spiritually pluralistic world of technology, of modern mass society, of unified planetary civilization, of constitutionally guaranteed freedom of thought, of propaganda—in brief, of all the characteristics which today qualify each individual's sphere of human existence. This Church lives therefore in an heretically or crypto-heretically structured world of cryptogamic heresies. Hence her members cannot help being infected also in a cryptogamic heretical way. For the Church is the Church of sinners, and it is an unquestionable fact that mutually contradictory principles can co-exist (even though on different levels of existential assent) in the same person, especially when we consider that they are to a certain extent not even explicitly formulated and do not need to be so formulated in order to be effectively present. This kind of heresy may be present in any member, even in those belonging to the hierarchical leadership of the Church. After all, there is no principle in the Church which would make it impossible for there to be unbelievers even among the members of the hierarchy, although this would be in a hidden way and without their admitting it to themselves. This unformulated, cryptogamic heresy does not need to be formal, culpable heresy. Particularly today, the elements of a person's spiritual sphere of existence are (less frequently than before) elements which have been passed by the explicit and reflex censorship of the theoretical and personal responsibility of the individual. Naturally, the Church always defends herself even against this cryptogamic heresy in her midst. The Church as a whole—in her members who pray and carry their cross, in her poor and in her forsaken (and yet patiently enduring) members, in brief, in all her great and small, known and unknown saints—lives the true and unfalsified gospel over and over again in such depth, existential decisiveness, genuineness and purity, that it is certain that she will not succumb to the heresy in her midst. Even though she is the Church of sinners, she is also—by the power of God and by that unconquerable grace of Christ promised to her as a whole which embraces all the weakness of man—the unconquerably holy Church and the Church who stands fast in the truth. This undoubtedly means not only that by her proclamation she always bears witness to God's truth as against the (explicit or latent) heretical error of the 'world', but also that she truly 'realizes' this truth testified to by her in the personal 'assent' of many (even though not all) of her members. She does this in such a way that even though cryptogamic heresy may indeed always remain present as a mortal danger to each individual in the Church, this heresy does not become so powerful in the Church as a whole as to make the Church pay merely lip-service to the gospel, when interiorly she has become heretical and has thus fallen away from this truth.

This also helps to make the second thesis understandable: this cryptogamic heresy exists also in the Church in and together with her explicit orthodox beliefs. The fact of belonging to the Church and of explicitly declaring oneself for her teaching is not an absolute and mechanically effective protection against heresy. Even in the Church, everyone is asked by God individually in his own, inalienable conscience as to whether deep down, underneath the outward appearances of orthodoxy (which can deceive not only others but even oneself), he is not unconsciously a heretic in the sense of cryptogamic heresy. For this is perfectly possible. One must not try to water down this statement by saying that the phenomenon referred to is simply a question of the well-known fact that someone may in his *practical* life offend against his theoretical principles, and that thus theory and practice may not conform to each other. Of course, this phenomenon also exists, and it is not always easy to distinguish it in the individual case from what we mean by cryptogamic heresy and its danger within the Church. There is an implicit, unformulated falsification of the standards of value themselves (and not merely a practical offending against right standards recognized as valid in themselves). This unformulated falsification of the standards of value themselves, this cryptogamic heresy—which naturally seems at first sight to be more active in the field of moral norms while it leads to the treating of the other norms of faith, which do not seem to be directly relevant to morality, merely with an existential indifference and with an uninterested acceptance—can certainly be accompanied by a verbal orthodoxy and a frightened, 'correct' care never to express 'views' which might come into conflict with the official norms of faith. It must be emphasized once more: there can be, not only 'practical' heresy, but also theoretical heresy, i.e. proper heresy (even though cryptogamic), under the appearance of orthodoxy. This phenomenon must not be confused with the (also occurring) phenomenon of conscious hypocrisy in faith for social or other similar reasons. In *that* case, the secret heretic (or apostate) is reflexly conscious of his lie; in this one, the heretic deceives himself (and not primarily others), for this self-deception is a constitutive element of the pheno-menon of cryptogamic heresy in the form in which it can and really does occur in the Church, so that no one is proof against this heresy by his well-intentioned belonging to the Church and by his explicit pro-fession of her doctrine.

The implicit nature of heresy in the member of the Church finds a strange ally in the man of today, in his reluctance to let himself be tied down to concepts in religious questions. The man of today is more likely to discuss quite freely the most intimate details of his sex life with a psychoanalyst than to carry on a 'religious discussion' with someone else from whom he cannot hope to get absolute agreement right from the start (since he is, for instance, the official representative of the Church), a discussion which prescinds entirely from himself and is concerned with purely theoretical matters. There may be many reasons for this strange phenomenon (at least in Central Europe): God's 'absence' as considered by modern philosophers (and not merely in fashionable talk), the feeling of insecurity in all these matters in view of the disruption in the world and in our time, caused by the incalculable number of religious world-views and standpoints—disruptions which each individual encounters in his own personal life with a sharpness and forcibleness unusual in previous ages—and above all, the feeling of the immeasurable distance between religious expression in human con-cepts and the reality signified by it, a feeling which is in itself quite correct and positive and is experienced almost as something killing all true dialogue. Whatever may be the precise reason, it remains an un-deniable fact that the man of today finds religious and theological reflection very difficult, and clear formulations of matters of faith are inclined to impress him as impious, smart and typically clerical. This need not yet be accompanied in any way by a flight from the institution-ally constituted practice of religion or even from the Church. On the contrary, this reticence in the face of clear concepts may quite easily result today in an instinctive attempt to avoid any conceptual formulation of religious matters as far as one's own existential attitude is concerned and hence may precisely in this way lead to a certain tolerance towards the traditional, conceptually formulated doctrine of the Church in the feeling that in any case one could not say 'it' any better, so that, as a result of this reticence which has become almost a taboo, even educated people will nowadays frequently allow themselves to hold on to the most childish formulations of faith. This attitude, however, becomes then the reason why one's heretical attitude does not become a theoretically expressed and exactly formulated heresy (as it did in the past): one lives in heresy but shrinks from formulating it as a 'system of doctrine' and from placing it before the Church for mutual discussion. One lives, for instance, in a religious, metaphysical agnosticism, yet timidly avoids maintaining that the first Vatican Council was wrong in teaching that man can recognize God's existence by the light of reason. One prefers not to ask about what is and what is not the real meaning of this statement made by the Vatican Council, one does not formulate and thus also does not come into conflict with formulae. Yet one is nevertheless a cryptogamic heretic in this case right in the midst of the Church, and this perhaps in spite of a not insignificant 'practice' of one's religion.

This already explains also the next, previously stated proposition: cryptogamic heresy is not merely *de facto* a reflexly non-articulated heresy, but also has a positive tendency to remain such. Certainly man has basically the impulse (one of the most essential existentials of his existence) to give an account of himself to himself, to objectify what he is and to retrace what in the first place is merely actual (both in being and in action) to the necessary grounds of nature. But man has also the opposite impulse, and this not merely because of more general considerations such as the fact that fundamentally reflection never fully attains the whole of man's spiritual existence and man is always more (even spiritually and personally) than he explicitly says of himself in propositions gained by systematic reflection, or the fact that there is the phenomenon of self-deceit, of repression, of the false 'good conscience', etc., all of which is conceivable only if there is such a contrary basic impulse. There are also special reasons in this case for this phenomenon of a positively holding on to the unreflected state of this basic heretical attitude. We have already mentioned one of these reasons: the dread of religious reflection in general. But there are still other reasons for this.

One of these reasons is a certain strange good will towards the Church which is to be found in many educated people of the twentieth century, a good will greater than in the nineteenth century. This good will cannot be explained as it could be at that time—if it was still present at all—by a certain social link with tradition; it has quite different roots today (roots which in themselves, however, have just as little to do with a genuine religious decision as the aristocratic and bourgeois, social and religious traditionalism of the last century). In contrast to the age of self-conscious individualism and liberalism, the man of today no longer has as much confidence in his own opinions; above all, he is no longer convinced of the possibility of founding a religious community on such a private opinion, without thereby losing oneself in a hopeless sectarianism and religious fanaticism. If, however, one does not have much confidence in one's own opinion and is indeed very little convinced that someone else will be right (in this case, the authority of the Church) yet has nevertheless the more or less clear feeling that the religion (which one wants) must somehow entail also a religious community, then one will find that the easiest way to 'solve' the problem posed by these three positions is not to let it come to a conflict in the first place: one does not articulate one's sceptical or otherwise heretical or pseudo-heretical attitude, and thus 'manages to get by'. Furthermore, one perhaps adapts oneself in such a way that quite instinctively one carries on a certain formation of groups[15] within the universal Church, establishes a kind of special 'chapel' within the big Church, where one is 'amongst kindred spirits' and where therefore there is less danger from the very outset of subjects coming up for discussion which might force one to abandon the attitude of 'letting sleeping dogs lie'.

The actual tactics adopted by cryptogamic heresy in order to *remain* latent, vary in different cases. Frequently,[16] they simply consist in an attitude of mistrust and of resentment against the Church's *magisterium*,

[15] This of course does not imply anything against the legitimate formation of groups in an open and confident relationship to the whole Church and her hierarchical leadership. Every religious Order, for instance, with its own proper spirit different from other Orders, is also such a formation of groups which makes the individual's life in the universal Church more bearable.

[16] We repeat, in what follows, a few pages which we had already written earlier on, viz. in *Gefahren im heutigen Katholizimus* (Einsiedeln[3] 1955), pp. 75–78.

that widespread feeling of being controlled in a suspicious and narrow-minded way by the Church's *magisterium* in one's research and teaching, the opinion that one just 'cannot say what one thinks' (and deems it quite legitimate to think in 'good' conscience). Does one not here and there come up against the attitude that (at least among friends) one can say more than one could write? Or one is given the impression that one ought to be glad that this or that is being said by Protestant theologians outside the Church and that one must read it in their works, since it is dangerous to say it oneself. One may sometimes get the impression that the theoretical opinion of a theologian hides itself behind the forms and figures of his historical investigations in order to make itself known without becoming tangible. Is there not here and there something like an esoteric doctrine which is handed on orally? Is there not unformulated heresy which avoids definite theses, which works merely with omissions and one-sided perspectives, and which in the wrong spirit by-passes the thesis and goes straight into the practical field? Is something like this not present when, for instance, one assiduously avoids using the word 'hell' and where there no longer is any mention —or at least only with a great deal of uncertainty and embarrassment— of the Evangelical Counsels, vows and the Religious state, unless there is no other way out? How often do preachers, talking to educated people in our part of the world, still speak to their audience about temporal punishment, indulgences, angels, fasting, the devil (or at most speak only of the 'demonic' in man), of Purgatory, of prayer for the Holy Souls, and similar old-fashioned things? Whenever someone advises us to preserve our 'inner freedom' and 'to continue to live positively in the Church while treating the Confessional as something which in fact is not competent for us as long as it administers the sacrament of forgiveness in the service of the Moloch of legalism',[17] then this is a recommendation to practise such cryptogamic heresy and, with rather strange irony, it may affect especially those who are most proud of the untroubled orthodoxy of their time-tested views and doctrines: heresy in the garb of indifference.

God's truth is always one, always remains the same and is final; it is proclaimed by the *magisterium* of the Church. Whenever and wherever this *magisterium* has stated this truth entrusted to it by Christ, and has stated it in a form binding on the conscience of the believer, then this truth is true and valid in this form for all times; in

[17] Thus in E. Michel, *Die Ehe* (Stuttgart 1949), p. 128.

such a case, theology and the proclamation of the truth will always refer back to these formulations of revealed truth formed in the course of the history of the Church, with the assurance that the intended truth has really been correctly stated in these formulae (however true it may be that every formulation of the truths of the faith—since it is expressed in human words—never corresponds fully to the object referred to and so, at least in principle, can always be replaced by an even better and more comprehensive one); in such a case, an intellectual and conceptual formulation is never merely a subsequent reflex of an experience of faith which of itself would be a-rational (as is maintained by the modernistic understanding of the intellectual element of faith). Yet this divine truth expressed in human words is not given to us so that it may simply go on being repeated with everlasting monotony in the textbooks of dogmatic theology. No, it is meant to bring about a living encounter with man in the concrete, to enter into his mind and heart, by becoming flesh and blood, and to bring man to truth. For this, however, it is necessary that man makes it his own ever anew. Man, just as he is formed by his age, his experiences, his fate, his spiritual situation which is not merely the situation of ecclesiastical Christianity but is also the situation of his age in general, must hear this divine message ever anew in the whole of his characteristic situation. And since the faith of man cannot be constituted by a message which might be heard but only by the message which is actually heard—and since the truth of revelation cannot and will not exist on earth in an external 'in itself' of eternal validities, but only in its actually 'being believed'—the pure, eternally unchanging truth of the gospel must, for this very reason, bear in every age the imprint of that age within the concrete realizations of its knowledge and acknowledgement.

If it does not bear this imprint, or at least does not have it to a sufficient extent, then it does not thereby become less time-determined or more universally valid, but rather merely bears within itself the spirit of a bygone age to which one has become accustomed and which, on account of its age and well-known form, is wrongly regarded as the expression of the eternal validity of the truth of the gospel. In such a case, this freezing of the form in which the truth of the gospel is expressed, is itself nothing else than a dangerous symptom of the indifference towards the truth of the gospel under which a period suffers, whether it knows it or not, and a symptom of the lack of a power of appropriation and practical assimilation from which such pure 'traditionalists' suffer. Who would doubt the fact that this kind of heresy exists even in our own age, a heresy in which dead orthodoxy is merely the result and expression of an inner indifference towards truth, in which one lets something endure because basically it is so indifferent to oneself that one shrinks even from the effort of getting rid of it or of disputing it?

Anyone who thinks that all this has been stated to lead to a sniffing around for heresies in every corner and to starting a hunt for concealed heretics, has misunderstood what has been our intention in all this. We have drawn attention to the signs of the actual presence of such crypto-gamic heresies simply as an *a posteriori* confirmation of the *a priori* thesis that there must be such a change in form of heresy today. Anyone who wishes to draw practical conclusions from this theological specu-lation, should first of all fear this danger in himself and try to avoid it. For a mere desire for orthodoxy and for submitting obediently to the *magisterium* does not yet protect a person completely against heresy in the sense intended here.

From what has been said, it follows inevitably that the Church's *magisterium* can undertake only relatively little with the means used up till now, when it wishes to combat this danger of cryptogamic heresy. It can proclaim the truth; it can itself bring heretical tendencies to a conceptual formulation (as was done for the first time in Pius X's Encyclical on Modernism) and then condemn it in this form. It can do very little, however, against silent heresy itself; it is to a large extent helpless when faced with a heresy which gives open expression only to correct propositions and keeps quiet about those which do not suit it; it is to a large extent helpless in the face of the heresy of indifference and of theologically sterile integralism. The *magisterium* lives today even inevitably under the temptation of aggravating the difficulty, and this indeed for the same reason which has caused the change in form of heresy. For, since today (especially since the time of the Vatican Council) it has become aware of its own authority which is now acknowledged most reflexively as an object of faith, the *magisterium* may be tempted more than ever before to suppress heretical lines of thought merely by its formal authority without seeing to it that they are also overcome from within the inner nature of the matter itself. Thus there arises the temptation to combat heresy, as it were, merely through administrative channels (by placing certain works on the index, by removing suspect lecturers, etc.) instead of combating it in the proper manner of the *teaching* office, i.e. by a positive formulation of the true teaching so that error is really 'uprooted'. The *magisterium* may be tempted to command people to hold their peace and to keep silence, without saying or letting there be said also just the right word, and saying it or letting it be said in such a way that it is not merely actually true but also enters into the understanding and heart of men. As stated, this is not an insurmountable temptation, but it does exist (without necessarily being realized) and it is part of the situation of change in the form of heresy, since this danger springs from the same causes as this change in form itself. For instance, was there not silence for too long about certain questions of biblical theology during the period of modernism?

At any rate, there is a greater danger today than previously that where theological theses and opinions which seem questionable or immature, are too hastily suppressed by the *magisterium*, the heresy is not killed but simply takes on a new form and thus becomes even more 'resilient' against the measures taken by the Church's *magisterium*. For it seems to us that the development of the Church and of her formal teaching authority as a proper object of faith 'must' give rise to a form of heresy in the Church which was unknown in the past to the same extent.

The fight against this heresy of cryptogamic attitudes must, therefore, be carried on especially by the conscience of the individual. Where heresy does not objectify itself in theses but remains an unformulated heresy and hence one which is not put up for discussion and one which takes on the appearance of unquestionable inevitability, it becomes— and this in Christians who after all wish to be such—almost something like a sneaking heresy of false emphases. This means that all or most of the postulates of today or tomorrow will have something absolutely true or defensible or historically inevitable about them, even to the extent in which they signify a getting away from the style of life of earlier and even Christian generations. It is possible to make quite a legitimate demand for (or simply to realize tacitly in the concrete shaping of one's life) a greater tolerance than in the past, a more liberal attitude to the body and to sex, a greater understanding for social questions, more emphasis on the principles of an existential ethics and on the individual decisions of conscience, a greater distinction between the theological proposition in its historical and hence conditional 'garb' and what is actually meant by it, a more liberal attitude towards the modern world in general, etc. All this can indeed be advocated in such a way that one cannot be convicted of explicit heresy. Yet one may nevertheless be guilty of a cryptogamic heresy in all this, simply by the (although unverifiable) erroneous balancing of all these things.

'Balancing' may not sound very good and may give a primitive impression. One might say that the problems have not been thought through very well, for otherwise this idea that it is all a question of the right balance just would not arise. There are certainly plenty of cases where a problem cannot be solved by a compromise, by a certain give and take, by avoiding 'exaggerations' on both sides or by similar attitudes and measures, but where it can be solved only by working out exactly and clearly *one* principle in the light of which the right way of acting can then be clearly determined. Yet it still remains true that man, being finite and multidimensional, is unavoidably forced to act out of a plurality of principles which he *cannot* 'elevate' into a higher principle (by reconciling their content in a positive way) so as to give all his actions this one higher principle as their guiding principle and thus man would not require to respect several principles at the same time. Hence the problem of 'right balance'—i.e. of simultaneously and genuinely respecting several demands whose *content* cannot be reduced speculatively to a unique, higher court of appeal (of principle, of authority, etc.)—is an unavoidable human task which basically cannot be solved adequately (i.e. rationally and without consideration of historical factors) on the theoretical plane but only on the plane of practical life which cannot be fully theorized; in other words, this problem cannot be solved by science, but only by prudence and wisdom. Hence, cryptogamic heresy—especially when it wants to remain latent—likes to be a heresy of false emphases, of exaggerations, of one-sideness, but of course of false emphases etc., which can be proved only with difficulty, or even cannot be proved at all on the theoretical plane, and which consequently cannot be branded by the *magisterium* of the Church, or can be branded by it only with great difficulty, only very much later and only in extremely general terms (which no one feels are meant for him).

Who can, for instance, say exactly where the modern craze about sport starts to become a cryptogamic heresy in the form of a wrong balance between character training and body worship, i.e. the heresy of the implicit idolization of the human body? General warnings about this matter will simply make each adherent of this heresy (wherever it is present) think that they are meant only for someone else who is engaged in this idol worship in a still more one-sided and radical manner, or that a reactionary office bearer who is still living in the past, is using such warnings to throw suspicion on the sensible sports activities of today or to persecute it because he regards it as something unchristian. This whole situation is made even more difficult by the following circumstance: modern heresy, even where it expresses itself theoretically, will today have already expressed itself far too much in a great number of people and their experiences to appear very 'undialectic' and 'one-sided' in its formulation. When it declares its true meaning and praises its own particular idol, it will put forward the necessary provisos, counter-balances, restrictions, etc., so that innocent people will be deceived only too easily and will get the impression that this is a balanced system. Today, every systematic praise of sport as a *god* (to keep to our example) will also offer up a little incense to the 'spirit'. Materialism will emphasize that it must be understood in a 'dialectic' sense, so that the denial of the spirit, which is certainly part of materialism, is not at all so easy to prove. All this shows the importance today of accentuation, the proper balance and emphasis, and the difficulties facing the Church's *magisterium* in trying to fulfil this task. In this matter, the individual Christian is set and called to a task and responsibility which no one else can accomplish for him. The practical balancing in one's concrete attitudes of life cannot be fully determined theoretically. Yet it can be false and heretical, and the Christian is not relieved of his responsibility of having done something heretical in this sense, simply because he has not heard any objection from the *magisterium*. For instance, may it not have been true that, in the nineteenth and in the first part of the twentieth century, the *magisterium* stressed the justification of patriotism *and* the incorporation of this principle into higher norms, and that the individual Christians did not deny this dialectic doctrinal pronouncement theoretically, but in practice engaged nevertheless in a heretical nationalism, against which the *magisterium*—which is concerned with theoretical norms—did not and could not protest in any clear manner, with the result that the individual Christians—since they themselves were not watchful and sufficiently critical of themselves—thought that everything was in perfect order (apart from certain exaggerations by . . . the others)? Today, the question of building up atomic stock-piles provides us with an example of a question which theoretically must always end up simply in a weighing of pros and cons, beyond which even the *magisterium* cannot and must not go, and so this whole question (when it comes to the historically concrete question of deciding on a course of action) remains really an open question and yet is a question of *conscience*.

This watchfulness and mistrust in the face of cryptogamic heresy which must be the inalienable task and duty of each individual, since they cannot ever be taken completely off his shoulders by the *magisterium*, are of course *not* to be understood as the task of the individual conscience of each person—of his existential morality—in the sense that everyone lives in isolation and by himself as far as this task is concerned. The finding of concrete imperatives (which go beyond the dialectic of mutually balanced principles and which make clearer demands) is something which can take place also in the public forum of the Church, e.g. in the formation of a charismatically inspired 'public opinion'. Every great Christian movement, all the various spheres of life, can be understood in this sense and could therefore be brought forward as examples of what is meant here. The decisive factor, however, even for the always new and living formation of such attitudes against cryptogamic heresy in the Church, will always be that grace of God which gives the individual an insight into cryptogamic heresy and inspires his decision not to allow himself simply to 'be conformed to this world'; against this conformism St Paul has already warned (Rom 12.2).

INDEX OF PERSONS

SUBJECT INDEX